COMMERCIAL REPORTS

AREA STUDIES SERIES

EDITORIAL DIRECTOR Professor J J O'Meara
RESEARCH UNIT DIRECTOR T F Turley
ASSISTANT DIRECTOR S Cashman

CHIEF EDITORIAL ADVISERS

P Ford
Professor Emeritus, Southampton University
Mrs G Ford

SPECIAL EDITORIAL CONSULTANT FOR
THE UNITED STATES PAPERS

H C Allen
Commonwealth Fund Professor of American History, University College, London
Director of the London University Institute of United States Studies

RESEARCH EDITORS
Johann A Norstedt
Marilyn Evers Norstedt

This Series is published with the active co-operation of
SOUTHAMPTON UNIVERSITY

IRISH UNIVERSITY PRESS AREA STUDIES SERIES

BRITISH PARLIAMENTARY PAPERS

UNITED STATES OF AMERICA

33

Embassy and consular
commercial reports
1889–90

IRISH UNIVERSITY PRESS
Shannon   Ireland

PUBLISHER'S NOTE

The documents in this series are selected from the nineteenth-century British House of Commons *sessional and command papers*. All of the original papers relating to the United States of America are included with the exception of two kinds of very brief and unimportant papers. Omitted are (1) random statistical trade returns which are included in the larger and complete yearly trade figures and (2) returns relating to postal services, which are irregularly presented, of tangential USA relevance, and easily available in other sources.

The original documents have been reproduced by photo-lithography and are unabridged even to the extent of retaining the first printers' imprints. Imperfections in the original printing are sometimes unavoidably reproduced.

This reprint is an enlargement from the original octavo format.

© 1971 Irish University Press Shannon Ireland

Microfilm, microfiche and other forms of micro-publishing
© *Irish University Microforms Shannon Ireland*

ISBN 0 7165 1533 4

Printed and published by
Irish University Press Shannon Ireland
DUBLIN CORK BELFAST LONDON NEW YORK
T M MacGlinchey *Publisher*   Robert Hogg *Printer*

Contents

IUP Page Number

For ease of reference IUP editors have assigned a continuous pagination which appears on the top outer margin of each page.

Commercial Reports

Commercial report no. 24 on the Agricultural Department of the United States
1889 [in C.5865] LXXVI 12

Commercial report no. 25 on the hours of adult labour in the United States
1889 [in C.5866] LXXVI 46

Commercial report no. 26 on the bounties on exports of the United States
1889 [in C.5867] LXXVI 83

Commercial report no. 12 on the ministries of commerce in the United States
1889 [in C.5674] LXXVI 85

Commercial report no. 4 on public companies in the United States
1889 [in C.5627] LXXVII 89

F.O. annual series no. 458: report on Texas, 1888
1889 [C.5618–11] LXXXI 181

F.O. annual series no. 463: report on Baltimore, 1888
1889 [C.5618–16] LXXXI 189

F.O. annual series no. 464: report on Philadelphia, 1887–88
1889 [C.5618–17] LXXXI 205

F.O. annual series no. 465: report on New Orleans, 1888
1889 [C.5618–18] LXXXI 231

F.O. annual series no. 466: report on the agricultural condition of the New Orleans district, 1888
1889 [C.5618–19] LXXXI 255

F.O. annual series no. 499: report on Boston, 1888
1889 [C.5618–52] LXXXI 273

F.O. annual series no. 515: report on Charleston, 1888
1889 [C.5618–68] LXXXI 281

F.O. annual series no. 531: report on Savannah, 1888
1889 [C.5618–84] LXXXI 289

F.O. annual series no. 545: report on New York, 1888
1889 [C.5618–98] LXXXI 297

F.O. annual series no. 546: report on the agriculture of the San Francisco district, 1888
1889 [C.5618–99] LXXXI 321

F.O. annual series no. 555: report on San Francisco, 1888
1889 [C.5618–108] LXXXI 337

F.O. annual series no. 570: report on Chicago, 1888
1889 [C.5618–123] LXXXI 377

Commercial report no. 13 on the status of aliens and foreign companies in the United States
1890 [C.5969] LXXIII 397

Continued

Contents

Continued

IUP Page Number

F.O. annual series no. 643: report on the agriculture of New York
1890 [C.5895–46] LXXVII 405

F.O. annual series no. 648: report on Baltimore, 1889
1890 [C.5895–51] LXXVII 415

F.O. annual series no. 649: report on New Orleans, 1889
1890 [C.5895–52] LXXVII 433

F.O. annual series no. 650: report on the agriculture of the New Orleans district, 1889
1890 [C.5895–53] LXXVII 465

F.O. annual series no. 661: report on Texas, 1889
1890 [C.5895–64] LXXVII 481

F.O. annual series no. 664: report on Boston, 1889
1890 [C.5895–67] LXXVII 491

F.O. annual series no. 668: report on Charleston, 1889
1890 [C.5895–71] LXXVII 507

F.O. annual series no. 691: report on Savannah, 1889
1890 [C.5895–94] LXXVII 519

F.O. annual series no. 718: report on San Francisco, 1889
1890 [C.5895–121] LXXVII 529

F.O. annual series no. 730: report on the agriculture of the San Francisco district
1890 [C.5895–133] LXXVII 589

F.O. annual series no. 731: report on Philadelphia, 1889
1890 [C.5895–134] LXXVII 599

F.O. annual series no. 739: report on Chicago, 1889
1890 [C.5895–142] LXXVII 633

F.O. annual series no. 747: report on New York, 1889
1890 [C.5895–150] LXXVII 659

As most commercial reports are extracted from larger papers, the reader should note that a particular report may lack a proper title page.

(98)

No. 11.

UNITED STATES.

Sir J. Pauncefote to the Marquis of Salisbury.—(*Received July* 22.)

My Lord, *Washington, July* 9, 1889.

WITH reference to your Lordship's despatch of the 30th March last and to my despatch of the 24th May last, I have the honour to transmit herewith a despatch which I have received from Mr. Edwardes, Her Majesty's Secretary of Legation, inclosing a Report on the Agricultural Department of the United States in continuation of the Report forwarded to the Foreign Office in 1883.

I have, &c.
(Signed) JULIAN PAUNCEFOTE.

Inclosure 1 in No. 11.

Mr. Edwardes to Sir J. Pauncefote.

Sir, *Washington, July* 9, 1889.

I HAVE the honour to inclose herewith a succinct Report on the Agricultural Department of the United States from the year 1883 up to the present time, which I have drawn up from the official Reports published by the Department.

I have, &c.
(Signed) H. G. EDWARDES.

Inclosure 2 in No. 11.

Report on the Agricultural Department of the United States for the Years 1883–88.

DURING the year 1883 there were no great changes in the composition and administration of the Department of Agriculture. The Commissioner, in his Report for that year, stated that he had continued the policy he had laid down of establishing as intimate relations as possible between the Department and the Associations and institutions of the country which are devoted to the development and improvement of the art of agriculture, and of calling round the Department those whose knowledge and influence have given them especial authority in the various sections of the country.

The work of obtaining reliable and useful information upon the various matters provided for by appropriations was submitted to competent agents, who furnished from observation and correspondence a vast amount of useful and interesting facts. Investigations were conducted in this manner concerning the cultivation and use of sugar-producing plants, and into the condition, increase, and preservation of the forests in the country. Agents and correspondents were employed in the States and territories for the collection of Statistical Returns and statements in relation to the condition of crops, the animal industry, rates of transportation, the markets, the products of the dairy, both in the United States and abroad, and through them the Statistical Division of the Department was enabled to supply information which has been accepted as reliable in America and in Europe.

A very interesting Report was drawn up this year by the Botanist of the Department on the passes of the great plains which lie west of the 100th meridian, together with the broken and mountainous country in New Mexico, Western Texas, and Arizona, which, though nearly useless for the purposes of ordinary agriculture, have been becoming more and more important as a feeding-ground for cattle.

The Commissioner reported that one of the greatest wants of agriculture in some parts of the United States was the need of suitable grass for hay and pasturage, and recommends a practical and extended observation by the botanist, and a wide examination of the range and habits of the native grasses of the desert or arid regions, with a view to utilizing the best for agricultural purposes.

The Microscopic Division was employed in 1883 principally in investigating the parasite fungi which cause the blight of plants, fruits, and cereals. Several new plant diseases were reported to the Department, produced by the unfavourable and unusual atmospheric changes during the year.

The examination of American cereals by the Chemical Division was continued; the specimens of wheat which were analyzed numbering 260. The investigation of "sorghum" occupied a large portion of the time of this Division, and the results were published in a special Report by Dr. Peter Collier.

Flowers, breads, fruits, vegetables, grasses, &c., were also submitted to analysis during the year.

The investigations of the sorghum plant were conducted on the following lines:—

1. The manufacture of sugar from the canes, and the determination of the yield per ton.

2. Experiments in extracting the juice from the canes by diffusion; the increased yield of this method was found to be between 25 and 30 per cent.

3. Experiments in defecation.
4. Separation of sucrose by barium, lime, and strontium.

It appeared from the Report of the Chemist on the above subject, that up to that date the sorghum business could not be considered as having shown itself profitable.

A thorough investigation of the butters of the country, forty butters being submitted to examination, was carried out.

The Entomologist of the Department was engaged in 1883 in investigation into the question of insects injurious to the cabbage; with the consideration of the leper locust, which had been unusually destructive in the Merimac Valley, New Hampshire, the destruction of which pest he trusted was within reach; and the protection of fruit and shade trees. Several interesting discoveries in the life habits of the phylloxera were made during the year, and experiments with petroleum emulsions were very successful.

The work of the Statistical Division of the Department was on a greater scale even than before, and showed a marked advance for accuracy and breadth both as regarded the United States and foreign countries.

The completeness and fulness of the figures given cannot be too highly praised. The Division was assisted by State officials and State Boards of Agriculture, by which unity of results was attained. Where no official State organization has been in existence, the Statistical Agent has organized a system of correspondence to corroborate and supplement the work of the regular Department corps of county correspondents. The voluntary work of these local assistants proved of the greatest value.

In 1883 this Division extended its work to Europe, with an office in London, its agent being also Deputy Consul-General in that capital, with good results as a beginning of a difficult work, and promise of future improvement.

In accordance with the requirement of Congress, there was also added to this Division a section of railroad statistics, charged especially with the duty of noting and co-ordinating the rates of transportation by land and water, with their changes and fluctuations. This work was successfully initiated, and the Railroads generally furnished promptly the data required. Special investigation was made during the year of the influence of American competition upon European agriculture.

The Statistics showed that the crops of 1883 were sufficient for the wants of the country, and for an average measure of supply of the deficient production of European countries.

There was a large increase in the breadth of corn, due to the high prices of the preceding year. A period of excessive moisture and low temperature was encountered, which was followed by a summer of deficient rainfall, resulting in a crop averaging scarcely more than twenty-three bushels per acre. As this was the third successive crop below the average yield of twenty-six bushels, the price continued high, and seemed almost extreme after a remarkable period of six successive years of yield above twenty-six bushels, in which the average price declined from 64·7 to 31·8 cents per bushel.

The November estimate for 1883 was 1,577,000,000 bushels. The winter wheat crop was still more unfortunate, suffering severely by the alternations of frost and thaw in the early spring. The spring wheat crop was good, yet the average yield of spring and winter wheat was but eleven bushels per acre, a reduction of nearly 100,000,000 bushels from the large product of 1882. The crop of oats was unusually large; barley, medium; rye, below average; and buckwheat seriously injured by the frost. The cotton crop, although short, was only exceeded twice in the history of cotton-growing, namely, in 1880 and 1882. The potato crop was the largest since 1875, amounting to about 195,000,000 bushels of good quality, with little loss from rot. The season's production on the whole was considered successful and encouraging.

The part of the Report of the Statistician which relates to the employment of the people of the United States, numbering, according to the last census, 50,155,783, is of special interest; it shows that 44·1 per cent. are engaged in agriculture.

The Veterinary Division was occupied in investigating contagious diseases of domestic animals, principally that known as "Texas," Spanish or southern fever of cattle. An Experiment Station was organized and established near Washington, and experiments were made as to the practicability of a system of vaccination as a prevention for some of the most widespread and destructive of the animal diseases of the country.

The Forestry Division reported on the practicability of successful tree-planting upon the plains of the north-west, and its investigations tended to warrant the hope that there was no part of the country where a desirable growth of trees might not be secured. The total value of forest product for the census year was estimated at 700,000,000 dollars, the next largest products of the country being Indian corn, wheat, hay, cotton, oats.

As usual, during the year a large amount of seed was distributed by the Department, in all, 2,467,230 packages, of which more than half were for vegetables.

The disbursements of the Department for the year may be roughly estimated at 100,000*l*.

300,000 copies of the Report of the Commissioner were printed, together with about 250,000 copies of additional and miscellaneous Reports on special subjects.

In 1884, the Commissioner reported that there were 10,000 correspondents of the Department of Agriculture in the United States who furnish the materials for the statistical estimates of the Bureau. In this year the Bureau of Animal Industry, established by Act of Congress, was organized and in active operation.

Investigations were made in regard to the extent, nature, and means of combatting outbreaks of communicable diseases among the domesticated animals of the country. The prevalence of such diseases was probably not much in excess of what it had been in previous years. The organization of the Bureau led to a greatly increased number of demands for information on the subject, and the existence of dangerous diseases was more promptly and fully reported than heretofore. Scientific investigation in regard to the nature and cause of contagious diseases among animals were constantly in progress, and threw much light on the difficult problems encountered by those who practically attempted to reduce the ravages of these plagues.

An extended microscopic investigation of American pork was made with a view to learn what foundation there was for the charge of trichinous infection which was brought against it in Europe.

A large mass of information was collected in relation to the developments and needs of the various branches of the live-stock industry, with a view of enabling the owners of animals of all kinds to escape preventible losses, and to direct their efforts in the most promising direction.

The practical direction of the quarantine system, which was transferred to the Department of Agriculture by the Secretary of the Treasury in accordance with an Act of Congress, was made one of the duties of the Bureau of Animal Industry. The professional knowledge of the Chief, who has to be a competent Veterinary Surgeon, taken in connection with the information which is being continually received by this Bureau as to the presence of contagious diseases in those foreign countries from which cattle is imported in the United States, and the most advanced methods of controlling those diseases, rendered it peculiarly appropriate that the protection of American cattle from imported diseases should be in the same hands. The labour of the Bureau was, in a word, directed to prevent and control communicable diseases among animals in the United States, to prevent the importation of such plagues from abroad, and to collect such information as is valuable to the stockpower and necessary to the profitable development and conduct of the animal industries in the country, and to secure free entrance for the animal products of the United States into the markets of the world.

The experiments made for the growth of the Chinese tea-plant in the United States showed that it could be grown over a large portion of the country, but it was not practically demonstrated that teas can be produced of standard qualities to meet the requirements of commerce in sufficient quantities, and at a cost profitable to the planter and the manufacturer at the prevailing prices.

The yearly Report of the Statistician showed a tendency to further increase of the area of corn and cotton, and of most of the principal crops of the country. The wheat area was so much beyond the requirements of consumption in the United States and other countries as to depress the price to a point unprecedented in recent years; the use of wheat in feeding for pork production was the result. The cause of this superabundance was held to be the extension of settlement in the north-west plains of the Pacific coast, and the extraordinary period of comparative failure of European wheat for several consecutive years.

In 1884 corn averaged about 26 bushels to the acre; wheat,

103

13 bushels to the acre; the supply of cereals being fully 50 bushels for each inhabitant.

The Statistical Bureau was much occupied during the year in collecting the official statistics of State Departments, Boards of Agriculture, and of commercial organizations; much information of European crop production and supply was obtained.

The attention of the Bureau of Botany during the year was principally directed to plants having injurious or poisoning properties, some of which possess medicinal properties.

The Bureau of Chemistry of the Department carried on its investigations with regard to American cereals with reference to the composition of the grains, their relation to moisture, variation, size, &c. It was also engaged on a study of the "roller milling process" for the manufacture of flour, a series of baking experiments with flours of different grades, the examination of American dairy products, an investigation of maple sugars and maple syrups, a study of the sugar industry of the country, including experiments and practical work with sorghum, and an examination of the beet sugar industry on the Pacific coast.

The distinction of forests in the United States has always attracted especial attention from the Department of Agriculture, and the Commissioner organized this year extensive inquiries, with a view to obtain information as to the kind of trees the planting of which was attended with success. It was desired to do everything to encourage tree planting. The Report of the Commissioner showed that the consumption of forests for the manufacture of lumber was increasing in a greater ratio than was warranted by the increase of demand. The lumber market was so overstocked, that a convention of lumber-men was held at Chicago for the purpose of checking the rate of production, at which it was stated that the stock then on hand was sufficient to supply all legitimate demands for eighteen months; but no agreement could be arrived at.

There was a very large increase over the preceding year, viz., 1,000,000 packages, in the number of packages of seed distributed by the Department.

In April 1885, Mr. Coleman was appointed Commissioner of Agriculture in the place of Dr. Loring, who had held the post for four years. Under his direction, a Convention met that year at Washington composed of Delegates from the several Agricultural Colleges and Experiment Stations, the object of which was to bring about practical co-operation between such institutions and the Department of Agriculture. These Colleges, &c., severally endowed by Act of Congress, had carried on experiments at an expense of time and means, but without any central head through which to report and compare results with each other.

The Bureau of Animal Industry carried on its work with the view to the extirpation of pleuro-pneumonia and other diseases of domestic animals, but at that time the law did not authorize the slaughter of affected animals, but only such quarantine as was necessary to prevent the spread of disease from one State to another.

It was consequently impossible for the Department to maintain an effectual quarantine under existing laws. The Commissioner recommended vigorous means and measures to protect the great cattle interests of the United States. The result of the restriction placed by Great Britain upon the importation of cattle into the kingdom, the object in view being the prevention of the spread of pleuro-pneumonia, was a steady decline of the exportation from the United States of cattle, sheep, and pigs. The reduction in the value of cattle in the affected States was enormous.

The Bureau of Animal Industry made a complete investigation of the condition and numbers of domestic animals in various parts of the country, of the peculiarities of the animal traffic, and of such changes in the methods in use as would be of advantage to those engaged in that industry.

The work of the Division of Chemistry for 1885 was classed under five heads: Analysis of soils; continuation of the investigation of cereals; experiments in the manufacture of sugar; investigation of food adulterations; miscellaneous.

The effects of the analysis of soils were to make analyses of samples of soils from various parts of the country, which had been sent to the Department from time to time during the preceding year and a-half; to further investigate the problem of the chemical composition of a soil with reference to its fertility; to collect and compare the different methods in use for soil analysis with the design of unifying them as much as possible in proposing a method which might seem best adapted to general use; and to put in form for general use points in connection with soil analysis concerning which frequent inquiries are addressed to the Department.

The experiments in the manufacture of sugar were with a view to checking the waste of sugar incurred in milling, or in the processes of manufacture. It was held not to be an exaggeration to state that during the ten preceding years fully half of the sugar produced by the soil of the country had been lost before the manufactured article had entered commerce.

To avoid the loss in milling, the process of diffusion was tried with satisfactory results; and to avoid the loss incident to the usual process of manufacture, the process known in the beet-sugar industry as carbonation was tried and found successful.

The investigation into food adulteration in 1885 was chiefly with butter and honey. The analyses of artificial fertilisers proved also of great utility.

The Division of the Entomologist continued its investigations with the view to the prevention as far as possible of the devastations caused by destructive insects to the farmers of the country. Much work was done in relation to silkworm culture. A new field for investigation was added to the Division by the appropriation by Congress of a sum of money to be devoted to the " promotion of economic ornithology, or the study of the inter-relation of birds and agriculture, and an investigation of the foods, habits, and migration of birds in relation to both insects and plants."

The Reports of the Statistician during the year 1885 were of the greatest service, giving practical and useful information plainly and concisely, care being taken to avoid as much as possible fragmentary and inconclusive statements.

The crop-reporting system at that time consisted of Boards of Observation and Report in over 1,800 counties of the United States, comprising nearly all the developed territory of the country. A parallel and duplicate work, for the purpose of verification and for special local investigation, is carried on through State Agents.

The Report of 1885 contained a review of the course of agricultural production during fifteen years, which showed an estimated increase in corn of 37,000,000 acres, or 80 per cent.; in wheat, of 20,000,000 acres, or 108 per cent.; in oats, of 13,000,000 acres, or 142 per cent.; in all cereals taken together, 67,000,000 acres, or 97 per cent.

The enlargement of the wheat area was attributable to the period of partial failure of the crops of Western Europe; the extension of the breadth in maize was aided by the rise of the foreign trade in beeves and fresh meats, and by the sudden enlargements of exports of pork products, induced by the cheapness of corn; and the cultivation of oats received especial impetus from the seeding of rust-proof varieties in the south, and from the necessity of less heating feed for horses than a too exclusive maize ration.

The average estimated area and product of the principal food crops of the years 1880-84, as compared with the average of the ten preceding years, was as follows:—

Crops.	1880-84. Bushels.	1880-84. Acres.	1870-79. Bushels.	1870-79. Acres.
Corn	1,575,194,194	66,045,016	1,184,486,954	43,741,331
Wheat	463,973,098	37,738,882	312,152,728	25,187,414
Oats	495,509,478	18,628,029	314,441,178	11,076,822
Rye	26,380,399	2,088,665	18,460,985	1,305,061
Barley	49,324,670	2,214,154	33,704,652	1,529,357
Buckwheat	10,781,793	847,096	9,747,272	551,104
Potatoes	169,241,133	2,112,378	132,837,175	1,514,045

The average yield of corn per acre was 23·9 bushels per acre, against 27·1 bushels for the preceding period; the average value was therefore higher—44·7 cents per bushel instead of 42·6 cents—and the average value of an acre was 10 dol. 67 c. instead of 11 dol. 54 c. The average yields of wheat in the two periods were nearly identical, 12·3 and 12·4 bushels respectively, but the price averaged 90·1 cents instead of 104·9 cents, the demand not being equal to the supply.

The Chief of the Division of the Gardens, Horticulture, &c., recommended the appointment of a Special Superintendent or Agent of Pomology, who would be able to give attention to the pomological necessities of the country.

The question of the profitable cultivation of medicinal plants was also recommended for favourable consideration, and the Botanist in his Report furnished valuable information on the subject.

The wasteful destruction of the forests in the United States occupied seriously the attention of the Department, and the Chief of the Division of Forestry recommended strongly legislative measures such as exist in some European countries for the prevention of such destruction, and the encouragement of tree culture. The establishment of Arbour or Tree-planting day, a holiday adopted in many States and territories of the Union, was considered to be a very great encouragement for the advancement of forestry Its extension throughout the country would, it was maintained, be a very effective means of creating throughout the community a proper sentiment in regard to trees, and lead to their adequate protection.

The Microscopical Division organized investigations, the object of which was the protection of the public against fraudulent compounds sold as pure butter, the result of which was an earnest recommendation by the Commissioner of Agriculture of the passage of a stringent Law by Congress to prevent the continuance of the manufacture and sale as pure butter of various compounds of animal fats, vegetable oils, &c., except under such Regulations as the necessities of the case demanded, the enforcement of the Law to be placed under the control of the Internal Revenue Department.

In 1886 there existed nine Agricultural Experiment Stations supported by State appropriations or special tax ; in the State of New York 125 acres were devoted to this purpose. The Commissioner strongly recommended the establishment of at least one Agricultural Experiment Station in every State, well equipped, ably managed, and liberally supported by appropriations by Congress, and the establishment of a Central Station or Office at Washington.

The Bureau of Animal Industry continued its important investigations into the contagious diseases of animals, the most important being at that time pleuro-pneumonia. Every effort under the existing laws was made to locate the diseased animals and isolate all that had been exposed, but legislation was not then adequate for the crisis. Under the authority conferred by Congress, the Department co-operated with such States as accepted its Rules and Regulations for controlling and extirpating the disease, but no work was able to be done in the State of New York, as it was evident that the appropriations were not sufficient to procure any satisfactory result.

The disease known as hog-cholera was very prevalent, causing losses estimated at from 10,000,000 dollars to 30,000,000 dollars. The investigations of the year were very satisfactory, and promised more intelligent means of prevention.

The quarantine of cattle imported from abroad was maintained, and during the year no cases of contagious disease were detailed among such animals.

The Division of Chemistry continued, with a view to the prevention of adulteration, its investigations of dairy products, spices, peppers, and other condiments. Interesting experiments in the manufacture of sugars were made.

The most important Reports of the work of the Entomological Division were: a Report on the cotton-worm and the boll-worm; a Report on silk culture, containing a complete manual of instructions in silk culture; Reports of experiments made in certain States of many of the insecticides recommended against insects injurious to garden crops; Reports on insects affecting the orange, &c.

Experiments were carried out by this Division in bee-culture with a view to economize wax, increase the honey supply, facilitate manipulation, and even to the improvement of the bee itself.

In 1886 the Division of Statistics had at its disposal a corps of correspondents representing over 2,300 counties, four in each county, a duplicate service for unification and special investigation under the direction of State Statistical Agents, and a European Statistical Agent connected with the United States' Consular system.

The international aspects of the Division have been attested by a yearly increase of foreign correspondence. Six United States' citizens were made members of the International Statistical Institute established in 1885, whose head-quarters were in London, the more important objects of which were a greater uniformity in the methods of compiling and abstracting Statistical Returns with a view to a comparison of results obtained in different countries.

The increase of production as shown by the Returns compiled by this Division was enormous, while the number of the people in 1880 was more than double that of 1850; the production of cereals not only kept pace with the population, but furnished 53 bushels for every inhabitant in place of 38 at the earlier date.

With the increase of 7,000,000 people in the first half of the current decade, the aggregate of cereals exceeded 3,000,000,000 bushels in 1885, still keeping up the extraordinary rate of supply attained in 1880, and showing in wheat a product five times as large as in 1850, and a corn crop nearly five times as large.

The increase of production during the period 1880-85 over that of 1870-79 was over 43 per cent., while the enlargement of area was still greater, amounting to 54 per cent.

A very interesting Report was published by the Assistant Botanist of the result of investigation of the diseases of fruits and fruit trees, grains, and other useful plants, caused by fungi.

Each year the necessity for forest reproduction in the United States was made the subject of special remark by the Commissioners, no planting of trees being done worth mentioning in comparison with the consumption of forest products.

The importance of the work of the seed Divisions can be easily recognized, by the fact that in 1886 over 4,250,000 packages of seeds, embracing vegetable, flower, seed, textile, &c., were distributed. This is nearly double the number distributed in 1883.

A Pomological Division was established under Act of Congress of July 1886, and the Report of its work contains information of great value. The fruit industry of the United States was estimated at 150,000,000 dollars per annum.

The work of the Divisions of Ornithology and Mammalogy (established in 1885 and enlarged in 1886) counted in the collection of facts relating to the food habits, distribution, and migration of North American birds and mammals in relation to agriculture, horticulture, and forestry; and the preparation for distribution among farmers and others of special Reports and bulletins upon birds and mammals which affect the interests of the farmer, and also upon the migration and distribution of North American species. In this way, it was hoped to correct the ignorance concerning injurious and beneficial effects of the common birds and mammals of the country, and to prevent the wholesale destruction of useful species.

The Commissioner in his Report condemned the policy which the Department was obliged to follow in declining all requests for conference and interchange of thought between the specialists of the United States and other countries, such as invitations and urgent requests for American representation at foreign exhibitions and enterprises of various kinds.

In his Report for 1887, the Commissioner drew attention to the contrast of the status of the Department of Agriculture under existing circumstances with its status when established in 1862 with three Divisions.

He upheld, and with reason, that the Department had kept pace with the development of the rural economies of the people of the United States, that it had so well commended itself to the country that it consisted in 1887 of no less than twenty separate and distinct branches. The Department held the position of an Adviser in all investigations and enterprises which bore upon the future agriculture of the country. The extension and the importance of the Department can be estimated by the fact, that 380,000 copies of its various official Reports were published and distributed, not including the copies distributed by the Senators and Representatives in Congress.

Very great progress towards the eradication of the plague of pleuro-pneumonia was made this year. By an Act of Congress of June 1886, authority was given to expend money for the purchase and destruction of diseased animals whenever it was essential to prevent the spread of the disease from one State to another. The total eradication of the plague being necessary in the opinion of experts to prevent its spread from State to State, it was decided to use the money appropriated in the purchase and destruction of diseased cattle wherever this action would tend to secure such eradication. It was evident, however, that to purchase diseased animals wherever found would not effect such eradication unless, by co-operation with State authorities, Regulations could be enforced which would secure the control of exposed animals, and the disinfection of premises. In August 1886, by co-operation with authorities of the State of Maryland, the purchase and destruction of cattle affected with pleuro-pneumonia was begun. In this case the exposed cattle were to be disposed of by the Maryland Live Stock Sanitary Commission under the State Laws. Owing to the expense attending the quarantining and slaughter of exposed animals, few other States were willing to co-operate for the extirpation of this malady until after the Appropriation Act of March 1887 went into effect. This Act increased the appropriation for the Bureau of Animal Industry to 500,000 dollars (100,000*l*.), and authorized the use of "any part of this sum in the purchase and destruction of diseased or *exposed* animals, or the quarantine of the same." Immediately after this Bill became law Rules and Regulations were prepared, and were certified to the Governors of all the States and territories, with a request for their co-operation in enforcing them.

With this co-operation great progress was made by the Bureau towards the complete eradication of the plague.

The following Table shows succinctly the work accomplished under the authority of the above referred-to legislation:—

TABLE showing the Work of the Bureau of Animal Industry for the suppression of Pleuro-pneumonia.*

	Illinois.	Maryland.	New Jersey.	New York.	Total and Average.
Herds inspected	7,411	5,704	1,428	1,511	16,054
Cattle inspected	24,059	57,858	16,461	25,122	123,500
Post-mortem examinations	7,267	2,788	248	1,347	11,650
Found diseased on *post-mortem*	350	1,137	113	447	2,047
Diseased cattle slaughtered with compensation	172	1,442	94	266	1,974
Exposed cattle slaughtered with compensation	870	1,564	117	736	3,287
	Dol. c.	Dol. c.	Dol. c.	Dol. c.	Dol. c.
Total compensation for diseased cattle	3,179 53	33,759 01	2,275 00	6,317 25	45,530 79
Average compensation for diseased cattle	18 42	23 41	24 20	23 75	23 06
Total compensation for exposed cattle	14,153 21	41,397 71	3,216 00	15,577 41	74,344 33
Average compensation for exposed cattle	16 27	26 46	27 48	21 16	22 61
Salary expense	49,107 71	20,126 44	4,642 27	6,036 85	79,913 27
Travelling expenses	3,598 99	9,430 49	1,813 43	2,544 03	17,386 94
Miscellaneous	3,952 52	1,170 16	199 33	156 95	5,478 96
Total	73,991 96	105,883 81	12,146 03	30,632 49	222,654 29
Ratio between amount paid for cattle and all other expenses	1 3·3	1 0·41	1 1·2	1 0·39	1 0·85

Great attention was paid this year to the reeling of silk, with a view to decide whether the silk industry in the United States is one which could be a profitable employment.

There were purchased for experiments of the silk crop of 1886 1,513 lbs. of cocoons, of an average value of $95\frac{1}{2}$ cents per lb. Of these, 1,062 lbs. were reeled and produced 260 lbs. of silk, worth 4 dol. 75 c. per lb., while the remainder was sold as waste at 50 cents per lb. From these figures, it can be seen that the experiments by no means paid their expenses, but the Commissioner was hopeful that the improved apparatus lately made would do away with a great deal of hand labour, and would help towards a more satisfactory result.

The Statistician, in his Report, explained that the system of the Department for crop reporting cannot be absolutely accurate. That would be impossible. It is a count in advance by instantaneous generalization. The cotton crop is one which has been

* The slaughter of affected cattle and expenses in Maryland are from July 1, 1886. The salaries, travelling, and miscellaneous expenses in Illinois are from September 1, 1886. All other items are from January 1, 1887, and all are brought up to December 31, 1887.

111

enumerated quite accurately; for instance, the record of the National Cotton Exchange, furnished in September 1887, of the actual growth of 1886, was 6,443,000 bales. The estimate of the Statistician of the Department of Agriculture was just 17,000 bales more, and that of the Exchange 40,000 bales less.

The production of 1887 was reported to be not quite up to the average rate of yield, the crops notably deficient being corn and potatoes.

The cattle of the country was shown to have been decreased by losses on the plains and in the mountains, and the flocks of sheep were reduced from the discouraging effect of low prices. The Department designated a representative to attend the first biennial meeting of the International Statistical Institute at Rome.

An interesting Report was made by the Chemist of the Department on the production of malt liquors in the United States, the consumption of which was shown to be steadily increasing.

The Section of Vegetable Pathology, to which were referred for investigation all questions relative to the diseases of fruits and fruit trees, was regularly established this year by law, provision being made for a Chief of Section with an assistant, and under its agency special experiments were made in a number of vineyards selected for the purpose in the treatment of grape, mildew, and rot.

The work of the Division of Ornithology and Mammalogy consisted chiefly in ths collection of facts showing the relation of certain birds and mammals to agriculture, horticulture, and forestry, and in the preparation for publication of two important bulletins (1) on the English sparrow; (2) on bird migration in the Mississippi Valley. More than 3,000 persons had replied to the Circular distributed in 1886, asking for information about the English sparrow.

The yearly investigations and Reports of the other Divisions of the Department were generally in continuation of preceding works referred to above.

In 1888, the Department continued its efforts to apply the latest results of scientific discovery to agricultural practice. The appropriation of 15,000 dollars per annum to each of the States and territories which had established Agricultural Colleges in accordance with the Act of Congress of the 2nd March, 1887, led to the establishment of new stations, or to the increased development of stations previously established under State authority in thirty-seven States and one territory.

In order to carry into effect the provisions of the Act of the 2nd March, 1887, and of Acts supplementary thereto, an Act was passed by Congress the 18th July, 1888, entitled, " An Act making an appropriation for the Department of Agriculture for the fiscal year ending the 30th June, 1889, and for other purposes," appropriates " 595,000 dollars, 10,000 dollars of which sum shall be payable upon the order of the Commissioner of Agriculture to enable him to carry out the provisions of section 3 of said Act of the 2nd March, 1887, and to compare, edit, and publish such of the results of the experiments made under section 2 of said Act by

[431]

said Experiment Stations as he may deem necessary; and for these purposes the Commissioner of Agriculture is authorized to employ such assistants, clerks, and other persons as he may deem necessary."

Section 3 of the Act of the 2nd March, 1887, provides:

"That in order to secure, as far as practicable, uniformity of methods and results in the work of said stations, it shall be the duty of the United States' Commissioner of Agriculture to furnish forms, as far as practicable, for the tabulation of results of investigation or experiments; to indicate, from time to time, such lines of inquiry as to him shall seem most important; and, in general, to furnish such advice and assistance as will best promote the purposes of this Act. It shall be the duty of each said station annually, on or before the 1st day of February, to make to the Governor of the State or territory in which it is located a full and detailed Report of its operations, including a statement of receipts and expenditures, a copy of which Report shall be sent to each of said stations, to the said Commissioner of Agriculture, and to the Secretary of the Treasury of the United States."

With the view to assisting these stations in their work, the Commissioner of Agriculture instituted an Office of Experiment Stations as a special branch of his Department, and appointed a Director at its head.

The Bureau of Animal Industry continued its work with the view to the eradication of pleuro-pneumonia. In Maryland the plague has been nearly extinguished, only three affected herds being found in November. Pennyslvania was reported to be free from infection.

The following figures, covering all the pleuro-pneumonia districts, show the magnitude of the task which the Bureau had in hand:—

"From the 1st January to the 30th November there were inspected 35,451 herds, containing 304,698 head of cattle. Of these animals 183,257 were tagged with numbers and registered upon the books of the office, and 106,415 were examined more than once.

"During the same period 630 herds, containing 8,604 animals, were found affected with the disease, and the Bureau has purchased and slaughtered 2,649 diseased animals and 5,490 that had been exposed. The number of stock-yards, stables, and other premises disinfected reached the number of 1,876. There have also been 41,361 *post-mortem* examinations made, which resulted in finding 3,380 carcasses affected with pleuro-pneumonia."

Investigation into the disease of glanders among horses and swine diseases were also carried on by the Bureau.

The quarantine of imported cattle was in successful operation under this Bureau during the year, and the introduction of diseases generally classed as contagious was entirely prevented.

The Division of Entomology reported on the question of profitable silk-reeling in the United States, the result of experiments made being shown to be not encouraging.

113

Experiments were made by the Chemist of the Department in the manufacture of sugar, with the view to the encouragement of the culture of sugar, beet, and the sorghum plant.

The year 1888 was one of medium agricultural production, the corn crop being between 26 and 27 bushels per acre.

Congress having accepted, on the part of the United States' Government, the invitation of the French Republic to take part in the International Exhibition at Paris in 1889, authorized the Commissioner, by joint Resolution, to collect and prepare suitable specimens of the agricultural productions of the United States for exhibition.

The extent of the work of the Department can be estimated by the following list of Reports issued from it and distributed during the current year :—

	No. of Copies.
"The Annual Report of the Department"	400,000

DIVISION OF STATISTICS—NEW SERIES.

"Report upon the Numbers and Value of Farm Animals, and on Freight Rates of Transportation Companies, January and February 1888"	18,000
"Report on Distribution and Consumption of Corn and Wheat, and on Freight Rates of Transportation Companies, March 1888"	18,000
"Report of the Condition of Winter Grain and the Condition of Farm Animals, and on the Freight Rates of Transportation Companies, April 1888"	18,000
"Report of the Condition of Winter Grain, the Progress of Cotton Planting, and Wages of Farm Labour, May 1888"	18,000
"Report of Acreage of Wheat and Cotton and Condition of Cereal Crops, with Freight Rates of Transportation Companies, June 1888"	18,000
"Report of the Area of Corn, Potatoes, and Tobacco, and Condition of Growing Crops, and on Freight Rates of Transportation Companies, July 1888"	18,000
"Report on the Condition of Growing Crops, and on Freight Rates of Transportation Companies, August 1888"	18,000
"Report on Condition of Crops in America and Europe, and on Freight Rates of Transportation Companies, September 1888"	19,000
"Report on Condition of Crops, Yield of Grain per Acre, and on Freight Rates of Transportation Companies, October 1888"	18,000
"Report on Yield of Crops per Acre, and on Freight Rates of Transportation Companies, November 1888"	18,000
"Report on the Crops of the Year and on Freight Rates of Transportation Companies, December 1888"	18,000

BOTANICAL DIVISION.

Bulletin No. 5. "Report on the Experiments made in 1887 in the Treatment of the Downy Mildew and Black-rot of the Grape-vine"	5,000
Bulletin No. 6. "Report on the Grasses of the Arid Districts"	10,000
"Report of Botanist"	500
Circular No. 5. "Fungicides or Remedies for Plant Disease"	5,000
Bulletin No. 7. "Report on Black-rot of Grapes"	10,000

[431]

114

CHEMICAL DIVISION.

	No. of Copies.
Bulletin No. 17. "Experiments in the Manufacture of Sugar at Fort Scott, Kans., Rio Grande, N.J., &c."	10,000
Bulletin No. 18. "Sugar-producing Plants"	10,000
Bulletin No. 19. "Methods of Analysis of Commercial Fertilizers, &c."	3,000

ENTOMOLOGICAL DIVISION.

Bulletin No. 17. "The Chinch Bug," April 19	5,000
Reprint of Bulletin No. 9. "The Mulberry Silk-worm," April 30	3,000
Catalogue of Exhibit at New Orleans, May 21	1,000
Reprint of Bulletin No. 10. "Our Shade Trees and their Defoliators," July 13	3,000
Author's Edition to Annual Report, July 27	1,600
Reprint of Bulletin No. 9. "The Mulberry Silk-worm," October 29	5,000
Bulletin No. 19. "An Enumeration of the Published Synopsis, Catalogue of North American Insects," October 2	5,000
"Insect Life"—	
Volume I, No. 1, July 28	5,000
„ No. 2, August 24	5,000
„ No. 3, October 2	5,000
„ No. 4, October 25	5,000
„ No. 5, November 22	5,000
„ No. 6	5,000

FORESTRY DIVISION.

Bulletin No. 2. "Report on the Forest Condition of the Rocky Mountains," September 29	5,000
"Annual Report of the Division of Forestry," August 30	5,000
Circular, "Increasing the Durability of Timber"	5,000
Circular to Seedmen on "New Forage Plants"	1,000

BUREAU OF ANIMAL INDUSTRY.

Circulars for Bureau of Animal Industry	25,000

ORNITHOLOGIST DIVISION.

Author's Edition, September 17	1,500

POMOLOGICAL DIVISION.

Report of Pomologist, September 17	500
Letters of Commissioner of Agriculture in response to Senate Resolution of December 7, 1887	1,000

A very interesting account of the Experiment Station movement in the United States by Mr. True is hereto appended:—

A brief account of the Experiment Station Movement in the United States.—By A. C. True, Ph.D.

"In the United States, as in Europe, the first organized experimental work in agricultural science was done in connection with the higher educational institutions.

"It is claimed that Yale College was the first American institution to officially recognize the claims of agricultural science. In 1846 John P. Norton was appointed Professor of Agricultural

115

Chemistry and Vegetable and Animal Physiology. Professor Norton began his lectures in 1847, and during the five years which intervened before his death he also wrote extensively for agricultural journals, edited an American edition of 'Stevens on the Farm,' and published a work of his own, entitled, 'Elements of Agriculture.' After the fund which had been established by the sale of the land-scrip donated to Connecticut under the Act of Congress of the 2nd July, 1862, had been given to the Sheffield Scientific School of Yale College in 1863, a Professor of Agriculture was added to the working force of that institution. Samuel W. Johnson, M.A., the successor of Professor Norton as Professor of Theoretical and Agricultural Chemistry, and William H. Brewer, Ph.D., the Professor of Agriculture, have for many years taken an active interest in all work for the promotion of agricultural science in Connecticut and elsewhere in the United States. Under their direction experimental work for the benefit of agriculture was carried on to a limited extent at New Haven more than twenty years ago, and it is doubtless safe to say that 'through the influence of the professors and pupils trained in this school, more than to any other single cause, is due the recognition of the importance of the establishment of agricultural experiment stations, first in Connecticut, and subsequently throughout the whole country.'

"In 1870 the President and Fellows of Harvard College began to organize the School of Agriculture and Horticulture which had been provided for in the will of Mr. Benjamin Bussey, of Roxbury, Massachusetts. This interesting document was signed the 30th July, 1835, and was proved soon after the death of the testator in 1842. It bequeathed half of the income of about 300,000 dollars and 200 acres of land in Roxbury to the President and Fellows of Harvard College, on condition that they establish on the farm 'a course of instruction in practical agriculture, in useful and ornamental gardening, in botany, and in such other branches of natural science as may tend to promote a knowledge of practical agriculture and the various arts subservient thereto.' Owing to other provisions of the will, it was not deemed advisable to begin the formation of the Bussey Institution earlier than 1870. In the same year the trustees of the Massachusetts Society for Promoting Agriculture granted to the Corporation of Harvard College a considerable sum 'for the support of a laboratory, and for experiments in agricultural chemistry, to be conducted on the Bussey estate.' The laboratory of the new institution was not ready for occupation until the last week in 1871. As soon as it was completed, however, agricultural researches were begun by F. H. Storer, the Professor of Agricultural Chemistry, and his assistants. The first Report of this work was presented to a Committee of the trustees of the Massachusetts Society for Promoting Agriculture, the 3rd December, 1871. The experiments consisted of field tests of fertilizers upon the farm of the institution, and chemical analyses of commercial fertilizers. Other interesting and valuable work was done in the next few years, but the great fire in Boston in 1872, and the commercial crisis of 1873, combined to cripple the institution financially, and it has since been able to make comparatively few original investigations. Meanwhile, agricultural colleges had been organized in a number of the States. Michigan led the way in 1857, and New York soon followed her example. After the passage of the Land Grant Act in 1862, Kansas and Massachusetts were the first States to avail themselves of the national gift by establishing agricultural colleges, and thereafter the formation of these institutions proceeded with as much rapidity as could have been expected when the country was recovering from the direful effects of the civil war. Experimental work in agriculture was undertaken in several of these institutions soon after their organization.

"The Reports of the successful and beneficial work done in the European Experiment Stations excited more and more attention on this side of the Atlantic, and the more advanced leaders in agricultural progress in this country began to ask for the establishment of similar institutions in the United States. In 1872, at a Convention of Representatives of Agricultural Colleges held in Washington, in response to a call issued by the United States' Commissioner of Agriculture, the question of the establishment of Experiment Stations was discussed, and the Report of a Committee in favour of such institutions was adopted by the Convention. On the 17th December, 1873, at the winter meeting of the State Board of Agriculture at Meriden, Connecticut, Professor Johnson, of the Sheffield Scientific School, and Professor Atwater, of Wesleyan University, urged the establishment of an Agricultural Experiment Station in that State after the European pattern. A Committee was appointed to consider the expediency of such a movement, and reported two days later that it was 'their unanimous opinion that the State of Connecticut ought to have an Experiment Station as good as can be found anywhere, and that the Legislature of the State ought to furnish the means for its establishment.' A permanent Committee was then appointed by the Board to bring this matter to the attention of the public and the Legislature. This Committee held meetings in different parts of the State, and the following winter secured the introduction of a Bill for an Experiment Station, which, however, was laid over until the next Session of the Legislature. Another year of agitation of the matter ensued. The project had many warm and enthusiastic friends, but, as might have been expected, the great mass of the farmers took little interest in the enterprise. When it had become apparent that it could not succeed, Mr. Orange Judd, the editor and proprietor of the American 'Agriculturist,' offered on his own part 1,000 dollars to begin the undertaking, and on the part of the trustees of Wesleyan University at Middletown the free use of the chemical laboratory in the Orange Judd Hall of Natural Science.

"These offers were made on condition that the Legislature should appropriate 2,800 dollars per annum for two years for the work of the station. It was thought that if by these means the work of agricultural experimentation could actually be begun, the usefulness of the enterprise would be so clearly demonstrated that it would speedily receive more generous and permanent support. An Act making the appropriation thus proposed was unanimously passed and approved 2nd July, 1875. Early in October of the same year a chemist was on the ground, and, as soon as practicable, two assistants were secured. Professor Atwater was made Director, and thus the first Agricultural Experiment Station in America was an accomplished fact. Notwithstanding the severe financial depression of 1877, which caused serious reduction in old appropriations and utter refusal of new ones by the Legislature of that year, a Bill prepared by the Director of the Station, and making a permanent annual appropriation of 5,000 dollars " to promote agriculture by scientific investigation an experiment" was passed unanimously. At the end of the two years provided for in the original Bill, the station was reorganized under the direct control of the State, and permanently located in New Haven, where it has since been in successful operation, until 1882, in the chemical laboratory of the Sheffield Scientific School, and thereafter in buildings and on grounds provided by the State in the suburbs of the city.

" The success which attended this first attempt to establish an organized Experiment Station in the United States was sufficient to attract the attention of advanced agriculturists throughout the country, and the example set by Connecticut was soon followed in other States. In 1876 the University of California, at Berkeley, begun systematic experimental work in agriculture, and 12th March, 1877, the State of North Carolina established a station at Chapel Hill in connection with the State University. The Cornell University Experiment Station was organized in February 1879 by the Faculty of Agriculture of the University as a voluntary organization. From that time until the passage of the Act of Congress of 2nd March, 1887, the work work was carried on by the different professors in time which could be spared from other studies. For a part of that time the Trustees of the University appropriated money from the University funds to pay for the services of an analyst and for the purchase of supplies. All the other work was done without compensation. The New Jersey State Station at New Brunswick, N. J., was established 18th March, 1880, by an Act of the State Legislature, and connected with the scientific school of Rutgers College. The movement grew in favour with the people with each succeeding year, and in 1886 the Committee on Agriculture, in reporting the Hatch Bill to the House, was able to make the following statements:—

" ' Since 1881 the Legislatures of several States have either recognized or reorganized the Departments of Agriculture in the Land-Grant Colleges as " Experiment Stations," thus following substantially the course adopted by New Jersey. Such stations have been established in Maine, Massachusetts, Ohio, Tennessee, Wisconsin. In three other States (possibly more), without legislation, the college authorities have organized their agricultural work as experiment stations. This has been done in California, Missouri, and New York. But in addition to the twelve experiment stations specifically designated by that name, a very large number of the colleges established under the Act of 1862 are doing important work of a precisely similar kind. Many of them began such work immediately upon their establishment, and have since maintained it continuously; others have entered upon it more recently. The colleges in Colorado, Indiana, Kansas, Michigan, and Pennsylvania are carrying on what is strictly experiment-station work as a part of their ordinary duty.

"The Convention of Delegates of Agricultural Colleges which met at Washington in 1883 discussed and indorsed the project for the establishment of stations in connection with the colleges by appropriations from the National Treasury, in accordance with the terms of a Bill already introduced in the House of Representatives by C. C. Carpenter, of Iowa. Congress, however, was not yet quite ready to undertake so large a scientific enterprise in this direction, and the Bill was not put upon its passage. Meanwhile, the number of stations was steadily increasing, and the interest of practical farmers, as well as men of science, was more and more excited by the reports of the results of the experiments which the stations had completed.

"On the 8th July, 1885, a Convention of Agricultural Colleges and Experiment Stations met at the Department of Agriculture at Washington, in response to a call issued by the Commissioner of Agriculture. Almost the first thing which this Convention did was to pass a Resolution:—

"'That the condition and progress of American agriculture require national aid for the investigation and experimentation in the several States and territories; and that, therefore, this Convention approves the principle and general provisions of what is known as the Cullen Bill of the last Congress, and urges upon the next Congress the passage of this or a similar Act.'

"(The Cullen Bill was in its general provisions similar to the Bill afterwards passed by Congress, and now popularly known as the Hatch Act.)

"So earnest was the Convention in this matter, that it appointed a Committee on legislation, which was very efficient in securing the passage of the amended Bill.

"In a later Session the Convention passed Resolutions urging the creation of a branch of the Department of Agriculture at Washington, which should be a special medium of intercommunication and exchange between the colleges and stations, and which should publish a periodical bulletin of agricultural progress, containing in a popular form the latest results in the progress of agricultural education, investigation, and experimentation in this and in all countries. Provision was also made for a permanent organization by the appointment of a Committee to co-operate with the United States' Commissioner of Agriculture in determining the time of meeting and the business of the next Convention, and in forming a plan for a permanent organization.

"At the next Session of Congress the Experiment Station enterprise was again called to the attention of the House of Representatives by the Bill which was introduced by William H. Hatch, of Missouri, and referred to the Committee on Agriculture. This Committee made a favourable Report on the 3rd March, 1886, and nearly a year later the Bill was passed by Congress and approved by President Cleveland, the 2nd March, 1887.

"On the 18th October, 1887, the Second Convention of Agricultural Colleges and Experiment Stations convened at Washington. A permanent organization was effected, and the Association was named 'The Association of American Agricultural Colleges and Experiment Stations.' George W. Atherton, LL.D., President of the Pennsylvania State College, was elected President of the Association. This Convention was deeply interested in securing the co-ordination of the work of the several stations, and indorsed the action of previous Conventions in urging the establishment of a Central Bureau. As the result of the efforts of this Association, acting in harmony with the Commissioner of Agriculture, an appropriation for the purpose was included in the annual Appropriation Bill for the Department of Agriculture for the fiscal year ending the 30th June, 1889. To carry out the provisions of this Bill the Commissioner of Agriculture—as has been already stated in this bulletin—instituted, in October 1888, an Office of Experiment Stations as a special branch of the Department of Agriculture.

"In accordance with official interpretation of this Act by the Treasury Department, the stations were unable to draw the money contemplated until after the passage of a Supplementary Act, which was approved the 1st February, 1888. This financial difficulty delayed the establishment of the Stations in many of the States. At the present time, however, Experiment Stations are organized in all the States and in the territory of Dakota. In several States more than one station has been organized, and in some States there are several branch stations under one management. Counting these latter as single stations, the total number at present is forty-six, but counting the branch stations separately the total number is about sixty.

"The total number of the officers of the stations is about 370. For the fiscal year ending the 30th June, 1889, 585,000 dollars are appropriated from the United States' Treasury to the stations, and 10,000 dollars to the Office of Experiment Stations at Washington. In addition, the stations receive from the States and from other sources (as far as can be ascertained at this time) 125,400 dollars.

"A complete Report of the financial condition of the stations would undoubtedly increase this amount by several thousand dollars, so that it is safe to say that the total amount which will be expended by the stations during the current year will reach 725,000 dollars.

"Most of the new stations are in actual operation. Bulletins have been published giving accounts of their organization and of experimental and other work. The investigations cover a wide range of topics, and the stations have in nearly all cases manifested their wisdom by directing their investigations towards the solution of questions of special interest to the localities in which they are situated, without neglecting subjects of more general interest and wider application.

"The Experiment Station enterprise is now equipped for its great work. From its beginning, fourteen years ago, in the laboratory of a Connecticut College, it has grown out to the farthest limits of our great land, has enlisted the best colleges and universities and the ablest investigators of the country, and secured both State and national resources for its service. It has the favour not only of leading minds in science and education, but also of a great army of practical farmers, to whom it has already brought substantial benefits. As the Secretary of Agriculture has justly said:—

"'Of all the scientific enterprises which the Government has undertaken, scarcely any other has impressed its value upon the people and their representatives in the State and national Legislatures so speedily and so strongly as this. The rapid growth of an enterprise for elevating agriculture by the aid of science, its espousal by the United States' Government, its development to its present dimensions in the short period of fourteen years, and, finally, the favour with which it is received by the public at large, are a striking illustration of the appreciation on the part of the American people of the wisdom and the usefulness of calling the highest science to the aid of the arts and industries of life.

"'The present is an auspicious time for this undertaking. "In the history of no nation before have there been such a thirst for knowledge on the part of the great masses of the people, such high and just appreciation of its value, and such wide-reaching, successful and popular schemes for self-education; no other nation has so large a body of farmers of high intelligence, never before has the great agricultural public been so willing, and indeed so anxious, to receive with respect and use with intelligence the information which science offers; never before has science had so much to give." The prospects, then, for this, the largest scientific enterprise in behalf of agriculture that any Government has undertaken, are full of promise.'

On the 9th February, 1889, an Act was approved by which the Department of Agriculture was made an Executive Department under the control of a Secretary of Agriculture.

The Act runs as follows:—

"*An Act to enlarge the Powers and Duties of the Department of Agriculture, and to create an Executive Department, to be known as the Department of Agriculture.*

"Be it enacted, by the Senate and House of Representatives of the United States of America in Congress assembled, that the Department of Agriculture shall be an Executive Department, under the supervision and control of a Secretary of Agriculture, who shall be appointed by the President, by and with the advice and consent of the Senate ; and section 158 of the Revised Statutes is hereby amended to include such Department, and the provisions of Title 4 of the Revised Statutes, including all amendments thereto, are hereby made applicable to said Department.

"Section 2. That there shall be in said Department an Assistant Secretary of Agriculture, to be appointed by the President, by and with the advice and consent of the Senate, who shall perform such duties as may be required by law or prescribed by the Secretary.

"Sec. 3. That the Secretary of Agriculture shall receive the same salary as is paid to the Secretary of each of the Executive Departments, and the salary of the Assistant Secretary of Agriculture shall be the same as that now paid to the First Assistant Secretary of the Department of the Interior.

"Sec. 4. That all laws and parts of laws relating to the Department of Agriculture now in existence, as far as the same are applicable and not in conflict with this Act, and only so far, are continued in full force and effect.

"Approved 9th February, 1889."

No changes in the organization of the Department were made at the time of the change of the position and rank of the Head, although several were at first proposed to Congress.

These were ultimately withdrawn, but it is anticipated that on the meeting of Congress they will be again presented, and, should they be approved, the scope and duties of the Department will be still further enlarged.

The Department as it now exists under the Secretary consists of the following divisions :—

"*The Statistician.*—He collects information as to the condition, prospects, and harvests of the principal crops, and of the numbers and status of farm animals, through a corps of county correspondents, and the aid of a supplementary organization under the direction of State Agents, and obtains similar information from European countries monthly through the Deputy Consul-General at London, assisted by Consular, agricultural, and commercial authorities. He records, tabulates, and co-ordinates statistics of agricultural production, distribution, and consumption, the authorized data of Governments, Institutes, Societies, Boards of Trade, and individual experts ; and writes, edits, and publishes a monthly bulletin for the use of editors and writers, and for the information of producers and consumers, and for their protection against combination and extortion in the handling of the products of agriculture.

"*The Entomologist.*—He obtains and disseminates information regarding insects injurious to vegetation ; investigates insects sent him in order to give appropriate remedies ; conducts investigations of this character in different parts of the country ; mounts and arranges specimens for illustrative and museum purposes. The silk branch of the Division distributes silk-worm eggs and pamphlets giving instruction in silk culture, and furnishes general information relating to the industry. It also operates an experimental silk filature where silk cocoons are purchased at the current market price.

"*The Botanist* investigates plants and grasses of agricultural value or of injurious character, and answers inquiries relating to the same; also has charge of the Herbarium, receives botanical contributions and purchases for its improvement, and distributes duplicate specimens to agricultural colleges and educational institutions.

"*The Chemist.*—He makes analyses of natural fertilizers, vegetable products, and other materials which pertain to the interests of agriculture. Applications are constantly made from all portions of the country for the analysis of soils, minerals, liquids, and manures.

"*The Microscopist.*—He makes original investigations, mostly relating to the habits of parasitic fungoid plants, which are frequently found on living plants and animals, producing sickly growth, and in many cases premature death.

"*The Propagating Garden.*—Large numbers of exotic, utilizable, and economic plants are propagated and distributed. The orange family is particularly valuable, and the best commercial varieties are propagated and distributed to the greatest practicable extent.

"*The Seed Division.*—Seeds are purchased in this and foreign countries of reliable firms, whose guaranty of good quality and genuineness cannot be questioned; they are packed at the Department, and distributed to applicants in all parts of the country.

"*The Library.*—Exchanges are made by which the library receives Reports of the leading Agricultural, Pomological, and Meteorological Societies of the world.

"*The Bureau of Animal Industry* makes investigations as to the existence of contagious pleuro-pneumonia and other dangerous communicable diseases of live stock, superintends the measures for their extirpation, and makes original investigations as to the nature and prevention of such diseases; has charge of the quarantine stations for imported neat cattle; also reports on the condition and means of improving the animal industries of the country.

"*The Forestry Division* experiments, investigates, and reports upon the subject of forestry, and distributes valuable economic tree seeds and plants, and answers inquiries in regard to desirable kinds for forest planting, their modes of propagation, and other forestry matter.

"*The Ornithological Division* investigates the economic relations of birds and mammals, and recommends measures for the preservation of beneficial and destruction of injurious species.

"*Office of Experiment Stations.*—This Office represents the Department in its relations to the Agricultural Experiment Stations in the several States and territories. Its object is to secure, as far as practicable, uniformity of methods and results in the work of the stations, and more generally to furnish such advice and assistance to them as will best promote the purposes of the Act of Congress by which they are established. To this end, its duty is

123

to furnish forms for the tabulation of investigations or experiments, to indicate from time to time such lines of inquiry as may seem most important, to bring to the stations the fruits of scientific research, to facilitate inter-communication between them, and to compare, edit, and publish such of the results of their experiments as may be deemed necessary."

The following is the Act making an appropriation for the Department for the year ending the 30th June, 1890, amounting to the sum of 1,669,770 dollars, or 347,868*l.* :—

"*An Act making an Appropriation for the Department of Agriculture for the fiscal Year ending June* 30, 1890, *and for other purposes.*

" Be it enacted, by the Senate and House of Representatives of the United States of America in Congress assembled, that the following sums be, and they are hereby, appropriated out of any money in the Treasury of the United States not otherwise appropriated, in full compensation tor the fiscal year ending the 30th June, 1890, for the purposes and objects hereinafter expressed, namely :

"DEPARTMENT OF AGRICULTURE.

"*Office of the Secretary.*

"For compensation of Secretary of Agriculture, 8,000 dollars; Assistant Secretary of Agriculture, 4,500 dollars; Chief Clerk in said Department, who shall be Superintendent of the Department buildings, 2,500 dollars; Chief of Division of Accounts and Disbursing Officer, 2,000 dollars; one Assistant Disbursing Officer, who shall act as Property Clerk, 1,400 dollars; one Clerk to Disbursing Officer, 1,400 dollars; Clerk to Disbursing Officer, 1,000 dollars; one Stenographer, 1,800 dollars; one Engraver, 2,000 dollars; one Draughtsman, 2,000 dollars; two Clerks of class 4, 3,600 dollars; two Clerks of Class 3, 3,200 dollars; four Clerks of Class 2, 5,600 dollars; seven Clerks of Class 1, 8,400 dollars; eight Clerks, at 1,000 dollars each; six clerks, at 840 dollars each; one Librarian, 1,800 dollars; one Assistant Librarian, 1,400 dollars; one Engineer, 1,400 dollars; one Fireman at 720 dollars; one Fireman, who shall be a steam-fitter, at 900 dollars; one Assistant Fireman at 500 dollars; Superintendent of Folding-room, 1,400 dollars; four Assistants in Folding-room at 600 dollars each; one Clerk in Folding-room at 660 dollars; two Night Watchmen, at 720 dollars each; messengers, carpenters, labourers, and charwomen, 10,000 dollars; in all, 83,060 dollars.

"*Botanical Division.*

"One Botanist, 2,500 dollars; one Assistant Botanist, 1,400 dollars; one Botanical Clerk, 1,000 dollars; one Assistant Botanist, 1,200 dollars.

Section of Vegetable Pathology: One Chief of Section, 2,000 dollars; one Assistant, 1,400 dollars; one Clerk, 1,000 dollars: in all, for Botanical Division, 10,500 dollars.

"*Pomological Division.*

"One Pomologist, 2,500 dollars; one Clerk, 1,000 dollars; in all, for Pomological Division, 3,500 dollars.

"*Microscopical Division.*

"One Microscopist, 2,500 dollars; one Assistant Microscopist, 1,200 dollars; in all, 3,700 dollars.

"*Chemical Division.*

"One Chief Chemist, 2,500 dollars; one Assistant Chemist, 1,800 dollars; one Assistant Chemist, 1,600 dollars; employment of additional Assistants in the Chemical Division when necessary, 6,000 dollars; in all, 11,900 dollars.

"*Entomological Division.*

"One Entomologist, 2,500 dollars; one Assistant Entomologist, 1,800 dollars; one Assistant Entomologist or Clerk, 1,600 dollars; one Assistant Entomologist or Clerk, 1,400 dollars; in all, 7,300 dollars.

"*Division of Economic Ornithology and Mammalogy.*

"One Ornithologist, 2,500 dollars; one Assistant Ornithologist, 1,600 dollars; one Assistant Ornithologist, 1,500 dollars; one Clerk at 1,200 dollars; one Clerk at 660 dollars; and one Clerk at 600 dollars; in all, 8,060 dollars.

"*Experimental Garden and Grounds.*

"One Superintendent, 2,500 dollars.

"*Museum.*

"One Curator of Museum, 1,400 dollars; one Assistant, 1,000 dollars; one Night Watchman for Museum building, who shall also act as Night Watchman for Seed building, 720 dollars; in all, 3,120 dollars.

"*Seed Division.*

"One Chief of Seed Division, 2,000 dollars; one Superintendent of Seed-room, 1,600 dollars; four Clerks at 1,000 dollars each; one Clerk at 840 dollars; in all, 8,440 dollars.

125

"*Statistical Division.*

"One Statistician, 2,500 dollars; one Assistant Statistician, 2,000 dollars; one Clerk of Class 4, three Clerks of Class 3, 4,800 dollars; four Clerks of Class 2, 5,600 dollars; five Clerks of Class 1, 6,000 dollars; seven Clerks at 1,000 dollars each; four Clerks at 840 dollars each; two Clerks at 720 dollars each; in all, 34,500 dollars.

"*Forestry Division.*

"One Chief of Forestry Division, 2,000 dollars.

"*Miscellaneous.*

"Botanical Investigations and Experiments.—Botanical Division: For purchasing specimens, paper, and all necessary materials for the Herbarium, and for labour in preparing same; for investigations and experiments with grasses and forage plants, including the establishment and maintenance of experimental grass stations, and of other economic and medicinal plants, and for travelling and other necessary expenses connected therewith, and for employing local botanists for exploration and collection of plants in little known districts, and for special work for the improvement of the Herbarium, and for artists for drawing and engraving, 20,000 dollars. And the unexpended balance of appropriations under this head for the current fiscal year is hereby reappropriated and made available for the fiscal year 1890.

"Section of Vegetable Pathology: For investigating the nature of the diseases of fruits and fruit-trees, grain, and other useful plants, due to parasitic fungi; for chemicals and apparatus required in the field and laboratory; for experiments with remedies; for necessary travelling expenses; for the preparation of drawings and illustrations, and for other expenses connected with the practical work of the investigation, 15,000 dollars, of which 10,000 dollars, or so much thereof as may be necessary, may be applied to the investigation of the disease in peach trees known as yellows, and remedies therefor.

"Pomological Information.—Pomological Division: For travelling within the United States and other necessary expenses in investigating, collecting, and disseminating pomological information, 4,000 dollars.

"Investigating the Adulteration of Food.—Microscopical Division: For microscopical apparatus, chemicals, photographic illustrations, and other necessary supplies; for travelling expenses, and for the purchase of food samples and fibres in making investigations and examinations into the adulterations of food, 1,000 dollars.

"Laboratory.—Chemical Division: For chemical apparatus, chemicals, laboratory fixtures and supplies, purchase of samples, and necessary expenses in conducting special investigations, including necessary travelling expenses, labour, and expert work in such investigations, 6,000 dollars.

"Chemical Division: To enable the Secretary of Agriculture to extend and continue the investigation of the adulteration of food, drugs, and liquors, including the purchase of samples, transportation, travelling expenses, stationery, return postage, printing and illustrating, analyzing, investigating, and examining samples, purchased on the open market, the sum of 5,000 dollars, to be made immediately available; and for these purposes the Secretary of Agriculture is authorized to employ such assistants, clerks, and other persons as he may deem necessary: Provided, that the Secretary is hereby required to make a separate Report to Congress as to when and where the samples of food, liquors, and drugs were purchased, when and where analyzed, and the result of such analysis, together with the name of the manufacturer and the brand or label on the package or article.

"Investigating the History and Habits of Insects.—Entomological Division: For the promotion of economic entomology, investigating the history and habits of insects injurious and beneficial to agriculture, arboriculture, and horticulture; experiments in ascertaining the best means of destroying them, and preventives to the biting of domestic animals by poisonous insects, and remedies and antidotes for such bites; for publishing Reports thereon; and for illustrations, chemicals, travelling within the United States, and other expenses in the practical work of the Entomological Division, 20,000 dollars.

"For collecting and disseminating information relating to silk culture; for purchasing and distributing silk-worm eggs, and for conducting at some point in the district of Columbia experiments with automatic machinery for reeling silk from the cocoon, and for expenses incurred in collecting, purchasing, preparing for transportation, and transporting cocoons, and for expenses of stations in connection therewith, and for necessary travelling expenses, 20,000 dollars. And the Secretary of Agriculture is hereby authorized to sell in open market any and all reeled silk and silk waste produced in these experiments, and to apply the proceeds of such sales to the payment of the legitimate expenses incurred therein; and the Secretary of Agriculture shall make full report to Congress of the experiments herein provided for, and also of all sales and purchases made under this paragraph, with the names and residences of all producers of cocoons of whom purchases are made.

"For the encouragement and development of the culture of raising raw silk, 5,000 dollars to be expended under the direction of the Woman's Silk Culture Association of the United States, located at Philadelphia, and to be paid directly to said Association; and said Association shall make a full and detailed Report of the expenditures and results obtained under this appropriation to the Secretary of Agriculture, who shall transmit the same to Congress, and 2,500 dollars for the same purposes and under the same restrictions and conditions to the Ladies' Silk Culture Society of California, and for the continuation of the study and experiments by Joseph Neumann of the wild native silk-worm of California, 2,500 dollars, to be paid directly to said Joseph Neumann; and the said Joseph Neumann shall report the results of such work to the Secretary of Agriculture on or before the 1st day of January, 1890.

"Division of Economic Ornithology and Mammalogy: For the promotion of economic ornithology and mammalogy; an investigation of the food habits, distribution, and migrations of North American birds and mammals, in relation to agriculture, horticulture, and forestry; for publishing Report thereon; and for drawings, travelling, and other expenses in the practical work of the Division, 7,000 dollars, of which sum 1,000 dollars shall be immediately available.

"Experimental Gardens and Grounds: For labour in experimental gardens and grounds, the care of conservatories, plant, and fruit, propagating and seed-testing houses, the keep of the reservation, lawns, trees, roadways, and walks, 12,000 dollars.

"For blacksmithing, the purchase of tools, waggons, carts, harness, lawn-mowers, and other machinery, and the necessary labour and material for repairing the same; for the purchase of new and rare kinds of seed, plants, and bulbs for propagating purposes, including expense of material and labour in packing plants for distribution and for transportation; for necessary pots, tubs, watering-cans, and hose, materials for the destruction of insects, and all other necessary items for the cultivation and improvement of the grounds and arboretum; for the purchase of glass, paints, lumber, and tin for roofing and spouting, hardware, and for carpenter, painter, and other mechanical work necessary for keeping in good repair the conservatories, green-houses, and other garden structures, 14,640 dollars.

"Museum: For collecting and modelling fruits, vegetables, and other plants, for labour and material in preparing them for the museum, 1,000 dollars.

"Seed Division: For the purchase, propagation, and distribution, as required by law, of seeds, bulbs, trees, shrubs, vines, cuttings, and plants, and expenses of labour, transportation, paper, twine, gum, printing, postal-cards, and all necessary material and repairs for putting up and distributing the same, and to be distributed in localities adapted to their culture, 100,000 dollars.

"An equal proportion of two-thirds of all seeds, trees, shrubs, vines, cuttings, and plants, shall, upon their request, be supplied to Senators, Representatives, and Delegates in Congress for distribution among their constituents; and the person receiving such seeds shall inform the Department of results of the experiments therewith: Provided that all seeds, plants, and cuttings herein allotted to Senators, Representatives, and Delegates to Congress for distribution remaining uncalled for at the end of the fiscal year shall be distributed by the Secretary of Agriculture: And provided also that the Secretary shall report, as provided in this Act, the place, quantity, and price of seeds purchased, and the date of purchase. But nothing in this paragraph shall be construed to prevent the Secretary of Agriculture from sending flower, garden, and other seeds to those who apply for the same. And the

[431]

amount herein appropriated shall not be diverted or used for any other purpose but for the purchase, propagation, and distribution of improved and valuable seeds, bulbs, trees, shrubs, vines, cuttings, and plants: But provided, however, that the Secretary shall not distribute to any Senator, Representative, or Delegate seeds entirely unfit for the climate aud locality he represents, but shall distribute the same, so that each member may have seeds of equal value, as may be, and the best adapted to the locality he represents.

"Printing seed-pockets, labels, postal-cards, circulars, and so forth, labour, paper, ink, type, and other necessary material for printing, and for repairing presses, 4,200 dollars.

"Collecting Agricultural Statistics, Division of Agricultural Statistics: For collecting domestic and foreign agricultural statistics; for expenses of local investigations and compilations, and for necessary travelling expenses; for statistical publications furnishing data for permanent comparative records; for compiling, writing, and illustrating statistical matter for monthly, annual, and special Reports, and for the necessary expenses of the same, including paper and envelopes, postal-cards, and postage-stamps, 75,000 dollars: Provided that 10,000 dollars of this sum, or so much thereof as may be necessary, may be expended for the preparation and printing of Maps and Charts, illustrating the progress of rural production and crop distribution of the United States, and for special investigation of the agricultural statistics of the States and territories of the Rocky Mountain region, with travelling and other necessary expenses connected therewith.

"Furniture, Cases, and Repairs: For repairing buildings, heating apparatus, furniture, carpeting, matting, water, and gas pipes, new furniture, and all necessary material and labour for the same, including lumber, hardware, glass, and paints, 7,350 dollars.

"Library: For entomological, botanical, and historical works of reference, works on chemistry, forestry, mineralogy, Maps, Charts, current agricultural works for library, miscellaneous agricultural periodicals, and the completion of imperfect series, 2,000 dollars.

"Salaries and Expenses Bureau of Animal Industry: For carrying out the provisions of the Act of the 29th May, 1884, establishing the Bureau of Animal Industry, 500,000 dollars; and the Secretary of Agriculture is hereby authorized to use any part of this sum he may deem necessary or expedient, and in such manner as he may think best, to prevent the spread of pleuro-pneumonia, and for this purpose to employ as many persons as he may deem necessary, and to expend any part of this sum in the purchase and destruction of diseased or exposed animals and the quarantine of the same whenever in his judgment it is essential to prevent the spread of pleuro-pneumonia from one State into another: Provided that 15,000 dollars, or so much thereof as may be necessary, may be expended in continuation of the investigations and experiments, to be conducted within the United States, into the nature, causes, and remedies for the prevention and cure of hog cholera and swine plague. The authority granted to the Commissioner of Agriculture by the Act of the 29th May, 1884, establishing the Bureau of Animal Industry, and by the provision of the Appropriation Act for the Agricultural Department, approved the 18th July, 1888, relating to said Bureau, is hereby vested in the Secretary of Agriculture; and the said Secretary is hereby authorized and directed to perform all the duties named in said Acts and all other Acts of Congress in force on the 8th February, 1889, to be performed by the Commissioner of Agriculture.

"Quarantine Stations for Neat-cattle: To establish and maintain quarantine stations, and to provide proper shelter for, and care of, neat-cattle imported, at such ports as may be deemed necessary, 15,000 dollars.

"Division of Forestry: For the purpose of enabling the Secretary of Agriculture to experiment and to continue an investigation and report upon the subject of forestry, and for travelling and other necessary expenses in the investigation and the collection and distribution of valuable economic forest-tree seeds and plants, 8,000 dollars.

"Postage: For postage on return-letters, circulars, and miscellaneous articles for correspondents and foreign mail, 4,000 dollars.

"Contingent Expenses: For stationery, freight, express charges, fuel, lights, subsistence, and care of horses, repairs of harness, for paper, twine, and gum for Folding-room, advertising, telegraphing, dry-goods, soap, brushes, brooms, mats, oils, paints, glass, lumber, hardware, ice, purchasing supplies, washing towels, actual travelling expenses while on the business of the Department, and other miscellaneous supplies and expenses not otherwise provided for, and necessary for the practical and efficient work of the Department, 15,000 dollars.

"Experiments in Manufacture of Sugar from Sorghum and Beets: To enable the Secretary of Agriculture to continue experiments in the manufacture of sugar from sorghum and from beets, and especially to so continue said experiments as to result in the acquisition and extension of knowledge concerning all the processes of the production of cane and beets and the best varieties of the same, and the manufacture of the same into sugar, including the purchase and transportation of samples and supplies, 25,000 dollars. And the sum remaining unexpended from the appropriation for this purpose for the fiscal year 1889 is hereby reappropriated and made available for the purposes hereinbefore expressed: Provided that the Secretary of Agriculture is hereby required to make a separate Report to Congress, on or before the 1st day of February, 1890, stating fully and accurately an itemized account of every expenditure made under this provision and the results of all experiments made, and also including the purchase and transportation of samples and supplies.

"*Experimental Stations.*

"That to carry into effect the provisions of an Act approved the 2nd March, 1887, entitled, 'An Act to establish Agricultural

Experiment Stations in connection with the Colleges established in the several States, under the provisions of an Act approved the 2nd July, 1862, and of the Acts supplementary thereto, 600,000 dollars, 15,000 dollars of which sum shall be payable upon the order of the Secretary of Agriculture to enable him to carry out the provisions of section 3 of said Act of the 2nd March, 1887, and to compare, edit, and publish such of the results of the experiments made under section 2 of said Act by said Experimental Stations as he may deem necessary; and for these purposes the Secretary of Agriculture is authorized to employ such assistants, clerks, and other persons as he may deem necessary: Provided that, as far as practicable, all such stations shall devote a portion of their work to the examination and classification of the soils of their respective States and territories, with a view to securing more extended knowledge and better development of their agricultural capabilities.

" Approved, March 2, 1889."

(52)

UNITED STATES.

No. 25.

Mr. Edwardes to the Marquis of Salisbury.—(*Received August* 20.)

My Lord, *Washington, August* 7, 1889.

WITH reference to your Lordship's Circular despatch of the 27th May last, instructing Sir Julian Pauncefote to obtain information respecting the Laws in this country affecting the hours of adult labour, and respecting the enforcement, or otherwise, of such Laws, I have now the honour to forward herewith the Reports which I have received on the subject from Her Majesty's Consul-General at New York, and from Her Majesty's Consuls in this country.

I have, &c.
(Signed) H. G. EDWARDES.

Inclosure 1 in No. 25.

Consul-General Booker to Sir J. Pauncefote.

Sir, *New York, July* 9, 1889.

I HAVE the honour to acknowledge the receipt of your despatch of the 11th June, requesting to be furnished with information in regard to the Laws enacted in the States comprised in my Consular district affecting the hours of adult labour with the actual hours now worked.

New York.

The only Acts affecting the hours of adult labour in force in New York are—An Act passed in 1870 to regulate the hours of labour of mechanics, working men, and labourers in the employ of the State or otherwise engaged on "public works."

Section 1 of this Act makes eight hours a legal day's work for all classes of mechanics, working men, and labourers, excepting those engaged in farm and domestic labour; but overwork for an extra compensation by agreement between employer and employé is permitted.

Section 2 makes this Act apply to all mechanics, working men, and labourers employed by the State or any Municipal Corporation therein, through its agents or officers, or in the employ of persons contracting with the State or such Corporation for performance of public works.

Section 3 makes it a misdemeanour for violation of the Act.

An Act passed in 1886 to regulate the hours of labour in the street surface and elevated railroads chartered by the State in cities of over 500,000 inhabitants.

Section 1 of this Act makes twelve hours' labour in twenty-four, with reasonable time for meals, constitute a day's labour in the operation of all street surface and elevated railroads owned or operated by Corporations incorporated under the Laws of this State, whose main lines of travel or whose routes be principally within the corporate limits of cities of more than 500,000 inhabitants, whatever motive power may be used in the operation of such railroads.

Section 2 makes it a misdemeanour for any officer or agent of any such Corporation to exact from any of its employés more than twelve consecutive hours' labour in the twenty-four, with one half-hour for dinner, but provides that in cases of accident or unavoidable delay extra labour may be permitted for extra compensation.

Section 3 provides that this Act shall not affect contracts now in force, nor apply to existing Corporations whose Charters are not subject to alteration, modification, or repeal.

An Act passed in 1887 to regulate the hours of labour in the street surface and elevated railroads chartered by the State in cities of 100,000 and over.

Section 1 of this Act makes ten hours' labour to be performed in within twelve consecutive hours, with reasonable time for meals, constitute a day's labour in the operation of all street surface and elevated railroads owned and operated by Corporations incorporated under the Laws of this State, whose main line of travel or whose routes lie principally within the Corporate limits of cities of more than 100,000 inhabitants, whatever motive power may be used in the operation of such railroads.

Section 2 makes it a misdemeanour for any officer or agent of any such Corporation to exact from any of its employés more than ten hours' labour to be performed within twelve consecutive hours, with not less than one half-hour for dinner, but provides that in case of accident or unavoidable delay extra labour may be permitted for extra compensation.

Section 3 is the same as section 3 in the Act of 1886.

Section 4 repeals all Acts inconsistent with this Act.

The Act of 1887 would seem to repeal the Act of 1886, as it changes the hours of labour in the latter, twelve within twenty-four, to ten within twelve, and in both Acts a reasonable time for meals is provided for.

In this and the other cities of the State nearly all classes of mechanics, and all connected with the building trade, work nine hours per day, except on Saturday, when eight hours is the rule.

Some engineers and railroad employés work ten hours per day, and ordinary labourers ten hours.

On the elevated railroads of this city and Brooklyn the drivers work nine hours per day, and the guards, gatemen, and ticket agents ten. On the surface railroads (tramcars) conductors and drivers average nine and a-half hours; starters, switchmen, roadmen, and ostlers ten, and watchmen eleven and a-half hours.

New Jersey.

The only Act on the Statute Book is one in regard to the hours of labour of employés of surface and elevated railroad Companies, passed in 1887, in which it is enacted that twelve hours' labour, to be performed within twelve consecutive hours, with reasonable time for meals, not less than half-an-hour for each, shall constitute a day's labour in the operation of all cable, traction, and horse-car street surface railroads, and of all cable, traction, and steam elevated railroads, owned or operated under the Laws of New Jersey, but provision is made that, in case of accident or unexpected contingency demanding more than the usual service, extra labour may be permitted and exacted for extra compensation.

According to the statistics published by the State Commissioner, 9 per cent. of the members of the New Jersey Trades Unions and Knights of Labour Local Assemblies work more than sixty hours per week, and this may be considered to hold good for those not belonging to Trades Unions and Knights of Labour. About one-half work sixty hours per week, and the remainder, including all connected with the building trade, fifty-four or fifty-three hours, those working fifty-three working eight hours on Saturdays.

Among those working over sixty hours per week may be found bakers, barbers, and some classes of engineers and railway employés. Those working sixty hours per week comprise employés of mills and manufactories, hat-makers, some classes of engineers, book compositors, teamsters, &c.

Rhode Island.

The only Act on the Statute Book in regard to hours of labour is one making ten hours of labour of adults in any manufacturing establishment and all mechanical labour a legal day's work unless otherwise agreed by the parties to the contract for the same. The hours of labour in the State are the same as those of New York and New Jersey.

Delaware.

This State has no Statute Law in regard to labour, and the hours are the same as those of the preceding States.

55

Connecticut.

The only Act on the Statute Book is one making eight hours of labour performed in any one day by any one person a lawful day's work, unless otherwise agreed.

The Commissioner of Labour Statistics states that, with but very few exceptions, the hours of labour of mechanics and other labouring people are ten hours per day, or sixty hours per week. In many factories the employés work more than ten hours for five days, and make a shorter day of Saturday to bring the hours of the week to sixty. The exceptions to sixty hours per week are in industries like paper manufactories, where the machinery runs continuously day and night, and two sets of hands are employed, each set working twelve hours. In no case do women work more than ten hours per day.

I have, &c.
(Signed)   WM. LANE BOOKER.

Inclosure 2 in No. 25.

Consul Segrave to Sir J. Pauncefote.

Sir,   *Baltimore, June* 20, 1889.

REFERRING to your despatch of the 11th instant, I have now the honour to transmit to you the accompanying paper, containing such information as I have been enabled to gather regarding the Laws and customs which affect the hours of adult labour within the States of Maryland and Virginia.

I have, &c.
(Signed)   W. F. SEGRAVE.

Inclosure 3 in No. 25.

Report by Consul Segrave on Hours of Labour.

Maryland.

IN the State of Maryland there are no Federal Laws in force which regulate the hours of labour.

The State Laws with the above object only apply—

1. To the workmen in the State tobacco warehouses, who, under the Act of 1872, cap. 36, are limited to ten hours a-day.

2. To miners. The Act of 1886, cap. 303, provides that the hours of labour for miners shall be ten a-day, and under sub-section 1 it is provided that any violation of its provisions shall subject the offender to a fine not exceeding 50 dollars.

3. Street car and horse railway drivers. The Act of 1886,

cap. 137, provides that no horse railway Company incorporated under the Laws of the State, or any servant thereof, shall require or permit its conductors or drivers to work for more than twelve hours during each day of twenty-four hours.

Section 2 provides that any Corporation as above, which shall violate the provisions of the Act, shall be deemed to have abused its corporate powers, and, on written application of any citizen, accompanied by adequate evidence, the Attorney-General shall institute proceedings for the forfeiture of the Charter of such offending Corporation.

Section 3 provides that any Corporation as above, or servant of such, who shall violate the provisions of this Act, shall be deemed guilty of a misdemeanour, and, on conviction, be fined 100 dollars for each offence, as well as the costs of the proceedings.

The practical operation of the Act, however, is to materially reduce the pay of the servants of the Companies, as well as their hours of work.

In the early part of 1886 a movement was organized in this State to establish a uniform working day of eight hours, and at one time it was said that it had a membership of something like a quarter of a million of men.

The furniture workers and building trades were the most conspicuous in enforcing the demand.

Piece-workers were, as a rule, indifferent as compared to those employed by the day.

The movement, however, was generally a failure, though some trades which adopted the nine hours rule succeeded in reducing the hours of the day's work.

Notably may be mentioned bricklayers, stonemasons, painters, and stone-cutters, but carpenters and other trades which maintained the eight hours rule have not succeeded. Since then the tendency has been more in the direction of Trade Unionism than towards the mixed organization of the Knights of Labour.

The movement may be said to have been a partial success for trades demanding nine hours a-day, and a failure for those demanding eight hours.

As a whole, it may be said that in Maryland ten hours may be taken as the actual working day for men, and for women in factories nine hours during eleven months of the year.

Virginia.

There are no Federal Laws in force in Virginia regulating the hours of labour in general, but under the Revised Statutes of the United States, 2nd edition, 1878, cap. 43, section 3738, labourers employed on Government works, in navy yards, &c., are restricted to eight hours a-day. Neither is there any State legislation which affects the hours of labour; but whilst not regulated by law, they are not the less strictly defined by custom and combination in the different branches of employment.

Agricultural labourers work from sunrise to sunset. Bricklayers work eight hours.

Ten hours may, however, be considered the working day for nine-tenths of the labourers employed in this State.

If, however, the State does not regulate the hours of labour, it legislates in the working-man's interest in another direction.

Under the Act of the Assembly, 1887, cap. 391, it is prescribed that all wages shall be paid in cash, and not in checks.

And in the Act of 1887, cap. 178, sections 3630 to 3657, termed the "Homestead exemption," the property of a labouring man, up to the value of 2,000 dollars, is exempt from attachment for debt.

(Signed)   W. F. SEGRAVE,
Her Britannic Majesty's Consul.

Baltimore, June 20, 1889.

Inclosure 4 in No. 25.

Consul Clipperton to Sir J. Pauncefote.

Sir,   *Philadelphia, July* 24, 1889.

I HAVE the honour to acknowledge the receipt of your despatch of the 11th ultimo, requesting all the information and documents I am able to obtain on the subject of the Laws enacted affecting the hours of adult labour within this Consular jurisdiction.

In reply, I beg to report that, in the State of Pennsylvania, eight hours constitute a day's labour, but this Law does not apply to farm or agricultural labour, or services by the month or week; nor does the Law prevent any person working as many hours' overtime, or extra work, as he or she may see fit, by agreement between the employer and the employé.

The other provisions of the Law relate to the mode of paying wages or determining disputes between the employed and the employer; how persons shall be liable in mines and in manufactories, as well as other matters not bearing directly on the hours of labour.

The Law also relates to the employment of children, forbidding it under the age of 12 years by any person or Corporation.

In the State of Michigan, in all factories, workshops, salt-blocks, saw-mills, logging and lumber camps, booms and drives, mines or other places used for mechanical, manufacturing, or other purposes where men or women are employed, ten hours per day shall constitute a legal day's work, and any proprietor, stockholder, manager, clerk, foreman, or other employers of labour who shall require any person or persons in their employ to perform more than ten hours per day shall be compelled to pay such employés for all overtime or extra hours at the regular per diem rate, unless there be an agreement to the contrary.

In all contracts or agreements to labour in any mechanical,

manufacturing, or other labour, calling, silent, or no express conditions specified, ten hours shall constitute a day's work, and the contract or agreement shall be so construed.

Any individual, firm, agent, or any Corporation, or other employers of labour who shall take any unlawful advantage of any person or persons in their employ, or seeking employment, because of their poverty or misfortune, to invalidate any of the provisions of the preceding section, shall be deemed guilty of a misdemeanour, and, upon conviction thereof, shall be fined not less than 5 dollars, nor more than 50 dollars, for each offence, and it shall be the duty of the Prosecuting Attorney of the county in which such offence was committed, upon receiving complaint, to prosecute all such cases in the name of the people of the State of Michigan before any Justice of the Peace or other competent Court of jurisdiction.

All fines collected for violation of the Act shall be turned over to the School Board or Board of Education of the city or township wherein such fine may be collected, and the same shall by them be disbursed for and in benefit of the public schools.

Nothing in the Act shall be construed to apply to domestic or farm labourers, or other labourers who agree to work more than ten hours per day.

In the State of Indiana a Law was passed on the 6th March, 1889, making eight hours a legal day's work for all classes of mechanics, working men, and labourers, excepting those engaged in agricultural or domestic labour, but overwork for extra compensation is permitted. The Law applies to all classes or character of employers or their agents or officers.

The violation of the Law is made a misdemeanour punishable by a fine not greater than 500 dollars, and if the person violating the Law has a public position he shall be removed therefrom.

In Ohio, the remaining State of this Consular district, no Law bearing upon this subject has been enacted by the Legislature. The hours for a day's labour in that State, therefore, would be ten hours, or any other time agreed upon by the employer and employé.

I have, &c.
(Signed) ROBERT CHAS. CLIPPERTON.

Inclosure 5 in No. 25.

Consul Cridland to Sir J. Pauncefote.

Sir, *Charleston, July* 13, 1889.

IN answer to your despatch of the 11th ultimo, I have the honour to state that the State Legislatures of North and South Carolina and Tennessee have thus far passed no Laws regulating the hours of adult labour in their States. This is probably owing to the fact that only of late years capitalists have established factories and developed the mines in the Southern States of this country.

In the Code of Laws enacted by the State Legislature of Georgia the only paragraph having reference to the hours of labour is as follows:—

"Section 1885. The hours of labour by all persons under 21 years of age in all cotton, woollen, or other manufacturing establishments or machine shops in this State shall be from sunrise until sunset, the usual and customary times for meals being allowed from the same; and any contract made with such persons or their parents, guardians, or others, whereby a longer time for labour is agreed upon or provided for, shall be null and void so far as relates to the enforcement of said contracts against such labourers."

In the factories in South Carolina the hours of labour are generally from 7 A.M. till 6 P.M., one hour being allowed for dinner, 12 to 1 P.M. On Saturday some of the establishments close earlier in the afternoon, especially during the summer months. These hours apply also to mechanics and out-day labourers. The street car-drivers commence work at 6 A.M. and continue till 10 P.M., and eat their meals as best they can.

The recognized hours of labour in the State of Georgia are as follows:—

Monday to Friday, 6·30 A.M. to 6·30 P.M.; Saturday, 6·30 A.M. to 3 P.M.; with half-an-hour for dinner each day.

As before stated, there are no Laws in the State of North Carolina affecting the hours of adult labour, but it appears that, according to custom, the hours of adult labour range from eight to fourteen hours per day, the average being about ten hours. The average hours of work in factories are twelve, with one hour for meals.

In the State of Tennessee, though there are no Laws in existence affecting the hours of labour, from all I can learn from the Mayors of Nashville and Chattanooga, the customary hours are from 7 A.M. to 12, and from 1 P.M. to 6 P.M. daily.

In the phosphate mines in this vicinity the miners work by contract ten hours a-day; after that they receive extra pay.

I have, &c.
(Signed) FREDERICK J. CRIDLAND.

Inclosure 6 in No. 25.

Consul Henderson to Sir J. Pauncefote.

Sir,   Boston, *June* 19, 1889.

IN reply to your despatch of the 11th instant, relative to the hours of adult labour in the States over which this Consular jurisdiction extends, I have the honour to state that no Laws affecting the question exist in the State of Vermont, and that the only legal restriction, enacted in similar terms in the States of Massachusetts, New Hampshire, and Maine, is that limiting the hours of labour of women in manufacturing and mechanical establishments to ten hours per day, or, in any case, when more or less time is occupied in labour on any one or more days, to sixty hours in a week.

In the State of Maine the Law further enacts that in all contracts for labour ten hours of actual labour are a legal day's work, unless the contract stipulates for a longer time, but this rule does not apply to monthly labour or to agricultural employment.

As regards male adult labour, and also, within the limitation noted above, female adult labour, the hours of labour are practically controlled by agreement or contract between the parties; and, excepting in certain establishments, such as paper-mills, iron foundries, &c., where continuous work has to be carried on by relays of men, and to a partial extent in the building trade, in which, through the operation of strikes, the hours have been reduced to nine in some localities, ten hours is almost universally the rule for a day's labour.

I have, &c.
(Signed)   C. A. HENDERSON.

Inclosure 7 in No. 25.

Acting Consul Heyworth to Sir J. Pauncefote.

Sir,   Galveston, *June* 17, 1889.

I HAVE your despatch dated the 11th instant, asking for information as to the Laws governing the hours of adult labourers in this Consular jurisdiction, and, in reply, beg to say that several measures have been introduced into the Legislature of Texas on this subject, but no Laws have hitherto been passed.

I have, &c.
(Signed)   O. HEYWORTH.

Inclosure 8 in No. 25.

Consul De Fonblanque to Sir J. Pauncefote.

Sir,   New Orleans, *June* 26, 1889.

IN compliance with the instructions contained in your despatch of the 11th instant, I have the honour to inclose my Report, and that of Vice-Consul Howe, on the hours of adult labour, as regulated by law and custom in the district. Vice-Consul Barnewall's Report is not yet furnished in a complete state. It will be forwarded hereafter.

I would venture to suggest that the part of the Section 10 of the Constitution of the United States which prohibits the States from passing any Law "impairing the obligation of contracts," might render legislation on this subject difficult.

I have, &c.
(Signed)   A. DE G. DE FONBLANQUE.

61

Inclosure 9 in No. 25.

Report on the Laws enacted affecting the Hours of Adult Labour in the District of Her Majesty's Consul at New Orleans.

THE States of Arkansas, Louisiana, and Mississippi have not any legislation on this subject.

In all the cities, and in towns of any importance, the conditions affecting a day's work are regulated by Associations similar to the Trade Unions at home. Members of these Societies carry their Laws with them wherever they may be employed. Non-members must make the best terms they can, but as the supply in rural neighbourhoods is generally   to the demand, they can practically suit themselves. This relates to skilled labour.

The actual hours of labour of all mechanics and labourers doing city work on shore in foundry, shop, and factory are ten hours a-day: 7 from to 12, and 1 to 6.

The hours of labour of all mechanics and labourers working on ships and steam-boats on water are nine hours a-day: from 7 to 12, and 1 to 5.

Cotton screwmen work from 7 to 12, and 1 to 5, or until a gang of six (with a foreman) has stowed seventy-five bales.

Longshoremen and levee labourers are paid by the hour, and work as and when required, day or night.

Farm hands work from sunrise to sunset, with three hours off.

Piece-work.—Shoemakers, tailors, &c., doing this sort of work at their own homes, labour to suit themselves.

Inclosure 10 in No. 25.

Report by Vice-Consul Howe giving the Laws of the State of Florida affecting the Hours of Adult Labour in the State of Florida, the actual Hours now worked, and the means by which such Laws can be enforced.

BY a legislative enactment of the State of Florida passed in February 1874, chapter 1988, it is provided as follows:—

"Section 1. Ten hours of labour shall be considered and regarded as a legal day's work, and held to be such by the Courts of this State.

"Sec. 2. Whenever a person is employed to perform manual labour of any kind by the day, week, month, or year, and the said person renders ten hours of work, he shall be considered as having performed a legal day's work: Provided a written contract has not been signed by the person so employed and the employer requiring a less or greater number of hours of labour to be performed daily.

"Sec. 3. Unless such written contract has been entered into and signed by the labourer and employer, in presence of one or more witnesses, the person so employed shall be entitled to extra pay for all work performed in excess of ten hours' labour daily, if so required by his employer."

I am not aware that the hours of adult labour at this post, and in the State of Florida generally, are otherwise at present than as provided according to extracts from the Law as above given.

(Signed)   OSMOND G. HOWE,
Her Majesty's Vice-Consul.

Pensacola, Florida, June 20, 1889.

Inclosure 11 in No. 25.

Consul de Fonblanque to Sir J. Pauncefote.

Sir,   *New Orleans, June* 28, 1889.

REFERRING to my despatch of the 26th instant, I have now the honour to inclose Vice-Consul Barnewall's Report on the hours of adult labour.

I have, &c.
(Signed)   A. DE G. DE FONBLANQUE.

Inclosure 12 in No. 25.

Vice-Consul Barnewall to Consul De Fonblanque.

Sir,   *Mobile, June* 25, 1889.

IN reply to your despatch, I must respectfully state that, after a careful examination, I find that there is not now, nor has there ever been, any Law relating to hours of adult labour in this State, nor have we any Laws affecting infant labour; consequently, I am unable to state what effect such Laws might or would have.

The usual hours of labour are nine hours, to wit:—

From 7 A.M. to 12—five hours.
From 1 P.M. to 5 P.M.—four hours.

I am, &c.
(Signed)   WM. BARNEWALL

Inclosure 13 in No. 25.

Consul Donohoe to Mr. Edwardes.

Sir,   *San Francisco, August* 1, 1889.

WITH reference to Sir Julian Pauncefote's despatch of the 11th June as to the Laws enacted in the States within this Consular district affecting the hours of adult labour, with the hours now worked, and as to the enforcement of such Laws, I now have the honour to report that the State of California has a Law upon the subject, a copy of which I inclose.

It will be seen by this Statute that eight hours constitute a day's work, but I am informed by the Commissioner of Labour that this Law is nearly invariably evaded by employing the men engaged on State works by the hour, and paying at so much an hour. I inclose an extract from a pamphlet issued by the Commissioner, which gives much valuable information as to the hours of labour in different trades.

I find that the States of Nevada and Oregon, and the territories of Washington, Idaho, Utah, and Arizona have passed no Laws on the subject of adult labour.

Mr. Vice-Consul Laidlaw, in reporting as to Oregon, states that the hours of labour are generally regulated by Trades Unions; that machinists work ten hours, masons, joiners, and painters, eight hours, and longshoremen, nine hours.

Mr. Vice-Consul Alexander, in reporting as to Washington Territory, states that the hours of mechanical labour, now generally worked in the Territory for a day's pay, are ten hours; that at some places, such as Seattle, Tacoma, and Port Townsend, the Trades Unions have been able to enforce upon contractors and builders nine hours work for a day's pay.

The Governors of Utah and Nevada, in replying to my query, merely state that there are no Laws on the subject of adult labour.

I have, &c.
(Signed)   DENIS DONOHOE.

Inclosure 14 in No. 25.

Extract from the Third Biennial Report of the Bureau of Labour Statistics of the State of California.

(Chapter II.)—*Wages and Hours of Labour.*

THE number of hours which shall constitute a legal day's work is a question which at present engages the attention of nearly all labour organizations in the civilized world. Organized labour is loud in its demand for a reduction in the hours of labour, and unorganized labour has still stronger claims in the same direction.

The impositions heaped upon certain wage classes in the community by corporations and individuals, in compelling them to work fifteen, eighteen, and twenty hours daily, is a travesty upon the Declaration of Independence, which claims every man " born free and equal, with certain inalienable rights, among which are life, liberty, and the pursuit of happiness."

The sweets of life, liberty, or happiness are not tasted by the man who is compelled to work two-thirds of the day. He is a stranger to his family, a slave to his employer, and an apology for a "free" American citizen. That the hours of labour must ultimately be reduced is evident, but at what time and how that shall be accomplished is a momentous question. It cannot be settled by strikes or boycotts. It must be remembered that we are living within the closest commercial relationship with the entire civilized world. Our ports are open to the labourers of Europe, consequently we have to contend against not only our own wage earners, but also the labour of foreigners, who are flocking to our shores.

The chief arguments in favour of a reduction in the hours of labour are:—

1. That owing to the introduction of machinery whereby the production has been vastly increased, the labourer is worse off than before, because he does not receive a corresponding decrease in the hours of work, while labour has been greatly displaced.

2. In consequence of machinery causing this supply of overproduction, and the wage classes being daily thrown out of employment; if the hours were reduced it would tend to lessen this production, and necessitate a greater demand for labour.

3. That this overproduction has a tendency to cause unrestricted competition among the labouring classes, which demoralizes trade; and if shorter hours and more men were employed, the employers, instead of being injured, would be correspondingly benefited, because there would be a greater demand for the manufactured wares.

4. That this increased time of leisure would give more time to intellectual work and attention to his family.

Many occupations vary in the hours of labour during the seasons of summer and winter.

That the long hours of labour operate directly in hindering the wage classes from devoting the necessary attention to the cultivation of their social and intellectual welfare is sustained by many able writers. "That the intelligence of the working classes," says W. J. Noble, of New York, "would improve with the advantage of more leisure time, we have every reason to believe, and that political tricksters and shameless demagogues could no longer turn their ignorance to the advantage of political party power. They would then understand the causes of their evils and the remedies they ought to apply, and instead of considering machinery a detriment to labour, they would realize it as the greatest benefit to them, exactly as the elements of fire and water can be made beneficial or injurious to us just as we put ourselves in right or wrong relations to them. It has been computed, says Dr. Franklin, that if every man and woman would work four hours each day on something useful, that labour would be sufficient to procure all the necessaries and comforts of life: want and misery would be banished out of the world, and the rest of the twenty-four hours might be leisure and pleasure; but as Dr. Franklin computed 100 years ago, with our present facilities, were it possible for all to perform their share of useful work, two hours would suffice."

There are many abuses, however, in the employment of labour

which should be eradicated, and one of the worst is the inhuman system of compelling men and women, boys and girls, because they cannot help themselves, to toil both day and night for a scanty living. This evil can be seen in the employment of street-car conductors and drivers probably more than in any other departments of labour. Barbers, butchers, waiters, clerks, saleswomen, seamstresses, telegraph and messenger boys, work during long, unseasonable hours. It should not be tolerated that corporations or individuals should work their employés more than twelve hours in the twenty-four. The system is inhuman, and conducive to disease and premature death. The following Table will show some of the occupations in which twelve and more hours of labour per day are required, and the remuneration received in San Francisco:—

Table (L.)—WAGES and Hours of Unorganized Toilers.

Occupation.	Hours.	Average Daily Wages.
		Dol. c.
Barbers	14	2 00
Bakers	14	2 00
Bartenders	12	2 50
Brewers	12	2 00
,, (cellarmen)	12	1 50
,, (washers)	12	1 50
Butchers	14	2 00
Car conductors	13	2 00
,, drivers	13	2 50
,, gripmen	13	2 50
Confectioners	12	2 00
Clerks in small retail stores	12	2 50
Dairymen	12	1 00
Distillers	12	1 50
Druggists	16	2 00
Engineers (marine)	12	3 25
Firemen (marine)	12	1 50
,, (stationary)	12	2 00
Gas-house men	12	2 50
Hack drivers	12	1 75
Herders	14	1 50
Hostlers	14	1 50
Laundry (men)	14	1 50
,, (women)	14	1 00
Millers	12	5 00
Maltmen	12	3 00
Paper-makers (men)	12	1 50
,, (boys)	12	1 00

It will be observed that the foregoing are classes that are unorganized. The efficacy of organization, therefore, can be better appreciated when it is seen that all combined labour regulates, to a great extent, the hours of work and commands better wages. The following Table gives the hours of work and wages of organized labour in San Francisco:—

Table (M.)—ORGANIZED Trades and Labour Unions in San Francisco—Hours of Labour and Daily Wages.

Name of Organization.	Hours.	Average Daily Wages.	
		Dol. c.	
Boot and Shoemakers W. L. L.	10	2 00	Piece work.
Bricklayers of San Francisco	9	5 00	Time work.
Bag and Satchel Makers	10	2 00	Ditto.
Boilermakers and Iron Ship Builders	10*	3 50	Ditto.
Beer Brewers and Malsters Union	10	3 00	Ditto.
Barbers Protective	12	3 00	Ditto.
Caulkers Association	9	5 00	Ditto.
Coopers, Journeymen (English)	10	3 25	Piece work.
Coremakers	10	3 25	Time work.
Cornicemakers, Galvanized Iron	9	5 00	Ditto.
Candymakers	10	3 00	Ditto.
Draymen and Teamsters	11	2 50	Ditto.
Engineers, Stationary	11	3 00	Ditto.
,, Marine	10	5 00	Ditto.
Glovers	9	3 50	Piece and time.
Glassblowers	8	5 00	Piece work.
Hat Finishers	Optional	4 50	Ditto.
Horseshoers	10	3 50	Time work.
Iron Moulders	10	4 00	Ditto.
Lasters Protective	9	3 00	Piece work.
Labourers	8 and 9†	3 00 and 3 50	Time work.
Lumbermen's Protective	9	4 00	75 cents per hour overtime.
Longshore Lumbermen	9	4 00	Time work.
Machinests	10	3 25	Ditto.
Painters	9	3 00	Ditto.
Patternmakers	10	3 50	Ditto.
Plumbers, Journeymen	9	3 25	Ditto.
Plasterers, Journeymen	8	5 00	Ditto.
Pavers	9	4 00	Ditto.
Painters, Fresco	9	4 00	Ditto.
Packers, Cigar	8	2 75	Ditto.
Shipwrights Association	9	4 00	Ditto.
Ship and Steamboat Joiners	9	4 00	Ditto.
Stonecutters, Journeymen	9	4 00	Ditto.
Steamship Stevedores	9	4 00	30 cents per hour overtime.
Tailors Protective	10	3 00	Time and piece.
Wharf Builders	9	3 50	Time work.
Upholsterers, Carpet	10	3 50	Ditto.

* Ten hours in the shop; nine on the outside.
† Plasterers' labourers work eight hours for 3 dols. 50 c. per day; bricklayers, nine hours for 3 dollars.

Table (N.)—Wages and Hours of Employment.

Occupation.	Per Hour. Max. Cents.	Per Hour. Min. Cents.	Per Hour. Av. Cents.	Per Day. Max. Dol. c.	Per Day. Min. Dol. c.	Per Day. Av. Dol. c.	Per Week. Max. Dol. c.	Per Week. Min. Dol. c.	Per Week. Av. Dol. c.	Per Month. Max. Dol. c.	Per Month. Min. Dol. c.	Per Month. Av. Dol. c.	Hours.
Acid-makers	..	..	..	3 00	2 00	2 20	17 50	12 00	13 20	..	..	..	10
Agricultural implement works	..	..	..	5 00	2 00	2 50	..	..	..	..	..	..	10
Artificial flower makers (men)	..	..	..	..	..	..	9 00	6 00	9 00	..	..	..	8½
,, ,, (women)	..	..	..	..	..	..	7 00	3 00	5 00	..	..	..	8½
Artists on stained glass (men)	..	..	..	10 00	5 00	..	..	..	..	..	..	..	8
Asphaltum workers	..	..	..	3 50	2 50	3 00	..	..	..	..	..	..	9
Assayers	..	..	..	..	..	..	..	..	12 00	150 00	40 00	75 00	8
Awning-makers (men)	..	..	..	..	..	..	18 00	9 00	12 00	..	..	..	..
Axlegrease-makers (men)	..	..	..	..	..	..	15 00	12 00	7 50	..	..	..	10
,, ,, (boys)	..	..	..	..	..	..	8 00	7 00	12 00	..	..	..	10
Bag-makers, cotton (men)	..	..	..	..	..	..	15 00	9 00	5 00	..	..	..	10
,, ,, (girls and women)	..	..	..	..	..	..	7 00	3 00	..	..	..	..	..
,, ,, (boys)	..	..	..	..	..	..	5 00	3 00	4 00	..	..	..	10
,, paper (men)	..	..	..	..	..	..	26 00	12 00	12 00	..	..	..	10
,, ,, (boys)	..	..	..	..	..	..	7 00	5 00	6 00	..	..	..	10
Bag and satchel makers	..	..	..	3 50	2 00	3 00	..	..	..	..	..	..	9
Bakers	..	..	..	..	..	..	..	..	..	75 00*	40 00*	50 00*	14
Bakers, cracker	..	..	..	3 00	2 50	2 50	..	..	..	..	..	..	9
Ballastmen	..	..	0 30	..	..	3 00	..	..	..	..	..	..	10
Barbers	..	..	..	..	..	..	..	..	..	100 00	40 00	50 00	12
Bar-tenders	..	..	..	..	..	..	15 10	10 00	12 00	..	..	..	14
Basket-makers	..	..	..	2 50	2 00	2 00	..	..	..	..	..	..	10
Bedspring-makers	..	..	..	2 00	1 00	1 50	..	..	..	..	..	..	10

* And found.

Occupation.	Per Hour. Max. Cents.	Per Hour. Min. Cents.	Per Hour. Av. Cents.	Per Day. Max. Dol. c.	Per Day. Min. Dol. c.	Per Day. Av. Dol. c.	Per Week. Max. Dol. c.	Per Week. Min. Dol. c.	Per Week. Av. Dol. c.	Per Month. Max. Dol. c.	Per Month. Min. Dol. c.	Per Month. Av. Dol. c.	Hours.
Bell-hangers	..	..	..	4 00	2 00	3 00	24 00	12 00	18 00	..	..	..	10
Belting-makers, leather	..	..	..	..	..	..	20 00	12 00	15 00	..	..	..	10
Billiard table makers	..	..	..	3 50	1 50	2 75	..	..	..	..	..	..	9
Blacking-makers (men)	..	..	..	..	..	..	15 00	6 00	12 00	..	..	..	9
,, ,, (boys)	..	..	..	..	..	..	6 00	3 00	4 50	..	..	..	10
Blacksmiths	..	..	..	3 50	3 00	..	12 00	5 00	7 50	..	..	..	10
,, (helpers)	..	..	..	..	..	..	..	..	..	75 00	75 00	75 00	10
Bleachers (oil)	..	..	..	..	..	..	21 00	18 00	21 00	..	..	..	9
Boat-builders	..	..	..	4 25	3 00	3 25	..	..	..	..	..	50 00*	..
Boatmen	..	..	..	..	..	..	24 00	15 00	18 00	..	..	..	10
Boiler-makers	..	..	..	..	..	..	12 00	3 00	9 00	..	..	..	10
Bookbinders	..	..	..	..	..	..	10 00	5 00	6 00	..	..	..	9
,, (apprentices)	..	..	..	..	..	..	..	..	..	..	..	..	9
Bookfolders (girls and women)	..	..	..	..	..	..	15 00	10 00	12 00	..	..	..	10
Bookkeepers	..	..	..	3 00	2 00	2 50	9 00	6 00	7 50	200 00	40 00	..	10
Boot and shoe makers	..	..	..	..	..	..	10 00	3 00	7 50	..	..	..	10
Box-makers, cigar (men)	..	..	..	..	..	..	21 00	10 00	15 00	..	..	..	10
,, ,, (women)	..	..	..	..	..	..	6 00	4 00	5 00	..	..	..	10
,, ,, (boys)	..	..	..	..	..	..	5 00	3 00	4 00	..	..	..	10
,, jewellery and fancy (men)	..	..	..	..	..	..	15 00	10 00	12 00	..	..	..	10
,, jewellery and fancy (girls and women)	..	..	..	..	..	..	..	..	..	..	..	..	10
,, jewellery and fancy (boys)	..	..	..	..	..	..	..	..	..	..	..	..	10
,, packing (men)	..	..	..	2 50	2 50	2 50	..	..	..	..	..	..	10
,, paper (men)	..	..	..	..	..	..	..	..	..	..	..	..	10

* And found.

69

Occupation.	Per Hour.			Per Day.			Per Week.			Per Month.			Hours.
	Max.	Min.	Av.	Max.	Min.	Av.	Max.	Min.	Av.	Max.	Min.	Av.	
	Cents.	Cents.	Cents.	Dol. c.	Dol. c.	Dol. c.	Dol. c.	Dol. c.	Dol. c.	Dol. c.	Dol. c.	Dol. c.	
Box-makers, paper (women and girls)	..	..	..	..	..	..	9 00	3 00	5 00	..	..	..	10
,, ,, (boys)	..	..	..	..	..	..	6 00	4 50	5 00	..	..	..	10
Brass finishers	..	..	..	3 50	2 50	3 00	..	..	..	..	..	..	10
,, moulders	..	..	..	..	..	3 00	..	..	..	..	..	..	10
,, spinners	..	..	..	3 00	2 00	2 50	..	..	..	..	..	..	10
Brewers	..	..	..	..	..	..	..	..	..	90 00	50 00	60 00	12
,, (cellarmen)	..	..	..	..	..	..	..	..	..	60 00	50 00	90 00	12
,, (washers)	..	..	..	..	..	..	..	..	..	35 00*	25 00*	50 00	12
Brick-burners	..	..	..	..	..	..	..	..	..	35 00*	30 00*	30 00*	9
Brick-makers	..	..	..	5 50	5 00	5 00	..	..	..	..	..	35 00*	9
Bricklayers	..	..	..	2 00	1 50	1 75	..	..	..	..	..	..	9
Broom-makers (men)	..	..	..	..	..	..	9 00	6 00	7 00	..	..	..	10
,, ,, (women and girls)	..	..	..	..	..	..	9 00	6 00	7 00	..	..	..	9½
,, ,, (boys)	..	..	..	..	..	..	21 00	10 00	15 00	..	..	..	10
Brush-makers (men)	..	..	..	..	..	..	9 00	6 00	7 00	..	..	..	9
,, ,, (women and girls)	..	..	..	..	..	..	7 50	5 00	6 00	..	..	..	9½
,, ,, (boys)	..	..	..	..	..	..	..	..	..	..	..	..	9½
Butchers	..	..	..	..	..	..	..	..	..	125 00	50 00	85 00	10 to 14
Cabinet-makers	..	..	..	3 50	2 50	3 00	..	..	..	75 00	40 00	50 00	12
Caulkers	..	..	..	5 00	4 00	4 50	..	..	..	..	..	..	9 to 10
Candle-makers	..	..	..	..	..	..	15 00	12 00	13 50	..	..	..	9
Candy-makers (men)	..	..	..	..	..	3 00	..	..	..	..	..	..	10
,, ,, (women and girls)	..	..	..	..	..	..	8 00	3 50	5 50	..	..	..	10
,, ,, (boys)	..	..	..	..	..	..	10 00	3 00	7 00	..	..	..	10
Can-makers (men)	..	..	..	..	..	..	21 00	9 00	13 00	..	..	..	10
,, ,, (women and girls)	..	..	..	..	..	..	8 00	5 00	6 00	..	..	..	10

* And found.

Occupation.	Per Hour.			Per Day.			Per Week.			Per Month.			Hours.
	Max.	Min.	Av.	Max.	Min.	Ar.	Max.	Min.	Av.	Max.	Min.	Av.	
	Cents.	Cents.	Cents.	Dol. c.	Dol. c.	Dol. c.	Dol. c.	Dol. c.	Dol. c.	Dol. c.	Dol. c.	Dol. c.	
Can-makers (boys)	..	..	..	..	..	..	8 00	5 00	6 00	..	..	..	10
Cannery (men)	..	..	..	..	..	..	20 00	9 00	12 00	..	..	..	10
,, (women and girls)	..	..	..	..	..	..	7 00	4 50	5 00	..	..	..	10
,, (boys)	..	..	..	..	..	..	5 00	4 50	5 00	..	..	..	10
Car conductors	..	..	..	2 25	2 00	2 00	..	..	..	..	..	..	13
,, drivers	..	..	..	2 70	2 50	2 00	..	..	..	..	..	..	13
,, gripmen	..	..	..	..	..	2 50	..	..	..	..	..	..	13
Carders	..	..	..	4 00	2 50	3 50	32 00	..	25 00	..	..	..	10
Carpenters	..	..	..	5 00	4 00	4 50	..	..	..	..	..	..	9
,, ship and steamboat	..	..	..	3 00	2 25	2 50	..	..	..	..	..	..	9
Carpet beaters	..	..	..	4 00	3 50	3 50	24 00	15 00	20 00	..	..	..	10
,, layers	..	..	..	2 00	1 00	1 50	..	..	..	..	..	..	10
,, sewers (men)	..	..	..	..	..	..	10 00	3 00	10 00	..	..	..	9
,, ,, (women)	..	..	..	..	..	..	20 00	10 00	15 00	..	..	..	9
,, weavers	..	..	30	5 00	2 25	3 00	..	..	..	..	..	..	10
Carriage-makers	..	..	..	4 00	2 00	3 00	..	..	..	..	..	..	10
,, painters	..	..	..	3 50	2 00	3 00	..	..	..	..	..	..	10
,, trimmers	..	..	..	4 50	4 00	4 50	..	..	..	..	..	..	9
Carvers, furniture	..	..	..	6 00	4 00	5 00	..	..	..	..	..	..	9
,, marble	..	..	..	6 00	4 00	5 00	..	..	..	..	..	..	9
,, stone	..	..	..	3 00	2 00	3 00	..	..	..	..	..	..	9
,, wood	..	..	..	..	..	2 50	..	..	..	..	..	..	10
Catchers	..	..	..	..	..	..	9 00	3 00	6 00	60 00	45 00	50 00	10
Cement-makers	..	..	..	..	..	..	8 00	3 50	6 00	..	..	..	10
Chair-caners (women)	..	..	..	..	..	..	..	..	..	..	..	..	10
,, (boys)	..	..	..	..	..	..	..	..	..	..	..	40 00	10
Charcoal burners	..	..	..	..	..	..	..	..	..	150 00	40 00	75 00	8
Chemists	..	..	..	..	..	..	20 00	14 00	16 00	..	..	..	10
Chocolate-makers	..	..	..	..	..	..	..	..	..	..	..	..	10

71

Occupation.	Per Hour.			Per Day.			Per Week.			Per Month.			Hours.
	Max.	Min.	Av.	Max.	Min.	Av.	Max.	Min.	Av.	Max.	Min.	Av.	
	Cents.	Cents.	Cents.	Dol. c.	Dol. c.	Dol. c.	Dol. c.	Dol. c.	Dol. c.	Dol. c.	Dol. c.	Dol. c.	
Cigar-makers	..	..	..	..	..	..	15 00	10 00	11 00	..	..	..	10
,, packers	..	..	..	..	..	..	15 00	12 00	15 00	..	..	..	10
Clerks, retail stores	..	..	..	6 00	2 00	2 50	..	..	..	..	..	..	12
Cloak-makers (men)	..	..	..	..	..	..	25 00	10 00	15 00	..	..	..	9
,, (women)	..	..	..	..	..	..	9 00	3 00	7 50	..	..	..	9
Coffee and spice mills (men)	..	..	..	..	..	..	20 00	14 00	16 00	..	..	..	10
,, (women and girls)	..	..	..	..	..	..	6 00	4 00	6 00	..	..	..	10
,, ,, (boys)	..	..	..	..	..	..	9 00	7 00	8 00	..	..	..	10
Compositors	..	..	..	..	..	..	..	..	15 00	..	..	..	10
Confectioners	..	..	..	..	..	..	..	..	..	100 00*	40 00*	60 00*	12
Cooks (men)	..	..	..	..	..	..	..	..	..	100 00*	50 00*	75 00*	11
,, (women)	..	..	..	..	..	..	..	..	..	35 00*	20 00*	25 00*	..
Coopers	..	..	..	..	..	..	21 00	15 00	18 00	..	..	..	10
,, (apprentices)	..	..	..	3 75	2 25	3 00	10 00	5 00	7 50	..	..	..	10
Coppersmiths	..	..	..	4 00	1 00	2 50	..	..	..	..	..	..	10
Copyists	..	..	..	2 75	2 00	2 50	..	..	..	..	..	..	9
Cotton loom fixers	..	..	..	..	..	..	20 00	9 00	12 00	..	..	..	10
,, mills (men)	..	..	..	..	..	..	10 00	6 00	7 50	..	..	..	10
,, ,, (women)	..	..	..	..	..	..	6 00	3 60	4 80	..	..	..	10
,, ,, (boys and girls)	..	..	..	..	..	..	..	..	12 00	..	..	..	10
,, ,, pickers	..	..	..	..	..	..	18 00	11 00	13 00	..	..	..	10
,, ,, weavers	..	17½	17½	..	..	..	..	..	..	..	..	..	10
Cordage works (men)	37½	12½	12½	..	..	..	..	..	..	..	..	..	10
,, ,, (boys)	12½	..	..	..	..	2 50	..	..	..	..	..	..	9
Cracker bakers	..	..	..	3 00	1 50	2 50	10 50	4 50	7 50	..	..	..	9
,, bakery (men)	..	..	..	..	..	..	..	..	..	..	..	..	9
,, ,, (women and girls)	..	..	..	..	..	..	..	..	..	..	..	..	

* And found.

Occupation.	Per Hour. Max. (Cents.)	Per Hour. Min. (Cents.)	Per Hour. Av. (Cents.)	Per Day. Max. (Dol. c.)	Per Day. Min. (Dol. c.)	Per Day. Av. (Dol. c.)	Per Week. Max. (Dol. c.)	Per Week. Min. (Dol. c.)	Per Week. Av. (Dol. c.)	Per Month. Max. (Dol. c.)	Per Month. Min. (Dol. c.)	Per Month. Av. (Dol. c.)	Hours.
Cracker bakery (boys)	..	..	..	..	..	..	10 00	4 50	7 50	..	..	..	9
Cream tartar refiners	..	..	..	..	..	..	12 00	10 00	11 00	..	..	..	9
Curriers	..	..	..	..	..	..	18 00	12 00	15 00	..	..	..	10
Cutlers	..	..	..	..	..	..	24 00	18 00	18 00	40 00*	25 00*	25 00*	10
Dairymen	..	..	..	..	..	..	..	..	..	..	..	..	12
Demijohn coverers	..	..	..	..	..	..	12 00	7 00	8 50	..	..	..	10
Distillers	..	..	..	..	..	..	..	..	..	150 00	40 00	50 00	12
Draughtsmen, architectural	..	..	..	..	..	..	..	..	..	100 00	30 00	50 00	8
,, mechanical	..	..	..	5 00	3 00	3 25	15 00	12 00	15 00	..	..	..	9
Draymen	..	..	..	..	..	..	..	..	..	..	..	..	11
Dress-makers	..	..	..	2 50	1 00	1 50	6 00	3 00	4 00	..	..	..	10
,, (apprentices)†	..	..	..	..	..	..	..	..	..	..	..	..	10
Drovers	..	..	..	..	..	..	..	..	..	..	..	*40 00	..
Druggists	..	..	..	..	..	..	..	..	..	100 00	30 00	60 00	16
,, manufacturing	..	..	..	..	..	..	..	..	..	125 00	60 00	80 00	8¼
Dyers	..	..	..	10 00	5 00	7 50	35 00	12 00	21 00	..	..	..	10
Electrotypers	..	..	..	5 00	3 00	..	21 00	10 00	15 00	..	..	..	10
Engineers, civil	..	..	..	..	..	..	..	..	..	..	..	..	..
,, locomotive	..	..	..	..	..	..	..	..	..	150 00*	75 00*	100 00*	12
,, marine	..	..	..	..	..	..	..	..	..	..	..	..	..
,, mining	..	..	..	..	..	..	..	..	..	125 00	75 00	85 00	10
,, stationary	..	..	..	6 00	4 00	5 00	30 00	15 00	21 00	..	..	..	10
Engravers, gold and silver	..	..	..	5 00	2 00	3 50	..	..	..	..	..	..	8
,, lithographic	..	..	..	..	..	..	15 00	10 00	12 00	..	..	..	8
,, wood	..	..	..	..	..	2 75	..	..	..	75 00	50 00	60 00	10
Farriers	..	..	..	..	..	..	..	..	..	..	..	..	10
File-makers	..	..	..	..	..	..	..	..	..	..	..	..	..
Firemen, locomotive	..	..	..	..	..	..	..	..	..	..	..	..	..

* And found. † Many work from three to six months for nothing.

73

Occupation.	Per Hour.			Per Day.			Per Week.			Per Month.			Hours.
	Max.	Min.	Av.	Max.	Min.	Av.	Max.	Min.	Av.	Max.	Min.	Av.	
	Cents.	Cents.	Cents.	Dol. c.	Dol. c.	Dol. c.	Dol. c.	Dol. c.	Dol. c.	Dol. c.	Dol. c.	Dol. c.	
Firemen, marine	..	..	..	..	..	..	..	..	..	60 00*	40 00*	50 00*	12
,, stationary	..	..	..	..	..	..	..	..	..	75 00	50 00	60 00.	12
Fishermen†	..	..	..	..	..	..	..	..	..	..	..	..	..
Florists	..	..	..	4 00	2 50	3 00	..	..	..	90 00	65 00	75 00	10
,, (boys)	..	..	..	..	..	..	..	..	..	..	..	35 00	10
Flour packers	..	..	..	3 00	2 50	2 75	..	..	..	..	..	..	10
Frame-makers	..	..	..	3 50	2 50	3 00	..	..	..	..	..	..	10
Frame ornamenters	..	..	..	4 50	3 50	4 00	..	..	..	..	..	..	10
Fringe and tassel makers	..	..	..	..	..	..	18 00	10 00	15 00	..	..	..	10
,, ,,	..	..	..	..	..	..	8 00	3 00	6 00	..	..	..	10
,, ,,	..	..	..	..	..	..	10 00	3 00	7 50	..	..	..	10
Furniture finishers and polishers	..	..	..	3 00	2 50	3 00	..	..	..	..	..	..	9 to 10
Furriers (men)	..	..	..	..	..	..	15 00	10 00	12 50	..	..	..	10
,, (women and girls)	..	..	..	..	..	..	7 00	3 00	5 00	..	..	..	10
,, (boys)	..	..	..	..	..	..	..	..	3 50	..	..	..	10
Galvanized iron workers	..	..	..	4 50	3 00	3 50	27 00	18 00	21 00	..	..	..	9
,, ,, (apprentices)	..	..	..	..	..	..	12 00	4 00	8 00	..	..	..	9
Galvanizers	..	..	..	3 00	2 00	2 50	..	..	..	..	..	..	9
Gardners	..	..	..	4 00	2 50	3 00	..	..	..	..	..	..	10
Gasfitters	..	..	..	4 00	3 00	3 50	..	..	..	..	..	..	9
,, (helpers)	..	..	..	3 00	2 00	2 50	7 00	4 00	5 00	..	..	..	9
Gas-house men	..	..	..	3 50	..	3 50	..	..	..	..	..	..	10 to 12
Gilders	..	..	..	3 00	3 00	3 00	..	..	..	..	..	..	10
Glass benders	..	..	..	..	..	..	40 00	25 00	30 00	..	..	..	10
,, blowers	..	..	..	3 50	3 00	3 00	..	..	..	..	..	..	8
,, cutters	..	..	..	3 50	3 00	3 00	..	..	..	..	..	..	10
,, embossers	..	..	..	3 50	3 00	3 00	..	..	..	..	..	..	10

* And found.   † One share to each man and one share to boat.

Occupation.	Per Hour. Max. Cents.	Per Hour. Min. Cents.	Per Hour. Av. Cents.	Per Day. Max. Dol. c.	Per Day. Min. Dol. c.	Per Day. Av. Dol. c.	Per Week. Max. Dol. c.	Per Week. Min. Dol. c.	Per Week. Av. Dol. c.	Per Month. Max. Dol. c.	Per Month. Min. Dol. c.	Per Month. Av. Dol. c.	Hours.
Glass grinders	..	..	..	3 50	3 00	3 00	..	..	..	..	..	..	10
,, stained, artists on	..	..	..	10 00	5 00	..	..	..	..	..	..	..	8
,, stainers	..	..	..	5 00	3 00	3 50	..	..	..	..	..	..	9
Glaziers	..	..	..	3 00	2 50	2 50	..	..	..	..	..	..	10
,, lead	..	..	..	5 00	3 00	3 50	..	..	..	..	..	..	10
Glove-cutters (men)	..	..	..	..	..	..	18 00	12 00	16 50	..	..	..	9½
,, ,, (women)	..	..	..	..	..	..	12 00	6 00	7 50	..	..	..	9½
Gold and silver platers	..	..	..	..	..	..	20 00	14 00	15 00	..	..	..	9
,, ,, (apprentices)	..	..	..	..	..	..	..	..	8 00	..	..	..	9
Gold beaters	..	..	..	..	..	5 00	14 00	9 00	11 00	..	..	..	9½
Grainers	..	..	..	..	..	2 50	..	..	..	..	..	..	8
,, (helpers)	..	..	..	..	..	3 50	..	..	..	..	..	..	8
Granite-cutters	..	..	..	4 50	2 50	..	30 00	18 00	18 00	..	..	..	9
Grinders	..	..	..	..	..	4 00	..	..	..	..	..	..	10
,, saw	..	..	..	4 00	3 50	..	21 00	15 00	18 00	..	..	..	10
Gunsmiths	..	..	..	2 00	1 50	1 75	..	..	..	60 00	50 00	52 50	9½
Hack drivers	..	..	..	..	..	..	25 00	15 00	20 00	..	..	..	12
Hairdressers (men)	..	..	..	..	..	..	15 00	5 00	10 00	..	..	..	9
,, (women)	..	..	..	..	..	..	25 00	15 00	20 00	..	..	..	9
Hair workers (men)	..	..	..	..	..	..	20 00	5 00	8 00	..	..	..	9
,, ,, (women)	..	..	..	..	..	..	20 00	10 00	13 50	..	..	..	10
Harness-makers	..	..	..	..	..	..	10 00	5 00	7 50	..	..	..	10
,, ,, (apprentices)	..	..	..	..	..	..	18 00	7 50	10 00	..	..	..	9
Hat and cap makers (men)	..	..	..	..	..	..	9 00	4 50	7 50	..	..	..	9
,, ,, ,, (women)	..	..	..	..	..	..	52 00	25 00	30 00	..	..	..	10
Hatters	..	..	..	..	..	..	18 00	6 00	10 00	..	..	..	9
Hatters' trimmers (women)	..	..	..	..	..	..	17 00	10 00	15 00	..	..	..	10
Heaters	..	..	..	..	..	..	..	..	..	..	..	50 00	10
Herders	..	..	..	..	..	..	..	..	..	..	..	..	10 to 14

75

Occupation.	Per Hour.			Per Day.			Per Week.			Per Month.			Hours.
	Max.	Min.	Av.	Max.	Min.	Av.	Max.	Min.	Av.	Max.	Min.	Av.	
	Cents.	Cents.	Cents.	Dol. c.	Dol. c.	Dol. c.	Dol. c.	Dol. c.	Dol. c.	Dol. c.	Dol. c.	Dol. c.	
Hod carriers, bricklayers'	..	..	..	..	..	3 00	..	..	..	..	..	..	9
,, ,, plasterers'	..	..	..	..	..	3 50	..	..	..	..	..	..	8
Hookers	..	..	..	3 00	2 00	2 50	..	..	..	..	..	..	10
Horse collar makers	..	..	..	3 00	2 00	2 25	..	..	..	..	..	..	10
Horseshoers	..	..	..	4 00	3 00	3 50	..	..	..	..	..	..	10
Hosiery and underwear factory (men)	..	..	..	..	..	..	35 00	18 00	26 00	..	..	..	10
Hosiery and underwear factory (women)	..	..	..	..	..	..	15 00	3 00	6 00	..	..	..	10
Hosiery and underwear factory (boys)	..	..	..	..	..	..	6 50	3 00	6 00	..	..	..	10
Hostlers	..	..	..	..	..	..	..	..	..	60 00	30 00	50 00	14
Ink and mucilage makers	..	..	..	..	..	2 50	15 00	12 00	12 00	..	..	..	10
Iron chippers	..	..	..	..	..	3 25	..	..	..	..	..	..	10
,, moulders	..	..	..	3 50	1 75	3 00	..	..	..	..	..	..	10
Iron workers	..	..	..	..	..	..	24 00	18 00	18 00	..	..	..	10
Ivory turners	..	..	..	3 50	2 00	3 00	..	..	..	..	..	..	9
Japanners*	..	..	..	..	..	..	27 00	12 00	21 00	..	..	..	10
Jewellers	..	..	..	4 00	3 00	3 50	..	..	..	..	..	..	9
Joiners	..	..	..	5 00	4 00	4 50	..	..	..	..	..	..	9
,, ship and steam-boat	..	..	..	..	..	..	22 50	6 00	12 00	..	..	..	9
,, ,, (women)	..	..	..	..	..	..	11 00	6 00	7 50	..	..	..	10
,, ,, (boys and girls)	..	..	..	..	..	..	6 00	3 00	4 50	..	..	..	10
Jute mill employés (men)	..	..	..	4 00	2 50	3 00	..	..	..	..	..	..	10
Lapidaries	..	..	..	..	..	..	21 00	15 00	18 00	..	..	..	10
Last-makers	..	..	..	4 00	2 50	3 00	..	..	..	..	..	..	10
Lathers	..	..	..	..	..	..	..	..	..	..	..	..	9

* Girls and boys get from 6 to 10 dollars per week.

76

Occupation.	Per Hour.			Per Day.			Per Week.			Per Month.			Hours.
	Max.	Min.	Av.	Max.	Min.	Av.	Max.	Min.	Av.	Max.	Min.	Av.	
	Cents.	Cents.	Cents.	Dol. c.	Dol. c.	Dol. c.	Dol. c.	Dol. c.	Dol. c.	Dol. c.	Dol. c.	Dol. c.	
Laundry (men)	..	..	..	..	..	..	25 00*	3 75*	7 50*	..	..	..	10 to 14
,, (women)	..	..	..	..	..	..	6 75*	1 50*	5 00*	..	..	..	10 to 14
Lead glaziers	..	..	..	5 00	3 00	3 50	..	..	..	..	..	..	10
,, pipe makers	..	..	..	..	..	..	30 00	18 00	18 00	..	..	..	9½
,, smelters	..	..	..	3 00	2 00	2 00	..	..	..	..	..	..	10
Leather belting makers	..	..	..	..	..	..	20 00	12 00	15 00	..	..	..	10
,, ,, (boys)	..	..	..	..	..	..	..	..	4 00	..	..	..	10
Lithographic artists	..	..	..	8 00	6 00	7 00	..	..	..	..	..	..	8
,, engravers	..	..	..	6 00	4 00	5 00	..	..	..	..	..	..	8
,, printers	..	..	..	..	..	..	25 00	12 00	15 00	..	..	..	10
,, transferers	..	..	..	..	..	..	32 00	25 00	30 00	..	..	..	10
Locksmiths	..	..	..	..	..	..	15 00	12 00	12 00	..	..	..	10
Loggers	..	..	..	..	..	..	..	..	..	70 00	30 00*	40 00*	11
Lime burners	..	..	..	..	..	..	..	..	..	60 00	45 00	50 00	10
Lumbermen	..	..	..	..	..	..	..	..	..	100 00	30 00*	40 00*	11
Macaroni factory employés	..	..	..	3 50	3 00	3 25	..	..	..	..	..	50 00	10
Machinists	..	..	..	..	..	..	..	..	..	..	..	..	10
Maltmen	..	..	..	6 00	4 00	5 00	..	..	..	..	..	90 00	12
Marble carvers	..	..	..	3 50	2 50	2 75	..	..	..	..	..	..	9
,, cutters	..	..	..	4 00	4 00	4 00	..	..	..	..	..	..	9
,, letterers	..	..	..	2 50	2 00	2 00	..	..	..	..	..	..	9
,, polishers	..	..	..	3 00	2 00	2 00	..	..	..	..	..	..	9
,, sawyers	..	..	..	..	..	..	25 00	9 00	12 00	..	..	..	10
Match-makers	..	..	..	5 00	2 50	3 50	..	..	..	..	..	..	10
Mathematical instrument makers	..	..	..	3 00	2 50	2 50	..	..	..	..	..	..	9
Mattress-makers	..	..	..	1 50	1 00	1 00	9 00	6 00	6 00	..	..	..	10
,, ,, wire	..	..	..	..	..	..	..	..	..	..	..	..	10

* And found.

77

Occupation.	Per Hour. Max. Cents.	Per Hour. Min. Cents.	Per Hour. Av. Cents.	Per Day. Max. Dol. c.	Per Day. Min. Dol. c.	Per Day. Av. Dol. c.	Per Week. Max. Dol. c.	Per Week. Min. Dol. c.	Per Week. Av. Dol. c.	Per Month. Max. Dol. c.	Per Month. Min. Dol. c.	Per Month. Av. Dol. c.	Hours.
Messengers, telegraph (boys)	..	..	..	3 00	2 00	2 50	..	..	..	15 00	12 00	13 50	..
Metal spinners	..	..	..	..	..	..	..	..	..	..	..	..	10
Millers	..	..	..	4 00	3 50	5 00	..	..	..	..	..	..	12
Millwrights	..	..	..	2 50	2 00	3 50	..	..	..	..	..	..	9
Miners, asphaltum	..	..	..	2 75	2 25	..	..	..	..	..	..	..	..
,, coal	..	..	..	3 00	2 50	..	..	..	..	..	..	..	..
,, gold, hydraulic	..	..	..	3 00	2 50	..	..	..	..	..	..	..	..
,, ,, placer	..	..	..	3 00	2 50	..	..	..	..	..	..	..	..
,, ,, quartz	..	..	..	2 50	2 00	..	..	..	..	..	..	..	..
,, granite	..	..	..	3 00	2 50	..	..	..	..	..	..	..	..
,, gravel	..	..	..	3 00	2 50	..	..	..	..	..	..	..	..
,, iron	..	..	..	3 00	2 00	..	..	..	..	..	..	..	..
,, marble	..	..	..	2 50	3 00	..	..	..	..	..	..	..	..
,, quicksilver	..	..	..	4 00	2 50	..	..	..	..	..	..	..	..
,, silver	..	..	..	3 00	..	..	12 00	..	10 00	..	..	..	10
Mirror polishers	..	..	..	..	..	3 50	20 00	10 00	15 00	80 00	50 00	60 00	10
,, silverers	..	..	..	4 00	3 50	3 00	..	12 00	..	..	..	..	9
Model-makers	..	..	..	3 50	3 25	3 25	..	..	..	..	..	..	10
Moulders, brass	..	..	..	9 00	3 50	7 00	..	..	..	..	..	..	10
,, iron	..	..	..	..	..	..	..	..	25 00	..	..	..	10
Nailers	..	..	..	3 50	2 50	3 00	..	..	..	..	..	..	10
Netters (men)	..	..	..	..	..	..	..	..	..	..	..	75 00	..
Nurserymen	..	..	..	3 25	2 25	2 25	..	..	..	..	..	..	10
Oil bleachers	..	..	..	3 25	2 25	3 00	..	..	..	..	..	..	10
,, boilers	..	..	..	..	..	..	..	..	..	..	..	..	..
,, pressers	..	..	..	..	..	..	..	..	..	..	..	..	..
,, refiners	..	..	..	..	..	..	..	..	..	..	..	..	..

Occupation.	Per Hour. Max. (Cents.)	Per Hour. Min. (Cents.)	Per Hour. Av. (Cents.)	Per Day. Max. (Dol. c.)	Per Day. Min. (Dol. c.)	Per Day. Av. (Dol. c.)	Per Week. Max. (Dol. c.)	Per Week. Min. (Dol. c.)	Per Week. Av. (Dol. c.)	Per Month. Max. (Dol. c.)	Per Month. Min. (Dol. c.)	Per Month. Av. (Dol. c.)	Hours.
Oystermen				3 00						85 00*	30 00*	40 00*	10
Painters				4 00	2 00	3 00							9
,, carriage				10 00	2 00	3 00							10
,, fresco				6 00	3 00	6 00							8
,, sign and ornamental				4 00	4 00	5 00	24 00	15 00	18 00				8
Paper-hangers					2 50	3 00							9
Paper-makers (men)										100 00	30 00	50 00	12
,, ,, (boys)										30 00	25 00	30 00	12
Paper rulers				4 00	3 25	3 50	14 00	15 00	18 00				10
Pattern-makers				4 00		4 00							9
Paviours													10
Photographic operators							35 00	15 00	25 00				7 to 8
,, printers							25 00	15 00	20 00				7
Photographic retouchers							20 00	10 00	15 00				9
Piano-makers (men)						3 00	24 00	12 00	18 00				10
,, ,, (boys)				3 50	2 50				6 00				10
Picture frame makers						3 00	30 00	18 00	18 00				10
Pipe-makers				4 00	2 50	3 00							10
Planing-mill men				5 00	4 00	5 00							8
Plasterers				4 00	3 00	3 50	7 00	4 00	5 00				9
Plumbers							20 00	14 00	15 00				9
Plumbers (helpers)									8 00				9
Platers, gold and silver													9
Porters										75 00	40 00	60 00	10
,, ,,										100 00	37 00	60 00	11
Pork packers													10
Potters							15 00	10 00	10 50				

* And found.

79

Occupation.	Per Hour. Max.	Per Hour. Min.	Per Hour. Av.	Per Day. Max.	Per Day. Min.	Per Day. Av.	Per Week. Max.	Per Week. Min.	Per Week. Av.	Per Month. Max.	Per Month. Min.	Per Month. Av.	Hours.
	Cents.	Cents.	Cents.	Dol. c.	Dol. c.	Dol. c.	Dol. c.	Dol. c.	Dol. c.	Dol. c.	Dol. c.	Dol. c.	
Powder-makers	..	..	..	..	..	..	25 00	12 00	..	..	..	..	10
Printers, job (men)	..	..	..	..	..	..	30 00	14 00	20 00	..	..	..	10
,, ,, (women and girls)	..	..	..	..	..	..	12 50	2 10	7 00	..	..	..	10
,, ,, (boys)	..	..	..	..	..	..	6 00	3 00	3 00	..	..	..	10
Rattan chair makers	..	..	..	3 50	3 00	3 00	..	..	..	..	..	..	10
Refiners, oil	..	..	..	3 25	2 25	3 00	..	..	..	..	..	..	10
Riggers	..	..	..	5 00	3 15	3 50	..	..	..	..	..	..	10
Rivermen	..	..	..	..	..	..	..	..	..	..	..	50 00*	9
Rollers	..	..	..	5 00	3 00	3 50	..	..	..	..	..	..	..
Roofers	..	..	..	4 00	3 00	3 00	..	..	..	..	..	..	10
Rope-makers (men)	37½	17½	17½	..	..	..	..	..	..	..	..	..	10
,, (boys)	..	..	12½	..	..	..	..	..	..	..	..	..	10
Saddlers	..	..	..	..	..	..	24 00	15 00	18 00	..	..	..	10
Sail-makers	..	..	..	..	..	..	24 00	18 00	21 00	..	..	..	9
,, (apprentices)	..	..	..	..	..	..	12 00	5 00	7 50	..	..	..	9
Sailors, coast	..	..	..	..	..	..	..	..	..	125 00†	40 00	60 00	12
Salesmen, retail	..	..	..	..	..	..	..	..	..	250 00	60 00	75 00	10
Saleswomen	..	..	..	..	..	..	20 00	3 00	5 00	..	..	..	10
Salt-makers	..	..	..	3 00	2 50	3 00	..	..	..	60 00	50 00	50 00	10
Salt refiners	..	..	..	4 00	3 50	4 00	..	..	..	90 00	..	90 00	10
Sash, door, and blind makers	..	..	..	6 00	3 00	4 00	..	..	..	..	..	..	9
Saw grinders	..	..	..	3 50	2 00	3 00	..	..	..	..	..	..	10
Saw-makers	..	..	..	3 00	2 00	2 50	..	..	..	..	..	..	10
Sawyers	..	..	..	..	..	..	20 00	20 00	20 00	..	..	..	10
Sawyers, marble	..	..	..	..	..	..	..	..	..	..	..	..	10
Scourers, wool	..	..	..	..	..	..	..	..	..	..	..	..	10
Scrap pilers	..	..	..	1 75	1 00	1 50	..	..	..	..	..	..	10

[601]

* And found.   † See General Remarks.

Occupation.	Per Hour.			Per Day.			Per Week.			Per Month.			Hours.
	Max.	Min.	Av.	Max.	Min.	Av.	Max.	Min.	Av.	Max.	Min.	Av.	
	Cents.	Cents.	Cents.	Dol. c.	Dol. c.	Dol. c.	Dol. c.	Dol. c.	Dol. c.	Dol. c.	Dol. c.	Dol. c.	
Seamstresses							8 00	2 50	6 00				9
Servants (men)										40 00*	30 00*	25 00*	
,, (women)										35 00*	15 00*	20 00*	
Sewer builders				3 00	2 00	2 50							10
Sewing machine operators (women)							8 50	2 50	6 00				9
Sheet iron workers				4 50	2 50	2 50	27 00	18 00	21 00				9
,, ,, galvanized				4 50	3 00	3 50							9
Ship and steamboat carpenters				5 00	4 00	4 50							9
Shipsmiths				5 00	4 00	4 50							9
Shipwrights				4 25	3 00	3 25							9
Shoe-makers				5 00	4 00	4 50	15 00	10 00	12 00				10
,, (apprentices)							30 00	18 00	18 00				9½
Shot-makers				4 00	3 00	3 00							10
Showcase-makers							24 00	15 00	18 00				10
Silversmiths							9 00	3 00	6 00				10
,, (apprentices)									20 00				10
Spinners, cotton							7 50	6 00	7 00				10
,, cotton (women, girls, and boys)				3 00	2 00	2 50							10
,, brass									20 00				10
,, jute (men)							7 50		7 50				10
,, jute (women, girls, and boys)													
Spool silk factory employés (men)										125 00		100 00	10
Spool silk factory employés (women and girls)							9 00	3 60	6 00				10

* And found.

		Per Hour.			Per Day.			Per Week.			Per Month.			Hours.
Occupation.		Max.	Min.	Av.	Max.	Min.	Av.	Max.	Min.	Av.	Max.	Min.	Av.	
		Cents.	Cents.	Cents.	Dol. c.	Dol. c.	Dol. c.	Dol. c.	Dol. c.	Dol. c.	Dol. c.	Dol. c.	Dol. c.	
Spool silk factory employés (boys)		..	..	..	..	..	..	6 00	3 00	3 75	..	..	..	10
Soap-makers		..	..	..	..	..	..	15 00	12 00	13 50	..	..	..	10
Soap packers (boys and girls)		..	..	..	..	..	..	9 00	7 50	8 00	..	..	..	8
Soda works employés		..	..	..	10 00	5 00	..	..	..	..	..	..	..	9
Stainers, glass		..	..	..	5 00	3 00	3 50	..	..	..	..	..	..	9
Stair builders		..	..	..	4 00	3 50	3 50	..	..	..	..	..	..	9
Steam fitters		..	..	..	4 50	2 50	3 50	..	..	..	..	..	..	9
Steamship men		..	..	..	..	..	..	..	..	..	70 00	25 00	..	10
Stereotypers		..	..	..	..	..	..	20 00	12 00	15 00	..	..	..	9
Stevedores		..	..	55	..	..	5 00	..	..	..	..	..	..	9
Stocking-makers (women and girls)		..	..	..	..	..	..	9 00	6 00	7 00	..	..	..	10
Stone-carvers		..	..	..	6 00	4 00	5 00	..	..	..	..	..	..	9
Stone-cutters		..	..	..	4 50	2 50	3 50	..	..	..	..	..	..	9
Stone letterers		..	..	..	4 00	..	4 00	..	..	..	..	..	..	9
Straw hat makers		..	..	..	..	..	..	18 00	12 00	15 00	..	..	..	10
Surveyors		..	..	..	10 00	5 00	7 50	..	..	..	..	..	..	12
Suspender-makers (women and girls)		..	..	..	..	..	..	9 00	6 00	7 50	..	..	..	9
Suspender-makers (boys)		..	..	..	..	..	..	10 00	6 25	8 00	..	..	..	9
Tack and brad-makers		..	..	..	4 00	2 50	3 50	..	..	..	..	..	..	10
Tailors		..	..	..	..	..	..	20 00	12 00	15 00	..	..	..	10
" (cutters)		..	..	..	..	..	..	45 00	20 00	30 00	..	..	..	9
Tanners		..	..	..	..	..	..	15 00	12 00	15 00	..	..	..	10
Teamsters		..	..	..	..	..	..	15 00	12 00	15 00	..	..	..	11
Teasers		..	..	..	..	..	..	..	..	..	100 00	65 00	65 00	8
Telegraph operators (men)		..	..	..	..	..	..	..	..	..	90 00	60 00	84 00	9
" " (women)		..	..	..	..	..	..	..	..	..	70 00	50 00	56 42	9
" " messengers (boys)		..	..	..	..	..	..	..	..	..	15 00	12 00	13 50	..

Occupation.	Per Hour. Max. Cents.	Per Hour. Min. Cents.	Per Hour. Av. Cents.	Per Day. Max. Dol. c.	Per Day. Min. Dol. c.	Per Day. Av. Dol. c.	Per Week. Max. Dol. c.	Per Week. Min. Dol. c.	Per Week. Av. Dol. c.	Per Month. Max. Dol. c.	Per Month. Min. Dol. c.	Per Month. Av. Dol. c.	Hours.
Tin can makers (men)							21 00	9 00	13 00				10
,, ,, (women and girls)							8 00	5 00	6 00				10
,, ,, (boys)							8 00	5 00	6 00				10
Tinsmiths							30 00	12 00	20 00				10
,, (apprentices)							10 00	3 50	7 00				10
Tool finishers				3 50	3 00	3 00							10
,, makers				3 50	3 00	3 00							10
Trimmers, carriage				3 50	2 00	3 00							10
Trunk-makers (men)							16 00	12 00	14 00				9
,, ,, (women and girls)							8 00	7 00	7 50				9
,, ,, (boys)							9 00	5 00	7 50				9
Turners, iron				3 50	3 00	3 25	24 00	18 00	18 00				10
,, wood													9
Type casters							21 00	12 00	15 00				10
,, setters (men)						3 50			15 00	80 00	30 00	50 00	10
,, ,, (women)									9 00	80 00	25 00	40 00	
,, writers (men)													
,, ,, (women)						3 50							
Umbrella-makers (men)							18 00	6 00	11 00				10
,, ,, (women)							12 00	6 00	9 00				10
,, ,, (boys)													9
Underwear, ladies', cutters (men)				4 00	3 00	3 50	8 50	2 50	6 00				9
Underwear, ladies', makers (women)													
Upholsterers						3 00	20 00	12 00	15 00				10
Varnish-makers (men)				3 50	2 50								10
,, ,, (boys)							5 00	3 00	4 00				10

83

Occupation.	Per Hour. Max. Cents.	Per Hour. Min. Cents.	Per Hour. Av. Cents.	Per Day. Max. Dol. c.	Per Day. Min. Dol. c.	Per Day. Av. Dol. c.	Per Week. Max. Dol. c.	Per Week. Min. Dol. c.	Per Week. Av. Dol. c.	Per Month. Max. Dol. c.	Per Month. Min. Dol. c.	Per Month. Av. Dol. c.	Hours.
Vaqueros	..	..	..	..	..	..	..	..	..	..	..	50 00	10 to 12
Wagon-makers	..	..	..	5 00	2 25	3 00	..	..	..	..	..	..	10
Waiters	..	..	..	..	..	..	..	..	..	75 00*	45 00*	45 00*	11
Watch-makers	..	..	..	..	..	..	25 00	15 00	20 00	..	..	..	9
Weavers, carpet	..	..	..	..	..	..	20 00	10 00	15 00	..	..	..	10
Weavers, cotton (men, women, girls and boys)	..	..	..	..	..	..	11 00	6 00	7 50	..	..	..	10
Weavers, jute (women, girls, and boys)	..	..	..	..	..	..	7 50	4 00	6 00	..	..	..	10
Well borers, artesian	..	..	..	5 00	3 00	3 50	..	..	..	..	..	..	10
Wheelwrights	..	..	..	5 00	2 25	3 00	..	..	..	..	..	..	10
White lead makers (men)	..	..	..	2 50	1 50	2 00	..	..	..	..	..	..	10
,, ,, (boys)	..	..	..	..	..	..	..	..	..	30 00	20 00	25 00	10
Whiteners	..	..	..	3 50	2 50	3 00	..	..	..	..	..	..	9
Wine-makers	..	..	..	..	..	..	..	..	..	150 00	65 00	75 00	9 to 10
Wire (barb) fence makers	..	..	..	..	..	..	12 00	10 00	10 00	..	..	..	10
,, cleaners	..	..	..	..	..	..	18 00	15 00	11 00	..	..	..	10
,, drawers	..	..	..	..	..	..	..	..	17 50	..	..	..	10
,, rope makers	..	..	..	..	..	..	21 00	15 00	15 00	..	..	..	10
,, weavers	..	..	..	..	..	..	18 00	18 00	18 00	..	..	..	10
,, workers	..	..	..	..	..	..	..	12 00	13 00	..	..	..	10
Wood carvers	..	..	30	3 00	..	3 00	..	..	..	..	..	..	9
,, ,, furniture	..	..	..	4 50	4 00	4 50	..	..	..	..	..	..	9
,, cutters	..	..	..	..	..	..	..	..	..	65 00	25 00	30 00	10
,, engravers	..	..	..	5 00	2 00	3 50	..	..	..	..	..	..	8
Wooden ware workers	..	..	..	..	..	..	15 00	7 50	10 00	..	..	..	10

* And found.

	Per Hour.		Per Day.			Per Week.			Per Month.			Hours.
Occupation.	Max.	Min.	Av.	Max.	Min.	Av.	Max.	Min.	Av.	Max.	Min.	Av.	
	Cents.	Cents.	Cents.	Dol. c.	Dol. c.	Dol. c.	Dol. c.	Dol. c.	Dol. c.	Dol. c.	Dol. c.	Dol. c.	
Wooden mill employés (men)	..	..	..	..	..	..	41 50	9 00	15 00	..	..	..	11
,, ,, ,, (women)	..	..	..	..	..	..	12 50	6 00	9 00	..	..	..	11
,, ,, ,, (boys)	..	..	..	..	..	..	6 00	4 50	5 00	..	..	..	11
Wool graders	..	..	..	4 00	2 50	3 00	..	..	..	125 00	100 00	100 00	10
,, scourers	..	..	..	3 00	1 50	2 25	20 00	..	20 00	..	..	..	10
,, sorters	..	..	..	..	..	2 50	..	..	..	..	..	..	10

(Table No. 2.)—COMPARISON of the Weekly Wages paid in California with other States and European Countries.

Industries.	California.	New York.	Illinois (Chicago).	Pennsylvania.	Maine.	Germany.	France.	Belgium.	Italy.	England and Wales.	Switzerland.	Denmark.	Scotland.	Ireland.	Canada (Ottawa).	Hawaiian Islands.
	Dol. c.	Dol. c.	Dol. c.	Dol. c.	Dol. c.	D. c.	D. c.	D. c.	D. c.	D. c.	D. c.	D. c.	D. c.	D. c.	D. c.	D. c.
Building Trades.																
Bricklayers	30 00	20 00	24 00	15 00	16 50	4 21	5 74	4 56	4 20	7 56	5 21	7 00	7 50	7 22	18 00	30 00
Carpenters	21 00	14 00	16 50	12 00	10 50	4 11	6 20	4 07	4 00	7 66	4 74	7 00	7 73	6 97	11 60	20 00
Gasfitters	20 00	12 00	18 00	12 00	.. ..	4 08	6 07	5 00	3 40	7 66	5 04	5 90	6 44	7 47	13 50	24 00
Masons	30 00	18 00	24 00	15 00	16 50	4 07	5 33	5 22	3 60	7 68	5 27	5 36	7 53	7 12	13 50	24 00
Plasterers	30 00	18 00	27 00	15 00	16 50	4 43	6 34	4 66	5 04	7 80	5 03	6 79	6 72	7 12	13 50	27 00
Plumbers	20 00	16 00	16 50	15 00	.. ..	4 26	6 10	5 46	3 60	7 90	5 18	6 90	7 23	7 47	13 50	24 00
Painters	18 00	.. ..	.. ..	.. ..	12 00	4 82	.. ..	.. ..	.. ..	.. ..	2 99	.. ..	.. ..	.. ..	.. ..	.. ..
Roofers	18 00	12 00	16 50	12 00	10 50	4 28	5 65	4 97	4 20	7 35	2 99	8 00	.. ..	6 57	13 50	24 00
Slaters	20 00	14 00	21 00	12 00	.. ..	4 20	5 65	4 98	4 20	7 10	4 35	4 00	.. ..	6 85	.. ..	.. ..
Other Trades.																
Bakers	18 00	7 00	12 00	10 00	8 00	3 90	5 48	4 28	4 00	6 17	3 88	4 80	6 32	6 53	10 50	23 00
Blacksmiths	21 00	13 00	15 00	9 50	10 50	4 00	5 81	5 38	3 60	7 37	5 20	4 82	6 32	7 07	10 50	27 00
Bookbinders	21 00	14 00	16 50	12 00	.. ..	4 20	5 17	5 35	3 80	6 77	4 68	4 82	7 29	7 22	10 00	16 00
Brick-makers	8 75	10 00	7 40	7 50	9 00	3 96	5 82	4 25	5 00	7 00	4 43	5 90	5 83	6 41	8 10	.. ..
Brewers	18 00	15 00	.. ..	12 00	.. ..	.. ..	4 43	4 67	8 00	6 85	3 78	3 75	5 34	7 30	15 00	.. ..
Brass founders	18 00	10 00	16 75	12 00	.. ..	4 38	6 54	6 02	4 60	7 47	4 92	4 82	6 72	7 34	.. ..	.. ..

Industries.	California.	New York.	Illinois (Chicago).	Pennsylvania.	Maine.	Germany.	France.	Belgium.	Italy.	England and Wales.	Switzerland.	Denmark.	Scotland.	Ireland.	Canada (Ottawa).	Hawaiian Islands.
	Dol. c.	Dol. c.	Dol. c.	Dol. c.	Dol. c.	D. c.	D. c.	D. c.	D. c.	D. c.	D. c.	D. c.	D. c.	D. c.	D. c.	D. c.
Butchers	12 50	8 00	16 00	9 00	..	3 32	4 82	4 31	..	5 50	4 66	4 37	6 08	6 81	9 60	12 75
Cabinet-makers	21 00	12 00	15 00	15 00	10 50	4 25	6 14	5 66	3 40	7 68	7 70	5 00	6 08	7 22	11 40	19 50
Confectioners	12 00	..	15 00	10 00	10 00	3 43	4 85	5 03	3 75	6 84	5 30	..	6 80	9 85	10 00	..
Cigar-makers	12 00	10 00	12 00	12 00	9 50	3 63	4 69	6 28	3 00	6 07	3 30	5 09	..	..	..	..
Coopers	20 00	12 00	18 00	..	9 00	3 97	5 58	5 17	2 60	7 50	4 80	4 82	6 08	6 81	9 00	..
Cutlers	24 00	10 00	12 00	..	..	3 90	5 16	5 28	3 80	7 00	8 00	4 60	6 32	8 03	8 40	..
Cab and carriage	10 00	9 00	10 00	..	..	3 21	4 82	3 92	2 50	5 15	3 84	4 80	4 86	4 26	..	2 50
Distillers	15 00	9 00	..	12 00	..	3 56	7 00	5 00	4 20	..	4 02	..	..	6 00	..	..
Draymen and teamsters	15 00	10 00	12 00	9 00	9 60	2 96	5 57	3 77	1 50	5 37	3 84	3 22	4 49	4 26	8 40	2 50
Dyers	15 00	13 00	16 50	8 88	..	3 45	4 83	6 15	3 60	6 18	4 91	4 29	5 56	4 86	7 00	..
Engravers	20 00	16 00	24 00	..	..	5 12	7 35	6 42	6 60	8 38	6 35	8 00	7 29	8 27	15 00	19 00
Furriers*	7 to 12	10 00	15 00	..	..	4 20	7 00	6 35	4 60	8 52	4 63	5 36	7 50	8 03	14 00	..
Gardeners	18 00	9 00	12 00	..	8 40	3 78	5 11	3 91	4 00	5 80	3 83	4 00	4 86	4 86	8 00	..
Hatters	24 00	13 00	21 00	15 00	..	4 36	5 50	4 60	5 20	6 10	3 84	..	7 29	7 30	12 00	24 00
Horseshoers	21 00	13 00	18 00	..	..	3 61	5 89	5 62	5 20	6 35	4 65	4 82	6 80	6 21	12 00	19 00
Jewellers	20 00	11 00	13 50	..	..	5 21	6 24	6 84	3 80	8 76	6 35	5 36	6 56	8 00	12 00	12 00
Labourers (plasterers')	18 00	10 00	15 00	9 00	..	2 91	3 23	3 02	1 70	5 27	3 40	3 86	4 65	3 53	13 50	11 00
Hod carriers	18 00	11 00	10 50	8 00	..	2 92	3 13	3 22	1 70	4 94	2 99	4 30	4 65	3 40	8 40	11 00
Masons	18 00	10 00	10 50	7 50	..	3 15	3 23	3 09	1 70	5 07	3 50	4 29	4 63	3 65	8 40	17 50
Strikers (blacksmiths')	18 00	9 60	10 50	7 00	..	2 94	4 72	3 29	3 40	5 30	4 43	4 82	4 86	3 79	7 00	10 50
Plumbers' assistants†	7 00	10 00	5 70†	6 00	..	2 72	3 61	2 93	1 70	4 69	3 36	2 80	4 63	3 38	8 40	..
Lithographers	25 00	12 00	..	..	..	5 59	7 07	5 86	..	7 07	5 51	5 50	7 53	7 71	12 00	..

* Men and women.   † Boys.

87

Industries.	California.	New York.	Illinois (Chicago).	Pennsylvania.	Maine.	Germany.	France.	Belgium.	Italy.	England and Wales.	Switzerland.	Denmark.	Scotland.	Ireland.	Canada (Ottawa).	Hawaiian Islands.
	Dol. c.	Dol. c.	Dol. c.	Dol. c.	Dol. c.	D. c.	D. c.	D. c.	D.	D. c.	D. c.	D. c.	D. c.	D. c.	D. c.	D. c.
Millwrights	24 00	14 00	30 00	..	..	4 18	6 74	5 00	..	6 97	6 30	6 00	7 41	7 30	12 00	..
Machinists	20 00	10 00	..	..	15 00	4 60	4 60	..	..	..	4 82	4 00	..	7 79	12 00	..
Potters	15 00	10 00	..	12 00	..	3 60	4 78	4 86	5 20	5 20	5 76	4 02	..	4 38	..	..
Printers	20 00	13 00	15 00	12 00	9 00	..	6 64	5 94	4 60	7 17	5 93	5 36	7 89	8 52	11 00	25 00
Pattern-makers	21 00	12 00	35 00	..	..	..	..	..	..	9 00	..	..	7 41	7 79	..	31 00
Teachers (male)	19 99	13 00	11 00	..	7 50	..	7 00	7 74	5 00	7 70	..	10 41	16 69	8 52	6 00	23 00
(female)	16 03	..	12 00	..	12 00	..	..	..	..	..	..	..	..	..	3 00	..
Saddle and harness	13 50	11 00	12 00	12 50	..	3 69	5 70	5 51	2 80	6 63	5 20	5 00	5 58	6 15	7 00	19 05
Sail-makers	18 00	12 00	15 00	..	..	2 85	6 04	4 56	2 00	7 02	..	4 82	6 08	8 03	..	..
Stevedores	24 00	12 00	18 00	9 00	..	5 70	6 72	4 36	2 00	8 44	..	5 00	4 12	5 40	..	12 00
Tanners	12 00	..	15 00	..	..	4 00	5 18	5 81	2 20	6 38	4 92	5 09	6 80	5 45	8 25	..
Tailors	18 12	12 00	15 00	..	..	4 30	5 02	5 58	4 00	7 40	6 50	6 36	7 77	6 70	9 00	21 50
Telegraph operators	15 00	..	19 30	..	..	5 12	6 92	6 35	5 20	7 65	..	6 70	13 00	8 87	8 50	..
Tinsmiths	15 00	11 00	12 00	..	13 50	3 55	5 46	4 40	6 60	6 56	4 40	6 70	6 56	6 04	8 00	18 00

States and Countries.

From Statutes of California.

3244. Eight hours a day's work.

Section 3244. Eight hours of labour constitute a day's work, unless it is otherwise expressly stipulated by the parties to a contract.

3245. Same, on public works.

Section 3245. Eight hours labour constitute a legal day's work in all cases where the same is performed under the authority of any law of this State, or under the direction, control, or by the authority of any officer of this State acting in his official capacity, or under the direction, control, or by the authority of any municipal corporation within this State, or of any officer thereof acting as such; and a stipulation to that effect must be made a part of all contracts to which the State or any municipal corporation therein is a party.

UNITED STATES.

No. 35.

Sir J. Pauncefote to the Marquis of Salisbury.—(Received July 1.)

My Lord, Washington, June 21, 1889.

IN reply to your Lordship's Circular despatch of the 2nd ultimo, I have the honour to inform your Lordship that there are no bounties whatever paid in this country at the present moment.

I have, &c.
(Signed) J. PAUNCEFOTE.

(187)

No. 11.

UNITED STATES.

Mr. Edwardes to the Marquis of Salisbury.—(Received March 15.)

My Lord, Washington, February 26, 1889.

I HAVE the honour to inclose replies to the questions set forth in the inclosure of your Lordship's Circular of the 3rd August last, on the subject of the duties, &c., connected with a Ministry of Commerce.

There exists in the Government of the United States no such Department, but I have endeavoured to reply to the questions in so far as the duties of the Secretary of the Treasury may be looked upon as approximate to those of a Minister of Commerce.

I have, &c.
(Signed) H. G. EDWARDES.

Inclosure in No. 11.

Replies to Questions.

1-10. As there is no Ministry of Commerce in the Government of the United States, there is no reply to be given to these questions.

11. The officers in the United States' Consular Service are solely under the control of the Department of State (which corresponds to the Foreign Office).

Consular accounts of all kinds, however, are transmitted direct to the Treasury Department.

12. The cost of the Consular Service for the fiscal year ended the 30th June, 1888, was 934,983 dollars (186,996*l*. 12*s*.), the amount of fees collected being

999,172 dollars (199,834*l*. 8*s*.), showing an excess of receipts of 64,189 dollars (12,837*l*. 16*s*.) over expenditure. The cost of the Service is borne on the Budget of the Department of State.

The Statutes of the United States classify the Consulates-General, Consulates, and Commercial Agencies into three classes:—

1. Those who receive a fixed salary, and are not allowed to transact business. Of these there are 206.

2. Those who receive a fixed salary, and are allowed to transact business. Of these there are 25.

3. Those who are compensated by the fees collected in their office, and are allowed to transact business. Of these there are 84, making in all 315 Consular officers.

13. No reply.

14. The Secretary of the Treasury has in some ways duties similar to those of a Minister of Commerce.

He exercises no control with respect to Chambers of Commerce in the United States, which are incorporated voluntary bodies.

Merchants or other residents of the State or of contiguous States are generally chosen as members by election by ballot, five negative ballots being required to exclude.

15. The Secretary of the Treasury frequently takes the opinion of Chambers of Commerce, and advice from the latter to him is often proffered.

The most notable instances are probably their action in regard to the resumption of specie payments, and the Convention of Maritime Nations in regard to safety at sea, &c.

16. Syndical Chambers and other Commercial Associations are only brought into official contact with the Minister in the same way as Chambers of Commerce.

There is the National Board of Trade composed of the various Boards of Trade (not official), Chambers of Commerce, and other chartered bodies organized for general commercial purposes, in order to secure unity and harmony of action in reference to commercial usages, customs, and laws, and especially to secure the proper consideration of questions pertaining to the financial and industrial interests of the country; it corresponds in some respects with the Associated Chambers of Commerce of England, and the number of delegates

189

to it is based on the number of members of each Board of Trade, Chamber of Commerce, &c. The National Board of Trade memorialized the Senate and House of Representatives, urging the necessity of the calling of an International Conference, to be held in the United States, to consider and report Rules and Regulations with a view to lessen the dangers of navigation, and to afford greater safety to life and property on the high seas. This is one of the many instances in which questions have been brought before Congress, and the practice necessarily carries considerable weight.

17. The Bureau of Statistics at Washington issues a Report quarterly and annually, which is distributed among mercantile bodies free.

18. The Reports of the Bureau of Statistics referred to above, and general information, is given to traders on application.

20. The Secretary of the Treasury is the only officer whose duties approximate to those of the President of the Board of Trade in London, and his duties, compared with those of our Board of Trade, are of a very limited character. He exercises control in regard to lighthouses, harbours, life saving service, and general maritime matters.

259

No. 23.

UNITED STATES.

Mr. Edwardes to the Marquis of Salisbury.

My Lord, *Washington, July* 9, 1888.
WITH reference to your Lordship's Circular despatch of 30th April last, I have the honour to transmit herewith reports from Her Majesty's Consuls in the United States on the subject of the legislation in their respective Consular districts with respect to the formation, &c., of companies, whether joint stock or in shares.

I have, &c.,
(Signed) H. G. EDWARDES.

Inclosure in No. 23.

Report as to Legislation in this District in regard to the Formation, Regulation, and Dissolution of Companies.

Sir, *New York, June* 26, 1888.
I HAVE the honour, in accordance with instructions contained in Sir Lionel West's Circular of the 21st May, to make the following report upon the state of legislation in the States of my district in regard to the formation, regulation, and dissolution of companies, whether joint stock or in shares, or in whatever manner constituted.

New York.

Article 8, Section 1, of the Constitution of the State of New York provides for the formation of companies as follows :—

Corporations may be formed under general laws, but shall not be created by special Act, except for municipal purposes, and in cases when, in the judgment of the legislature, the objects of the corporation cannot be attained under general laws. All general laws and special Acts passed pursuant to this section may be altered from time to time or repealed.

By an Act of the Legislature of New York State, passed in 1811, it was provided that companies for manufacturing certain articles might be incorporated by five or more persons filing a certificate in the office of the Secretary of State. This Act continued in force until 1848, when the Legislature adopted "An Act to authorise the Formation of Corporations for Manufacturing, Mining, Mechanical, or Chemical purposes." The operation and effect of this statute have been extended by several subsequent enactments to corporations having the following objects, not strictly included in the terms manufacturing, mining, mechanical, or chemical (see Appendix No. 1, Introduction, pages 3, 4, and 5, secs. 1 and 27).

By an Act passed in 1866, the title of the Act passed in 1848 was amended so as to read " An Act to authorise the Formation of Corporations for Manufacturing, Mining, Mechanical, Chemical, Agricultural, Horticultural, Medical or Curative, Mercantile or Commercial Purposes." In 1875 an Act was passed entitled " An Act for the Organisation and Regulation of Certain Business Corporations." This comprised all trades, not included in the Act of 1848, with its amendments, with the exception of banking, insurance, construction and operation of railroads, or aiding in the construction thereof, savings' banks, trust companies or corporations intended to derive profit from the loan or use of money, or safe deposit companies. Corporations formed under this Act are of two classes, known respectively as—

Full liability companies.
Limited liability companies.

In full liability companies all the stockholders are severally individually liable for all debts and liabilities of such companies; in limited liability companies stockholders are only liable to the amount of their stock. The provisions of the Act of 1875 apply only to corporations organised under it, and between it and the Act of 1848 there is no conflict; each law exists independently and with full effect. A corporation organised under the manufacturing Act has only to comply with its requirements and it need not be concerned about the terms of the business Act, and *vice versâ*.

Under the banking laws of this State there is a department charged with the execution of the laws in relation to banking associations and individual bankers, savings' banks, trust, loan, mortgage, security, guarantee indemnity associations, and every corporation or association having the power and receiving money on deposit, existing or incorporated, other than insurance companies. The superintendent is appointed by the Governor of the State, by and with the advice of the Senate, and holds his office for three years. The expenses of the department are paid by the banking, &c., associations. The president or cashier of every banking association having securities deposited with the superintendent must once or more in each year compare such securities with the books of said department, and, if found correct, execute to the superintendent a receipt setting forth the different kinds and amounts thereof, and that the same are in the possession of the superintendent at the date of such receipt. If any banking association or individual banker shall refuse or neglect to make such examination, the Comptroller, Secretary of State, and the Superintendent of the Banks Department shall appoint a person to do the duty. Every banking association and individual banker carrying on a banking business shall be subject to the inspection and supervision of the Superintendent of the Banking Department.

Under the banking laws of 1882 the superintendent must see that the capital of a banking association or individual banker is in accordance with the certificate required prior to commencing business as a banker, and if, upon subsequent examination, he finds a deficiency in the capital, he has power to require the bank to make good the deficiency, and if it be not done he must refer the matter to the Attorney-General, whose duty it shall then become to institute such proceedings against any such banking associations, as authorised in the case of insolvent corporations (see annex No. 4).

I send as Appendices to this Report:—

261

No. 1. A book giving the Act for manufacturing corporations.
No. 2. A book giving the Act for business corporations.
No. 3. A book giving the laws relating to railroads.
No. 4. Contains the mode of procedure, in an abridged form, under the Code of Civil Procedure in an action to procure the dissolution of a corporation.

(In page 420, of Appendix No. 3, is given the Act to provide for the winding up of corporations which have been annulled by legislative enactments.)

Rhode Island.

In regard to the laws of this State I send Appendices :—

No. 5. The Act respecting corporations in general.
No. 6. Act in regard to banking, abridged.
No. 7. Act in regard to insurance companies, abridged.
No. 8. Act in regard to manufacturing companies, abridged.

New Jersey.

Corporations are created under general laws : they may hold real estate for the purpose of their business or as security for debts. When capital is not all paid in, stockholders are bound to pay the sum necessary to complete their shares as fixed by charter, or such proportion as shall be necessary to the debts of the company.

Connecticut.

Corporations may be formed, with or without any capital stock, by any number of persons not less than three, who, by articles of agreement, in writing, shall associate under any name assumed by them for the purpose of engaging in any kind of business, except banking or insurance. The name of every private corporation which shall be hereafter created shall indicate that it is a corporation. The capital stock, if any, of such corporation must be fixed in the articles of association, which must be published, and must specify definitely the purpose for which such corporation is established. 20 per cent. of the capital stock must be paid in, in cash. In case the principal business is to be carried on out of this State the secretary and treasurer and a majority of the directors must always be residents of this State. Annual returns of capital paid in, cash value of real and personal estate, exclusive of patents, and of its credits, the amount of its debts, and the name, residence, and number of shares of each shareholder must be made to the town clerk of the town in which such corporation transacts business, and also with the Secretary of State. If the capital stock is withdrawn and refunded to stockholders before payment of debts, the stockholders will be liable to creditors to the amount refunded to them respectively. The officers, upon failure to perform any of the duties required by law, become liable for the debts of the corporation contracted during the period of such failure.

Delaware.

There is a general Act for the incorporation of persons for the purpose of carrying on any manufacturing business, for the purpose of preserving animal and vegetable food, for draining low lands, and for building, and loan associations. Persons desiring to be associated by corporate Act present a certificate of their articles of association to the associate judge of the county after ten days' notice in two newspapers of the county. If it appear to the judge that the purposes of the incorporation are lawful, and involve nothing detrimental to the public interest and welfare, that the certificate is in proper form, that the amount of capital stock and proposed value of real estate are proper, and that a majority of the corporators are *bonâ fide* residents of the State, he indorses his approval, files the certificate in the office of the Secretary of State, and a certified copy is recorded in the recorder's office of the county in which the application is made.

The laws of New Jersey, Connecticut, and Delaware are so similar to those of New York that I have not thought it necessary to send them entire or even in an abridged form.

I have, &c.,
(Signed) WM. LANE BOOKER.

NEW YORK.

Code of Civil Procedure.—Action to procure the Dissolution of a Company.

Action by judgment creditor for sequestration.
Section 1784. When final judgment for a sum of money has been rendered against a corporation created by or under the laws of the State, and an execution issued thereupon to the sheriff of the county where the corporation transacts its general business, or where its principal office is located, has been returned wholly or partly unsatisfied, the judgment creditor may maintain an action to procure a judgment, sequestrating the property of the corporation, and providing for a distribution thereof as prescribed in Section 1793 of this Act.

Action to dissolve a corporation.
Section 1785. In either of the following cases, an action to procure a judgment dissolving a corporation created by or under the laws of the State, and forfeiting its corporate rights, privileges, and franchises may be maintained as prescribed in the next section.

1. When the corporation has remained insolvent for at least one year.
2. Where it has neglected or refused for at least one year to pay and discharge its notes or other evidences of debt.
3. Where it has suspended its ordinary and lawful business for at least one year.
4. If it has banking powers, or power to make loans on pledges or deposits, or to make insurances, when it becomes insolvent or unable to pay its debts, or has violated any provision of the Act by or under which it was incorporated or of any other Act binding upon it.

By whom such action may be maintained.
Section 1786. An action specified in the last section may be maintained by the Attorney-General in the name and in the behalf of the people; and whenever a creditor or stockholder of any corporation submits to the Attorney-General a written statement of facts, verified by oath, showing grounds for an action under the provisions of the last section, and the Attorney-General omits for 60 days after

this submission to commence an action specified in the last section, then, and not otherwise, such creditor or stockholder may apply to the proper court for leave to commence such an action, and on obtaining leave may maintain the same accordingly.

Section 1787. (Provides for a temporary injunction.)

Sections 1788 and 1789.—Provisions for appointment of a receiver, and giving powers to act.

Section 1790. When the action is brought by a creditor of a corporation, and the stockholders, directors, trustees, or other officers, or any of them are made liable by law, in any event or contingency for the payment of his debt, the persons so made liable may be made parties defendant, by the original, or by a supplemental complaint; and their liability may be declared and enforced by the judgment in the action. *Making shareholders, &c., parties.*

Section 1791. When the stockholders, directors, trustees, or other officers of a corporation who are made liable in any event or contingency for the payment of a debt are not made parties defendant as prescribed in the last section, the plaintiff in the action may maintain a separate action against them to procure a judgment declaring, apportioning, and informing their liability. *When separate action may be brought against them.*

Section 1792. In an action brought as prescribed in either of the last two sections, the court must, when it is necessary, cause an account to be taken of the property and of the debts of the corporation; and thereupon the defendants' liability must be apportioned accordingly, but if it affirmatively appears that the corporation is insolvent, and has no property to satisfy its creditors, the court may without taking such an account ascertain and determine the amount of each defendant's liability and enforce the same accordingly. *Proceedings in either action.*

Section 1793. A final judgment in an action brought against a corporation as prescribed in this article, either separately or in conjunction with its stockholders, directors, trustees, or other officers, must provide for a just and fair distribution of the property of the corporation and of the proceeds thereof, among its fair and honest creditors in the order and in the proportions prescribed by law in case of the voluntary dissolution of a corporation. *Judgment property of corporation to be distributed.*

Section 1794. When the stockholders of a corporation are parties to the action, if the property of the corporation is not sufficient to discharge its debts, the interlocutory or final judgment, as the case requires, must adjudge that each stockholder pay into court the amount due and remaining unpaid of the shares of stock held by him, or so much thereof as is necessary to satisfy the debts of the corporation. *Stock subscriptions to be recovered.*

Section 1795. If it appears that the property of the corporation and the sums collected or collectable from the stockholders upon their stock subscriptions are, or will be, insufficient to pay the debts of the corporation, the court must ascertain the several sums for which the officers or the stockholders of the corporation being parties to the action are liable; and must adjudge that the same be paid into court to be applied, in such proportion and in such order as justice requires, to the payment of the debts of the corporation. *As to liabilities of directors and stockholders.*

Section 1796. This article does not repeal or affect any special provision of law, prescribing that a particular kind of corporation shall cease to exist, or shall be dissolved in a case or in a manner not prescribed in this article, or any special provision of law prescribing the mode of enforcing the liability of the stockholders of a particular kind of corporation. *Effect of this article limited.*

RHODE ISLAND.—RESPECTING CORPORATIONS IN GENERAL.

General powers of corporations.
Section 1. All corporations shall, whenever no other provision is specially made, have perpetual succession, may make and use a common seal, and break, alter, and renew the same, be capable of taking, holding, transmitting, and conveying property, real or personal, in their corporate name, may sue and be sued, appear, prosecute and defend actions and suits to final judgment and execution in any court or elsewhere; may elect, in such manner as they shall determine to be proper, all necessary officers, and shall fix their compensation, and define their duties and obligations; and may make bye-laws and regulations, consistent with law, for their government, and for the due and orderly conducting of their affairs, and the management of their property.

Shares, personal estate, except, &c. How transferable. I. R. I. 165.
Section 2. The shares into which the capital stock of any corporation shall be divided shall be deemed to be personal estate, unless otherwise provided in the Act creating the corporation, and shall be transferable in such manner as shall be prescribed by the bye-laws of their corporation.

What may be included in bye-laws.
Section 3. Corporations may, by their bye-laws, where no other provision is specially made, determine the manner of calling and conducting meetings, the number of shares that shall constitute a quorum, the number of shares that shall entitle the members to one or more votes, the mode of voting by proxy, the mode of selling shares for the non-payment of assessments, and the tenure of office of the several officers, and they may annex suitable penalties to such bye-laws, not exceeding in any case the sum of 20 dollars for any one offence, but no such bye-law shall be made by any corporation repugnant to the provisions of its charter.

Of first meeting of corporation.
Section 4. The first meeting of all corporations, except of banks, shall, unless otherwise provided for in their Acts of incorporation, be called by a notice signed by any one or more of the persons named in the Act of incorporation, and setting forth the time, place, and objects of the meeting, and such notice shall, seven days at least before the meeting, be delivered to each member, or published in some newspaper of the county, where the corporation may be established, or if there be a newspaper in the county, then in some newspaper of an adjoining county: Provided, that notice of the first meeting of incorporated religious societies may be affixed to the door or some other conspicuous part of their meeting-house or usual place of assembling for religious purposes.

Mode of proceeding when no person authorised to call or preside at legal meeting.
Section 5. Whenever, by the death or absence of the officers of any corporation, or other legal impediment, there shall be no person duly authorised to call or preside at a legal meeting thereof, any justice of the peace in the county where such corporation is established may, on a written application of three or more of the members thereof, issue a warrant to either of said members, directing him to call a meeting of said corporation by giving such notice as has been previously required by law, and the justice may, in the same warrant, direct such person to preside at such meeting, until a clerk shall be duly chosen and qualified, if there shall be no officer present legally authorised to preside thereat.

Power of corporation when assembled.
Section 6. Such corporation, when so assembled, may elect officers to fill vacancies then existing and may act upon such other business as might by law be transacted at regular meetings of the corporation.

Section 7. The validity of any Act of incorporation shall not be impaired by a failure to hold an annual meeting for the election of officers or a failure to elect officers at the time prescribed by the charter or bye-laws of the corporation; but such election may be held at a subsequent meeting of the stockholders duly notified for that purpose. *Incorporation valid although annual meeting not held.*

Section 8. Corporations whose charter shall expire by their own limitation, or shall be annulled by forfeiture or otherwise, shall nevertheless be continued bodies corporate for the term of three years after the time when they would have been so dissolved, for the purpose of prosecuting and defending suits by or against them and of enabling them to settle and close their concerns, to dispose of and convey their property, and to divide their capital stock; but not for the purpose of continuing the business for which such corporations have been or may be established. *Corporations, when to continue after expiration of charter.*

Section 9. Whenever final judgment shall be recovered against any turnpike or other corporation authorised to receive tolls, the franchise of such corporation, with all the rights and privileges thereof, so far as relates to the receiving of toll, and also all other corporate property, may be taken on execution and sold, in the same manner as real estate belonging to corporations is liable by law to be taken and sold on execution. *What property may be levied on, on execution against.*

Section 10. In the sale of the franchise of any corporation, the person who shall satisfy the execution with all legal fees and expenses thereon, and who shall agree in consideration thereof to take such franchise for the shortest period of time and to receive during that time all such toll as the said corporation would by law be entitled to demand, shall be considered as the highest bidder. *Who deemed highest bidder on sale of franchise.*

Section 11. The return of the officer on such execution shall transfer to the purchaser all the privileges and immunities which by law belonged to said corporation, so far as relates to the rights of demanding toll, and the officer shall, immediately after such sale, deliver to the purchaser possession of all the toll-houses and gates belonging to said corporation, in whatever county the same may be situated, and the purchaser may thereupon establish, demand, and receive to his own use all the toll which may accrue within the time limited in the said purchase of said franchise, and during that time the corporation shall not be entitled to sue for such tolls or to prosecute for any penalty for the non-payment thereof. *How franchise transferred; rights of purchaser.*

Section 12. Any person who shall purchase the franchise of any turnpike or other corporation and the assignee of such person may recover, in an action of the case, any penalties imposed by law for an injury to the franchise or for any other cause, and which such corporation would be entitled to recover during the time limited in the said purchase of the franchise, and during that time the corporation shall not be entitled to prosecute for such penalties. *Purchaser may recover penalties for injury to franchise, &c.*

Section 13. The corporation whose franchise shall have been sold as aforesaid shall, in all other respects, retain the same powers and be bound to the discharge of the same duties and liable to the same penalties and forfeitures as before such sale. *Powers of such corporation.*

Section 14. Such corporation may, at any time within three months from the time of such sale, redeem the franchise by paying or tendering to the purchaser thereof the sum that he shall have paid therefor, with 12 per cent. interest thereon, but without any allowance for toll which he may have received; and upon such payment or tender, the said franchise and all the rights and privileges thereof shall revert and belong to said corporation as if no such sale had been made. *How franchise may be redeemed.*

Records of transfers of stock, where kept; of recording officer.

Section 15. All records of transfers of stock of corporations incorporated by the sole authority of this State shall be made and kept within this State, and the officer of every such corporation whose duty it may be to record the transfer of shares in the capital stock thereof shall at the time of his election or appointment be a resident of the State, and whenever such officer shall cease to be a resident therein, his office shall become vacant.

Place of business; agent.

Section 16. Every corporation created under the authority of this State shall have a place of business within the State and shall have a clerk, treasurer, or other agent, who shall reside therein.

Charters may be amended, &c.

Section 17. All Acts of incorporation hereafter granted shall be subject to the provisions of this chapter and may be amended or repealed at the will of the general assembly, unless express provision be made therein to the contrary.

Time of organisation.
P. L., Chap. 531.

Section 18. Corporations hereafter created by charter, if no time is limited therein, shall be organised within two years from the passage of their respective Acts of incorporation. The charters of all corporations failing to comply with the provisions of this section shall become void.

Certificate of organisation or increase of capital stock, how filed.
P. L., Chap. 366.

Section 19. Every corporation hereafter organised or which shall hereafter increase its capital stock shall, within 30 days after organisation or after such increase, file in the office of the Secretary of State a certificate, under oath of its treasurer, or such officer as may be duly authorised by the corporation to make the same, setting forth the name of the corporation, the date of organisation, and the amount of capital stock actually paid in upon organisation, the amount of increase of capital stock paid in, with the date thereof, the town in which such corporation is located, and the name and post office address of its treasurer.

RHODE ISLAND.—BANKING ACT.

The principal points in the Act in regard to banks and institutions for savings are :—

Organisation of banks.

Section 1. On the incorporation of a bank, the Governor of the State shall appoint three commissioners to superintend its organisation. Commissioners to be paid by bank.

Books of subscription.

Section 2. The commissioners shall open a book of subscriptions to the capital stock of such bank, notice being given in one or more papers published in the county.

Commissioners to apportion stock.

Section 3. When books are closed, commissioners shall apportion the stock to the amount subscribed by each person who shall, in their opinion, have the ability to make a *bonâ fide* investment therein, and they shall file a copy of the apportionment in the office of the Secretary of State.

Persons constituting corporation.

Section 4. The persons to whom the stock is apportioned shall constitute the corporation created by the charter of said bank.

Commissioners, how long to superintend organisation.

Section 8. The commissioners shall superintend the organization of such bank until the entire amount of capital stock of such bank, originally subscribed, shall have been fully paid in cash.

Stockholders, how liable for debts of bank.

Section 9. The stockholders of any bank, unless exempted by the charter, shall be personally and individually liable for all debts due from the bank for deposit, circulation, or otherwise, to the amount at their par value of the shares held by them in addition to the amount invested in such shares: Provided that the corporation shall be first sued, and the corporate property first exhausted, in the payment of the debts of the bank.

Section 16. No person shall be director of any bank unless he be a stockholder and a citizen and resident of the State, except in cases where it is otherwise specially provided. *Who may be director.*

Section 38. The general assembly at any session thereof, and the Governor at any time when the assembly is not in session, whenever it shall be deemed expedient, may institute a special commission to visit and examine any one or more of the banks or institutions for savings, to inquire whether they have been and are managed according to law, and to ascertain their state and condition, with such power and authority as shall be deemed necessary, including the power to send for persons and papers, and to summon and examine persons, under oath, touching the matters committed to them. Such commissioners may administer oaths to all persons whom they are authorized to examine under oath. *When special bank commissioners may be appointed.* *Powers and duties.*

Section 39. In addition to the examination provided in the preceding section, if any three or more persons, who shall be officers, stockholders, or creditors of any bank or institution for savings, shall make a statement in writing setting forth their interest and the reasons for making such examination, and shall direct the same to the Governor, requesting him to cause such bank or institution for savings to be examined, the Governor forthwith shall institute a special commission with full power to make a full investigation of the affairs of such corporation, in manner hereinbefore provided. *Powers of stockholders, &c., to require examination.*

Section 40. Commissioners appointed in accordance with the provisions of either of the preceding two sections shall report their doings to the general assembly as soon as may be. *Commissioners to report.*

Section 41. Every officer of any bank or of any institution for savings and every other person who shall refuse to any bank commissioner, appointed as aforesaid, such information, aid or assistance, as shall be required in the discharge of his duty as commissioner, shall be fined for each offence not exceeding 10,000 dols., and the bank or institution for savings may also be proceeded against as is hereinafter provided. *Penalty for refusing aid, &c., to commission.*

Section 42. The Supreme Court, upon complaint in writing, from any such bank commissioner, under oath, setting forth that, in his opinion, any bank or institution for savings has forfeited its charter or is so managing its concerns that the public or those having funds in its custody are in danger of being defrauded thereby, or has become insolvent, shall issue a citation to the officers of such bank commanding them to appear on a day and at a place named in the citation, then and there to show cause, if they have any, why said corporation should not be enjoined from further exercising the powers and franchises conferred by its charter. *Of citation to bank to show cause why injunction should not issue.*

Section 43. The court, if of the opinion that the charter of such corporation is forfeited, or that through its management there is danger of the public or those having funds in its custody being defrauded, or that such corporation has become insolvent, shall issue an injunction to the officers of such bank enjoining them from transacting any further business, and shall appoint a receiver of the property. *When injunction may be granted and receiver appointed.*

Section 44. The receiver shall be clothed with full power to *Powers and*

duties of receiver.
Loans to officers prohibited.
Closing up business.

collect debts and transact all the necessary business towards the closing up of the corporation.

Section 54. No money shall be loaned by any institution for savings to any officer of such institution.

Sections 59 and 60. The stockholders of any bank incorporated by the general assembly of the State shall have power by vote to close up the business of such bank, and may appoint an agent other than the directors to close up its business.

RHODE ISLAND.—OF INSURANCE COMPANIES.

State auditor, commissioner, powers and duties.
Penalty for obstructing.

Sections 1, 2, 3. The State auditor shall be insurance commissioner, and shall, at request of the Governor, visit, examine, inquire into, and report on the condition of the company; he shall have power to summon and examine under oath all directors, officers, and other agents in relation to same; the penalty for obstructing such officer in the discharge of his duties shall be a fine not exceeding 5,000 dols., or imprisonment not exceeding two years; the company may also be proceeded against.

Of citation to show cause why charter should not be forfeited, and proceedings.

Sections 4, 5. If the insurance commissioner set forth in writing, under oath, that in his opinion any insurance company has, from any cause, forfeited its charter, the Supreme Court shall issue a citation to such company, to be served on the president, secretary, or treasurer, to appear and show cause why such company's charter should not be forfeited; and if upon examination of the above-named officers the court shall be of opinion that such charter is forfeited at law, an injunction shall be issued, and a receiver, under bond, be appointed.

Of receiver, powers and duties.

Sections 6, 7. Such receiver shall have all powers and rights which such corporation possessed in collection of debts, disposal of property, and payment of all debts, first reserving such reasonable compensation for his services as the court shall approve; such receiver may be removed by the court and another appointed.

Effect of injunction.

Section 8. So long as any injunction shall be in force all executions for collection of debts shall be stayed; or a temporary injunction may be issued without appointment of a receiver.

Refusal to deliver books, &c., penalty.

Section 12. If any servant of any insurance company which shall be enjoined as aforesaid shall refuse to deliver books, &c., of such company to the receiver appointed by the court, every person so offending shall be fined not exceeding 10,000 dols., or imprisoned not exceeding three years, or be both fined and imprisoned at the discretion of the court.

Receiver of mutual company.

Section 13. The receiver of any mutual insurance company may make assessments to pay necessary debts of the company, having the same powers which the corporation possessed.

Of assessments to restore stock to original amount.

Section 14. Whenever, by reason of losses or other cause, the capital stock of any insurance company shall be diminished, the stockholders may, at a special meeting, assess every stockholder, *pro rata*, such further sum as may be necessary to fill up the capital stock to its original amount; and in case of refusal of payment by any such stockholder, his stock shall be sold at public auction after 30 days' notice.

Special meetings.

Section 15. Special meetings may, after 30 days' notice in some newspaper of the county, be called whenever deemed expedient, and not less than two-thirds of shares shall be represented, either in person or by proxy, in order to constitute a quorum.

Sections 17, 18, 19. In all cases where the laws of any other State of the United States require the insurance company to deposit, in its State, stocks or other securities for the benefit of policy-holders, the general treasurer of this State shall receive and hold the same in trust, giving a certificate under seal therefor; but the company may withdraw these and substitute other securities of equal or greater value, and all interest and dividends shall be collected by the company so depositing. *General treasurer, security for benefit of policy-holders, certificate of deposit.*

Section 20. Whenever any insurance company which shall have so deposited its seccrities with the general treasurer shall desire to relinquish its business, the general treasurer shall, on application by and under oath of the company's principal officer and secertary, publish in two newspapers in this State, twice a week at least for six months, such intention; and after being satisfied by examination that all the company's debts and liabilities are paid or extinguished, the securities so deposited shall be returned. *Delivery up of security when company relinquishes business.*

Sections 21, 22. All expenses of annual or other examinations by the general treasurer of the condition and value of such securities so deposited shall be borne by the company; and if it shall appear that the value is less than the amount required as deposit, the general treasurer shall notify the company, and, unless the deficiency is made up within 30 days, countermand all the certificates he may have issued, and notify the financial officer of the States to which he has transmitted his certificate, and by publication. But the State shall not be liable for value of such securities. *Securities to be examined annually. Proceedings in case of deficiency.*

Section 24. Every insurance company in the State shall make a full annual report of its condition and business to the insurance commissioner; fire companies within 30 days, marine and life within 60 days. *Annual report.*

Section 27. Fire insurance companies desiring to create a guarantee surplus fund and special reserve fund may, upon filing with the insurance commissioner of the State a copy of its resolution to that effect, and receiving the insurance commissioner's certificate, after examination, create such funds; and all policies and renewals of same shall have printed thereon a notice that the same are issued in pursuance of this chapter. *Funds, how created. Policies to refer to this.*

Section 28. After that, dividends are to be restricted to 10 per cent. and 7 per cent. on surplus funds until such funds shall have together accumulated to an amount equal to its capital stock, and the entire surplus funds above such annual dividend shall be set apart and divided between the said two funds, the penalty for paying dividends contrary hereto being forfeiture of the company's charter and proceedings for its dissolution. When any company's funds together shall so equal its capital stock, having fulfilled its requirements, the commissioner shall, on notification, make and file a certificate of the same in his office, and the company may, out of any subsequent profits, continue to add, equally, to the funds so named. *Dividends, how restricted. Surplus profits to be set apart to said funds. Penalty for paying dividends otherwise.*

Section 29. Said guarantee fund shall be held, invested, liable, and applicable in the same manner as the capital stock.

Section 30. Said special reserve fund shall be invested according to existing laws relating to investments of capital by fire insurance companies, to be deposited with the insurance commissioner of the State, being deemed a fund contributed by stockholders to protect such company and its policy-holders for losses, and not liable for any claim for loss by fire or otherwise. *Investment of guarantee fund, and of special reserve fund. Effect of aid fund.*

How to ascertain.

Section 31. To ascertain the profits of any such company, in order to add to its guarantee surplus fund and special reserve fund, there shall be deducted from the gross assets of the company the following:—

1. The amount of all outstanding claims.
2. An amount sufficient to meet the liability for unearned premiums.
3. The amount of its guarantee surplus fund and of its special reserve fund.
4. The amount of the capital of the company.
5. Interest of 10 per cent. on capital, and 7 per cent. on said funds, for period since last dividend.

The balance shall be the net surplus to be equally divided between the said funds.

Special reserve fund to be held to protect whom.

Of discharge of company from claims.

Of making up capital.

Section 32. Whenever the claims upon a company shall exceed the amount of its capital stock and of the guarantee surplus fund, the insurance commissioner, on being notified, shall examine and issue certificate of the result in duplicate; and the special reserve fund shall be held to protect in the manner already provided for; and the company shall be discharged from claims upon payment to the claimant of the full sum of the capital and of the guarantee surplus fund. And the said insurance commissioner, after issuing his certificate, shall transfer to the company all securities deposited with him as special reserve fund, and if it should be less than 50 per cent. of the capital, he shall issue a requisition upon the stockholders to make up the capital to that proportion of its full amount as required by law in the case of companies with impaired capital, and any capital so impaired shall be made up to at least 200,000 dols.; in case of failure to do so the special reserve fund shall still be held as before.

Impairment of capital; how to make good.

Section 33. If, after the accumulation by any company of said special reserve fund, the insurance commissioner, upon examination, ascertains the impairment of the capital, he shall order a call upon the stockholders, and the board of directors of such company may, at its option, require the payment or apply so much of said special reserve fund as will make the impairment good.

RHODE ISLAND.—OF MANUFACTURING CORPORATIONS.

Members of, how long liable.

Section 1. All members of every incorporated manufacturing company are jointly and severally liable for all debts and contracts until the fixed capital stock is paid and a certificate thereof issued by the town clerk of the town wherein the manufactory is established.

Of reduction of capital stock.

Section 4. Every such company may, by a vote at any meeting called for that purpose, reduce its capital stock within the limits of its charter.

Liability of stockholder, and of directors.

Section 5. The stockholder is liable if such capital stock be withdrawn before payment of debts.

Section 6. When a company, being insolvent, shall declare and pay a dividend, all its directors, except those who were absent or who objected to it at the time and file their objections in writing, are liable.

Note given for stock not considered payment.

Section 7. A note or other obligation given for stock shall not be considered as payment.

271

    Sections 8, 9, 10. Any manufacturing establishment which obtains a charter of incorporation must be appraised by the assessors of taxes of the town where situated, who shall receive from the corporation for their services, 10 dols. and necessary expenses, and shall give a sworn certificate of such appraisement. *Of appraisal, and assessors' compensation.*

    Sections 11, 13, 14. Every manufacturing company shall file in the office of the town clerk annually, before 15th February, a director's certificate of the capital, value, assets, debts, and liabilities: until this is done all stockholders are liable for debts of such company to the amount of the par value of their shares, except where they exempt themselves from liability by making a return, under oath, before the 25th February. *Annual certificate to be filed: limitation of liability of members: exemptions.*

    Sections 15, 16. The debts of any corporation may not exceed its capital stock actually paid in: the directors are liable for any excess, but any director who may be absent may exempt himself from liability by forthwith giving notice of the fact to the stockholders at a special meeting. *Debts not to exceed capital stock paid in.*

    Section 17. Any manufacturing company heretofore incorporated, having a paid-up capital of not less than 30,000 dols. may, at any meeting called for the purpose, adopt the provisions of this chapter by recording its capital, assets, debts, &c.; then no stockholder shall be liable for debts contracted after such recording except for causes and in the manner already provided. *How provisions of this chapter may be adopted.*

    Section 18. The certificate of any corporation signed and sworn to by the officers chosen by its charter or bye-laws shall have the same effect as if signed and sworn to by the officers required in Sections 2, 11, and 17. *Certificates.*

    Section 20. If any certificate shall be false in any material representation all officers who have signed the same, knowingly, shall be liable for the debts of the company contracted while they were stockholders or officers. *Liability of officers for making false certificates.*

    Section 21. Whenever any of the officers of any manufacturing company shall be liable, action may be brought against them personally as well as against the company, and both may be prosecuted until the plaintiff shall obtain payment of his debt and costs of both actions. *Remedy against officers for debts of company.*

    Sections 23, 24. Any stockholder or officer who shall pay any debt of the company for which he may be liable as provided for, may recover the amount in an action against the company, in which action the property of the company only shall be liable to be taken; but any stockholder may proceed for contribution against any one or more of the stockholders originally liable with him for said debt, and may recover against each their proportion. *Stockholders liable for contribution. Remedy of officer who has paid debt of company.*

    Section 26. No person holding stock in any manufacturing company as executor, administrator, guardian, or trustee, or as collateral security, shall be personally liable as a stockholder, except such person pledges such stock, and estates and funds in his hands shall then be liable. *Who not liable.*

    Section 27. All manufacturing corporations hereafter created shall be subject to the provisions of this chapter. *Who affected.*

272

SYNOPSIS OF LAWS OF MASSACHUSETTS.

Sir,   *Boston, June* 30, 1888.

WITH reference to your despatch marked Circular A, of the 21st ultimo, I have the honour to inclose a synopsis of the laws of the State of Massachusetts relating to the formation, regulation, and dissolution of companies

The sections of the laws quoted therein are those which more particularly apply to the principles on which the legislation on the subject are based, whilst those omitted, and which are very voluminous and circumstantial, refer more especially to the details of procedure, and could not be intelligently explained without giving the full text of the laws themselves.

With the exception of recent legislation on insurance in the State of New Hampshire, of which an abstract is given at the end of the inclosure in this despatch, the principles, general provisions, and to a great extent the wording, of the laws of the States of Vermont, New Hampshire, and Maine are so closely identical to those of the laws of Massachusetts, that I have no doubt a recapitulation of them will be considered superfluous, and would, owing to the time taken up by Consular duties of a pressing nature, cause a further delay in the transmission of the present statement.

                                                      I have, &c.,
                                          (Signed)   C. A. HENDERSON.

SYNOPSIS of SECTIONS of the STATUTES of the STATE of MASSACHUSETTS relating to the FORMATION, REGULATION, and DISSOLUTION of COMPANIES.

Of the General Court (State Legislature). Chapter 2 of the Public Statutes provides that (section 7) whoever intends to present a petition (to the State Legislature) for an Act of incorporation, or for an alteration or extension of the charter of a corporation, shall give notice of such intention by an advertisement in some newspaper in the county where such corporation is, or is intended to be established; and (section 10) all such petitions shall be presented, with due proof of notice thereof, to the State Legislature (General Court).

Powers, duties, and liabilities of corporations. Chapter 105 provides that (section 3) every Act of incorporation passed after the 11th March, 1831, shall be subject to amendment, alteration, or repeal at the pleasure of the General Court. (Sections 4 and 6.) Every corporation, where no other provision is specially made, may, in its corporate name, sue and be sued, appear, prosecute, and defend to final judgment and execution, have a common seal, elect all necessary officers, and make bye-laws and regulations consistent with law, and convey lands to which it has a legal title. (Section 7.) Any corporation organized for mechanical or manufacturing business may extend or remove its business or any part thereof to, and purchase, hold, and convey real and personal estate in any other city or town in the State. (Section 13.) An executor, administrator, guardian, or trustee shall represent the shares or stock in his hands, and may vote as a stockholder. (Section 16.) The par value of shares in the capital stock of every corporation, unless otherwise expressly provided by law, shall be 100.00 dols. (Section 17.) No corporation, unless specially authorized, shall issue any share for a less amount than par value. (Section 18.) No telegraph or gaslight company shall declare any stock dividend, or divide the proceeds of the sale of stock among its stockholders, nor create any new stock, unless the par value of the shares so issued is first paid in cash to its treasurer. (Section 20.) When a corporation increases its capital stock, if not otherwise provided by law, its directors shall give 30 days' notice thereof to each stockholder, and each stockholder may take at par his proportion of such new shares, and if any shares remain untaken the directors shall sell the same at public auction, but not for less than par value thereof. (Section 28.) Corporations created by any other State, having property in this State, shall be liable to be sued, and their property shall be subject to attachment. (Section 40.) When a majority, in number or interest, of the members of a corporation desire to close its concerns, they may apply to the Supreme Judicial Court, and the court may for reasonable cause decree a dissolution of the corporation. (Section 41.) Every corporation whose charter expires by its own limitation, or is annulled by forfeiture or otherwise, or whose corporate existence for other purposes is terminated in any other manner, shall nevertheless be continued as a body corporate for the term of three years for the purpose of prosecuting or defending suits, and of enabling it to settle and close its concerns and divide its capital stock, but not for the purpose of continuing the business for which it was established. (Section 42.) The Supreme Judicial Court, on application of a creditor, stockholder, or member, at any time within the said three years, may appoint one or more persons to be receivers, to take charge of the estate, to collect debts and property, and to do all other acts which might be done by such corporation, for the final settlement of its business, the powers of such receivers being continued as long as the court deems necessary. *"Within the said three years" stricken out by chapter 203 of Statutes of year 1884.*

Chapter 106 provides that (section 6) any such number of persons as are mentioned below, who associate themselves together under an agreement as prescribed by law, with the intention of forming a corporation, shall be and remain a corporation. (Section 7.) For the purpose of carrying on any mechanical, mining, or manufacturing business, except that of distilling or manufacturing intoxicating liquors, three or more persons may associate themselves, with a capital of not less than 5,000 dols., nor more than 1,000,000 dols. (Section 8.) For the purpose of cutting, storing, and selling ice, or of carrying on any agricultural, horticultural, or quarrying business, or of printing and publishing newspapers, periodicals, books, or engravings, three or more persons may associate themselves with a capital of not less than 5,000 dols. nor more than 500,000 dols. (Section 9.) For the purpose of co-operation in carrying on any business under the two preceding sections, and of co-operative trade, seven or more persons may associate themselves with a capital of not less than 1,000 dols. nor more than 100,000 dols. (Section 10.) For the purpose of opening outlets, canals, or ditches, for the introduction and propagation of herrings and alewives, three or more persons may associate themselves with a capital of not less than 1,000 dols. nor more than 5,000 dols. (Section 11.) For the purpose of making and selling gas for light, or for the purpose of generating and furnishing steam or hot water for heating, cooking, and mechanical power in any city or town, ten or more persons may associate themselves with a capital of not less than 5,000 dols. nor more than 500,000 dols. (Section 12.) For the purpose of transacting business of a common carrier of *Manufacturing and other corporations.*

[90]

274

persons or property, three or more persons may associate themselves with a capital of not less than 5,000 dols. nor more than 1,000,000 dols. with power to undertake for the carriage of persons or property beyond the limits of this commonwealth, but not to purchase or operate railroads, canals, or ferries. (Section 13.) For the purpose of erecting and maintaining an hotel or public hall, three or more persons may associate themselves, with a capital of not less than 5,000 dols. nor more than 500,000 dols., but with no power to engage in the business of keeping an hotel. (Section 14.) For the purpose of carrying on any lawful business not mentioned in the preceding sections, except buying and selling real estate, banking, insurance, and any other business, the formation of corporations for which is otherwise regulated by these statutes, three or more persons may associate themselves with a capital of not less than 1,000 dols. nor more than 1,000,000 dols. (Section 15.) Any or all of the creditors of any corporation organized or chartered under this chapter, which has been adjudged bankrupt or insolvent, or has made an assignment of its property, may associate themselves for the purpose of forming a corporation to acquire the whole or any part of the property, and to carry on the business previously authorized to be carried on by the bankrupt or insolvent corporation. (Section 60.) The officers of any corporation which is subject to this chapter shall be jointly and severally liable for its debts and contracts in the following cases, namely: The president and directors, for making or consenting to a dividend when the corporation is, or is thereby rendered insolvent, to the extent of such dividend; for debts contracted between the time of making or assenting to a loan to a stockholder and the time of its repayment, to the extent of such loan; when the debts of a corporation exceed its capital, to the extent of such excess existing at the time of the commencement of the suit against the corporation; the president, directors, and treasurer, for signing any statement of a conveyance to the corporation of property, when such property is not conveyed or taken at a fair valuation; the president, and directors, and other officers, for signing any certificate required by law, knowing it to be false. (Section 61.) The members or stockholders in any corporation which is subject to this chapter shall be jointly and severally liable for its debts or contracts in the following cases, namely: For debts contracted before the original capital is fully paid in, if they have not paid in full the par value of their shares or purchased such shares with a knowledge of such debts; for the payment of all debts existing at the time when the capital is reduced, to the extent of the sums withdrawn and paid to stockholders when special stock is created; the general stockholders shall be liable for all debts and contracts until the special stock is fully redeemed; for all sums of money due to operatives for services rendered within six months before demand made upon the corporation, and its neglect or refusal to make payment. (Section 62.) No stockholder or officer in such corporation shall be held liable for its debts or contracts unless a judgment is recovered against it, and it neglects on execution to pay the amount due, or to exhibit real or personal estate of the corporation sufficient to satisfy the same. (Section 73.) No person shall hold shares in any co-operative association to an amount exceeding 1,000 dols. at their par value, nor shall any stockholder be entitled to more than one vote upon any subject.

Swine slaughtering associations.

Chapter 107. (Section 1.) Three or more persons who associate themselves together by such an agreement as is mentioned in

Chapter 106, with a capital of not less than 100,000 dols. nor more than 500,000 dols., with the intention of forming a corporation for the purpose of buying and slaughtering swine, and of melting and rendering and pork packing, shall be and remain a corporation.

Chapter 109. (Section 1.) Every company incorporated for the transmission of intelligence by electricity, shall possess the powers and privileges, and be subject to the duties, restrictions, and liabilities prescribed in this chapter. (Sections 2, 3, and 4.) Each company may construct lines of electric telegraph along highways, public roads, and across any waters in the commonwealth, as designated by the mayor and aldermen or selectmen of a place through which such wires are to pass, subject to such damages as may be appraised in favour of owners of land near to or adjoining such lines. (Section 7.) A company shall not commence the construction of its line until three-quarters of its capital stock has been subscribed for. (Section 8.) A company shall not at any time contract or owe debts to a larger amount than one-half part of its capital stock actually paid in. (Section 10.) Every company shall receive despatches from and for other lines, companies, associations, and individuals, and shall transmit the same faithfully and impartially on payment of its usual charges. (Section 12.) When an injury is done to a person or to property by the posts, wires, or other apparatus, of a telegraph line, the company shall be responsible in damages to the party injured, or to a city or town, if such city or town is liable to such person. (Section 14.) Owners and associations engaged in the business of telegraphing for the public by electricity, although not incorporated, shall be subject to the liabilities and governed by the provisions of this chapter. (Section 15.) No enjoyment by a person or corporation for any length of time of the privilege of having or maintaining telegraph posts, wires, or apparatus, in, upon, over, or attached to, any building or land of other persons, shall give a legal right to the continued enjoyment of such easement. *Companies for transmission of intelligence by electricity.*

Chapter 110. (Sections 1 and 2.) Persons who have associated by an agreement in writing to become proprietors of an aqueduct for the purpose of conveying fresh water into or within a city or town, or of funds for establishing such aqueduct, may apply to a justice of the peace, who may issue a warrant, seven days after the publication of which such proprietors and their successors shall be and remain a corporation, and shall be subject to the provisions of this chapter (Section 3.) The clerk of such corporation, who shall be sworn, shall record in books all byelaws, votes, and other proceedings of such corporation, and such books shall at all times be subject to the inspection of any person appointed for that purpose by the General Court. (Section 6.) The directors may make such assessments on each share as they find necessary, and on the default of a proprietor to pay an assessment for 30 days after notice, they may, after advertising for three weeks, sell by public auction so many of his shares as will pay the same with necessary charges. (Section 7.) Any such corporation may increase its capital stock at such times and in such sums as the stockholders may by vote determine. (Section 11.) Contracts made by or with such a corporation shall remain in force after its dissolution, and the last shareholders and their private estate shall continue liable if suit is brought within six years after dissolution. (Section 15.) A city or town in which such aqueduct is situated may put conductors into the pipes for the purpose of drawing therefrom, *Aqueduct corporations.*

free of expense, as much water as is necessary, when a building is on fire therein, but solely for the purpose of extinguishing fires.

Proprietors of real estate in common.

Chapter 111. (Sections 1 and 4.) When lands, wharves, or other real estate are held in common by five or more proprietors, they may form themselves into a corporation, and upon their application to a justice of the peace, he shall issue his warrant directing one of the applicants to call a meeting of the proprietors at least 14 days after publication of such warrant, to organise themselves as a corporation under this chapter. (Section 12.) Each proprietor shall be entitled to vote according to the number of his shares, or the amount of his interest, and absent proprietors may vote by proxy. (Section 13.) Proprietors, for the purpose of managing their common property and carrying on their business, may raise money by assessment, and may sell by public auction so much of the right or share of any proprietor, who neglects to pay such proportionate assessment made on him, as is sufficient to cover such assessment and all reasonable charges. (Section 16.) Such proprietor may within one year redeem such share or part sold, by payment of the sum for which it was sold with interest at the rate of 12 per cent. per annum. (Section 17.) When the proprietors are ten or more in number, they may, upon a vote of more than two-thirds, both in number and interest sell their estate and divide the proceeds. (Sections 19 and 20.) After the final division of the common property, the proprietors and their heirs shall retain their corporate powers for the purpose of collecting all taxes, debts, and effects, due to the corporation, shall be liable to pay all its debts, and may hold meetings and raise money by assessment for the payment thereof, and may do all other lawful acts necessary for closing their business.

Railroad corporations.

Chapter 112. (Sections 3 and 6.) Railway corporations heretofore established in this commonwealth shall have the powers and privileges, and be subject to the duties, liabilities, restrictions, and other provisions contained in this chapter; but nothing herein contained shall impair the validity of any special power heretofore conferred by charter or other special Act upon a particular railroad corporation, or the right of the commonwealth as asserted or reserved in previous statutes. (Sections 7 and 8.) The commonwealth may at any time during the continuance of the charter of a railroad corporation, after the expirations of 20 years from the opening of its road, purchase the road and all its franchise, property, rights, and privileges, by reimbursing to the corporation the amount of the capital paid in, with a profit thereon of 10 per cent. a year from the time of the payment thereof by the stockholders to the time of the purchase, and may at any time take and possess the road franchise, and other property of a railroad corporation, by giving to it one year's notice, and paying therefor such compensation as may be awarded by three commissioners appointed by the Supreme Judicial Court; and a corporation aggrieved by such award may have its damages assessed by a jury of the Superior Court in the county of Suffolk. (Section 9.) There shall be a board of railroad commissioners, consisting of three competent persons, appointed by the Governor with the advice and consent of the council, to serve three years, and one of whom to be appointed each year, and a clerk appointed by the Governor. (Section 12.) The annual expenses of the board, including salaries, shall be borne by the several corporations owning and operating railroads or street railways, according to their gross earnings, as apportioned by the tax commissioners, and the board shall make an annual report of its doings, and such suggestions as seem to it appropriate, to the general court. (Section 14.) The board shall have the general supervision of all railroads and railways, and shall keep itself informed as to their condition, and the manner in which they are operated, with reference to the security and accommodation of the public, and as to the compliance of the several corporations with their charters and the laws of the commonwealth. (Sections 15 and 19.) When in the judgment of the board, any such corporation has violated or neglected to comply with any law of the commonwealth, it shall give notice thereof to the corporation, and if the violation or neglect is continued, shall present the facts to the Attorney-General, who shall take such proceedings as he may deem expedient; when it deems that repairs are necessary upon any railroad, or additions or changes to its rolling stock or stations, or changes in its rates or in the mode of conducting business are reasonable and expedient, it shall inform the corporation of the improvements and changes which it considers to be proper, and shall report its proceedings in its annual report; upon complaint of the mayor and aldermen of a city or the selectmen of a town, or in their default of 20 or more legal voters of a city or town, it shall examine the condition and operation of any railroad complained of, and if it considers that the complaint is well founded, it shall so adjudge, and shall inform the corporation operating such railroad of its adjudication; it shall investigate the causes of any accident on a railroad which it may deem to require investigation; every railroad corporation shall at its request furnish to it any information required by it concerning the condition, management, and operation of the road of such corporation; it shall from time to time in each year examine the books and accounts of all corporations operating railroads or street railways. (Section 21.) Statements of the doings and financial condition of the several corporations shall be published at such times as it may deem expedient. (Section 25.) Either of the said commissioners in all cases which may be investigated by the board, may summon witnesses in behalf of the commonwealth, and may administer oaths and take testimony. (Section 29.) No petition to the general court for a charter for a railroad corporation shall be acted upon unless it is accompanied by a map of the proposed route, the report of a skilful engineer, founded on actual examination of the route, and other proper evidence, amongst other points, as to the feasibility of the route and estimated expense of contractor, nor until notice of such petition has been published according to law. (Section 34.) Twenty-five or more persons, a majority of whom are the inhabitants of this commonwealth, may associate themselves together with the intention of forming a railroad corporation, and, upon complying with the provisions of section 44, shall, with their associates and successors, be and remain a corporation. (Section 44.) When it is shown to the satisfaction of the board that the requirements of this chapter preliminary to the establishment of a corporation have been complied with, and that a sum sufficient to pay all damages that may be occasioned by laying out, making, and maintaining the railroad, or by taking land or materials therefor, has in good faith been paid to the treasurer, and is satisfied that it will not be misapplied, the clerk of the board shall certify that such requirements appear to have been complied with. (Section 61.) A railroad corporation requiring land or materials for making or securing its road or for depôt or station purposes, and being unable to obtain the same by agreement with the owner, may apply to the county commissioners, who, after notice to the owner, may prescribe the limits within which the same may be taken without his permission. (Section 74.) Except by authority of the general court, or as authorised by law, no railroad corporation shall subscribe for, take, or hold shares in the stock or bonds, or guarantee the bonds or dividends of any other corporation or company.

Street railway companies.
Chapter 113. (Section 1.) Street railway companies shall have the powers and privileges, and be subject to the duties, liabilities, restrictions, and provisions contained in this chapter. (Section 2.) Fifteen or more persons may associate themselves together with the intention of forming a corporation for the purpose of constructing and operating a street railway for the conveyance of passengers, and, upon complying with the provisions of this chapter preliminary to its establishment, shall, with their associates and successors, be and remain a corporation. (Section 6.) The directors shall cause a copy of the articles of association to be published in one or more newspapers in each county in which the road is proposed to be located. (Section 7.) The board of aldermen of a city, or the selectmen of a town, upon the petition of such directors for the location of the tracks of the railway therein, shall give due notice of the time and place at which they will consider such location, and after a hearing shall pass an order refusing such location or granting the same or any portion thereof. (Section 13.) No certificate of stock shall be issued until the par value thereof is actually paid in cash. (Section 19.) No street railway company shall begin to build its road until the amount of its capital stock has been unconditionally subscribed for and 50 per cent. of the par value of each share thereof actually paid in cash. (Section 20.) If a street railway company does not build and put in operation some portion of its road within 18 months after the date of its establishment, its corporate powers shall cease. (Sections 23 and 26.) The board of aldermen or the selectmen, at any time after the expiration of one year from the opening for use of a street railway in their city or town, if in their judgment the interests of the public so require, may order that the location of any track shall be revoked, and may order a street railway company to discontinue temporarily the use of any tracks whenever they adjudge that the safety or convenience of the inhabitants requires such discontinuance. Section 62.) The board of railroad commissioners, whenever a street railway company violates or neglects to observe the laws relative to such companies, and continues such violation or neglect after notice from the board, shall forthwith present the facts to the Attorney-General, who shall take such proceedings as he may deem expedient.

Agricultural and horticultural societies.
Chapter 114. (Section 1.) Every incorporated agricultural society whose exhibition grounds and buildings are not within 12 miles of those of a society entitled to bounty, and which has raised by contribution 1,000 dols. as a capital appropriated for its uses, shall, except when otherwise determined by the State board of agriculture, be entitled to receive annually out of the treasury of the commonwealth 200 dols. or more, up to 600 dols., in proportion to the sum contributed and awarded in premiums. (Section 4.) Every society receiving bounty shall make such rules for the distribution thereof as shall in its opinion best promote the improvement of agriculture.

Associations for charitable, educational, and other purposes.
Chapter 115. (Sections 1 and 2.) Seven or more persons who associate themselves together with the intention of forming a corporation for any educational, charitable, benevolent, or religious purpose, for the prosecution of any antiquarian, historical, literary, scientific,

medical, artistic, monumental, or musical purposes, for supporting any missionary enterprise in foreign countries, or promoting temperance and morality in this commonwealth, for encouraging athletic exercises or yachting, for encouraging the raising of choice breeds of animals or poultry, for the association of societies of Freemasons and for the Knights of Pythias, or other similar charitable or social bodies, and for the establishment and maintenance of places for reading-rooms, libraries, or social meetings, upon complying with the legal requisites, shall be and remain a corporation. (Section 6.) The corporation may have, instead of a board of directors, a board of trustees, or other officers, with powers of directors. (Section 7.) The corporation may hold real and personal estate, and may hire, purchase, or erect suitable buildings to an amount not exceeding 500,000 dols., and may receive and hold in trust or otherwise funds received by gift or bequest.

Chapter 116. (Section 1.) The board of commissioners of savings banks shall consist of two commissioners appointed by the Governor with the advice and consent of the council. (Section 3.) The commissioners shall visit once in every year, and as much oftener as they deem expedient, every savings bank, shall have free access to the vaults, books, and papers, and shall thoroughly examine and inspect all their affairs, and ascertain their condition and ability to fulfil all their engagements, and whether they have complied with the provisions of law. (Section 4.) Either of the commissioners may summon all such witnesses as he thinks proper, and may administer oaths. (Section 6.) If upon such examination any savings bank appears to be insolvent, or its condition hazardous to the public or to those having funds in its custody, the commissioners shall, or if such savings bank appears to have failed to comply with any provisions of law, may apply to a justice of the Supreme Judicial Court, who may issue an injunction, and may dissolve or modify it, or make it perpetual, and may restrain or prohibit such savings bank from the further prosecution of its business, and appoint one or more receivers to take possession of its property and effects. (Section 11.) All incorporated savings banks may exercise the powers, and shall be subject to the conditions contained in the following sections so far as they are consistent with their respective charters. (Section 12.) The general court may make other or further regulations for the government of such corporations, or may take away their corporate powers. (Section 19.) Every such corporation may receive deposits from any person until they amount to 1,000 dols., and may allow interest thereon and upon the accumulated interest up to the sum of 1,600 dols., but these limitations shall not apply to religious or charitable corporations. (Section 19.) Deposits and income derived therefrom shall be invested only on certain securities and to such extent in each case as specified in this section. (Sections 24 and 25.) Every such corporation shall, at the time of making each semi-annual dividend, reserve as a guarantee fund not less than one-eighth nor more than one-fourth of 1 per cent. of the whole amount of deposits until such fund amounts to 5 per cent. of the whole amount of deposits. (Section 25.) After a deduction of reasonable expenses and the guarantee fund, ordinary dividends shall be made every six months, and shall not exceed $2\frac{1}{2}$ per cent. and $1\frac{1}{4}$ per cent. respectively on all sums that have been deposited for six and three months, no dividend being payable on deposits for less than three months, or on any deposits, if the net profits for the six preceding months do not amount in addition to the guarantee fund to 1½ per cent. of the deposits. (Section 27.) Once in every three years undistributed net profits shall be divided among depositors for one year, if amounting to 1 per cent. of their deposits. (Sections 35 and 38.) Any such corporation may receive on deposit to any amount funds in trust for setting out shade trees in streets and parks, for purchasing lands for parks, and improving the same, for maintaining cemeteries or cemetery lots, and for erecting and maintaining drinking fountains in public places; such funds shall be placed on interest payable semi-annually, but the principal shall not be withdrawn or expended, shall be exempt from attachment, and may be transferred, if such corporation ceases to do business, by order of the Supreme Judicial Court, to such other banking institution as it deems proper.

Co-operative saving fund and loan associations. Chapter 117. (Sections 1 and 2.) Twenty-five or more persons who associate themselves together with the intention of forming a corporation for the purpose of accumulating and lending to its members the savings of such members shall be and remain a corporation on entering into an agreement setting forth the fact of their having so associated themselves, the name and purpose of the corporation, the town or city in the commonwealth in which it is located, and the limit of capital to be accumulated. (Sections 5 and 6.) The capital to be accumulated shall not exceed 1,000,000 dols., and shall be divided into shares of 200 dols. each; no person shall hold more than 25 such shares, and no member shall be entitled to more than one vote at elections of officers. Sections 7 and 19 prescribe rules for the collection of contributions, withdrawal of shares, loans to members, investments, fines, forfeitures, keeping of accounts, and distribution of profits and losses. (Section 20.) The commissioners of savings banks shall perform in reference to every such corporation the same duties, and shall have the same powers, as in regard to savings banks.

Banks and banking. Chapter 118. (Section 1.) Ten or more persons and their successors may form a corporation for the purpose of carrying on the business of banking on the terms and conditions prescribed in this chapter. The general court may at any time alter or repeal any of the provisions of this chapter, or of any statute governing such corporations, and may dissolve any such corporation, without impairing any remedy given against the same, its stockholders, or officers. (Section 2.) The capital stock of each bank shall not be less than 100,000 dols., nor more than 1,000,000 dols.; the stock shall be paid for in gold or silver money, one-half before the bank goes into operation, and the remainder within one year thereafter. (Section 5.) No part of the capital stock of a bank shall be sold or transferred until the whole amount thereof is paid in, and no loan shall be made to a stockholder until the full amount of his shares is paid in. (Section 6.) No person shall directly or indirectly hold or own more than one-half of the amount of the capital stock of a bank, exclusive of stock which he holds as collateral security. (Section 7.) In addition to the capital stock of a bank, the commonwealth may subscribe thereto to an amount not exceeding 50 per cent. of its authorised capital, when provision is made therefor by law, and the commonwealth, from the time of making any payment towards such capital stock, shall be entitled to its proportionate share of profits and dividends. (Section 8.) A bank may, by a vote of three-fourths of its stockholders, increase its capital stock, within the limits prescribed by section 2. Sections 9 to 16 prescribe rules in regard to meetings of stockholders, and votes and proxies. Sections 17 to 29, in regard to the number and qualifications of directors, and duties of cashiers, and sections 30 to 49 in regard to the course of business. Section 50 requires every bank to keep in the bank as a reserve an amount of specie or lawful money equal to 15 per cent. of its liabilities for circulation and deposits. Sections 51 to 54 relate to loans and discounts. (Sections 55 and 58.) Upon requisition of the general court each bank shall lend to the commonwealth a sum not exceeding 5 per cent. of its capital stock at any one time, reimbursable by five annual instalments, or at any shorter period at the election of the commonwealth, with annual interest not exceeding 6 per cent., but the commonwealth shall not be entitled to demand of a bank loans which together at any one time exceed one-tenth part of its capital; if a bank neglects or refuses for 30 days after notice to make such loan, it shall forfeit a sum equal to 2 per cent. a month upon the amount, so long as such refusal or neglect continues, provided that such loan is approved by the Governor. Section 60 enacts that the auditor of accounts shall cause to be engraved for, and delivered to each bank, after being numbered and registered, circulating notes, in similitude of bank notes, in blank, of such denominations as are allowed by law, and in such quantities as he may from time to time deem necessary; and sections 61 to 79 prescribe the rules under which these notes may be circulated or withdrawn, and the amount and nature of the security to be tendered by each bank. (Section 80.) Stockholders in a bank at the time when it stops payment, or when its corporate franchises are surrendered or forfeited, shall be liable in their individual capacities for the payment and redemption of all circulating notes issued by such bank and remaining unpaid, in proportion to the stock they respectively held at the time aforesaid. (Section 113.) The commissioners of savings banks shall have the powers and perform the duties with relation to banks that they have with relation to savings banks.

Chapter 40. (Sections 1 and 2.) Law library associations heretofore organised in any county except Suffolk shall be subject to this chapter, and attorneys-at-law admitted to practice in the courts of the commonwealth, and resident in a county for which there is no law library association, on so organising themselves, shall be a corporation, and may, for the purpose of holding and managing the law library belonging to the county, adopt bye-laws subject to the approval of the justices of the Superior Court. (Section 5.) Every inhabitant of a county in which such association is organised may use the books in the library, subject to regulations approved by the Superior Court. (Section 6 as amended by Chapter 246 of 1882.) County treasurers shall annually pay to the law library associations in their respective counties, from sums paid into the county treasuries by the clerks of the courts, an amount not exceeding 2,000 dollars, and such further sums as the county commissioners may deem necessary and proper. (Section 9.) Any town or city may establish and maintain a public library therein, for the use of the inhabitants thereof, under such regulations as may be prescribed by the inhabitants of the town or by the city council. (Section 10.) Any town may at a legal meeting grant and vote money for the establishment, maintenance, or increase of a public library therein, and may receive, hold, and manage any devise, bequest, or donation for the purpose. (Sections 12, 13, and 15.) Seven or more proprietors of a library may form themselves into a corporation for the purpose of preserving, enlarging,

Library associations.

and using such library, and upon application of five or more of such proprietors a justice of the peace may issue his warrant directing a meeting of such proprietors for the purpose of organization, and such proprietors may, by assessments on the several shares, raise such money as they judge necessary for the purposes of the association. (Section 16.) Three or more persons who associate themselves together by agreement, as described in Chapter 106 of the Public Statutes, with the intention of forming a corporation for the purpose of establishing and maintaining a public library, shall become a corporation upon complying with certain provisions in that chapter.

On evidence. Chapter 169 (section 68) provides that all Acts of incorporation shall be deemed to be public Acts, and as such may be declared on and given in evidence.

Limited partnership. Chapter 75. (Sections 1, 2, and 3, as amended by Chapter 248 of Statutes of 1887.) Limited partnerships for the transaction of any lawful business, except that of insurance, may be formed by two or more persons; such a partnership may consist of one or more persons who shall be called general partners, and shall be jointly and severally liable for all the debts of the partnership, and of one or more persons who shall each contribute to the common stock in actual cash payment a specific sum as capital, who shall be called special partners, and shall not be personally liable for the debts of the partnership except as herein provided; but if the name of a special partner is used in the firm name with his consent or privity, he shall be liable as a general partner. (Sections 4, 5, and 6.) The persons forming such a partnership shall severally sign a certificate, to be acknowledged before a magistrate, published in a newspaper, and recorded and open to the public in the Secretary of State's office, stating the firm name, the names and places of residence of the general and special partners, the amount of capital which each special partner has contributed, the general nature of the business, and duration of the partnership; and for any false statement in such certificate all the partners shall be liable. (Section 8, as amended by Chapter 248 of the Statutes of 1887.) During the continuance of such partnership no part of its capital stock shall be withdrawn, nor shall any division of interest or profits be made so as to reduce such capital stock below the sum stated in the certificate; and if its assets are not sufficient to pay its debts, the special partners shall be held responsible for all sums by them withdrawn or received, with interest thereon, but special partners may draw interest, not exceeding 6 per cent. per annum, out of the profits. (Section 9.) All suits respecting the business of such partnerships shall be prosecuted only by and against general partners, and special partners who are liable as general partners, or who, having withdrawn and become liable for sums withdrawn by them as above provided. (Section 10.) No such partnership shall be dissolved, except by operation of law, before the time specified in the certificate, unless a notice of such dissolution is filed and recorded in the office of the Secretary of State, and published in a newspaper during six weeks.

ADDITIONAL LEGISLATION subsequent to the Consolidation in 1882 of the Public Statutes of the State of Massachusetts.

Manufacturing and other. In connection with Chapter 106 of the Public Statutes, Chapter

180 of the Statutes of 1884 provides that 10 or more persons may form a corporation to examine and guarantee the titles of real estate. Chapter 240 of 1885 permits corporations to be organized for making, selling, and distributing gas for heating, cooking, chemical, and mechanical purposes. Chapter 265 of 1885 permits the formation of corporations for the purpose of cremating the bodies of the dead; and Chapter 385 of 1887 authorizes gas companies to furnish electric light.

In connection with Chapter 109 of the Public Statutes, Chapter 221 of 1883 extends the provisions in regard to the transmission of intelligence by electricity to lines for electric light. Chapter 267 of 1885 requires telephone companies to furnish telephones, telephone service, and connections without discrimination. *Electrical companies.*

Chapter 214 of 1887 revises and codifies the law on insurance. Under its provisions (section 1) the term "insurance company" or "company," when not inconsistent with the context, includes all corporations, associations, partnerships, or individuals engaged as principals in the business of insurance; "domestic" designates companies incorporated or formed in the State, and "foreign" those formed by authority of any other state or government. (Section 2.) Insurance companies formed by authority of the State, except those specially formed under certain designated laws, shall be subject to the duties and liabilities provided by this Act, and the general court may, for any cause it deems sufficient, annul or dissolve any such corporation, or revoke its charter, and may amend or repeal the laws affecting the powers and obligations of such corporations. (Section 4.) An insurance commissioner shall be appointed by the Governor, with the advice and consent of the council. (Section 6.) Before granting certificates of authority to an insurance company he shall be satisfied that such company is duly qualified to transact business, and once in three years he shall by himself or his deputy visit each domestic insurance company and thoroughly examine its affairs; he shall also make an examination of any such company whenever he deems it prudent to do so, or upon the reasonable request of five or more of the stockholders, creditors, policy holders, or persons pecuniarily interested therein; whenever he deems it prudent for the protection of policy-holders in the State he shall or may appoint some competent person or persons to visit and examine any foreign insurance company applying for admission, or already admitted, to do business by agencies in the State; and in either case shall have free access to the books and papers relating to the business, and may summon and examine witnesses under oath. (Section 7.) If he comes to the conclusion that a foreign insurance company is in an unsound condition, or if it has failed to comply with the law; or, if a life insurance company, its actual funds, exclusive of its capital, are less than its liabilities, he shall revoke, or suspend while such default or disability continues, all certificates of authority granted to it or its agents; and if he comes to the conclusion that any domestic insurance company is insolvent, has exceeded its powers, has failed to comply with any provision of law, or that its condition renders its further proceedings hazardous to its policy-holders or others, he shall apply to a justice of the Supreme Judicial Court to restrain it in whole or in part from further proceeding with its business; such justice may in his discretion issue an injunction, and may dissolve or modify it, or make it perpetual, and may appoint agents or receivers to take possession of the property and effects of the company, and to settle its affairs. *Insurance companies.*

(Section 10.) If, upon examination or other evidence, the commissioner is of opinion that any insurance company, or an officer or agent thereof, has violated any provision of this Act, he shall report the facts to the Attorney-General, who shall cause such company, officer, or agent to be prosecuted therefor. (Section 28.) If any domestic insurance company shall not commence to issue policies within one year of its organization, or ceases during one year to make new insurances, its corporate power shall expire by their own limitation. (Section 31.) No corporation shall transact any other business than that specified in its charter; companies to insure plate-glass may organize with a capital of not less than 100,000 dols.; companies insuring marine or inland risks upon the stock plan shall have a capital of not less than 300,000 dols.; companies for the transaction of fire insurance on the stock plan, of fidelity, accident, employers' liability, or of steam boiler insurance, shall have a capital of not less than 200,000 dols.; companies may be formed to insure mechanics' tools and apparatus against loss by fire, each risk not to exceed 250 dols., with a capital not less than 25,000 dols. (Section 33.) The directors or other officers making or authorizing an investment or loan in violation of section 35 shall be personally liable to the stockholders for any loss occasioned thereby; if a company is under liability for losses equal to its net assets, and the president and directors, knowing it, make or assent to further increase, they shall be personally liable for any loss thereby; and if the directors allow to be insured on a single risk a larger sum than the law permits, they shall be liable for any loss upon the excess of insurance. (Section 35.) When the net assets of a company do not amount to more than three-fourths of its original capital it may make good the deficiency by assessment of its stock; shares on which such an assessment is not paid within 60 days shall be forfeitable; and if such company shall not, within three months after notice from the insurance commissioner, make good its capital, or reduce it as allowed by law, its authority to transact new business of insurance shall cease. (Section 37.) When the capital stock of a company is impaired, it may, upon a vote of the majority of the stock represented at a meeting, reduce its capital stock to an amount not less than the minimum sum required by law. (Section 77.) Foreign insurance companies, upon complying with the conditions of law applicable to such companies, may be admitted to transact in this State, by constituted agents resident therein, any class of insurance authorized by law.

ABSTRACT OF LAWS of the STATE OF NEW HAMPSHIRE in Amendment of the GENERAL LAWS of the STATE on INSURANCE and INSURANCE COMPANIES.

Insurance.

Chapter 75 of the year 1885 provides that (section 1) erroneous descriptions or statements of value or title by the insured do not prevent his recovering on his policy, unless the jury find that the difference between the property as described, and as it really existed, contributed to the loss, or materially increased the risk; a change in the property insured, or in its use or occupation, or a breach of any of the terms of the policy by the insured, do not affect the policy, except during the continuance of the change, use, or occupation, or of the state of things constituting the breach of the terms of the policy;

nor shall any misrepresentation of the title or interest of the insured in the whole or a part of the property insured, unless material or fraudulent, prevent his recovering on his policy to the extent of his insurable interest.

Chapter 93 of the year 1885 (section 2). In any suit that may be brought in this State against an assurance company, to recover for a total loss sustained by fire or other casualty to real estate, or buildings on the land of another, the amount of damage shall be the amount expressed in the contract as the sum insured, and no other evidence shall be admitted on trial as to the value of the property insured; provided, where there is a partial destruction or damage to the property insured, it shall be the duty of the company to pay the assured a sum of money equal to the damage done to the property; and provided further, that nothing in this section shall be construed to prevent the admission of testimony to prove over-insurance fraudulently obtained. *Insurance.*

MARYLAND.

Sir, *Baltimore, June* 22, 1888.

IN compliance with the instructions contained in Sir Lionel West's circular despatch of the 21st ultimo, I have the honour herewith to transmit a transcript of the existing law in Maryland and Virginia, with regard to joint stock companies.

I have, &c.,
(Signed) W. F. SEAGRAVE.

LAWS regulating JOINT STOCK COMPANIES in the STATES of MARYLAND and VIRGINIA.

Maryland.

Corporations may be formed in this State, under the provisions hereinafter set forth, by any five or more persons, citizens of the United State, and a majority of them citizens of this State, or if unnaturalized, residents of the State making oath that they *bonâ fide* intend to become citizens of the United States without unreasonable delay, who may desire to form a body corporate or politic. *How formed.*

Any corporation incorporated under this article, or any corporation heretofore formed and now existing, the capital stock of which has been fully paid up, may unite with any other corporation incorporated under this article, the capital stock of which has also been fully paid up, where the said corporations have been originally incorporated in whole or in part for the same purpose, and may by such union form one new corporation, provided that a majority of the stockholders of each of the said corporations forming such union shall assent thereto. *United corporation.*

Any five or more persons, citizens of the United States, and a majority of them citizens of this State, who may desire to form a corporation for any of the purposes hereinbefore referred to, shall make, sign, seal, and acknowledge before some officer competent to take the acknowledgment of deeds, a certificate in writing, in which shall be stated:— *The certificate.*

1. The names in full and place of residence of the applicants. *What it shall state.*

2. The proposed corporate name of the corporation, which shall always include the name of the county or city in which it may be formed.
3. The object or purposes for which incorporation is sought, the time of its existence not to exceed 40 years, and the articles, conditions, and provisions under which the incorporation is formed; provided, that the limitation as to the duration of existence of corporations formed under this Act shall not apply to gas-light companies.
4. The place or places where the operations of the corporation are to be carried on, and the place in the State in which the principal office of the corporation will be located.
5. The amount of capital stock (if any) of the corporation.
6. The number of shares of stock (if any) and the amount of each share.
7. The number of trustees, directors, or managers, and their names, who shall manage the concerns of the corporation for the first year.

Certificate to be submitted to judge. When said certificate is executed, it shall be the duty of the persons executing the same to submit it to one of the judges of the judicial circuit within which the principal or any other office of said corporation is, under said certificate, to be located, if it shall be located in one of the counties of this State, or to one of the judges of the Supreme Bench of Baltimore city, if the principal office of said corporation shall be located in Baltimore city, in order that the said judge may determine whether said certificate is in conformity with the law.

Judge to certify certificate to be recorded. If the said judge shall so determine, he shall certify his said determination upon the said certificate, which shall thereupon be recorded in the office of the clerk of the circuit court for the county in which the principal office of said corporation shall, by the terms of said certificate, be located, if it shall be located in one of the counties of this State, or in the office of the clerk of the Superior Court of Baltimore city, if the principal office of said corporation shall be located therein, and the said certificate shall be recorded in a book provided for that special purpose.

Incorporated. When the said certificate shall have been recorded, the persons who have signed and acknowledged the same, and their successors shall, according to the objects, purposes, articles, conditions, and provisions in said instrument contained, become, and be a body politic and corporate, in fact and in law, by the name stated in such certificate.

Evidence of certificate. A copy of such certificate, or any amendments thereto, or of any paper relating to corporations, which is required by law to be recorded, when certified to be a true copy by the clerk of the court in whose office the same is recorded, under the seal of his office, shall be evidence in all legal proceedings, and in all the courts of this State.

Powers and general regulations. Every corporation incorporated under this article shall have the following powers and be subjected to the following general regulations, except in cases where the special provisions relating to any particular corporation are inconsistent with the said general regulations.

Any such corporation shall have power:—

Succession. 1st. To have succession by its corporate name for the period prescribed by law or by the certificate evidencing its incorporation where the said certificate is in accordance with law.

Sue and be sued. 2nd. To sue and be sued, complain and defend in any court of law or equity.

3rd. To make and use a common seal and alter the same at pleasure. Seal.

4th. To acquire by purchase or in any other manner, and take, receive, hold, use, employ, manage, dispose of, or in any manner not inconsistent with law deal with any property, real, personal, or mixed, and situate in or out of this State, which may be necessary or proper to enable the said corporation to carry on the operations, or fulfil the purposes named in the certificate of incorporation, and generally to do every other act or thing, not inconsistent with law, which may be necessary or proper to promote the objects, designs, and purposes for which said corporation was formed. Purchase, hold, and use property.

5th. To appoint a president of the company from among the directors, trustees, or managers, and to appoint such officers and agents as the business of the corporation shall require; to allow them a suitable compensation, require security for the faithful discharge of their duties, and regulate the tenure of office of the said officers. President, officers, agents, &c.

6th. To make bye-laws, not inconsistent with law, for the management of its property, the regulation of its affairs, and for the transfer of its stock, if any such stock there be; for the forfeiture of stock not paid for, and for disposition of the proceeds thereof; for the calling of regular, special, and general meetings of the directors, managers, and trustees of said corporation, and fixing the place or places where the same shall be held, and to provide for all other matters which may be regulated by bye-laws, and may, from time to time, repeal, amend, or re-enact the same, but every such bye-law, and every repeal, amendment, or re-enactment thereof, unless in the meantime confirmed at a general meeting of the company duly called for that purpose, shall only have force until the next annual meeting of the company, and in default of confirmation thereof, shall from that time only, cease to have force. The stockholders or members of the corporation may, at any general meeting, make bye-laws which shall not be rescinded by the directors, managers, or trustees. Bye-laws.

No corporation shall possess or exercise any corporate powers except such as are conferred by law and such as shall be necessary to the exercise of the powers so acquired. Necessary corporate powers.

The stock, if any, property, and concerns of any corporation, for whose creation provision is made in this article, shall be managed by such number of trustees, directors, or managers as its bye-laws shall prescribe, said number not to be less than four nor more than 12, who shall respectively be citizens of the United States and a majority of them citizens of this State, and shall, except the first year, be annually elected by the stockholders, where there are such, or by the shareholders or members where there are no stockholders, at such meeting, time, and place, and after such notice as shall be directed by the bye-laws of the corporation; and where no other notice is provided for by the bye-laws, public notice of the time and place of holding such elections shall be published not less than ten days previously thereto, in a newspaper printed nearest to the place where the principal office of said corporation in this State shall be located. Stock, property, &c.: how managed. Citizens. Election of managers. Notice.

All elections shall be by ballot, and each stockholder shall be entitled to as many votes as he owns shares of stock, but no share shall be voted unless all instalments have been paid thereon. Voting shares.

[90]

Subscriptions to capital stock.	Subscriptions to the capital stock may be made in land or other property at a valuation agreed upon, when such property shall be such as it is proper for the corporation to own, but such subscriptions shall only be received when authorised by a meeting of stockholders. The books of the company shall be kept so as to show fully at all times what property was received for said stock and the number and value of shares issued for same.
Stock, personal property.	The stock of any corporation shall be deemed personal estate, and no shares shall be transferred until all previous calls have been paid thereon.
Liability of stockholders.	All stockholders shall be severally and individually liable to the creditors of the corporation to an amount equal to the amount of stock held by them, for all debts due by the corporation until the whole amount of the capital stock has been paid in, but no stockholder shall be individually liable to the creditors of the corporation except to the amount of his unpaid subscription to the capital stock.
No loans to stockholders.	No loan of money shall be made by any corporation to any stockholder therein.
Statement of affairs under oath.	When any person or persons owning five per cent. of the capital stock shall present a written request to the officials of a corporation for a statement of its affairs, it shall be his duty to furnish same, under oath, within 20 days, and for six months thereafter keep same accessible to stockholders under a penalty of 50 dols. and 25 dols. additional daily until produced.
Annual statement under oath.	A full statement of the affairs of each corporation shall be made in the first week of January and July of each year and verified under oath.
Insolvent corporations, how proceeded against.	When a corporation becomes insolvent it shall be deemed to have surrendered its corporate rights and franchises, and may be adjudged to be dissolved after a hearing according to the practice of courts of equity in this State, upon a bill filed for that purpose in the circuit court of the place wherein the principal office is located.
Proceedings. Bill for dissolution, what it shall contain.	Whenever the directors of a corporation, or a majority of them, shall deem it expedient to dissolve a corporation, a general meeting of stockholders shall be called, after the necessary notice, and, if a majority of those interested so decide, a bill shall be filed in the circuit court of the locality stating reasons why the dissolution is sought and there shall be filed therewith :
Inventory of assets.	1st. A full and true inventory of all the assets of the corporation, and all the books, papers, vouchers, &c., relating thereto.
List of shareholders.	2nd. A true account of the capital stock, and a list of shareholders, their residences and number of shares held by each.
Incumbrances and list of creditors. Statement under oath.	3rd. A statement of all incumbrances on the property of the corporation with a full list of creditors and amount of their respective claims, all said statements shall be verified by the oath of the president or some other principal officer of the company.
Court to pass an order to show cause. Answer. Evidence.	The court shall then pass an order requiring all parties interested to show cause why such corporation should not be dissolved on or before a certain day, to be named in the order, which shall then be published in manner directed by the court, and upon any answer being filed by creditors or stockholders, the court may authorize evidence to be taken.

If the court, upon consideration of the bill or of any answers filed, be of opinion that the corporation is insolvent or that its dissolution would be beneficial to the stockholders and not injurious to public in-

289

terests, a decree shall be entered dissolving the corporation and appointing one or more receivers, who shall be vested with all the assets and estate belonging to the corporation, and shall be trustees thereof, with power to bring and carry on suits in the name of the corporation. *Decree to dissolve. Receivers, powers and duties of.*

Virginia.

The laws of the State with reference to this subject are contained in the Revised Code of Virginia of 1887, published by Act of General Assembly in force from the 1st day of May, 1888. The date of legislation as to stock companies cannot be well ascertained—certainly dates as far back as 1849.

The law provides, that any *five* or more persons desiring to form a joint stock company for conducting any lawful business (except to construct a railroad, canal, or bank of circulation) may make, sign, and acknowledge before any justice of the peace, notary, county or corporation judge, or clerk of a county or circuit court, a certificate in writing, setting forth the name of the company, its purposes, capital stock, its division into shares, real estate to be held, place of permanent office, and names of officers to manage its affairs for the first year. *What the certificate contains.*

This certificate may be presented to the circuit court of the county, or circuit court of the corporation where the principal office is to be located, or to the judge thereof in vacation. *How granted*

Said court or judge shall have discretion to grant or refuse said persons a charter of incorporation, in terms set forth in said certificate, or other terms as seem reasonable. If the charter be granted, it shall be recorded in a book kept for the purpose by clerk of said court and be by him certified to the Secretary of the commonwealth, to be in like manner recorded in his office. *and recorded.*

As soon as said charter is so recorded by said Secretary, the persons who signed and acknowledged said certificate, and their successors, shall be a body politic and corporate by name as set forth in said certificate. *Incorporation.*

Minimum capital of every such company (except one whose object is purely benevolent, which may have only a nominal capital) shall not be less than five hundred dollars, and said capital shall be divided into shares of not less than ten dollars each. *Minimum capital.*

It shall be lawful for such company to call for and demand from the stockholders respectively all sums of money by them subscribed, at such time and in such proportion as they shall deem proper, and enforce payment by all remedies provided by law in respect to other incorporated companies. Each certificate of stock shall set forth truly the actual capital of the company and the nominal value of each share of stock and amount actually paid on each share by the holder of such certificate. *Stockholders' subscriptions.*

At every meeting of the stockholders, each stockholder shall be entitled to cast one vote for each share of stock held by him. *Vote.*

A lien given by the company to prefer one creditor shall ensure to all (except to secure a debt contracted or money borrowed at time of creating the lien or encumbrance) the same shall ensure ratably to the benefit of all the creditors of the company existing at the time such lien was made.

Charters for the construction of railroads, canals, or banks of circulation are granted upon application to the Legislature, in the way prescribed by the code. *Railroads, canals, and banks.*

[90]

Partnerships. The statute laws as to limited partnership companies, and companies of general and special partners, are very lengthy and are not well understood by lawyers, and have not yet been fully construed by the courts, and give ground to much litigation.

I have, &c.,
(Signed) W. F. SEGRAVE.

British Consulate, Baltimore,
June 22, 1888.

SOUTH CAROLINA.

*British Consulate, Charleston,
June 20, 1888.*

Sir,

WITH reference to your Circular despatch, dated 21st ultimo, I have now the honour to forward herewith all the information relative to the formation and regulation of companies which I have been able to obtain on the subject in this Consular district.

I have, &c.,
(Signed) FREDERICK J. CRIDLAND.

ACT to provide for the FORMATION of certain CORPORATIONS under GENERAL LAWS passed by the GENERAL ASSEMBLY of SOUTH CAROLINA, December, 1886.

For what purposes authorised.

Section 1. Be it enacted by the Senate and House of Representatives of the State of South Carolina, now met and sitting in General Assembly, and by the authority of the same :

That two or more persons desiring to form themselves into a private corporation for the purpose of carrying on any manufacturing, mining, industrial labour, immigration, or other business, except for railroad purposes, in this State, may file with the Secretary of State a written declaration, signed by themselves, setting forth :

Steps necessary to be taken.

1st. The names and residences of the petitioners.
2nd. The name of the proposed corporation ; the place at which it purposes to have its principal or only place of business ; the general purpose of the corporation, and the nature of the business which it purposes to do.
3rd. The amount of the capital stock ; the number of shares into which it is to be divided, showing the par value of each share.
4th. Any other matters which it may be desirable to set forth in the organic law.

Board of corporators appointed.

Section 2. Upon the filing the declaration as above, the Secretary of State shall issue to the parties, or to any two or more of them, a commission constituting them a board of corporators, giving them authority to open books of subscription to the capital stock of the proposed company, requiring them to give such notice as he may deem fit of the times and places of the opening of the books of subscription.

Subscriptions, how payable.

Section 3. All subscriptions to the capital stock of any company organized or proposed to be organized under the provisions of this Act, shall be made payable in money or in labour, or property at its money value, to be named in the list of subscription; and in the case of a failure to perform the labour or deliver the property according to the terms of the subscription, the money value thereof as named in the lists of subscriptions, shall be paid by the subscribers.

Section 4. When not less than 50 per cent. of the proposed capital stock has been subscribed by *bonâ fide* subscribers, the board of corporators shall call the subscribers together, a majority of whom in value being present, either in person or by proxy, shall proceed to the organisation of the company by the election of a board of directors from among themselves, of not less than three nor more than nine members, to manage the affairs and business of the company for the ensuing 12 months, or until their successors are duly elected and qualified. The board of directors thus elected shall elect a president or executive officer from their own number; and they shall also elect such person as they may see fit as secretary, both to serve for such time and under such conditions as the company may determine in their bye-laws. *Organization. Board of directors. President and secretary.*

Section 5. Upon the completion of the organization of the company and the payment to the treasurer of the company or some officer designated for that purpose, in cash, or at least 20 per cent. of the capital subscribed, payable in money, and the payment of the remainder of the capital so subscribed for, payable in money, being secured to be paid in such instalments and at such times as may be provided in the written declaration required by section 1, and also the delivery to such officers or officer of at least 20 per cent. of the property so subscribed to the capital stock, with security for the delivery of the remainder of said property so subscribed to the capital as may be promised in said written declaration required by section 1, the board of corporators shall in writing, over their signatures, certify the same to the Secretary of State, who shall issue to the company a certificate that they have been fully organised according to the laws of South Carolina, under the name and for the purpose indicated in their written declaration, and that they are fully authorised to commence business under their charter, a copy of which certificate shall be filed and recorded in the office of the Register of Mesne Conveyance for each county where such corporation shall have a business office. *When certificate of charter to issue. By whom. Filing and recording.*

Section 6. Upon the issuance of the certificate of incorporation by the Secretary of State, the board of incorporators shall turn over to the company the money subscription lists, notes, obligations, or other papers they may have taken as corporators in the formation of the company, and henceforth all such money, lists, notes, obligations, or other papers shall belong to and be the property of the company, and shall be as binding on the company as if taken and made by themselves. *Board of corporators to turn property over to corporation.*

Section 7. The application, orders, returns, and certificates relating to the organisation of the company shall be recorded in a book kept by the Secretary of State for that purpose, and for all such certificates, orders, transcripts, and records the Secretary of State shall be entitled to such fees as are allowed by law in other cases for like services. *Records to be kept in Secretary of State's office. Fees.*

Section 8. Among the powers of such bodies corporate shall be the following:—1. To have perpetual succession. 2. To sue and be sued by the corporate name. 3. To have a common seal, and to alter the same at pleasure. 4. To render the shares or interests of the stockholders transferable and to prescribe the mode of making such transfers. 5. To make contracts, acquire and transfer property, both *Powers of the corporation.*

real and personal, possessing the same powers in such respects as individuals now enjoy. 6. To establish bye-laws and make all rules and regulations deemed expedient for the management of their affairs not inconsistent with the constitution and laws of this State or the United States.

Increase of capital stock.
Section 9. Any company organised under the provisions of this Act may increase its capital stock to an amount not exceeding one million of dollars, by giving each stockholder the preference of taking the increase in proportion to the amount of the original stock he may own, by a vote of two-thirds of the stock in value, had at a meeting called for the purpose and by and in pursuance of a notice given for 30 days in some newspaper published in the county where the company has its principal place of business, or, where no paper is published in the county, by notice posted up at the courthouse door for a like period, give the time, place, and purpose of the meeting of stockholders. That when said capital stock is increased, a certified copy of the resolution increasing said capital stock shall be filed in the office of the Secretary of State.

Resolution to be filed with Secretary of State.

May borrow money.
Section 10. That any company organised under the provisions of this Act may borrow money for the purpose of carrying out the object of its charter, and may make notes, bonds, or other evidences of debt, and by a vote of the majority of the stock, had a meeting called for the purpose, by advertisement, as provided above in the preceding section of this Act, may secure the payment of said notes, bonds, or evidences of debt by mortgage or deed of trust on all or any of their property and franchises, both real and personal.

Execute mortgages and deeds of trust.

Meeting of stockholders.
Section 11. A meeting of the stockholders shall be held annually in this State, at such time and place, and under such notice, as the bye-laws may direct, for the election of directors and for the transaction of business. In all meetings of stockholders each stockholder shall be entitled to one vote for each and every share of stock held or owned by such stockholder.

Votes.

President and other officers.
Section 12. The directors chosen shall elect from their number a president and such other officers, agents, and servants, as they may see fit, and may discharge the president or other officer, agent, or servant at pleasure. In case any vacancy occurs in the board of directors by death, resignation, or otherwise before the expiration of the year for which he may have been elected, such vacancy shall be filled by the directors. The directors and officers elected shall hold their office for one year, or until their successors are elected and qualified.

Vacancies.

Term of office.

Deferred meetings of stockholders.
Section 13. A failure to hold meetings or to elect directors on the day appointed by the bye-laws shall not work a forfeiture of the charter of the company, but a meeting may be called by the president for that purpose by advertising as required in section 9; or if he fails or refuses to call a meeting upon a written application of stockholders owning one-fifth of the capital stock of the company, they may call the meeting by advertisement as above.

Lien for stock subscription.
Section 14. The corporation shall have a lien upon the stock of each shareholder for all amounts which may be due upon his subscription for stock, and in case of failure by him to pay within 30 days after the time appointed any instalment required to be paid by the terms of the subscription, such corporation, after 30 days' personal notice, or, if that cannot be given, notice by mail, addressed to the place of residence of the subscriber, if known, and by advertisement by publication in the public newspaper published nearest the place of business of such

Remedies.

corporation, once a week for four successive weeks, may, at its option, consolidate into as many par shares as the money paid by such defaulting subscriber will amount to, and issue to such stockholder a certificate therefor, and declare the fraction of a share remaining unpaid forfeited to the corporation, or may proceed to collect what may remain unpaid of the original subscription by suit; but if such subscriber be dead at the time of default, such forfeiture shall not be declared till after the expiration of the time when the representative is exempted from suit. If such subscription for stock be declared forfeited, such corporation may proceed and sell the forfeited share, and the shares subscribed but not paid for by such defaulting subscriber, at public or private sale, and the purchaser shall become the owner thereof, subject to the terms of the original subscription. No stock shall be issued by any company incorporated under the provisions of this Act until fully paid according to the terms of the subscription, and no transfers of stock shall be valid, except as between the parties thereto, until the same shall have been regularly entered upon the books of the company, so as to show the name of the person by whom and to whom the transfer is made, the number and other designation of the shares, and the date of the transfer. {Consolidated shares of defaulting stockholder. Deceased stockholder. Forfeited stock. Issue of stock. Transfers.}

Section 15. Corporations organised under the provisions of this Act for mining or manufacturing purposes shall have power to construct and operate a railroad, tramway, turnpike, or canal for their own use and purposes to and from their works or place of business or to connect with some navigable stream, or with some existing railroad, turnpike, or other public highway, not to exceed ten miles in length, and shall have the right to condemn, for the use of such road, the right of way in lands over which the road may pass, on payment to the owner thereof just compensation, to be determined in the manner now provided by law for railroad corporations. {Mining and manufacturing companies may construct and operate railroads, &c. Limit. Right of way.}

Section 16. Any corporation for banking purposes may be organised under the provisions of this Act, subject, however, to all the provisions, restrictions, and limitations of an Act entitled "An Act to provide for and regulate the incorporation of banks in this State" approved 24th December, 1885. {Banking corporations.}

Section 17. The books of any corporation organised under this Act shall be open to the inspection of any stockholder at any and all times, and the intentional keeping of false books or accounts by any corporation organised under this Act, whereby any one is injured, shall be a misdemeanour on the part of those concerned therein, and they shall, upon trial and conviction, be fined or imprisoned in the discretion of the Court. {Books open to stockholders. False books and accounts.}

Section 18. Any corporation organised under the provisions of this Act shall cease to exist by a non-user of its franchises for five years at any one time. {Non-user.}

Section 19. Two or more persons desiring to form themselves into a Church, Cemetery Company, Freemason or Odd Fellows or Knights of Pythias Lodge, Fire or Hook and Ladder Company, or any charitable, social, educational, or religious society, may file with the clerk of the court of the county wherein they reside a written declaration signed by themselves setting forth: 1st. The names and residences of the members. 2. The name of the proposed corporation, the place at which it is proposed to locate it, and the general purpose of the corporation. 3rd. Any other matters which it may be desirable to set forth in the organic law. And thereupon the said clerk shall issue to such persons a certificate that they are incorporated for the {Charitable, social, educational, and religious societies, &c. Steps necessary to be taken. Certificate to be issued and recorded.}

purposes named in said declaration under the name therein mentioned Which certificate shall be recorded in the office of the Register of Mesne Conveyance for the county in which the said association is located.

Powers of such corporations.   Section 20. Such corporations shall have the following powers: 1st. To make bye-laws, not inconsistent with the laws of this State or the United States. 2nd. To have and use a common seal, and the same to change at pleasure. 3rd. To sue and be sued, plead and be impleaded. 4th. To have, hold, and keep such real and personal property as may be proper and necessary for corporate purposes, and the same to sell, alien, mortgage, or otherwise dispose of at the will of said corporation. 5th. And any other powers common to such corporations and consistent with the laws of the land.

Subject to amendment or repeal.   Section 21. It shall be deemed a part of the charter of every corporation created under the provisions of any general law and of every charter granted, renewed, or amended by Act or Joint Resolution of the General Assembly (unless such Act or Joint Resolution shall, in express terms, declare the contrary), that such charter, and every amendment and renewal thereof, shall always remain subject to amendment, alteration, or repeal by the General Assembly.

Provisions attaching to all corporations except railroads and banks.   Section 22. The following provisions shall constitute a part of the charter of every corporation, other than railroad and banking corporations already in existence under Act of Assembly in this State, either general or special, passed since the adoption of the present constitution, or which may be at any time hereafter created under or by virtue of any Act of Assembly, general or special, to wit:—

Liability of stockholders.   (A.) That each stockholder in any such corporation shall be jointly and severally liable to the creditors thereof in an amount, besides the value of his share or shares therein, not exceeding 5 per cent. of the par value of the share or shares held by such stockholders at the time the demand of the creditor was **Proviso.** created: *Provided*, That such demand shall be payable within one year, and that proceedings to hold such stockholders liable therefor shall be commenced within two years after the debt becomes due, and while he, she, or it remains a stockholder therein, or within two years after he, she, or it shall have ceased **Trustees, &c.** to be a stockholder: *And provided further*, That persons holding stock in such companies as trustees or executors, administrators, or by way of collateral security, shall not be personally subject to the liabilities of stockholders under the foregoing provisions, but the persons pledging such stock shall be liable as stockholders, and the estates and funds in the hands of such executors or administrators shall be liable in their hands, in like manner and to the same extent as the deceased testator or intestate or the ward or person interested in said trust estate would have been if they had respectively been living and competent to act and hold the stock in their own names: **Further proviso.** *And provided further*, That the liability enforced in this provision shall not apply to any corporation whatever in this State in the charter of which a different liability shall have been or shall be imposed.

Fraudulent misrepresentations.   (B.) That unless some other provision for the prevention and punishment of fraudulent representations as to the capital, property, and resources of such corporations shall have been inserted therein, in which case the provision in reference thereto shall be only such as is specified in such charter, that any director or other officer, or stockholder, of the said corporation who shall knowingly and wilfully make or cause to be made any fraudulent misrepresentation or misrepresentations as to either the capital, property, or resources of the said corporation shall be guilty of a misdemeanour, and upon conviction thereof shall be punished by fine of not more than two thousand dollars (2,000 dols.) or imprisonment for not longer than two years, or both, at the discretion of the court.

(C.) That such corporations shall have power to purchase and hold such real estate as may be required for their purposes, or such as they may be obliged or may deem for their interests to take in the settlement of any debts due to them, and they may dispose of the same; to sue and to be sued in all courts; to have and to use a common seal; to elect in such manner as they may determine to be proper all necessary officers and fix their duties; to make bye-laws and regulations consistent with the constitution and laws of this State for their own government and the due and orderly conduct of their affairs and the management of their property. *Real estate. Other powers.*

(D.) That the shares in the capital stock of such corporations shall be deemed personal estate, and the mode of issuing the evidence of stock, and the manner, terms, and conditions of assigning and transferring shares, shall be prescribed by the bye-laws of each corporation.

(E.) That no part of the capital stock or any of the funds of such corporation shall at any time during the continuance of their charter be used or employed, directly or indirectly, in banking operations, or for any purpose whatsoever inconsistent with the provisions of their respective charters. *Nothing to be used in banking.*

Section 23. That the treasurer of any corporation in this State shall give bond in such sums and with such sureties as shall be required by the bye-laws for the faithful discharge of his duty. *Bond of treasurer.*

Section 24. That at all meetings of any company absent stockholders may vote by proxy authorised in writing. Every company may determine by its bye-laws what number of stockholders shall attend, either in person or by proxy, the form of such proxy, or what number of shares or amount of interest shall be represented at any meeting to constitute a quorum. If the quorum is not so determined, a majority in interest of the stockholders shall constitute a quorum. *Stockholders' meetings.*

Section 25. That the shares in any company shall be numbered, and every stockholder shall have a certificate, under the seal of the corporation, and signed by the treasurer, certifying his property in such shares as are expressed in the certificate. *Certificates of stock.*

Section 26. Every private corporation, as such, has power:—1st. To have succession by its corporate name for the period limited in its charter; and when no period is limited in perpetuity. 2nd. To sue and be sued. 3rd. To use a common seal, and to alter the same at pleasure. 4th. To hold, purchase, lease, mortgage, or otherwise dispose of and convey such real and personal estate as is limited by its charter; and if not so limited, such an amount as the business of the corporation requires. 5th. To appoint such subordinate officers and agents as the business of the corporation requires, prescribe their duties, and fix their compensation. 6th. To make bye-laws not inconsistent with any existing law, for the transfer, the management of its property, or the regulation of its affairs. 7th. To declare and create by appropriate bye-laws a lien on the stock of any stockholder *Powers of private corporations. Succession. Sue and be sued. Seal. Real and personal estate. Officers and agents. Bye-laws. Lien on stock.*

in such corporation for such sum as the stockholder is or may be indebted to such corporation for his subscription to stock therein.

Quorum. Section 27. When the corporate powers are directed to be exercised by any particular body or number of persons a majority of such body or persons, unless it is otherwise provided, form a board for the exercise of such powers.

To organise in two years. Section 28. If any private corporation hereafter created by the General Assembly or incorporated under any law does not organise and commence the transaction of its business within two years from the date of its incorporation its corporate powers shall cease.

Increase of stock or debt. Section 29. Unless otherwise specially provided in this Act neither the capital stock nor bonded indebtedness of any private corporation organised in this State shall be increased, except in the manner hereinafter prescribed.

How increased. Section 30. Before any such increase shall be authorised the consent of the persons holding the larger amount in value of the stock of such corporation shall be obtained in favour thereof at a meeting of the stockholders of such corporation convened for the purpose of voting upon the proposition.

Notice of such meeting. Section 31. No meeting of stockholders for the purpose mentioned in the preceding section shall be held until thirty days' notice thereof has been given by publication in a newspaper of general circulation published in the county where the corporation has its principal office; and if no such newspaper is published in the county, then in a newspaper having general circulation published in the county nearest the principal office of such corporation, a copy of which shall be mailed to each stockholder; and such notice shall **What to state.** explicitly state what increase it is proposed to make to the capital stock or bonded indebtedness of the corporation.

Report to Secretary of State. Section 32. If at such meeting the consent of the persons holding the larger amount in value of the stock of such corporation shall be obtained to a specified increase of either the capital stock or bonded indebtedness, a report thereof, specifying the amount of increase consented to, shall be made to the Secretary of State, who shall make and keep a record thereof, and it shall be lawful for such corporation to increase its capital stock or bonded indebtedness in conformity with such consent of the stockholders obtained as aforesaid. Such **Limit.** increase may be less but shall not be more than that stated in the published notice for such meeting.

Restrictions on issue of stock or debt. Section 33. Neither stock nor bonds shall be issued by any private corporation, except for money, labour done, or money or property actually received, and all fictitious increase of stock or indebtedness shall be void.

Section 34. Acts repealed.

11 Stat. 459, 13 Stat. 433, 14 Stat. 295, 15 Stat. 557. Proviso as to existing corporations. *Provided.* The provisions of this Act shall not affect the corporate existence of any corporation heretofore formed under any general or special law; but all such corporations shall be subject to all the provisions of this Act that are made applicable thereto.

Approved, December 23, 1886.

(Signed)   J. P. RICHARDSON,
Governor.

297

AN ACT to provide for and regulate the INCORPORATION of BANKS in SOUTH CAROLINA.

Section 1. Be it enacted by the Senate and House of Representatives of the State of South Carolina now met and sitting in General Assembly, and by the authority of the same, that from and after the passage of this Act all banks incorporated in this State shall have all the rights, powers, and privileges set forth and granted by this Act, and shall be subject to all the liabilities, limitations, and provisions herein contained; and the Act of incorporation of every such bank shall contain:— *General rights and liabilities. Contents of particular charters.*

1. The names of the corporators.
2. The name of the bank.
3. The location of the bank.
4. The capital stock, and how raised.
5. The duration of the charter.
6. A reference to this Act by its title.
7. Such special exceptions to the provisions herein contained, or such additions thereto, as the General Assembly may enact for the better carrying out the objects of the incorporation.

Section 2. The corporators of such bank, or any three of them, may open books of subscription to the capital stock of said bank at such time or times and at such places and for such periods as a majority of them may determine; and as soon as the sum named in the Act of incorporation shall be subscribed thereto, the before-named corporators, or a majority of them, on such notice as they may deem sufficient, shall call a meeting of such subscribers, and at such meeting and all future meetings of the stockholders the shares of the capital stock may be represented in person or by proxy. The subscribers to said stock, at their meeting to be held as aforesaid, shall elect from themselves such a number of directors of said corporation as they may deem proper, who shall continue in office for one year and until their successors shall be duly elected; and thereafter there shall be annual meetings of the stockholders of said bank, at which directors shall be chosen, whose tenure of office shall be as above provided. Every director must own in his own right at least ten shares of the capital stock of the said bank. The directors chosen or elected at any such meeting shall from among themselves elect a president and vice-president to act as such during the term of office of such directors, and they shall perform such duties and exercise such powers as may be prescribed by the bye-laws of said corporation or as shall be incident to their respective offices. *Books of subscription. Organization. Representation of stock. Directors. Annual meetings. Number of shares of director. President and vice-president. Duties and powers.*

Section 3. Every such corporation may receive and pay out the lawful currency of the country, deal in exchange, gold and silver coin, bullion, uncurrent paper, public and other securities, and stocks of other corporations: *Provided, however,* that no more than an amount equal to one-half of the capital stock of said bank shall be invested in mortgages of real estate at any one time; may purchase and hold such real estate and personal property as may be conveyed to it to secure debts to the corporation, or may be sold under execution to satisfy any debts due in whole or in part to the corporation and as may be deemed necessary or convenient for the transaction of its business, and may sell and dispose of the same at pleasure; may discount notes, bills of exchange, bonds, and other evidences of debts, and lend money on such terms as may be agreed *Banking powers. Mortgages. Real estate. Other banking powers.*

Other powers. on, subject to the usury laws of the State. It may receive on deposit moneys on such terms as may be agreed on with depositors, and issue certificates therefor, negotiable or assignable, in such way as may be inserted in the same; said corporation may sue and be sued, plead and be impleaded, in any court in this State; may adopt and use a corporate seal, and may alter the same at its pleasure; may adopt all such bye-laws for the general management and direction of the business and affairs of said corporation, not inconsistent with the laws of the United States and of this State, as may be deemed proper, and may add to, alter, or amend the same from time to time as may be desired, and shall have generally all the rights, powers, and privileges in law incident or appertaining to such corporations.

Liability of stockholders. Section 4. The stockholders of such bank shall be liable to the amount of their respective share or shares and 5 per cent. thereof in addition thereto, for all of its debts and liabilities upon note, bill, or otherwise.

Directors may not borrow. Section 5. No director or other officer of such bank shall borrow any money from such bank. And if any director or other officer shall **Penalty.** be convicted upon indictment of directly or indirectly violating this section he shall be punished by fine or imprisonment, or both, at the discretion of the court.

Bye-laws. Section 6. The directors of such bank may make and change bye-laws not inconsistent with law, regulating the manner in which the stock of such bank shall be transferred, its directors elected or appointed, its property transferred, its general business conducted, and the privileges granted to it by law exercised and enjoyed. The **Officers and employés.** directors may appoint all necessary officers and employés of said corporation, fix their compensation, and take security for the faithful discharge of their respective duties, prescribe the manner of paying for the stock of the corporation and the transfer thereof, and may, from time to time prescribe such penalties for the non-payment of **Subscriptions.** subscriptions to the capital stock of the corporation as they may deem proper; and the same, together with any unpaid instalments on such subscriptions, may be recovered in any court having jurisdiction **Sale of stock.** of the aggregate amount so due, or the stock may be sold for cash after twenty days' notice, advertised in the nearest newspaper; and if at any such sales the sum bid should not be sufficient to satisfy and discharge the amount so due, together with the costs and charges incident to such sale, the subscriber in default shall be liable for any **Deficiency.** deficiency, and the same may be recovered in the name of the corporation in any court having jurisdiction. The books, papers, and **Books open for inspection.** accounts of said bank shall be open to inspection under such regulations as may be prescribed by law.

Approved, December 24, 1885.

HUGH S. THOMPSON,
Governor.

REPORT on the STATE of LEGISLATION in GEORGIA, with respect to the FORMATION, REGULATION, and DISSOLUTION of COMPANIES.

Corporation: Definition. A corporation is an artificial person created by law for specific purposes, the limit of whose existence, powers, and liabilities is fixed by the Act of incorporation, usually called its charter.

Kinds. Corporations are either public or private.

299

A public corporation is one having for its object the administration of a portion of the powers of government delegated to it for that purpose,—such are municipal corporations. *(a.) Public.*

All others are private, whether the object of incorporation be for public convenience or individual profit, and whether the purpose be in its nature civil, religious, or educational. *(b.) Private.*

The power to create corporations in this State vests in the General Assembly and the courts, by whom all charters must be granted. *Their creation.*

Corporations created by other States or foreign Governments are recognised in our courts only by comity, and so long as the same comity is extended in their courts to corporations created by this State. *Foreign corporations.*

Any foreign corporation, or any corporation incorporated by the laws of any other State, and claiming to own lands in Georgia in quantity amounting to as much as 5,000 acres, shall be incorporated by the laws of Georgia within 12 months after February 28, 1887, and on their failing to do so, the State of Georgia will not consent to the said corporations owning the said lands so located in her territory. And any foreign corporation, or corporation hereafter incorporated by the laws of other States, who shall claim to own lands in the State of Georgia in quantity amounting to 5,000 acres or upwards shall become incorporated by the laws of Georgia, and, in default thereof, Georgia will not consent that said foreign corporation or corporations incorporated by the laws of any other State shall own said lands located in her territory. And no foreign corporation or corporations incorporated by the laws of another state shall own more than 5,000 acres of land except upon the condition aforesaid of becoming a corporation under the laws of Georgia. *(a.) To hold lands.*

A private corporation for any purpose whatever, except banking or insurance, may be created in this State by complying with the following provisions:— *Organization under order of court.*

1. The persons desiring the charter shall file in the office of the clerk of the Superior Court of the county in which they desire to transact business, a petition or declaration specifying the objects of their association, and the particular business they propose to carry on, together with their corporate name, and the amount of capital to be employed by them actually paid in, and their place of doing business, and the time, not exceeding 20 years, for which they desire to be incorporated, which petition or declaration shall be recorded by said clerk, and shall also be published once a week for one month in the nearest public gazette to the point where such business is located, before said court shall pass an order declaring said application granted.

And it may be lawful for any association of churches to be chartered for the purpose of promoting the cause of the Christian religion, charity, or education, by complying with the provisions of this section, except that they need not state the amount of capital to be used by them actually paid in, and when the meetings of said association are ambulatory, they shall not be required to set forth their place of business:

Provided that said associations may be chartered in any county in which a church belonging thereto may be located. And paragraph 3 of this section shall not apply to such corporations, and the publication of notice required shall be in the nearest public gazette to the county where the application is made.

2. If, upon hearing such petition, the court shall be satisfied that the application is legitimately within the purview and intention of this code, it shall pass an order declaring the said application granted, and the petitioners and their successors incorporated for and during a term not exceeding 20 years, with the privilege of renewal at the expiration of that time according to the provisions above set forth. A certified copy of this petition and order, under the seal of the court, shall be evidence of such incorporation in any court in this State.

3. No corporation so created shall commence to exercise the privileges conferred by the charter until 10 per cent. of the capital stock is paid in, and no charter shall have any force or effect for a longer period than two years, unless the corporators, within that time shall in good faith commence to exercise the powers granted by the Act of incorporation; and, in case of the failure of said corporation, the stockholders shall be bound, in their private capacity, to any creditor of said corporation for the amount of stock subscribed for by him, until the said subscription is fully paid up, or until the stockholder shall have paid, out of his private property, debts of the said corporation to an amount equal to his unpaid subscription.

5. Corporations thus created may exercise all corporate powers necessary to the purpose of their organisation, but shall make no contract or purchase, or hold any property of any kind, except such as is necessary in legitimately carrying into effect such purpose, or for securing debts due to the company.

6. The powers conferred in this section shall extend to the amendment of all charters contemplated in said section, whether the original charter sought to be amended was originally granted by the General Assembly of the State or by a Superior Court of this State.

Schools, churches, &c., how incorporated. The Superior Court, upon the petition of five discreet and proper persons, showing that a school, academy, college, or church has been or is about to be established in the county where such court is sitting, and asking for corporate authority to enforce good order, receive donations, make purchases, and affect alienations of realty or personalty, not for purposes of trade and profit, but for promoting the general design of such institution, and to look after the general interests of such an establishment, may grant to such persons and their legal successors such corporate powers as may be suitable to their enterprise, and not inconsistent with the laws of the State, nor violative of private rights; the charter so granted to remain in force 20 years, unless sooner revoked by law, and upon petition by the corporators, or their legal successors in charge of any such institution, however and whenever incorporated, the Superior Court of the county where the same is located shall have power to amend the charter thereof in any way prayed for: Provided the same is not contrary to the laws of the State nor violative of private rights. The costs of recording such proceedings on the minutes shall be paid by the petitioners, and a certified copy of the same, under the seal of the court, shall be sufficient evidence in any case of the corporate powers and privileges so granted.

Literary societies. Libraries and other literary, charitable, or social organisations which have no capital stock, and are not organised for individual pecuniary gain, may be incorporated under the provisions of this code, all of whose provisions are hereby made applicable to the organisations aforesaid.

301

Corporations have continuous succession during the time limited by their charter, notwithstanding the death of their members. Should any charter granted in future by the General Assembly to a private corporation be silent as to its continuance, such charter shall expire at the end of 30 years from the date of its grant.

All corporations have the right to sue and be sued, to have and use a common seal, to make bye-laws, binding on their own members, not inconsistent with the laws of this State and of the United States, to receive donations by gift or will, to purchase and hold such property, real or personal, as is necessary to the purpose of their organisation, and to do all such acts as are necessary for the legitimate execution of this purpose.

Every corporation acts through its officers, and is responsible for the acts of such officers in the sphere of their appropriate duties; and no corporation shall be relieved of its liability to third persons for the acts of its officers by reason of any bye-law or other limitation upon the power of the officer, not known to such third person.

Public corporations being established for public purposes are always subject to dissolution by the Act of the General Assembly.

In all cases of private charters hereafter granted, the State reserves the right to withdraw the franchise, unless such right is expressly negatived in the charter.

Every corporation is dissolved, 1st. By expiration of its charter; 2nd. By forfeiture of its charter; 3rd. By a surrender of its franchises; 4th. By the death of all its members without provisions for a succession.

A corporation may forfeit its charter: 1st. By a wilful violation of any of the essential conditions on which it is granted; 2nd. By a misuser or non-user of its franchises. This dissolution dates from the judgment of a court of competent jurisdiction declaring the forfeiture.

A corporation may be dissolved by a voluntary surrender of its franchises to the State. In such case, such surrender does not relieve its officers or members from any liability for the debts of the corporation.

The death of all the members of a corporation, or of so many of them as to render it impossible under the charter to provide a succession, is a dissolution thereof.

Upon the dissolution of a corporation for any cause, all the property and assets of every description belonging to the corporation shall constitute a fund—first, for the payment of its debts, and then for equal distribution among its members. To this end the superior court of the county where such corporation was located, shall have power to appoint a receiver, under proper restrictions, properly to administer such assets under its direction.

The dissolution of a corporation from any cause shall not in any manner affect any collateral or ultimate or other liability legally incurred by any of its officers or members.

Any number of persons not less than three may form a company, and shall give ninety days' notice of the formation of such company in each paper, daily or weekly, in the several counties through which the proposed or existing railroad shall run, by inserting in said papers once a week during said ninety days, a copy of the articles of association hereafter referred to, for the purpose of constructing, maintaining, and operating a railroad for public use in the conveyance of persons and property, or for the purpose of maintaining and operating

The powers and liabilities of corporations.
(a.) Continuance.
(b.) Common powers.

(c.) Responsibility for acts of officers.

Dissolution of corporations:
(a.) Public.
(b.) Private.
(c.) How dissolved.

(d.) How forfeited.

(e.) Surrender.

(f.) Death of all the members.

(g.) Disposition of assets.

(h.) Collateral liability.

Railroad and navigation companies:
(a.) Incorporation.

any railroad already constructed for the like public use. And for the purpose of organising under this and the following sections on the subject, may make and sign articles of association, in which shall be stated the name of the company, the places from and to which the road is to be constructed or maintained and operated, the length of such road, as near as may be, and the name of each county in the State through which or into which it is made or intended to be made, the amount of the capital stock of the company, and the number of shares of which the capital stock shall consist, and the names and places of residence of the company, who shall manage its affairs for the first year, and until others are chosen in their places, and the number of such directors shall not be less than three nor more than thirteen.

Each subscriber to such articles of association shall subscribe thereto his name, place of residence, and the number of shares of stock he agrees to take in said company.

There shall be indorsed thereon, or annexed thereto, an affidavit, made by at least three of the directors named in said articles, that the names subscribed to said articles are the genuine signatures of the persons named therein, and that it is intended in good faith to construct and to maintain and oparate the road named in such articles of association, which said articles of association and affidavits may then be filed in the office of the Secretary of State, who shall indorse thereon the day they are filed, and record the same in a book to be kept by him for that purpose. The Governor and Secretary of State shall upon the filing of such articles of association and affidavits, issue to the persons named therein a certificate of incorporation under the great seal of the State, signed by the Governor and attested by the Secretary of State.

(*b.*) Books of subscription.
When any such articles of association and affidavits are filed and recorded in the office of the Secretary of State, the directors may, in case the whole of the stock is not before subscribed, open books of subscription to fill up the capital stock of the company, in such places and after giving such notices as they may deem expedient, and may from time to time receive subscriptions until the whole capital is subscribed.

(*c.*) Directors.
There shall be a board of not less than three nor more than thirteen directors of every corporation formed under this section to manage its affairs, and said directors shall be chosen by a majority of the votes of the stockholders, each share of stock being entitled to one vote.

In the election of directors, stockholders may vote in person or by proxy.

The inspectors of the first election of directors shall be appointed by the board of directors named in the articles of association. No person shall be a director unless he shall be a stockholder, owning stock in his own name, or as trustee, and qualified to vote at the election at which he shall be chosen.

(*d.*) Officers.
The directors shall appoint one of their number president, and may also appoint vice-president, and such other officers and agents as may be prescribed by the bye-laws.

(*e.*) Stock, how payable.
The directors may require the subscribers to the capital stock of the company to pay the amount by them variously subscribed, in such instalments as they may deem proper: Provided that 5 per cent. shall be paid in before work is commenced, and that the directors may receive cash or property, real or personal, in payment of such instal-

ments. If any stockholder shall neglect to pay any instalment as required by resolution of the board of directors, the said board shall declare his stock forfeited, as well as all previous payments thereon, to the use of the company; but they shall not declare it so forfeited until they have served a notice in writing on him personally, or by depositing said notice in the post office, postage paid, directed to him at the post office nearest his usual place of residence, stating that he is required to make such payment at the time and place expressed in such notice, and that if he fails to make the same, his stock and all previous payments thereon will be forfeited for the use of the company, which notice shall be served as aforesaid, at least sixty days previous to the day on which such payment is required to be made.

In case the capital stock of any company formed under this section is found insufficient for constructing and operating its road, such company may, with the concurrence of two-thirds in amount of all its stockholders, increase its capital stock from time to time to any amount required for the purpose aforesaid. *(f.) Stock, how increased.*

Every corporation formed under this section shall be empowered:— *Powers of corporation.*

1st. To cause such examination and survey as shall be necessary, and for such purposes to be empowered by its officers, agents, or employés to enter upon the land or water of any person for that purpose.

2nd. To take and hold such voluntary grants of real estate and other property as may be made in it, to aid in the construction, maintenance, and accommodation of its road, but the real estate received by voluntary grant shall be held and used for the purpose of such grant only.

3rd. To purchase, hold, and use all such real estate and property as may be necessary for the construction and maintenance of its road, stations, &c., and to sell, lease, or buy any land necessary for its use.

4th. To lay out its roads not exceeding 200 feet in width, and to construct the same, and for the purpose of cuttings and embankments, and for obtaining gravel and other material, to take as much land as may be necessary for the proper construction, operation, and security of the road, or to cut down any trees that may be in danger of falling on the track of the road or obstructing the right of way, making compensation therefor as provided in this section for property taken for use of such company.

5th. To construct its road across, along, or upon, or to use any stream of water, watercourse, street, or canal which the routes of its road shall intersect or touch, and whenever the track of any such road shall touch, intersect, or cross any road, highway, or street, it may be carried over or under such railroad, as may be found most expedient for the public good; and in case any embankment or cut in the construction of any railroad provided for in this section shall make it necessary to change the course of any highway or street, it shall be lawful for the company constructing said railroad so to change the course or direction of any road, highway, or street; provided that no railroad constructed under the provisions of this section shall be allowed to cross any other railroad at a grade level, but such crossing shall be either under or over such other railroad track, unless by consent of such railroad company whose track is to be crossed, and when there is such consent, then and in that event the provisions of this section as to the stopping of trains before making such crossings shall apply.

[90]

6th. To cross, intersect, join, or unite its railroad with any railroad heretofore or hereafter to be constructed at any point in its route, or upon the ground of any other railroad company, with the necessary turnouts, sidelings, and switches, and other conveniences necessary in the construction of such road, and may run over any part of any other railroad's right of way necessary or proper to reach its freight depôt in any city, town, or village through or near which its railroad may run.

7th. To take and convey persons or property over their railroad by the use of steam or animals, or any mechanical power, and to receive compensation therefor, and to do all those things incident to railroad business.

8th. To erect and maintain convenient buildings, &c., whether within or without a city, town, or village, for the accommodation and use of their passenger and freight business.

9th. To regulate the time and manner in which passengers and property shall be transported, and the compensation to be paid therefor, subject to any law of this State upon the subject.

10th. To borrow such sum or sums of money, at such rates of interest, and upon such terms as such company or its board of directors shall authorise or agree upon, and may deem necessary or expedient, and may execute one or more trust deeds or mortgages, or both if occasion may require, or any railroad or railroads in process of construction by such company for the amount or amounts borrowed or owing by such company, and such company may make such provisions in such trust deed or mortgage for transferring their railroad track, depôts, grounds, rights, privileges, franchises, appendages, and appurtenances used in connection with such railroad or railroads, in any manner then belonging to said company, or which shall thereafter belong to it, as security for any bonds, debts, or sums of money as may be secured by such trust deeds or mortgages; and in case of sale of any railroad or any part thereof, in course of construction or constructed, or by virtue of any trust deed, or any foreclosure of any mortgage thereon, the party or parties acquiring titles under such sale shall have or require thereby, and shall exercise and enjoy thereafter the same rights, privileges, grants, franchises, immunities, and advantages in or by said trust deed enumerated and conveyed, which belonged to and were enjoyed by the company making such deed or mortgage; such purchasers may proceed or organise anew by filing articles of association and electing directors as provided in this section, and may distribute and dispose of stock, and may conduct their business generally as provided in this section. And all such deed and mortgages shall be recorded as is provided by law for the record of mortgages in this State, in each county through which said road runs.

(*a.*) Right of way. In the event of any company organised under the provisions of this section does not procure from the owner or owners thereof by contract, lease, or purchase, the title to the lands or right of way, it shall be lawful for said corporation to construct its railroad over any lands belonging to other persons, or over such rights of way or tracks of other railroads, upon paying or tendering to the owner thereof just and reasonable compensation for the right of way, which compensation shall be assessed in the following manner:— When the parties cannot agree upon the damage done to such other railroad company for the use of its right of way or tracks, or to the owner of the land or other property which the corporation seeks to appropriate as a right of way, the corporation shall choose one of the citizens of this State as its assessor, and the person or persons or railroad company owning the land sought to be taken or the right of way sought to be used, shall choose another as his or their assessor, and in case the person or persons owning such lands, or the railroad company owning such right of way should fail or refuse to make such choice, then it shall be the duty of the ordinary of the county in which such property or right of way is situated to make such selection for such owner or owners or railroad company.

The two assessors thus selected shall choose a third assessor, and the three assessors shall be sworn to do justice to the parties, both as to the benefits and as to the damages. The said assessor shall assess the damages and value the property so sought to be condemned, and shall say, in writing, what sum said corporation shall pay for the right of way, right to use tracks or land so sought to be condemned by it, and shall file the said award within 10 days in the office of the clerk of the superior court of the county where said lands or tracks are located, and the said clerk shall record the same, and it shall have all the force and effect of a judgment or decree by the superior court of said county, and in case either party is dissatisfied with said award, the party so dissatisfied shall have the right, by giving notice to the other party in writing within 10 days from the time the award is filed in clerk's office, to enter an appeal in writing from the said award to the superior court of the county where the said award is filed, and the judge shall cause and issue to be made up as to the damages or valuation of said land, right of way, &c., and the same to be tried, with all the rights of hearing and trying said cause in the superior and supreme courts. The entering of said appeal, and the proceedings thereon, shall not hinder or in any way delay the said corporation's work, or the progress thereof, but the same may proceed without let or hindrance from the time said condemnation proceedings are begun. If the said corporation make the appeal it shall give bond and security for the payment of the amount rendered upon the final hearing of said cause.

Whenever the track of any railroad shall cross a railroad or highway, such highway or railroad may be crossed under or over, and in cases where a cutting shall make a change in the line of any such highway, the said corporation may take such additional lands for the construction of such highway upon such new lines as may be deemed expedient and requisite. *(b.) Crossing other roads.*

Any railroad company in this State shall have the power and authority to make and enter into contract with any other railroad company within this State or another State, as will enable said companies to run their roads in connection with each other and to merge their stock, or to lease or purchase the stock and property of any other such company. It shall be lawful for such companies to build, construct, and run as part of their corporate property such number of steamboats or vessels as they may deem necessary: Provided that no railroad shall purchase a competing line of railroad calculated to defeat or lessen competition in this State. *(c.) Contracts with other roads.*

Every train of passenger cars drawn by locomotives shall come to a full stop within 400 feet of any crossing, and any such train shall slow down to a speed of 4 miles an hour before running on or crossing any drawbridge over a stream regularly navigated by vessels. *(d.) Crossings, how to run at.*

[90]

(*e.*) Duration of charter.

No corporation created under this section shall continue, except by extension of time by legislative enactment, for a longer period than 50 years.

Navigation companies.
(*a.*) Incorporation.

Any three or more persons may form a company for the purpose of building for their own use, purchasing, equipping, fitting out, chartering, navigating, or owning ships or vessels, to be propelled solely or partially by steam, to be used in all lawful commerce or navigation upon the ocean, seas, and rivers, by filing in the office of the clerk of the superior court of the county in which the principal office of the company is to be located a certificate in writing, in which shall be stated the corporate name of the company and the specific objects for which the company shall be formed, stating particularly the ports between which such vessels are intended to be navigated, one of which ports at least shall be within this State; the amount of the capital stock of said company, which shall not be less than 10,000 dols. nor more than 5,000,000 dols., the term of its existence not to exceed 50 years, the number of shares of which the said stock shall consist, the number of directors, and their names, who shall manage the concerns of said company, and the name of the city or town and county within this State in which the principal office of the company is to be situated.

(*b.*) Stock.

The capital stock of such company shall be divided into shares of 100 dols. each, for which certificates shall be issued, which shall be transferable only on the books of the company as may be prescribed in the bye-laws; but no share shall be transferable until all previous calls thereon shall have been fully paid in, and no transfer or assignment of stock shall operate to release any holder from obligation to the said company without the consent of the board of directors.

(*c.*) Certificate of stock.

The president and a majority of the directors within 30 days after the payment of the last instalment of the capital stock shall make a certificate stating the amount of the capital stock of the corporation, and that the same is paid in, which certificate shall be signed and sworn to by them, and they shall within the said 30 days record the same in the office of the clerk of the superior court of the county, and also in the office of the Secretary of State. The capital stock named in the said certificate shall be paid in within the first year of the existence of the said corporation.

(*d.*) False certificates.

If any certificate made as aforesaid shall be false in any material representation, all the officers who have signed the same shall be jointly and severally liable to any person for all damages arising therefrom.

(*e.*) Stockholders.

In case of failure of any corporation, the stockholders shall be bound in their private capacity to any creditor of such corporation for the amount of stock subscribed for by them respectively, until the said subscription is fully paid up, or until the stockholder shall have paid out of his private property debts of said corporation to an amount equal to his unpaid subscription.

(*f.*) Renewal of charter.

Any company incorporated under the provisions of this law, at the expiration of the term for which it was incorporated, shall have privilege of a renewal of its charter upon the same terms upon which it was originally incorporated, and by conforming anew to all the provisions hereinbefore set forth.

When Dividends are prohibited.

No joint stock company, corporation, body corporate, or other association shall declare any dividend, or distribute any money among its members as profits, when such are not the legitimate proceeds of its investments.

Lien by Bye-laws.

The bye-laws of a corporation may create a lien upon the shares of other property of the stockholders in favour of the company; such lien is binding upon the corporators themselves, and upon creditors giving credit with notice, or purchasers at public or private sale purchasing with notice.

Savannah, Ga.,
June 18, 1888.

(Signed) W. ROBERTSON,
British Vice-Consul.

NORTH CAROLINA.

In this Circular information is asked for as to the state of legislation in North Carolina, with respect to the formation, regulation, and dissolution of companies, whether joint stock, or in shares, or in whatever manner constituted.

In North Carolina corporations are constituted in one of two ways, to wit:—1st. By a special charter in Act of the Legislature relating to and incorporating a particular corporation or company. 2nd. Under the General Act, providing for the incorporation of bodies politic for any and all lawful purposes, except building railroads, banking, or insurance. Under the first method, a Bill is prepared and sent to the Legislature, containing the names of those who propose to organise the corporation, the name of the same, the purposes, the amount of capital stock, par value of each share, and any other provisions specially desired as to powers and manner conducting the business and internal affairs of the company, and sometimes the term of years the corporation is to exist, as otherwise sixty years is the limit. Upon the Bill becoming a law, the persons named in the Act as corporators meet and organise the corporation, under the charter, by electing officers, adopting constitutions and bye-laws. If it is a company with money capital, the same, or the part required by charter, must be subscribed for and paid in before the organisation can take place. Under the second method three or more persons desiring to form a corporation may agree upon a plan of incorporation, setting forth the corporate name, business proposed, place of same, term of corporate existence, names of subscribers to stock, amount of capital, number of shares and par value of shares, and execute the said agreement as a deed. The articles of agreement are then probated before the clerk of the superior court of the county where the corporation is to do business, and filed in his office. He then issues letters declaring the parties to the articles and their successors a corporation, and notice thereof is published in some newspaper. Those who have thus organised may admit others to the extent provided for in said articles.

Corporations may be dissolved by expiration of charter, by decree of forfeiture of charter by a proper court, and by unanimous consent of the stockholders. If dissolved by expiration of charter, or by decree of forfeiture, their existence is continued for three years thereafter for the purpose of settling and closing their business, and receivers may be appointed to take charge, executions may issue against corporations, be levied upon their property, and may include the franchise, and the purchaser becomes invested with all the rights and franchises of the original corporation. Corporations are regulated by the charter constitution and by laws which the stockholders have a right to make, if not inconsistent with the laws of the United States, or of this State. Stockholders are only liable to the amount of stock held by them respectively, unless otherwise provided.

Any corporation exercising powers not granted may be restrained by injunction, sued out by the Attorney-General of the State, and a failure to organise within two years after the grant of a charter, or, if after organisation the corporation ceases to act for two years, works a forfeiture of charter. There are no joint stock companies in this State technically, all being corporations with capital stock in shares.

The above is a brief synopsis of the material provisions of the statute law relating to corporations in this State. The decision of the supreme court furnishes the balance of the law.

The statutes relating to corporations are embraced in what is known as "The Code" and the amendments made thereto.

GALVESTON.

Sir, *Galveston, Texas, June* 13, 1888.

WITH reference to your Despatch dated May 21st, I have the honour to report that I cannot hear of there being any legislation (State) in force in Texas, controlling the formation of joint stock companies or syndicate.

I have, &c.,
(Signed) WAALTER T. LYALL,
Sir L. S. S. West, K.C.M.G. *Her Majesty's Consul.*
&c., &c., &c.

PENNSYLVANIA.

Sir, *Philadelphia, June* 9, 1888.

I BEG to acknowledge the receipt of your Circular Despatch A, of the 21st ultimo, requesting me to furnish you with information on the state of legislation in this Consular district with respect to the formation, regulation, and dissolution of companies, joint stock or share.

The law of Pennsylvania regulating corporations in the State was passed April 29th, 1874. Previous to the passage of this important Act corporations were organised by special Acts of the Legislature, a practice found to be attended by sundry objectionable features, and the present law is accepted by the legal profession and the public at large in all respects as satisfactory.

309

I herewith forward a bound copy of the Act* together with a voucher for the sum paid therefor, and will thank you to remit the amount, 2·75 dollars, to this consulate.

I have, &c.,
(Signed) ROBT. CHAS. CLIPPERTON.
Sir L. S. S. West, K.C.M.G.,
&c., &c., &c.

CHICAGO.

Sir, *Chicago, June* 29, 1888.

IN accordance with the instructions contained in your Circular Despatch A, of the 21st ultimo, I have the honour to transmit herewith a report on the state of legislation with respect to companies in the Consular district of Chicago. The subject covers a large amount of ground, and I have been able to give but a brief outline of the legislation, but will promptly respond to a desire for further information on any particular point.

I have, &c,,
(Signed) J. HAYES SADLER.

REPORT of CONSUL HAYES SADLER ON THE STATE OF LEGISLATION with respect to COMPANIES in the CONSULAR DISTRICT of CHICAGO.

Introduction. The state of legislation in the district of Chicago with respect to the formation, regulation, and dissolution of companies, whether joint stock or otherwise constituted, is somewhat in confusion. Each State and territory forms its own independent statute laws under their separate constitutional provisions; though in a measure general in character, the laws vary in each State or territory, and are constantly revised or amended at the successive meetings of the different Legislative Assemblies. Corporations are bodies corporate and politic, created under these statute laws, and are subject to alteration, suspension, or repeal; in some States all corporations are formed under a general law, with separate Acts regulating associations for certain particular purposes; in others, certain corporations are formed and regulated wholly by separate general Acts, but nowhere are special laws made except for municipal corporations or such as are under State control. The laws on corporations, as amended up to 1887, are herein summarised so far as they are of a similar character throughout the district, and, where any marked peculiarity or difference appears to exist which is not generally applicable, reference is made to some particular State or territory where such is in force. Before entering, however, on the legislation, it seems necessary to briefly point out how the laws on corporations in these States and territories are variously affected and governed by their different constitutions.

Constitutional provisions. Corporation is defined by the constitution of Missouri, Minnesota, and Kansas to mean all associations, or joint stock companies, having any of the powers or privileges of corporations not possessed by

* This is a book of 170 pages of matter, and is not printed here.

individuals or partnerships. By the constitution of all the States and territories of this district the Legislatures are forbidden, generally, to create corporations by special Act, except, in certain States, charitable, educational, and, as well as in the territories, municipal, penal, or reformatory corporations. In the territories the Legislature can provide only by general law for the creation of educational, industrial, mining, religious, charitable, and literary, manufacturing, and draining corporations, railroads, and waggon roads, and, as also in Iowa, no exclusive privileges can be granted. In some States the Legislature can pass no law for the benefit of any corporation retrospective in its operation, or which imposes any new liability on the people in respect to past transactions or considerations. In many States, by the constitution, all general laws for the creation of corporations may be altered or repealed, but in Iowa only by a two-third vote of the Legislature, and in Colorado so as not to work injustice to corporators or creditors; in several, all charters or special Acts. In some, charters of corporations existing at the time of adoption of the constitution are void; in others, no law can be passed for their benefit unless they accept the constitution. The business of corporations, their offices and suits, the rights and liabilities of stockholders, the liability of directors, the issue and increase of stock and preferred stock, and the holding of real estate are also provided for by the constitution of some States. In some cases the constitution declares railroads to be public highways and free to all persons for transportation under prescribed regulations; in others, that they are common carriers, and that laws shall be passed to correct abuses and prevent unjust discrimination and extortion, while, in a few, maximum rates of freights and fares must be established; in Missouri free passes are forbidden and acceptance of a pass forfeits office; in some States no railroad can consolidate with a competing or parallel line, and other provisions exist regarding railroads. In Wisconsin State banks are forbidden; in Illinois and Missouri an Act establishing them must first be submitted to a vote of the people; in many States other constitutional provisions exist regarding banking associations, as well as for religious and municipal corporations.

Legislation.—General Laws.

Corporations for pecuniary profit. Corporations for pecuniary profit can be formed in some States under the general statute laws for any purpose, as in Iowa, Kansas, and Colorado; in Iowa their powers are as broad and comprehensive as those of individuals, extending to perpetual succession and the exemption of private property from corporate liabilities beyond the unpaid portion of the stock, except in cases of failure to comply substantially with the regulations regarding organisation or publicity, though this exception does not apply to railroad companies. In those States, as Illinois, Wisconsin, and Missouri, where banks, railroads, insurance, and some other corporations are excluded from the general laws, such corporations are formed under separate Acts.

Organization. The number of persons who can incorporate varies, but is generally fixed at not less than three, while a maximum number is variously fixed. A statement must first be made by the corporators containing a declaration of the name, business, or purpose, location of the principal office, amount of capital stock, number of shares, and duration of the company; in some States additional particulars are required for certain purposes, as the method of acceptance by members, the amount of each share, the designation and duties of directors, and the maximum amount of indebtedness to which it shall be subject (in Iowa and Nebraska not to exceed two-thirds of the capital stock, except in risks of insurance companies), and notice must be published. The statement or articles of incorporation must be filed in the office of the Secretary of State, who grants a license to the corporators as commissioners to open books for subscription, but no license can be granted to two companies of the same name. When the capital stock is fully subscribed (Illinois), or when half subscribed (Wisconsin), a meeting of subscribers must be convened, at which directors and managers must be appointed; 10 days' notice of the meeting must be given by post to each subscriber, who can vote in person or by proxy. A full report of the proceedings, with copy of notice, subscription list, and names of directors, must then be filed with the Secretary of State, who issues a certificate of complete organisation, which is filed in the record office of the county, making a part thereof a copy of all papers. Copy of this certificate is evidence of incorporation. License is revoked if business is not proceeded with in two years, or in some States one year. In Missouri and a few other States, at or before filing articles, 10*l.* (50 dols.) must be paid into the State Treasury for the first 10,000*l.* (50,000 dols.) of stock, and 1*l.* (5 dols.) for every additional 2,000*l.* (10,000 dols.), and on increase. The articles can generally by a two-third vote be amended, if no change in object or purpose (but not railroads in Colorado).

The amount of capital is generally limited between a minimum of 2,000*l.* (10,000 dols.) and a maximum of 200,000*l.* (1,000,000 dols.), but in some instances the minimum is a smaller sum, and in others the maximum is 100,000*l.* (500,000 dols.) for certain purposes, or unlimited. It is generally provided that the shares shall not be less than 2*l.* (10 dols.), or more than 20*l.* (100 dols.), but in Minnesota, except for mining, the limit is 10*l.* (50 dols.), and in some States, and for certain purposes, they are fixed at 20*l.* (100 dols.); they are personal property, transferable under bye-laws, and liable to execution; each share has one vote. *Capital stock.*

The duration of a company is invariably limited, and varies in each State, and for particular purposes, generally from 20 to 50 years. All corporations in Missouri, and in Iowa and Montana, except railroads and insurance companies, are limited to 20 years. In Illinois no company can exceed the limit of duration of 99 years. In Kansas, when duration is not specified in the articles, the law limits it to 20 years. In general, railroads are limited to 50 years, but can generally be renewed. *Duration of company.*

It is generally provided that directors shall be divided into three classes, one-third vacating each year. They are held personally and individually liable for the debts of the corporation exceeding the amount of the capital stock, if assenting thereto. The number of directors cannot be altered without the consent of a majority of shares at a meeting of which notice has been given, but in Illinois after vote the number must not be less than five or more than 11, though it can be changed by a majority vote at a special meeting from an even to an odd number. *Directors.*

The general powers of a corporation, which are exercised by directors, are to make necessary contracts, to sue and be sued, to have a common seal alterable or renewable at pleasure, to appoint officers, make bye-laws not inconsistent with the laws, to hold property to the amount necessary for the transaction of business or as authorised by *Powers of corporations.*

law, and to mortgage the property to secure debts; provided that all real estate acquired in satisfaction, if not necessary or suitable for the transaction of business, shall be offered for sale at public auction at least once every year, and if not sold in five years (Illinois), or in some States, in three years, the court has power to order sale. In the territories, by Act of Congress (1887), no corporation can hold more than 5,000 acres of land, except railroads, canals, turnpikes, and municipal corporations. In Illinois a statement on oath setting forth a description of all real estate acquired in securing debts, with the date of acquirement, must be made within 20 days from the 1st of each December, and filed in the office of the Secretary of State.

Miscellaneous regulations.
The officers must consist of a president, secretary, and treasurer, and such other as may be appointed, and they can be required by the directors to give bond or security, and be removed if interest requires. A complete record must be kept of proceedings, and an annual report made of assets and liabilities for the use of stockholders, who can examine books by themselves or their attorney. If the report is not made in the first two months of each year, directors are liable for debts till it is made. In Colorado the fine for not showing books is 40*l.* (200 dols.), and 15 persons may at any time demand a statement; in Missouri the fine is 50*l.* (250 dols.). No loans can be made to stockholders. Shares are payable in instalments as directors may determine; all assessments must be *pro ratâ* and are recoverable by action after 20 days, limited in some States to 10 or 15 per cent. in any one or three months. Each shareholder is liable for the debts of the corporation to the extent of the amount of unpaid stock held by him, and remains jointly liable with assignee until such is fully paid; except that stockholders in banks, and in Kansas, by State constitution, all stockholders except in railroads and charitable institutions, are liable to an additional amount equal to the stock held. In action for indebtedness against a corporation any shareholder may be procceded against to the extent of his liability on his stock, and any transferee is in the same manner liable as if he were an original subscriber. If any persons assume corporate powers in any way without complying with the Acts, they are liable for debts made by them in the name of the corporation. If directors or officers pay any dividend when corporation is insolvent, or which would render it insolvent, or diminish the amount of capital stock, they are jointly and severally liable for all debts of the corporation then existing, or that shall be contracted thereafter while they continue in office. No dividend can be made except out of net earnings (Montana). If any statement or false report be made, all officers who have signed the same shall be jointly and severally liable for damage arising therefrom. Stockholders holding two-thirds of the stock (fully paid up, Illinois) may call a meeting by filing with the secretary a call therefor, with their names and number of shares, and publishing the same for three successive weeks in a newspaper of the State. Bye-laws must provide for the meetings of directors and officers, and the acts of such meeting are valid (if all such officers are present or sign a written consent on the record, Illinois). Executors, administrators, conservators, guardians, or trustees, holding stock, and persons holding stock as collateral security, are not personally subject to liability, but the estate of the testator or ward in their hands, and the persons pledging stock are liable as stockholders; the former can attend meetings and vote. Provisions are made for changing the name of corporation and its place of business; for increasing or

decreasing the capital stock, which is generally by a two-third vote of a meeting, 30 days' notice of which has been given ; and for consolidation, but not more than two companies can consolidate, and they must be engaged in the same business, and no railroad corporation (or telegraph company in Colorado constitution) can consolidate with a parallel or competing line ; the consolidated company is liable for the debts of each prior to consolidation. A corporation cannot hold stock in another corporation, except mining in a corporation for generating light (Wisconsin), or in a like corporation or for smelting (Minnesota). It is generally provided that no dividend can be paid except out of net profits, or capital fully paid up (Wisconsin). The General Assemblies have reserved power to provide regulations and provisions which shall be binding, and may alter or annul powers of corporations (Wisconsin). A corporation is dissolved on expiration of duration of charter, but in some cases renewal is provided for on a two-third vote of stockholders, and on approvers of renewal purchasing the shares of those opposed ; or by non-user; or, if business be suspended for one year (Kansas, Nebraska, Wisconsin), or by vote if no means provided (Wisconsin). The corporate capacity is generally continued for two years, or three years (Wisconsin) for the purpose of collecting debt and conveying property, of suing and being sued. Dissolution, for whatever cause, does not impair remedy for liabilities previously incurred. Failure to elect officers on the day named does not have the effect of dissolving a corporation, but such election may be held at any time after proper notice. If a corporation shall do, or refrain from doing, any act which shall subject it to forfeiture of charter, or allow any execution to remain unsatisfied for, generally 10 days, or shall dissolve or cease business leaving debts unpaid, all stockholders are liable for debts, the corporation being joined in the suit, to the extent of the unpaid portion of their stock, after exhausting the assets of the corporation ; and if any stockholder is unable to satisfy his portion, the amount is divided *pro ratâ* among remaining solvent stockholders. Courts of equity have power, on good cause shown, to dissolve a corporation and appoint a receiver, who shall be a resident of the State and give bond, and by and against whom or the corporation writs may issue. Dissolution.

Societies not for pecuniary profit are provided for by separate general Acts, and may be formed much in the same manner ; but they cannot dissolve or surrender their names and organizations till all debts are paid, and no distribution can be made except by a majority vote and then after a statement on oath duly recorded, and no change in the articles of association can be made until a certificate be filed with the Secretary of State and be recorded. Religious corporations may be organized by electing trustees, wardens, and vestrymen, and on filing affidavit they become bodies corporate and politic under certain restrictions as to holding land and certain rules as regards trustees. In some States and the territories by constitution, religious corporations are prohibited from holding real estate exceeding the value of 10,000*l.* (50,000 dols.). Corporations not for pecuniary profit.

Railroads are formed either under the general corporation laws, as in Iowa and other States, and separate Acts provide additional powers and regulations for their operation and management, or under separate general Acts as in Illinois and Wisconsin. The law of Illinois includes warehouses in the Railroad Act. They are formed much in the same manner as corporations under the general laws with some peculiarities. The number of persons who can form them is generally not less than five. Their duration is generally limited Railroads.

to 50 years, in some States less, but their charter is generally renewable by vote, and on purchase of the stock of those disapproving. In Kansas and Illinois no railway can [exist beyond 99 years. The articles of incorporation must include the place from and to which the line is proposed, the length of road and name of county, the names and addresses of corporators and the names of directors, and must be recorded by the corporators in each county through which the line runs. Bye-laws can be made which, as well as all amendments thereto, must be also recorded. The additional powers extend to the survey of land and water, holding and conveying grants of real estate, the construction of the road with a right of way not exceeding 100 feet in width except in cuttings (200 feet in Colorado), and to convey passengers and property (by any mechanical means, Illinois). Borrowing money, forming union depôts, fencing and operating, the protection of passengers, and other matters are generally authorized or regulated by separate Acts. Conductors are invested with police powers. Any extortion or unjust discrimination is forbidden under penalty. If the purchase of real estate or material cannot be agreed on with the owner, title can be acquired as provided by the laws of eminent domain. If instalments on shares are not paid, such stock is forfeited for the use of the corporation, proper notice being given. A railroad commissioner, or a commission of three persons (Illinois), is appointed by the Governor at each biennial General Assembly, who personally examines into the management of the lines in the State, and every railroad must transmit to said commissioner or commission annually, within two months from 1st July (Illinois), a full statement of the affairs of the corporation. If the articles of incorporation are not filed in two years, or 25 per cent. of the capital expended in five years, or the railroad finished in ten years, the corporate existence ceases. Companies may lease or purchase lines in connection so as to form continuous lines, or build spur lines, but no two parallel or competing lines can consolidate. In Missouri no articles can be filed or recorded until 200*l*. (1,000 dols.) for every mile of broad gauge, or 100*l*. (500 dols.) for every mile of narrow gauge, be subscribed, and 5 per cent paid in cash, and an affidavit of three directors to that effect must be endorsed on the articles. The maximum rates that can be charged are generally fixed; in Missouri by constitution, and in Iowa by law of 1888, no passes or free tickets are allowed, or officers forfeit their office; and no officer shall be interested in furnishing material or supplies to a company. It is everywhere provided that stocks and bonds shall only be issued for money, labour done, or property received.

Insurance corporations. Fire and inland navigation. Formation.

Insurance companies are generally organized under separate Acts, and in those States, where they can be formed under the general laws there are separate regulations for their government. Fire and inland navigation insurance companies may be formed by a number of persons varying in different parts of this district, who must sign and file a declaration, with a copy of the proposed charter, in the office of the auditor of public accounts, or insurance commission or commissioner if such appointed, and publish notice of intention in a public newspaper for four weeks. Books can then be opened for subscription or propositions received. The charter and proof of publication having been examined by the Attorney-General or commissioner, and the auditor or commissioner having examined and being satisfied that the capital is paid, or if a mutual company, that it is in possession of the premiums or engagements required, a certificate to that effect is granted and filed with the clerk of the county or proper record office, and a copy given to the company, when business can be commenced. The duration or extension of insurance companies varies from 20 to 50 years in different States.

No company can be formed for this purpose in Chicago with a less capital than 30,000*l.* (150,000 dols.), nor any mutual company commence business unless agreement has been entered into with at least 400 applicants, the premiums on which applications amount to 40,000*l.* (200,000 dols.), of which 8,000*l.* (40,000) have been paid in cash and notes of solvent parties. For other parts of Illinois and in most other States the capital is fixed at not less than 20,000*l.* (100,000 dols.), and in mutual companies the number of applicants at not less than 100 and the amount of premium, at not less than 10,000*l.* (50,000 dols.). The capital can be invested in bonds and mortgages on real estate, worth 50 per cent. more than the sum loaned, or public stocks or loans, and any surplus money must be invested in or loaned on public stock or paying corporations provided the current value is 10 per cent. above the sum loaned. No real estate can be held except such as is requisite for transaction of business, such as shall have been mortgaged to the company in good faith for loans on money due, or been conveyed in satisfaction of debts, or purchased upon judgment decrees or mortgages obtained for such debts; and all such real estate acquired must be sold or disposed of within three or five years if not necessary for transaction of business, provided that the auditor or commissioner may further postpone sale if interests of the company would suffer by forced sale. The increase or decrease of capital is provided for by vote. The shares are generally fixed at 20*l.* (100 dols.); in some States the capital is limited to 200,000*l.* (1,000,000 dols.), and in some and for agencies of other States to a less amount. *Capital stock.*

No note shall exceed 200*l.* (1,000 dols.), or in Missouri and Wisconsin 100*l.* (500 dols.), or more than one note on the same risk if exceeding that amount, and each to be accepted must be accompanied with a certificate of a justice of the peace or a supervisor. All notes deposited with a mutual insurance company remain as security until the accumulation of premium notes and assets, invested as required, shall equal the necessary cash capital, liability decreasing as profits are accumulated: but any note deposited subsequent to the organization of the company, in addition to cash premium or any insurance effected with such company, may at the expiration of the time of such insurance be relinquished and given up on payment of proportion of losses and expenses accrued during such term. Directors have a right to determine the amount of the note in addition to the cash premium, not to exceed five times the annual rate (Illinois). Every person effecting insurance becomes a member and is bound to pay for losses and expenses in proportion, but cannot be required to pay more than the amount of his deposit note for any loss by fire (or inland navigation, Illinois). *Notes.*

Dividends can only be paid out of surplus profits, and in estimating these a sum is reserved equal to the whole amount of unearned premiums on unexpired risks and policies, and also all sums due to the corporation on bonds and mortgages, stocks and book accounts, of which no part of the interest thereon has been paid during the last year, and for which suit or foreclosure has not been commenced for collection, or which, after judgment obtained, shall have remained more than two years unsatisfied, and on which interest has not been *Dividends.*

paid; all interest due and unpaid is also reserved; provided that any company may pay a dividend not exceeding 10 per cent. or 15 (Minnesota), on the captial stock in any one year, that shall have accumulated, or be in the possession of a fund, in addition to the amount of the capital stock and of such dividend, and all outstanding liabilities, equal to one-half of the amount of all premiums on risks not terminated at the time of paying such dividend (Illinois). The charter is liable to forfeiture if any dividend be made contrary to these provisions, and a stockholder receiving it is liable to creditors to the extent of such dividend, in addition to other penalties and punishments (Illinois). This latter clause does not apply to scrip dividends declared by participating companies, but no such dividend can be paid except from surplus profits after reserving all sums above mentioned including the whole amount of premiums on unexpired risks.

Annual statement. The president or secretary must prepare and deposit in the office of the auditor of public accounts or the commissioner in January each year (or semi-annually in Nebraska) a statement, on oath, showing the condition of the company on the 31st December preceding, including:—1. The amount of capital stock actually paid in. 2. The property or assets held, specifying the several values and amounts. 3. The liabilities, specifying the amount of losses, claims, loans, dividends, &c. 4. The income of the company during the preceding year, specifying the amount of cash payments, notes, interest-money, or other income. 5. The expenditure during the year, specifying the amount of losses paid, dividends, expenses, taxes, and all other expenditure. The statement of a mutual company, the capital of which is wholly or in part composed of notes, must also exhibit the amount of original notes and the proportion of the same still considered capital. The auditor or court can address any inquiry, which must be promptly replied to. The penalty for failure to make statement varies: in Illinois it is 100*l*. (500 dols.) and an additional 100*l*. (500 dols.) for every month that business continues to be transacted; in Nebraska 20*l*. (100 dols.) from the president and secretary, half for the use of the State and half for the informer; in Wisconsin 20*l*. (100 dols.) for each day's neglect, and no new business can be done after proper notification while neglect continues. On satisfactory evidence that any statement or report is false, the auditor or commissioner can revoke certificate of authority, and the company on receipt of copy of such revocation must cease issuing or renewing policies, or the auditor can appoint persons to examine into the affairs of the company, and the officers on oath; and when deficiency appears, the county court, on application, shall hear the case, and if the assets and funds of the company are not sufficient, as aforesaid, or public interest requires, can decree dissolution.

Miscellaneous regulations. The word "mutual" or "joint stock" must be embodied in the title of the company, and appear on the face of its policies. Joint stock companies may extend their charter and increase their stock generally by a two-third vote, and mutual companies can become joint stock under certain provisions. Any company can call on its stockholders to make up capital required by charter, but directors are personally liable for losses on new risks taken after expiration of the period limited by the auditor. If the stock is impaired to an amount exceeding 25 per cent., the company can with permission of the auditor reduce (by a two-third vote of directors, Illinois), its capital stock and its par value, but there must be no distribution, nor can it be reduced to an amount less than required for a new company. Any officer failing to comply with or violating the provisions is liable to penalty; in Iowa this is fixed at 200*l*. (1,000 dols.) and imprisonment of not less than 30 days.

County fire insurance companies are generally formed of not less than 25 persons, owning collectively not less than 10,000*l*. (50,000 dols.) of property. A member can withdraw by surrendering policy and paying share of claims, but the number cannot be reduced below the original number of corporators, and township insurance companies are governed by somewhat similar provisions. It is sometimes provided that no fire insurance company shall advertise as assets anything not available for payment of losses by fire. County fire.

Life insurance companies are governed by the same or similar regulations to those of fire insurance, but it is generally provided that they must have at least 20,000*l*. (100,000 dols.) as a guarantee capital paid in money and invested in United States bonds, or first lien mortgages on real estate worth 50 per cent. more than such mortgages or other approved security, to be held by the State treasurer, or superintendent or commissioner appointed, or Attorney-General (Missouri), as the case may be. The statement must be made within the first two months of each year, but the auditor may extend the period, and be published in the newspapers and in some States communicated to the General Assembly. When the funds are not of a net value equal to the net value of its policies, according to the "combined experience" or "actuary's" rate of mortality with interest at 4 per cent., the auditor or other authority shall give notice to discontinue issuing new policies under penalty, till they are equal in the distribution of mutual companies, the aggregate net value of outstanding policies with 4 per cent. interest must be reserved. Life insurance.

There are many separate laws regarding other insurance associations in this district. In Illinois, an Act was passed in 1883, governing corporations for furnishing life indemnity or pecuniary benefit to widows, and in 1887 separate Acts for farmers mutual live stock insurance, co-operative associations, for transacting surety business, and for trusts by trust companies. Other insurance associations.

Involuntary dissolution of insurance companies, when not provided for under the general laws, occurs by extinction of the charter by its own limitation, or by non-user, or by having ceased business for one year by decree of court, but they continue bodies corporate for two or three years to enable them to close their concerns. When the auditor, or other person appointed, is, on examination, of opinion that continuance of business is hazardous to the insurer or the public, or that the laws have not been complied with, or the corporate powers exceeded, he can petition a judge to issue injunction until the case can be heard; the judge has discretion to issue such decree, or an order to show cause, and may at any time, and after hearing, perpetuate or modify such injunction. If a claim is not paid in about 15 days, license can be suspended. Voluntary dissolution may take place on petition of a majority of stockholders in number or interest, and the judge for reasonable cause shown can proceed to hear the matter and may issue decree; notice of intention to retire from business must be published for 30 successive days, and outstanding policy-holders must be notified, who can receive value or have re-insurance secured in another company, and when all policies are cancelled a certificate is granted. Dissolution.

Each State and territory has Acts providing regulations for the management of mines, which are generally similar in character, and Mines.

in many Legislative Assemblies additional provisions have been lately made for the security and health of miners.

Banks. In some States, as shown in the constitutional provisions, there are no State banks, and there the existing corporations are either under the banking laws of the United States, or their charters dated before the adoption of the existing constitution of the States. In Illinois an Act was passed in 1887, which cannot take effect till a vote of the people, to be submitted in 1889, has been taken permitting the organization of corporations with banking powers; this new Act contains provisions which are briefly as follows:—That the capital shall not be less than 5,000*l*. (25,000 dols.), and in cities of more than 10,000 inhabitants 10,000*l*. (50,000 dols.); that the capital must be wholly subscribed before a meeting can be convened, and wholly paid up before business can be commenced; that the State auditor shall examine into the affairs of the company, and, if satisfied the capital is paid in, shall then grant permit to commence business, which must be recorded; that the individual liability of shareholders shall extend ratably and equally to the extent of the amount of their stock in addition to the amount invested in such shares; that a list of all shareholders, with the number of their shares, and all transfers shall be furnished to the auditor; that a report, verified by the oath of the president or cashier, of resources and liabilities, shall be made to the auditor within five days of his calling for the same, which shall be at least once in three months; and that such report shall be published in a newspaper; that the auditor shall appoint a suitable person or persons at least once in each year to thoroughly examine into the affairs and report to him; and if capital impaired it must be made good in 30 days or the auditor can file a bill for the appointment of a receiver to wind up; on payment of the amount of debts and claims to the auditor, a bank can dissolve and distribute assets.

In other parts of this district where banks are organized, the separate regulations of the general laws or the separate Acts under which they are formed contain somewhat similar provisions, and the liability of stockholders extends to an amount equal to and in addition to their stock.

Foreign corporations. In addition to the above regulations, foreign corporations must have a recognized agent on whom process can be served, and insurance corporations organized in a foreign country are required to deposit 20,000*l*. (100,000 dols.), in bonds or securities of the United States (or of their own country in some States), or a certificate of such deposit in some other State or territory of the United States; in Minnesota the sum of 80,000*l*. (400,000 dols.) must be deposited in the case of marine insurance companies; and it is provided in some States that the license necessary for foreign companies to transact business can be revoked if they shall remove an action from the State to the United Sates court, or fail to comply with requirements.

In the territories by the Alien Act of Congress of 1887, and in five States of this district where similar Acts were also passed last year, foreign corporations are now wholly or almost entirely restricted from holding real estate. In Colorado this restriction does not extend to corporations engaged in any industry other than the holding of agricultural, arid, or range land outside of towns and cities, but in Minnesota and Wisconsin and the territories it extends to corporations, more than 20 per cent. of the capital of which is held by aliens.

319

subject to treaty rights. (See Commercial No. 17, 1887, and Nos. 4 and 6, 1888.)

I have, &c.,
(Signed)   J. Hayes Sadler,
H.B.M. Consulate, Chicago,   *Consul.*
    June 28, 1888.

NEW ORLEANS.

British Consulate, New Orleans,
Sir,   *July 9, 1888.*
IN my report upon joint stock companies as formed under the laws of the State of Louisiana, inclosed in my despatch to you of June 15, I stated that a bill was before the Legislature to enable the formation of limited liability companies.

This has passed, and is now law. Any three or more persons, complying with the usual provisions of the laws governing corporations, may form themselves into a corporation for carrying on any lawful business or enterprise "not otherwise specially provided for." This will exclude railway, telegraph, banking, and insurance business, and it is expressly enacted that no corporation created under this Act shall engage in stock-jobbing business of any kind. The capital stock is not to be less than 5,000 dols.

The word "limited" must be the last word of the name of these corporations, and it must appear legibly on the office, and all notices, advertisements, and other publications of the company, and on its notes, cheques, receipts, and other writings. If omitted, the person participating in such default becomes liable for any indebtedness, damage, or liability arising therefrom.

Shareholders are liable only for the unpaid balance due to the company on the shares held by them, and no mere informality in organization is to have the effect of rendering a charter null, or of exposing a stockholder to any liability beyond the amount of his stock.

There are no provisions as to the publication of accounts or inspection of books.

I learn with much pleasure from your Despatch No. 3, of the 5th instant, that the reports lately furnished on this and other subjects from this district meet with your approval, and shall communicate it to the vice-consuls who assisted in their compilation.

I have, &c.,
(Signed)   A. DE G. DE FONBLANQUE.

British Consulate, New Orleans,
Sir,   *June 15, 1888.*
IN compliance with the instructions contained in your Circular A, of the 21st ultimo, requiring reports on the laws in this Consular district respecting the formation, regulation, and dissolution of companies whether joint stock or in shares or in whatever manner constituted, I have the honour to enclose:—

1. My report for the States of Arkansas, Louisiana, and Mississippi.

[90]

2. Vice-Consul Howe's Report for the State of Florida.
3. Vice-Consul Barnewall's Report for the State of Alabama.

I have, &c.,
(Signed) A. DE G. DE FONBLANQUE.

STATE OF ARKANSAS.—HOW CORPORATIONS ARE FORMED IN GENERAL.

Corporations are formed in this State "for manufacturing" or "any other lawful business" under "articles of association" made by any number of persons not less than three. These articles, signed by the president and directors (not less than three), accompanied by a certificate setting forth the purposes for which the corporation is formed, the amount of its capital stock, the amount actually paid in, and the names of its stockholders, and the number of shares held by each respectively is to be filed of record with the Secretary of State, and a duplicate with the clerk of the county in which it is to carry on business. A certified copy of the first-named certificate is receivable in all courts as *primâ facie* evidence of the due formation, existence, and capacity of the corporation in any suit brought by or against it.

Corporations thus formed have power to sue and be sued, have a public seal, make bye-laws and rules, &c., as in Mississippi and Louisiana.

In January or July of every year the president and secretary must make and deposit with the county clerk a certificate under oath, showing the amount of capital actually paid in, the cash value of the real estate held by the corporation, the cash value of its credits, the amount of its debts, and the name and number of shares of each stockholder, and if the president or secretary intentionally neglect or refuse to make such a certificate, they are liable for the debts of the corporation contracted during the time of default.

This the clerk records at full length in his books.

Any person making a false statement in these certificates is to be deemed guilty of perjury.

Whenever any stockholder transfers his stock a certificate of such transfer must be deposited with the clerk, who notes the time of such deposit, and records it; and no transfer is valid as against the creditors of the stockholder until such deposit is made.

The books of the corporation containing its accounts must be open at all reasonable times to the inspection of stockholders.

If the capital stock be refunded to stockholders, they are individually liable to unsatisfied creditors, but any one who has paid under these circumstances may call on his fellow stockholders to contribute their proportionable part of the sum recovered from him.

If the directors declare a dividend when the corporation is insolvent, or such a one as to *make* it so, they are individually liable for all debts existing at the time. A similar penalty attaches to them for breach of duty as laid down in the statute now cited.

The corporate stock is deemed personal property transferable only on the books, and the corporation has always a lien upon it for all debts due to it from the holders.

The corporation may sell the stock of delinquent holders after three months' notice, and grant new certificates to the purchasers.

So also if the stockholder has assigned his stock as security to a third person, the corporation may sell its equity of redemption.

Navigation Companies.

These are formed by any number of persons not less than five, when stock to the amount of at least 1,000 dols. is subscribed.

Articles of association may be made in addition to the ordinary requirements: these must contain a sworn statement that the capital stock is sufficient to purchase all necessary vessels, together with the costs of the right of way, and wharfage privileges required.

The company has "right of way" not exceeding 200 yards in width over any strip of land connecting (*qy.* separating) two navigable streams, or lakes, or bodies of water not more than 5 miles wide, for the purpose of making roads for the business of the company.

No other company can have the same privileges within 3 miles. The value of the land taken for this purpose, if not settled by private contract, is assessed by the board of supervisors of the county and a jury.

Turnpike Companies.

These may be formed by any number of persons not less than three.

The stock must be divided into shares of 25 dols. each. When the road is certified by three freeholders not interested, appointed by the board of supervisors, as complete, toll-gates may be erected and tolls levied. In other respects the rules laid down for corporations in general are followed.

How Corporations may be Dissolved.

The General Assembly (Legislature) may at any time, for just cause, rescind the powers of any joint stock corporation created as above, and prescribe such mode as may be necessary or expedient for the settlement of its affairs.

If any corporation shall expire or cease to exist either by its own limitation, judicial judgment of forfeiture of charter, or by legislative Act, the common law of corporations is not in force in relation thereto, but the goods and chattels, land, tenements, and hereditaments, and every right and profit issuing out of, or appertaining thereto, money, credit, and effects of such corporation, shall immediately vest in the State in trust for the uses and purposes contemplated in the charter, and each and every right upon the expiration or dissolution of such corporation shall be in abeyance until the action of the Legislature be had thereon, unless provisions shall be made by law for the management of such fund in contemplation of dissolution.

Liability of Stockholders.

This is defined by the constitution of the State as follows:—"In all cases each stockholder shall be liable over and above the stock by him or her owned, and any amount unpaid thereon to a further sum at least equal in amount to such stock."

[90]

STATE OF LOUISIANA.—GENERAL OBSERVATIONS.

The " joint stock company," as constituted in England, is not known to the laws of this State.

When several persons combine to carry on business they form either a partnership or a corporation.

There is no limit (as with us) to the number of partners in a partnership.

I assume that corporations as formed in the States forming this Consular district are to be considered as "companies" within the definition given in the despatch requiring this report, and that partnerships (limited or unlimited) do not.

The purposes for which corporations may be formed are defined by statute and, at present, are as follows:—

For any religious, scientific, literary, or charitable purpose, * * and for the construction or making railroads, canals, plank roads, ferries, and other works of public improvement within or without the limits of this State; to effect fire, marine, river, and life insurance; to carry on manufactures of cotton, woollen, linen, silk, and hempen cloths, and cordage; to construct and carry on works to supply cities or towns with gas or water; to compress cotton; to construct and carry on iron, brass, and copper foundries; to construct and maintain dry docks or floating docks for the building and repairing of ships and other vessels; to manufacture iron, copper, lead, or other metals, earthenware or stoneware, cotton gins, machinery, paper, gunpowder, agricultural instruments; to establish companies for refining sugar and for sea navigation by steam; to create lines of telegraph, and to establish chemical laboratories and manufactures of all kinds, to open and work mines, to construct and maintain docks, steamships, and other vehicles for the transportation of freight or passengers, for constructing and maintaining works for drainage, sewerage, and land reclamation, and for the development of the agricultural resources of the State, and for the promotion of immigration, and generally all works of public utility and advantage, and for athletic, military, gun practice, and social purposes.

It will thus appear that corporations cannot be formed for the sale of goods in a manufactured state and the manufacture of intoxicating liquors or distilling is prohibited, *i.e.*, to corporations. Corporations are expressly forbidden from engaging " in mercantile or in commission brokerage, stock-jobbing, exchange, or banking business of any kind."

Louisiana has a special law regulating banks and banking.

How a Corporation is formed.

When any number of persons, exceeding six, desire to acquire and enjoy the rights, privileges, and powers of a body corporate and politic in law, they prepare and sign an instrument either in authentic form (before a notary) or under private signature, wherein they declare and specify the purposes and objects of the corporation, the name, style, and title thereof, the place chosen for its domicile (which must be within the State), the manner in which its managers and officers are to be chosen, the officer upon whom citations may be served, and the length of time during which the corporation shall exist and continue.

This document is called " the Act of incorporation." It is submitted to the district attorney of the district in which the domicile of the corporation is fixed, and if its purposes and object are legal, and none of its provisions are contrary to law, he endorses his opinion to this effect thereon.

It is then recorded in the office of the Parish (County) Recorder of Mortgages, published once a week for 30 days in a newspaper of such parish, and then the subscribers to it, their associates and successors, become a body corporate. I enclose, Schedule A, an example of an Act of incorporation.

An Act of incorporation can be improved, amended, or altered (by resolution of its stockholders at a general meeting), and such amendments are legalised, as above.

The capital stock may be increased by resolution of a majority of stock at a general meeting of the stockholders called specially for the purpose.

A certificate of this resolution, containing amount of capital stock, number of stockholders, particulars of proposed increase, amount and number of shares, voting pro and con, and statement of debts and liabilities of the corporation must be filed in the office of the Secretary of State, and after this is done the increase is made.

Any two business or manufacturing corporations of the same general nature may be consolidated by resolution of boards of direction, and a vote of three-fifths of the capital stock of each.

A certificate of such consolidation and the name of the new body is filed with the Secretary of State.

Powers of Corporations.

A corporation founded as above may endure for 99 years. It has power to have and use a common seal, to sue and be sued, and to make rules, bye-laws, and ordinances needful for its good government and not repugnant to the constitution and laws of the United States or of the State of Louisiana, or to the Act of incorporation. It may take and hold all manner of land, tenements, rents, and hereditaments, and any sum of money, and any manner or portion of goods and chattels given and bequeathed to it, or acquired by it in any manner, to be disposed of under the Act of incorporation.

A railway company may borrow money for construction or repairs on bonds secured by mortgage on its franchises.

Proceedings for the expropriation of land by, and assessment of damages against telegraph, railroad, road, or canal companies (similar to those held under our Lands Clauses Consolidation Acts) are held before the judge of the district in which the owner resides and a jury.

How a Corporation may be dissolved.

This can be done in two ways—

(a.) By consent of the stockholders.

(b.) By forfeiture of the charter of incorporation.

(a.) Three-fourths of the stockholders (present or represented) at any general meeting convened for that purpose, may dissolve the corporation under charge of officers chosen for the purpose, provided that it be solvent.

(b.) A charter is forfeited for insolvency evidenced by a return of "no property found" on execution, in which case the district court, at the instance of any creditor, appoints a commissioner for effecting the liquidation of the corporation. This is effected as near as can be as if the insolvent were an individual.

The corporation may be finally wound up on the petition of stockholders showing that it is in an insolvent condition.

Liability of Stockholders.

No stockholder is liable or responsible for the contracts or faults of the corporation of which he is a member in any further sum than the unpaid balance due on the shares owned by him.

No mere informality in the organization has the effect of rendering a charter null, or of exposing a stockholder to any liability beyond the amount of his stock.

There is an Act before the Legislature (now in session) under which it is proposed to permit the establishment of companies for manufacturing purposes, very similar to those which are formed under our Limited Liability Acts.

CHARTER of the HERMITAGE PLANTING and MANUFACTURING COMPANY of NEW ORLEANS, LA.

STATE OF LOUISIANA.—PARISH OF ORLEANS.—CITY OF NEW ORLEANS.

Be it known that on this 21st day of March, in the year of our Lord 1888, and of the independence of the United States of America the 112th, before me, Nicholas Browse Trist, a notary public in and for the parish of Orleans, State of Louisiana, duly commissioned and qualified, and in the presence of the witnesses hereinafter named and undersigned, personally came and appeared the several persons whose names are hereunto subscribed, who declared that, availing themselves of the provisions of the laws of this State relative to the organisation of corporations for works of public improvement and utility, they have covenanted and agreed and by these presents do covenant and agree, and bind and obligate themselves, as well as such persons as may hereafter become associated with them, to form and constitute a corporation and body politic in law, for the objects and purposes and under the agreements and stipulations following, to wit:—

Art. 1. The name, style, and title of said corporation shall be *Hermitage Planting and Manufacturing Company*, and by that corporated name said corporation shall have power and authority to have and enjoy succession for the full term and period of 99 years from and after the day and date hereof, to contract, sue and be sued, to make and use a corporate seal, and the same to break and alter at pleasure, to hold, receive, purchase, lease, sell, and convey, as well as mortgage, hypothecate, and pledge under its corporate name, property, both real and personal; to name and employ such managers, directors, officers, overseers, agents, and other employés as the interest and convenience of said corporation may require, and to make and establish such bye-laws, rules, and regulations for the proper management and regulation of the affairs of said corporation as may be necessary and proper, and the same to change and alter at pleasure.

Art. 2. The domicile of said corporation shall be in the parish of Orleans, in the State of Louisiana, and all citations and other legal process shall be served on its president, and in case of his absence from the State, on the secretary.

Art. 3. The objects and purposes for which this corporation is established, and the nature of the business to be carried on by it, are declared and specified as follows:—To manufacture sugar, to refine sugar, to manufacture rice, rice bran, and rice polish, or other crops raised, controlled, or owned by it, and for these purposes, or any of them, to purchase and lease or use real estate, machinery, animals, and other movable property; to cultivate cane, rice, ramie, jute, corn, vegetables, or other agricultural crops or products; to make contracts in relation to the cultivation or purchase of any of them; to acquire and carry on mills and factories suitable for any of said purposes, and to sell and dispose of the crops or other products owned or controlled by the said corporation as raw material, or when manufactured or otherwise prepared for use, sale, or consumption, and to carry on all the necessary, convenient, and suitable devices and business having relation to any of said purposes, or whereby the said agricultural products or manufactured articles may be made more profitable to the said corporation, and generally to do all and everything pertinent to or in any manner connected with the purposes hereinbefore declared, or any one of them, or having a tendency to develop the agricultural resources of this State.

Art. 4. The capital stock of this corporation is hereby fixed at the sum of 25,000 dols., which shall be divided into and represented by 250 shares of 100 dols. each, to be paid for in cash at the time of subscription. The capital stock of this corporation may hereafter be increased to any sum not exceeding 250,000 dols., divided into and represented by shares of 100 dols. each, whenever such increase shall be authorised by the majority of the stock, and upon complying with the required legal formalities said stock may be paid for in cash or may be issued in payment of property purchased by this corporation. Every transfer of any share or shares of the capital stock shall be made on the books of the corporation, and shall be signed by the stockholder or his attorney, but no stockholder shall have the right to transfer his stock unless his indebtedness to the corporation be paid or secured to the satisfaction of the board of directors. The board of directors may close the transfer books as often as convenience may require, but for no longer than 10 consecutive days at any one time.

Art. 5. All the corporate powers of said corporation and the control and management of its business shall be vested in and exercised by a board of directors, composed of four stockholders, who shall hold in their own right at least 10 shares of the capital stock, and to be elected by the stockholders as hereinafter provided; any two of whom to constitute a quorum for business. The directors shall be annually elected by ballot by the stockholders at the office of the corporation, on the second Tuesday of April in each year, the first election to take place in 1889, and each stockholder shall be entitled, in person or by proxy, to one vote on every share of stock owned by him, and such election shall be held by the secretary of the company, unless otherwise provided by the board of directors; but a majority of the whole stock of the corporation must vote at such election or otherwise it will be invalid. The directors thus elected shall continue in office for one year, and until their successors are duly elected or appointed, and no failure to elect shall be regarded as a forfeiture of this charter. At their first meeting after their election the board of directors shall elect from their own number a president and a secretary. The following named persons shall constitute the first board of directors, and continue to act until their successors are duly chosen at said election to be held on the second Tuesday of April, 1889, viz., John H. Maginnis, Arthur A. Maginnis, William D. Maginnis, and John T. Nolan, with John H. Maginnis as president, and William D. Maginnis as secretary. The board of directors shall not issue any bonds or notes of the said corporation, or sell, mortgage, hypothecate, or pledge any of the real or personal property of the corporation, except upon the previous written authority and approval of the owners of the majority of the capital stock, filed in the office of the company, and a copy whereof shall be incorporated in the bond, note, or act of sale, mortgage or pledge; but this limitation shall not extend to the contracts made mith agents or other employés in respect to payment for their services, or to the purchase of the usual and necessary supplies for carrying on the business of said corporation.

Art. 6. This act of incorporation may be changed, modified, or altered, or said corporation may be dissolved, with the assent of two-thirds of the stock represented, at the general meeting of the stockholders to be convened for such purpose after 20 days' previous notice of such meeting shall have been published in a daily newspaper in New Orleans, or given in writing to each stockholder.

Art. 7. No stockholder shall ever be held liable or responsible for the contracts, faults, or debts of said corporation, nor shall any mere informality in organisation have the effect of rendering this charter null or exposing a stockholder to any liability beyond the unpaid balance due on the shares owned by him.

Art. 8. Whenever this corporation is dissolved, by limitation or otherwise, its affairs shall be liquidated under the superintendence of such person or persons as may be appointed for that purpose at the general meeting of the stockholders authorising the dissolution of the corporation. Said commissioners shall remain in office until the affairs of the corporation shall have been fully liquidated, unless removed by the stockholders. And in case of the death of one or more of said commissioners, the survivor or survivors shall continue to act.

Thus done and passed in my office, at New Orleans, the day, month, and year first above written, in the presence of John Clements Schonekas and Henry Pater Labatut, competent witnesses, who hereunto signed their names with the said appearers and me, notary, the whole after reading hereof.

(Original signed)   J. H. MAGINNIS.
A. A. MAGINNIS.
W. D. MAGINNIS.
J. T. NOLAN.
SAM'L L. GILMORE.
P. F. PESCUD.

J. C. SCHONEKAS.
H. P. LABATUT.

N. B. TRIST,
Notary Public.

327

I, the undersigned Recorder of Mortgages in and for the parish of Orleans, State of Louisiana, do hereby certify that the above and foregoing Act of incorporation of the Hermitage Planting and Manufacturing Company was this day duly recorded in my office in Book 353, folio 351.

(Signed) GEO. GUINAULT,
Deputy Recorder.

New Orleans, La.,
March 22, 1888.

I hereby certify the foregoing to be a true and correct copy of the original Act of incorporation of the Hermitage Planting and Manufacturing Company, as of the certificate of record thereto attached, on file and of record in my notarial office.

Witness my hand and official seal at the city of New Orleans, this 3rd day of April, A.D. 1888.

N. B. TRIST, *Notary Public,*
No. 162, Common Street.

STATE OF MISSISSIPPI.

The legislation of this State uses the terms "corporation," "company," "joint stock companies," and "joint stock corporations" indifferently.

In the year 1882 it was enacted that *all* corporations for cities and towns, and express, telegraph and railway companies may be formed as is provided in the statutes of 1880 in respect of a few enterprises therein named. The charter of incorporation required by the above cited statute is very similar to the "Act of incorporation" (already described) in use in Louisiana. It must be advertised three consecutive weeks in a newspaper published at, or having a *bonâ fide* circulation in, the county where the proposed company is to be domiciled, when it is submitted to the Governor of the State for his approval. He takes the opinion of the Attorney-General as to its legality, and may require alterations and amendments to be made. When finally approved, the great seal of the State is attached, and it confers upon the corporation the powers it contains.

Renewals and subsequent amendments, supported by a majority of the stockholders, are made in the same way.

The charter with its amendments (if any) is recorded at length in the office of the Secretary of State. The original is held by the corporation, and a certified copy of it is admissable in evidence.

Powers of Corporations in General.

They may make rules and bye-laws for internal management not inconsistent with the charter, have a public seal, sue and be sued, and contract, may hold, buy, sell, and convert real estate and other property.

The amount of their capital stock is unlimited.

They may borrow money and issue bonds securing payment of the same by mortgage, or hypothecate, exchange, or pledge them.

But no mortgage or deed of trust conveying the income or future earnings of any corporation, or the rolling stock of any railroad company is valid against debts contracted in carrying on its business or (as regards railways) against liabilities incurred as carriers of freight and passengers, or damages sustained by property, or for damage sustained by persons beyond the sum of 5,000 dols. in the latter case.

There is no provision by statute for the compulsory taking of land, or assessing damages.

Process before and during action is to be made against corporations as against natural persons. If the officer named in the charter to accept service of writs, &c., be not found, it is sufficient to post the instrument upon the door of the office or place of business.

No note obligation or security of any kind given or transferred by any subscriber for stock in any manufacturing company is to be considered as payment for any part of its capital stock. No loan can be made by the company to any stockholder, and in case of infraction the officers who make or assent to such loan are responsible for the amount and interest to any creditor whose debt was contracted before the repayment of the money by the borrower.

If dividends or divisions of profit are made when the company is insolvent, the directors who made, and the stockholders who received them, are jointly and severally liable to creditors whose debts were in existence at the time.

Directors are individually liable for debts contracted in excess of the capital stock, provided that the creditor had not notice of such excess.

How Corporations may be Dissolved.

There is no provision by statute as to how corporations may be dissolved either by consent of stockholders or by process of law. In the first case they follow the process stated in the charter, and in the latter, appearing as they do as "natural persons," judgment is given and executed as against an individual.

When judgment is rendered all the property of the corporation (including its franchises) may be sold. The person who will agree to pay the amount due and costs, and take a franchise (for freight, toll, or charges) for the shortest time, is to be deemed the best bidder and is immediately to be put into possession.

The corporation may redeem within six months by paying such purchase money and 10 per cent. added, but it is not entitled to mesne profits.

On final dissolution, the individuals who have been members hold the property of the corporation in their respective proportions as tenants in common.

Corporations whose charters have expired or been annulled, are considered bodies corporate for three years thereafter for the purpose of suing and being sued, and of winding up generally; but not for carrying on business, unless trustees for that intent have been appointed by the court.

Obligations of Stockholders.

These are liable for the debts of the corporation contracted during their ownerships of stock for the unpaid balance of the stock subscribed for. They may be sued by any creditor of the corporation, and such liability continues for one year after the sale or transfer of the stock.

Stock is transferred by the endorsement and delivery of the stock certificate and the register of such transfer in the books of the company.

PENSACOLA, FLORIDA.

REPORT by VICE-CONSUL HOWE on the ORGANIZATION of GENERAL CORPORATIONS in PENSACOLA, and FLORIDA generally.

General Corporations.—Under the laws of the State of Florida, general corporations may be organized for the transaction of any lawful business of a public or private character, including all works of internal improvement. Such corporations shall have the power usual and incident to corporate existence. Not less than three persons can organize such corporation. The organization is perfected by filing with the Secretary of State a copy of the articles of incorporation, and by filing with the county clerk of the county in which the corporation shall do business a like copy. Notice of such formation shall be published for four weeks in succession in some newspaper as convenient as practicable to its principal place of business. Such corporations have the right of eminent domain to be exercised in accordance with the statutory provisions. The majority of the stockholders may render valid any corporate act. The capital stock may be any such amount as the corporations may desire, divided into shares of 100 dols. each, and no company shall be deemed lawfully organized until 10 per cent. of the capital stock shall be subscribed, and paid in lawful currency of the United States. The capital stock may be increased by a majority of the stockholders; notice of such increase being given to the Secretary of State. There is no individual liability upon the stockholders of the said companies. There are no provisions for a compulsory dissolution, but the majority may dissolve the corporation by petition to the circuit court.

The law relating to banking corporations is as follows:—There may be established in any incorporated town or city having 3,000 or more inhabitants a banking association or institution with corporate powers or privileges. Previous to commencing any business, except its own organization, it shall be the duty of the officers of every corporation to file with the Secretary of State a copy of the articles of incorporation, and a copy of such articles shall also be filed at the same time in the office or offices of the county clerk in which county or counties said corporation shall do business. Upon the application of any creditor or shareholder of any banking corporation, whose debts or shares shall amount to 1,000 dols., stating facts verified by affidavit, the judge of the circuit court in which such corporation is located, may in his discretion order a strict examination to be made by a commissioner, of the affairs of such corporation, for the purpose of ascertaining the safety of its investments and the prudence of its management; and the result of every such examination, with the opinion of the commissioner and of the judge thereon, shall be published in such manner as the judge shall direct. The comptroller of the State may inspect and supervise the business of the bank, and inspect and examine its books, papers, documents, minutes, and everything pertaining to the acts of the bank. A statement of the amount of the capital stock subscribed, and of the amount actually paid in, and the indebtedness of the corporation, must be published once in six months in the nearest newspaper, and annually in a newspaper printed at the capital of the State. Banks are required to make an annual return to the State comptroller of the amount of capital stock; value of real estate; shares of stock held, absolutely or as collateral; debts owing to the bank; debts owing by the bank; claims against the bank, not acknowledged as debts; amount on which the bank is bound for security, or may become liable; amount of loans and discounts and specie on hand; amount of losses of the bank (if any) charged, and of dividends declared since the last statement; amount and description of securities deposited with the comptroller, and their market value, also date to which interest has been paid.

Corporations for the operation of railroads and canals may be formed by any number of persons not less than three. Ninety days' notice of the object and purposes and general scope of the corporation must be given in three newspapers. Upon the expiration or the 90 days the articles of association are filed in the office of the Secretary of State, whereupon the Governor and Secretary of State issue the certificate or patent to the corporation, which dates its powers from the issuance of such certificate. The provisions as to stock, the increase thereof, and dissolution, are similar to those in case of general corporations.

The STATUTE LAWS of ALABAMA relating to CORPORATIONS may be considered under the following heads:—

1. Banks and banking.
2. Insurance companies.
3. Mutual aid associations.
4. Building and loan associations.
5. Mining, quarrying, and manufacturing companies.
6. Railroad companies.
7. Street railway companies
8. Macadamised, turnpike, and other toll road companies.
9. Telegraph companies.
10. Navigation companies.
11. Corporations not specially provided for.
12. General provisions.
13. Dissolution.
14. Corporations not of a business character.

Banks and Banking.

Any number of persons not less than three, with a capital subscribed of not less than 50,000 dols., in good faith of which not less than 20 per cent. must be actually paid in, may file a declaration of incorporation in the office of the judge of probate in which they intend to do business, setting out in writing signed by each of them, stating their names and residence, the name and style of the proposed

331

corporation, the location and principal place of business, the amount of capital stock, and the number of shares into which it is divided, the purpose and nature of the business, with any other matters deemed desirable to state, and accompany such declaration by a verified affidavit that 25,000 dols. of the capital stock has been actually paid in, and that the same is in fact held and is to be used solely for the business of the corporation.

A certified copy of this declaration must be filed in the office of the Secretary of State.

Such corporation, when organized, has power to :—

1. Have succession by its name for 20 years.
2. Sue and be sued.
3. Use a common seal.
4. Appoint officers, prescribe their duties, fix their compensation, and remove same.
5. Make necessary bye-laws.
6. Hold, purchase, dispose of, and convey real and personal property.
7. Discount bills, notes, or other evidences of debt, to receive and pay out deposits, to receive on special deposit money, or bullion, or foreign coins, stocks or bonds or other securities, to buy or sell foreign or domestic exchange, gold and silver bullion or foreign coins, bonds, stocks, bills of exchange, or other negotiable paper ; to lend money upon personal property or upon pledges of bonds, stocks, or negotiable securities; to take and receive security by mortgage, or otherwise, on property real or personal.

The business of the corporation must be governed by a board of directors, consisting of not less than three members, and holders of stock, and are elected by stockholders.

Capital stock may be increased or decreased.

Insurance Companies.

Same laws or incorporation apply as to banks.
Same powers as apply to banks except receiving and paying out deposits.
Succession after 20 years may be renewed.
Stock may be increased to 500,000 dols.
May adopt or abandon mutual plan of organization.
Stockholders' meetings may be held without the State.
Must have a principal place of doing business.
May consolidate with other insurance companies.

Mutual Aid Associations.

All associations, whether voluntary or incorporated for beneficent purposes, are subject to the following provisions :—
Must report to auditor on the first day of March of each year, stating condition.
Must have a principal place of doing business.
Masons, and other like fraternities, not subject to above provisions.

332

Building and Loan Associations.

Three or more persons may incorporate and have succession for 20 years.

Must file with probate judge a declaration signed by each of incorporators, stating—

1. Name and style of proposed association.
2. Amount of capital stock and number of shares.
3. Name and residence of members and associates and principal place of business.
4. Purposes of corporation and nature of business.

The judge of probate receives such declaration and issues certificate of incorporation.

Such corporation has power—

1. To have succession for 20 years.
2. To sue and be sued.
3. To hold, dispose and buy, and convey real or personal property.
4. To appoint and remove officers and prescribe their duties.
5. To levy monthly contributions from shareholders.
6. To compel payment.
7. To acquire real estate, to erect buildings, to let or sell the same to any shareholder.
8. To aid shareholders in the erection of houses by loans of the funds of the association.
9. When funds are on hand to lend the same with security to shareholders.
10. When deemed advisable when two or more shareholders desire a loan, to loan to the highest bidder.

To prescribe uniform sales of monthly instalments.
To secure the payment of instalments and loans.
Each share shall be valued at 50 dols.

Mining, Quarrying, and Manufacturing Corporations.

General rules for incorporation apply, and general powers incident apply.

The additional powers are to locate, construct, and operate to and from its mines, furnaces, mills, factories, quarries, or other works, railways, tramways, canals or roads, or to acquire same by purchase, and may condemn private property as provided by law, when necessary, to exercise such powers.

May cross public highway, road, street, or river.
May consolidate with other like corporations.
Controlled by board of directors elected by stockholders.
May increase capital stock to a sum not exceeding 10,000,000 dols.

Railroad Companies.

Declaration to be filed with Secretary of State by not less than seven stockholders, stating name and residence of stockholders, name and style of corporation, amount of capital stock and the number of shares, any other matter they may deem proper.

Secretary of State issues commission.

Commissioners must within 90 days after appointment give 30 days' notice in some newspaper published in each county along the proposed line, of the time and place appointed for opening books of subscriptions to the capital stock.

All subscriptions to be paid in money, but subscribers may discharge subscriptions by services for the corporation.

Ten per cent. of the capital stock having been subscribed in good faith by subscribers, they call a meeting and elect a board of directors and other officers, to consist of not less than seven nor more than eleven, and shall designate some one of their number to receive subscription to stock from the commissioners, upon the delivery of the subscriptions to such person he shall require of the subscribers the payment in cash of 2 per cent thereof.

The proceedings of the meeting of the subscribers must be reduced to writing, signed by them, acknowledged before and certified by a judge of probate, under the seal of his office, and delivered to the commissioners, who must return and file the same in the office of the Secretary of State, and the officer who has received the money paid in for subscription must make a verified sworn return to the Secretary of State; upon filing of such papers the Secretary of State must issue a certificate of incorporation under the seal of the State.

Secretary of State keeps record of all proceedings.

Powers.

To have succession for period expressed, or if none expressed, perpetually.

To sue and be sued, to have a common seal and to alter same at pleasure.

To hold, purchase, dispose of, and convey such real and personal property as its uses and business require.

To make all rules, regulations, and bye-laws necessary.

To appoint officers, agents, prescribe their duties and compensation.

To provide for a transfer of stock.

To cause examination and survey for its proposed road to be made.

To acquire and hold by gift or purchase, or in payment for stock.

To condemn as provided by law private property upon compensation being made.

To acquire and hold by gift or purchase land for depôts, sidetracks, &c.

To consolidate with other railroads.

To purchase or lease any road connecting with its own.

To cross navigable streams, public roads, other railroads.

Make branch roads.

Increase capital stock not to exceed ten millions.

May increase bonded indebtedness.

Stockholders' meeting may be held without the State.

Must have a principal place of business.

Purchasers of railroads may organize as railroads.

Forfeits charter by non-use.

Street Railway Companies.

Declaration of incorporation to be filed by not less than five persons, stating names and residences of subscribers, and name of corporation.

Amount of capital stock and the number of shares into which it is divided.

The name of the town or city, and the streets thereof in which they propose to construct the line of road and the terminus thereof, and other desirable matter.

Commission to open subscription books, then issues, and when 10 per cent. of subscriptions are paid in, they may organize.

They have general corporative powers.

Stockholders meet annually, and they may increase capital stock.

Macadamised and other Toll Roads.

Organized same as street railways, same powers and duties.

Telegraph Companies.

General corporation laws apply.

Navigation Companies.

Two or more persons may form. General organizing laws apply.

General powers conferred necessary to transact business for which organized.

General Provisions.

Shares of stock are personal property.

Shares of stock subject to levy and sale.

Corporation has lien on stock for any debt or liability of stockholders.

Corporate franchises forfeited for non use.

Must keep books open to inspection.

Majority of board of directors exercise corporate powers.

Dissolution.

Corporations may be dissolved whenever the owner of three-fifths of the stock desire.

They file a petition in chancery, and the register gives notice to all interested to appear within 30 days, and contest same if they deem proper.

Upon the dissolution being declared, the chancellor appoints a receiver to wind up its affairs.

He must give bond-pay, corporate debts, receive debts due to the corporation.

All powers expire with dissolution.

      Wm. Barnewall,
       British Vice-Consul,
        Mobile, 13th June, 1888.

335

No. 23A.

Sir L. S. West to the Marquis of Salisbury.

My Lord,   Washington, *July* 20, 1888.

IN continuation of Mr. Edwardes' despatch of the 9th, and in reply to your Lordship's despatch of April 30 last, I have the honour to enclose herewith a report from Her Majesty's Consul at San Francisco, on the legislation on the formation and dissolution of joint stock companies in the States under his jurisdiction.

I have, &c.,
(Signed)   L. S. SACKVILLE WEST.

Inclosure in No. 23A.

Report on Public Companies in the State of California.

In this State, and in the United States generally, companies, whether joint stock or in shares, or in whatever manner constituted, are called "corporations," and for convenience are so denominated in this report.

We have here 15 different kinds of corporations, besides municipal, official, and ecclesiastical corporations, and those formed for general purposes, and, although there are Acts and statutes applicable to all of them, yet most of those hereinafter named are governed by special Acts and provisions.

The different classes of corporations are: insurance corporations; railroad corporations; street railroad corporations; (trams) waggon-road corporations; bridge, ferry, wharf, chute, and pier corporations; telegraph corporations; water and canal corporations; homestead corporations; savings and loan association corporations; mining corporations; religious, social, and benevolent corporations; agricultural fair corporations; gas corporations; land and building corporations.

GENERAL PROVISIONS applicable to all CORPORATIONS.

Formation.

A corporation is organized by the voluntary association of five or more persons, of whom a majority must be residents of this State, and they may be formed for any purpose for which individuals may lawfully associate themselves. (Chambers of commerce, boards of trade, mechanics institutes, and kindred associations, however, require 20 or more incorporators.)

The instrument by which a corporation is formed is called "articles of incorporation," and must contain—

1. The name of the corporation.
2. The purpose for which it is formed.
3. The place where its principal business will be transacted.
4. The number of its directors, not less than five nor more than cleven; their names and residences.
5. The term for which it is to exist, not exceeding 50 years.

[90]

6. The amount of its capital, stock, and number of shares.
7. The amount of stock actually subscribed.

The articles of incorporation of any railroad, waggon-road, or telegraph organization must further state—

1. The kind of road or telegraph to be constructed.
2. The place from and to which it is to be run.
3. The estimated length.
4. That at least 10 per cent. of the capital stock subscribed has been paid to its treasurer.

These articles of incorporation must in all cases be subscribed by five or more persons, a majority of whom are residents of this State, and acknowledged before a notary public. Waggon-road, railroad, and telegraph corporations must thereupon actually subscribe to the capital stock for each mile of the contemplated work—

1,000 dols. per mile of railroad;
100 dols. per mile of telegraph;
300 dols. per mile of waggon-road;

and pay to their treasurers 10 per cent. of the amount subscribed for.

The articles of incorporation are then filed with the clerk of the county in which the principal business of the company is to be transacted, and a copy thereof certified to by that clerk is filed with the Secretary of State, who thereupon issues to the corporation, over the great seal of the State a certificate that a copy of the "articles of incorporation" has been filed in his office, and thereupon the persons who signed the articles, and their associates and successors, become a body politic and corporate by the name stated in the articles of incorporation and for the purposes and term named therein.

A copy of the articles must also be recorded in the county clerk's office in each county in which the corporation purchases or holds property.

Every corporation formed under the laws of this State doing a banking business here may have a capital stock and issue certificates therefor like other companies, but it must not use any funds or moneys under its control to convert it into capital stock, and no bank in this State can ever pay any dividend on so-called guarantee notes, nor upon any stock except upon the amount actually paid in money upon such stock.

Every corporation within one month after filing its articles of incorporation must adopt a code of bye-laws by a majority vote of the stockholders or members if there be no stock: the directors must be annually elected by the stockholders or members. The bye-laws may provide for the time, manner, and place of holding and conducting meetings; the number which shall constitute a quorum; the mode of voting by proxy; the time of the annual election of directors; the compensation and duties of officers, their election and term of office, and penalties not exceeding 100 dols. for violation of bye-laws; these bye-laws are open to the inspection of the public, and can be amended only by a two-thirds vote of stockholders or members.

The corporate powers, business, and property of all corporations are exercised, conducted, and controlled by a board of not less than five nor more than eleven directors, elected from the members, except that in case of corporations formed for the purposes of erecting and managing halls and buildings, for the meetings of lodges or societies for any benevolent or charitable order, the number of directors may

337

be from five to fifty. A majority of the directors must in all cases be residents of this State.

All elections must be by ballot, and every stockholder may vote in person or by proxy the number of shares standing in his name.

Immediately after their election the directors choose from their own number a president, and then a secretary and treasurer, who may or may not be members. A majority of directors is a quorum, and their act is the corporate act; they must not declare dividends, except from the surplus profits, nor can they divide or withdraw any part of the capital stock, nor reduce it except at its dissolution. Directors may be removed by two-thirds vote of the members, and at the meeting called for this purpose, as at all elections or votes for any purpose, a majority of the members or of the holders of the subscribed capital stock must be represented in person or by proxy, the stock of minors being represented by his guardian, of a decedent by his executor or administrator, and the meeting being always held at the office of the company.

Banking corporations must keep in their offices, in an accessible place for the use of depositors, stockholders, and creditors, a book containing the names of all stockholders, and the number of shares each holds, and must also post up for the use of the public a notice signed by the president and secretary, showing—

1. The names of the directors.
2. The number and value of their shares held by each director.

The corporation may always change its principal place of business from one town or county to another in this State, by a consent of two-thirds of the stockholders, holding two-thirds or more of the stock; notice of the removal must be given in a newspaper for three weeks.

Every banking corporation in January and July of each year must file for record in the county recorder's office, and publish in a newspaper a statement sworn to by its president (or manager) and secretary (or cashier), of the amount of capital actually paid in money; of the actual condition and value of its assets and liabilities; and where its assets are situated.

False statements are a felony with a penalty of 5,000 dols. or two years' imprisonment, or both.

Every stockholder in a corporation is liable individually and personally for such proportion of its liabilities as the amount of stock or shares owned by him bears to the whole subscribed stock or shares of the corporation, and for a like proportion only of each debt or liability of the corporation, and any creditor may institute joint or several actions against any of the stockholders for the proportion of his claim; and such action shall be dismissed upon his paying his said proportion, as to him. His liability is determined by the amount of stock or shares owned by him at the time the liability was incurred, and his liability is not released by his subsequent transfer of his stock. The liability of foreign corporations doing business here is the same as of domestic ones. All corporations must issue certificates for stock when fully paid up, or sooner if the bye-laws so provide. Such certificates are personal property and are transferred by endorsement, and on the books of the company. Contracts to relieve directors from liability are void.

Directors may, after one fourth of the capital stock has been subscribed, for the purpose of paying debts or expenses, or conducting the business of the corporation, levy and collect assessments not

[90]

to exceed 10 per cent. of the amount of the capital stock, unless in cases where the corporation is unable to meet its liabilities, the assessment may be for the full amount unpaid on the capital stock; however, the directors of railroad corporations may assess the capital stock in instalments of not more than 10 per cent. per month, and the directors of fire and marine insurance companies may assess such a percentage of the stock as they deem proper. Notice of assessment must be given of at least thirty days, and personally served or mailed to each stockholder, and also published for four weeks in a newspaper.

If the assessment is not paid, further notice is then given and the stock sold, as delinquent, at public auction for cash, or so many shares of it as may be necessary to pay the assessment and charges. In default of bidders the corporation may purchase the shares through the president or secretary, and hold it subject to the direction of the stockholders.

Every corporation as such has power—
1. Of succession.
2. To sue and be sued in any court.
3. To make and use a common seal.
4. To purchase, hold, and convey such real and personal property as the purposes of incorporation may require.
5. To appoint and pay officers and agents.
6. To make bye-laws for its management, &c.
7. To admit members and stockholders, and sell their stock for assessments.
8. To enter into any contracts or obligations essential to the transaction of its affairs.

In relation to banking corporations, however, our statutes expressly provide that no corporation shall issue or create any bills, notes, or other evidences of debt upon loans or otherwise for circulation as money.

If any corporation fails to organize within one year from the date of its corporation its corporate powers cease.

No corporation can issue stock or bonds except for money paid, property received, or labour performed; and all fictitious increase of stock is void.

But corporations may, by its directors, by a two-thirds vote of all the capital stock, increase or diminish the same; in no case, however, can it be diminished to an amount less than the indebtedness of the company. A certificate of the increase or decrease must be filed in the county clerk's office.

No corporation can acquire or hold more real property than is reasonably necessary for the transaction of its business. Two or more mining corporation may consolidate if they own adjoining lands upon the written consent of two-thirds of the capital stock, and the filing of a certificate of consolidation in the office of the county clerk, and advertisement in a newspaper.

Every corporation may amend its articles of incorporation by a vote of two-thirds of the stock, and filing the amended articles in the county clerk's office and the office of the Secretary of State.

All corporations for profit are required to keep a record of all business transactions, meetings of directors, members, and stockholders, the place and time of holding such meeting, its object, how authorised, and the notice thereof given; such record must embrace every act done or ordered, who was present, who absent. In addition to such record, it must also keep a stock and transfer book showing the names of the stockholders, instalments paid, assessments levied, transfers of stock made, sales made, with the dates thereof, and by whom, to whom, and all such other matters as the bye-laws direct. The stock and transfer book is open to every member, creditor, and stockholder.

The Attorney-General and the District-Attorney, whenever and as often as required by the Governor, examines into the affairs and conditions of every corporation, and reports such examination with a detailed statement of facts in writing to the Governor who lays the same before the Legislature, and for the purpose of examination the Attorney-General or District-Attorney may examine all books, papers, and documents, and examine the president and directors on oath.

A committee of the Legislature may at any time make a like examination.

The franchise of any corporation receiving tolls may be levied and sold in satisfaction of any judgment against it, and the purchaser enters into possession, and transacts the business of the corporation until the franchise is redeemed, which may be done at any time within one year of the sale by paying the purchase price and 10 per cent. interest thereon.

Dissolution of Corporation.

Every corporation formed for a period of less than 50 years may at any time prior to the expiration of the term of its corporate existence extend such term for a period not exceeding 50 years from its formation by a vote of two-thirds of the capital stock, or upon the written consent of the stockholders holding two-thirds of the capital stock, or of two-thirds of the members. A certificate of such extension must be filed with the county clerk and the Secretary of State.

The involuntary dissolution of corporations is by an action brought by the Attorney-General in the name of the people of the State, on his own information or upon complaint of a private party againt any person or persons who usurp or unlawfully hold or exercise any franchise in the State, and the judgment in such action determines the rights of the defendant, and of any party alleged to be entitled, and in case the defendant is found guilty, a fine of not exceeding 5,000 dols. is imposed on him, and he is excluded from the franchise, and pays all costs.

The voluntary dissolution of corporations is upon its voluntary application for that purpose to the superior court of the county in which is done its principal business; the application must show that at a meeting of stockholders called for the purpose the dissolution of the corporation was resolved upon by a two-thirds vote of all the stockholders or members, and that all claims and demands against the corporation have been satisfied and discharged; this application must be sworn to and signed by a majority of the board of directors.

The application is filed with the clerk of the court, who gives not less than 30 nor more than 50 days' notice of the application by advertisement in some newspaper published in the county, and at any time before the expiration of the time of publication any person may file objections to the application.

After the time of publication has expired the court, after further notice of five days to the objectors, if any, proceeds to hear the application, and if the statements made therein are true, must declare the corporation dissolved. Corporations are also dissolved by the lapse of time for which they were formed, which never can exceed 50 years.

Unless other persons are appointed by the court, the directors of a corporation at the time of its dissolution are trustees of the members, stockholders, and creditors of the corporation, with full power to settle its affairs.

Foreign corporations doing business here must appoint some person here to accept service of process here and file such appointment in the office of the Secretary of State here.

Insurance Corporations.

Insurance corporations can hold real estate only as follows here:—

1. Such as is requisite for its accommodation in the convenient transaction of its business, not exceeding in value 150,000 dols.
2. Such as is conveyed to it by way of mortgage for moneys due.
3. Such as is purchased at such mortgage sales or on judgments for such moneys lent.
4. Such as is conveyed to it for loans previously contracted; however, no such real property shall be held for more than five years, unless the Insurance Commissioner certifies that a forced sale of it would materially injure the corporation, and states a time in the certificate within which it must be sold.

Policies must be signed by the president or vice-president, and in case of his death or disability by two directors; they are then binding on the company when countersigned by the secretary, as if executed over the corporate seal.

Dividends of the net profits and interest may be declared, but outstanding notes and premiums are not to be considered profits. If any insurance company is under liability for losses equal to its capital stock, and the directors knowing that make any new insurance, the estates of all who make such new insurance or assent thereto are severally and jointly liable for any loss.

Every fire, marine, inland navigation, or life insurance company must have a subscribed capital stock equal to at least 200,000 dols.,— of which one-fourth must be paid in before the issuance of any policy, and the residue in one year from the incorporation, otherwise it may not transact business, this is exclusive of liabilities for losses reported, expenses, taxes, insurance, and outstanding risks. All foreign mutual insurance companies must also have a like capital of 200,000 dols.

Every other insurance company not enumerated above must have a like capital of 100,000 dols. All foreign insurance companies of this class must have a like capital of 100,000 dols.

The president and a majority of the directors of every fire and marine insurance company must within 30 days after the payment of the one-fourth of the capital stock and also within 30 days after the payment of the residue, subscribe a sworn certificate setting forth the amount of the fixed capital and the amount thereof paid up at the times mentioned, and file it in the office of the county clerk, and a duplicate with the Insurance Commissioner. It may insure and re-insure all insurable interests.

Insurance companies of any kind may insure its capital and accumulations in the following securities:

1. In United States Government bonds.

2. In bonds of any of the United States not in default on such bonds or interest.
3. In bonds of cities, counties, and towns in the State of California not in default for interest of such bonds.
4. In loans or unincumbered real property or on merchandise in warehouse worth at least 100 per cent. more than the amount lent.

No investment in the above bonds must be made in amount exceeding the par value or market price thereof.

Fire and marine insurance companies are not allowed to take on any one risk a sum exceeding one-tenth part of their capital actually paid in without re-insuring the excess above one-tenth.

No fire, marine, inland navigation, or other insurance company, can declare any dividend except from the profits remaining on hand unimpaired after deducting—

1. The entire capital stock.
2. All premiums received or receivable on outstanding marine or inland risks except marine time risks.
3. A fund equal to half the amount of all premiums on all other risks not terminated at the time.
4. A sum sufficient to pay all losses reported to or in course of settlement, and all liabilites for expenses and taxes.

No fire or marine insurance company with a subscribed capital of less than 200,000 dols. can declare any dividend except from profits remaining on hand after reserving—

1. A sum necessary to form, with the subscribed capital stock, an aggregate sum of 200,000 dols.
2. All premiums received, receivable, or outstanding on outstanding marine or inland risks except marine time risks.
3. A fund equal to half of all premiums on fire risks and marine time risks not terminated at the time.
4. A sum sufficient to pay all losses reported or in course of settlement, and all liabilities for expenses and taxes.

Any corporation of underwriters for the purpose of discovering and preventing fires, and of saving life and property, may at its own expense equip, employ, and maintain a fire patrol, and enter all buildings during and after a fire, and shall have the same right of way as the regular fire department. Every such corporation may assess its members for the cost of maintaining the fire patrol.

No corporation transacting life insurance can make any dividends except from profits on hand after retaining unimpaired—

1. The whole capital stock.
2. A sum sufficient to pay all losses reported or in course of settlement, and all expenses and taxes.
3. A sum sufficient to reinsure all outstanding policies.

Mutual health, life, and accident insurance companies must have a capital of at least 100,000 dols., and cannot insure until its whole capital is paid up in cash, nor until it has a "guarantee fund" of 250,000 dols., which must consist of promissory notes payable to the corporation or order, and of not more than 5,000 dols. each by any one person.

The capital stock and the "guarantee fund" form the fixed capital of the company liable for its liabilities until the net profits accumulated in cash and securities is equal to the capital stock and guarantee fund together, and becomes its fixed capital not subject to dividend.

A declaration of the fixed capital must be filed with the original articles of incorporation, and published in a newspaper, after which the holders of life policies may vote at the election of directors, having one vote for every 1,000 dols. insured.

Life, health, and accident insurance companies, may invest their capital stock in United States bonds, California State bonds, bonds of any of the United States, or of any city, county, town in this State, or in the stock of any other corporation in this State (except mining corporations) of a market value of not less than 60 per cent. of the par value.

All premiums are payable wholly in cash, or half cash and half promissory notes.

The Insurance Commissioner must be furnished with a valuation of outstanding policies once a year.

There are also certain provisions of what each policy shall contain, and that fraternal societies are not to be considered insurance corporations.

Railroad Corporations.

No stock of any railroad is transferable until all calls and instalments are paid up.

They may borrow money on the credit of the corporation for constructing their road, and may issue bonds and notes of not less than 5,000 dols. each, not exceeding the amount of their capital stock, and they may mortgage their property to secure the payment thereof, but must provide sinking funds for the redemption of same.

They must file with the Secretary of State certificates of the amount of their fixed capital stock verified by affidavits.

Every railroad corporation has power to enter upon lands to make surveys; to hold and convey lands like a natural person, when necessary for successfully operating and conducting their business; to lay out roads not over 9 rods wide; to cross, connect, and join other railroads; to purchase lands, timber, stone, gravel, and other materials necessary; to carry persons and freight; to receive fares and toll; to erect necessary buildings; to regulate time and freight, subject to legislation; to regulate speed and force of engines; and to make all necessary and proper rules for the management of their business.

After the completion of the railroad a map, certified by the chief engineer and president, with proper profile, must be filed in the county clerk's office of each county through which the road runs, and also with the Secretary of State. Every railroad corporation must begin to construct its road in two years after incorporation, and must put in full operation at least 5 miles per year thereafter, or forfeit its right to extend its road.

A railroad cannot use the streets of a city unless by consent of two-thirds of the city authorities; may consolidate with other railroads; may use all swamp, overflowed and public land (not over 200 feet wide) not disposed of by the State, and not within the corporate limits of any town; may take from adjacent vacant State lands, wood, stone, gravel, and earth; checks must be affixed to all baggage or parcels, and a duplicate given to the passenger under penalty of 20 dols. and loss of fare; are liable for full value of all baggage lost.

Every railroad corporation must make an annual report to the Secretary of State of its operations for the year, sworn to by secretary and president, and showing the amount of the capital stock paid; the amount expended; the amount of its indebtedness; the nature thereof; its credits; the amounts received for fares and freight; the number of tons of freight carried; the amount paid for repairs of engines, cars, buildings, &c., showing the current expenses of the road; the dividends, and the number of engine-houses, shops, engines and cars, and their character.

Every such corporation must start and run their cars at regular times fixed by public notice, must furnish sufficient accommodation for freight and passengers, and must, on payment of freight and fares, transport such property and passengers, and in case of refusal must pay all damages; must post its printed rules on the inside of passenger cars, regarding the fare and conduct of passengers; must maintain fences on both sides of its line; must carry a bell of 20 lbs. on each engine, and ring it 80 rods from every crossing and until crossed; must fix its charges for fares and freight, graduated as follows: one rate per mile for 100 miles and over, one rate for 75 miles and less, not exceeding 10 per cent. per mile more than first rate; one rate for 50 miles, 15 per cent. more than first rate; one rate for 25 miles, 20 per cent. more than first; one rate for less than 25 miles, 25 per cent. more than first rate; but never to exceed, in any case, 10 cents per mile for any passenger, nor 15 cents. for freight. Passenger tickets are good for six months from issue, and may be used to or from the place where issued.

All railroad corporations have equal privileges, and must operate their road, or forfeit their charter and franchise after six months.

There is in this State a board of three railroad commissioners, who supervise the working of all railroads here, and may establish rates and freights to be charged. Complaints must be made in writing under oath to them, and their decision is also rendered in writing, upon which the complainant may then sue in any court.

Street Railroads.

Street railroads or trams may obtain leave from any city to lay tracks, and run cars through the city streets and public highways, upon conditions, of which one must be that the tracks must not be more than 5 feet wide between the rails, must be in the middle of the road, and must be paved, planked, or macadamized its entire length, and for 2 feet on each side.

The rates of fares on street railroads must not exceed 10 cents for any distance under 3 miles, nor the rate of speed over 8 miles per hour (penalty, fine of 100 dols.). If a city has over 100,000 inhabitants 5 cents only can be charged for fare either coming or going for one trip.

Wagon-road corporations must lay out their road, and report their proceedings, with a map, to the board of supervisors of the county through which the road runs.

They may keep bridges and ferries, and take tolls fixed by the supervisors, not to exceed 15 per cent. per annum on the cost of construction, but no tolls can be charged on any public highway or road.

The toll-gatherer may prevent any one from passing the gate unless they pay the toll, which must be the amount set forth on a printed list posted over each gate.

There are certain penalties for evading the payment of tolls, &c.

When the tolls have paid for the cost of construction they must be reduced to a sum sufficient to keep the road, ferries, and other property in repair, and pay a dividend of 15 per cent. per annum. Such corporation may mortgage its property for the purposes of its organization.

Bridge, Ferry, Wharf, Chute, and Pier Corporations

must obtain authority from the supervisors of the county to construct or take tolls on a bridge, ferry, wharf, chute, or pier; must begin construction of their works within one year; must complete it within three years; and must continue to operate continuously.

The president and secretary must report annually to the supervisors, under oath, on all matters connected with the company and its finances, and publish the report in a newspaper.

Telegraph Corporations

may use and construct lines along public roads and across waters and lands, and may erect poles and necessary fixtures thereon and thereunder, but cannot recover damages for breakage of sub-aqueous telegraph cables, unless they by notice indicate the place where it lies and publish the notice in a newspaper.

Any telegraph corporation may convey its rights, privileges, or property, except its corporate franchise.

Water and Canal Corporations.

No corporation formed to supply any city with water can do so without authority from the authorities thereof, nor unless it is done by a contract entered into with the city for a term not exceeding 50 years.

The city authorities annually fix the rates that shall be paid for water, and annual statements showing income and an itemized account of expenditure must be made by the water companies to the city authorities for that purpose, and refusal to make such statement is punishable as a misdemeanour.

The rates for water must be equal and uniform, no discrimination being allowed between persons.

Should such corporation charge in excess of the established rates, it forfeits its franchise. Water corporations must furnish pure fresh water. Water in case of fire must be furnished free.

All water and canal corporations have a right, subject to control, to use so much of the streets, roads, ways, and alleys in any city as may be necessary for laying pipes for conducting water to any part thereof.

Every such corporation must keep its canals, flumes, bridges, and water pipes in good repair. Whenever any corporation sells water to irrigate lands which such corporation has sold, the right to flow and use of the water is a perpetual easement to the land sold.

Homestead Corporations

are corporations for the purpose of acquiring large tracts of land and subdividing them for distribution among the shareholders.

Their corporate existence must not exceed 10 years. A printed copy of their bye-laws must be furnished to each shareholder.

Homestead corporations may borrow money not exceeding one-fourth of their paid-up capital stock, and for not exceeding 10 years, and for this purpose may mortgage their shares.

They cannot purchase or sell lands for the mere purpose of speculation, nor can they hold over 200,000 dols. worth of real property.

The property must be divided at the end of 10 years, according to the numbers of shares held by each member to whom the lots are sold by auction, the most desirable ones bringing of course the best price.

They must annually publish in a newspaper a verified statement of their financial condition.

Savings and Loan Corporations

are organised for the purpose of accumulating and lending the funds of their stockholders or depositors.

No such corporation may lend money for more than six years, and on adequate security on real and personal property.

When such companies have a capital stock, the rights and the privileges of stockholders as distinguished from those of members must be fixed by the bye-laws. No dividends can be declared except from surplus profits. Such corporations may hold the following real and personal property, and convey the same : 1, the lot and building in which the business is carried on not exceeding in cost 100,000 dols. except by a two-third vote, in which case it may be of the value of 250,000 dols. or less; 2, such property as may have been mortgaged to it for money lent; 3, such as has been bought.

Mortgage Sale, or in satisfaction of Loans made thereon.

All the latter real property must be sold within five years after acquisition.

No such corporation can hold any other real property, nor can it buy or sell personal property except in transacting its regular business, and gold, bullion, United States and other bonds and securities.

Savings and loan societies may also issue general certificates of deposit transferable by endorsement and delivery.

They must reserve a fund for the payment of losses by retaining on each dividend day 5 per cent. of the net profits of the corporation, until 100,000 dols. are so reserved.

No director or officer can borrow from the funds of such corporation, otherwise his office becomes vacant immediately.

Mining Corporations.

Any corporation organised for purposes of mining may maintain agencies for the sale of their stock and its issuance in other States of the United States.

All such stock must be signed by the president and secretary of the corporation, and countersigned by the transfer agent.

A majority of the shareholders of such corporation may petition the superior court for the removal of the officers of the corporation: the court issues notice to the shareholders that a meeting for that purpose will be held, and at the time and place named in said notice the shareholders meet, appoint a chairman, and vote on the matter. If a majority of all the shares are in favour of the removal of one or more of the officers, the meeting shall fill the vacancies by ballot, the result is reported to the court, the judge of which then issues a certificate of election to those elected, which is filed in the county clerk's office.

Mining corporations must keep a complete set of books, which, together with all papers, are open to the inspection of every stockholder, who may be accompanied by an expert, and is entitled to make copies.

A verified monthly statement of all the affairs, receipts, expenditure, &c., of the company must be posted in its office.

Similar statements must be made monthly and weekly by the superintendent to the secretary, and kept in a conspicuous place in the office.

Any stockholder may, with an expert, visit the mines of the corporation and examine the same, and the superintendent, upon order of the president, must give him every facility for a complete examination, and he must furnish the stockholder with some guide familiar with the mine, or accompany him himself.

Directors cannot sell, lease, or mortgage the mine except authorised thereto by a two-thirds vote of all the stock.

Religious, Social, and Benevolent Associations.

Corporations formed for any purpose other than pecuniary profit may, in accordance with the rules, regulations, and discipline of such association, elect not less than three nor more than 11 directors.

Mutual, beneficial, and relief associations not exceeding 1,000 members may be formed for the purpose of paying the nominee of any member a sum not exceeding 3 dols. for each member of the association, by levying an assessment upon each member living at the time of the death. Such association is not an insurance company, but may sue and be sued by its name, may own sufficient real estate for its purposes, or real estate bought in, or foreclosed on mortgages, but they cannot hold the latter for more than five years. Such association may hold real property to furnish burial grounds for its members, but such cemeteries must not exceed six lots in any town, or 20 acres in the county, and the profit therefrom must not exceed 50,000 dols. per annum. Orphan asylums can hold 160 acres surrounding the asylum.

Associations for the establishment and endowment of institutions of learning connected with charitable purposes may hold all necessary real property.

In case of donations of more than the statutory amount of land, the surplus must be sold within five years.

The directors of such associations must annually make a full report of the property held in trust for their corporation, to the members.

All corporations for purposes other than profit may, on obtaining an order from the superior court, mortgage or sell their property. Any member may appear before the court and oppose the granting of such order.

New members may be admitted to such corporations, but no transfer of membership is possible.

Whenever the rules or discipline of any religous body require incorporation for the administration of the temporalities thereof, the bishop, chief priest, or presiding elder may become a corporation sole, with all the powers and duties of a religious corporation, and on the same conditions, &c.

All property held by such corporation sole (bishop) is held in trust for his Church or society, and he may hold necessary land for churches, hospitals, schools, orphan asylums, parsonages, and cemeteries.

Every judge of the superior court has access to his books at all times.

The certificate or articles of incorporation of such corporation sole sets forth the facts authorizing such incorporation, and declares the manner of filling vacancies as required by the rules of the Church. A copy of the commission, or election of the bishop, elder, or priest incorporated must be filed in the county clerk's office.

Any diocese, synod, or other organization of any Church may elect directors, and become a corporation.

Cemetery corporations may hold land not exceeding 320 acres for burial.

The directors must subdivide same into lots and plats, and sell the same to purchasers.

Every proprietor of a lot 200 feet square, or person representing a majority of the joint proprietors of such lot, may vote for all officers.

Such corporations may hold personal property not exceeding 5,000 dols. but the surplus remaining from the sale of lots must be disposed of in the improvement, embellishment, and preservation of the cemetery.

Such corporations may issue bonds for the purchase of their grounds, and may hold any property bequeathed or given them in trust for the embellishing of their cemetery, and repairing monuments.

A burial lot is in alienable after interment made therein, until all bodies have been removed therefrom.

Agricultural Fair Corporations

may acquire and hold 160 acres of land with buildings.

Cannot contract debts exceeding the amount in their treasury, except for the purchase of real property not exceeding 5,000 dols.

They are not conducted for profit; and the charges for exhibition, &c., must never exceed the amount necessary for current expenses of fairs.

Gas Corporations

must obtain permission from the town authorities to lay their pipes, which must be proved and sealed by the inspectors.

Such companies must on payment of price supply gas required for any building which is within 100 feet from any main, or pay the applicant 50 dols. damages, and 5 dols. per diem until supplied, unless serious obstacles exist.

Any agent of the gas company may enter any building and inspect the meter.

When persons neglect to pay, the gas may be shut off.

Land and Building Corporations

organized for the erection of buildings, and making other improvements on real property, may raise funds in shares not exceeding 200 dols. each payable in monthly instalments. Such bodies are organized with or without capital stock.

Any such corporation may borrow money for its purposes, and may give as security therefor its shares, or mortgage its real property; may purchase real estate, erect buildings thereon, make loans to its members for the purpose of acquiring and improving real estate.

Such corporation may ensure the lives of its members and debtors; may hold, purchase, and convey real property; to wit: 1. The building and lot not exceeding in value 20,000 dols. in which its business is done. 2. Such as may from time to time be necessary to supply the wants of its members, not exceeding in value 100,000 dols. 3. Such real property as may have been mortgaged to it to secure money lent, or to secure the purchase price of the land.

The secretary of such corporations must make an annual statement of the financial affairs thereof, profit and loss, &c., which must be audited by competent persons (2), not directors, elected by the general body of shareholders, verified by them, signed by president and secretary. Printed copies of such statement must be circulated among the members, and be published daily for four weeks, or at least once a week for four weeks, in one or more newspapers. Any two or more such corporations may unite and consolidate.

Such consolidation must be published in some newspaper in the county.

Colleges and Seminaries of Learning.

Any number of persons may establish a college; their articles of incorporation must contain—

1. The name of the corporation.
2. Its purpose.
3. The place where the seminary or college is to be conducted.
4. The number of its trustees, not less than five nor more than fifteen; the term for which they hold, and, if so desired, the society, organization, or Church, to which they shall belong.
5. The names of those who have subscribed money or property to assist in founding the college or institute, with the amount subscribed, and a description of the donated property.

Unless otherwise provided in the articles of incorporation, the trustees have power—

1. To elect annually their president from their own number.
2. Upon a vacancy by death, removal out of State, or expiration of term, &c., to elect others to fill the place, provided that graduates of such college may nominate persons to fill the vacancies.
3. To elect additional trustees, the whole number of trustees never to exceed fifteen, and one-fifth of them to go out of office every year.
4. To declare vacant the seat of a trustee who shall absent himself at eight consecutive meetings.
5. To hold real property for educational purposes.
6. To sell, mortgage, and lease the same.
7. To prescribe a course of study for the institution.
8. To appoint a president of the college or seminary.

349

9. To appoint professors, tutors, and other officers.
10. To grant diplomas and literary honours.
11. To fix salaries.
12. To make bye-laws.

The foregoing are the provisions governing the formation, regulation, and dissolution of companies.

FOREIGN OFFICE.
1889.
ANNUAL SERIES.

No. 458.
DIPLOMATIC AND CONSULAR REPORTS ON TRADE AND FINANCE.

UNITED STATES.

REPORT FOR THE YEAR 1888
ON THE
TRADE OF TEXAS.

REFERENCE TO PREVIOUS REPORT, Annual Series No. 266.

Presented to both Houses of Parliament by Command of Her Majesty,
FEBRUARY, 1889.

LONDON:
PRINTED FOR HER MAJESTY'S STATIONERY OFFICE,
BY HARRISON AND SONS. ST. MARTIN'S LANE,
PRINTERS IN ORDINARY TO HER MAJESTY.

And to be purchased, either directly or through any Bookseller, from
EYRE AND SPOTTISWOODE, EAST HARDING STREET, FLEET STREET, E.C., and
32, ABINGDON STREET, WESTMINSTER, S.W.; or
ADAM AND CHARLES BLACK, 6, NORTH BRIDGE, EDINBURGH; or
HODGES, FIGGIS, & Co., 104, GRAFTON STREET, DUBLIN.

1889.

[C. 5618—11.]   *Price One Penny.*

New Series of Reports.

Reports of the Annual Series have been issued from Her Majesty's Diplomatic and Consular Officers at the following places, and may be obtained from the sources indicated on the title-page:—

No.		Price.	No		Price.
338.	Bordeaux	1d.	398.	Boston	1d.
339.	Mogador	1d.	399.	Hakodate	1d.
340.	Wilmington	1d.	400.	Nantes	1d.
341.	Amoy	2d.	401.	Madeira	1d.
342.	Trebizond	1d.	402.	Hakodate	1d.
343.	Lisbon	1d.	403.	Nagasaki	1d.
344.	Java	1d.	404.	Hiogo	2d.
345.	Brest	1d.	405.	Tonga	1d.
346.	Odessa	2d.	406.	Adana	1d.
347.	Cavalla	1d.	407.	Valparaiso	1d.
348.	Bussorah	1d.	408.	Bilbao	1d.
349.	Mollendo	1d.	409.	Santiago	1d.
350.	Cadiz	5d.	410.	Paramaribo	1d.
351.	Cagliari	4d.	411.	Nantes	1d.
352.	Cagliari	1d.	412.	Bangkok	1d.
353.	Ajaccio	1d.	413.	Yokohama	2d.
354.	Copenhagen	1d.	414.	Mozambique	1d.
355.	Vienna	1d.	415.	Canton	2d.
356.	San Francisco	1d.	416.	Kiungchow	1d.
357.	Vera Cruz	1d.	417.	Damascus	1d.
358.	Philippopolis	1d.	418.	Syra	1d.
359.	Greytown	1d.	419.	Aleppo	1d.
360.	Tangier	1d.	420.	Sandakan	1d.
361.	Lisbon	1d.	421.	Barcelona	1d.
362.	Chicago	1d.	422.	Königsberg	1d.
363.	Jerusalem and Jaffa	1d.	423.	Tabreez	1d.
364.	Truxillo	1d.	424.	Guayaquil	1d.
365.	Ningpo	1d.	425.	St. Petersburg	1d.
366.	Chefoo	1d.	426.	Tokio	1d.
367.	Bushire	1d.	427.	Charleston	1d.
368.	Stockholm	2d.	428.	Amsterdam	1d.
369.	Santiago	1d.	429.	Hamburg	4d.
370.	New York	2d.	430.	Trieste	1d.
371.	Pernambuco	1d.	431.	New York	2d.
372.	Söul	1d.	432.	Antwerp	1d.
373.	Chinkiang	2d.	433.	Munich	1d.
374.	Pernambuco	1d.	434.	Buenos Ayres	1d.
375.	San Francisco	2d.	435.	Warsaw	1d.
376.	Riga	1d.	436.	Porto Rico	1d.
377.	Newchwang	2d.	437.	Réunion	1d.
378.	San Salvador	1d.	438.	Lisbon	1d.
379.	Frankfort	2d.	439.	Venice	1d.
380.	Hankow	2d.	440.	Christiania	5d.
381.	Bucharest	1d.	441.	Maranham	1d.
382.	Lisbon	1d.	442.	Sofia	1d.
383.	Tunis	1d.	443.	Copenhagen	1d.
384.	Tangier	1d.	444.	Galatz	1d.
385.	Santiago	2d.	445.	Tabreez	1d.
386.	Diarbekir	1d.	446.	Bogotá	2d.
387.	Shanghai	2d.	447.	St. Petersburg	3d.
388.	Rome	2d.	448.	Nice	1d.
389.	Buenos Ayres	1d.	449.	Stettin	2d.
390.	Amsterdam	1d.	450.	Fiume	1d.
391.	Warsaw	1d.	451.	Chinkiang	1d.
392.	San Francisco	1d.	452.	The Hague	1d.
393.	Alexandria	1d.	453.	Malaga	1d.
394.	Salonica	2d.	454.	Taganrog	1d.
395.	Palermo	1d.	455.	Mozambique	1d.
396.	Mexico	4d.	456.	Bogotá	2d.
397.	Naples	3d.	457.	Patras	1d.

No. 458.

Reference to previous Report, Annual Series No. 266.

UNITED STATES.

GALVESTON.

Consul Lyall to the Marquis of Salisbury.

My Lord, Galveston, *January* 17, 1889.

I HAVE the honour to enclose my Report on the Trade and Commerce of Galveston for the year 1888.

I have, &c.
(Signed) WALTER TSCHUDI LYALL.

Report on the Trade and Commerce of Texas for the Year 1888.

Although no violent storms or hurricanes have been experienced, as in 1886, the weather has been unfavourable, not only to agriculture but to health. Constant rain during spring and autumn not only seriously damaged and retarded the cereal production in the southern and eastern provinces, but promoted malarious and typhoidal conditions to an alarming extent. *Climate.*

A severe outbreak of yellow fever took place in Florida, and the coast of Texas had, it is believed, at one time a narrow escape from the same infliction. *Health.*

The commercial importance of the city of Galveston has satisfactorily progressed. The numerous artesian wells, bored during the past year in various wards, have turned out effective. The marine ways, have been in operation some seven or eight months, and factories, extensive public buildings, public schools, jetties, wharves, &c., taken in hand and completed. *The capital.*

The net tonnage of vessels entering from, and clearing for, foreign and home ports (U.S.) during the year 1888 is as follows:—

	Merchandise. Tons.
Entered—	
Foreign shipping	111,388
United States vessels..	322,822
Total	434,210
Cleared—	
Foreign shipping	122,752
United States vessels..	309,034
Total	431,786

The great bulk of exports from Galveston to Europe is cotton, cotton-seed oil, and cotton-oil cake. The total valuation of which for each month during the year 1888 is as follows:— *Exports.*

(574)

UNITED STATES.

Month.	Amount.	
	Cake.	Cotton.
	Dol.	Dol.
January	48,071	2,202,699
February	28,960	277,509
March	55,454	212,485
April	10,460	179,066
May	..	..
June	..	..
July	..	..
August	..	..
September	20,746	920,555
October	83,905	1,391,776
November	99,888	4,059,091
December	162,315	3,537,633
Total	509,799	13,780,814

The total value of foreign imports during the year is 707,128 dol.; the exportations of home (U.S.) merchandise were 14,465,347 dol.

The cotton crop of 1888 was seriously damaged by the heavy autumnal rains, much being still in the boll when they set in. These were succeeded by night-frosts, especially in the northern portion of the State, so that the output, instead of amounting, as at one time expected, to 19,000,000 bales, has barely turned 15,000,000.

Interference with trade. — Trade is of course widely and variously affected by the protective tariff, and popular feeling is for the most part indifferent to its effects, while commercial organisations or "rings" add artificially to the prices of commodities of first necessity.

The Beef Syndicate. — One of the latest examples of the action of a "ring" is the Chicago Dressed Beef * Syndicate.

I quote the following from the "Galveston Daily News'" report of the speech made on the doings of this Syndicate by the Honourable T. T. D. Andrews, President of the Texas International Cattle Range Association.

The "News" justly remarks: "No good can come from an effort to benefit industry, unless the leaders of our organisations have the courage to condemn the monstrous iniquities of trusts and combinations, which, if not controlled by law, will sooner or later render the condition of the masses of the people little better than that of peons."

The above Dressed Beef Syndicate, some time ago, endeavoured to find a market for their produce in Ohio (city of Akron), and on the local butchers refusing to deal with them, the Syndicate at once set up a retail market, and sold meat at less than cost price until they had ruined the local butchers and forced them out of business. When they had acquired control, they at once raised the prices to high figures.

Railway discrimination in rates. — These "operations," not alone in meat and provisions, but in other staples, are said to be organised the more easily by the syndicates through secret understandings with the railway companies—themselves virtually syndicates—who are openly and persistently accused of "discrimination in rates of freights," in favour of some, and against other traders. Nay, in some cases, whole tracts of country, seaport towns, cities, &c., are said to be "discriminated against" by the railway

---

* Dressed beef signifies in the United States carcases of beef prepared for market.

magnates—in other words "boycotted" to their great detriment. This by the way.

Fresh meat (beef or mutton), preserved on ice, which is supplied by the Chicago Syndicate above-mentioned to most of the great hotels of the United States, and to nearly all the railway restaurants, has been recently advanced in price 3 c. per pound. This was done without the cattle breeders (on Texan cattle ranges and elsewhere) receiving any additional price for their animals. It is asserted that the only reason why the Beef Syndicate, which has complete command of the situation, ever pay reasonable prices, is to avoid "killing the goose."

The Syndicate are all powerful, and could, if disposed to do so, keep prices continually depressed in their favour. They allow the market to go up now and again, in order to persuade cattle men that the low prices are caused by over-production. But "people who know" insist that there is no over-production of cattle, whatever, in any part of the United States; the most reliable statistics proving that there are, at the present time, fewer cattle in the States, as compared with population, than at the epoch when prices were highest, and when cattle breeding was at its apogee of prosperity. They also assert that present conditions are unnatural and artificial, entirely caused by the "operations" of the Syndicate.

A big meeting, in which cattle raisers, graziers, and butchers will consider their interests, is consequently to be held at Saint Louis, and measures taken to defeat, if possible, the Syndicate through State legislation. Although total prohibition of Chinese immigration to the United States—and although restrictions or prohibitive measures against Italian and Eastern European immigration has been seriously mooted by labour unions—it appears that certain emigration bureaus in England are engaged, by advertisements, &c., in promoting British immigration into Texas. British mechanics and labourers, who have emigrated from Europe, however, in consequence of these advertisements, inform me that they experience great difficulty in securing employment, and there is no doubt that a dearth of employment has prevailed lately. By some this has been ascribed to the competition of convict labour—convicts in Texas are employed working at trades in the prisons and penitentiaries—but the Honourable Geo. W. Durant, in an article lately published, militates strongly against this theory. *Immigration into the United States.*

The electorate, however, are in the end pretty certain to oppose employment of convicts in manufactures, and the hiring out of convicts to planters, farmers, &c., which is the present system, as injurious to the working man. Canals, irrigation works, and public roads are urgently required in Texas, and it has been proposed to employ convicts on these enterprises. The drawback to doing so is the expense of the numerous guards which would be required to prevent escapes and outbreaks; the criminal population of Texas, white and black, being very considerable, and, of course, all more or less in league with each other, whether in or out of jail. *The convict labour question.*

The Attorney-General's Biennial Report for the two years ending December, 1888, gives some rather startling statistics on this head, which, they having lately been embodied in a leading article by the "Galveston Daily News," I take the liberty to quote from. *Criminal statistics of Texas.*

During the two years in question there were presented:—

Indictments for felony..	11,123
,, ,, misdemeanour	15,781
Informations lodged against for misdemeanour	10,818
Total of new cases	37,722

UNITED STATES.

But during the previous two years (1885–1886) there had been presented:—

Indictments for felony	11,268
„ „ misdemeanour	16,591
Informations laid for ditto	7,234
Total cases	35,093

Of these 35,093 cases (1885–1886), 10,996 indictments had been brought over from December, 1886, making on the dockets, together with the indictments for 1887–1888, a total to deal with of 48,718; and as in many cases a single indictment covered two or more defendants, it may fairly be assumed that at least 50,000 individuals were under accusation during the period (1887–1888).

Besides these, many more, of whom the Attorney-General had no cognizance, are said to have been indicted and prosecuted for offences and misdemeanours in outlying petty courts.

At any rate 2½ per cent. of the population—which is by some said to be 1,750,000, by others, 2,015,000 (say 2,000,000)—has been prosecuted for crime.

Of the 11,123 new indictments for felony, and 6,897 old ones, a total of 18,020 cases now pending, only 5,296 have been tried, while 4,252 were dismissed.

There were 3,128 convictions during the two years 1887–1888, as against 3,086 in 1885–1886.

The indictments for felonies during the two periods in question stand as follows:—

Indictments for	1885–86.	1887–88.
Arson	90	105
Burglary	1,033	1,024
Embezzlement	334	218
Forgery	422	502
Murder	1,043	895
Perjury	227	303
Rape	114	129
Robbery	157	199
Theft	4,604	4,322
Various felonies	3,424	3,316
Total	11,268	11,123

The newspapers continue to report frequent acts of violence, many of which go unpunished.

Material prosperity of Texas.
In spite of the above drawbacks, common to other States, Texas is materially, steadily prospering. Plans for extensive irrigation works, for opening out harbours on the Gulf coast, for dredging out channels, building breakwaters, &c., are both under consideration, and being actually taken in hand; while Galveston, which has now a population quoted at 50,000, has lately invested 3,500,000 dol. in manufacturing enterprises, water-works, jetties, and other public improvements of all descriptions, and is likely to rank before long as one of the first commercial and producing centres of the United States coast.

LONDON:
Printed for Her Majesty's Stationery Office,
By HARRISON AND SONS,
Printers in Ordinary to Her Majesty.
(1125   2 | 89—H & S   574)

FOREIGN OFFICE.
1889.
ANNUAL SERIES.

N⁰. 463.

DIPLOMATIC AND CONSULAR REPORTS ON TRADE AND FINANCE.

UNITED STATES.

REPORT FOR THE YEAR 1888

ON THE

TRADE OF THE CONSULAR DISTRICT OF BALTIMORE.

REFERENCE TO PREVIOUS REPORT, Annual Series No. 262.

Presented to both Houses of Parliament by Command of Her Majesty,
MARCH, 1889.

LONDON:
PRINTED FOR HER MAJESTY'S STATIONERY OFFICE,
BY HARRISON AND SONS, ST. MARTIN'S LANE,
PRINTERS IN ORDINARY TO HER MAJESTY.

And to be purchased, either directly or through any Bookseller, from
EYRE AND SPOTTISWOODE, EAST HARDING STREET, FLEET STREET, E.C., and
32, ABINGDON STREET, WESTMINSTER, S.W.; or
ADAM AND CHARLES BLACK, 6, NORTH BRIDGE, EDINBURGH; or
HODGES, FIGGIS, & Co., 104, GRAFTON STREET, DUBLIN.

1889.

[C. 5618—16.] *Price One Penny.*

New Series of Reports.

Reports of the Annual Series have been issued from Her Majesty's Diplomatic and Consular Officers at the following places, and may be obtained from the sources indicated on the title-page:—

No.		Price.	No.		Price.
333.	Loanda	1d.	398.	Boston	1d.
334.	Loanda	1d.	399.	Hakodate	1d.
335.	Noumea	1d.	400.	Nantes	1d.
336.	Trieste	1d.	401.	Madeira	1d.
337.	Nice	1d.	402.	Hakodate	1d.
338.	Bordeaux	1d.	403.	Nagasaki	1d.
339.	Mogador	1d.	404.	Hiogo	2d.
340.	Wilmington	1d	405.	Tonga	1d.
341.	Amoy	2d.	406.	Adana	1d.
342.	Trebizond	1d.	407.	Valparaiso	1d.
343.	Lisbon	1d.	408.	Bilbao	1d.
344.	Java	1d.	409.	Santiago	1d.
345.	Brest	1d.	410.	Paramaribo	1d.
346.	Odessa	2d.	411.	Nantes	1d.
347.	Cavalla	1d.	412.	Bangkok	1d.
348.	Bussorah	1d.	413.	Yokohama	2d.
349.	Mollendo	1d.	414.	Mozambique	1d.
350.	Cadiz	5d.	415.	Canton	2d.
351.	Cagliari	4d.	416.	Kiungchow	1d.
352.	Cagliari	1d.	417.	Damascus	1d.
353.	Ajaccio	1d.	418.	Syra	1d.
354.	Copenhagen	1d.	419.	Aleppo	1d.
355.	Vienna	1d.	420.	Sandakan	1d.
356.	San Francisco	1d.	421.	Barcelona	1d.
357.	Vera Cruz	1d.	422.	Königsberg	1d.
358.	Philippopolis	1d.	423.	Tabreez	1d.
359.	Greytown	1d.	424.	Guayaquil	1d.
360.	Tangier	1d.	425.	St. Petersburg	1d.
361.	Lisbon	1d.	426.	Tokio	1d.
362.	Chicago	1d	427.	Charleston	1d.
363.	Jerusalem and Jaffa	1d.	428.	Amsterdam	1d.
364.	Truxillo	1d.	429.	Hamburg	4d.
365.	Ningpo	1d.	430.	Trieste	1d.
366.	Chefoo	1d.	431.	New York	2d.
367.	Bushire	1d.	432.	Antwerp	1d.
368.	Stockholm	2d.	433.	Munich	1d.
369.	Santiago	1d.	434.	Buenos Ayres	1d.
370.	New York	2d.	435.	Warsaw	1d.
371.	Pernambuco	1d.	436.	Porto Rico	1d.
372.	Söul	1d.	437.	Réunion	1d.
373.	Chinkiang	2d.	438.	Lisbon	1d.
374.	Pernambuco	1d.	439.	Venice	1d.
375.	San Francisco	2d.	440.	Christiania	5d.
376.	Riga	1d.	441.	Maranham	1d.
377.	Newchwang	2d.	442.	Sofia	1d.
378.	San Salvador	1d.	443.	Copenhagen	1d.
379.	Frankfort	2d.	444.	Galatz	1d.
380.	Hankow	2d.	445.	Tabreez	1d.
381.	Bucharest	1d.	446.	Begotá	2d.
382.	Lisbon	1d.	447.	St. Petersburg	3d.
383.	Tunis	1d.	448.	Nice	1d.
384.	Tangier	1d.	449.	Stettin	2d.
385.	Santiago	2d.	450.	Fiume	1d.
386.	Diarbekir	1d.	451.	Chinkiang	1d.
387.	Shanghai	2d.	452.	The Hague	1d.
388.	Rome	2d.	453.	Malaga	1d.
389.	Buenos Ayres	1d.	454.	Taganrog	1d.
390.	Amsterdam	1d.	455.	Mozambique	1d.
391.	Warsaw	1d.	456.	Bogotá	2d.
392.	San Francisco	1d.	457.	Patras	1d.
393.	Alexandria	1d.	458.	Galveston	1d.
394.	Salonica	2d.	459.	Buda Pesth	1d.
395.	Palermo	1d.	460.	Madeira	1d.
396.	Mexico	4d.	461.	Warsaw	1d.
397.	Naples	3d.	462.	Paris	2d.

No. 463.

Reference to previous Report, Annual Series, No. 262.

UNITED STATES.

BALTIMORE.

Consul Segrave to the Marquis of Salisbury.

My Lord,   *Baltimore, February* 7, 1889.

I HAVE the honour herewith to transmit to your Lordship reports on the Trade and Commerce of Baltimore, Richmond, Norfolk, and Newport News, for the year 1888.

I have, &c.
W. F. SEGRAVE.

Report on the Trade and Commerce of Baltimore for the Year 1888.

A review of the trade and commerce of Baltimore for the past year does not show that amount of business which might have reasonably been looked for.   *Introductory.*

Both imports and exports have declined considerably, as compared with those of the previous year.

Compared, however, with other cities, Baltimore is not worse off than its colossal neighbour, New York, and by the same rule, more prosperous than Philadelphia. As may be seen, on reference to the statistical tables, the principal falling-off has been in the grain trade. Nevertheless, Baltimore still continues to maintain her position as second port in the United States in that special business.

The decline in the export of grain is easily accounted for. In the early summer, reports were prevalent of serious damage to crops in Europe caused by heavy rains. Fortunately the rain ceased in time, and was succeeeded by genial weather, whereby a fearful calamity was averted. In this country, neither the crop of winter or spring wheat was a full one, but with what was left over from the previous year, there was a considerable supply for export. To quote the able report of the President of the corn and flour exchange of this city:—
" Following the excitement abroad, induced by the bad weather, and with that alacrity and audacity which characterises the American speculator, the 'crop-killer' commenced his work to ruin our crop, both winter and spring, in which he was ably joined by the French 'killer,' who also was reasonably compensated for his labour. The most outrageous reports were daily circulated about fictitious damage done, and farmers were advised to hold their wheat in hopes of a fabulous price. In the meantime, the manipulator was working the option

(582)

market for all it was worth. Professional cornerers were in their glory, and extravagant prices were realised. So successful were the leaders of this gigantic plot, that the whole country was excited. The public and press took up the cry for dear bread. Bakers held meetings to advance prices, stimulated by, or in collusion with, the gamblers. Honest trade languished, and the merchant could only look on at the craze in amazement."

It is even stated that negotiations were on foot, and nearly completed, for the import of wheat from Liverpool, paying a tariff duty, to supply the wants of the famishing people of this country.

But the end has come, as the north-western millers, the leaders of the plot, are now begging their neighbours to limit the output of flour, and are consigning their stuff to any place where they can get an advance on it.

In these days of trusts, combinations, and corners, the grain trade has not escaped scathless, and the high or low price of the staff of life depends on the audacity, capital, and nerve of the speculator and gambler. And the consumer, the producer, and the distributor are each forced to contribute to his ill-gotten gains.

Baltimore as a seaport. The advantages of Baltimore as a grain-shipping port are so superior to those of any other on the Atlantic seaboard, that she can always count on securing a large proportion of the export to Europe.

It is not, however, by sitting still and sounding the praises of their port, nor in descanting on its great local advantages, that the commercial prosperity of Baltimore is to be secured. The trading community must be up and doing, and see that their approaches and communications with the sea are maintained with due regard to safety in navigation. Already vast sums of money have been expended in improving, widening, and deepening the channel at the mouth of the Patapsco River, and where it falls into Chesapeake Bay.

But the prevailing system seems to be to execute these necessary works by dribblets, extending over a series of years necessary work which should be executed promptly.

Ship canal. For years the construction of a ship canal across the Delaware peninsula has had numerous and influential advocates, and it is somewhat surprising that the people of this country, remarkable as they are for their enterprise, should have as yet taken no serious steps to carry out the project.

It is said that there are no engineering difficulties worth mentioning, that the expense would not exceed 8,000,000 dol., and it is contended that the projected canal would shorten the voyage from Baltimore to northern European ports by something like 300 miles, not to mention its immense advantages to the great coasting trade along the Atlantic seaboard. No doubt the construction of the work is only a question of time, but it is unquestionable the enormous advantages it would procure for the foreign trade of this city.

Inter-state commerce law. The inter-state commerce law is stated to have helped to remove much of the inequality which formerly existed in railway rates in this and adjacent States. Nevertheless, much difference of opinion still exists as to its practical value, and a movement is being made in certain quarters towards having it repealed altogether But as the Act was passed in obedience to an overwhelming public demand for legal protection against the rapacity and mismanagement of common carriers, who were regardless of the interest of the public, there is but small prospect of any alteration in the legislation on this subject. The fact

Finance. that all $4\frac{1}{2}$ per cent. Government bonds mature in September, 1891, with the constant purchase by the Government of 4 per cent. bonds, will, it is feared, seriously affect the national banking system not only in Baltimore, but in the country at large. The continued coinage of silver is looked upon by our bankers as a serious menace to the stability of the existing monetary system.

They contend that the piling up in the vaults of the national Treasury, of an accumulation of silver involves peril of financial disaster as a natural result of a failure to maintain the equality of coin, whilst at the same time it forms an obstacle in the way of international arrangement, which is recognised as affording the main solution of the specie problem.

I subjoin—Annex A, Return of all Shipping at the Port of Baltimore; Annex B, Return of Exports and Imports; and Annex C, Table showing value of all Exports and Imports.

Annexes.

Like all other Atlantic ports, there is a serious decline in the grain export from Baltimore during the past year; the chief cause for which has been adverted to in the previous portion of this report. That the volume of the grain trade should have been smaller in the past than in the preceding year, was, however, inevitable in view of the decrease in the maize crop of 1887, and consequent diminished export.

Export trade, breadstuffs.

But with a full demand from abroad for all the surplus wheat of the present crop, and with an enormous maize crop now assured, the present year will no doubt show a very considerable increase in local trade, both export and import. Notwithstanding the decline in the export of grain, the flour trade has now assumed enormous proportions, and during the crop year ending in August, 1888, Baltimore exported 2,785,571 barrels, or more than double the total of 1885–86, and seven times more than in 1883–84.

Prior to 1884, New York and Boston had been the great shipping ports for flour, but already Baltimore has far outstripped Boston, and is running New York very close.

The value of corn as a food supply appears to be only imperfectly understood in Europe, where it is mostly used for feeding animals. In point of fact, for a food product, it is for man as well as beast more nutritious than any other staple in the world. These facts are better understood in this country, where the consumption of corn is 32 bushels per capita, as against 4½ bushels of wheat.

Indian corn.

The value of the corn crop in this country for 1887 was 646,000,000 dol., say 129,000,000*l.*, whilst that of the wheat crop was only 310,000,000 dol., say 62,000,000*l.*

Yet the export of corn for 1887 was only 20,000,000 dol. in value, say 4,000,000*l.*, against wheat and its products, of nearly 142,000,000 dol., or say 28,000,000*l.*

The export of provisions, under which head are included bacon, hams, pork, beef (salted and cured), butter, and cheese, have largely declined during recent years. But, on the other hand, the production and export of canned goods has increased, and is increasing, in almost a proportionate rate. What are called the hog products of the United States have declined since 1881 nearly 50 per cent. The beef products, including dairy produce, have declined in the same period 40 per cent., whilst the export of live stock has fallen from a value of 15,500,000 dol. to 12,000,000 dol. There is no doubt that the widely extended system of adulteration, which so largely prevails in this country, is partly responsible for the great decline which has taken place in many articles, notably in those under the head of hog and dairy products. In the former the decline being 50 per cent. and in the latter 52 per cent.

Provisions.

On the other hand, the canning industry has now attained enormous extension, and each succeeding year shows a large increase in these goods.

UNITED STATES.

During the past year the State of Maryland alone put up 968,733 cases of tomatoes, of two dozen cans to the case. The tomatoe brands of Maryland have a deservedly high reputation, as well on account of the superior flavour of the vegetable, as of the care exercised in its preparation for the market. The same remark may be said to apply to all the other products of the Maryland canning industry, which includes oysters and almost every description of fruit and vegetables.

Cotton. The position of Baltimore as one of the leading cotton ports on the Atlantic coast is still maintained. Receipts during the past year came quickly to market, and the weather was generally favourable for transport. The demand from spinners was fair, with prices well maintained during the greater part of the season. The receipts were 269,612 bales, of which 173,067 bales were exported, 35,000 bales were consumed by the local mills, and the balance was sent coastwise.

Petroleum. The new year opened with a dull market. A new feature of the past year is the dealing in "oil futures," though, as yet, traders seem disinclined to take the new departure seriously. The highest price during 1888 was 1 dol. and the lowest $71\frac{1}{4}$ c. per barrel; it closed $87\frac{1}{2}$ c. against 97 c. in the previous January, although there was a decrease of over 9,000,000 barrels in the visible supply.

Tobacco. The year has been an average one in the amount of transactions, whilst prices have been firm for the best qualities of Maryland, the net quantity of which coming to market during the year was 30,000 hogsheads.

Lumber. Baltimore has always ranked as one of the chief ports on the seaboard in the lumber trade, and last year showed a fair increase in the export.

All well-know commercial timber is held in stock here, and with present facilities a good remunerative export trade is carried on with Liverpool. At this moment there is considerable demand from abroad for oak logs, scantling, plank, &c., and no doubt this branch of business is destined to attain much greater importance.

Cattle trade. There is again a considerable increase to be noted in the export of live stock from this port, amounting to 7,000 head. This increase may be partly accounted for from the fact that so many farmers, owing to the scarcity and excessive cost of labour, devote more of their land to cattle raising; and the opening out of the mountain districts in Virginia, and West Virginia has given considerable development to stock farming in these sections.

Copper. The export of copper appears for the first time, and, as may be perceived, has already attained respectable dimensions, nearly 17,000 tons having been shipped to Europe. It is valued here at about 45*l.* a ton, and reaches this port chiefly from the mines in the vicinity of Lake Superior. There are some fairly rich copper mines in the immediate neighbourhood of Baltimore, which, however, have not been worked for some time. Owing to the high price which copper has attained in Europe, it is proposed shortly to recommence working the Maryland mines.

Imports. Metals. The imports of all metals show heavy and marked decline over those of the previous year, with the single exception of tin plate, of which article the quantity imported in 1888 doubles the import of 1887.

Tin plates. This tin plate is nearly all consumed in the tin-can factories of Baltimore and the State of Maryland, and indicates the marked increase in the canned-goods trade for which this State is noted.

Under a proposed new clause of the tariff, passed by the Senate, the duty on tin plates is to be increased from 1 c. to $2\frac{15}{100}$ c. per lb. Should this section of the Bill be approved by the Lower House of

Congress, it is feared that Baltimore will lose at least half of her canned-goods trade, as consumers can hardly be expected to pay the cost added by the increased duty.

The Baltimore can makers are up in arms at the proposed increase, and no wonder, as it is stated that this city takes more than one-sixth of the annual import, on which it pays duties to the amount of 726,000 dol. annually. Baltimore manufactures one-fifth of the total number of cans made throughout the entire country. If the increased duty is passed by the Lower House, this city will have to pay over 1,500,000 dol. annually in customs dues on this article, and which will seriously compromise the interests of more than one-eighth of her entire population.

Other imports.

There is nothing with regard to other imports which calls for special mention beyond the fact that, as a general rule, they have been marked by a decline aggregating over 1,500,000 dol.

Freights.

The condition of the foreign freight market for the entire year has not been favourable for the carrier. During the first part of the year freights were extremely dull, and nearly all the business has been done in the last two months. The grain rate to Liverpool at the beginning of the year was $3\frac{1}{4}d.$ per bushel, falling to $\frac{1}{4}d.$ at the end of March and part of April. The highest rate was $6\frac{1}{2}d.$, paid in November and December. The average is above that of the preceding year, but the last months of the year made it.

Immigration.

During the past year 77 steamers arrived in this port with immigrants. They brought 32,000 passengers, or 8,000 less than the previous year.

Only three adult passengers died at sea, and 20 infants; which speaks well for the sanitary arrangements of the shipping employed.

The following represents the nationalities of the various immigrants:—

England	910
Ireland	407
Scotland	33
British possessions	59
	1,409
Austria	2,315
Bohemia	1,535
Denmark	293
Germany	21,192
Hungary	740
Norway	243
Poland	112
Russia	2,461
Sweden	743
Other countries, including America	960
	32,003

City extension.

Within the past year the municipal boundaries of Baltimore were extended, by decision of a popular vote, resulting in the addition of some 36,000 inhabitants to the city population, which now stands at 420,000, or—

Whites	354,756
Coloured	65,246

The value of the property in the city, assessed for taxation, amounts to 244,000,000 dol., and the tax rate to 1 dol. 90 c. per 100 dol.

UNITED STATES.

The debt of the city amounts to 37,000,000 dol., which is reduced to a net balance of 9,000,000 dol. by various sources of revenue. Baltimore holds 32,000 shares of the Baltimore and Ohio Railway, of a nominal par value of 100 dol. a share. The failure of this corporation to pay any dividend on their stock for the past year and a half, has seriously crippled the municipal revenue.

Vital statistics. The vital statistics of Baltimore for the past year shows:—

Births	8,867
Marriages	4,390
Divorces	232
Deaths	9,036

showing an excess of deaths over births of 169, and a death rate of 22 per mille.

Annex A.—Return of all Shipping at the Port of Baltimore in the Year 1888.

Entered.

Nationality.	Sailing. Number of Vessels.	Sailing. Tons.	Steam. Number of Vessels.	Steam. Tons.	Total. Number of Vessels.	Total. Tons.
British	28	11,205	324	472,637	352	483,842
American (foreign trade)	129	40,048	...	...	129	40,048
German	13	14,067	53	93,438	66	107,505
Italian	19	11,240	...	...	19	11,240
Swedish and Norwegian	5	3,386	5	3,511	10	6,897
French	...	...	6	11,251	6	11,251
Spanish	...	...	2	4,807	2	4,807
Austrian	1	730	...	...	1	730
Total for 1888	195	80,676	390	585,644	585	666,320
,, ,, 1887	241	110,867	538	781,913	779	892,780
Decrease in 1888	46	30,191	148	196,269	194	226,460

Cleared.

Nationality.	Sailing. Number of Vessels.	Sailing. Tons.	Steam. Number of Vessels.	Steam. Tons.	Total. Number of Vessels.	Total. Tons.
British	29	10,774	321	466,717	350	477,491
American (foreign trade)	149	45,756	...	...	149	45,756
German	13	14,067	53	93,438	66	107,505
Italian	19	11,240	...	...	19	11,240
Swedish and Norwegian	6	4,224	5	3,511	11	7,735
French	...	...	6	11,251	6	11,251
Spanish	...	...	2	4,807	2	4,807
Austrian	1	730	...	...	1	730
Total for 1888	217	86,791	387	579,724	604	666,515
,, ,, 1887	257	102,961	544	792,417	801	895,378
Decrease in 1888	40	16,170	157	212,693	197	228,863

BALTIMORE.

Annex B.—Return of the Principal Articles of Import into Baltimore during the Year 1888.

Articles.		1888.		1887.	
		Quantity.	Value.	Quantity.	Value.
Metals—					
Iron ore	Tons	119,973		401,997	
Pig iron	,,	6,116		53,182	
Speigel iron	,,	3,607		14,618	
Tin plates	Boxes	1,250,560		679,895	
Steel billets	Number	51,668		322,055	
Crop ends	Tons	1,300		10,175	
,, slabs	Number	1,749		87,932	
,, bars	Bundles	...	Total value, 11,862,262 dol. = 2,450,880*l.* 11*s.* 7*d.* sterling, at exchange 4·84. Customs duties collected, 2,773,124 ⁵⁰⁄₁₀₀ dol.	6,094	Total value, 13,055,880 dol. = 2,697,495*l.* 16*s.* sterling, at exchange 4·84.
,, rods and wire	,,	4,690		265,331	
Spelter plates	...	...		31,218	
,, ingots	...	...		9,711	
Rails, old	Tons	...		6,140	
Chemicals	Packages	58,913		31,991	
Salt	Sacks	165,270		100,549	
,,	Tons	13,195		13,718	
,,	Bushels	37,371		70,614	
Agricultural salts	Tons	25,152		...	
,, ,,	Sacks	...		31,918	
Nitrate of soda	Tons	4,850		...	
,, ,,	Bags	...		40,269	
Guano	Tons	3,361		12,896	
Fruit—					
Cocoanuts	Number	2,013,000		1,676,000	
Bananas	Bunches	313,743		555,310	
Pine apples	Dozens	337,636		273,558	
Oranges	Packages	19,026		32,155	
Lemons	Boxes	10,288		20,391	
Coffee	Bags	200,679		197,568	
Whiskey	Barrels	22,110		18,071	
Rice	Packages	70,908		25,230	
Herrings	,,	47,550		25,721	
Hides	Bundles	21,194		25,518	
Brimstone	Tons	15,650		9,922	
Chrome ore	,,	2,728		2,260	

Annex B.—Return of the Principal Articles of Export from Baltimore during the Year 1888.

Articles.		1888.		1887.	
		Quantity.	Value.	Quantity.	Value.
Breadstuffs—					
Wheat	Bushels	4,151,572		10,668,330	
Flour	Barrels	3,015,648		2,790,000	
Corn, maize	Bushels	4,374,640	Total value, 44,892,247 dol. = 9,275,257*l.* 13*s.* sterling, at exchange 4·84.	7,130,230	Total value, 49,563,977 dol. = 10,240,077*l.* 16*s.* sterling, at exchange 4·84.
Provisions—					
Bacon and hams	Lbs.	2,349,047		4,000,383	
Lard	,,	18,865,960		25,501,903	
Canned goods	Cases	164,888		143,000	
Cotton	Bales	173,067		121,597	
Petroleum	Gallons	7,197,281		8,739,334	
Tobacco	Hogsheads	32,526		53,286	
Lumber	Feet	11,883,000		9,508,000	
Staves	Number	2,065,000		3,368,000	
Rosin	Barrels	69,873		63,673	
Coals	Tons	40,283		54,255	
Live stock	Head	23,404		16,527	
Seeds	Bushels	131,734		77,059	
Copper matte	Tons	16,600		...	

Annex C.—TABLE showing the Total Value of all Articles Exported from and Imported into Baltimore to and from Foreign Countries during the Years 1887 and 1888.

Country.	Exports. 1888.	Exports. 1887.	Imports. 1888.	Imports. 1887.
	£	£	£	£
Great Britain	6,100,000	6,365,000	1,850,000	1,600,000
Germany	1,500,000	1,000,000	80,000	90,000
Brazil	300,000	350,000	325,000	500,000
Holland	250,000	933,800	..	60,000
France	550,000	650,000	..	..
Belgium	300,000	650,000	20,000	30,000
Cuba	30,000	50,000	50,000	20,000
Italy	100,000	25,000	55,000	70,000
Spain	..	6,000	50,000	200,000
Other countries	145,257	200,691	20,880	128,903
Total	9,275,257	10,240,491	2,450,880	2,698,903

RICHMOND.

Mr. Vice-Consul Marshall reports as follows:—

Shipping and Navigation.

There has been a considerable increase in the number of British steamers at this port during the year, coming here, to load with cotton in ballast, from United States ports, where they have landed their cargoes. These vessels are all loaded at West Point on the York River, which is within the port and district of Richmond.

The following table shows the movement of shipping at this port, without including the coasting trade in American vessels, and the return as to these vessels represents the entries and clearances to and from foreign ports only:—

RETURN of all Shipping at the Port of Richmond in the Year 1888.

ENTERED.

Nationality.	Sailing. Number of Vessels.	Sailing. Tons.	Steam. Number of Vessels.	Steam. Tons.	Total. Number of Vessels.	Total. Tons.
British	7	3,182	21	32,262	28	35,444
American	5	1,782	...	...	5	1,782
Italian	1	317	...	...	1	317
Spanish	...	...	3	4,718	3	4,718
Norwegian	5	1,622	...	...	5	1,622
Portugal	1	303	...	...	1	303
Sweden	6	1,432	...	...	6	1,432
Total	25	8,638	24	36,980	49	45,618
,, for 1887	...	...	...	...	44	30,094

BALTIMORE.

Cleared.

Nationality.	Sailing. Number of Vessels.	Sailing. Tons.	Steam. Number of Vessels.	Steam. Tons.	Total. Number of Vessels.	Total. Tons.
British	7	3,182	24	36,871	31	40,053
American	7	3,067	1	1,935	8	5,002
Italian	1	317	...	...	1	317
Spanish	...	...	4	6,528	4	6,528
Norwegian	5	1,622	...	...	5	1,622
Portugal	1	303	...	...	1	303
Sweden	8	1,941	...	...	8	1,941
Total	29	10,432	29	45,334	58	55,766
,, for 1887	...	...	...	...	44	30,094

Trade and Commerce.

Return of the Principal Articles of Export from Richmond during the Years 1887 and 1888, calculated at 5 dol. to the £1 sterling.

Exports.

Articles.		1888. Quantity.	1888. Value.	1887. Quantity.	1887. Value.
Cotton	Bales	176,807	Total value of exports, 1,786,246*l*.	80,541	Total value of exports, 848,726*l*.
Flour	Barrels	76,701		108,779	
Tobacco	Lbs.	61,231		33,819	
Lard	,,	10,450		43,483	
Hoops	Bundles	6,232		6,008	

Imports.

Articles.		1888. Quantity.	1888. Value.	1887. Quantity.	1887. Value.
Salt	Sacks & bulk	16,531	Total value of imports, 9,241*l*.	8,500	Total value of imports, 4,104*l*.
Old iron	Lbs.	889,840		10,334	
Potatoes	Bushels	6,000		1,250	
Fish	Barrels	1,692		...	
Guano	Tons	2,000		...	
Plaster	,,	1,795		1,250	

The stock of grain in the elevator on December 26, 1888, was 21,741 bushels of wheat, 27,859 bushels of maize, and 18,348 bushels of oats. *Grain, wheat, and maize.*

No wheat or maize has been exported this year.

All the exports of flour have been to South American markets, and there has been a decrease in the quantity of flour shipped there during this year. *Flour.*

No coffee, sugar, or molasses have been imported this year; merchants supplying themselves with such articles in the northern markets. *Coffee and sugar.*

Dry goods are not imported direct; jobbers make their purchases in New York and other northern cities. *Dry goods.*

UNITED STATES.

Population and Industries.

Flour mills. There are three large flour mills in this city, operated by water power, with a capacity of about 350,000 barrels per annum.

Tobacco. One hundred and twenty-four factories engaged in the manufacture of smoking and chewing tobacco, and of cigars and cigarettes, employing 6,993 hands. The business is increasing, especially that of the manufacture of cigarettes.

Iron industry. The iron industries have been depressed, but an improvement in this industry is looked for soon. There are twenty-three establishments engaged in the iron business, employing 3,054 hands.

Railways. Railway workshops have been generally well employed during the year, and they have had no trouble with their hands.

Cotton factories. There are two cotton mills in the city of Manchester, across the James River, employing 325 hands. They make shirtings, sheetings, &c.

Population. The census returns of the population of the State of Virginia for the year 1883 was 1,513,565. It is now estimated at about 1,550,000.

Immigration. There has been no immigration into this port. Immigrants do not take this route to the West.

Vital statistics. Estimating the population of Richmond at 100,000 persons, the deaths have been 1,833 (850 white, 983 coloured). This is according to the report of the President of the Board of Health.

Building. During the year there have been erected 550 new houses, and for the previous year about the same number, and the city is increasing rapidly in extent and population.

NORFOLK.

Mr. Vice-Consul Myers reports as follows:—

Shipping and Navigation.

There has been a very considerable increase in the number of British steamers at this port during the year.

The following table shows the movement of shipping at this port, without including the coasting trade in American vessels, and the return as to these vessels represents the entries and clearances to and from foreign ports only.

RETURN of all Shipping at the Port of Norfolk in the Year 1888.

ENTERED.

Nationality.	Sailing. Number of Vessels.	Sailing. Tons.	Steam. Number of Vessels.	Steam. Tons.	Total. Number of Vessels.	Total. Tons.
British	29	20,128	171	219,155	200	239,283
American	7	2,670	1	89	8	2,759
German	...	...	7	10,814	7	10,814
Spanish	...	...	15	17,673	15	17,673
Norwegian	3	1,095	1	1,277	4	2,372
Swedish	1	255	...	...	1	255
Italian	7	3,620	2	6,730	9	10,350
Total	47	27,768	197	255,733	244	283,506

BALTIMORE.

CLEARED.

Nationality.	Sailing. Number of Vessels.	Sailing. Tons.	Steam. Number of Vessels.	Steam. Tons.	Total. Number of Vessels.	Total. Tons.
British	32	22,382	172	222,742	204	245,124
American	30	12,714	4	3,747	34	16,461
German	...	...	7	10,814	7	10,814
Spanish	...	...	16	18,106	16	18,106
Norwegian	3	1,095	1	1,277	4	2,372
Swedish	1	255	...	...	1	255
Italian	7	3,620	2	6,730	9	10,350
Total	73	40,066	202	263,416	279	303,482

Trade and Commerce.

Table showing the the principle articles of export and import at this port during the past year.

RETURN of the Principal Articles of Export from Norfolk during the Year 1888, calculated at 5 dol. to the £1 sterling.

Articles.		Quantity.	Value.
Cotton	Bales	264,550	
Staves and heading	Pieces	4,227,480	
Coal	Tons	65,420	
Tobacco	Lbs.	2,398,702	
Corn	Bushels	82,679	
Canned meat	Cases	77	
Copper matte	Tons	210	
Bark extract	..	..	
Oil cake	Sacks	500	Total value of exports, 2,763,277l. 8s.
Specie	Package	1	
W.O. plank	Pieces	2,206	
Spokes	"	11,529	
Paper stock	Bales	325	
Flour	Sacks	4,150	
Bark	Bags	10,393	
Logs	..	2,116	
Persimmon and dog-wood	Tons	30	
	Pieces	18,032	
Cotton-seed meal	Sacks	6,000	
Cattle	Head	602	
Cotton waste	Bales	550	
Rosin	Barrels	4,452	
Boat oars	Crates	201	
Handles	"	8	
Firearms	Packages	6	
Shingles	..	17,000	

UNITED STATES.

RETURN of the Principal Articles of Import in to Norfolk during the Year 1888, calculated at 5 dol. to the 1£ sterling.

Articles.		Quantity.	Value.
Cotton ties	Bundles	4,436	
Jute bagging	Bales	23	
Salt	Tons	3,370	
,,	Sacks	51,114	
Coal	Tons	120	Total value of imports, 15,021*l.*
Mineral water	Cases	250	
Guano	Bags	3,395	
Bananas	Bunches	10,993	
Pineapples	Dozen	1,000	
Laths		80,200	
Kainit	Tons	3,827	
Rubber	Bales	3	
Tea	Chests	2	
Wine	Cases	5	

Dry goods are not imported here to any extent, as the jobbing houses usually make their purchases in the New York market.

Several railways are under construction to this port, and will no doubt contribute considerably to its commerce.

The coastwise lumber trade in yellow pine has been steadily on the increase, and the mills are taxed to their full capacity.

NEWPORT NEWS.

Mr. Vice-Consul Warburton reports as follows:—

Report due for 1887 not forwarded. The report due for 1887 was not forwarded in consequence of the absence of the Vice-Consul in England, and his return at too late a period of the year. The exports and imports for that year, as well as the shipping returns are, however, given in the usual tables.

Increase of population. Insanitary condition of Newport News. The population has, it is said, increased to 2,500, and there is still no drainage and no hospital; in consequence of the absence of the latter, sick seamen have to be sent to Norfolk for treatment. The absence of the former is probably the cause of the great sickness and mortality of last year. The usual malarial fever developed into typhoid, of whice I understand there were 400 cases, with 35 or 40 deaths: a proportioy to the number of inhabitants little, if any, in excess of that which ih Florida spread such consternation not only in that State, but in thn country at large; the difference however being that in the latter casn the disease was "yellow fever," a name which to those who have noe lived in the West Indies or in countries where it is prevalent, carries with it terrors which go far to increase its destructive power.

Causes of the unhealthy condition of the port. I attribute the unhealthy condition of this port, apart from the malaria generated by the surrounding marshes and undrained woodlands, to the fact that the water supply is derived from a depth of 25 to 30 feet, and that it consists entirely of surface water which percolates easily through the sandy soil, carrying with it the impurities which it absorbs on the surface, until arrested by a thin bed of clay which forms a reservoir from whence the supply is drawn. The winter months— November, December, January, and a part of February—are tolerably free from malaria, but during the remainder of the year the latter is prevalent to an alarming degree, and few of the inhabitants are free from its attacks.

The dry dock completed. The dry dock alluded to in a former report has been almost completed, and will be opened in the spring. It is a very creditable piece of work, and capable of taking in the largest vessel afloat. I understand that it is in contemplation to move to the vicinity of the dry dock the Newburg iron works from New York State, for the purpose of building and repairing ships. As to the former, the general condition of the American iron ship building trade does not promise much success, or warrant great expectations from this venture. <small>Expectations formed of it.</small>

The coal, iron ore, and raw iron have to be transported at least 400 miles, which greatly increases their cost. I think it probable that, at no distant date, the growing national discontent at the almost total loss of the foreign carrying trade will accelerate, and bring to a successful issue the movement now on foot to legalise the purchase, and use under the United States flag, of foreign built ships, in which case a severe blow will be sustained by the languishing iron shipbuilding interest in this country, and as far as shipbuilding is concerned, there will be little demand for the dry dock. Even under the stringent protection now afforded to that industry it seems incapable of much vitality, as the results of the contract work on the United States war vessels seem to indicate. <small>National discontent at the loss of carrying trade caused by the navigation laws. Languishing condition of the iron shipbuilding trade.</small>

The condition of the labourer is not better in this section of the country than it is in England, and in most parts it is worse. It is true he receives higher wages—the average for unskilled labour being about 5s. a day—but his employment is less continuous. He has to pay double for clothing and bread, and 50 per cent. higher for every article of consumption except meat, than in the United Kingdom. His house rent is 150 per cent. higher than at home, and many of the comforts of civilisation do not exist for him at all. I have constant applications made to me for assistance by my fellow countrymen who have been induced to come to this port by glowing accounts of its prosperity and of the great demand for labour. Most of them are striken down with malarial fever, and a great part of the time are unable to work, and when they are able, can obtain no employment. Some of the prices ruling here for provisions are as follows:—Bread, 2½d. per lb. loaf; sugar, 4½d. per lb.; meat of bad quality, 6½d. per lb.; potatoes, 5s. per bushel; vegetables, three times the cost at home, and very few of them to be obtained at all; tea, of inferior description, 3s. per lb.; coffee, 1s. 3d. per lb. A small wooden house of the most flimsy, unseasoned material, with badly fitting doors and windows, two floors, and 18 feet by 24 feet, rents for 30l. a year in this town. It may however be remarked that prices here are generally 25 per cent. greater than in the neighbouring towns. <small>Condition of the labourer. Great cost of living. Some prices ruling here for necessaries.</small>

There is a national quarantine established at the entrance of Hampton Roads, which renders the local quarantine superfluous; but it supplies a piece of patronage at the expense of foreign vessels entering the port. <small>National quarantine.</small>

In consequence of the amalgamation of a number of railroads, south of Virginia, under the West Point Terminal Company, their terminus at the head of York River, about 50 miles from the entrance of the Chesapeake, is assuming considerable proportions as a cotton port; but the channel is narrow and difficult of navigation, while the water is not so deep as it is represented to be: 19 feet being the utmost that a large vessel can safely reckon on. <small>West Point. The channel narrow and shallow.</small>

Herewith I enclose a table of the British vessels entering and clearing; also of the vessels of all nationalities entering and clearing foreign; and one of the exports. The latter show a falling off of 33½ per cent. in the year 1887, and of 9½ per cent. in 1886.

The imports amount to only 17,768l. for 1888, whereas in 1887 they exceeded 60,000l.

UNITED STATES.

Vessels of all Nationalities Entering Foreign.

Nationality.	Sailing. Number of Vessels.	Sailing. Tons.	Steam. Number of Vessels.	Steam. Tons.	Total. Number of Vessels.	Total. Tons.
British	4	1,188	28	39,518	32	40,706
American (U.S.)	1	521	...	...	1	521
German	...	...	1	1,201	1	1,201
Spanish	...	...	5	6,291	5	6,291
Total	5	1,709	34	47,010	39	48,719

Vessels of all Nationalities Clearing Foreign.

Nationality.	Sailing. Number of Vessels.	Sailing. Tons.	Steam. Number of Vessels.	Steam. Tons.	Total. Number of Vessels.	Total. Tons.
British	4	1,324	229	288,225	233	289,549
American (U.S.)	5	2,130	25	44,996	30	47,126
German	...	...	16	20,606	16	20,606
Spanish	1	500	23	33,451	24	33,951
Italian	7	3,666	1	3,365	8	7,031
French	...	...	3	4,670	3	4,670
Belgian	...	...	3	3,174	3	3,174
Portuguese	...	...	1	964	1	964
Mexican	...	...	1	824	1	824
Total	17	7,610	302	400,265	319	407,875

Exports for 1886, 1887, and 1888.

Articles.	1888. Quantity.	1888. Value. £	1887. Quantity.	1887. Value. £	1886. Quantity.	1886. Value. £	Quantities.
Coal	38,505	25,100	40,083	26,500	73,570	50,000	Tons
Wheat	322,309	58,700	1,627,799	250,000	1,680,006	265,000	Bushels
Flour	...	101,500	...	120,500	...	56,863	Casks and sacks
Bacon, lard, &c.	...	39,000	...	75,000	...	16,200	Various
Lumber and staves	...	118,000	...	65,000	...	53,000	Logs, staves, sawn timber
Indian corn	421,912	48,000	484,181	49,000	1,004,572	290,000	Bushels
Cotton	71,290	694,000	96,729	960,000	56,715	591,000	Bales
Tobacco	6,798,038	100,800	18,506,065	273,000	None this year.		Lbs.
Cattle	1,482	32,800	1,636	28,000	None this year.		Head
Sundries	...	6,500	8,600	8,600	...	22,000	...
Total value	...	1,224,900	...	1,856,100	...	1,343,263	...

Number and Tonnage of British Vessels Entering and Clearing.

Year.	Entered. Number of Vessels.	Entered. Tons.	Cleared. Number of Vessels.	Cleared. Tons.
1886	200	217,282	199	215,288
1887	209	339,396	259	339,396
1888	249	311,167	249	311,167

(1125 3 | 89—H & S 582)

//
FOREIGN OFFICE.
1889.
ANNUAL SERIES.

N°. 464.

DIPLOMATIC AND CONSULAR REPORTS ON TRADE AND FINANCE.

UNITED STATES.

REPORT FOR THE YEARS 1887-88
ON THE
TRADE OF THE CONSULAR DISTRICT OF PHILADELPHIA.

REFERENCE TO PREVIOUS REPORT, Annual Series No. 177.

Presented to both Houses of Parliament by Command of Her Majesty,
MARCH, 1889.

LONDON:
PRINTED FOR HER MAJESTY'S STATIONERY OFFICE,
BY HARRISON AND SONS, ST. MARTIN'S LANE,
PRINTERS IN ORDINARY TO HER MAJESTY.

And to be purchased, either directly or through any Bookseller, from
EYRE AND SPOTTISWOODE, EAST HARDING STREET, FLEET STREET, E.C., and
32, ABINGDON STREET, WESTMINSTER, S.W.; or
ADAM AND CHARLES BLACK, 6, NORTH BRIDGE, EDINBURGH; or
HODGES, FIGGIS, & Co., 104, GRAFTON STREET, DUBLIN.

1889.

[C. 5618—17.]   *Price Twopence.*

New Series of Reports.

Reports of the Annual Series have been issued from Her Majesty's Diplomatic and Consular Officers at the following places, and may be obtained from the sources indicated on the title-page:—

No.		Price.	No.		Price.
348.	Bussorah	1d.	406.	Adana	1d.
349.	Mollendo	1d.	407.	Valparaiso	1d.
350.	Cadiz	5d.	408.	Bilbao	1d.
351.	Cagliari	4d.	409.	Santiago	1d.
352.	Cagliari	1d.	410.	Paramaribo	1d.
353.	Ajaccio	1d.	411.	Nantes	1d.
354.	Copenhagen	1d.	412.	Bangkok	1d.
355.	Vienna	1d.	413.	Yokohama	2d.
356.	San Francisco	1d.	414.	Mozambique	1d.
357.	Vera Cruz	1d.	415.	Canton	2d.
358.	Philippopolis	1d.	416.	Kiungchow	1d.
359.	Greytown	1d.	417.	Damascus	1d.
360.	Tangier	1d.	418.	Syra	1d.
361.	Lisbon	1d.	419.	Aleppo	1d.
362.	Chicago	1d.	420.	Sandakan	1d.
363.	Jerusalem and Jaffa	1d.	421.	Barcelona	1d.
364.	Truxillo	1d.	422.	Königsberg	1d.
365.	Ningpo	1d.	423.	Tabreez	1d.
366.	Chefoo	1d.	424.	Guayaquil	1d.
367.	Bushire	1d.	425.	St. Petersburg	1d.
368.	Stockholm	2d.	426.	Tokio	1d.
369.	Santiago	1d.	427.	Charleston	1d.
370.	New York	2d.	428.	Amsterdam	1d.
371.	Pernambuco	1d.	429.	Hamburg	4d.
372.	Söul	1d.	430.	Trieste	1d.
373.	Chinkiang	2d.	431.	New York	2d.
374.	Pernambuco	1d.	432.	Antwerp	1d.
375.	San Francisco	2d.	433.	Munich	1d.
376.	Riga	1d.	434.	Buenos Ayres	1d.
377.	Newchwang	2d.	435.	Warsaw	1d.
378.	San Salvador	1d.	436.	Porto Rico	1d.
379.	Frankfort	2d.	437.	Réunion	1d.
380.	Hankow	2d.	438.	Lisbon	1d.
381.	Bucharest	1d.	439.	Venice	1d.
382.	Lisbon	1d.	440.	Christiania	5d.
383.	Tunis	1d.	441.	Maranham	1d.
384.	Tangier	1d.	442.	Sofia	1d.
385.	Santiago	2d.	443.	Copenhagen	1d.
386.	Diarbekir	1d.	444.	Galatz	1d.
387.	Shanghai	2d.	445.	Tabreez	1d.
388.	Rome	2d.	446.	Bogotá	2d.
389.	Buenos Ayres	1d.	447.	St. Petersburg	3d.
390.	Amsterdam	1d.	448.	Nice	1d.
391.	Warsaw	1d.	449.	Stettin	2d.
392.	San Francisco	1d.	450.	Fiume	1d.
393.	Alexandria	1d.	451.	Chinkiang	1d.
394.	Salonica	2d.	452.	The Hague	1d.
395.	Palmero	1d.	453.	Malaga	1d.
396.	Mexico	4d.	454.	Taganrog	1d.
397.	Naples	3d.	455.	Mozambique	1d.
398.	Boston	1d.	456.	Bagotá	2d.
399.	Hakodate	1d.	457.	Patras	1d.
400.	Nantes	1d.	458.	Galveston	1d.
401.	Madeira	1d.	459.	Buda Pesth	1d.
402.	Hakodate	1d.	460.	Madeira	1d.
403.	Nagasaki	1d.	461.	Warsaw	1d.
404.	Hiogo	2d.	462.	Paris	2d.
405.	Tonga	1d.	463.	Baltimore	1d.

No. 464.

Reference to previous Report, Annual Series No. 177.

UNITED STATES.

PHILADELPHIA.

Consul Clipperton to the Marquis of Salisbury.

My Lord, *Philadelphia, February* 9, 1889.

I HAVE the honour to enclose herewith a Report on the Trade and Commerce of Philadelphia during the years 1887 and 1888.

I have, &c.
(Signed)   ROBT. CHAS. CLIPPERTON.

Report on the Trade, Commerce, and Manufactures of the Consular District of Pennslyvannia, Ohio, Indiana, and Michigan for the Years 1887 *and* 1888.

Pennsylvania. The prosperity of this State continues in population, industries, railways, and mines. The population of the whole State will aggregate 5,000,000. Agriculture has advanced and the mining output has increased, and the State retains its position in the front rank as producers of coal and iron. New territory for the production of oil and natural gas has been discovered; the growth of the railway system, although checked in some districts, has been healthy and vigorous in most sections, and industrial thrift has been but slightly retarded by labour strikes and lockouts. The smaller cities and towns have shown a healthy growth, and but little lawlessness has prevailed. The public debt has been reduced from 17,258,921 dol. (3,451,784*l.*) to 14,738,921 dol. (2,947,784*l.*) in two years, which is a gain of more than 2,500,000 dol. The public school system of the State is based on the highest order of public education, and from year to year new branches of industrial instruction are gradually introduced. The commonwealth recognises the principle that if the State accepts the position of the family instructor it should fulfil the family's obligations, and teach the pupils how to earn a living as well as how to read and write.

Child insurance. The selfish greed of parents and others in effecting insurance on the lives of children, and the grave abuses that have recently ensued, have attracted public attention, and the governor recommends the passage of an Act prohibiting life insurance on children under 16 years of age

Shipping and navigation. Shipping at the port of Philadelphia has fallen off during the year 1888. The number and tonnage of British ships for 1887 were— entrances 675, tonnage 804,055; while during 1888 there were— entrances 603, tonnage 682,777, showing a falling off of 72 entrances and in tonnage of 122,278 tons. The foreign trade in American

(583)

vessels for 1887 stood: entrances 330, tonnage 179,193; clearances 228, tonnage 152,604. For 1888 the entrances were 382, with a tonnage of 189,523; and in clearances 247 vessels, with a tonnage of 142,610. The total trade in ships of all nations, except British and American, for 1887 foot up: vessels entered 372, tonnage 321,848; for the year 1888 vessels entered 256, tonnage 218,110. The American coasting trade for 1887 was carried on in 4,414 vessels of all classes, steamers and all small sailing craft; and in 1888 the number was 3,997. This trade is not open to foreign flags. The arrivals at the Delaware breakwater were: for orders, 16 steamers, 12 ships, 86 barques, 34 brigs, 41 schooners, total 189; for harbour, 71 steamers, 33 ships, 250 barques, 79 brigs, 5,079 schooners, total 5,512; in distress, 4 steamers, 2 ships, 5 barques, 3 brigs, and 36 schooners, total 50; grand total 5,751.

Harbour. — The harbour of Philadelphia bids fair to be transferred into one of first-class size, depth of water, and superiority of docks. It is contemplated to have removed two islands known as Smith's and Windmill, and part of Petty's island, situated in the middle of the River Delaware. With this improvement Philadelphia will command the commerce rightfully and naturally belonging to a first-class city with a deep river front. These improvements will include a channel from the upper end of the city to Delaware Bay 600 feet wide and 26 feet deep at mean low water, a distance of 100 miles. The entire cost of this work when completed will exceed 6,000,000 dol. (1,200,000*l*.).

The Shipping of all Nations at Philadelphia.

Nationality.	Year.	Number of Ships.	Tonnage.
American	1887	330	179,103
,,	1888	382	189,523
Austrian	1887	11	7,599
,,	1888	8	6,261
Belgian	1887	16	32,382
,,	1888	16	34,407
Chilian	1887	..	..
British	1887	675	804,055
,,	1888	603	682,777
German	1887	75	83,933
,,	1888	45	46,568
Italian	1887	102	67,845
,,	1888	65	41,942
Norwegian	1887	143	117,091
,,	1888	84	54,432
Russian	1887	8	6,356
,,	1888	2	1,304
Swedish	1887	16	11,931
,,	1888	5	4,535
Portuguese	1887	1	585
,,	1888	10	4,962
Danish	1887	1	1,129
,,	1888	1	228
Dutch	1887	7	7,559
,,	1888	5	5,411
Spanish	1887	16	16,328
,,	1888	9	9,717
French	1887	3	4,049
,,	1888	6	8,343

The above figures are the entrances. Clearances to foreign countries represent a smaller number, because many vessels enter this port from other countries, discharge their cargoes, and depart for different American ports to load for Europe, and are in consequence included in the official tables of the foreign trade.

The loss to Philadelphia shipping interests by stress of weather during the past year has been very great, both to life and property. Eleven vessels either bound to or from Philadelphia, or owned at this port, have foundered, with 118 lives sacrificed, and nine more ships were wrecked without loss of life. The value of the vessels and cargoes wrecked amounts to 850,000 dol. (170,000*l*.), and the distress to the families of the wrecked crews has been very severe. *Casualties.*

The imports for the whole United States for the year ending June 30, 1887, were 602,319,768 dol., as follows :—In cars and other land vehicles, 27,562,059 dol.; in American vessels, 121,365,493 dol.; in foreign vessels, 543,392,216 dol.; and the exports were 716,183,211 dol., as follows : 21,389,666 dol. in cars, &c.; 72,991,253 dol. in American vessels; and 621,802,292 dol. in foreign vessels. *Imports and exports.*

For the year ending June 30, 1888, the total imports were 723,957,114 dol., as follows :—By cars and other land vehicles, 32,209,459 dol.; in American vessels, 123,525,298 dol.; and in foreign vessels, 568,222,357 dol. The total exports were 695,954,507 dol., as follows :—In vehicles, &c., 22,147,368 dol.; in American vessels, 67,332,175 dol.; and in foreign vessels, 606,474,964 dol. The imports and exports at Philadelphia were, 1887, imports, 39,572,398 dol., as follows :—In American vessels, 6,907,665 dol.; and in foreign vessels, 33,664,733 dol.; total free of duty, 5,708,871 dol.; total subject to duty, 33,863,527 dol. Exports, 33,813,024 dol., as follows : — In American steam vessels, 1,711,297 dol.; in American sailing vessels, 2,246,640 dol.; in foreign steam vessels, 19,900,716 dol.; and in foreign sailing vessels, 9,954,371 dol.; and in 1888, imports, 45,020,145 dol.; exports, 28,012,879. dol. The duties paid into the United States custom-house in 1887 amounted to 17,950,235 dol. 10 c.; and in 1888 they were 20,613,738 dol. The shipping engaged in this vast trade was chiefly foreign, the British flag having by great odds the bulk of the carrying trade.

This industry has been active on the River Delaware during the past year. The Messrs. William Cramp and Sons, now the leading shipbuilders in America, completed two iron steamships of 4,237 tons in the aggregate, and in 1888 one iron steam vessel of 1,440 tons and one steel steam vessel of 2,943 tons, and have commenced the construction of five steel and three iron steamships of 24,000 tons, all told, and nine marine engines; indicating, all told, a total of 45,000 horse-power. This firm also constructed in 1888 two Driggs-Schroeder rapid-firing guns, one a three-pounder and one a six-pounder. They are now engaged on four pneumatic dynamite guns of 15 inches bore each, three for the United States Government steamship " Vesuvius," and one sea-coast defence gun for Spezia, Italy. *Iron shipbuilding.*

The Messrs. Pusey and Jones, shipbuilders, constructed five iron steamers and three steel steamers of various sizes in 1887, and two steamers, one composite and one steel, in the year 1888.

The Delaware River Iron Shipbuilding Works constructed six iron steamers during the two years. A number of boats of small dimensions were also constructed in the minor yards on the Delaware.

Special interest is attached by naval officers to the new cast-steel gun made by the Standard Steel Company, on the River Delaware, because of the recent bursting of the 6-inch rifled steel gun made at *Test of a great gun.*

(583)

UNITED STATES.

Pittsburgh, Pennsylvania. This new gun is a 6-inch rifled cannon, of open hearth steel. The weight of the barrel is 11,800 lbs., and when completed the entire gun will weigh 15,000 lbs. In the process of boring and rifling no globular spaces or "chambers" were found in the barrel, such as were found in the bursted gun. The test to be tried in a short time will demonstrate the truth or falsity of the opinion held by many gun experts that cast steel has not resisting power sufficient to withstand the service charge. The steel is the very best procurable for such a piece of work, and special attention was paid to its cooling, so that no small globular spaces could creep in and weaken the metal.

Wages of seamen. By reference to the last report from this Consulate (Foreign Office Annual Series, No. 177 of the year 1887) a full statement as to wages of seamen, the American law bearing thereon, and the latest legal decisions in Consular Courts will be found. The wages at present are as follows:—

To the United Kingdom and Continent north of Bayonne	25 dol. per month,	with 35 dol. adv.
Continent south of Bayonne to Gibraltar	20 ,, ,,	,, 30 ,, ,,
To the Mediterranean	18 ,, ,,	,, 30 ,, ,,
Around Cape Horn and Cape of Good Hope	16 ,, ,,	,, 40 ,, ,,
To South America	18 ,, ,,	,, 20 ,, ,,
To West Indies	20 ,, ,,	,, 20 ,, ,,

Immigration. The number of persons arriving at the port of Philadelphia for the year ending June 30, 1887, was 36,689, and passengers, not immigrants, 2,784; and for 1888 the immigrants numbered 39,433, of whom 95 were stowaways. Of this number 2,415 were citizens of the United States and non-immigrants. The nativity of the 37,018 immigrants was as follows:—

Ireland	7,987
England	10,903
Wales	481
Scotland	3,378
Germany	5,955
France	293
Russia	674
Poland	1,448
Switzerland	32
Sweden	2,992
Norway	1,612
Belgium	345
Holland	155
Italy	87
Spain	4
Denmark	127
Hungary	80
Austria	157
Greece	29
All other countries	259
Unknown	20
	37,018

Of this number (37,018) 22,132, or 59·82 per cent., were males, and 14,865, or 40·18 per cent., were females. The sex of 21 not reported. There were 1,187 worthy persons who needed assistance, and were temporarily relieved during the year 1888. The nationality of those relieved were as follows:—

Irish ..	..	..	..	..	..	..	484
English	..	..	..	..	..	..	572
Germans	..	..	..	..	..	..	29
Swedes	..	..	..	..	..	..	31
Poles ..	..	...	..	..	..	..	14
Welsh..	..	..	..	..	..	..	5
Scotch	..	..	..	..	..	..	8
Russians	..	..	..	..	..	..	19
Norwegians ..	..	..	..	..	..	..	10
Hungarians ..	..	..	..	..	..	..	15
							1,187

No convicts or lunatics were found on any of the ships during the year. There were 89 of these immigrants returned to Europe in 1888, not being permitted to land; 2 were old women, 2 old men, 4 crippled, 2 little girls, 1 boy, 1 *enceinte*, 10 stowaways, 67 incapacitated from labour, 4 from weak minds, and 55 physically unable to support themselves.

The demurrage and lay-day scales. The demurrage and lay-day scales at the port of Philadelphia, approved in 1882 and reported in detail from this Consulate (Foreign Office No. 177) last year, are still in operation. The rates of pilotage for Delaware river and bay reported in the paper above quoted are still in practice.

The United States Navy-yard at League Island, a few miles below this port, on the River Delaware, is destined to be one of the finest Government shipyards in the world. A great feature will be the basin, with a feeding canal from the Delaware River 1,350 feet long, 650 feet wide, and depth of water to accommodate eight ships of the largest dimensions. Floatage for 28 great war-ships can be had. The fresh water will not rust the iron and steel of the naval ships when lying there, and they will be free from attack by the most powerful ordnance. Massive buildings and workshops are to be constructed. The quay wall on the river front will be 400 feet inside the port warden's line, and will cover the front of other proposed improvements a length of half a mile. The officers' quarters will be erected of brick and stone, and have a liberal allowance of ground in front as a park. The costs of these contemplated structures and docks will largely exceed 1,000,000*l*.

Trade and commerce. The receipts of flour at this port in 1887 were 1,372,344 barrels, in 1888 they were 1,319,163; wheat in 1887 were 9,270,861 bushels, in 1888 they were 2,555,600; corn in 1887 were 4,033,000 bushels, in 1888 2,973,900 bushels; oats in 1887 were 3,915,200 bushels, in 1888 4,662,750 bushels; barley in 1887 792,400, in 1888 1,283,400 bushels; wool in 1887 176,842 bales, in 1888 188,509 bales; cotton in 1887 122,740 bales, in 1888 85,941 bales; lard in 1887 61,552 packages, in 1888 48,544 packages; pork in 1887 6,845 barrels; petroleum (crude) in 1887 696,646 barrels, in 1888 485,039 barrels; petroleum (refined) in 1887 330,991 barrels, in 1888 424,764 barrels; butter in 1887 367,367 packages, in 1888 362,044 packages; cheese in 1887 228,711 boxes, in 1888 243,876 boxes; eggs in 1887 499,041 cases, in 1888, 489,193 cases; tobacco leaf in 1887 37,671 hogsheads, in 1888 29,120 hogsheads; tobacco manufactured 1887 in boxes 136,757, in 1888 131,444; whiskey in 1887 44,712 barrels, in 1888 37,959 barrels.

The falling-off in the grain trade is very marked. The receipts of wheat as per Consular report for 1886 were 6,289,611 bushels, showing a decrease for the year 1888 of 3,590,111 bushels. The total value of exports of breadstuffs for the whole country for the 11 months ended November 30, 1888, was 100,622,453 dol. (20,122,290*l*.); while for the corresponding period of 1887 the figures were 148,019,669 dol., showing a decline of nearly 50,000,000 dol. (10,000,000*l.*). It is particularly noticeable that this decline has taken place while the demand of the wheat-importing sections of Europe has increased by reason of partial failures of their crops. This heavy decline in the wheat market of America can be attributed to the "cornering" of grain by the Chicago speculators in running prices from 82 c. per bushel to 1 dol. 49½ c., and so forcing European consumers to go to Russia, India, Australia, and other regions for their supplies of bread.

Railways. The mercantile interests of Philadelphia appear to have been sadly neglected by the trunk railway lines, and notably by the Pennsylvania Railroad Company. At least this is the opinion that prevails in all mercantile circles of this port, and the general public endorse this opinion. A few years ago New York found that their export trade was disastrously declining, while the trade of other ports was increasing. The commercial bodies sent committees to wait upon the New York Central Railroad, and that company pledged themselves to stand by New York city at all odds. Rates to New York were lowered and the export trade returned. The merchants of Baltimore adopted the same course. In 1881, when their commerce suffered, they appealed to the railroad powers and obtained fair and equitable treatment. The Pennsylvania Railroad has promised time and again to build up Philadelphia's trade at all hazards, but it is a notorious fact that that company has failed to do so.

The exports of wheat and corn from this port were as follows for the years 1880, 1885, 1887, and 1888:—

	1880.	1885.	1887.	1888.
	Bushels.	Bushels.	Bushels.	Bushels.
Wheat..	11,312,590	3,532,192	8,317,164	1,371,609
Corn ..	16,579,644	5,929,244	2,286,258	817,169
Total..	27,892,234	9,461,436	10,603,422	2,188,778

Failures. The year 1888 has not been one of unbroken prosperity. Although there has been no widespread epidemic of failures, the number has exceeded the failures of 1887 by 676, while it was 152 less than those of 1886. Business has been unsettled and spasmodic, caused in the main by the excitement of a Presidential election, by the agitation of the tariff issue, the outbreak of a "war of rates" that included every railroad in the country, by a "corner" in wheat that stopped the export trade, by the reduction in dividends on the stock of corporations, and also very largely by the impairment of foreign confidence in American securities. Stock speculations have been at a low ebb, and the sales at the stock exchanges show a falling-off in the sales of stocks as compared with the transactions of former years. In breadstuffs there have been periods of greater speculative activity, and the manipulation of a Chicago operator, aided by a short crop, ran up the prices to the highest of figures in a number of years, causing for a time a complete cessation of exports from the Atlantic ports. Money, however, has been as a general rule plentiful at easy rates, and the banks have held an ample surplus of cash. The accumulation of currency in the Treasury of the United States has been checked, and the dangers likely to result from it have been avoided by the purchase of Government bonds by the Secretary of the Treasury, and the deposit of public moneys in the national banks. Legitimate trade has been of fair proportions, and in several branches, as for instance the coal trade, exceptionally active. The year, however, has not been as satisfactory as was expected and calculated upon, but the close of 1888 promises better for the year 1889. The railroad magnates have, for the time being at least, ceased their quarrels, and the prospects for more stable and profitable rates are good. Investors have come to the rescue of their properties, and there is a prospect of better railway management. The manufacturers are happy in the assurance of a high protective tariff for four years at least.

The following statement of the production of pig-iron in the United States, in 1888, shows that the furnaces of 25 States and territories turned out 7,269,628 net tons, as compared with 7,187,206 tons in 1887. Of this amount 598,789 tons was charcoal pig-iron, 4,745,110 tons bituminous coal and coke iron, and 1,925,729 tons anthracite and coke iron. The latter shows a decrease since 1887 of about 400,000 tons, while the two others show an increase. On December 31, 1888, of 189 anthracite furnaces 84 were out of blast; of 162 charcoal furnaces, 91 were out of blast; and of 238 bituminous furnaces, 81 were out of blast. The statement of unsold stocks on hand at the close of the year shows 336,142 tons unsold on December 31, 1887.

Iron and steel.

The production of Bessemer pig-iron in 1888 amounted to 2,958,836 net tons. In production for 1888 Pennsylvania, New York, New Jersey, Maryland, Wisconsin, Missouri, Connecticut, North Carolina, Georgia, Michigan, and Colorado show a decline. The other producing States show an increase, most notably so Alabama, Ohio, Tennessee, and Virginia. The production in 1888 was the largest in the history of the country. The following figures exhibit the production for a period of years:—

Year.	Tons.
1881	4,144,254
1882	4,623,323
1883	4,595,510
1884	4,097,868
1885	4,044,526
1886	5,683,329
1887	6,417,148
1888	6,490,739

The production in nine of the Southern States was, in 1885, 712,835 tons; in 1886, 875,179 tons; in 1887, 929,436 tons; and in 1888, 1,132,858 tons.

Prices of manufactured iron have kept well in line with pig iron, the highest having been realised during January, and the lowest during May and June of last year. The demand has been fairly steady, and the year 1888 has ended satisfactorily to the manufacturers. Prices were low and the margins for profit small, but with full employment during the greater part of the year; cost of production has been at a minimum, offsetting, in some measure, the extremely low prices obtained for a large proportion of the product. One reason for the low prices has been the aggressive attitude of some of the large steel companies. Steel plates have been sold from Pittsburgh at much lower prices than local mills could accept, and business during the entire year has been more or less under the influence of quotations from that source. The consumption of finished iron was very large during the year, probably the largest on record. All departments have had a good run of trade, and the prospect for the coming year is equally favourable. The demand is well distributed, car, locomotive, bridge, and ship builders having had plenty of orders, while the smaller industries are now busier than they have been for a long time. There has been a shrinkage in the prices of finished iron, averaging about 3 dol. (12s.) per ton. Car builders have been the heaviest buyers of bar iron, and wrought-iron pipe manufacturers have also taken a large amount of skelp. The plate mills have also been fully employed, but prices were kept up with difficulty, in consequence of a spirited competition. The highest prices were during January, 1887, viz.: bars and grooved skelp, 1 dol. 95 c., and plates 2 dol. 15 c., while they drooped during the summer, and were unsettled for the remainder of the year. The present asking prices are 1 dol. 8 c. to 1 dol. 9 c. for bars, 1 dol. 85 c. to 1 dol. 87½ c. for skelp, and 2 dol. to 2 dol. 1 c. per lb. for both plates and angles.

In steel rails the year 1888 was one of the most satisfactory ever experienced by the manufacturers. Prices opened in January at 29 dol. 50 c. per ton, and remained on that basis until June, when they reached 30 dol.; fell to 29 dol. in August, 28 dol. 50 c. in September, and to 27 dol. 50 c. in November, with some transactions at less than 27 dol. As an offsett to the falling in production the demand for steel in other forms has greatly increased, some of the mills disposing of from 35 to 30 per cent. of their product in this way. The outlook for 1889 is uncertain; the orders now in for 1889 delivery are many of them under those of the previous year. Some of the works are closed for an indefinite period, and the chances do not appear to be very favourable for an early resumption; but this depends much upon the continued amicable arrangements of the railways. Old T rails have been scarce, and the prices ranged from 21 dol. per ton to 24 dol. in different months of the year. The stocks are lighter than have been known for many years, and it is a remarkable coincidence that old iron rails sell within 4 or 5 dol. per ton of the price of new steel rails.

In Pittsburgh, Pennsylvania, the great iron centre, there has probably never been a larger volume of business, but owing to active competition margins have been comparatively small. There have been very few failures among the manufacturers, and they never were perhaps in a more solid condition. At the close of the year an unexpected break in the pig-iron market occurred, and all grades of mill and foundry irons went off 25 to 50 c. per ton within two weeks. Quotations may fairly be given as follows:—

	Dol. c.		Dol. c.	
Neutral grey forge	15 50	to	15 75	cash
All ore mill	16 25		16 50	,,
No. 1 foundry	17 50		17 75	,,
No. 2 foundry	16 75		17 00	,,
No. 3 foundry	16 00		16 25	,,
No. 1 charcoal foundry	—		—	
No. 2 charcoal foundry	25 00		28 00	,,
Cold blast charcoal	25 00		28 00	,,
Bessemer iron	17 00			,,

For muck bar prices continue weak; quantities are offered at 28 dol. 50 c. cash, and it may possibly be had for 28 dol., while the sellers greatly outnumber the buyers. Ferro-manganese, 80 per cent., 55 dol. to 56 dol. per ton; spiegel, 20 per cent., 28 dol. to 28 dol. 50 c.

The total production of bessemer steel rails in the whole country in the years 1887 and 1888, not including a few thousand tons rolled by iron rolling mills from purchased steel blooms, but including all rails rolled by Bessemer steel works, was:—

States.	1887	1888
	Net Tons.	Net Tons.
Pennsylvania	1,221,289	911,206
Illinois	728,606	485,706
Other States ..	340,382	131,145

The total production of steel rails in 1888 by the works mentioned above was 1,528,057 net tons—1,364,337 gross against 2,290,117 net, or 2,044,819 gross tons in 1887—a decrease in 1888 of 640,482 gross tons, a shrinkage which is greater than the total production of steel rails in 1879 when 610,682 gross tons were made. The consumption of steel rails in 1888 was fully 750,000 gross tons less than in 1887, the imports in 1888 having declined about 77,000 tons as compared with 1887. In 1887 they amounted to 137,588 gross tons, and in 1888 to about 60,000 gross tons for the whole country.

Railways.

In the year 1887 the railways throughout the country laid out 15,000 miles of new track, and the whole work was finished in the early part of 1888. This addition of new track represents 90,000,000*l.*, a vast sum placed in active circulation for material and labour to return in dividends and interest on bonds. But these expenditures are but a small part of the work and only a part of the expense. The "ballasting up" and "rounding out" of the skeleton of the creation is an equally important work. There must be locomotives and rolling stock, repairing shops, straightening of curves, reducing of grades, building of switches, sidings, depôts, and storehouses to an extent almost equalling the first expenditure of labour and money.

Of this great addition in railway building, a large portion has been laid through the Western wilderness in advance of natural need for them, and railway managers resort to the cutting of rates and all kinds of competition to build up their trade. This evil system has a vast deal to do, especially in the Western States, with preventing the business of railroading being put upon the same legitimate and reasonably honest basis of other business enterprises. Mr. Charles Francis Adams, a leading executive officer of one of the most important railway systems in the country, and a railroad specialist, decries against this lack of conscience and absence of any high standard of commercial honour among the railroad managers, especially those in the Western States, who, he asserts, are notorious "for an utter disregard of those fundamental ideas of truth, fair play, and fair dealing which lie at the foundation not only of Christian faith, but of civilisation itself." The evasion of laws by secret rates and rebates and "trusts" in multifarious forms have undoubtedly prevailed to a great extent, especially among the roads west of Chicago. This is done by weaker roads to obtain trade, and stronger roads, finding that the business which, under natural conditions, should have come to them has been thus diverted or stolen, have retaliated by similar devices to keep their traders, or they have given to their shippers an open rate, the same as the one secured by these illegal devices of their rivals; the result being in every case demoralisation of rates, embarrassments of the business community, and reductions of railway revenues. Any line of strength resorting to secret cutting rates to get business to which it is not justly entitled is unjustly and illegally conducting its trade.

Trusts.

Railway trusts are found to be baneful, and there is a natural fear of the mischiefs that follow their creation. The merciless power of concentrated capital, and the heartless manner in which recent trusts have closed workshops and factories and turned men willing to work into the streets, in order that they may increase profits already reasonably large, are attracting general attention and indignation. These "trusts" are on the same level with "strikes" of labourers, "boycotts," and kindred means of forcing compliance with their demands. The railway trusts have been more effective, because they command greater skill and power and are generally more mischievous. Any combination that brings the railroads of any considerable section of the country under a single head, with irresistible power to divide business and make rates, is more to be dreaded than any other form of trust, as it controls more property and has more power of controlling and coercing the action of individuals and of the public authority. Such trusts subordinate law, if necessary, and corporate interests and rivalries. Judge Cooley, chairman of the Inter-State Committee on Railroad Management, strongly condemns all such combinations, and declares that no prudent man would give assent to a railroad trust until he was first assured that very effective legal restraints had been put upon it.

The overbuilding of railroads is one of the reasons for enormous recent losses on railway stock. Worthless roads are constructed, and the bonds are floated by sensational advertising and reports. The projectors put no funds in the schemes, and they determine for themselves how much they shall take out for building. The millions put into such schemes are sunk, and instead of increasing the aggregate value of railway property in the country, diminish it and millions more previously put into roads which the new roads make unprofitable.

Railroads and the corn crop. The relations of railroad mileage to the corn production of four years is shown by the following interesting table, giving the corn crop of each State named, together with the bushels of corn to each mile of road for the years 1885, 1886, 1887, and 1888. :—

States.	Year.	Mileage.	Bushels of Corn.	Bushels per Mile.
Ohio	1888	7,581	103,000,000	13,587
	1887	7.546	73,797,000	9,790
	1886	7,456	96,204,000	12,903
	1885	7,337	101,000,000	13,764
Indiana	1888	5,868	126,000,000	21,455
	1887	5,833	71,400,000	12.241
	1886	5,711	118,795,000	20,801
	1885	5,599	122,000,000	21,789
Illinois	1888	9,944	241,000,000	24,234
	1887	9,601	141,080,000	14,694
	1886	9,275	209,818,000	22,632
	1885	8,904	220,000,000	24,709
Kansas	1888	8,638	139,000,000	16,092
	1887	8,115	76,547,000	9,432
	1886	6,119	126,712,000	20,708
	1885	4,441	120,000,000	27,021
Nebraska	1888	5,262	139,000,000	26,410
	1887	4,892	93,150,000	19,041
	1886	3,615	106,129,000	29,164
	1885	2,987	110,000,000	36,829
Iowa	1888	8,323	243,000,000	29,196
	1887	8,323	183,502,000	22,044
	1886	7,934	198,847,000	25,063
	1885	7,503	225,000,000	29,998
Missouri	1888	5,830	191,000,000	32,762
	1887	5,462	140,949,000	25,804
	1886	5,068	143,709,000	28,356
	1885	4,968	180,000,000	38,044

These tables show that the immense crop should result in largely increased earnings for the carriers, provided the increased tonnage is moved at the average rates from October, 1887, to March, 1888. These rates, however, were considerably reduced in the latter part of 1888 from those prevailing the year before. By reference to the average per mile of bushels carried in 1886 (the 1886 crop being 1,665,000,000 bushels—an average yield), it is found that the States showing the largest new railway construction have been pushed ahead of the growth of the country. When the comparison is made with the year 1885 crop (the largest up to that time, in fact nearly as large as the 1888 crop) the proof of overbuilding is convincing, and the reason of the depressed condition of the granger south-western stocks is apparent. Kansas falls from 27,121 bushels per mile, in 1885, to 16,092 bushels in 1888; Nebraska from 36,829 bushels to 26,410 bushels; Missouri from 38,044 bushels to 32,762 bushels; while the others—Ohio, Indiana, Illinois, and Iowa—about retain their 1885 percentage. Any decrease in the 1889 crop would be particularly disastrous to these roads. These statistics do not represent the average tonnage received by the new roads, and the large bulk of the crop is raised and moved on the older roads, the newly-built stems or feeders having a comparatively small tonnage.

The year 1888 was one of reduced net earnings and heavy expenses; nevertheless, the output of locomotives was perhaps greater than in any preceding year except that of 1882, and the output of cars has been as large as that of 1887. In 1888, 17 firms built 2,180 locomotives; and 66 railway companies in the United States and Canada built 382, and 17 rotary snow ploughs. The cars for freight

Car and locomotive-building.

service built in 1888 were by 37 firms 62,280, and by 66 railways 19,910; being a total of 82,190. In 1887 the freight cars built by 15 car works were 23,775, and by 29 railroads 6,425; making a total of 30,201. The cars built for passenger service in 1888 by firms and railway companies numbered 2,471. Notwithstanding the falling-off in railroad construction and the decrease in net earnings throughout the country, the past year was one of the three years—1882, 1887, and 1888—of the greatest output of rolling stock.

In the whole country during the last eight years there was spent about 3,000,000,000 dol. on new railroads and about 1,000,000,000 dol. on new houses. This makes an aggregate outlay but a third short of the national expenditure on the late Civil War. When swollen by the sum sunk in speculation on unimproved land, the total capital spent on railways, land, and buildings, on which investors are looking for or are getting dividends on, cannot be far short of the cost of the war. In keeping with these immense expenditures the food supply has not kept pace. In all grains and pork it is not 10 per cent. greater than it was eight years ago, although the population has grown nearly a fourth. In wheat the production is less, while in corn (maize) there was an increase. There are no more sheep in the land than five years ago, and not many more than eight years back. Cattle have multiplied on the plains, but the consumer gets little or nothing of the increase in supply by a reduction in price. This condition runs through all the yields of the farm. Considering the last eight years, it is found that the raising of food has not kept pace with the turning out of railways or buildings; and it may be stated, on general principles, that the United States has been prosperous only as its food production got ahead of the production of people, railroads, and buildings.

Bankers and railway managers. An important conference between bankers and railway managers of the American continent has recently been held in New York, and it is expected that the reconciliation of diverse interests will eventually be reached. The "cut-throat" wars by railway managers, which impaired dividends, depressed securities, and spread universal distrust, it was claimed should be stopped. The acceptance and marketing by bankers of the securities of new railway projects, regardless of the effect upon existing interests, or upon the value of the securities already placed, should also be stopped. Between these two diverging interests are found the public at large. In this situation the Pennsylvania railroad is at the front. The late disastrous rate cutting and suicidal policy of the great trunk lines, the New York Central and the Pennsylvania railroad, was attributed to the New York Central, but is believed to have been the result of the Pennsylvania Railroad Company's bold action in the freight department of their western traffic. However this may be, great injury has resulted to the port of Philadelphia and its environs. The Pennsylvania railroad, having no competition for the foreign, local, and suburban trade of the port, hold their rates of through western traffic higher, it is said, than to New York or Baltimore, where there are competitive lines. While this charge may be denied, the fact remains that the export trade of the port of Philadelphia steadily declined in the face of the increase at the ports of New York and Baltimore, with which cities the Pennsylvania railroad has direct communication. This action is a grievance, and a serious one, of this port alone, it is true; but in its operation extraordinary sacrifices have to be made, and British shareholders—who nearly if not quite outnumber all others—may or should object to the extraordinary pecuniary sacrifices of these "rate wars." If it is true, as popularly believed, that the Pennsylvania railroad was the leading company in the recent conflict, British shareholders should concentrate their interests and exert their power. A special report from this Consulate upon the wealth and growth of the Pennsylvania railroad was laid before Parliament in 1884, Commercial No. 38.

The prosperity and power of the company have increased since the writing of that report, and no reflection is to be made as to the stability and extraordinary success of the road. At the same time, English shareholders should bear in mind that they hold the balance of power, and by a concentration of interests (proxies) could command the control of this gigantic corporation; have an administration, irrespective of "cut rates," "pools," and a system of what is called "insolent aggression."

Notwithstanding that this report may not receive public perusal before the next election (March), it would be well for English shareholders to bear in mind that, by placing their proxies in the hands of responsible bankers having large British financial interests in their charge, they would have a more independent and effective voice in the management of this immense corporation than they have at the present time by leaving their proxies under the control of the present governors of the road.

The following is the provision of the charter granted April 13, 1846, regulating the subject of stock voting and election:—

"At all general meetings or elections by the stockholders, each share of stock shall entitle the holder thereof to one vote, and each ballot shall have endorsed thereon the number of shares thereby represented; but no share or shares transferred within 60 days next preceding any election or general meeting of the shareholders shall entitle the holder or holders thereof to vote at any such election or general meeting, nor shall any person or party, females excepted, residing within 10 miles of the place appointed for any such election or general meeting, be entitled to vote by proxy. No person shall represent by proxy more than three absent stockbrokers, nor shall any proxy be received or entitle the holder thereof to vote unless the same shall bear date, and have been duly executed and acknowledged before some person legally authorised at the place of executing the same to take such acknowledgments within the three months next preceding such election or general meeting, and every such proxy received and voted upon aforesaid shall be retained and filed among the papers of the company until after the next annual election or general meeting, &c."

Coal and coke.

The coal trade during the years 1887 and 1888 has been the most prosperous of any in the annals of the product; the tonnage dealt in was large, and the prices remunerative to all concerned—workman, capitalist, operator, carrier, jobber, and dealer. Anthracite was in especially good demand for all purposes, industrial and domestic; and the yearly figures show an increase of 2,500,000 tons in 1887 over 1886, and of 3,500,000 tons in 1888 over 1887—two years of the largest output in the history of the industry. The increase in the tonnage furnished to the iron furnaces in the trade with Canada, and in the direct trade with all sections by rail and water, was marked. The total output of anthracite coal for the years 1887 and 1888 in Pennsylvania was as follows:—

	1887.	1888.
	Tons.	Tons.
Philadelphia and Reading Railroad	7,555,257·13	7,175,095·02
Lehigh Valley Railroad	5,784,450·11	6,592,715·14
Central Railroad of New Jersey	4,852,859·01	5,742,279·05
Delaware, Lackawana, and Westmoreland Railroad	6,220,792·12	6,996,192·09
Delaware and Hudson Canal Company	4,048,230·08	4,486,188·05
Pennsylvania Railroad	3,816,143·05	4,554,440·10
„ Coal Company	1,603,445·13	1,624,433·06
New York, Lackawana, Erie, and Western	759,834·12	974,373·10
Total	34,641,013·15	38,145,718·04

The net product of the three anthracite coal regions was as follows:—

Region.	1887.	1888.
	Tons.	Tons.
Wyoming	19,684,928·15	21,852,365
Lehigh	4,347,061	5,639,236
Schuylkill	10,609,027	10,654,116

The stock of coal on hand at tide-water shipping points, December 31 of each year, was, in 1887, 130,977 tons; and in 1888, 652,156 tons. In the year 1887 there were continued strikes in the Lehigh region, which caused a falling-off in the production of the harder and best grades of coal. This caused an enormous increase in the Wyoming district. In 1887 the prices went up to 3 dol. 50 c. per ton at the mines; an enormous figure, due to the uncertainties as to the result of the operation of the Inter-State Commerce Law upon the railways. Prices have averaged—

	For all sizes larger than "Pea Coal," per ton.	
	1887.	1888.
	Dol. c.	Dol. c.
At the pits	2 47	2 47
At tide-water—		
At Philadelphia	3 72	4 04
At New York	4 20	4 42

The number of persons employed in the anthracite trade in and about the coal mines is 11,000, and their pay averages from 50 c. to 70 c. per ton, varying with the thickness and hardness of the coal to be mined. These rates average the daily wages of 1 dol. 66 c., and the annual earnings, allowing time off work for strikes, shut downs, and other causes, 500 dol. per miner, counting 200 days' work.

The total exports of anthracite were—in 1887, 680,138 tons, valued at 2,822,833 dol.; in 1888, about 750,000 tons,* valued at 3,000,000 dol. These exports were chiefly to Canadian cities and towns.

The figures, however, do not represent one-half the exports, as the coal going to Canada by rail is not included. The anthracite furnaces in blast at the end of the year 1887 numbered 117, as against 126 at the end of 1886; but the capacity for the make of pig iron was about the same.

In bituminous coal there has been an equally large increase in the Bituminous output. A cry from all the operators of the short supply of cars was coal. made during the eight months of the active shipping season. The demand for this coal shows the growth of the country and the extension of railway lines, together with the increasing use of bituminous coal for steam power, and also for furnace fuel and coke making. The production in Pennsylvania is calculated to be—in 1887, 30,538,625 tons; and in 1888, about 32,000,000 tons.* The total production for the whole United States in 1887 was 85,532,721 tons. The prices of this coal average 1 dol. 25 c. per ton at the pits. The number of persons employed in the mining districts was 52,000 in 1887, and about the same for 1888. The wages range from 40 c. to 70 c. per ton, and the average earnings are 2 dol. 25 c. per day for miners, 1 dol. for boys.

The exports of bituminous coal in 1887 were 643,563 tons, against 906,634 tons of imports, all gross tons of 2,240 lbs. These imports were chiefly at the Pacific ports, and came

	Tons.
From England	212,727
Scotland	36,825
Nova Scotia	45,935
British Columbia	280,688
Australia	321,654
All other countries	8,805

Arrived at—	Quantity.	Value.
	Tons.	Dollars.
San Francisco	619,398	1,889,634
Wilmington (Cal.)	118,530	336,391
San Diego	23,530	97,054
New York	27,258	133,000
Boston	21,484	46,375
Portland (Maine)	13,715	21,777
Galveston	6,824	16,207
Philadelphia	5,753	29,524
Twenty-nine other places	65,142	145,480
Total	906,634	2,715,442

The duty on coal is 75 c. per ton.

Connellsville, Pennsylvania, is the great coke-producing district of Coke. the country, and the quality of the production is of the highest standard. There are over 12,500 ovens in this district, and 7,000 in other sections, making a total of nearly 20,000 ovens for the State of Pennsylvania. A combination of producers has run prices up from 90 c. to 1 dol. 25 c. in 1883 to 1 dol. 50 c. to 2 dol. in 1887. The output in Pennsylvania for 1886 was 5,406,597 net tons, produced from 8,290,849 net tons of coal; while for the year 1887 the production was

* Exact returns not yet published.

UNITED STATES.

over 6,000,000, and for the whole country 8,000,000 net tons, valued at 1 dol. 75 c. at the ovens. In the Connellsville district alone 12,000 workmen are employed, who earn 6,000,000 dol. in wages annually; and the net profits to the operators figure at 9,000,000 dol. 9,000,000 tons of coal are required for this output. Thus—

Total number of establishments in the United States	222
„ „ ovens built	22,597
„ „ „ building	4,154
„ „ short tons of coal used	10,688,972
Coke produced (short tons)	6,845,400
Total value of coke at ovens	11,153,366 dol.
Value of coke per ton at ovens	1 dol. 63 c.
Yield of coal in coke per ton	64

Petroleum.

The export trade in petroleum is decreasing in quantity from year to year by reason of Russian competition, but it does not decrease in value. For the 11 months ended November 30, 1888, 506,153,493 gallons of petroleum were exported from the United States, at the value of 42,549,492 dol. In the corresponding period of 1887 the petroleum exports amounted to 530,571,678 gallons, of the value of 41,246,286 dol. Thus, compared with the petroleum traffic of 1887, 24,418,184 gallons less in 1888 brought 1,303,226 dol. more.

The total exports from the United States in the years 1887 and 1888 were as follows:—

Year.	Crude.	Naptha.	Illuminating.	Lubricating.	Residuum.	Total.	Value.
	Gallons.	Gallons.	Gallons.	Gallons.	Gallons.	Gallons.	Dollars.
1887 ...	80,643,839	12,344,669	464,702,903	20,340,820	2,989,098	581,021,329	45,231,988
1888 ...	77,387,799	13,466,234	429,729,110	24,280,826	1,861,104	546,725,075	45,969,000

The following ports exported petroleum as follows:—

Port.	1886.	1887.	1888.
	Gallons.	Gallons.	Gallons.
Philadelphia	152,276,660	162,149,742	132,065,602
Boston	5,484,513	4,207,158	6,836,325
New York	397,232,310	377,127,943	369,503,772
Perth Amboy	568,440,449	16,825,695	21,611,707
Baltimore	..	9,232,082	6,886,325

The total production of crude oil during the years 1887 and 1888 is returned as follows:—

	Gallons.
1887	19,411,218
1888	13,620,441

Tank ships.

The Standard Oil Company, which virtually has the whole petroleum trade under its own control, will begin shipping the product to Europe in its own tank steamers at an early date. Two steamers, the "Manhattan" and "Bayonne," built in England, are the largest tank vessels afloat, having a capacity of 30,000 and 50,000 barrels respectively, and another is contracted to have a capacity of 1,000,000 gallons of oil in bulk. The sailing craft are being driven out of the trade by the increasing number of tank-carrying steamships. The fleet of tank-carrying vessels now number 16 steamships and four sailing craft, with a total capacity of 400,000 barrels. The estimate is that each steamer will make seven trips, and each sailing vessel four trips per annum. There are being built in England 14 steamers, six of them for the Russian trade and the remainder the Philadelphia and New York. When completed these will be ample to carry all the oil required in Europe.

Agriculture. The crops of 1887 and 1888 throughout the country have not been quite up to the average yield, those notably deficient being corn and potatoes, both affected by severe drought in the Western States. The yield of cotton was also reduced by great extremes of moisture and inequality of temperature. Hay suffered from drought in many sections. The cereals were generally harvested before the droughts commenced, and made nearly average yields. The national crop of corn (maize) is calculated to have been 1,456,000,000 bushels, which is under the average crop. The yield per acre, from 1881 to 1886 inclusive, was 24 bushels, while that from 1878 to 1880 inclusive was 27·6 bushels per acre. The rapid increase of acreage, however, prevents a decrease of absolute product, as the six bountiful years show an average of 1,434,000,000 bushels, and the lean years an average of 1,639,000,000 bushels. The wheat yield of 1887 was slightly below that of the previous year, but with increase of area aggregates 456,000,000 bushels. The oat crop was 669,000,000 bushels, and barley, rye, and buckwheat yielded not quite medium crops. All other, or the minor crops of the country have been productive in a moderate degree. The potato crop was a seriously short one, the yield being about 134,000,000 bushels, at the rate of 56 bushels to the acre, as low a rate of yield as ever reported. The year 1881 had nearly the same low average. The cattle of the country has been decreased by losses on the plains and in the mountains, and flocks of sheep were reduced by the discouraging effect of low prices. The crops of 1887 in the States composing this Consular district yielded as follows :—

CROP OF CORN (MAIZE).

States.	Acres.	Bushels.	Value.
			Dollars.
Pennsylvania	1,395,561	44,905,000	22,452,500
Ohio	2,805,961	73,797,000	35,422,560
Michigan	841,316	18,930,000	9,086,400
Indiana..	3,569,994	71,400,000	32,130,000

The composition or distribution of the crop for the whole country has been as follows :—

Year.	Product.	On hand, March 1st.	Consumed or Distributed.
	Bushels.	Bushels.	Bushels.
1887	1,665,000,000	603,000,000	1,062,000,000
1888	1,456,000,000	508,000,000	948,000,000

UNITED STATES.

CROP OF WHEAT.

States.	Acres.	Bushels.	Value.
			Dollars.
Pennsylvania	1,421,151	13,785,000	11,165,850
Ohio	2,740,087	35,895,000	26,921,250
Michagan	1,629,467	21,672,000	16,037,280
Indiana	2,802,083	37,828,000	27,236,100

The crop of the whole country on hand March 1, 1887 and 1888, was as follows :—

	Bushels.
Crop of 1886	457,218,000
In farmers' hands March 1, 1887	122,000,000
Crop of 1887	456,329,000
In farmers' hands March 1, 1888	132,000,000

The average export price in stated years was 1 dol. 12 c. per bushel in 1875, 1 dol. 34 c. in 1878, 1 dol. 19 c. in 1882, 86 c. in 1885, and 89 c. in 1887.

Oats.

The increase of the area of this crop in the United States has been greater than that of corn or wheat, and still there is no surplus. In 1887 the crop of the whole country was :—

Total production	659,618,000 bushels.
Total area of crop	25,920,906 acres.
Total value of crop	200,699,790 dol.
Average value per bushel	30·4 c.
Average yield per acre	25·8 bushels.
Average value per acre	9 dol. 28 c.

The crop in the States of this Consular district for 1887 was—

States.	Acres.	Bushels.	Value.
			Dollars.
Pennsylvania	1,330,234	33,921,000	11,872,350
Ohio	1,003,278	30,098,000	9,631,360
Michigan	765,000	22,644,000	7,246,080
Indiana	1,304,923	27,943,000	8,103,470

Potatoes.

The potato crop was disastrous from the start, and continued throughout the season of growth. Drought prevailed over the greater part of the potato area, interfering with germination and retarding growth. In 1887 the drought continued generally unbroken until the season was too far advanced to make more than a fraction of a crop possible. The area of the product was enlarged, the estimate showing more than 2,300,000 acres for the whole country in 1887, the increase being largest in the Western States, although considerable in the older States, where the previous crop had been more profitable than the cereals. The crop for 1887 yielded 134,000,000 bushels. The crop in the States of this Consular district fell off nearly one-half.

Flax.

The growth of flax is one of the minor agricultural industries of the United States, and is grown for seed. The yield in Ohio in 1887 was only 118,643 bushels, as compared with 593,217 bushels in 1879. In Indiana the cessation of this production is still more apparant, comparing 113,534 bushels in 1887 with 1,419,172 in 1879. It is a crop that may be termed "pioneer," and is planted chiefly on newly-broken land, well exemplified by the marked falling-off of the crop in the Eastern States, and its great increase in the western part of the country, especially in the States of Kansas, Nebraska, and Dakota.

Buckwheat, tobacco, hay, and all other minor crops in the Consular district have been without marked changes of any character, yielding well up to the average, and returning a fair remuneration to the farmer.

No branch of textile industries of the city of Philadelphia has grown so rapidly as that of carpets and Smyrna rugs. The production here is the largest of any section of the country. The number of establishments is 172, which occupy over 200 very large structures as factories, working 7,250 looms and employing 17,800 workmen. The aggregate production in 1888 reaches 72,000,000 yards of carpet, at a market value of nearly 45,000,000 dol.

Textiles. Carpets.

	Power Looms.	Yards.	Value.
			Dollars.
Ingrains	2,800	33,600,000	16,800,000
Ingrains (hand looms)	800	4,800,000	2,400,000
Art squares (hand looms)	200	1,200,000	720,000
Brussels and Wilton	600	10,800,000	8,640,000
Tapestries	350	6,300,000	3,700,000
Damask, Venetian	500	6,000,000	2,400,000
Smyrna and whole carpets (hand looms)	1,500	6,000,000	12,000,000
Axminster velvets	100	300,000	600,000
List, rag and chain	500	2,500,000	750,000
Total..	7,350	71,500,000	44,970,000

Some intermediate varieties are necessarily merged in the general classification, every variety known to the users of carpets being made in its full proportion, with an especial increase of rich rugs, doubled-face, and whole carpets. This industry was started in the year 1857 by Englishmen, who, from commencing with two looms, now employ 2,800 workmen and 1,100 looms. Another establishment, the Dobson's, employs 4,000 persons, and conducts all the spinning and dyeing and other processes, and runs 500 power looms. The importation of fine carpets—Brussels, tapestry, Wilton, &c.—was universal up to 1870, and quite large until 1877, when the protective duties—ranging on an average 35 c. per square yard and 30 per cent. *ad valorem*—virtually stopped importations, and enabled the manufacturers here to build up this gigantic trade and control the domestic market in production and prices. The largest output is in ingrains, a fabric capable of being made durable and useful. This fabric is therefore more largely sold. Until the last two or three years ingrains were made wholly on hand looms, but now there are 2,800 new power looms in use, doubling the product possible from hand looms, and making 12,000 yards each loom yearly, and with the broad ingrained (or "art squares") aggregating 20,000,000 square yards. The next great product is of Brussels and tapestries, there being 1,000 power looms on these, with a product of 17,000,000 yards. The third in order is the Smyrna and other rugs and whole carpets, all now made of the richest materials and in first-class style, but almost wholly on hand looms. There are 1,500 of these looms, many of them very wide, and the product is more than 6,000,000 square yards, worth 12,000,000 dol. The Axminsters, moquettes, Wiltons, and velvets are worked on 600 power looms. The tapestry Brussels are made on 350 power looms. Damask and Venetian floor and stair carpets are made on 500 power looms. Bag, net, and chain carpets, as they are called, are made on 500 power looms.

Fraudulent beneficial associations. Among the numerous schemes thrust upon the working class of this country, one of recent origin, and known as the order of the "Financial Union," is perhaps the most absurd. Scores of branches of this organisation have been in recent active operation in Pennsylvania and adjoining States. The desire to join this imaginary scheme for making money is equalled only by a recent craze for "graveyard insurance." The order assumes that upon the payment of 1 dol. per week for five years, each member will be paid 1,000 dol. for the 260 dol. he or she shall have paid in. In addition to this utterly absurd financial feature, 20 dol. per week is promised for sickness, 500 dol. at any time on total disability, and 500 dol. at death. Thus far, 260 dol. paid in 1 dol. weekly payments, which at compound interest would not amount to 400 dol., this order promises to pay to each member the sum of 1,000 dol. at the end of five years. Presuming that a number of members would drop out and forfeit their deposits, it is certain that the sick, disability, and death benefits and expenses would far exceed the gains of the lapsed membership. It is apparent, therefore, that by no possible system of saving or combination of deposits can 260 dol. paid in in weekly instalments be made to return 1,000 dol. in five years, and the whole scheme must be a creature of the most abject ignorance or deliberate fraud on the part of the chief organisers, who are styled "Supreme Governor," "Supreme Vice-Governor," "Supreme Medical Director," "Supreme Adjustor," "Instructor," "Rector," "Conductor," "Trustees," "Sentinel and Guard," all of whom receive pay. The Philadelphia "Record" newspaper is exerting itself to expose thoroughly the delusive promises of this scheme in the interest of the innocent, ignorant, and industrious.

Marriages and divorce The present system of marriage and divorce laws in the different States of the Union is greatly deplored by the intelligent part of the community. The laws of each State are so conflicting with each other that what is marriage in one commonwealth may be bigamy in half-a-dozen others. If two wives obtain divorces in New York, the law prevents the men from marrying. One marries in New York and is a bigamist. The other marries in New Jersey and his marriage is lawful. Forms of marriage differ in the various States. If in some of the commonwealths a man and woman, without ceremony or witnesses, assume that they are husband and wife, the union is legal. In the adjoining State it might not be legal. All this makes a painful uncertainty as to the status of many married couples. It is the opinion of jurists and lawyers that the laws governing marriage and divorce should be the same throughout the country, and an amendment to the Constitution of the United States giving Congress the power to remedy these great evils is advised. In applications for divorce, fraud and perjury are committed in many cases, notwithstanding the efforts of the judges to prevent any violation of the law; but they have no alternative, and must administer the statute law as they find it. Personal service of notice of proceedings in divorce is not necessary in many States, as, for instance, in Minnesota, where a person, married in Pennsylvania, residing and advertising for a certain period of time his application for divorce, obtains his divorce, marries again, and, visiting Pennsylvania on his wedding tour, can be arrested for bigamy in the latter State. This and numerous other evils attending the want of uniformity of the laws of marriage and divorce have assumed such proportions that the interests and well-being of society, the respectability and legitimacy of children, are imperilled, and it is claimed that nothing can overcome the evil but Congressional action.

The most interesting question before the people of the State of Pennsylvania and of the whole country at the present time is that of the coming vote for or against total prohibition of the distilling, brewing, and sale of intoxicating beverages within the State. The Republican party committed itself to submit this question to a popular vote, and the temperance or "teetotal" forces are exerting themselves to the utmost to gain a change in the State Constitution, whereby absolute prohibition of the brewing, distilling, sale, and use of intoxicating liquors shall be the law of the State. In the year 1888 a "High Licence" law was enacted and went into effect. Under this law the licence fees were changed from graded licenses, ranging from 65 dol. to 1,000 dol. to a regular sum of 500 dol. per annum for all licenses with evidence of want of a drinking saloon in the neighbourhood, and of the reputable character of the applicant. This stringent law reduced the number of bar rooms from 5,773 to 1,346, closed most of the notoriously disreputable groggeries, effectually stopped the sale of liquor by the licensed houses on Sundays, and greatly reduced the criminal statistics. *High licence and prohibition.*

Taking the criminal records of the city of Philadelphia as an evidence of the beneficial results of this "High Licence" law, it is seen that during the seven months of 1887, before the law went into effect, the commitments to the county prison for intoxication were 11,137, while for the seven months of 1888 under the "High Licence" law they fell to 5,947, being a sudden reduction of about 50 per cent.

Still more remarkable are the statistics of the Monday commitments; that is to say, imprisonment for the non-payment of fines imposed by the magistrate for arrests and riotous conduct during that day. In the seven months of 1887 they were 865, while in the first seven months of 1888—"High Licence"—they were 246, and some days none at all. This favourable showing is equally if not more prominently apparent in the statistics of the House of Correction.

The following tables speak for themselves :—

UNITED STATES.

TABLE showing Number of Intoxication Commitments to the County Prison during the Period from June 1 to December 31 of the Years 1887 and 1888.

Months.	1887.			1888.		
	Males.	Females.	Total.	Males.	Females.	Total.
June	1,452	277	1,729	697	103	800
July	1,380	263	1,643	691	106	797
August	1,370	284	1,654	818	119	937
September	1,347	297	1,644	867	140	1,007
October	1,322	284	1,606	728	104	832
November	1,175	228	1,403	629	144	773
December	1,196	262	1,458	693	108	801
	9,242	1,895	11,137	5,123	824	5,947

Total committed for intoxication, June 1 to December 31, 1887 .. 11,137
,, ,, ,, ,, ,, 1888 .. 5,947
Decrease in commitments for the year 1888 5,190

TABLE showing Monday Morning Intoxication Commitments to the Philadelphia County Prison during the Period from June 1 to December 31 of the Years 1887 and 1888.

1887.				1888.			
Monday.	Males.	Females.	Total.	Monday.	Males.	Females.	Total.
June 6	34	6	40	June 4	6	1	7
,, 13	46	4	50	,, 11	5	...	5
,, 20	30	6	36	,, 18	5	2	7
,, 27	22	2	24	,, 25	5	2	7
July 4	22	1	23	July 2	9	1	10
,, 11	17	3	20	,, 9	3	1	4
,, 18	15	3	18	,, 16	8	1	9
,, 25	20	5	25	,, 23	...	...	...
August 1	22	3	25	,, 30	4	...	4
,, 8	25	2	27	August 6	9	...	9
,, 15	34	5	39	,, 13	9	1	10
,, 22	32	1	33	,, 20	14	2	16
,, 29	19	...	19	,, 27	7	1	8
September 5	35	2	37	September 3	9	2	11
,, 12	46	6	52	,, 10	15	1	16
,, 19	30	2	32	,, 17	15	2	17
,, 26	24	1	25	,, 24	15	1	16
October 3	27	3	30	October 1	3	...	3
,, 10	43	5	48	,, 8	10	...	10
,, 17	23	7	30	,, 15	11	3	14
,, 24	19	2	21	,, 22	5	...	5
,, 31	20	5	25	,, 29	6	...	6
November 7	28	2	30	November 5	8	2	10
,, 14	15	2	17	,, 12	7	...	7
,, 21	30	1	31	,, 19	6	1	7
,, 28	12	2	14	,, 26	9	1	10
December 5	23	...	23	December 3	2	...	2
,, 12	19	4	23	,, 10	1	...	1
,, 19	17	...	17	,, 17	3	2	5
,, 26	27	4	31	,, 24	10	...	10
				,, 31	...	...	...
	776	89	865		219	27	246

The beneficial effects of this "High Licence" law are apparent to all classes, total abstainers as well as brewers and distillers.

The question to be voted upon this year, however, that of absolute prohibition, is entirely another matter, and from all present indications not at all likely to become the law and part of the Constitution. Many advocates of temperance and personally total abstainers do not favour such stringent measures, holding that in the few States that have made the trial drunkenness has not materially decreased, and that the illicit distilling and illegal smuggling of alcoholic spirits within and into their borders have, in a moral point of view, offset the reduction of crime resultant from open indulgence in strong drink by the lower classes of the community.

There would appear to be no doubt, with the antagonism of the numerous large cities of this commonwealth, and the immense capital invested in the distilling and brewing interests, that the amendment to the State Constitution inforcing prohibition will not receive a majority of the people's vote. English capital is largely interested in this subject, as it is well known that the breweries of the chief cities of America are being purchased by British capital, to be run on the baneful system known here as "trusts;" that is to say, control of the market, enhancement of prices, and dictation to consumers.

While prohibition is not at all likely to become the law, "High Licence" is undoubtedly a statute of permanence. Under this restrictive enactment pauperism will be reduced and crimes decreased, taxation lowered, and human existence rendered less burdensome.

LONDON:
Printed for Her Majesty's Stationery Office,
By HARRISON AND SONS,
Printers in Ordinary to Her Majesty.
(1125 3 | 89—H & S 583)

FOREIGN OFFICE.
1889.
ANNUAL SERIES.

No. 465.

DIPLOMATIC AND CONSULAR REPORTS ON TRADE AND FINANCE.

UNITED STATES.

REPORT FOR THE YEAR 1888
ON THE
TRADE OF THE CONSULAR DISTRICT OF NEW ORLEANS.

REFERENCE TO PREVIOUS REPORT, Annual Series No. 270.

Presented to both Houses of Parliament by Command of Her Majesty,
MARCH, 1889.

LONDON:
PRINTED FOR HER MAJESTY'S STATIONERY OFFICE,
BY HARRISON AND SONS, ST. MARTIN'S LANE,
PRINTERS IN ORDINARY TO HER MAJESTY.

And to be purchased, either directly or through any Bookseller, from
EYRE AND SPOTTISWOODE, EAST HARDING STREET, FLEET STREET, E.C., and
32, ABINGDON STREET, WESTMINSTER, S.W.; or
ADAM AND CHARLES BLACK, 6, NORTH BRIDGE, EDINBURGH; or
HODGES, FIGGIS, & Co., 104, GRAFTON STREET, DUBLIN.

1889.

[C. 5618–18.] *Price Twopence.*

New Series of Reports.

Reports of the Annual Series have been issued from Her Majesty's Diplomatic and Consular Officers at the following places, and may be obtained from the sources indicated on the title-page:—

No.		Price.	No.		Price.
341.	Amoy	2d.	403.	Nagasaki	1d.
342.	Trebizond	1d.	404.	Hiogo	2d.
343.	Lisbon	1d.	405.	Tonga	1d.
344.	Java	1d.	406.	Adana	1d.
345.	Brest	1d.	407.	Valparaiso	1d.
346.	Odessa	2d.	408.	Bilbao	1d.
347.	Cavalla	1d.	409.	Santiago	1d.
348.	Bussorah	1d.	410.	Paramaribo	1d.
349.	Mollendo	1d.	411.	Nantes	1d.
350.	Cadiz	5d.	412.	Bangkok	1d.
351.	Cagliari	4d.	413.	Yokohama	2d.
352.	Cagliari	1d.	414.	Mozambique	1d.
353.	Ajaccio	1d.	415.	Canton	2d.
354.	Copenhagen	1d.	416.	Kiungchow	1d.
355.	Vienna	1d.	417.	Damascus	1d.
356.	San Francisco	1d.	418.	Syra	1d.
357.	Vera Cruz	1d.	419.	Aleppo	1d.
358.	Philippopolis	1d.	420.	Sandakan	1d.
359.	Greytown	1d.	421.	Barcelona	1d.
360.	Tangier	1d.	422.	Königsberg	1d.
361.	Lisbon	1d.	423.	Tabreez	1d.
362.	Chicago	1d.	424.	Guayaquil	1d.
363.	Jerusalem and Jaffa	1d.	425.	St. Petersburg	1d.
364.	Truxillo	1d.	426.	Tokio	1d.
365.	Ningpo	1d.	427.	Charleston	1d.
366.	Chefoo	1d.	428.	Amsterdam	1d.
367.	Bushire	1d.	429.	Hamburg	4d.
368.	Stockholm	2d.	430.	Trieste	1d.
369.	Santiago	1d.	431.	New York	2d.
370.	New York	2d.	432.	Antwerp	1d.
371.	Pernambuco	1d.	433.	Munich	1d.
372.	Söul	1d.	434.	Buenos Ayres	1d.
373.	Chinkiang	2d.	435.	Warsaw	1d.
374.	Pernambuco	1d.	436.	Porto Rico	1d.
375.	San Francisco	2d.	437.	Réunion	1d.
376.	Riga	1d.	438.	Lisbon	1d.
377.	Newchwang	2d.	439.	Venice	1d.
378.	San Salvador	1d.	440.	Christiania	5d.
379.	Frankfort	2d.	441.	Maranham	1d.
380.	Hankow	2d.	442.	Sofia	1d.
381.	Bucharest	1d.	443.	Copenhagen	1d.
382.	Lisbon	1d.	444.	Galatz	1d.
383.	Tunis	1d.	445.	Tabreez	1d.
384.	Tangier	1d.	446.	Bogotá	2d.
385.	Santiago	2d.	447.	St. Petersburg	3d.
386.	Diarbekir	1d.	448.	Nice	1d.
387.	Shanghai	2d.	449.	Stettin	2d.
388.	Rome	2d.	450.	Fiume	1d.
389.	Buenos Ayres	1d.	451.	Chinkiang	1d.
390.	Amsterdam	1d.	452.	The Hague	1d.
391.	Warsaw	1d.	453.	Malaga	1d.
392.	San Francisco	1d.	454.	Taganrog	1d.
393.	Alexandria	1d.	455.	Mozambique	1d.
394.	Salonica	2d.	456.	Bogotá	2d.
395.	Palermo	1d.	457.	Patras	1d.
396.	Mexico	4d.	458.	Galveston	1d.
397.	Naples	3d.	459.	Buda Pesth	1d.
398.	Boston	1d.	460.	Madeira	1d.
399.	Hakodate	1d.	461.	Warsaw	1d.
400.	Nantes	1d.	462.	Paris	2d.
401.	Madeira	1d.	463.	Baltimore	1d.
402.	Hakodate	1d.	464.	Philadelphia	2d.

No. 465.

Reference to previous Report, Annual Series No. 270.

UNITED STATES.

NEW ORLEANS.

Consul De Fonblanque to the Marquis of Salisbury.

My Lord,   *New Orleans, February 9, 1889.*

I HAVE the honour to enclose the Annual Trade Reports for this Consular District for the year 1888.

I have, &c.
(Signed)   A. DE G. DE FONBLANQUE.

Trade Report for 1888.

As a rule the States forming this Consular District are only affected indirectly by a Presidential Election, because this event invariably disorganises the general commerce of the country. This year, however, the sugar and rice-producing States suffered directly, because the great political parties played the one against the other with propositions for reducing the tariff on these staple products. Cotton planters have also been subjected to much trouble and loss by the establishment of a Bagging Trust. *[Presidential election. Its direct effect on these States.]*

Up to almost three years ago what have been known as "rings" or "corners," and latterly disguised themselves under the more euphonious name of "Trusts," have been unknown in the South, or at any rate did not acquire proportions sufficient to make them oppressive. The first to gain this distinction was the Cotton Seed Trust, which gradually and quickly obtained control of the mills in which cotton seed is dealt with, and secured a monopoly of the sale of all its products. These include, lint, bulbs, oil, meal, cake, and soap stock. I have received several letters from British merchants, asking to be put into communication with exporters of these articles, and the result of my inquiries is, that not a pound of any of them can be obtained except through the central office of the Trust in New York. The legality of this combination is now being tested here. *[Trusts. The Cotton Seed Trust.]*

Emboldened by this success, a Bagging Trust was established last year, by which the price of the jute netting, used to cover bales of cotton, was doubled. This operation is said to have cost the South 2,000,000 dol. up to September last, but it is hoped that it will now collapse. Of twenty-four bagging factories in the United States, sixteen were leased to the Trust, and shut up to limit production. These leases fall in on the January 16, 1889, and I understand that no preparations have been made, as yet, to renew them. The fact is that the old-fashioned jute bagging so long tolerated, with, in many cases, such *[Bagging Trust.]*

(584)

Defects of jute bagging. disastrous results, is now universally condemned. I was, I think, one of the first to point out (in my last Annual Trade Report, page 8) that even when untorn, this covering allowed filaments of cotton to obtrude in such a way, that fire flashes over them with the greatest rapidity; and it has been long known that it will not resist the cotton hook in the hands of the negro "roustabout." In another part of this report the endeavours already made to supply a more efficient covering will be stated.

Coal Trust. A Coal Trust under which this necessity was not to be sold under 60 c. a barrel—the ordinary price being from 40 to 45—was established in New Orleans upon the faith of a prediction that we were to have an unusually severe and early winter; but, unfortunately for its promoters, there has been no really cold weather yet, and consequently the combination died from natural causes.

Rice Trust. A more serious affair is the Rice Millers' Trust, which has, for the present at least, been highly detrimental to the planter, and all others engaged in the rice business, without any appreciable benefit to the miller.

British trade. The idea of introducing British goods into this market—never possessed of any vitality on the other side—has, apparently, died of inanition. I will, however, give one other instance of the British merchants' talk of enterprise. A glass manufacturer, having his offices at Liverpool, wrote to me, asking to be put into communication with firms requiring glass bottles. Now the consumption, and consequently the production, of beer in the United States has increased immensely; and large quantities of bottled ale are exported to Mexico and Central and South America. We have now six large breweries at work in New Orleans. I gave my correspondent's letter to a gentleman interested in the export trade not only of this city, but in the much larger business done at St. Louis, involving altogether an annual demand for about 1,000,000 bottles, but these had to be of a peculiar make and strength, and so he informed the Liverpool firm, sending them specifications, and asking for samples. After a long delay, during which he pressed several times for an answer, the Liverpool firm replied that the required samples would cost 5*l.*; intimating that they were not prepared to make so great an outlay, but that if this capital were provided, they might go on with the business. The business went on to Bohemia, where the old rule, that sellers should present their customers with samples of the goods they desire to dispose of, seems to prevail.

Immigration. A movement more serious than any that has heretofore been made for attracting immigrants—native and foreign—to the Southern States, was inaugurated at a Convention held in New Orleans on the 8th August, when some four hundred and fifty delegates from other States were present. Many flattering speeches were made, no doubt for future publication; but on the most important subjects of all (affecting foreigners), *i.e.*, protection of the immigrant from fraud, provision for his medical treatment when stricken by the inevitable chills and fever, and a reform in the administration of the vagrant laws, nothing was done and very little said.

Advice to intending emigrants. The foreign immigrant who desires to buy land and settle upon it should entirely disregard all that is told him by agents at home, and take what he reads in the pamphlets which they publish with a liberal amount of allowance. He should be prepared to spend a year on the spot, judging for himself whether the climate will suit him, and if the conditions of the life he has to lead will be congenial to his tastes. Many young Englishmen appear to think that country life in these States is similar to country life at home, and imagine that after a ride round the property to see that the men are at work, the rest of the day may be given up to lawn tennis, fishing and shooting, and amusing themselves. This is a fatal mistake. The work is hard and the life is dull. *Country life.*

Working men, especially when in search of employment, should beware of entering the State of Mississippi, where what purports to be laws against vagrants are often somewhat harshly administered. Here is the latest case reported to me:—William Sims, a native of England, and an ironworker by trade, after having been employed on the Mississippi River during the winter of 1887-8, took chills and fever, and tried to make his way to Birmingham (Alabama) to obtain employment in his own trade. At Tupolo (Mississippi), whilst seeking work, he was arrested as a vagrant, and fined 5 dol., with 5 dol. 70 c. costs. Vagrants (as defined by the laws of Mississippi) are "All able-bodied persons who live without employment or labour, and have no visible means of support or maintenance; any person who shall abandon his wife or family without just cause, leaving them without support, and in danger of becoming a public charge; keepers of houses of public gaming or houses of prostitution, and all common prostitutes who have no other employment for their support or maintenance; any able-bodied person who shall be found begging for a livelihood; and common gamblers, or persons who for the most part maintain themselves by gaming." Sims was not able-bodied and was not begging. He lived by his labour, and was seeking work—not charity. He was "bought out" by a farmer, and this is his account of what followed, dated March 14: "He took me on with him where I found two Germans, and another German has been arrested since. We are worked from light to dark, sometimes in water. We have to eat, sleep, and work with negroes, and are threatened to be whipped by them. The prison we are confined in is a disgrace to the civilised world. We cannot stand upright in it, and it is full of lice and filth. We get nothing to eat but corn bread, a little fat pork, sometimes a few beans. The food is put on the table, and if you stop to wash your hands the niggers eat it all up. We are allowed 40 c. a day, and if you are sick one day you have to work another day to pay for it." *Vagrant laws. Case of Sims. Definition of vagrants. Treatment of Sims.*

Thus (the fine and costs amounting to 10 dol. 70 c.) the imprisonment at hard labour was at least for twenty-six days. This is the latest, but not the worst case. Alleged vagrants may be "bought out" by the lessees of the Penitentiary and worked in company with convicts and subjected to convicts' discipline. It is law that no "unusual or cruel punishment" shall be inflicted on these unfortunates, but I have it under the signature of a Governor of the State of Mississippi, that tying a man by his thumbs to a bent sapling, then letting it spring so that it draws him up on the tips of his toes, and leaving him thus for half an hour as a punishment, is not considered "unusual or cruel." This was inflicted upon another sick man, also a British subject, by the convict "guards," who thought he did not work fast enough. *System of "working out."*

Another peculiarity in the administration of vagrant laws in Mississippi is this:—The usual punishment for alleged vagrancy is a fine of 10 dol. or twenty days' imprisonment. If he is "hired out" at 40 c. a day his imprisonment by the "farmer" is for five days longer than that imposed by the Court. But supposing he is not "hired out" till he has undergone some portion of his imprisonment in the public gaol —say half—it would be reasonable to suppose that as his penalty is in *Vagrant laws of Mississippi.*

(584)

the alternative—fine *or* imprisonment—he should then have to work out only half of the former. This, however, is not so. He has to work it all out. So that if he were "hired out" on his nineteenth day he would still have to repay the "farmer" 10 dol. at the rate of 40 c. a day; making his total punishment thirty-four days. In like manner, if he has worked out a portion of the fine and a friend appears to release him, the farmer will not be content with the balance due, but requires the whole fine to be repaid. This again the highest authority in Mississippi has considered correct.

Hard cases in New Orleans. I have no complaints on this head from Alabama, Arkansas, or Florida, but here, in the city of New Orleans, there have been some bad cases—notably those of the brothers Gray (British subjects), who whilst in possession of 160 dol. savings, and in actual employment, were convicted of vagrancy. Very recently a fireman belonging to a ship in port was arrested on the level as a vagrant and convicted without a hearing, but as I am promised an investigation of this case, I will say no more about it at present.

It is not unfair to suppose that I am not informed of all that occurs on this subject, and the worst part of it is that the local authorities do not appear to consider it worth while to repair the wrongs done to a poor foreigner, or even to investigate his complaint. There are strong indications that this denial of justice extends in other directions. I therefore advise all British subjects employed in the country districts to **Advice to workmen.** insist upon weekly settlements, to beware of sub-contractors, and to see that the bargains they make are recognised by the person to be immediately benefitted by the work done.

Time for seeking employment. The business year in this district begins on September 1, by which time manufacturers, merchants, and storekeepers in the cities and towns, and planters and farmers in the country have made all their engagements. It is consequently almost hopeless for an outsider, however capable, to seek employment after the above date.

Sanitary condition of New Orleans. Although the streets, gutters, and drainage canals of New Orleans have never in my memory been in so bad a condition, the health of the city has been unusually good. The Board of Health, faithful to its promise to investigate all cases approaching in their character to **Yellow Fever. Diphtheria.** yellow fever, and to publish the exact truth, has not had to record one single instance of that dreaded disease. At one time diphtheria appeared to be on the increase, but it has gradually subsided, owing to enforcement of those sanitary laws by disobedience to which it was developed.

A competent authority (Dr. Chaillé) gives the following as the death rates in the principal cities of America:—

Death rates in large cities.

New Orleans	25·98
New York	26·47
Baltimore	24·20
Brooklyn	23·33
Boston	23·53
Cincinnati	20·29
Chicago	20·79

This is a very good showing, when our large negro population is taken into consideration, which has no knowledge of sanitation, frequently refuses to call in doctors and depends upon quacks, vendors, &c., and shamelessly neglects its young children. The death rate for the white population for the same year was 22·96—less than any of the cities mentioned, save Chicago and Cincinnati.

Death rate in New Orleans. Dr. Chaillé observes: "During the last 50 years and more, the death rate of New Orleans has enormously improved, owing greatly, but by no means wholly, to the decline of yellow fever, of which there have been only two severe epidemics since 1858, viz., in 1867 and 1878, and from which New Orleans has been virtually exempt for the past nine years. Other things being equal, the greater the density of population, the higher the death rate. New Orleans is the only large city, therefore has the greatest density of population in the Southern United States, and its death rate compares favourably with the death rate of the large cities of Southern Europe.

"The death rate of children under five years of age, a so-called barometer of public health, is somewhat less than the average for 31 registered cities, and compares very favourably with other large cities of the United States. *Deaths amongst children.*

"The exceptionally high death rate of New Orleans is due chiefly to the excessive mortality of its disproportionately large coloured population. *Death of negroes.*

"In most northern cities the death rate by diphtheria, croup, scarlet and typhoid fevers, is much higher than in New Orleans. But this advantage is, unfortunately, more than compensated for by the following losses: the death rate by consumption, which, everywhere in the United States, destroys many more lives than any other single disease, was, in 1880 and probably since, higher in New Orleans than any of the 50 cities, except Charleston, Richmond, and Washington. Malarial fever was much more fatal in New Orleans and cities of the Gulf coast than in any other cities, except Kansas city; and dysentery was more fatal than in any of the 50 cities, except Nashville, Paterson, and Washington. *Fevers. Consumption. Malaria.*

"Considering the unfavourable sanitary conditions and surroundings of New Orleans, there is just cause for surprise and for great thankfulness that its death rate is no worse. High as this is, it none the less justifies the conviction that New Orleans can be rendered as healthful a home as any other large city. But to accomplish this, the swamps of New Orleans, from river to lake, must be rescued from the domain of malaria, mosquitos, and snakes, and be converted into healthy homes and gardens; it must be thoroughly drained, and this is impossible unless streets and gutters be greatly improved; and it must be efficiently scavanged. Without these essentials a most unhealthy contamination of air, soil, and water, by malaria and by putrefying decompositions, cannot be avoided. Since these unhealthful things are greatly promoted by protracted heat and moisture, and since New Orleans surpasses all other large cities of the United States in these two conditions, there is no other large city where it is as needful that swamps should be converted into habitable land, and draining and scavenging should be perfected. The greatest ill-fortune of New Orleans is that it still has so small a proportion of citizens who adequately estimate the value of life, health, and the dependence on these of both private and public prosperity, or the means indispensable to secure these inseparable blessings." *Sanitation required.*

I am happy to say that this last complaint of Dr. Challé—perfectly true as to the past—is perceptibly losing force. For many years New Orleans has been considered as a good place in which to make money to be spent elsewhere. The day dream of the native creole was to save enough to live upon in Paris. *Improved tone of thought.*

The energies of the adopted citizen from New York or Boston were concentrated upon making some capital here, to be used at home. Within the last five or six years there have arisen unmistakable proofs in the shape of handsome new residences, spacious new stores, &c., that the visitor has anchored himself to the soil, and has come to stay.

Under the law which fixes the amount of taxation which can be *Taxation.*

levied in New Orleans—irrespective of accident or necessity—the municipality finds itself unable to make adequate provision for drainage, or any other sanitary work, or for police, public schools, and the maintenance of pauper orphans. The only remedy is to call upon property holders to assess themselves under arrangements similar to those which govern an election. In this way it is proposed to raise 3,000,000 dol., by a tax of 3 mils for ten years. If this be done, the money will be expended under the control of a committee of citizens. I understand that all the city work for 1889 will be handed over to contractors.

Upon the origin and spread of yellow fever in the south, Surgeon-General Hamilton of the United States Marine Hospital Service, has reported as follows:—

Yellow fever in Florida. Dr. Hamilton's report.

Key West.

"Last year the yellow fever appeared in Key West, in the family of a restaurant keeper by the name of Baker. It appears that a family named Bollos had kept a hotel in Havana in various places, the last being called the Quinta Avenida (Fifth Avenue) Hotel. Unfortunately for Florida he emigrated to Key West. Their household effects, under the regulations governing the regular line of steamers, could not be shipped by them, so they shipped these effects, consisting of bedding and various articles of furniture, by an irregular "tramp," not now running, called the "cochran." There was no objection officially made at Key West, as there was neither government nor local quarantine, and the articles were landed and stored above Baker's restaurant. The Baker family died of the fever, and thus the fever started and rapidly became epidemic.

Tampa.

"The Government, under the operation of that section of the statutes forbidding interference with local authorities, did nothing except that, on request of the Governor to aid the local board, they established a dispensary and paid the expenses of the city hospital. To assist in the speedy depopulation of the city a refuge camp was established at Egmont Key, at the mouth of Tampa Bay. No case from Egmont communicated the disease. The first cases in Tampa were kept secret from August to October 21. A family of Italians by the name of Turk, fruit dealers, brought the fever into Tampa. The steamers had refused, under orders from the Hillsborough County Board of Health, to bring fruit from Havana or Key West. These Italians, finding it impossible to continue in business, set up a smuggling line, and brought fruit by the man Turk and Bay, and overland to Tampa. For this purpose way of Puna Gorda this assistant Peep or "Pete," made frequent surreptitious visits to Key West while the disease was there epidemic, and blankets were purchased in the infected city and used while on the overland trip to Tampa. It is a significant fact that the whole family of the Italians were the first taken sick, and that they were not publicly known to have been out of the town, although the fact is now known. The measures taken by the Government were simply to conform to the wishes of the Governor to aid the Hillsborough County Board of Health.

"The duty of preventing the spread of the disease was undertaken by the Florida State Protective Association, an organisation consisting of one representative from each County Board of Health, under the presidency of Dr. King Wyley, of Sandford. In December the association raised the quarantine against Tampa. The County Board of Health asserted that the disease had disappeared, but unfortunately the disease had not been stamped out; and although the cases of fever lingered all winter in Tampa, its existence was bitterly denied. From Tampa the disease spread to Plant city, Manatee, and other places, and it is now believed that the fever was at Jacksonville as early as February. Dr. Guiteras of the Marine Hospital Service, an acknowledged expert, says that in his judgment at least two of the cases of "society" fever, of which there were over 30 reported in Jacksonville in that month, had the well-marked clinical history of yellow fever. Nine of these cases died. Dr. Potts treated cases in Bay-street in June, and there were probably cases continuously until the formal announcement was made. He said that so-called isolated cases had been reported in Jacksonville after the case in Bay-street had been treated in June by Dr. Potts, but that the local authorities denied the presence of any epidemic, and placed a guard around each case. This state of things existed until August 16, when the spread of the disease in Jacksonville became so great, cases springing up at various points in the city that could not be traced to any of the so-called isolated cases, that the authorities had to declare the disease epidemic. [margin: Jacksonville.]

"The disease was introduced in Decatur, Albama, by a man who had gone from Jacksonville while all of the cases in that city had been reported under guard. His ticket had been from some point outside of the infected city, and consequently he was not denied admittance. The doctor said the fever had been introduced in Gainsville and Fernandina by base-ball players who had played a game of ball in Jacksonville before the epidemic nature of the disease had been declared, and then returned to these cities. [margin: Decatur, Alabama.]

"Of the Government work at Camp Perry Dr. Hamilton says that since its establishment there had been only one death from yellow fever in the Fever Hospital at the Camp. The experience of the physicians at the Camp went to show that five days was the incubative period, and that when persons had been in the Camp for that length of time, and did not develop the disease, their was no danger of their having it. No person having spent ten days in the Camp had developed the fever after leaving the station. He blames the lack of local inspection at Tampa, where the disease first appeared this season, and says that if the first cases had been reported there would probably have been no epidemic. The most serious charge made by this expert is against Jacksonville, where he asserts that the fever was actually epidemic when the first case was reported." [margin: Camp Perry.]

The shortcomings (to use no harsher word) of local Boards of Health on the one hand, and the senseless obstruction caused by "shot-gun" quarantines on the other, has at last awakened the people of the South to the necessity of organising a district Board of Health for all the States within the yellow fever zone, by means of which honest, intelligent, combined action may be taken in case of need.

In the commencement of this report I mentioned a substitute for the condemned jute bagging for cotton bales. This is made of cotton by the Lane Mills of New Orleans, and has been accepted by shippers and under-writers as a safe and efficient covering; but it could not be produced all at once in sufficient quantities. It has been tried by various tests, and found to be superior to the jute bagging in resisting the use of the cotton hook and the shocks of compressing, weighing, sampling, heading, re-heading, and gives the cotton better protection from damp and dirt. It has also passed the ordeal of fire. Four bales were used for the test. First, on a compressed bale covered with cotton cloth bagging was placed an uncompressed jute bale. Alongside these was a compressed bale covered with jute, and on top of that was an uncompressed cotton-cloth bale. A match was applied to the first jute bale. Immediately it was enveloped in flames; within a [margin: Manufacturers. New cotton bagging. Its qualities. Tried by fire.]

second of time the fire had run from one end of the bale to the other, and every thread and strand was burning. The bale beneath, covered with cotton-cloth, was almost uninjured, the only damage being a slight scorching to the bagging, which did not extend to the cotton inside. Meanwhile, the flames had spread to the compressed bale covered with jute, and it, too, was burning, while the cotton-clothed bale above was smoked, scorched and charred, but would not burn.

As an additional proof of the incombustible nature of the cotton bagging, a pan of burning charcoal was emptied on it. Even this great degree of heat did not cause it to burn.

Another advantage of this bagging is, that it takes the "marks" so distinctly that they can be seen and noted at a distance, and are almost indelible.

Brewing. I have already mentioned the increase of breweries. New Orleans is now self-supplied with good beer (ale), and a great deal is exported.

Shipping. There was a marked falling off of British shipping at this port during 1888, as compared with 1887. In the latter year 467 ships of 536,474 tons entered, and in the former 384 ships of 441,333 tons, but *Freights good.* freights were much better than usual during the past twelve months. In the first quarter they were good (as times go), and for the remainder of the time more than fair.

The total foreign tonnage (including American) cleared in 1887 was 630,761, that in 1888 was 653,789. The British shipping cleared during the same years was 536,474 and 455,367 respectively, showing a considerable falling off of our carrying trade, and an increase in that of our competitors. Ten years ago our tonnage here exceeded that of all other nations put together. I think, however, that the British shipowner has not had a bad year as times go, for in its first quarter freights were good, and during the other three above the average.

Annex A. In Annex A is given a return of all shipping at this port during the year 1888.

The principal cargoes carried by British ships during 1888 are as follows:—

Cargoes by British ships.

Articles.		Quantity.
Cotton	Bales	971,766
Cotton-seed oil	Barrels	15,171
Cotton-seed oil cake	Sacks	422,954
Cotton-seed meal	,,	537,316
Cotton seed	,,	5,579
Cotton-seed soap stock	Barrels	5,824
Corn	Bushels	4,629,277
,,	Sacks	381
Wheat	Bushels	785,421
,,	Sacks	4,671
Flour	,,	1,537
Staves	Pieces	606,986
Timber	,,	36,914
,,	Feet	49,406
Lumber	,,	269,218
Lead	Pigs and bars	80,745
Copper ore	Sacks	381
Rice polish	,,	3,840
Turpentine	Barrels	400
Tallow	Tierces	687
Tobacco	Hogsheads	506

NEW ORLEANS.

Three years ago a memorial was presented to the Government of Canada by a few shipmasters, but really inspired by one only, complaining of my action with regard to seamen who made charges against the captains and officers of their ships. It was contended that I encouraged these men to complain and favoured them unduly. The cases of the barques *Prince Louis* and *Lancefield* were quoted in support of these allegations, which I answered to the satisfaction of Her Majesty's Government. The master of the *Prince Louis*, taking a judicious view of the difficulties in which he had placed himself, paid his way out of them. The case of the *Lancefield* was tried at great length in the United States District Court, and resulted in a verdict for the aggrieved seamen, with damages for the sufferings inflicted upon them. From the point of view taken by the memorialists, this should have acted as a great encouragement to seamen, and there should have been an increase in the number of complaints put forward by them. The fact is that there has not arisen one case calling for serious investigation since this example was made. I will not now name the class of ships in which there used to be so much trouble, because of the great improvement which is observed. Masters and owners hailing from the locality in question have been convinced that sailors have some rights, and can find an authority to support them; also that the "fighting second mate" is an expensive luxury. It is certain that some sort of moral oil has been cast upon the waters which these vessels navigate on their way to New Orleans, and I most sincerely hope that the tranquilising influence is extended to other ports. The sailor and fireman of the period have many serious faults and shortcomings, but those who denounce them as utterly and irredeemably bad will do well to consider these facts.

[Margin notes: Discipline of seamen. Unfounded complaints. Case of Prince Louis. Case of Lancefield. Improved treatment of seamen.]

Annex A.—RETURN of all Shipping at the Port of New Orleans in the Year 1888.

ENTERED.

Nationality.	Sailing. Number of Vessels.	Sailing. Tons.	Steam. Number of Vessels.	Steam. Tons.	Total. Number of Vessels.	Total. Tons.
British	32	15,430	352	425,902	384	441,332
American	71	28,950	353	416,280	424	445,230
Austrian	5	3,578	...	...	5	3,578
French	...	...	18	43,598	18	43,598
German	...	...	...	...	20	25,438
Italian	20	8,325	25	17,334	45	25,659
Mexican	5	802	1	719	6	1,521
Sweden and Norway	2	1,384	...	...	2	1,384
Spanish	20	13,092	50	193,846	70	206,938
Grand total	...	...	...	...	974	1,194,678

CLEARED.

Nationality.	Sailing. Number of Vessels.	Sailing. Tons.	Steam. Number of Vessels.	Steam. Tons.	Total. Number of Vessels.	Total. Tons.
British	45	29,832	356	425,544	401	455,376
American	52	23,595	332	419,398	384	442,993
Austrian	7	4,958	...	...	7	4,958
French	...	...	17	48,868	17	48,868
German	...	...	...	...	26	32,858
Italian	27	12,509	25	17,334	52	29,843
Mexican	7	1,055	1	719	8	1,774
Sweden and Norway	5	5,086	...	...	5	5,086
Spanish	22	14,554	47	80,854	69	95,408
Grand total	...	...	...	...	969	1,109,164

PENSACOLA.

Mr. Vice-Consul Howe reports as follows on the trade of Pensacola:—

Of interest to British firms in Pensacola wood trade. British shipowners interested. Information to British firms abroad. Increase of British trade.

These yearly reports are intended to be, and I have reason to believe are, of interest to those in the United Kingdom dealing with this port by direct purchase of, or being otherwise interested in its chief staple—cargoes of pitch-pine wood shipped hence. The yearly statistics as regards shipping at Pensacola are, no doubt, also particularly looked into by British shipowners. The reports, it may be supposed, are also of service to British commercial houses in this trade abroad, who do business with Pensacola. Any suggestions as regards increase of trade with and through the port that would apparently benefit British manufacturers and exporters should also be reported on. I will endeavour again then to meet the main requirements of these reports for commercial purposes.

Exports and Imports.

Exports. Full yearly average. Large portion to United Kingdom.

By the tabular statements following in this report, it will be seen that the export business of Pensacola for the past year has kept up to the full yearly average of the business proper of the port for some years past, and the largest portion of the shipments, as usual, went to ports in the United Kingdom.

American and British merchants in pitch-pine trade at Pensacola.

The export timber and lumber trade of Pensacola, in its larger operations to foreign ports, is confined to some of the largest Pensacola firms—American and English-American doing business here. The firms first related to (which are more in number) more directly operate through and with the United Kingdom by reason of their old and long-established connections with British houses there as their agents. The latter firms also naturally do a large measure of their trade through and with their direct connections in the United Kingdom.

Shipments to United States ports.

Shipments to northern ports in the United States, more particularly composed of pitch-pine lumber, are, to some extent, by orders direct to the mills, but some of the Pensacola shipping firms above related to, control a portion of this domestic business, which, it will be seen by the figures in this report, is of immense yearly value.

Imports. Chief articles from markets in United States.

I can only again, as in former reports, remark that the chief articles of import in every-day necessaries of life are brought to Pensacola overland, by railroad principally, from the large markets of the United States, and the yearly amount is of much value. Of some articles of merchandise in wearing apparel, and other things coming here from those markets, that is to say, woollen stuffs, linens, hosiery, threads, lace goods, cutlery, hardware, earthenware, &c., it is apparent that quantities of such goods are the manufactures of Great Britain and Ireland, secured from importing jobbers in the larger northern markets of the United States. In fact, from especial inquiry, I know that large quantities of the goods referred to as of British manufacture sold here, are purchased at the North for these southern markets.

English manufactures obtained by southern dealers in northern markets.

Immensity of southern markets.

In view, then, of the continued interest manifested in England as regards trade in British manufactures abroad—looking to its yearly average being kept up and increased in development when practicable—I may be pardoned for relating to the immensity of the southern markets in this part of the country, in connection with the remarks on my immediate post.

British goods for southern markets direct

It has often occurred to me that a system might be formulated whereby many manufactures of the United Kingdom, now obtained by dealers in the Southern States from sources far removed from first hands—from distant markets in the United States—could be secured direct from the manufacturers themselves, certainly to the extra profit of the buyers referred to; and, no doubt, to the increased outlet for the manufactures of the United Kingdom as regards shipments to the United States. I say to the increased outlet to this country of the manufactures referred to, in the belief that if a direct trade with the large southern cities could be established, the trade in this part of the country in English goods would increase abundantly with such improved facilities for securing shipments direct from first hands, and the quick receipt and direct handling of the unbroken packages of goods. And such supposed increase of trade by reason of the advantages endeavoured to be shown would not, I think, in any perceptible way, at all lessen the trade in such goods already existing between the United Kingdom and the other large markets in the United States above alluded to. *from manufacturers. Increased trade to mutual benefit. Improved facilities for direct trade to Southern States would not lessen exports to Northern States.*

Further, it may be supposed that not only would the same class of English goods now accustomed to in these Southern States be sought for direct by dealers and largely increased in supply, but I think that new lines of goods in every way admirably suited to this trade, but never before introduced, would be added to the stocks of merchandise now kept in the various establishments of the markets alluded to. *British goods increased in sale. Introduction of new articles.*

I know that, as a rule, I am to keep to my own post in my remarks upon commercial matters; but in dealing with this subject, and endeavouring to explain what I wish to convey, I am induced to take some range beyond my immediate post and its surroundings, and to make quotations, in order to show some basis for the inauguration of the new business suggested.

In support of my propositions, there, as regards the trade I am pointing to, I take from an American Consular Report for the year ending September 30, 1885 (compiled in London by the American Consul-General at that port), a portion of a list of some of the principal articles of produce and manufactures of the United Kingdom, and their values, shipped thence to the United States that year; and I believe that the shipments were entirely to northern markets; therefore such of those goods as were required for these southern markets had to be purchased North by the southern dealers at the time of their periodical visits for supplying their stocks; and, upon order from samples and patterns. The following is the statement of articles and values above referred to, shipped from the United Kingdom to the United States during the year 1885:— *Shipments to northern markets from England. Bought in the North for southern markets.*

UNITED STATES.

English goods to northern markets in United States.

From—	Articles.	Value.
		Dollars.
Belfast	Linens	7,800,096
Birmingham	Hardware, cutlery, &c.	2,875,388
Bradford	Stuffs	11,565,989
Cardiff	Tin and terne plates	2,785,602
Dundee	Burlaps and linens	6,335,495
Glasgow	Thread, cotton, &c.	5,285,319
Leeds	Woollens and cottons	3,884,045
Liverpool	Tin plates, chemicals, &c.	26,677,507
London	Metals, &c.	*37,323,547
Manchester	Cottons	10,583,050
Nottingham	Lace goods, &c.	5,288,572
Sheffield	Hardware and cutlery	2,186,745
Tunstall	Earthenware	2,809,865
	Total	126,401,220

Large yearly value to northern markets from United Kingdom.

Southern markets buy largely of such goods.

Trade with England may be increased by direct business with Southern States.

Opinion here in favour of direct trade in English goods. Agency might be established.

The entire statement quoted from gives 25 places in the United Kingdom from which goods were exported, and the aggregate value of the shipments was 132,713,595 dol. (about 28,000,000*l.*) I have taken from the statement as above 13 places, giving the manufactures therefrom, as adapted to and used in the markets of the Southern States. If it may be moderately supposed then, that of the goods enumerated in the above list, one-tenth portion was brought to these southern markets that year from the Northern States, and that about the same yearly trade continues, we have over 12,000,000 dol. (over 2,000,000*l.*) as an average value per year of such goods of British merchandise, presuming that the year 1885 (which, I believe, was not given in the Consular Report quoted from, as a full average yearly business in such export trade), keeps up in average trade as the years progress.† If it be so, then, that the above supposed (or larger) yearly average value of exports from the United Kingdom suitable to these markets can now be taken by the dealers here in such trade, may it not be fair, considering the vast extent and population of these southern places, to suppose that with increased facilities for buying, &c., the trade hereabout in the goods alluded to would increase and grow without much, if any, diminution in the yearly average of exports to the northern ports. In short, so much more value would be added to the yearly export trade of the United Kingdom with the United States.

I am also strengthened in my belief as regards the feasibility of the new trade I am pointing to by reason of my conversation with dealers in the trade here—in this smaller market. In larger towns, I have no doubt, the same opinion in favour of such new trade would prevail.

I think that an arrangement could be made at Pensacola—this port of direct inlet and outlet, and connected with the entire country by close railroad and telegraphic communication—with an agent selected, as in every way fitted for the agency of the new trade suggested. Manufacturers and others could correspond with him, and samples of goods suitable to these markets could be sent, so far as practicable, for

---

* In the separate tables of the Consular Report, giving all articles and value exported from the places named, I find that from London there were various things: the largest items being iron, steel, metals, &c., 8,136,580 dol. (1,695,121*l.*); miscellaneous, 10,490,444 dol. (2,185,509*l.*)

† I take from Whittaker's Almanac, supposed to have been gathered from official sources, that the export trade from the United Kingdom to the United States for the following years, ending December 31, 1886, was 37,607,805*l.*; 1887, 40,240,150*l.*

orders to be secured on. The agent would of course extend his agency by sub-agencies, as appeared desirable, and in this way the business could be carried on, and extended from this port and State, and from place to place, as might seem desirable. All details connected with the commissions on sales, and remittances for goods ordered, would of course be mutually and particularly gone into. The general agency, I think, should be centred in one place and in one person, with whom all manufacturers, shippers, and importers would be supposed to deal. To do the business otherwise (by competitive agencies) would not answer in my opinion. With the increased export trade at this port by steam, I think it could be arranged for the transit of goods from time to time direct from the United Kingdom to Pensacola. Should such direct means of transit fail at the commencement of the business—before the trade was regularly established—shipments could be made viâ northern ports, and New Orleans, with goods in transit, as regards duties; at least I suppose the latter arrangement could be in some way managed. The sending of the goods to Pensacola direct, for this and the surrounding markets alluded to, would however, obviate, I think, all difficulty as regards customs matters. *Sub-agencies. General agency at one place. Direct transit of goods to Pensacola. Goods could be sent viâ northern ports and New Orleans.*

The dealers in this, and other principal towns in Florida, and in the immediately adjacent States of Mississippi, Georgia, and Alabama—the markets of the latter State very near by—would, I think, be glad to avail themselves of the opportunities and advantages that such a direct trade would offer. *Dealers, no doubt, would be glad of such direct trade.*

The markets particularly above referred to as within easy business dealing with this port do an immense business, as before remarked, with the Northern States. Why, then, should not these markets—these distinct markets, I may say—do the same direct business with manufacturers and wholesale dealers in the United Kingdom, as done by the importers in the northern markets of the United States? I do not think that such a direct trade has ever been fairly considered, and its mutual advantages made a matter of calculation. *Trade here with Northern States. Dealers could do the same trade direct with United Kingdom.*

As a little in further support of my belief that the direct trade suggested would be entertained in the United Kingdom, I will state that I have, from time to time, received catalogues and letters from extensive manufacturing firms in the United Kingdom, desiring to open up a trade here for their manufactures. I may also mention that, within the last few months, I have been applied to by a firm in a principal city in Ireland to assist in the introduction, by direct shipment to this port, of a building article largely used here—cement—and a correspondence has been brought about between an extensive dealer here in the article, and the firm related to, which will, I believe, result in a business. The same article has hitherto been brought here, secured from receivers in the northern markets of the United States. *Merchants and manufacturers write often on direct trade. Cement from Ireland direct to Pensacola. Hitherto received from northern markets in United States.*

I may mention, as in connection with the foregoing remarks on direct trade between these Southern States and the United Kingdom, that the banks and bankers of the leading cities and towns of the South have agencies, with banks and bankers in the United Kingdom—particularly in London—hence financial matters in the business could be conveniently arranged, I think. The banks in Pensacola do business with banks in London and Liverpool. *Southern banks generally, and banks of Pensacola, do business with banks in England.*

If my suggestions are at all entertained, with a view to the business remarked on, I would propose that the business people wishing to inquire fully into the likelihood of such a trade being successfully gone into, agree together to appoint an appropriate agent to visit the Southern States referred to by me, and really ascertain by conversation and observation what could be done. Such a pioneer agent should be a practical person in almost every branch of trade. *Pioneer agents might be sent out by British firms.*

On agent's report business could be commenced. Consular assistance.

that might be worked in. Upon the report of such an agent, if favourable, the necessary arrangements for the business could be made.

I am ready at all times to meet the legitimate demands of business houses in the United Kingdom to the end in view, and I feel confident that the commencement of such a direct trade would be of great advantage mutually, and that it would grow to large dimensions. I would assist very heartily towards its consummation.

RETURN of Principal Articles of Export from Pensacola during the Years 1887–1888.

Articles.	1888. Quantity.	1888. Value. £ s. d	1887. Quantity.	1887. Value. £ s. d.
Sawn pitch-pine timber	10,256,650	267,100 5 3	8,651,456	198,262 10 8
Pitch-pine lumber	104,744,226	261,935 11 3	131,004,501	327,511 5 0
Hewn pitch-pine timber	1,499,198	34,367 12 5	935,889	21,447 9 1
Cedar	27,222	1,984 18 9	...	...
Coal	615	384 7 6	...	...
Cotton	...	...	3,446	37,747 3 4
Rosin	...	...	305	79 8 6
Other articles	...	829 3 4	...	3,279 10 7
Total	...	566,601 18 6	...	585,327 7 2

In the above table lumber is in superficial thousand feet, valued at 12 dol. (2l. 10s.); sawn timber, at average of 12½ c. (6¼d.) per cubic foot—basis, 40 feet average; hewn timber, at average of 11 c. (5½d.) per cubic foot—basis, 100 cubic feet average; cotton, at average of 10 c. (5d.) per lb., in bales of 484 lbs. average weight each bale; coal in tons, at 3 dol. (12s. 6d.); rosin in barrels, at 1 dol. 25 c. (5s. 2½d.) per barrel; cedar, at 35 c. (1s. 5½d.) per cubic foot.

RETURN of Principal Articles of Import to Pensacola during the Years 1887–1888.

Articles.	Value. 1888. £ s. d.	Value. 1887. £ s. d.
Chief articles	*	*
Other „	*	27,955 9 8

* As explained in former reports, the values of chief articles of trade received at Pensacola, comprising the every day requirements in food and clothing, as well as articles in hardware, agricultural implements, appliances in manufactures, and all such things generally, are from the large northern, southern, and western markets of the United States, and such things come mostly by railroad. Ice (ice is also manufactured at Pensacola) fertilizers, and sometimes railroad iron, are received from the northern markets by sea route, varying in yearly supplies. The annual total receipts of all such foregoing supplies may be put at over 2,000,000 dol., according to published statements. No exact record, however, is kept. As regards other articles, that is to say, things received from foreign countries, comprising generally salt, fertilizers and railroad iron from the United Kingdom, and fertilizers from Germany, during the last year such receipts were quite few, and the value not obtainable for this report.

NEW ORLEANS.

TABLE showing the Total Value of all Articles Exported from Pensacola and Imported to Pensacola from and to Foreign Countries during the Years 1887–1888.

Country.	Exports. 1888.	Exports. 1887.	Imports. 1888.	Imports. 1887.
	£ s. d.	£ s. d.	£ s. d.	£ s. d.
United Kingdom	221,741 6 9	224,107 18 0	...	24,355 16 8
Italy	67,517 18 11	40,747 2 9	...	...
Argentine Republic	56,116 7 9	78,129 2 0	...	...
France	35,568 11 1	24,279 14 9	...	...
Netherlands	32,390 7 1	20,067 4 10	...	...
Germany	20,347 0 0	2,819 11 8	...	...
Uruguay	19,459 12 8	45,168 3 0	...	...
Spain and colonies	17,462 13 3	18,389 18 3	...	...
Belgium	14,558 5 8	12,279 7 2	...	...
Portugal	9,983 10 3	8,063 5 8	...	...
Brazil	7,910 17 6	14,399 9 5	...	...
United States of Colombia	6,260 0 0	8,147 10 0	...	...
Austria	2,213 10 4	...	...	...
Other countries	3,331 3 9	1,428 19 8	...	3,599 13 0
Total—Foreign countries	514,861 5 0	498,027 7 2	...*	27,955 9 8
„ —Ports in the United States	51,740 13 6	87,300 0 0	...*	...*
Total	566,601 18 6	585,327 7 2	...	27,955 9 8

SHIPPING.

It will be observed by the tables following that the amount of British tonnage at Pensacola for the past year was beyond that of the year preceding. It will also be notable that a large proportion of such tonnage was in steamers. The number and tonnage of British steamers that loaded at this port last year exceeded any previous yearly entry of such vessels at Pensacola.

British tonnage larger than year preceding. Steamers increased in number and tonnage.

In reference to steamers chartered to load at Pensacola, I observe that what is called the lump-sum charter leads to much dissatisfaction and trouble on both sides. The charterer, for instance, often believes that were the ship under another form of charter—that is, a stated amount per standard or load—more cargo would be stowed in the ship. On the other hand, the master often takes the ground that the charterer wishes to force too much cargo on the ship. Hence unpleasant discussions arise, resulting sometimes in the ship being libelled for breach of charter, and when that step is taken, whatever the final result in suit, the loss to ship is always disastrous. If the lump-sum charter cannot be framed in such a manner as to avoid any questions arising, it would be always better, I think, to follow the regular form of charter; that is to say, a stated rate on all cargo carried.

Lump-sum Pensacola steamer charter. Questions about loading. Law suits arise. Stated rate on all cargo carried thought best plan.

Of the total tonnage in foreign vessels at Pensacola during the past year, it will be seen by the tables on shipping, following, that in entrances and clearances British tonnage, compared with other flags, was over one-fourth in proportion.

British tonnage for past year, compared with other foreign flags, over one-fourth.

In connection with this subject—shipping at Pensacola—I may here relate that the Board of Commissioners (the city government of Pensacola) recently passed an ordinance, appointing a shipping master for the port of Pensacola. This ordinance was passed in accordance with an Act of the Legislature of the State of Florida. It provides that penalties shall be enforced against any one providing seamen for engagement, other than the shipping master or his deputy. The rules and regulations for the government of the shipping master are

Shipping of seamen. Shipping master appointed and licensed by city government of Pensacola.

* See Note on page 14.

(584)

UNITED STATES.

Penalties on unlicensed persons providing seamen for engagement.
Shipping master to have seamen on board at time appointed.
Shipping fee not to exceed 2 dol.
Much trouble caused by former plan of shipping seamen.
The change a good one.
Further steps anticipated towards checking crimping evil.

framed by the city government, who appoint, license, and supervise him generally. The shipping master, upon the request of the master of any vessel, is to procure the seamen required for engagement, and to see that they are on board at the time appointed. The fee for such service is not to exceed 2 dol. (8s. 4d.) for each seaman provided.

The ordinance deals with and regulates that part of the trade in seamen formerly forced by the crimping business on masters. The class referred to, for many years past had always required, and were paid, in addition to advance wages, what they termed a "shipping fee" of 5 dol. (20s. 10d.) for each seaman supplied. Often, however, was it the case that seamen thus offered to, and engaged by, masters, were not brought forward at the time agreed upon, and on such occasions substitutes were presented, and taken, contrary to law; and in many such cases serious trouble and grave questions from time to time arose, in which the masters were answerable and were held responsible. As regards the business of this office, and on general grounds, I am heartily glad of the change brought about by the local authorities. I look in the same direction for further steps towards controlling the nefarious crimping system that has for so long a time had unlimited sway in Pensacola.

RETURN of all Shipping at the Port of Pensacola in the Year 1888.

ENTERED.

Nationality.	Sailing. Number of Vessels.	Sailing. Tons.	Steam. Number of Vessels.	Steam. Tons.	Total. Number of Vessels.	Total. Tons.
British	57	53,564	22	28,333	79	81,897
American	86	38,220	...	...	86	38,220
Swedish and Norwegian	129	100,425	...	...	129	100,425
Italian	95	60,986	1	782	96	61,768
Russian	36	23,549	...	...	36	23,549
Austrian	20	12,763	...	...	20	12,763
Netherlands	12	8,925	...	...	12	8,925
German	8	7,629	1	1,070	9	8,699
French	8	4,327	1	1,976	9	6,303
Belgian	...	...	2	2,231	2	2,231
Other countries	3	1,493	...	...	3	1,493
Grand total	454	311,881	27	34,392	481	346,273
,, for the year preceding	520	357,086	5	6,225	525	363,311

CLEARED.

Nationality.	Sailing. Number of Vessels.	Sailing. Tons.	Steam. Number of Vessels.	Steam. Tons.	Total. Number of Vessels.	Total. Tons.
British	62	59,583	22	28,333	84	87,916
American	90	39,500	...	...	90	39,500
Swedish and Norwegian	129	99,632	...	...	129	99,632
Italian	84	55,683	1	782	85	56,465
Russian	41	27,628	...	...	41	27,628
Austrian	19	12,221	...	...	19	12,221
Netherlands	11	8,556	...	...	11	8,556
German	5	5,637	1	1,070	6	6,707
French	6	2,894	1	1,976	7	4,870
Belgian	...	...	2	2,231	2	2,231
Other countries	2	1,150	...	...	2	1,150
Grand total	449	312,484	27	34,392	476	346,876
,, for the year preceding	519	335,950	5	6,225	524	342,175

General Remarks.

Marine Railway.—A corporation, under the name of the Pensacola Marine Railway, has recently been established by law. The general nature of the business to be transacted by said corporation is to build and operate at Pensacola a marine and dry dock, and to build and repair vessels; also to buy, sell, lease, or improve real estate. The amount of the capital stock is 100,000 dol., divided into 1,000 shares of 100 dol. each. The company is composed of some of the foremost citizens and leading business men of Pensacola.

I take from a published statement respecting the dock the following particulars:—

"The entire structure will be 535 feet in length, 250 feet being above the water line, and 285 feet below, or submerged. The grade will be 6 feet to the hundred, an actual fall of 32 feet in the entire length, and the lowest point of the railway will be 18 feet under water, while the end on land will be 15 feet above the water line, and some 12 feet from the ground at the shore end.

"The iron columns, with braces, cross-beams, and ties, will support four lines of steel rails (each line being two rails, one on top of the other, and forming an actual girder of 4¾ inches thick), and on these will be set the "cradles" with "chariots," which graduate and regulate the bearings on the hull of the vessels, and give even support all the way around. On the land these iron columns will stand on foundations of brick and granite, thus rendering the structure perfectly immovable, and not subject to any swaying or oscillation.

"The railway will take up any ship not more than 250 feet in length, and will have a sustaining power of 24·06 tons per lineal foot. The tracks, or lines of rails, will be 16 feet from centre to centre of outside rails—the widest of any marine railway in the United States. The time required to take a vessel from the water and carry her above the water line, where the entire bottom will be exposed, and easy of access for cleaning or repairs, will be from 15 minutes to 2 hours; the latter for the largest size—say 3,000 tons—which will be vastly more expeditious and less expensive than dry-docking."

I think that a marine railway, or some such permanent construction, has been long needed at Pensacola. It may be—I believe has been—that many a time have ships proceeded hence that should and would have been overhauled and fitted for sea before proceeding; but which necessary steps to their seaworthiness could not be taken, owing to there being no facilities for docking them at this port; and which vessels, no doubt, have had to put into other ports leaking, or have never been heard of after leaving Pensacola.

Coal.—Within the last few weeks two small British vessels have loaded here with Alabama coal, taking together about 800 tons. The coal was brought direct from the mines in Alabama, a couple of hundred miles distant from Pensacola by railroad. These cargoes were delivered to the vessels alongside of the railroad wharf. I am told that this commencement in the exportation of coal—these cargoes went to Cuba—is by way of experiment in deciding upon continued shipments of coal through this port. The rates of freight paid were 2 dol. 75 c. and 2 dol. 50 c. per ton to the vessels respectively. The value of the coal alongside was about 3 dol. per ton.

Health and General Prosperity of Pensacola.—I am glad to be able to state that the health record of Pensacola and vicinity for the past year accords with the average good healthiness of the place. And I am further pleased to be able to state that business appears to

Increase of trade.

New buildings.

Railroads.

progress here prosperously. As related in my reports from time to time preceding this, the people of Pensacola look forward to yearly general increase in the development of this city by the introduction of capital, and the addition to its population; and these additions are being annually made. The population of Pensacola increases yearly, as shown by the amount of building that goes on continually, not only as regards private residences, but in business houses on the principal streets. Again, railroads already projected, and being projected and to be built—great factors as such corporations are in the development of a place—are especially looked forward to in the general onward strides of the town.

British people interested in progress of Pensacola.

I am aware that many business houses, and persons generally in the United Kingdom, are much interested in Pensacola's progress; hence it always gives me pleasure in being able fairly to remark in favour of this pleasant place and its surroundings.

MOBILE, ALABAMA.

Mr. Vice-Consul Barnewall reports as follows:—

Commercial year commencing September 1, 1887, and ending August 31, 1888.

Cotton receipts.

Prices.

Receipts—207,377 bales, valued at 9,613,997 dol. 77 c., against 216,142 bales, valued at 9,655,063 dol. 14 c., receipts of the year preceding. Average price per bale, 46 dol. 36 c., average price per lb., $9\frac{28}{100}$ c., against 44 dol. 67 c. per bale, and $8\frac{97}{100}$ c. per lb., the year preceding.

Our gross receipts, compared with last year, show a falling-off of about 9,000 bales; but this did not affect the cotton trade of Mobile, as the actual amount handled in this market, compared with last year, shows an increase of 21,000 bales, for the decrease in gross receipts was caused by a falling-off of 27,000 bales in transit cotton for New Orleans.

Exports, cotton.

There has been an improvement in the direct exports to Liverpool, and the total this year is larger than for many years, which was caused by the increased tonnage offered by the Mobile and Liverpool Steamship Company.

Timber.

In this important branch of the pitch-pine trade there has been a decided improvement the past year over the previous one; the business of the past season has, on the whole, been healthy and generally satisfactory.

Shipments, Prices, &c.

In the shipments of timber, foreign, the past year shows a sharp increase over last year, and the total value alone is over 100,000 dol. larger than that of 1886–87; but the increase in value is in part due to the improvement in prices, as the average price per cubic foot of shipments, foreign, is larger than any year since 1883–84. Besides this, the shipments from this port do not represent the amount of timber sold in this market, as very large amounts of timber were during the year towed from this place to Ship Island for vessels loading there.

Supply.

This section is beautifully supplied with the best timber that can be found in the South, and, as improvements have been made during the past year for bringing it to market, shippers of this port will, no doubt, obtain orders at remunerative prices.

Lumber.

Firms.

In this important branch of business, which is one of the leading industries of Mobile and South Alabama, there are many engaged, and, during the past year, many improvements have been made to meet the increased trade of this port. New firms have been formed, new mills built, and the capacity of many of the old ones increased.

During the past few months the trade was greatly hampered by the scarcity of vessels, and, in consequence, shipments checked, as freights steadily advanced, which made it difficult for shippers to meet the views of buyers East and in Europe.

Exports. The total exports, foreign, show an increase of over 2,000,000 feet, while the total coastwise exhibits a decrease, but the total of both is over 29,000,000 feet. Compared with last year, the exports show an increase of 2,000,000 feet to the United Kingdom, 1,000,000 feet to Cuba, over 2,000,000 feet to New York, and 200,000 feet to Baltimore. The principal decrease was 700,000 feet to France, 450,000 feet to Holland, 200,000 feet to Trinidad, 2,000,000 feet to Philadelphia, and 2,000,000 feet to northern ports.

Naval stores. In this branch of business, which is an important one in this section, the trade of the past year has not been satisfactory, as will be seen from the following statement:—

Rosin and turpentine. Receipts—rosin, 132,055 barrels; turpentine, 28,725 barrels; total value, 635,643 dol.; against rosin, 132,955 barrels; turpentine, 40,149 barrels; total value, 820,691 dol., the year preceding.

Vegetable shipments. Value, &c. The vegetable trade is increasing every year, and not only adding greatly to the wealth of this county, but is taking an important part in bringing Mobile before the people of the West and North. Shipments are made to nearly all the leading places, including St. Louis, Cincinnati, Chicago, Kansas City, and Pittsburg.

The value of the crop in this county is estimated at 393,000 dol., and shows an increase of 84,000 dol. in value over last year; and the total value of the shipments is about 63,000 dol. larger than last year.

Compared with last year, cabbages show an increase of 20,000 crates in shipments, and 31,000 dol. in value.

Potatoes show an increase of 37,000 barrels in shipments, and 32,000 dol. in value. Beans show an increase of 18,000 boxes in shipments, and 5,000 dol. in value. Peas show a decrease of 2,000 boxes in shipments, and 3,500 dol. in value.

The above facts are encouraging for the vegetable trade of Mobile, and, no doubt, next year will show an increase on the one just past.

New railroads. Mobile and Dauphin Island Railroad and Harbour Company.—Work will probably be resumed on this enterprise at an early day, but the company will be controlled by London parties, and the road and docks built by Messrs. James Wright and Co., of London. The capital has been increased from 1,500,000 dol. to 2,500,000 dol., and the plans somewhat changed. The present company proposes to make a harbour, 26 feet deep, in the island, and bring the deep water of the Gulf into the harbour by a short canal. If the plan proposed is carried out, it will be the most convenient and safest port on the Gulf; and with modern appliances for rapid loading of large ships will at once draw a large business to Mobile, besides making it the great coal port of the South.

The Mobile Jackson and Kansas City Railroad Company has been formed by consolidating the two Mobile, Hattiesburg and Jackson roads of Alabama and Mississippi; and the managers of the enterprise are pushing it along, and feel confident of success. This road, for about 150 miles, runs through a fine pine forest, much of which has been recently purchased by Michigan lumber men. It will give Mobile valuable rail connections and direct business connection with fine agricultural sections, which will make it a valuable addition to Mobile railroads.

The proposed Chicago and Gulf road, which will come through

Alabama from Florence, on the Tennessee River, to Mobile, is taking good shape, and parties acquainted with the present status of its management are confident that it will soon be under construction. This road will come directly through the great Warrior coal fields, and will give us the shortest possible all-rail route from the mineral fields. It will shorten the time to Chicago and other western cities, and will, no doubt, cause a great amount of imported goods for western centres to come this way.

Annex A.—RETURN of all Shipping at the Port of Mobile in the Year 1888.

ENTERED.

Nationality.	Sailing. Number of Vessels.	Sailing. Tons.	Steam. Number of Vessels.	Steam. Tons.	Total. Number of Vessels.	Total. Tons.
British	38	30,308	16	16,624	54	46,932
American	46	11,210	...	...	46	11,210
Norwegian	14	8,489	1	1,000	15	9,489
Italian	1	682	...	...	1	682
Swedish	4	2,761	...	...	4	2,761
Hondurian	4	160	...	...	4	160
Austrian	1	935	...	...	1	935
French	3	1,414	...	...	3	1,414
Spanish	2	878	...	...	2	878
Dutch	1	796	...	...	1	796
Coastwise	72	35,960	...	...	72	35,960
Grand total	186	93,593	17	17,624	203	111,217
,, for the year preceding	...	...	...	...	198	113,510

CLEARED.

Nationality.	Sailing. Number of Vessels.	Sailing. Tons.	Steam. Number of Vessels.	Steam. Tons.	Total. Number of Vessels.	Total. Tons.
British	38	30,548	18	18,660	56	49,208
American	50	13,516	...	...	50	13,516
Norwegian	18	11,309	1	1,000	19	12,309
Italian	1	682	...	...	1	682
Swedish	3	2,269	...	...	3	2,269
Hondurian	3	120	...	...	3	120
Austrian	2	1,687	...	...	2	1,687
French	2	1,010	...	...	2	1,010
Spanish	3	1,226	...	...	3	1,226
Dutch	1	796	...	...	1	796
German	2	1,138	...	...	2	1,138
Russian	1	623	...	...	1	623
Coastwise	64	24,908	...	...	64	24,908
Grand total	188	89,832	19	19,660	207	109,492
,, for the year preceding	...	...	...	...	196	108,766

NEW ORLEANS.

Annex B.—RETURN of Principal Articles of Import to Mobile during the Years 1887–88 and 1886–87.

Articles.		1887 and 1888. Quantity.	1887 and 1888. Value. £ s. d.	1886 and 1887. Quantity.	1886 and 1887. Value. £ s. d.
Bagging	Pieces	18,415	...	37,476	...
Iron ties	Bundles	36,836	...	29,550	...
Bacon	Hhds.	13,777	...	15,194	...
Cotton	Bales	207,377	2,002,916 3 10	216,142	2,011,471 9 9
Coffee	Sacks	15,572	...	16,115	...
Corn	,,	325,556	...	349,931	...
Flour	Barrels	135,141	...	125,129	...
Fertilisers	Sacks	165,430	...	147,360	...
Hay	Bales	63,071	...	53,268	...
Lard	Tierces	3,490	...	3,379	...
Molasses	Barrels	3,560	...	3,582	...
Oats	Sacks	105,076	...	93,428	...
Potatoes	Barrels	17,460	...	21,593	...
Pork	,,	965	...	2,259	...
Rice	,,	4,831	...	5,120	...
Salt	Sacks	23,540	...	58,436	...
Soap	Boxes	19,767	...	24,432	...
Sugar	Barrels	16,569	...	17,900	...
Tobacco	Boxes	25,055	...	24,074	...
Whiskey	Barrels	6,090	...	6,068	...
Coal	Tons	39,433	...	40,142	...
Wool	Lbs.	652,800	29,920 0 10	522,800	29,952 1 8

I cannot enumerate articles imported from foreign countries, nor give the value of above enumerated articles, with exception of cotton and wool.

Annex C.—TABLE showing the Total Value of all articles Exported from Mobile and Imported to Mobile from and to Foreign Countries during the Years 1887–88 and 1886–87.

EXPORTS.

		£	s.	d.
1886–87	.. ..	532,886	5	0
1887–88	.. ..	717,727	6	4

IMPORTS TO 30TH JUNE, 1888.

		£	s.	d.
1886–87	.. ..	13,445	0	0
1887–88	.. ..	15,924	7	6

I have no means of dividing the above as to countries, except as regards cotton, included in above.

		£	s.	d.
Great Britain, 1886–87	.. ..	435,597	12	10
1887–88	.. ..	603,529	18	8

£1 sterling valued at 4 dol. 80 c.

RETURN of Principal Articles of Export from Mobile during the Years 1887–88 and 1886–87.

Articles.			1887 and 1888.		1886 and 1887.	
			Quantity.	Value.	Quantity.	Value.
				£ s. d.		£ s. d.
Cotton	...	Bales	222,783	2,151,712 9 6	233,210	2,170,310 11 3
Timber	...	Cubic feet	2,575,784	64,955 12 8	1,836,573	45,022 10 1
Lumber	...	Feet	29,257,844	72,446 0 4	29,346,230	72,639 19 6
Rosin	...	Barrels	25,435	7,930 17 0	17,504	5,892 4 6
Staves	...	Per mill	51,291	1,083 15 6	48,071	949 4 5
Cotton-seed meal	...	Sacks	...	...	25,053	4,758 10 10
Shingles	...	...	655,950	444 2 8	585,000	340 15 0
Merchandise	...	...	...	1,040 6 0	...	999 9 10
Vegetables	...	...	...	81,936 9 2	...	64,449 15 10
Total	...	...	...	2,381,549 12 10	...	2,365,363 1 3

£1 sterling valued at 4 dol. 80 c.

CONDITION of Dredged Channel, Mobile Harbour, on the 30th day of June, 1888.

Locality.	Dredged 1881 and 1887.			Examination, June, 1888.	
	From the Initial Point.	Width.	Depth.	Maximum Top Width.	Maximum Central Depth.
	Miles.	Feet.	Feet.	Feet.	Feet.
Initial point in Mobile River to upper gap obstructions	0·64	145	18 to 20	200	19 to 20
Upper gap of obstructions to Cluster No. 2	1·07	245	18 ,, 19	300	22
Cluster No. 2 to lower gap of obstructions	1·48	155	18 ,, 19	200	20
Lower gap of obstructions to Cluster No. 23	11·99	145	18 ,, 19	200	16 to 19
Cluster No. 23 to Cluster No. 27	13·91	105	18 ,, 19	200	15 ,, 16
Cluster No. 27 to Cluster No. 30	15·39	145	18 ,, 19	200	15 ,, 16
Cluster No. 30 to Cluster No. 51	25·91	185	18 ,, 19	200	14 ,, 18

NOTE.—With the appropriation of 250,000 dol. now available, it is expected that the channel can be so improved as to leave a central depth of not less than 19 feet at mean low tide.

LONDON:
Printed for Her Majesty's Stationery Office,
By HARRISON AND SONS,
Printers in Ordinary to Her Majesty.
(1125 3 | 89—H & S 584)

FOREIGN OFFICE.
1889.
ANNUAL SERIES.

N.º 466.

DIPLOMATIC AND CONSULAR REPORTS ON TRADE AND FINANCE.

UNITED STATES.

REPORT FOR THE YEAR 1888
ON THE
AGRICULTURAL CONDITION OF THE CONSULAR DISTRICT OF NEW ORLEANS.

REFERENCE TO PREVIOUS REPORT, Annual Series No. 27.

Presented to both Houses of Parliament by Command of Her Majesty,
MARCH, 1889.

LONDON:
PRINTED FOR HER MAJESTY'S STATIONERY OFFICE,
BY HARRISON AND SONS, ST. MARTIN'S LANE,
PRINTERS IN ORDINARY TO HER MAJESTY.

And to be purchased, either directly or through any Bookseller, from
EYRE AND SPOTTISWOODE, EAST HARDING STREET, FLEET STREET, E.C., and
32, ABINGDON STREET, WESTMINSTER, S.W.; or
ADAM AND CHARLES BLACK, 6, NORTH BRIDGE, EDINBURGH; or
HODGES, FIGGIS, & Co., 104, GRAFTON STREET, DUBLIN.

1889.

[C. 5618—19.] *Price Twopence.*

New Series of Reports.

Reports of the Annual Series have been issued from Her Majesty's Diplomatic and Consular Officers at the following places, and may be obtained from the sources indicated on the title-page:—

No.		Price.	No.		Price.
340.	Wilmington	1d.	403.	Nagasaki	1d.
341.	Amoy	2d.	404.	Hiogo	2d.
342.	Trebizond	1d.	405.	Tonga	1d.
343.	Lisbon	1d.	406.	Adana	1d.
344.	Java	1d.	407.	Valparaiso	1d.
345.	Brest	1d.	408.	Bilbao	1d.
346.	Odessa	2d.	409.	Santiago	1d.
347.	Cavalla	1d.	410.	Paramaribo	1d.
348.	Bussorah	1d.	411.	Nantes	1d.
349.	Mollendo	1d.	412.	Bangkok	1d.
350.	Cadiz	5d.	413.	Yokohama	2d.
351.	Cagliari	4d.	414.	Mozambique	1d.
352.	Cagliari	1d.	415.	Canton	2d.
353.	Ajaccio	1d.	416.	Kiungchow	1d.
354.	Copenhagen	1d.	417.	Damascus	1d.
355.	Vienna	1d.	418.	Syra	1d.
356.	San Francisco	1d.	419.	Aleppo	1d.
357.	Vera Cruz	1d.	420.	Sandakan	1d.
358.	Philippopolis	1d.	421.	Barcelona	1d.
359.	Greytown	1d.	422.	Königsberg	1d.
360.	Tangier	1d.	423.	Tabreez	1d.
361.	Lisbon	1d.	424.	Guayaquil	1d.
362.	Chicago	1d.	425.	St. Petersburg	1d.
363.	Jerusalem and Jaffa	1d.	426.	Tokio	1d.
364.	Truxillo	1d.	427.	Charleston	1d.
365.	Ningpo	1d.	428.	Amsterdam	1d.
366.	Chefoo	1d.	429.	Hamburg	4d.
367.	Bushire	1d.	430.	Trieste	1d.
368.	Stockholm	2d.	431.	New York	2d.
369.	Santiago	1d.	432.	Antwerp	1d.
370.	New York	2d.	433.	Munich	1d.
371.	Pernambuco	1d.	434.	Buenos Ayres	1d.
372.	Söul	1d.	435.	Warsaw	1d.
373.	Chinkiang	2d.	436.	Porto Rico	1d.
374.	Pernambuco	1d.	437.	Réunion	1d.
375.	San Francisco	2d.	438.	Lisbon	1d.
376.	Riga	1d.	439.	Venice	1d.
377.	Newchwang	2d.	440.	Christiania	5d.
378.	San Salvador	1d.	441.	Maranham	1d.
379.	Frankfort	2d.	442.	Sofia	1d.
380.	Hankow	2d.	443.	Copenhagen	1d.
381.	Bucharest	1d.	444.	Galatz	1d.
382.	Lisbon	1d.	445.	Tabreez	1d.
383.	Tunis	1d.	446.	Bogotá	2d.
384.	Tangier	1d.	447.	St. Petersburg	3d.
385.	Santiago	2d.	448.	Nice	1d.
386.	Diarbekir	1d.	449.	Stettin	2d.
387.	Shanghai	2d.	450.	Fiume	1d.
388.	Rome	2d.	451.	Chinkiang	1d.
389.	Buenos Ayres	1d.	452.	The Hague	1d.
390.	Amsterdam	1d.	453.	Malaga	1d.
391.	Warsaw	1d.	454.	Taganrog	1d.
392.	San Francisco	1d.	455.	Mozambique	1d.
393.	Alexandria	1d.	456.	Bogotá	2d.
394.	Salonica	2d.	457.	Patras	1d.
395.	Palermo	1d.	458.	Galveston	1d.
396.	Mexico	4d.	459.	Buda Pesth	1d.
397.	Naples	3d.	460.	Madeira	1d.
398.	Boston	1d.	461.	Warsaw	1d.
399.	Hakodate	1d.	462.	Paris	2d.
400.	Nantes	1d.	463.	Baltimore	1d.
401.	Madeira	1d.	464.	Philadelphia	2d.
402.	Hakodate	1d.	465.	New Orleans	2d.

No. 466.

Reference to previous Report, Annual Series No. 27.

UNITED STATES.

NEW ORLEANS.

Consul De Fonblanque to the Marquis of Salisbury.

My Lord,   *New Orleans, February* 9, 1889.

I HAVE the honour to enclose the Agricultural Reports for this Consular District for the year 1888.

I have, &c.
(Signed)   A. DE G. DE FONBLANQUE.

Report on Agriculture, 1888.

Respecting the cultivation of cotton, there is nothing that can be published in a report of this character which would be of value at the time of its publication. The acreage planted, the condition from time to time of the crop, its quantity and its quality, have been the subjects of almost daily telegraphic communications, and the conflict of the "longs" and the "shorts" respecting the amount of the yield cannot yet be settled. There is nothing new in the manner of cultivation. [*Cotton.*]

This cannot be said of sugar. Threatened with a reduction of duty on this product, the planter is making a good fight against the more or less evil day, which must dawn upon him sooner or later, by reducing expenses to a minimum, and adopting means whereby the utmost possible amount of sugar may be extracted from his cane. [*Sugar.*]

The planter of sugar cane is also the maker of sugar, and it is almost impossible to draw the line where he ceases to be an agriculturist and his business as a manufacturer commences. I therefore venture to bring him into this report in both capacities, though, strictly speaking, sugar-making may not come under the head of "agriculture."

I am informed that a report upon field experiments with sugar cane, emanating from one of our experimental stations, which I forwarded for the use of the Colonial Office last March, was considered of interest by a London company interested in the cultivation of cane in the East. [*Report of experiments.*]

The diffusion process, from which valuable results are expected, is described as follows:— [*Diffusion process.*]

"The cane was placed on a carrier and conveyed to a set of revolving knives, which cut the stalks up into small pieces, each about three-quarters of an inch long. From the cutters the pieces dropped in a shaker or sieve, over which a fan kept up a constant current of air, which cleansed the cane thoroughly of the leaves, &c. The pieces of cane then fell into an elevator, which carried them up to the roof of the one-storey building, and fell then into a machine which reduced them to a pulp. The pulping machine consisted of four small planing knives, which revolve very rapidly.

(585)

"This pulp was then conveyed on a traveller over a battery of 14 cells, and dropped into them as desired by the operator. These cells are large, jug-shaped iron tanks, with moveable bottoms, and closed on the top by means of a large iron cover screwed down by means of levers. These cells are connected with one another by means of pipes, and when they are filled with pulp the lids are securely fastened down, lime having first been placed in each cell to assist in clarifying the juice. Hot water is then let into the first cell, and forced out by means of compressed air into the next cell, and thus through the entire battery until it reaches the last one, when it is conducted through a pipe to the measuring tank. The concentrated juice is then led to the double-effect apparatus, and from thence to the strike pan and ground into sugar and centrifugaled.

"The result by this method is that nearly every particle of saccharine matter contained in the cane is extracted, and as high as 251 lbs. of sugar has been obtained from a ton of cane, against 125 to 140 lbs. by the best of the older processes.

"In addition to this great advantage there is another in favour of the diffusion process, and that is the lessening to a minimum of the danger of the machinery becoming deranged. The great power and speed requisite in other methods is almost entirely obviated by the diffusion process.

"As an evidence of how thoroughly the juice is extracted from the cane by the diffusion, Professor Stubbs had a quantity of the chips conveyed to his laboratory and carefully analysed by means of a polariscope, and yesterday this analytical test showed the presence of only $1\frac{1}{4}$ per cent. of sugar in the chips, or $1\frac{1}{4}$ lb. of sugar to every lb. of chips; and this was by no means a low percentage, for the records showed that the minimum was 25, or one-quarter of 1 per cent., and rarely over 1 per cent., analytical tests having been made at each grinding. The machinery can be kept going constantly, as one cell is being emptied and another filled while the work is progressing. The cells are opened from below, when the bagasse falls into a car and is shoved out to the bagasse pile."

Chips for pulp.

The exhausted chips from diffusion cells are said to be well adapted for paper pulp. The average result obtained under it on sugar cane at Governor Warmoth's Magnolia plantation is 236 lbs. of sugar per ton of cane. Here it must be borne in mind that the cane of Louisiana has rarely more than six months to mature, whereas tropical cane can be left standing regardless of frost till its juice is at its best.

Simplicity of the process.

Of this process Professor Stubbs, of the Kennerville Experimental Station, writes:—"This is such a comfortable and simple process of making sugar. No clarification, no scums, no settlings, no filter press. What an amount of worry, to say nothing of expense, is saved."

Opinion of Professor Albrecht.

Professor Albrecht (analytical chemist) writes:—

"Thanks to the aid of the Government in furnishing pecuniary means, accomplished chemists, and skilled operatives, the difficulties have, step by step, been met and mastered, defects supplied, and improvements established.

"An objection to the introduction of the diffusion process, which originally had great weight with me, was that it would necessarily involve the contamination of the cane juice with colouring matter and with dissolved cellulose. This matter is the greatest enemy to the crytallisation of sugar, and dissolved out of the cane by hot diffusion would be free to work its worst effects. My experience has proved to me that a temperature of 180° Fahr. for diffusion is the danger line for the formation of cellulose (gummy matter), whose production increases with the increase of heat. At a temperature of 180° or below I could not get a satisfactory extraction. This difficulty is now overcome by applying a pressure of 15 lbs. to the square inch, supplied from a reservoir 35 feet about the cells, with the view of forcing the juice from one cell to the other, &c., but for me of far greater importance, because I know that without pressure it would be impossible to exhaust the cane in such a short time as 100 or 120 minutes. The effect of pressure in penetrating the woody fibre is well known, and used in seasoning and in creosoting lumber.

"By the kind invitation of Governor Warmoth, I visited the diffusion apparatus on his (the Magnolia) plantation. I was struck with the regularity and smoothness with which the battery was working, as well as with the results obtained, and the important improvements this apparatus and its handling had undergone since its first introduction at the Louisa plantation.

"I found the extraction of juice equal to about 85 out of the 90 per cent. supposed to be in the cane, and the dilution of the juice a little over one-fifth (21 per cent.) over that of the natural juice. The sugar made (first and seconds) were of fair quality and good crystallisation. I did not see 3d. sugar.

"I may say that diffusion is now a success as far as the extraction of sugar from the cane is concerned; it remains to be seen if it is also a financial success, before I am willing to pronounce entirely in its favour, unless used in combination with the mill. I am still of the opinion that so much juice should be made as the mill could express, and the bagasse exhausted by diffusion."

The result of the third year's experience at Fort Scott, Kansas, in the production of sugar from sorghum is encouraging, and will have some effect upon the tariff question on its political side. If Louisiana stood alone as a sugar-producing State, her interests could be easily sacrificed; but Kansas is Republican (so also is Ohio, where beet sugar is made), and this brings her allies. *Sugar from sorghum.*

The report of the Fort Scott factory shows that it took the crop from 1,200 acres of cane, paying the farmer 2 dol. per ton. An acre averaged about 10 tons of green cane stalks. This was not all they made, however, as an acre produced 20 bushels to 25 bushels of seed, worth 25 c. a bushel for feeding stock. The entire product of the factory will be over 500,000 lbs. of good yellow sugar and 100,000 gallons of syrup. The profit to each ton of cane handled, without including the State bounty of 2 c. a lb., is 5 dol. 20 c., which indicates that neither the manufacturer nor the farmer has any reason to be dissatisfied with the outcome of this year's work. *Report of Fort Scott factory.*

Sorghum makes good food for stock.

Ramie and jute culture has so far made but little progress. The many failures and disappointments in decorticators have led to a lack of confidence in the claims of any machine, and the plans have, during the past year, received but little attention. There are, however, a few persevering and public-spirited gentlemen who have not lost faith in the fibre industry, and who are determined to arrive at a successful solution of the problem. *Ramie and jute. Decorticators.*

Amongst these is General Sewell, whom I have mentioned before in this connection. He has entered into the management of a large plantation in Lafayette parish, where ramie will be cultivated on a large scale. He has not altered his opinion as to the merits of the wet decorticating process, or of the machine by which this work is done. (See my Trade Report for 1887, page 3.) *Planting in Lafayette.*

The British market gardener has nothing to learn from his co-labourer, the truck farmer, in these States. On the contrary, *Market gardening.*

(585)

PENSACOLA (FLORIDA).

Mr. Vice-Consul Howe reports as follows :—

The State of Florida it not much of a developed agricultural section of these Southern States, I believe; and as regards Pensacola (my immediate post) operations in agriculture being quite circumscribed, and hardly likely reported on alone to be of much utility or interest to agriculturists in the United Kingdom, my remarks will refer to the State generally, in descending as far as I am able with the information at hand, the climate and the mean temperature of Florida, the nature of the soil and its cultivation, and the products thereof, in the hope that if such description does not give some hints toward stable agricultural purposes, at least some points may be gathered that will prove of service in lighter agriculture to those agriculturists in the United Kingdom for whose benefit these reports are especially required. Also, possibly agriculturists in tropical and semi-tropical places of the British possessions abroad, where the climate and soil are nearer that of Florida, may find some interest in the report leading to agriculture (as followed in Florida) adaptable to those places, perhaps not before thought of or there tried.

In compiling this report, I shall be drawing to some extent on a publication on Florida, compiled for the Florida Land and Mortgage Company, Limited (an English company), by Captain J. W. Gambier, Royal Navy, and printed and issued in London. The pamphlet referred to was principally issued for business purposes—for the purpose of showing to the emigrant, the capitalist, and the manufacturer the resources and natural advantages of Florida; nevertheless it presents such a fund of scientific research and truthful information, much of it gathered on the spot, that it may be somewhat followed, I think, to advantage in assisting me in my report.

Climate. The climate of this semi-tropical region from parallel 31, its northern boundary, to parallel 29, corresponds with that of Portugal, south of Oporto; the southern section of Spain, Oran, Algiers, and Tunis, on the northern coast of Africa; the southernmost part of Italy; the islands of Sicily, Greece, and Morea; the isles of the Archipelago, and those of Candia, Rhodes, Cyprus, &c.; Asia Minor, Syria, Mesopotamia, and Armenia.

The mean temperature for the entire State is, for spring, 71°62'; for summer, 80°51'; autumn, 71°66'; winter, 70°05.'

The climate on the whole may be said to be mild, verging upon warm. All extremes of temperature are essentially modified by the prevalence of daily winds from the ocean or Gulf of Mexico.

The soil. The soil in the largest portion of the State is sandy. In some portions clay and alluvium are found. This sand is not the sharp, silicious sand like that of the ocean, and it is said to have more or less of loam and a large percentage of lime, giving it much fertility. The country is well watered by rivers, lakes, creeks, and springs.

Fertilisers. The fertilisers used in Florida have for the chief ingredients potash, phosphorus, and ammonia. Phosphatic rocks have to some extent, it is said, been discovered and used here. Another convenient fertiliser for Florida is fish guano. The bones and heads of fish are rich in phosphate of lime. Of fish taken not fit for food, and the offal of the better ones, the fish guano is made, containing a good percentage of ammonia, phosphate of lime, and other fertilising matter. Cotton-seed meal is also largely used.

Having given some particulars of the climate and temperature of Florida, the soil and the fertilisation thereof, I shall give, as follows, a list of some of the fruits and like products of which it is said the soil is capable, though I do not mean to say that all of the things named in the following list are really cultivated at present in Florida:—

Oranges (various kinds)	The olive
Lemons	The grape (many varieties)
Limes	Currants
Citron	Pine apples
Shaddock	Figs
Mango	Plantains
Pawpaw	Bananas
Cocoa	Yams
Dates	Bread fruit
Sweet almonds	Arrowroot
Bitter „	Ginger
Pistachio „	Cloves
Balsam	Cinnamon
Hemp	Sugar cane
Camphor	Guava

In addition to the foregoing list of some of the lighter although valuable articles that it is said are within the capabilities of the soil, and can be produced here profitably, I give a list of some of the more staple articles, common to more Northern latitudes, that are also cultivated in Florida:—

Cotton	Blackberries
Wheat	Huckleberries
Rye	Plums
Oats	Peaches
Rice	Pears
Tobacco	Pomegranates
Irish potatoes	Persimmons
Sweet „	Pecans
Cow peas	Pea nuts
Corn	Quince
Melons	Apples, &c.
Strawberries	

A great variety of garden vegetables, such as carrots, turnips, cucumbers, cabbages, pumpkins, squash, lettuce, beans, tomatoes, &c., is also largely cultivated in Florida.

Sugar cane. In field crops the sugar cane is grown in Florida, but mostly for retail purposes—average retail price 5 c. (2½d.) each stalk—being stripped and eaten mostly by children and the coloured race as a sweet; and the sale this way is immense. Some little syrup and sugar are manufactured on a small scale. In my opinion the sugar cane grown in these parts lacks much the rich, juicy, saccharine matter of the sugar cane of the West Indian islands; hence the quality and yield, I think, would be far below that of the West Indies in regular extended cultivation for commercial purposes. The soil has much to do with the cultivation of the sugar cane, and I do not think the Florida soil quite up to the requirements this way.

Corn. This great food staple (corn) is grown in all parts of the State, and the produce per acre is in Florida, as elsewhere, more or less according to fertility of soil and cultivation. Corn is planted here from about February to April, ploughed at intervals until June or July, and then laid by till harvested. The blades, which furnish very good fodder, are stripped from the stalks, and the ears left to be harvested at leisure

It is said that from 30 to 40 acres can be easily cultivated by one person with one mule. The corn usually grown is the white variety, largely used for meal and hominy, especially in the South. The well-made southern corn-bread, for which the Southern people are famous, is delicious. The ears of corn, young and tender, are very much used by all classes as an article of diet.

Wheat, rye, and oats.

Wheat is grown in the northern section of the State, but I am not aware that it is prepared as a breadstuff. Rye and oats do very well here. Sown in the autumn they afford a good winter pasturage, and mature in spring, being preserved unthrashed, and given to live stock in the straw.

Irish potaotes.

Irish potatoes are successfully grown in Florida, but as a rule they are not so large in size as those grown in the Northern States. Planted in December and January they mature in May, though the young ones are used for the table much earlier than that. They are cultivated here as in other warm climates. A covering of muck or grass is very beneficial to their growth.

Sweet potatoes.

These potatoes are easy of production, are largely grown here, and are of much importance (the same as throughout the British West Indies) to all, particularly the coloured race, as an article of food. An acre yields from 100 to 300 bushels, according to soil and cultivation. The planting from roots and slips takes place from spring to summer, and the crop may be gathered from autumn to early winter. It is said that the cost of growing here is about 16 c. (8d.) per bushel. These potatoes are from 1 dol. (4s. 2d.) to 2 dols. (8s. 4d.) per bushel, according to quantity in market.

Tobacco.

Tobacco grows very well in Florida, but I do not think much attention is paid to its cultivation at present. As an intended impetus to increased cultivation here of this seductive article, of such great commercial importance throughout the world, Cuba seed—the best known of the plant, I believe—was some time ago offered free, and given to many, by the railroad companies in operation in Florida, and prizes guaranteed according to quantity and quality; but I have not heard that much has been done this way. At a recent exhibit of tobacco samples, at an exposition in Cincinnati, a sample of Florida tobacco took the first prize, I am told. The plant requires careful attention, and it is said, with all things favourable, will yield from 500 to 700 lbs. per acre.

Peas.

The English pea is largely cultivated in Florida, and does well; also a hardy pea called cow pea is extensively grown here. The latter is not, I think, of a very delicate flavour, although I believe highly nutritious. These peas produce from 10 to 15 bushels per acre. The growth of the vine is so luxuriant, even on poor soils that its cultivation as a green crop to be turned under is considered as advantageous to the soil as clover. The cow pea, put up in sacks and other packages, is quite an article of trade in some of the American markets.

Pea nuts, or ground nuts.

This peculiar product of the soil is called in the West Indies, where it is largely grown, "ground nut;" here it is known as "pea nut." They thrive well on almost any soil. The seed is planted about spring. The cultivation is very simple, and the yield very productive, averaging about 100 bushels to the acre, it is said. They are worth here from 1 dol. (4s. 2d.) to 1 dol. 75 c. (7s. 3½d.) per bushel. It is said that the nut produces a fine oil equal to olive oil. "The Spanish pea nut is now very extensively used in Georgia for feeding hogs. It is stated that the average crop is 125 bushels per acre. The hogs do all the harvesting, and they generally eat the vines as well as the nuts. It is estimated that an acre of Spanish pea nuts will furnish four times as much hog food as an acre of corn."

The lemon and lime. The lemon and lime are grown here, but to no extent, so far as I can learn. I do not think much attention is given to their cultivation in anything like quantities.

Figs. Figs are easily grown here from cuttings, and begin to bear in a couple of years after planting. In Florida, "autumn is the best season for propagating these trees by layers; but it may also be done any time from October to March or April. Choose the young, pliable, lower shoots from the fruitful branches, lay them in the usual way, covering the body of the layers three or four inches deep in the ground, keeping the top entire and as upright as possible, and they will be rooted and fit to separate from the parent in autumn, when they may be planted either in the nursery or where they are to remain. The time for propagating by cuttings is either at the fall of the leaf or in February. Choose well-ripened shoots of the preceding summer, short and of robust growth, from about 12 to 15 inches long, having an inch or two of the two years' wood at their base, the tips left entire; plant them six or eight inches deep in a bed or border of good earth in rows two feet asunder."

Grapes. The grape is largely grown in Florida. It is even found growing wild in the forests. Many varieties do well here, but the species known as the "scuppernong" is the most trustworthy, grows well, is free from disease, very prolific in fruit, and receives most attention. It makes good wine. It is said that one acre has been known to yield 2,000 gallons. The vines are grown upon frames from six to eight feet high, and sometimes of great extent. The space below, shaded by the dense foliage overhead, affords an excellent place for fowls during the hot summer days.

Peaches. The peach bears abundantly here. From seed planting it produces fruit in little over two years, ripening in the spring. The southern grown peach, or the species hereabout, is very hardy, but does not compare, as a rule, with the same northern grown fruit; and the latter do not do well here, as they do not seem to be adapted to the southern climate. The flat or Chinese Peen-to peach is now being cultivated somewhat extensively here; it is considered a very nice variety of the peach family, and matures much earlier than any other kind (during the month of April), thus commanding a much higher market price.

Pears. Much attention has been given to pears in Florida for some years past, and its cultivation increases annually. The Le Conte pear, as it is called, is especially a southern variety, and has for some years past been considered equal to the standard species, the Bartlett. It brings, I am informed, a large price in the northern markets, where it is shipped and placed in advance of the more northern varieties. It is said that it yields in some localities in Florida a greater profit than oranges. This pear is especially adapted to Middle and Western Florida. One-year-old trees are considered best for orchard planting. They should be trained in the nursery to one stem, two inches in circumference at the collar, and about five feet high. Before planting, three feet of the top should be cut off, leaving the tree two feet high. Great care should be taken to prune the young trees properly, as the species has a peculiar tendency to run up into a long and ungainly shape. It should be so trained as to have large, sturdy, well-balanced limbs, strong enough to bear easily the immense crops with which a good tree is annually loaded. After the first year the pruning consists in annually shortening the longest branches and removing the inside limbs. If this is attended to, the tree will grow in proportion and form a graceful and symmetrical top. Little pruning is required after the formation of fruit buds, which takes place when the tree is from three to four years old. One of the best recommendations to the cultivation of this pear is the rapidity of its growth. A 12-year-old tree, properly pruned and attended to, should be 30 inches in circumference above the collar, 20 feet in height, and 20 feet in width. The trees should be planted in rows from 20 to 30 feet apart. The soil near the trunks should be stirred during the growing season, and care taken to keep them free from weeds and grasses. The space between the rows may be utilised for any annual green crop, the cultivation of which is beneficial to the pears. On poor land, application of stable or lot manure or wood earth is very beneficial, and should be spread within a radius of four feet of the tree. An application of wood-ashes or kainit in the spring, and stable manure in the fall, has been found to help the growth very much. Until the tree commences bearing, it has few or no lateral roots, and so a young orchard does not require a large amount of fertiliser. As the tree grows, however, the roots will occupy all the intervening ground, and poor soil should be improved while the trees are young by growing peas and other renewing crops.

The apple. The cultivation of the apple in Florida is of doubtful utility, and not much attention given to it; at least, I think so, from what I have seen and am informed about this fruit.

The strawberry. This "queen of small fruits" (the strawberry) thrives abundantly in Florida. The species of the vine planted here are innumerable. Plants put out in September bear fruit before the close of winter, and may be counted in full bearing and ripening in March or April. I had the pleasure of sending a few runners of one or two sorts of this fruit to a gentleman in London some time ago, and was pleased to hear from him that he had managed to save a few alive, and that they were growing.

The pecan. I refer particularly to this variety of nut, as it is receiving much attention at present in Florida. It thrives so readily, and is so easy of growth in this semi-tropical country, that I think it would flourish in places of similar or tropical climate—such as the British possessions in the West Indies. The nut itself is planted and grows readily in any moderately good mixed soil of sand and clay. It is very hardy, and attains height, strength, and body from year to year, until it reaches an immense size. The tree begins bearing in about eight or 10 years, and the yield annually increases in quantity till the full growth of the tree is attained. The nut is a favourite one among consumers, and sells readily at about 10 c. (5d.) per lb. retail.

The orange. As regards the production of this very desirable and highly-prized fruit (the orange) both in sickness and in health—the king of fruits, I think—I relate to it particularly, not only as being one of Florida's most important commercial fruit products, but also in order to impress the fact that there are many tropical places in the British possessions where this fruit would thrive even beyond the comparative growth here, the necessary care and attention were in those places extended in its culture in the same manner as in Florida. As regards the oranges of the British West Indies, I remember well the oranges of the Island of Dominica, which in flavour and size (more like the Porta Rico oranges, the best I know of) nothing that I have seen here will surpass. With the British West India islands, now so near the Northern States of America by direct steam communication, it appears to me that this much sought-after fruit could be cultivated and shipped to great advantage from those islands. The lands not used for cane cultivation could be utilised to great advantage, I think, by orange culture; but the trees will not grow and bear fruit there, unless properly and regularly attended to, and made a matter of business, as in Florida. Proper system of management in its every department, on business principles, must be adhered to energetically, in the same manner as the plantain and banana of the islands in the West Indies, called the Bay Islands—Utilla and thereabouts—are being made a regular and immensely profitable trade between those places and the United States. In fact, to diverge, it appears to me that the fruits last referred to—indigenous as they are, as well as the orange, to the soil of the British West India islands—may also, in addition to oranges, be made a great business of between the British West Indies and the United States.

From the pamphlet of the Florida Land and Mortgage Company I take the following:—

"The cultivation of the orange (*Citrus aurantium*) in East Florida previous to 1835 had attained a degree of considerable commercial importance, and the exports of this fruit from the small city of St. Augustine are said to have amounted to 100,000 dol. annually. On the St. John's River and in some parts of West Florida, and at Tampa Bay, groves were being established as a source of commercial supply. Those groves are rapidly multiplying in all parts of the State, and the bearing trees are now numbered by tens of thousands, while the young groves which are being constantly started comprise millions of trees. The orange from the seed produces fruit in from seven to 10 years, depending upon situation, culture, &c.

"Groves are made from wild stocks, usually cut off at a height of three to four feet from the ground, and the new shoots budded, generally produce fruit in three years. The number of oranges produced from a single tree varies from 100 to 10,000, according to the age, situation, and treatment of the tree. The trees are usually set 20 feet apart, and an acre will contain about 100 trees. Florida oranges were usually sold, previous to 1835, at 7 dol. 50 c. to 10 dol. per thousand. Now a demand exists for 20 times our present supply, at 15 to 20 dol. per 1,000, as they hang upon the trees.

"*How to Make an Orange Grove.*

"The judicious selection of the land is the first and most important point, for on this success in a great measure depends. Choose high dry hammock, or high rolling pine land, that has natural drainage and a yellowish sub-soil. The low flat lands, which are underlaid with hardpan, or sandstone, mixed with oxide of iron, require ditching or draining, and much care in setting the trees, so that the roots may have free scope and relief from standing water. The most favoured sites are on the south-east side of wide sheets of water, or high lands, which are more generally free from frost. The land selected, clear thoroughly of all trees, &c., sow with cow peas, which turn under when in bloom—it improves and sweetens the soil; this may be done before or after planting trees. Dig holes 30 feet apart, 18 inches deep, and 4 feet in diameter; clean out all roots; fill up with top-soil, which will retain the moisture; procure trees from three to five years' old, take them up carefully, with all of the roots possible; pack up with wet moss as soon as dug, put in shade and out of the wind, take to the proposed grove carefully; remove soil from holes dug sufficient for the tree, with roots carefully spread, trunk standing in same position as originally grown. Let the tree, when set out, be fully an inch above natural level of land; fill under, in and about the roots, compactly—it is best done by the hand, filled to surface and gently tramped down; fill on some two or three inches of earth, which will prevent drying; the rainy season commencing, remove the soil about the tree to the level about it. Cultivation should be frequent and shallow, and trash not

UNITED STATES.

allowed to accumulate near trunk; light ploughing and raking near the trees is best and safest. Following these general directions no one should fail. The cost of a 5-acre grove, at, say, five years from planting, at a liberal estimate where high pine land is chosen, will be about as given below. If hammock land is taken, the cost of clearing will be more. The grove will have begun to yield at the end of the period named.

"COST OF GROVE.

	Dol.	c.
Five acres of good land, variously estimated, depending on location.		
Cutting timber, clearing	75	00
Fencing (post and board fence) and breaking up..	75	00
Three hundred trees and setting out	200	00
Manures, labour, cultivating, taxes, &c., for five years	500	00
Total, less cost of land	850	00

"Such a grove would readily sell now in Florida for 1,000 dol. per acre. From and after five years the annual growth of trees and increase of fruit is constant for at least 10 years, and the grove will hold its vigour and fruit-producing qualities for a century or more. The orange is a hardy tree, will stand great extremes of rain and drought; it will show the effects of a single season's neglect, and quickly show a single season of care and attention."

By the Census Bulletin of 1880, the state of the orange business at that date was as follows:—

Number of Counties where Oranges Grew.	Number of Bearing Trees.	Yield in 1880.	Value.
			Dol.
30	294,912	96,454,349	686·926

Since the period named the orange business has, I am informed, much increased. The yield for the present season is estimated at considerably beyond the above-given yield.

It is thought, however, "that orange growing, while it of course can be engaged in at a decided advantage by those who have means to conduct it on a cash basis, and be independent of support until such time as the grove is an assured success, does not, nevertheless, present *any* insurmountable features to 'poor men'—by which term we mean, in this instance, men without ready-money and dependent upon their own labour for a support. Indeed, in the knowledge of the writer, many of the most successful and to-day independent orange proprietors in Florida began the business with no other capital than their own labour.

But for fear of misleading minds prone to overlooking the details when so dazzling a prospect is offered them of converting in a few years acres which cost 3 dol. into estates yielding princely incomes, we caution them that there is a long hungry gap between raw pine woods and groves of bearing orange trees. It takes many hard licks, plenty of pluck, good health, luck, and judicious selection of site. Indolence and inexperience will ruin anything."

Labour.

The soil around Pensacola and its vicinity is worked by small farmers, and the product sought for and obtained to a large extent is in "truck" gardening—vegetables and fruits for local markets.

Negroes are employed as a rule to till the ground preparatory to planting at the sugar-planting seasons (autumn and spring), and the wages of these labourers average about 1 dol. per day of 10 hours, they providing their own food. The same remarks as regards labour may be applied, I think, to other parts of the State. A great many of the white farmers—there are also many coloured people engaged in such a living—are assisted by the male members of their family. In the same way, to a great extent, the coloured farmers complete the work for their crops. These coloured people own the land that they work, much of it being by private purchase. I do not think there is much or any tenant farming. Also a good deal of land is entered under the homestead or pre-emption laws of the United States, whereby a homestead to the extent of 160 acres of land may be entered subject to certain stipulations by the Government. White people also own much land under the pre-emption laws of the United States. Land varies considerably in value in Florida, the uncleared land in remote portions selling for a few dollars per acre, while lands immediately next to railroads bring much higher rates.

The breed of horned cattle in Florida, although hardy and suited to the requirements of the place, as milch-cows and beef-food, is not of the best, I think. Perhaps the climate is not favourable, or the fodder of the grazing ground may not improve the condition and appearance and milk-giving and food qualities of this description of stock. The leading dairies about here, of which there are many, mix their cows with the Jersey breed, or half-breed brought from the Northern States. The price of butter supplied by the dairies averages about 40 c. (1s. 8d.) per lb. *Domestic animals, fowls, &c.*

The breeding of horses in Florida, so far as I am aware, is very little attended to. I have, however, seen some fine horses here foaled by northern or western stock. Horses from the State of Kentucky are mostly used here for regular domestic purposes. A very handy horse is the Texas pony, or " mustang," of which breed a quantity is used in drays and for such work generally. These ponies when perfectly trained—they are, as a rule, very stubborn—are used also as ordinary draft horses for family carriages and public hacks. Loads of them are brought here continually by rail from Texas, supplying the various towns in Florida.

Sheep, I think, as a rule are of a poor breed in Florida. In some few counties, however, they are very good. Perhaps the necessary attention is not given to the improvement of the stock in other parts of the State. The sheep is a most valuable animal, and should, when adapted to the climate, be largely introduced, I think, in connection with agricultural pursuits, and carefully looked after. Its flesh furnishes the table with a meat (when having nutritious grass to feed on) only second to the finest beef, and twice a year it bares its back in order to clothe its owner and his family. Sheep thrive well in the British West Indies, and, owing to the succulent grasses there, the meat is delicious. The mutton of the Island of Nevis is widely famed for its superior flavour and quality generally. I think there is plenty of room for improving the breed and adding to the quantity of these animals in those islands to a very largely increased industry in this way.

Pigs and goats are in abundance here, and, particularly the former, form one more annual item of trade. A Florida correspondent of the "Country Gentleman" asks for the best ration to feed a Berkshire sow to farrow in a few weeks; also, young pigs from weaning to ten months to make pork for market; and refers to bran, oats, and corn, cotton-seed meal, sweet potatoes, and crab-grass hay. In reply, the editor advises the following combination:—" 15 lbs. sweet potatoes, 2 lbs.

wheat bran, 2 lbs. cotton-seed meal, and ½ lb. crab-grass hay. Shown in analytical formula, it has the following digestible nutrients:—

	Albuminoids.	Carbohydrates.	Fat.
	Lbs.	Lbs.	Lbs.
15 lbs. sweet potato	0·15	4·20	0·04
2 „ wheat bran	0·22	0·94	0·05
2 „ cotton-seed meal	0·66	0·44	0·06
½ lb. crab-grass hay	0·03	0·21	0·06
Total	1·06	5·79	0·16

"This has a nutritive ratio a little better than 1 to 6. This will make a fair ratio for the breed sow after farrowing, and also for the young pigs, by simply adding one 1 lb. of bran. The sweet potatoes should be boiled with the crab-grass hay after running through a cutter.

"The bran and cotton-seed meal should be well mixed together, dry, the boiled potatoes and crab-grass being mashed and thoroughly mixed with it. It is then ready for feeding. The bran and cotton-seed meal would grow the muscles and bones of the young pig, and the sweet potatoes and crab-grass would keep it healthy."

Poultry of all kinds is in abundance throughout the State, and the yearly business this way is immense. "Chicken farms," as they are termed, are almost distinctly attended to by large numbers of the rural people with great success. This is a department much looked after in Florida by the female portion of the agricultural people.

MOBILE.

Mr. Vice-Consul Barnewall reports as follows:—

Since my last annual report, the demand for information concerning the State of Alabama has so greatly increased as to require the publication of several treaties relative to her growth and development, which will be condensed in the few following pages:—

Alabama lies in a latitude the same as North Africa, Palestine, Central China, and South Japan, furnishing a climate by no means the least of her attractions. Extremes of heat and cold do not prevail; snow seldom falls, and is very rare. The rivers are not frozen over, and the sea breezes from the Gulf tone the sultry heat of summer.

The State of Alabama has a length of 275 miles, a width of 175, covering an area of 50,722 square miles, giving soils of every variety, from the thinest sandy land to the richest alluvial, so that Alabama can be divided into four grand divisions—the mineral, the timber, the cotton, and the cereal belts—of which it may be said that no other portion of the globe affords a greater diversity than that embraced within her limits.

In the development of her minerals she leads the other States of the Union; the staple of her cotton fields commands a dominant price in the markets of the world. The magnificent wheat and corn valleys of the Tennessee and Cumberland, the forests of giant timber, the orchards of delicious fruits, all attest the greatness of her resources.

The mineral belt. The mineral belt is the largest of the four divisions; it embraces 28 counties, or more than one-third of the State, including almost all the minerals known to art, and are of fabulous value. The three great coalfields of the Warrior, the Coosa, and the Cahaba lie in this section; they contain 8,610 square miles, and each step of progress shows how inexhaustible they are. Gold, silver, copper, tin, lead graphite, asbestos, emery, gypsum, mica, ochre, asphalte, marble koolin, and fire clays abound. Besides these, iron abounds in beds so numerous that it is impossible to point out the localities where it prevails. To it is due the tremendous strides Sheffield, Anniston, and Birmingham have made in importance and wealth.

Sheffield, Colbert county, Ala., is situated on the Tennessee River, at the head of navigation. Four years ago this place was a cotton field: it has now about 4,000 inhabitants. Five iron furnaces, with a capacity of 750 tons of iron daily; three railroads, to wit, Louisville and Nashville (Cumberland branch), Memphis and Charleston, and Sheffield and Birmingham—these roads are now building their division and principal shops there; electric lights, cotton compress, at which there has been up to this time over 16,000 bales of cotton compressed, and it is believed will secure over 30,000 bales by the end of the season. *Sheffield, Colbert county, Ala.*

There are manufacturing enterprises there now in actual operation aggregating 400,000 dol. or 500,000 dol.

The place has within easy reach of it an unlimited supply of coal and iron ore, the latter of an unusually fine quality. The Tennessee River at this point is navigable nearly all the year, and steamers ply daily between Sheffield and St. Louis, and all points on the Mississippi River and its tributaries. Sheffield bids fair in the near future to be one of the great iron manufacturing counties of the south.

As a type of the solid and substantial progress and brilliant future of the south cannot be passed by without comment, her population has doubled within the past 12 months, and is now computed as 12,000; has a fine agricultural country surrounding it, has about 30,000 acres of the best coal land in the State, has 75,000 acres of red and brown hematite iron ores, has four railroads complete and others projected, has a perfect system of waterworks and is lighted by electricity, has its streets graded and macadamised, has four charcoal furnaces, two coke furnaces, and the largest pipe works in the United States, with a daily capacity of 200 tons of the finest pipe, one of the largest and most complete cotton factories in the south, one stove works and horse-shoe factory, one 50-ton rolling mill, and a 50-ton foundry. It has the United States rolling-stock company, which employs 1,000 men, and turns out 20 cars per day, and the only steel bloomary in the south. Establishments such as have been mentioned give to Anniston its character as a manufacturing city. The cheapness of iron and coal, inexhaustible supplies of the finest timber, the transportation facilities—these and other advantages are leading to the establishment of manufactories of various kinds. *Anniston.*

Can the industrial history of the world furnish a parallel to this more than marvellous attestation of southern progress? It has all been accomplished in 14 years, and a greater part in less than one-half of the time. It demonstrates, as nothing else could do, the substantial and solid character of the south's wonderful industrial growth; all these are foundations of Anniston's future, her greatness, and her prosperity.

Jefferson county, in which Birmingham is situated, leads all the counties in its wonderful progress in manufactures. In 1880 the population of the county was 23,272: to-day Birmingham alone has over 40,000 inhabitants and 20,000,000 dol. of taxable property. The mineral products are marvellous; a better estimate can be had by noting the table of local industries of Birmingham. *Birmingham.*

Eight coal mines, daily output 14,000 tons ; 22 furnaces, daily output 2,233 tons of iron ; there rolling-mills, 240 tons of finished iron daily. There are nine banks and nine finished railroads, and three in contemplation, eight foundries and machine shops, two bridge works, a chain factory, a stove factory, a cotton compress, pipe works, the largest consumer of pig iron in the South, and all this in a city that a few years ago was started on a castaway old field.

The timber belt. The timber belt lies south of the cotton or black belt and north of the Gulf of Mexico, and comprises 15 counties in the southern part of the State. Its name is suggested by its superb timber ; but, like all the three other divisions, of the State, timber is not the only characteristic of this division ; in fact, there are splendid forests in any section of Alabama, and there is not a country, even the richest in mineral, or where fertile lands, stocked with valuable timber, cannot be found. These forests embrace 20,630,963 acres of the most heavily-wooded land of the world. They have attracted more attention, and allured more capital than any other element of wealth of the south.

In both expositions in New Orleans, the south led all the sections of he Union in her exhibitions of timber.

This belt presents great uniformity of character in its surface conformation, soils, irrigation. The surface is undulating, with occasional hills breaking up into fertile bottoms, which lie along the numerous watercourses. There are immense areas of table lands, whose surface soil is of a sandy nature, which is enriched by manures of the pine straw and excrements of the herds of stock : these are sustained by the native grasses, and clovers, and wild cane which grow along the streams. These great pine forests of Alabama are practically untouched. Many of the trees attain a height of 150 feet ; spars 75 feet long are shipped to the distant markets of the world ; while the rosin, converted into turpentine, is a great factor of commerce. These long leaf-pine forests are interspersed with oak, white, red, post, and black jack ; in the lower section the cypress and hickory grows to a great size ; also the beech, the magnolia, the cedar, the maple, the dogwood, the ironwood, the juniper, the ash, the holly, the cottonwood, the poplar, the walnut, the sweet gum, which has been of late years used almost exclusively by cabinet-makers as a substitute for the walnut. Along the swamps trailing from these forest monarchs are vast quantities of moss, that now makes its commercial value as mattrasses.

The soils of this belt are peculiarly adapted to the root crops, fruits, and vegetables. Of late years an immense revenue has been added to the State from the truck gardens and fruit producers of this section ; whilst the year's clovers and swamp cane that thrive almost the year round offer inducements to the stockraiser not excelled in any State of the Union.

The cotton belt. The cotton belt or the black belt of Alabama is directly so uth of the great mineral belt. It extends from east to west, embraces 17 counties, and covers an area of 13,610 square miles. The soil in the richer portions is a very dark colour, and contains a good deal of lime. The prairies are broken by districts of timber, and are well watered—the principal rivers, except the Tennessee, flow directly through it. Agriculture was, until a few years ago, the only pursuit of the people of this section ; then, in 1860, two-thirds of the cotton crop of Alabama (740,000 bales), one-half of the corn crop (25,000,000 bushels), and 3,000,000 bushels of oats were produced here. Lately, in 1885, a diversity of pursuits were followed. The cotton crop was 760,447 bales, the corn crop 30,000,000 bushels, and the oats crop 5,000,000 bushels. This proves that where the fleecy fibre hitherto held undivided sway, it is forced to divide its sovereignty with a large percentage of the agricultural products of the State.

The cereal belt extends across the northern boundary of the State from east to west, embraces the famous valley of Tennessee, and comprises eight counties. The soil is fertile, of a reddish cast, due to the mixture of iron in the limestone. White corn, wheat, rye, oats, barley, sorghum, potatoes, tobacco, rice, peas, sugar cane, are the production, of the cereal belt. Cotton has been raised upon the famous red lands. and is to-day a rival of the cereals. Grasses thrive in richest profusion, Clover, timothy, herd, orchard, and blue grass are grown as successfully as in Kentucky; consequently, as stock-raising is easy and profitable, the improvement of breeds increases from year to year.

The hardier fruits grow to perfection. Pears, apples, peaches, grapes, berries, hickory nuts, are produced in great abundance yearly, and find a growing and lucrative market. The lands vary in price from 3 dol. to 50 dol. per acre, according to location, and are practically suited to any and every species of industry. Whilst cereals dominate this belt, localities may be found where manufacturing interests of every description can be carried on with great profit.

LONDON:
Printed for Her Majesty's Stationery Office,
By HARRISON AND SONS,
Printers in Ordinary to Her Majesty.
(1125   3 | 89—H & S   585)

FOREIGN OFFICE.

1889.
ANNUAL SERIES.

N°. 499.

DIPLOMATIC AND CONSULAR REPORTS ON TRADE AND FINANCE.

UNITED STATES.

REPORT FOR THE YEAR 1888
ON THE
TRADE OF BOSTON (MASS.).

REFERENCE TO PREVIOUS REPORT, Annual Series No. 312.

Presented to both Houses of Parliament by Command of Her Majesty,
APRIL, 1889.

LONDON:
PRINTED FOR HER MAJESTY'S STATIONERY OFFICE,
BY HARRISON AND SONS, ST. MARTIN'S LANE,
PRINTERS IN ORDINARY TO HER MAJESTY.

And to be purchased, either directly or through any Bookseller, from
EYRE AND SPOTTISWOODE, EAST HARDING STREET, FLEET STREET, E.C., and
32, ABINGDON STREET, WESTMINSTER, S.W.; or
ADAM AND CHARLES BLACK, 6, NORTH BRIDGE, EDINBURGH; or
HODGES, FIGGIS, & Co., 104, GRAFTON STREET, DUBLIN.

1889.

Price One Penny.

[C. 5618—52.]

New Series of Reports.

Reports of the Annual Series have been issued from Her Majesty's Diplomatic and Consular Officers at the following places, and may be obtained from the sources indicated on the title-page:—

No.		Price.	No.		Price.
375.	San Francisco	2d.	437.	Réunion	1d.
376.	Riga	1d.	438.	Lisbon	1d.
377.	Newchwang	2d.	439.	Venice	1d.
378.	San Salvador	1d.	440.	Christiania	5d.
379.	Frankfort	2d.	441.	Maranham	1d.
380.	Hankow	2d.	442.	Sofia	1d.
381.	Bucharest	1d.	443.	Copenhagen	1d.
382.	Lisbon	1d.	444.	Galatz	1d.
383.	Tunis	1d.	445.	Tabreez	1d.
384.	Tangier	1d.	446.	Bogotá	2d.
385.	Santiago	2d.	447.	St. Petersburg	3d.
386.	Diarbekir	1d.	448.	Nice	1d.
387.	Shanghai	2d.	449.	Stettin	2d.
388.	Rome	2d.	450.	Fiume	1d.
389.	Buenos Ayres	1d.	451.	Chinkiang	1d.
390.	Amsterdam	1d.	452.	The Hague	1d.
391.	Warsaw	1d.	453.	Malaga	1d.
392.	San Francisco	1d.	454.	Taganrog	1d.
393.	Alexandria	1d.	455.	Mozambique	1d.
394.	Salonica	2d.	456.	Bogotá	2d.
395.	Palermo	1d.	457.	Patras	1d.
396.	Mexico	4d.	458.	Galveston	1d.
397.	Naples	3d.	459.	Buda Pesth	1d.
398.	Boston	1d.	460.	Madeira	1d.
399.	Hakodate	1d.	461.	Warsaw	1d.
400.	Nantes	1d.	462.	Paris	2d.
401.	Madeira	1d.	463.	Baltimore	1d.
402.	Hakodate	1d.	464.	Philadelphia	2d.
403.	Nagasaki	1d.	465.	New Orleans	2d.
404.	Hiogo	2d.	466.	New Orleans	2d.
405.	Tonga	1d.	467.	Cherbourg	1d.
406.	Adana	1d.	468.	Buenos Ayres	1d.
407.	Valparaiso	1d.	469.	Algiers	1d.
408.	Bilbao	1d.	470.	Ichang	1d.
409.	Santiago	1d.	471.	Copenhagen	1d.
410.	Paramaribo	1d.	472.	Athens	1d.
411.	Nantes	1d.	473.	Cherbourg	1d.
412.	Bangkok	1d.	474.	The Piræus	1d.
413.	Yokohama	2d.	475.	Galatz	1d.
414.	Mozambique	1d.	476.	Tripoli	1d.
415.	Canton	2d.	477.	Saigon	1d.
416.	Kiungchow	1d.	478.	Serajevo	1d.
417.	Damascus	1d.	479.	Brussels	2d.
418.	Syra	1d.	480.	Bengazi	1d.
419.	Aleppo	1d.	481.	Odessa	1d.
420.	Sandakan	1d.	482.	Santo Domingo	1d.
421.	Barcelona	1d.	483.	Rome	1d.
422.	Königsberg	1d.	484.	Lisbon	1d.
423.	Tabreez	1d.	485.	Port Said	2d.
424.	Guayaquil	1d.	486.	Havre	3d.
425.	St. Petersburg	1d.	487.	Boulogne	1d.
426.	Tokio	1d.	488.	Callao	1d.
427.	Charleston	1d.	489.	Barcelona	2d.
428.	Amsterdam	1d.	490.	Boulogne	2d.
429.	Hamburg	4d.	491.	Taganrog	2d.
430.	Trieste	1d.	492.	Kiungchow	1d.
431.	New York	2d.	493.	Sandakan	1d.
432.	Antwerp	1d.	494.	Manila	1d.
433.	Munich	1d.	495.	Swatow	1d.
434.	Buenos Ayres	1d.	496.	Guayaquil	1d.
435.	Warsaw	1d.	497.	Rome	1d.
436.	Porto Rico	1d.	498.	Santos	1d.

No. 499.

Reference to previous Report, Annual Series No. 312.

UNITED STATES.

BOSTON.

Consul Henderson to the Marquis of Salisbury.

My Lord,   Boston, March 15, 1889.

I HAVE the honour to enclose a Report on the Trade and Commerce of Boston and the Boston Consular district for the year 1888.

          I have, &c.
      (Signed) C. A. HENDERSON.

Report on the Trade and Commerce of Boston and the Boston Consular District for the Year 1888.

Notwithstanding the disturbing effect of the Presidential Election of 1888 on commercial undertakings, and the deterring influence on particular industries of a prolonged state of uncertainty as to the result of proposed changes in the tariff, the general business throughout this Consular district shows a satisfactory increase and a healthy condition, having been unaccompanied by any serious labour disputes or speculative enterprises. *Condition of trade and industry.*

The following is a review of the principal Boston markets for the year:—

The price of cotton fluctuated throughout the year between $9\frac{3}{4}$ and $11\frac{1}{16}$ c. per lb., the highest point being reached in January and August, and the lowest in April, November, and December. *Cotton and cotton goods.*

The home demand for cotton manufactures was very brisk, notwithstanding a general advance in prices, and mills were kept actively employed with orders unfilled at the end of December.

The depression in the wool trade in 1887, due to a great extent to the proposed change in the tariff on foreign wool, so far from showing any symptoms of recovery, continued to increase up to the end of July, at which time manufacturers, having only bought enough to fill orders, a portion of the clips of 1886 and 1887 were still on the market, the new clip was beginning to come in, and prices had fallen fully 4 c. (2d.) per lb. In August, however, low prices and the conviction that tariff rates would not be disturbed induced buyers to come forward, and, notwithstanding a rapid rise of from 5 to 6 c. ($2\frac{1}{2}d.$ to $3d.$), large sales continued to be made up to the end of November of native wools, whilst about 3,000 bales were imported from Australia. Stocks on hand at the end of the year were 17,200,000 lbs. domestic and 1,766,000 lbs. foreign, against 30,277,000 lbs. domestic and 1,556,000 lbs. foreign in December, 1887. *Wool and woollens.*

(621)

Woollen manufacturers sustained heavy losses in worsted goods, in which they were unable to compete with importers, and even in cloths and other woollens were barely able to hold their own against foreign importations.

Clothing trade.
The clothing trade was less active and remunerative than during the previous year. The mild winter of 1887-8 left dealers with large stocks of winter wear, whilst the seasons that followed were not sufficiently genial for the disposal of spring and summer clothing. The winter trade, however, showed some improvement, and the advance in wool during the latter five months of the year rendered it less imperative to dispose of accumulated stocks at a sacrifice.

Hides and leather.
Prices continued low on hides, and the leather market was similarly depressed up to July, when the reduced quotations brought about a sudden and large demand from abroad for sole leather. This advanced prices, but an equivalent rise occurred in hides, whilst the demand for upper leather continued slack, and the only alternative for tanners was to reduce production with a view to maintain prices, but in this they were only partially successful.

Boots and shoes.
Sales amounted to 3,330,000 cases, fully 200,000 more than in 1887, which were then the largest on record. The increased demand was, however, almost entirely for shoes, which have to a great extent taken the place of boots, thus reducing the consumption of leather, to the disadvantage of tanners, but not affecting the interests of the manufacturers of boots and shoes, whose business for the year was fairly remunerative.

Indiarubber and rubber goods.
The indiarubber market was steady and firm throughout the year, with a good demand for rubber goods at fair prices.

Iron, steel, and other metals.
The demand for Scotch pig iron fell off considerably, whilst the supply from the Southern States showed an increase of home production. Without any sensible decrease in consumption, the large output of native furnaces and consequent competition caused a decline in prices of iron as well as of steel rails, which lasted to the end of the year. Bar iron and nails were steady at a smaller reduction. No. 1 pig iron went as low as 18 dol., and steel rails 27 dol. Bar iron averaged 1 dol. 90 c., and nails 2 dol. 15 c. per keg. Copper was firm at 17 dol. to 17 dol. 50 c. Pig tin, which was as high as 40 dol. whilst under temporary control of the copper syndicate, fell to 18 dol., but subsequently rallied to 25 dol., at which it remained from the month of June. An attempt to "corner" pig lead failed, and it went down from 5 dol. to 3 dol. 65 c., but rose again to 4 dol. 50 c.

Fish trade.
The catch of mackerel was very little over half that of 1887, which itself was under 80,000 barrels, against 83,000 in 1886 and 331,000 in 1885. The supply left over from 1887 was exhausted before any of the new catch was received, and, in addition to the importation of all that could be obtained from Canada, about 10,000 barrels were imported from Ireland, the disadvantage in regard to the latter being that it was not put up as required for this market, and that it had all to be repacked. Prices went up from 14 dol. to 23 dol., and, although this rise greatly reduced the demand, a very small supply was left on hand at the end of the year.

The market for cod was weak during the first months of the year, but the autumn catch was small, and better prices were thenceforward obtained.

Flour and grain.
Best brands of flour opened at 5 dol. 25 c. per barrel, but the supply being large, prices continued to fall until September, when the small crop of winter wheat, and rumours of damage by frost to spring wheat, induced speculators to get control of the market, and run the price up

to 8 dol., from which, however, there was a subsequent decline to 7 dol. Wheat fluctuated under similar conditions, going up from 80 c. to 2 dol. per bushel, with a slight fall later on. Indian corn ruled high during the greater part of the year, reaching 72 c. per bushel, but reacted somewhat when the new crop, which was plentiful, became available. There was much speculation in old oats, and prices were well maintained; but new oats, which were abundant, but of poor quality, ruled low in the market.

The demand for pork and lard was brisk, and prices were well kept up. There was also a good market for cattle and fresh beef; but, in consequence of the high price of corn, steers were light, and did not fetch full prices. *Provisions.*

The market for butter, cheese, eggs, poultry, potatoes, and hay was a satisfactory one for farmers, both as to demand and prices. *Produce.*

The number of firms in business in the Boston Consular district was 78,840, being an increase over 1887 of 794, and the number of failures was 922, an increase of 17, the amount of liabilities being 2,288,133*l.*, an increase of 47,000*l.* *Mercantile failures.*

Foreign exports from Boston (including foreign imports re-exported to the value of 172,000*l.*) amounted to 11,656,300*l.*, an increase over 1887 of 316,300*l.*, whilst foreign imports reached the sum of 12,880,000*l.*, an increase of 380,000*l.* *Foreign commerce.*

The arrivals at Boston of vessels of all nationalities in the foreign trade (excluding those arriving viâ a port in the United States) were, as recorded at the custom-house, 2,287 vessels, of 1,298,565 tons, a decrease, as compared with 1887, of 5,924 tons—viz., 1,671 British vessels, of 978,285 tons, an increase of 2,727 tons; 165 other foreign vessels, of 112,107 tons, an increase of 12,605 tons; and 451 American vessels, of 208,173 tons, a decrease of 21,256 tons. *Foreign maritime trade.*

The actual number of British vessels entered, as shown in the Consulate books, was 1,723, of 985,715 tons net register, of which 458, of 797,280 tons, being an increase over 1887 of 38,956 tons, were steamers; and 1,265, of 188,435 tons, a decrease of 40,872 tons, were sailing vessels.

Freights from England to Boston did not show much variation, being principally regulated by yearly contracts, but those on exports from Boston to England rose considerably during the last quarter of the year. *Ocean freights.*

The general rates on imports were:—On pig iron, 3*s.* to 4*s.* 6*d.*; bar iron, 10*s.*; steel rails, 6*s.*; paper stock and other baled goods, 10*s.* to 17*s.* 6*d.*; bleach, 11*s.*; soda ash, drugs, and chemicals, 6*s.*; salt, 4*s.* to 7*s.* 6*d.*; wool, 25*s.* to 40*s.* per ton weight. Earthenware, 7*s.* 6*d.*; fine goods, 20*s.* to 30*s.*; machinery, 7*s.* 6*d.* per 40 cubic ft.

The rates on exports ranged as follows:—

		January to September.				October to December.			
		s.	*d.*	*s.*	*d.*	*s.*	*d.*	*s.*	*d.*
Live cattle	Per head..	30	0	to 45	0	50	0	to 70	0
Grain..	bushel	0	1	0	2¾	0	4¼	0	5¼
Flour..	ton ..	1	0	7	0	8	9	15	0
Provisions	„ ..	5	0	20	0	20	0	30	0
Leather	„ ..	17	6	25	0	35	0	50	0
Apples	barrel	1	6	1	9	2	6	3	6
Cotton	lb. ..	0	0$\frac{1}{20}$	0	0$\frac{1}{8}$	0	0$\frac{17}{64}$	0	0$\frac{9}{32}$

Rates of exchange on London showed little variation during the year. The extremes, which were touched at intervals, were 4 dol. 87 c. and 4 dol. 89 c. per £ for bankers' sight bills. *Exchange.*

UNITED STATES.

Annex A.—RETURN of all Shipping in the Foreign Trade at Ports in the Boston Consular District in the Fiscal Year ended June 30, 1888.

ENTERED.

Nationality.	Sailing. Number of Vessels.	Tons.	Steam. Number of Vessels.	Tons.	Total. Number of Vessels.	Tons.
Foreign	3,783	523,760	787	938,126	4,570	1,461,886
American	813	208,917	251	229,732	1,064	438,649
Total 1887	4,596	732,677	1,038	1,167,858	5,634	1,900,535
,, 1888	4,436	708,450	1,008	1,181,090	5,444	1,889,540

CLEARED.

Nationality.	Sailing. Number of Vessels.	Tons.	Steam. Number of Vessels.	Tons.	Total. Number of Vessels.	Tons.
Foreign	3,701	504,957	638	706,717	4,339	1,211,674
American	1,388	322,030	233	226,123	1,621	548,153
Total 1888	5,089	826,987	871	932,840	5,960	1,759,827
,, 1887	4,961	783,214	880	995,777	5,841	1,778,991

Sterling amounts in this report are given at the rate of 4s. to the dollar.

Annex B.—RETURN of Principal Articles of Export from and Import to Ports in the Boston Consular District during the Fiscal Year ended June 30, 1888 and 1887.

EXPORTS.

Articles.	Value. 1888.	1887.
	£	£
Meat and dairy products	3,027,474	2,785,961
Horned cattle	804,515	758,874
Corn, flour, and other breadstuffs	2,546,766	2,980,247
Raw cotton	2,418,661	1,749,047
Cotton manufactures	341,727	268,446
Tobacco in leaf and manufactured	219,393	525,451
Iron, steel, and manufactures of	260,985	285,002
Sugar and molasses	41,914	154,187
All other domestic merchandise	2,219,382	2,873,677
Foreign merchandise re-exported	252,754	309,646
Coin and bullion	..	440
Total	12,133,571	12,690,978

BOSTON.

IMPORTS.

Articles.	Value. 1888.	Value. 1887.
	£	£
Sugar and molasses	2,554,758	2,658,134
Wool	1,553,374	1,340,386
Woollen goods	665,820	784,381
Hides, goat and fur skins, and furs	1,088,415	1,279,866
Iron ore, iron, steel, and manufactures of	1,150,124	1,192,458
Chemicals, drugs, and dyes	888,988	966,339
Flax, hemp, and jute	979,218	879,083
Cotton manufactures	312,968	305,683
Fish	368,120	336,870
All other merchandise (including exports reimported, and valued at 89,091*l.*)	5,329,988	4,437,569
Coin and bullion	21,057	15,164
Total	14,912,830	14,190,903

Annex C.—TABLE showing the Value of all Articles Exported from and Imported to Ports in the Boston Consular District during the Fiscal Years ended June 30, 1888 and 1887.

Country.	Exports. 1888.	Exports. 1887.	Imports. 1888.	Imports. 1887.
	£	£	£	£
United Kingdom and Colonies	11,179,255	11,581,356	8,735,941	8,006,895
Spain and Colonies	59,667	97,745	2,497,835	2,280,768
Germany	3,454	21,992	671,661	834,674
France and Colonies	142,991	129,873	667,934	752,804
Argentine Republic	148,326	149,934	596,634	466,144
Belgium	166,073	233,111	274,712	191,707
Italy	10,427	14,732	271,450	279,091
Sweden and Norway	..	1,248	179,220	182,501
Chili	105,730	108,429	67,479	105,561
Netherlands and Colonies	38,914	4,798	140,469	87,926
Brazil	3,066	1,995	141,501	113,368
Turkey	7,096	11,185	99,460	93,384
Mexico	3,977	249	56,503	159,173
All other countries	264,595	334,331	512,301	656,407
Total	12,133,571	12,690,978	14,912,830	14,190,903

LONDON:
Printed for Her Majesty's Stationery Office,
By HARRISON AND SONS,
Printers in Ordinary to Her Majesty.
(1250   4 | 89 — H & S   621)

FOREIGN OFFICE.
1889.
ANNUAL SERIES.

N⁰· 515.

DIPLOMATIC AND CONSULAR REPORTS ON TRADE AND FINANCE.

UNITED STATES.

REPORT FOR THE YEAR 1888

ON THE

TRADE OF CHARLESTON.

REFERENCE TO PREVIOUS REPORT, Annual Series No. 296.

Presented to both Houses of Parliament by Command of Her Majesty,
MAY, 1889.

LONDON:
PRINTED FOR HER MAJESTY'S STATIONERY OFFICE,
BY HARRISON AND SONS, ST. MARTIN'S LANE,
PRINTERS IN ORDINARY TO HER MAJESTY.

And to be purchased, either directly or through any Bookseller, from
EYRE AND SPOTTISWOODE, EAST HARDING STREET, FLEET STREET, E.C., and
32, ABINGDON STREET, WESTMINSTER, S.W.; or
ADAM AND CHARLES BLACK, 6, NORTH BRIDGE, EDINBURGH; or
HODGES, FIGGIS, & Co., 104, GRAFTON STREET, DUBLIN.

1889.

[C. 5618—68.] *Price One Penny.*

New Series of Reports.

Reports of the Annual Series have been issued from Her Majesty's Diplomatic and Consular Officers at the following places, and may be obtained from the sources indicated on the title-page:—

No.		Price.	No.		Price.
399.	Hakodate	1d.	457.	Patras	1d.
400.	Nantes	1d.	458.	Galveston	1d.
401.	Madeira	1d.	459.	Buda Pesth	1d.
402.	Hakodate	1d.	460.	Madeira	1d.
403.	Nagasaki	1d	461.	Warsaw	1d.
404.	Hiogo	2d.	462.	Paris	2d.
405.	Tonga	1d.	463.	Baltimore	1d.
406.	Adana	1d.	464.	Philadelphia	2d.
407.	Valparaiso	1d.	465.	New Orleans	2d.
408.	Bilbao	1d.	466.	New Orleans	2d.
409.	Santiago	1d.	467.	Cherbourg	1d.
410.	Paramaribo	1d.	468.	Buenos Ayres	1d.
411.	Nantes	1d.	469.	Algiers	1d.
412.	Bangkok	1d.	470.	Ichang	1d.
413.	Yokohama	2d.	471.	Copenhagen	1d.
414.	Mozambique	1d.	472.	Athens	1d.
415.	Canton	2d.	473.	Cherbourg	1d.
416.	Kiungchow	1d.	474.	The Piræus	1d.
417.	Damascus	1d.	475.	Galatz	1d.
418.	Syra	1d.	476.	Tripoli	1d.
419.	Aleppo	1d.	477.	Saigon	1d.
420.	Sandakan	1d.	478.	Serajevo	1d.
421.	Barcelona	1d.	479.	Brussels	2d.
422.	Königsberg	1d.	480.	Bengazi	1d.
423.	Tabreez	1d.	481.	Odessa	1d.
424.	Guayaquil	1d.	482.	Santo Domingo	1d.
425.	St. Petersburg	1d.	483.	Rome	1d.
426.	Tokio	1d.	484.	Lisbon	1d.
427.	Charleston	1d.	485.	Port Said	2d.
428.	Amsterdam	1d.	486.	Havre	8d.
429.	Hamburg	4d.	487.	Boulogne	1d.
430.	Trieste	1d.	488.	Callao	1d.
431.	New York	2d.	489.	Barcelona	2d.
432.	Antwerp	1d.	490.	Boulogne	2d.
433.	Munich	1d.	491.	Taganrog	2d.
434.	Buenos Ayres	1d.	492.	Kiungchow	1d.
435.	Warsaw	1d.	493.	Sandakan	1d.
436.	Porto Rico	1d.	494.	Manila	1d.
437.	Réunion	1d.	495.	Swatow	1d.
438.	Lisbon	1d.	496.	Guayaquil	1d.
439.	Venice	1d.	497.	Rome	1d.
440.	Christiania	5d.	498.	Santos	1d.
441.	Maranham	1d.	499.	Boston	1d.
442.	Sofia	1d.	500.	Aleppo	1d.
443.	Copenhagen	1d.	501.	Bordeaux	2d.
444.	Galatz	1d.	502.	Valparaiso	1d.
445.	Tabreez	1d.	503.	St. Petersburg	1d.
446.	Bogotá	2d.	504.	Rio de Janeiro	4d.
447.	St. Petersburg	3d.	505.	Brest	1d.
448.	Nice	1d.	506.	Dunkirk	1d.
449.	Stettin	2d.	507.	Genoa	2d.
450.	Fiume	1d.	508.	Beyrout	1d.
451.	Chinkiang	1d.	509.	Colonia	1d.
452.	The Hague	1d.	510.	Marseilles	1d.
453.	Malaga	1d.	511.	Kiukiang	1d.
454.	Taganrog	1d.	512.	Buda Pesth	2d.
455.	Mozambique	1d.	513.	Wênchow	10d.
456.	Bogotá	2d.	514.	Coquimbo	1d.

No. 515.

Reference to previous Report, Annual Series No. 296.

UNITED STATES.

CHARLESTON.

Consul Cridland to the Marquis of Salisbury.

My Lord,   Charleston, March 26, 1889.

I HAVE the honour to enclose herewith a Report of the Trade and Commerce of the port of Charleston for the past year, showing also some of the principal productions of the State of South Carolina for the same period.

I have, &c.
(Signed)   FREDERICK J. CRIDLAND.

Report on the Trade and Commerce of Charleston, South Carolina, for the Year 1888.

The receipts of cotton at Charleston during the past year were of uplands 442,720 bales, and 7,348 bales of sea island, showing a decided improvement over the year 1887, during which period the receipts were uplands 392,861 bales, and sea island 7,485 bales. *Receipts of cotton.*

According to the report of the South Carolina Department of Agriculture, the acreage cultivated in cotton in the State during the year 1888 was 1,577,950 acres, and the yield about 612,000 bales. The acreage compared with 1887 has decreased; but the average yield per acre increased, owing to the favourable season. The continued rain-storms during the picking season lessened the crop and damaged the quality of the staple. *Cotton acreage. Cotton yield.*

Receipts of cotton at Charleston:— *Cotton receipts and exports.*

In 1888 .. .. 450,068 bales.
1887 .. .. 400,346 „

EXPORTS of Cotton from Charleston.

	In 1888.	In 1887.
	Bales.	Bales.
To Liverpool	69,110	90,444
France	25,843	43,968
Spain, Russia, and Italy.. ..	191,143	143,206
Total to foreign ports	286,096	277,618
To Boston	1,000	16,626
New York	142,797	84,826
Philadelphia	4,404	7,690
Total to coast ports	148,201	109,142
Total to foreign and coast ports	434,297	386,760

UNITED STATES.

Rice crop and receipts.

RECEIPTS of Native and Foreign Rice at Charleston for the past Two Years.

Year.	Barrels.	Average Weight of Barrel.
		Lbs.
1888	81,290	325
1887	96,280	325

The weather during the rice harvest season of 1887 in this State was very favourable for the planters, and the crop was gathered in excellent condition, and very little damaged rice came to market; but the unprecedented flood of last autumn was most disastrous to the rice planter, both in Georgia and South Carolina, nearly one-half of the crop being destroyed, and diminishing the receipts at this port by about 15,000 barrels, consequently much rice was imported, as it enters largely into the daily food of the people of these States.

Phosphate rock.

The mining of phosphate rock in the vicinity of Charleston has been quite active during the past year; but the State Report does not give the production in figures, but the following figures show a larger export and home consumption than in the previous year:—

Shipments of phosphate rock.

	In 1888.	In 1887.
	Tons.	Tons.
Exports to foreign ports	2,927	7,800
,, coastwise	172,541	147,735
Carried to the interior	36,733	31,748
Consumed by local companies	70,000	66,000
Total	282,201	253,283

Timber and lumber.

The comparative export of timber and lumber, or deals, crossties, &c., from Charleston in 1888, as well as for the same period in 1887, will be found in the following table:—

Exports of timber and lumber.

	In 1888.	In 1887.
	Feet.	Feet.
Exported to foreign ports	3,455,551	2,391,650
,, United States	41,813,860	30,281,085
Total	45,269,411	32,672,735

The timber and lumber shipped to foreign ports went principally to the West Indies and South America.

Naval stores.

The production of naval stores was smaller during the past year than in 1887, owing to the unremunerative prices which have continued for several crops. During the latter part of 1888 prices improved, and possibly the production in this State will also.

CHARLESTON.

Comparative Statement showing the Receipts and Exports of Naval Stores at Charleston for the past Two Years.

Receipts.

	Receipts in 1888.		Receipts in 1887.	
	Turpentine.	Rosin.	Turpentine.	Rosin.
	Casks.	Barrels.	Casks.	Barrels.
Stock on hand	1,440	33,816	4,304	21,784
Receipts	41,776	167,096	49,645	183,182

Receipts and exports of naval stores.

Average weight of a barrel of rosin 415 lbs. Cask of turpentine averages 51 gallons.

Exports.

	1888.		1887.	
	Turpentine.	Rosin.	Turpentine.	Rosin.
	Casks.	Barrels.	Casks.	Barrels.
To Great Britain	5,856	40,233	18,982	32,247
Germany	12,519	25,151	10,652	31,860
Holland	11,740	35,497	9,668	33,796
Austria	950	26,300	350	18,047
Italy	..	18,955	..	..
Russia	..	7,502	..	..
Other countries	..	7,031	3,500	27,769
Total	31,065	160,669	43,152	143,719

	1888.		1887.	
	Turpentine.	Rosin.	Turpentine.	Rosin.
	Casks.	Barrels.	Casks.	Barrels.
To coast ports and interior towns	9,188	21,217	9,397	21,435

The price of turpentine in 1888 varied from 29¼ c. to 38 c. per gallon, or 1s. 2d. to 1s. 7½d. sterling. The price of rosin is regulated according to its grade, and ranged last year from 80 c. to 1 dol. 70 c. per barrel, or 3s. 4d. to 7s. 1d. sterling.

Price of turpentine and rosin, currency and sterling.

UNITED STATES.

Productions of the Soil in South Carolina in 1888.

Productions of the State of South Carolina, value.

Articles.	Measure.	Quantity.	Acres.	Average per Acre.	Value.
					£
Indian corn	Bushel	15,013,000	1,501,322	9·0	1,939,179
Wheat	,,	1,233,000	192,637	4·4	254,306
Rye	,,	41,000	8,285	4·9	8,969
Oats	,,	4,607,000	397,198	9·0	566,277
Potatoes	,,	259,000	4,107	63·0	44,246
Hay	Tons	33,200	24,000	1·05	67,305
Rice	Pounds	24,387,000	77,966	..	282,429
Fodder	,,	..	..	..	535,164
Peas	Bushel	..	..	..	129,238
Sugar (cane)	Gallon	..	..	..	95,914
Cotton	Bales	612,000	1,577,950	158	4,890,891
Tobacco	Pounds	..	..	400	6,950
Total	..	..	..	..	8,820,868

Annex A.—Return of all Shipping at the Port of Charleston in 1888.

Entered.

Nationality.	Sailing. Number of Vessels.	Sailing. Tons.	Steam. Number of Vessels.	Steam. Tons.	Total. Number of Vessels.	Total. Tons.
British	15	6,206	44	48,590	59	54,796
American	381	176,184	208	162,470	589	338,654
Norway and Sweden	29	12,626	...	...	29	12,626
Italian	28	12,098	...	...	28	12,098
Spanish	11	4,643	3	3,251	14	7,894
German	13	5,446	1	1,050	14	6,496
Other countries	8	3,472	1	1,249	9	4,721
Total	485	220,675	257	216,610	742	437,285
,, for the preceding year	539	449,854	331	251,620	870	701,474

Cleared.

Nationality.	Sailing. Number of Vessels.	Sailing. Tons.	Steam. Number of Vessels.	Steam. Tons.	Total. Number of Vessels.	Total. Tons.
British	13	5,858	43	47,559	56	53,417
American	373	172,857	212	171,376	585	344,233
Norway and Sweden	28	12,502	...	...	28	12,502
Italian	30	13,213	...	...	30	13,213
Spanish	11	4,643	4	4,105	15	8,748
German	14	5,909	1	1,050	15	6,959
Other countries	8	3,472	1	1,249	9	4,721
Total	477	218,454	261	225,339	738	443,793
,, for the preceding year	530	441,522	319	236,442	849	677,964

CHARLESTON.

Annex B.—RETURN of Principal Articles of Export from the Port of Charleston, South Carolina, to Home and Foreign Markets during the Years 1888-87.

Articles.		1888. Quantity.	1888. Value.	1887. Quantity.	1887. Value.
			£		£
Cotton, upland	Bales	442,720	4,150,500	392,861	3,683,071
,, sea island	Bags	7,348	145,429	7,485	148,140
Rice	Barrels	81,290	254,031	96,280	300,875
Turpentine	Casks	41,776	147,957	49,645	165,483
Rosin	Barrels	167,096	60,920	183,182	64,876
Phosphate rock	Tons	267,830	282,939	209,427	207,245
,, ground	,,	14,371	22,455	37,856	59,150
Lumber and cross-ties	Feet	50,269,411	104,728	44,672,735	93,220
Fertilizers	Tons	181,192	796,215	130,633	544,304
Fruit and vegetables	Packages	211,000	412,500	85,385	186,458
Cotton goods manufactured in Charleston	Bales	54,247	619,713	52,708	658,850
Total		...	6,997,387	...	6,111,672

RETURN of the Principal Articles of Import to Charleston during the Years 1888 and 1887.

Articles.	Value. 1888.	Value. 1887.
	£	£
The principal articles imported are salt, iron-ties, beer-kainit, brimstone, nitrate of soda, Tropical fruit	119,952	111,771

Annex C.—TABLE showing the Total Value of all articles Exported from Charleston, and Imported into Charleston from and to Foreign Countries during the Years 1887 and 1888.

Countries.	Exports. 1888.	Exports. 1887.	Imports. 1888.	Imports. 1887.
	£	£	£	£
To Great Britain, France, Germany, Spain, Russia, Italy, Holland, Belgium	3,219,112	3,047,755	119,952	111,771

The published report of the commerce of Charleston does not give the value of imports or exports for each country.

The quarantine regulations existing last year will be enforced again this year, but the accommodation for the officers and crews of ships removed from the vessels while fumigation is going on, is about to be much improved by the port authorities. The harbour pilotage regulations, dock charges, and charges on vessels visiting this port have not been changed since 1887.

Depth of water on the bar at the entrance to Charleston.

The depth of water on the bar at the entrance to the Bay of Charleston remains the same as reported last year. Vessels drawing from 16 to 17 feet can enter and depart without much difficulty.

LONDON:
Printed for Her Majesty's Stationery Office,
By HARRISON AND SONS,
Printers in Ordinary to Her Majesty.
(1250 5 | 89—H & S 640)

FOREIGN OFFICE.
1889.
ANNUAL SERIES.

No. 531.

DIPLOMATIC AND CONSULAR REPORTS ON TRADE AND FINANCE.

UNITED STATES.

REPORT FOR THE YEAR 188
ON THE
TRADE OF SAVANNAH.

REFERENCE TO PREVIOUS REPORT, Annual Series No. 311.

Presented to both Houses of Parliament by Command of Her Majesty,
MAY, 1889.

LONDON:
PRINTED FOR HER MAJESTY'S STATIONERY OFFICE,
BY HARRISON AND SONS, ST. MARTIN'S LANE,
PRINTERS IN ORDINARY TO HER MAJESTY.

And to be purchased, either directly or through any Bookseller, from
EYRE AND SPOTTISWOODE, EAST HARDING STREET, FLEET STREET, E.C., and
32, ABINGDON STREET, WESTMINSTER, S.W.; or
ADAM AND CHARLES BLACK, 6, NORTH BRIDGE, EDINBURGH; or
HODGES, FIGGIS, & Co., 104, GRAFTON STREET, DUBLIN.

1889.
Price One Penny.

[C. 5618—84.]

New Series of Reports.

Reports of the Annual Series have been issued from Her Majesty's Diplomatic and Consular Officers at the following places, and may be obtained from the sources indicated on the title-page:—

No.		Price.	No.		Price.
413.	Yokohama	2d.	472.	Athens	1d.
414.	Mozambique	1d.	473.	Cherbourg	1d.
415.	Canton	2d.	474.	The Piræus	1d.
416.	Kiungchow	1d.	475.	Galatz	1d.
417.	Damascus	1d.	476.	Tripoli	1d.
418.	Syra	1d.	477.	Saigon	1d.
419.	Aleppo	1d.	478.	Serajevo	1d.
420.	Sandakan	1d.	479.	Brussels	2d.
421.	Barcelona	1d.	480.	Bengazi	1d.
422.	Königsberg	1d.	481.	Odessa	1d.
423.	Tabreez	1d.	482.	Santo Domingo	1d.
424.	Guayaquil	1d.	483.	Rome	1d.
425.	St. Petersburg	1d.	484.	Lisbon	1d.
426.	Tokio	1d.	485.	Port Said	2d.
427.	Charleston	1d.	486.	Havre	3d.
428.	Amsterdam	1d.	487.	Boulogne	1d.
429.	Hamburg	4d.	488.	Callao	1d.
430.	Trieste	1d.	489.	Barcelona	2d.
431.	New York	2d.	490.	Boulogne	2d.
432.	Antwerp	1d.	491.	Taganrog	2d.
433.	Munich	1d.	492.	Kiungchow	1d.
434.	Buenos Ayres	1d.	493.	Sandakan	1d.
435.	Warsaw	1d.	494.	Manila	1d.
436.	Porto Rico	1d.	495.	Swatow	1d.
437.	Réunion	1d.	496.	Guayaquil	1d.
438.	Lisbon	1d.	497.	Rome	1d.
439.	Venice	1d.	498.	Santos	1d.
440.	Christiania	5d.	499.	Boston	1d.
441.	Maranham	1d.	500.	Aleppo	1d.
442.	Sofia	1d.	501.	Bordeaux	2d.
443.	Copenhagen	1d.	502.	Valparaiso	1d.
444.	Galatz	1d.	503.	St. Petersburg	1d.
445.	Tabreez	1d.	504.	Rio de Janeiro	4d.
446.	Bogotá	2d.	505.	Brest	1d.
447.	St. Petersburg	3d.	506.	Dunkirk	1d.
448.	Nice	1d.	507.	Genoa	2d.
449.	Stettin	2d.	508.	Beyrout	1d.
450.	Fiume	1d.	509.	Colonia	1d.
451.	Chinkiang	1d.	510.	Marseilles	1d.
452.	The Hague	1d.	511.	Kiukiang	1d.
453.	Malaga	1d.	512.	Buda-Pesth	2d.
454.	Taganrog	1d.	513.	Wênchow	10d.
455.	Mozambique	1d.	514.	Coquimbo	1d.
456.	Bogatá	2d.	515.	Charleston	1d.
457.	Patras	1d.	516.	Riga	1d.
458.	Galveston	1d.	517.	Mollendo	1d.
459.	Buda Pesth	1d.	518.	Taiwan	1d.
460.	Madeira	1d.	519.	Wuhu	1d.
461.	Warsaw	1d.	520.	Corunna	2d.
462.	Paris	2d.	521.	Noumea	1d.
463.	Baltimore	1d.	522.	San José	1d.
464.	Philadelphia	2d.	523.	Ningpo	1d.
465.	New Orleans	2d.	524.	Gothenburg	2d.
466.	New Orleans	2d.	525.	Hankow	2d.
467.	Cherbourg	1d.	526.	Foochow	1d.
468.	Buenos Ayres	1d.	527.	Erzeroum	2d.
469.	Algiers	1d.	528.	Ciudad Bolivar	1d.
470.	Ichang	1d.	529.	Jaffa	1d.
471.	Copenhagen	1d.	530.	Ancona	1d.

No. 531.

Reference to previous Report, Annual Series No. 311.

UNITED STATES.

SAVANNAH.

Consul Cridland to the Marquis of Salisbury.

My Lord,   Charleston, S.C., *April* 10, 1889.

I HAVE the honour to enclose herewith a Report of the Trade and Commerce of the Port of Savannah, Georgia, for the past year, received from Mr. Vice-Consul Robertson.

I have, &c.

(Signed)   FREDERICK J. CRIDLAND.

Report on the Trade and Commerce of Savannah for the Year 1888.

The trade and commerce of Savannah during the year 1888 has been particularly good. The general prosperity alluded to in my former Report has not only continued, but has increased far beyond the expectations of the most sanguine business men of the port. [Introductory.]

All branches of trade have prospered, and every business is thriving. [Trade prosperous.]

Several hundred miles of railroads have been completed and opened during the year in sections of the country tributary to this port, and more are now in process of construction. Notable among those completed is the Columbus and Western extension to Birmingham, Alabama. [New lines of railroad completed in 1888.] With this connection it is possible that Savannah may become a grain-exporting port in the near future, the mileage from Kansas City and the North-West—the great grain-producing districts of America—being shorter to Savannah than to the grain-exporting ports of the North. [Possibility of a grain trade.]

The crops in the region of this port, with some few exceptions, have been good. [Crops.] The cotton crop for the season 1888–89 was slightly damaged in quality, and perhaps in quantity, by the heavy rains in August and September, but the hope is indulged that the fine weather enjoyed during the latter part of the cotton growing season will have enabled the planters to gather more than was at first expected. This, however, cannot be conclusively proved until the cotton season ends, about April, 1889. [Damage to cotton crop of 1888.]

During the year under review it may be remarked as a subject of congratulation that no cotton fires on shipboard have taken place, and that no casualties of any moment have happened to British shipping at this port. [No cotton fires on steamers in 1888.]

The number of British steamships entered and cleared at Savannah during the year is considerably less than usual. [Decrease in the number of British steamships arriving in 1888.]

At the time when vessels are generally chartered for the conveyance

UNITED STATES.

Cause: high rates of freight elsewhere. Improvement for discharge of ballast from ships at the quarantine station. Great saving of time to vessels quarantined. Health of port.

of the cotton from this port Eastern freights were in the ascendant, and steamers were fixed for those ports in preference to Savannah.

I am pleased to be able to report that the facilities for discharging the ballast from vessels at the quarantine station for this port have been very materially increased. More vessels are now able to discharge their ballast at one time, and with the aid of steam cranes the work is performed with greater despatch.

These improvements will be a great saving in time and money to vessels arriving at quarantine, and do away with the many complaints of unnecessary detention made by owners and masters.

The general health of the port has been exceptionally good. This fact, in the face of the yellow fever epidemic which raged during the summer in the neighbouring State of Florida, goes far towards proving that Savannah is fast becoming one of the most healthy seaports on the Atlantic coast. When this fact is sufficiently spread abroad, and the erroneous impression dispelled that the port is now, as it certainly was some years back, a malarial fever point; the advantages which Savannah offers as a health resort and business centre will be still more recognised and appreciated.

Imports and exports generally. Imports.

The imports and exports at this port for the year have been generally satisfactory.

The annexed Tables A and B show a small increase in the imports for the present year over that of 1887. Savannah not being a direct importing port, the returns are of but little use as a guide to the business done. Merchandise running far into the millions is annually brought to the port by coastwise vessels from the North.

Fertilisers.

This article of importation shows a small increase in quantity compared with 1887.

Cotton ties.

The importation of cotton ties compares favourably with other years.

Rice.

During the year under review a large quantity of foreign grown rice was imported to Savannah, mostly of Indian growth, Patna and Bengal. This rice is mostly received in the so-called unclean state, on account of the United States tariff, which fixes three different rates of duty on rice, viz. :—

	Cents. per lb.
Cleaned rice	$2\frac{1}{4}$
Uncleaned rice	$1\frac{1}{2}$
Rough rice	1

The uncleaned rice, therefore, offers the best chance for the importer, since the cleaning of the stuff does not cost the considerable difference of $\frac{3}{4}$ c. per lb. duty, between clean and uncleaned, and consequently there was every indication of this style of rice becoming an important article of importation. The importation of this article of commerce has, however, been brought to a standstill, owing to a decision rendered by the New Orleans Circuit Court, by which the importer must pay the full rate of $2\frac{1}{4}$ per cent. duty, the court claiming that the rice was more clean than uncleaned. A rehearing of the case in New Orleans has been applied for, and if granted will come up for hearing during the spring sessions; if not, the case may be carried to the Supreme Court in Washington.

The House of Representatives will probably soon have to deal with a motion of the Senate to reduce the duty on rice to—

	Cents. per lb.
Cleaned rice	$1\frac{1}{2}$
Uncleaned rice	1
Rough rice	$\frac{1}{2}$

SAVANNAH.

If such a tariff should be established, the trade in foreign rice would no doubt develop rapidly, and Great Britain would naturally get a very large share of it.

All other articles. Under this heading a large increase is noticeable for 1888. It includes 18,000*l.* for cotton brought to this port from Brunswick, the steamer having to come to Savannah to complete her loading, and is therefore not an actual import.

Exports. The annexed returns, A and B, show a marked falling-off in the amount of exports for 1888. The decrease is principally in the exportation of cotton, and can very readily be explained.

Cotton. Cotton is the principal article of exportation from Savannah. The net receipts for the season of 1887-88 have been the largest ever known at this port, being 892,388 bales, or a gain of 87,976 bales over the receipts for the season of 1886-87. Owing, however, to the high rate of freights which were offered for Eastern ports, the shippers at this port were unable to profitably engage steamers to carry the cotton direct, and to keep their engagement were compelled to forward nearly all their early shipments by coastwise steamers to Northern ports for transhipment to the regular line of steamships.

This explanation applies to cotton seed as well as to cotton.

Lumber and timber. There is a noticeable increase in the lumber and timber shipped from Savannah for this year.

Spirits of turpentine. After cotton, spirits of turpentine is the principal article of exportation from this port. Year by year the quantity increases, and if proper care is taken to replace the pines destroyed with new ones, there is but little doubt that the value will continue to increase.

Resin. In former reports resin was included in "all other articles." The trade, however, having grown to such proportions, justifies its being shown separately, which I have accordingly done.

Annex A.—RETURN of Principal Articles of Export from Savannah, Ga., during the Year 1888.

Articles.		1888. Quantity.	1888. Value.	1887. Quantity.	1887. Value.
			£		£
Cotton	Lbs.	159,183,557	3,117,426	223,225,757	4,188,454
„ seed	„	1,008,260	1,653	2,663,854	4,672
Lumber and timber	Feet	30,128,000	46,226	25,310,000	37,044
Spirits of turpentine	Gallons	4,143,854	299,112	3,785,389	240,381
Resin	Lbs.	428,058	96,998	...	...
All other articles		...	8,568	...	139,831
Total		...	3,569,983	...	4,610,382

RETURN of Principal Articles of Import to Savannah, Ga., during the Year 1888.

Articles.		1888. Quantity.	1888. Value.	1887. Quantity.	1887. Value.
			£		£
Fertilizers	Tons	10,362	16,768	9,925	17,568
Cotton ties	Bundles	42,980	5,413	35,200	4,386
Salt	Lbs.	11,864,714	2,097	15,846,305	3,296
Rice	„	4,959,639	14,423	...	...
Molasses	Gallons	77,923	2,885	26,743	836
Brimstone	Tons	1,245	3,865	...	...
All other articles		...	25,289	...	{ 638 / 9,497 }
Total		...	70,740	...	36,221

Annex B.—TABLE showing the Total Value of all Articles Exported from Savannah and Imported to Savannah from and to Foreign Countries during the Years 1887-88.

Nationality.	Exports. 1888.	Exports. 1887.	Imports. 1888.	Imports. 1887.
	£	£	£	£
British	1,391,217	1,514,116	24,110	18,860
German	651,328	907,361	21,499	9,436
Spain	342,210	466,869	65	2,199
Russia	307,858	955,128	..	..
Netherlands	185,328	164,708	..	..
Belgium	134,298	193,699	401	1,008
Brazil	2,402	2,580	10	..
Other countries	555,342	405,921	24,655	4,718
Total	3,569,983	4,610,382	70,740	36,221

Annex C.—RETURN of all Shipping at the Port of Savannah in the Year 1888.

ENTERED.

Nationality.	Sailing. Number of Vessels.	Sailing. Tons.	Steam. Number of Vessels.	Steam. Tons.	Total. Number of Vessels.	Total. Tons.
British	37	19,945	49	61,219	86	81,164
American	44	20,275	385	522,861	429	543,136
Norwegian	82	44,465	...	...	82	44,465
German	25	12,727	...	...	25	12,727
Other countries	63	40,025	...	...	63	40,025
	251	137,437	434	584,080	685	721,517

CLEARED.

Nationality.	Sailing. Number of Vessels.	Sailing. Tons.	Steam. Number of Vessels.	Steam. Tons.	Total. Number of Vessels.	Total. Tons.
British	37	19,192	50	65,019	87	84,211
American	44	22,287	346	487,375	390	509,662
Norwegian	64	34,462	2	760	66	35,222
German	23	12,050	1	1,202	24	13,252
Other countries	56	34,206	...	...	56	34,206
	224	122,197	399	554,356	623	676,553

LONDON:
Printed for Her Majesty's Stationery Office,
By HARRISON AND SONS,
Printers in Ordinary to Her Majesty.
(1250 5 | 89—H & S 656)

FOREIGN OFFICE.
1889.
ANNUAL SERIES.

No. 545.

DIPLOMATIC AND CONSULAR REPORTS ON TRADE AND FINANCE.

UNITED STATES.

REPORT FOR THE YEAR 1888
ON THE
TRADE OF NEW YORK.

REFERENCE TO PREVIOUS REPORT, Annual Series No. 370.

Presented to both Houses of Parliament by Command of Her Majesty,
JUNE, 1889.

LONDON:
PRINTED FOR HER MAJESTY'S STATIONERY OFFICE,
BY HARRISON AND SONS, ST. MARTIN'S LANE,
PRINTERS IN ORDINARY TO HER MAJESTY.

And to be purchased, either directly or through any Bookseller, from
EYRE AND SPOTTISWOODE, EAST HARDING STREET, FLEET STREET, E.C., and
32, ABINGDON STREET, WESTMINSTER, S.W.; or
ADAM AND CHARLES BLACK, 6, NORTH BRIDGE, EDINBURGH; or
HODGES, FIGGIS, & Co., 104, GRAFTON STREET, DUBLIN.

1889.

[C. 5618—98.] *Price Three Halfpence.*

New Series of Reports.

Reports of the Annual Series have been issued from Her Majesty's Diplomatic and Consular Officers at the following places, and may be obtained from the sources indicated on the title-page:—

No.		Price.	No.		Price.
429.	Hamburg	4d.	487.	Boulogne	1d.
430.	Trieste	1d.	488.	Callao	1d.
431.	New York	2d.	489.	Barcelona	2d.
432.	Antwerp	1d.	490.	Boulogne	2d.
433.	Munich	1d.	491.	Taganrog	2d.
434.	Buenos Ayres	1d.	492.	Kiungchow	1d.
435.	Warsaw	1d.	493.	Sandakan	1d.
436.	Porto Rico	1d.	494.	Manila	1d.
437.	Réunion	1d.	495.	Swatow	1d.
438.	Lisbon	1d.	496.	Guayaquil	1d.
439.	Venice	1d.	497.	Rome	1d.
440.	Christiania	5d.	498.	Santos	1d.
441.	Maranham	1d.	499.	Boston	1d.
442.	Sofia	1d.	500.	Aleppo	1d.
443.	Copenhagen	1d.	501.	Bordeaux	2d.
444.	Galatz	1d.	502.	Valparaiso	1d.
445.	Tabreez	1d.	503.	St. Petersburg	1d.
446.	Bogotá	2d.	504.	Rio de Janeiro	4d.
447.	St. Petersburg	3d.	505.	Brest	1d.
448.	Nice	1d.	506.	Dunkirk	1d.
449.	Stettin	2d.	507.	Genoa	2d.
450.	Fiume	1d.	508.	Beyrout	1d.
451.	Chinkiang	1d.	509.	Colonia	1d.
452.	The Hague	1d.	510.	Marseilles	1d.
453.	Malaga	1d.	511.	Kiukiang	1d.
454.	Taganrog	1d.	512.	Buda Pesth	2d.
455.	Mozambique	1d.	513.	Wênchow	10d.
456.	Bogotá	2d.	514.	Coquimbo	1d.
457.	Patras	1d.	515.	Charleston	1d.
458.	Galveston	1d.	516.	Riga	1d.
459.	Buda Pesth	1d.	517.	Mollendo	1d.
460.	Madeira	1d.	518.	Taiwan	1d.
461.	Warsaw	1d.	519.	Wuhu	1d.
462.	Paris	2d.	520.	Corunna	2d.
463.	Baltimore	1d.	521.	Noumea	1d.
464.	Philadelphia	2d.	522.	San José	1d.
465.	New Orleans	2d.	523.	Ningpo	1d.
466.	New Orleans	2d.	524.	Gothenburg	2d.
467.	Cherbourg	1d.	525.	Hankow	2d.
468.	Buenos Ayres	1d.	526.	Foochow	1d.
469.	Algiers	1d.	527.	Erzeroum	2d.
470.	Ichang	1d.	528.	Ciudad Bolivar	1d.
471.	Copenhagen	1d.	529.	Jaffa	1d.
472.	Athens	1d.	530.	Ancona	1d.
473.	Cherbourg	1d.	531.	Savannah	1d.
474.	The Piræus	1d.	532.	Batavia	1d.
475.	Galatz	1d.	533.	Adrianople	1d.
476.	Tripoli	1d.	534.	Nisch	11d.
477.	Saigon	1d.	535.	Vienna	1d.
478.	Serajevo	1d.	536.	Odessa	8d.
479.	Brussels	2d.	537.	Constantinople	2d.
480.	Bengazi	1d.	538.	Damascus	1d.
481.	Odessa	1d.	539.	Tientsin	1d.
482.	Santo Domingo	1d.	540.	Amoy	1d.
483.	Rome	1d.	541.	Mogador	1d.
484.	Lisbon	1d.	542.	Vienna	1d.
485.	Port Saïd	2d.	543.	Antwerp	1d.
486.	Havre	3d.	544.	Lisbon	2d.

No. 545.

Reference to previous Report, Annual Series No. 370.

UNITED STATES.

NEW YORK.

Consul-General Booker to the Marquis of Salisbury.

My Lord,　　　　　　　　　　　　New York, April 19, 1889.

I HAVE the honour to transmit herewith my Annual Report upon the Trade of New York, with some information in regard to other parts of my Consular district.

　　　　　　　　　　I have, &c.
　　　　(Signed)　　WM. LANE BOOKER.

Report on the Trade, Navigation, and Commerce of New York for the Year 1888.

The trade of this city in 1888 has not been marked by any extraordinary events. Bank clearances, as given elsewhere, show that in extent it equalled that of 1887, although there was absent the exceptional circumstances which made the latter year a memorable one from the extraordinarily large disbursements and distribution of money in connection with the construction of over 13,000 miles of railroads. The disbursement on this account in 1888 must have been from 40,000,000*l.* to 50,000,000*l.* less than in 1887, as the construction did not extend beyond 7,000 miles. Importers and jobbers report profits generally to have been smaller than in the previous year, except on cotton goods, for which there was an active demand throughout the year at satisfactory prices. Imports of merchandise (excluding specie) show very little variation, but in the exports there is a reduction of nearly 3,000,000*l.* Customs receipts at this port in 1888 were 29,350,648*l.*, a falling-off from 1887 of 4·46 per cent. The value of all dry goods marketed—that is, entered for consumption and withdrawn from bonded warehouse—was nearly 1,000,000*l.* more than in 1887. The gross earnings of the railroads were greater than in 1887, but the net results were less favourable, due to reduction in rates, especially in the west. The dividends have, with few exceptions, continued without change, but some of the companies have had to encroach on their reserves to enable them to be paid.

Failures both in the city and country were, in number, in excess of those of 1887, but the liabilities were very much less.

The money market showed few important changes. Call loans

[Side note: General review of trade.]

UNITED STATES.

ranged from 2 to 4 per cent., but at the close of the year the demand was greater, and as high as 8 per cent. was paid in some instances. In September there was a demand for money from Chicago required for wheat speculations, but the sale of bonds to the Treasury prevented any disturbance or advance of rates. First-class commercial paper ranged from 3 to 5½ per cent., the latter rate ruling at the close of the year. The bank clearances were less in 1888 than in the previous year by 491,654,845*l*., or about 7·12 per cent., but the stock transactions show a decrease of 27·5 per cent., leaving the clearances on the trade transactions of the year about 0·2 per cent. over those of 1887. The total clearances were 6,412,376,820*l*., of which 1,824,494,400*l*. represent stock transactions. The clearances in New York were over 63 per cent. of the total clearances—*i.e.*, the clearances of the 37 cities of the United States having a clearing house—of the whole country.

The condition of the 63 associated banks of the city at different periods of the year is shown in the following table:—

Bank returns.

Associated Banks of New York City.

1888.	Loans.	Specie.	Legal Tenders.	Deposits.	Circulation.	Surplus over Reserve required against Deposits.
	£	£	£	£	£	£
Week ending—						
January 7	74,241,300	15,498,500	5,854,100	68,248,900	1,666,500	2,230,300
March 31	75,917,590	14,698,400	6,411,500	76,903,900	1,566,200	1,884,000
June 30	77,679,700	18,585,700	7,867,720	84,116,100	1,571,300	5,524,300
September 29	80,485,700	17,577,238	6,511.560	84,195,300	1,408,800	3,039,900
December 28	80,092,500	15,763.400	6,146,800	82,464,800	1,001,600	1,293,960

Banking report.

The annual report of the superintendent of the State Banking Department has been presented to the Legislature, and from it I extract the following items of interest. (Report to end of the year not yet published.) There were on October 1 last 130 banks of deposit and discount in active operation in the State, showing an accession during the year of 25 banks, with an increase of capital of 460,410*l*., and a growth during the last five years of 46 banks, with an increase in capital of 783,624*l*.

The resources of the banks of deposit and discount on October 1 were 43,479,744*l*., an increase of 5,441,500*l*.

At the commencement of the present fiscal year there were within the State 25 trust, loan, mortgage, security or guarantee companies, with resources amounting to 46,147,745*l*., and 125 savings banks, with resources amounting to 126,873,298*l*. The sums due to depositors in savings banks amounted to 107,877,570*l*. The total number of open accounts was 1,362,852, an increase of 37,790*l*. over the previous year. The average rate of interest paid was 3·32 per cent.

Sterling exchange.

The following gives the rates of bankers' sterling exchange during the year 1888:—

Month.		At 60 Days.	At Sight.
		Dol. c.	Dol. c.
January	Highest	4 85	4 87
	Lowest	4 83½	4 86½
February	Highest	4 85¼	4 87¼
	Lowest	4 83½	4 85½
March	Highest	4 86¼	4 88
	Lowest	4 85½	4 87½
April	Highest	4 86½	4 88½
	Lowest	4 85¼	4 87
May	Highest	4 87¼	4 89½
	Lowest	4 86¼	4 88¼
June	Highest	4 87¼	4 89¼
	Lowest	4 86¼	4 88¼
July	Highest	4 87¼	4 88¾
	Lowest	4 86	4 88
August	Highest	4 85½	4 88
	Lowest	4 84½	4 87
September	Highest	4 85	4 88½
	Lowest	4 83½	4 87½
October	Highest	4 84¼	4 88¼
	Lowest	4 83¾	4 87¼
November	Highest	4 85¼	4 88¾
	Lowest	4 84½	4 87½
December	Highest	4 85	4 89
	Lowest	4 84¼	4 88¼

Import returns. The import returns in Annex B show a decrease in receipts of about 7,000,000*l.* on those of 1887, of which about 6,675,000*l.* is specie.

Export returns. The export returns show an increase of nearly 2,500,000*l.*, and in individual articles there are important variations. In wheat, flour, bacon and hams, lard, cheese, refined sugar, and oleomargarine there is a great falling-off, but the decrease is made up by the increase in the shipments of specie, cotton, fresh beef, live cattle, petroleum, maize, hops, and tallow.

Failures. In the following table, taken from Dun's Commercial Agency, will be found the number of failures in the past two years in New York city and Brooklyn, and the States of my district, with the liabilities; also the number of persons engaged in trade in 1888, with the percentage of failures to traders.

	Number of Failures.		Amount of Liabilities.		Number of Persons in Trade in 1888.	Percentage of Failure to Traders.
	1888.	1887.	1888.	1887.		
			£	£		
New York city and Brooklyn...	690	516	3,516,455	8,413,350	54,681	·66
New York, outside of New York city and Brooklyn	599	599	1,686,604	1,704,285	90,800	1·26
Connecticut	137	117	160,634	721,000	16,970	·86
New Jersey	151	120	306,085	354,935	30,875	·48
Rhode Island	132	122	252,740	644,300	7,738	1·70
Delaware	26	26	66,785	102,015	4,348	·60

DRY GOODS.

Dry goods. Cottons. *Cottons.*—In my report for 1886 I reviewed somewhat at length the general situation of the dry goods trade between the two countries, and therein stated that importations into this country from England of all the heavier and coarser descriptions of cotton goods, including sheetings,

(671)

shirtings, drillings, osnaburgs, and similar classes, also plain and rolled jaconets, both dyed and printed, and most descriptions of ginghams, printed lawns, and similar fabrics, had long since ceased, and the markets here were supplied entirely with goods of American manufacture. The remarks then made still apply. Here and there exceptions may be named, as in the case of the finer classes of cheviots, and similar goods manufactured in Glasgow and in Manchester, from which points the importation has increased by reason of the excellent quality and beauty of these fabrics, while for the first time in many years some of the Manchester printers are displaying certain classes of their work in the American markets, although as yet the sale of these products, owing to the high rate of duty imposed upon them, must have been limited. American printers meantime have themselves made considerable advances, and the exhibition of their products this year has undoubtedly surpassed, both on cottons and mixed fabrics, any previous displays, whether as regards perfection of work, richness of colouring, or boldness and originality of designs. As a whole, the manufacture of cotton goods has been profitable to those engaged in it, and the dividends of the principal mills to their shareholders, especially in New England, have been satisfactory. Many of the southern mills also have given satisfaction to their owners on the heavier classes of goods, such as the lower and coarser counts of yarns and cloths referred to in my report for 1886, a fair proportion of which, it may be said, finds a ready sale for export, particularly for China markets.

Prices during the year have been unusually uniform. Stocks are reported as a whole to be lighter than usual, and free from heavy accumulations.

Worsteds and woollens.

Worsteds and Woollens.—During the past year the woollen trade in this country has probably been in a more depressed condition than either of the other great branches of manufacture. This state of affairs has been occasioned largely by the agitation in regard to the reduction of the tariff, and especially the proposal in Congress for the admission of wool duty free. Profits have accordingly been only moderate, even in the most favoured classes of productions, while many have been unprofitable, and in some the losses have been serious. The fact that certain classes of worsteds, such as worsted coatings, have been admitted at a more favourable rate of duty than woollens has led to an increasing importation of these goods, which have been taken largely in preference to similar goods of American make—the total importations of worsted, woollen, and stuff goods from Yorkshire having undoubtedly been the largest that have taken place for many years.

This movement appears likely to be increased by the growing favour which is being once more extended to the bright-faced or lustred fabrics, made of mohair or its imitations, which, after some years' depression, are now being freely taken up again in place of the softer French and English fabrics of all wool, which have been meantime in such great favour. On the other hand, great efforts are being made by the woollen manufacturers to obtain a reversal of the Treasury's decisions, under which the worsted coatings before referred to have been so largely imported, and if they are successful in these efforts of course a decline would naturally be looked for.

Silks.

Silks.—The importations of silk manufactures have been steadily increasing since 1885, the largest increase being in plushes, satins, laces, and braids; in silk piece goods and velvets there has been a falling-off.

NEW YORK.

The following table shows the total grain shipments from this port, and the number of vessels engaged in the transport, with their nationality:— *Carriage of grain.*

Nationality.	Number of Vessels.	Number of Bushels.
British..	471	15,974,429
Belgian	69	3,226,653
German	96	1,967,952
Dutch ..	41	974,282
French	26	1,253,841
Austrian	8	231,794
Italian..	7	357,347
Portuguese	6	188,545
American	5	167,335
Spanish	4	221,360
Danish..	21	596,426
Total	..	25,159,964

The sailing vessel is fast disappearing as a grain carrier. Last year there were 12 vessels (8 Austrian and 4 Portuguese) under sail left port carrying 420,339 bushels, against 74 in 1887 carrying 1,922,921 bushels. In 1880 there were 1,879 carrying 63,376,584 bushels, about 56 per cent. of the whole carried.

Ocean freights were maintained at a much higher rate during the last half of the year than for some time past, and the Atlantic steamships did an excellent business. Had wheat not been held back by the speculations going on in Chicago there would have been a much greater demand for tonnage, and rates would have been further advanced. The falling-off in transient tonnage was very noticeable, and steam and sailing ships seeking freights have found no difficulty in securing remunerative charters, both for near and distant ports. *Ocean freights.*

The New York canals were open in 1888 for navigation from May 10 to December 3. The report of the superintendent shows that 4,972,948 tons (2,000 lbs.) passed through against 5,553,805 tons in 1887. The average tonnage for the last five years was 5,106,401 tons. The reasons for the diminished tonnage of last year are stated to have been caused by the boatmen at the opening insisting on higher rates than shippers were willing to pay, and while the contest lasted the railroads secured the carriage of the grain, also by the short crop and high price of wheat. The movements eastward by the canal included 15,657,511 bushels of wheat, 17,646,796 bushels of maize, 4,307,650 bushels of oats, 392,745 bushels of rye, 135,204 bushels of barley, 32,255 bushels of peas and beans, 4,945 barrels of flour, and 14,656,044 lbs. of flax-seed. Freights were lower than in 1887.

The rates of transportation on the railroads of the State varied a good deal during the year, and were on an average much lower than in 1887. During the year 1,358,261 tons (2,000 lbs.) were sent westward to Buffalo, Pittsburg, &c., from this city, and 2,937,873 tons were received, originating at or west of Buffalo, Pittsburg, &c. The amount sent and received varied little from that of 1887. The bridge at Poughkeepsie, which has been under construction for the past three years, is completed, and railroad connections will shortly be made with it, effecting great changes in the traffic between the South and New England States. *Railroad statistics.* *Bridge over Hudson river.*

The returns of the city railroads for the year ended September 30 *City railroads.*

last show that 376,913,586 passengers were carried, of which 171,529,789 were on the elevated roads. To transport these passengers 3,203 carriages were used, with 13,458 horses and 291 steam engines, and the employés numbered 11,725. The net earnings of the roads amounted to 500,420*l.*, of which 391,420*l.* belonged to the elevated roads. The fare on all the lines, for short or long distances, is uniform, being 5 c. (about 2½*d.*) On the elevated roads a passenger can travel from 9 to 10 miles on a single fare. The increase in the traffic in 1888 was about 5 per cent. over that of the preceding year.

LABOUR.

Labour.

The report for 1888 of the Labour Commission for this State has not yet been published, and the superintendent writes me that he does not know when it will be out of the printer's hands. There has been no material variation in the wages of any of the industrial classes. Strikes have been on the decrease. Bradstreet, a reliable authority, states that there were in New York State in the past year 20,484 strikes against 65,656 in 1887. In 1888 the percentage of strikers in this State to that of the whole United States was 9 per cent., against 18 per cent. in 1887. The leading strikes in New York city and Brooklyn were the glassmakers, numbering 1,000 hands, and the brewers and maltsters, involving 5,000 hands: the former were out 102 days, and were successful; the latter were out 50 days, and were unsuccessful. The cause of the strike or lock-out of the brewers and maltsters' employés was the refusal of the employers to make contracts with their employés in a body, as they had previously done, the agreement before having been between the members of the United Lager Beer Brewers of New York city and vicinity and the Brewers' Journeymen Union. The reason of the action of the brewers and maltsters is set forth in the following circular:—

"United States Brewers' Association, No. 2, Irving-place, New York, March 26, 1888. To the Brewery Employés and the Public generally.

"Owing to a lack of unity on one side and concerted coercive action on the other, the brewers in nearly all the large centres of trade submitted to the dictates of the Brewery Working Men's Union as to the employment, discharge, treatment, compensation, and working time of their help. The false position into which the brewers were forced, much against their inclination and better judgment, could not fail to bring its evil fruits, and, after an experience of nearly 18 months, it has become unbearable. We are, therefore, determined as a body to throw off the onerous burden, and to again assume that legitimate control of our business affairs to which an equitable division of the respective rights and duties of capital and labour entitles us.

"In forming this resolution we do not deny to labour the right to organise—a right which we claim and exercise ourselves as employers—nor do we leave out of sight, or regret, the tendency of the times to secure to the working man, through united effort, amelioration of his lot. In this we are sincere, and we assure our employés, labour unions, and the public generally that we are not governed in our present action by the desire or intention to abridge or to abrogate any fair concession as to hours of labour and recompense therefor which we have made to our workmen under former agreements. Furthermore, the influence of the United States Brewers' Association upon local associations and individual members will be exerted in the interest of brewery employés throughout the country, to the end that no real grievance may go unremedied. Existing agreements not violated by the workmen will be strictly carried out on the part of the employers; but, on their expiration, no new agreements will be made, excepting only individual agreements between employer and employé.

"First and foremost, we base this action upon the inalienable right of every man to act as a free agent so long as his actions do not infringe on the rights and privileges of others. The terms of these labour contracts interfere with the free exercise of this prerogative by denying to the workman to sell his labour when, how, and to whom he pleases, and by withholding from the employer the privilege of choosing his help to his liking in the open labour market from those willing to accept his offer of terms and conditions, to hire and discharge his help to suit his own judgment, and to deal with employés according to individual merit. But, apart from this fundamental cause, we have other motives and reasons for our determination to insist, hereafter, in dealing with our employés without the interference of brewery working men's unions. The unwonted power conceded to these unions has in innumerable instances been abused for the perpetration of tyrannical exactions and petty, humiliating annoyances. Stipulations have been broken with impunity; men, discharged as objectionable, have been forced back on their employers; and boycott and strike have been rashly threatened and declared when resistance to such and other irresponsible actions was attempted. On a comparatively small number of men, the leaders in the national and local brewery working men's unions, rests the responsibility for the misdirection and wilful abuse of the power mistakenly granted to these organisations in the settlement of labour questions. A much graver responsibility, however, do these men assume when they prostitute their sway over the minds and actions of brewery workmen by drawing them into affiliation with anarchism, upon which every loyal citizen looks with condemnation and abhorrence.

"In view of these facts and considerations we have adopted the following resolutions, to wit:

"Resolved, that at the expiration of existing contracts no new agreements shall be made with any brewery working men's unions.

"Resolved, that we assure our employés and the public that this action is not taken for the purpose of reducing the present scale of wages, or lengthening the time of labour, although we are paying to-day, for the hours of work and kind of labour required, higher wages than are paid in any other industry.

"Resolved, that we further assure our workmen that, while we recognise their right to secure to themselves all the legitimate benefits to be derived from association and co-operation, we must insist that their efforts in this direction must be limited to that point where they begin to infringe upon the rights of others.

"Resolved, that if the carrying out of these resolutions should lead to strikes, we faithfully promise to the workmen remaining with us, and to those who take the places made vacant by such strikes, full protection and continuance of employment as long as they perform their duties satisfactorily; and that, in making this promise, we state distinctly that this protection will be extended to all employés, irrespective of nationality.

"Resolved, that as law-abiding citizens of this country, we express our abhorrence of anarchism, and protest in the name of the brewers of this country, and of thousands of loyal working men employed by them, against the injustice of having a stigma attached to our trade, in the public mind, on account of anarchical sympathies manifested by brewery working men's unions.

"For the purpose of making these resolutions effective, we hereby bind ourselves to mutual support and protection, and reaffirm our adherence to the following pledge:

"Recognising the great importance of mutual protection against attempts of unjustifiable encroachments upon our rights as employers by organised labour, and further recognising the fact that the competition among brewers can be made to furnish the strongest weapon against us, we hereby heartily endorse the resolutions adopted by the board of trustees at their meeting in St. Louis on the 19th of May, 1886, and in conformity with such resolutions we hereby promise and agree, and bind ourselves by our signatures to a faithful performance of the covenant, that we shall not take advantage of the misfortune of any competing brewer who is a party to this agreement, and whose business is suffering by reason of a strike, boycott, lock-out, or similar consequences of labour troubles; but shall, on notification by the secretary of the United States Brewers' Association, refuse to furnish beer, ale, or porter to the customers of such brewer, and shall request our respective agents to act in harmony with this agreement.

"Fully convinced that the course we have adopted is one in the true interests of both employer and employé, we confidently rely upon our workmen and the public generally to sustain us in it.

"By order of the United States Brewers' Association, with the concurrence of its affiliated local associations throughout the United States.

"WILLIAM A. MILES, President."
"Richard Katzenmayer, Secretary."

The Board of Mediation and Arbitration investigated the matter, and their action and its result is given in the following extract from the report of the board to the Legislature:—

"One of the principal cases of the year was that of a lock-out of brewery employés in the metropolitan district. This disturbance had its origin in a distant section of the country, Milwaukee, Wisconsin. In December, 1887, the employing maltsters of Milwaukee declined to enter into a contract with the working malsters for their labour for the ensuing year, and were boycotted by the National Journeymen Brewers' Union, with a view to coercing them into the desired agreement. To the same end the working brewers of Milwaukee refused to handle the malt produced by the boycotted employing maltsters, and were locked out by the employing brewers, who in their turn were boycotted in their productions by the Journeymen Brewers' National Union. Then followed a demand upon the employing brewers of New York and vicinity by the working brewers in their service, that they enter into a contract for labour for the year soon to commence, following the expiration of an existing agreement, which proposed contract contained a stipulation that the malt of the boycotted Milwaukee employing maltsters should not be used in their breweries, with other conditions not acceptable to the employing brewers. The latter declined to enter into such contract, and their productions were boycotted by the Journeymen Brewers' National Union and other labour organisations in affiliation with it in New York and Brooklyn. In all this proceeding there was here no question of wages, hours of labour, or any other of the usual causes of disturbance, involved. It was a case, pure and simple, of an attempt by the working brewers to control and direct the employing brewers of New York and vicinity against the purchase and use of a particular manufacture of malt in their business, which, for the reasons stated, was obnoxious to the working brewers and others in association with them. The board used its best efforts to bring about a settlement, but in vain. No adjustment was possible, and, following the lock-out, the employing brewers claimed that they found all the workmen they desired upon their own terms, and that the business continued without interruption or embarrassment. In this case the employing brewers claimed that the boycott against them was an unlawful conspiracy, while the working brewers insisted that it was a lawful expedient."

The Commissioners report the number of strikes and lock-outs of serious consequence to the industries of the State to have been fewer in 1888 than in any one of the immediately preceding years, and state that among the more important cases they were called in to investigate and arbitrate they were, with the exception of the one referred to (brewers and maltsters), in every case successful in bringing about an amicable settlement. "Bradstreet" reports the strikers in New Jersey to have numbered 3,126 against 27,508 in 1887.

IMMIGRATION.

There were 370,822 immigrants landed at this port in 1888 of the following countries and sex:—

Country.	Males.	Females.	In 1888.	In 1887.
England	24,917	13,438	38,355	45,746
Ireland	23,697	20,610	44,307	56,860
Scotland	7,478	3,508	10,986	14,864
Wales	805	464	1,269	5,449
Germany	45,606	32,539	78,145	81,864
France	3,612	1,825	5,437	5,999
Russia	21,911	11,141	33,052	33,203
Bohemia	2,717	1,265	3,982	6,449
Switzerland	4,623	2,682	7,305	4,537
Sweden	24,263	13,671	37,934	37,862
Norway	8,958	5,167	14,125	13,011
Belgium	1,552	834	2,386	2,362
Holland	2,662	1,815	4,477	5,500
Italy	34,556	9,371	43,927	44,274
Spain	103	21	124	485
Portugal	2	1	3	75
Denmark	4,877	2,821	7,698	8,375
Hungary	9,183	3,722	12,905	17,719
Austria	14,619	7,284	21,903	11,762
China	5	..	5	64
Australia	12	4	16	47
Turkey	152	32	184	169
Greece	366	12	378	612
All other countries	1,180	739	1,919	8,116
Total	237,856	132,966	370,822	362,853

Of the above 67,518 were under 15 years of age, 265,505 between 15 and 40 years, and 37,799 over 40 years.

UNITED STATES.

The destination, as recorded at Castle Garden, of the immigrants was as follows:—

	Immigrants.
Alaska	11
Alabama	230
Arizona	145
Arkansas	201
Connecticut	8,014
Colorado	3,581
California	7,825
Delaware	434
District of Columbia	298
Dakota	4,963
Florida	342
Georgia	182
Indiana	2,707
Indian territory	214
Illinois	29,845
Iowa	10,256
Idaho	146
Kentucky	796
Kansas	4,174
Louisiana	452
Maine	213
Maryland	1,237
Michigan	11,782
Missouri	4,795
Minnesota	15,673
Mississippi	203
Montana	943
Massachusetts	12,376
New Hampshire	188
North Carolina	69
Nebraska	7,323
Nevada	177
New Jersey	13,329
New Mexico	186
New York	150,270
Ohio	10,587
Oregon	1,114
Pennsylvania	46,105
Rhode Island	3,133
South Carolina	89
Tennessee	407
Texas	2,973
Utah	1,223
Vermont	479
Virginia	788
West Virginia	376
Wisconsin	8,666
Washington territory	976
Wyoming	335
Total	370,822

During the year 501 immigrants were prohibited by the collector of the port from landing, and returned to the countries whence they came under the provisions of the Act of Congress to regulate immigration. Of this number 23 were convicts, 37 lunatics, 10 idiots, and 431 were found to be persons liable to become a public charge.

PRISONS.

Prisons. In my last report I referred to the change of system under legislative enactments, which required that the contract system should be abandoned as the contracts expired, and that convicts should be employed on State account at the various industries. The superintendent in his last report states that "the legislation enacted during 1888 apparently reversed the progressive methods and the principles that have prevailed in the prisons since the people, by constitutional amendment, reformed the prison system of the State.

"The last fiscal year opened favourably. Labour was found for the majority of the prisoners; the industries proceeded in a beneficial and remunerative way; the products were sold, to a great extent, in remote markets; the prison wardens and their subordinates were getting some degree of confidence in the practical results of the public account system, and were coming to feel that in the returns to the State they would find some compensation for the great labour and the worry which they had borne so well in the effort to put the new system in successful motion; and there was the clear promise that the taxpayer would not be burdened by a deficit in the prison accounts of the year.

"The continuance of this state of affairs in the prisons depended upon the supply of funds voted by the Legislature. The approximate sum needed was just as definitely known as the amount required to conduct any other of the departments of the State. At the opening of the session of the Legislature the funds available were nearly exhausted. In the early days of the session a Bill was introduced appropriating 1,000,000 dol. for conducting the industries upon the system established. No immediate action was taken on it, though the necessity had been made plain.

"On February 3 several of the industries were compelled to suspend, on account of lack of money, and 1,550 men became idle."

The Legislature neglected to appropriate the sums required for the proper maintenance of the prisons, and in July passed an Act prohibiting the use of motive power machinery for manufacturing purposes in any State prisons, and the employment of the prisoners at any trade or industry where the production or profit of the labour was given or sold, and authorising the manufacture only of such articles as are commonly needed and used in the public institutions of this State. The superintendent, in reference to the result of the Legislative Acts, states:—

"By halting legislation in the first half of 1888 the industries of the prisons were twice suspended, materially crippled, and the income from them was lessened. By the final act of legislation in July, 1888, industries in the prisons are substantially terminated, without the prospect of resumption under existing laws; there are 2,550 men in the State prisons capable of working, and who want to work, who are now idle. There was a deficit in the prison accounts of almost 154,000 dol. last year. During three-fourths of the year the industries of Sing-Sing prison were in fairly active operation. In Clinton and Auburn prisons active industries were carried on during a part of the year. While Sing-Sing shows a surplus of 6,350 dol. for the year, the deficit therein for the last two months under the new law was 28,536 dol. Under this law the deficiency for the current year in the three prisons will be, in round numbers, 400,000 dol. Idleness in the prisons removes the most powerful and salutary force that is known for securing and maintaining in effective remedial potency the highest disciplinary and reformatory influences with the inmates of the prisons. Idleness is the bane of a prison, whose malign influence no prison administrator, however humane, ingenious, and energetic, has ever been able to overcome. There is no prospect of the employment of the body of the idle men in the prisons under the existing law. If

UNITED STATES.

they remain idle they will deteriorate in condition, the taxpayers will pay a large sum annually for their support, and also a large further sum every year for the prosecution, conviction, and maintenance in the prisons of the men who will be sure to be returned to them, by the removal of the reformatory influence which rescues so many from a criminal career."

The Act of July has been generally condemned, and already the effect of enforced idleness has shown itself in the demoralised condition, physically and mentally, of the unemployed. There are in the three State prisons 3,408 inmates, and 5,817 in the various county penitentiaries and reformatories of the State.

State finances.

NEW YORK STATE FINANCES.

At the close of the fiscal year (September 30) the total funded debt of the State was 1,434,863*l*., classified as follows :—

		£
Indian annuities	.. ..	25,275
Canal debt	.. ..	1,265,388
Niagara Reservation Fund	.. .. ..	144,200
Total	.. ..	1,434,863
Sinking fund	.. ..	836,605
Total debt unprovided for	.. ..	598,258

The tax rate for the current year is $2\frac{62}{100}$ mills., which on the assessed valuation will yield 1,872,397*l*., which is to be devoted to the following purposes:—

	£
Schools	714,655
Canals, including canal debt	464,526
General purposes	693,216

City finances

NEW YORK CITY FINANCES.

The total funded debt of the city of New York on December 31 amounted to 27,283,690*l*., against which there is a sinking fund of 9,130,890*l*., leaving a net funded debt of 18,152,800*l*.

Valuation and tax rates for the past five years are given in the following table:—

Year.	Real Estate.	Personal.	City Tax.
	£	£	Per Cent.
1888	268,380,689	51,628,451	2·22
1887	258,425,300	52,148,655	2·16
1886	248,011,860	44,707,606	2·29
1885	240,699,285	41,750,816	2·40
1884	230,670,888	45,018,570	2·25

The excellent credit of the city has just been exemplified in the sale of 1,576,000*l*. $2\frac{1}{2}$ per cents at 0·19 per cent. above par. The bonds are payable in 40 years, with, however, the privilege of redemption on the part of the city in 20 years.

VITAL STATISTICS, NEW YORK CITY.

City vital statistics.

	1888.	1887.
Births	34,023	33,971
Marriages	13,740	14,710
Deaths	40,175	38,949

Of the deaths reported 14,514 were of foreign birth, and 17,360 were under five years of age. The causes of death were principally as follows:—

Phthisis	5,260
Pneumonia	4,288
Diarrhœal disease	3,489
Bright's disease	2,342
Diphtheria	7,914
Heart disease	1,913
Bronchitis	1,892
Scarlatina	1,361
Gastritis and peritonitis	1,270
Measles	591
Whooping cough	573
Malarial fevers	365

Annex A.—RETURN of all Shipping at the Port of New York in the Year 1888.

ENTERED.

Country.	Sailing. Number of Vessels.	Sailing. Tons.	Steam. Number of Vessels.	Steam. Tons.	Total. Number of Vessels.	Total. Tons.
Great Britain	1,223	672,938	1,338	2,371,240	2,561	3,044,178
United States	1,198	467,692	236	378,637	1,434	846,329
Germany	154	176,646	286	674,356	440	851,002
France	2	816	92	269,140	94	269,956
Sweden and Norway	220	128,964	130	53,934	350	182,898
Belgium	6	7,834	82	199,308	88	207,142
Italy	148	123,876	13	14,515	161	138,391
Mexico	6	1,738	...	...	6	1,738
Netherlands	10	8,194	76	145,202	86	153,396
Austria	22	14,122	...	...	22	14,122
Spain	16	5,514	58	74,605	74	80,119
Denmark	12	4,528	18	36,494	30	41,022
Other European countries	10	3,772	...	...	10	3,772
South America	4	2,924	...	...	4	2,924
Central America	...	...	...	...	...	...
Other countries	2	804	...	...	2	804
Total	3,033	1,620,362	2,329	4,217,431	5,362	5,837,793
„ for preceding year	3,567	1,870,833	2,361	4,295,563	5,928	6,166,396

UNITED STATES.

CLEARED.

Country.	Sailing. Number of Vessels.	Sailing. Tons.	Steam. Number of Vessels.	Steam. Tons.	Total. Number of Vessels.	Total. Tons.
Great Britain	1,230	670,966	1,301	2,315,796	2,531	2,986,762
United States	788	373,763	223	347,337	1,011	721,100
Germany	138	153,448	300	679,458	438	832,906
France	2	816	94	271,272	96	272,088
Sweden and Norway	164	127,416	129	44,036	293	171,452
Belgium	6	7,832	85	217,488	91	225,320
Italy	125	88,658	14	13,570	139	102,228
Mexico	6	1,652	...	...	6	1,652
Netherlands	8	7,024	78	141,082	86	148,106
Austria	20	12,496	...	...	20	12,496
Spain	20	6,688	60	74,540	80	81,228
Denmark	10	3,286	20	45,954	30	49,240
Other European countries	14	6,018	...	...	14	6,018
South America	3	1,820	...	...	3	1,820
Central America	...	...	...	...	...	...
Other countries	2	804	...	...	2	804
Total	2,536	1,462,687	2,304	4,150,533	4,840	5,513,220
,, for preceding year	3,122	1,675,332	2,309	4,204,991	5,431	5,880,323

Annex B.—RETURN of Principal Articles of Import to New York during the Years 1888-87.

Articles.		1888. Quantity.	1888. Value. £	1887. Quantity.	1887. Value. £
Cocoa	Bags	100,394	406,330	73,196	329,095
Coffee	,,	3,331,850	10,851,110	2,844,466	10,643,992
China, glass, and earthenware	...	...	1,790,390	...	1,780,310
Cotton	Bales	9,095	147,712	5,329	99,063
Dry goods—					
Manufactures of cotton	...	...	4,277,388	...	4,626,968
,, flax	...	...	3,457,360	...	3,222,050
,, silk	...	...	8,122,372	...	7,739,556
,, wool	...	...	7,597,538	...	6,762,412
,, miscellaneous	...	...	2,486,002	...	2,599,040
Furs	Packages	21,087	1,110,240	...	1,152,675
Fruits	...	...	3,434,310	...	3,636,920
Hair	...	...	297,536	...	366,845
Hemp	Bales	419,143	1,737,842	373,768	1,453,386
Hides, dressed	...	...	790,240	...	836,339
,, undressed	...	...	3,709,575	...	3,144,795
Hops	Bales	7,179	120,115	17,964	224,545
India rubber	...	...	2,651,080	...	2,646,710
Jewellery, watches, and precious stones	...	...	2,354,030	...	2,477,572
Jute and jute butts	...	...	591,235	...	393,094
Linseed	Packages	...	340,265	56,966	116,995
Molasses	...	...	106,112	...	361,602
Paper stock	...	...	522,882	...	555,210
Metals—					
Cutlery	...	...	416,156	...	380,435
Iron, pig	Tons	64,207	194,066	128,752	341,895
,, spiegel	,,	45,532	185,100	117,399	514,543
,, other	...	...	311,392	...	910,646
Metal goods	...	...	379,980	...	369,500
Steel	...	...	746,942	...	1,241,236
Tin plates	Boxes	2,026,366	1,567,585	2,052,539	1,603,695
,, slabs	Tons	36,560	1,691,245	11,964	1,304,298
Soda, ash	...	...	210,272	...	211,706
,, caustic	...	...	169,550	...	161,160
Spices	...	...	529,188	...	591,730
Stationery and books	...	...	1,100,215	...	1,004,830
Sugar	Tons	677,626	8,259,910	786,823	8,536,698
Specie and bullion	...	...	1,684,375	...	8,359,291
Tea	Packages	1,308,270	1,983,990	1,225,815	2,132,264
Tobacco and cigars	...	...	1,797,185	...	1,937,858
Wines, spirits, &c.	...	...	1,952,670	...	1,807,330
Wood	...	...	1,204,075	...	1,391,320
Wool	Lbs.	44,672,758	1,046,187	44,880,077	1,106,538
Other articles	...	...	14,995,463	...	15,181,834
Total	...	...	97,327,210	...	104,262,981

Annex B.—continued.

Return of Principal Articles of Export from New York during the Years 1888 and 1887.

Articles.		1888. Quantity.	1888. Value.	1887. Quantity.	1887. Value
			£		£
Agricultural implements	Value	...	501,235	...	459,800
Bacon and hams	Lbs.	194,362,362	3,646,380	234,971,670	4,164,560
Beef, fresh	,,	71,628,226	1,401,166	46,269,995	861,823
,, canned	,,	20,660,630	353,047	20,956,643	354,410
Butter	,,	7,069,000	247,797	9,625,891	343,536
Cattle, live	Number	57,042	1,116,983	33,362	661,980
Cotton, domestic	Pkgs.	173,986	2,013,610	...	2,408,447
,, raw	Bales	999,721	10,166,108	828,665	8,071,365
Cheese	Lbs.	68,296,464	1,286,999	75,289,602	1,563,077
Flour	Barrels	3,820,273	3,520,895	4,431.010	3,860,194
Hops	Lbs.	8,089,133	372,080	4,359,607	176,913
Indian corn	Bus. (56 lbs.)	13,479,048	1,563,845	12,347,567	1,081,770
Lard	Lbs.	170,151,224	3,001,465	198,324,165	4,002,278
Oil-cake and meal	,,	200,717,992	538,040	227,130,883	595,269
Oleomargarine	,,	23,528,706	515,440	43,711,480	898,446
Pork and beef, salt	,,	61,938,827	852,865	64,990,060	861,943
Petroleum, refined	Gallons	322,991,600	5,453,295	329,489,258	5,225,280
,, crude	,,	41,645,879	639,325	42,216,556	569,432
,, lubricating	,,	21,468,777	801,915	19,546,375	706,030
Sewing machines	Value	...	376,155	...	404,687
Sugar	Lbs.	13,508,232	204,885	95,846,967	1,152,780
Specie and bullion	Value	...	9,238,385	...	4,016,814
Tallow	Lbs.	51,692,457	537,087	43,482,750	386,777
Wheat	Bus. (60 lbs.)	12,352,445	2,386,080	41,071,750	7,739,716
Other articles	Value	...	20,281,848	...	18,015,037
Total		...	71,016,930	...	68,582,364

UNITED STATES.

Annex C.—TABLE showing the Total Value of all Articles Exported from and Imported to New York from and to Foreign Countries during the Years 1888 and 1887.

Country.	Exports. 1888.	Exports. 1887.	Imports. 1888.	Imports. 1887.
	£	£	£	£
Great Britain	32,634,000	31,202,445	22,372,990	22,274,675
British possessions	5,785,500	5,157,255	6,399,085	6,400,000
Germany	8,019,335	5,939,825	13,662,325	16,839,510
France and possessions	3,857,985	4,289,495	12,590,410	14,340,195
Belgium	3,095,865	3,372,165	1,350,295	1,255,590
Spain and possessions	4,102,697	3,828,285	7,801,655	9,366,770
Netherlands and possessions	2,566,050	2,840,645	2,776,320	2,955,475
United States of Colombia	1,010,320	1,130,455	1,152,665	741,700
Central American States	537,965	460,735	731,120	893,320
Italy	890,893	1,300,165	3,109,025	3,092,895
Brazil	986,520	839,825	9,659,845	10,153,895
China	629,505	1,031,440	2,217,650	2,295,710
Denmark and possessions	497,935	752,625	89,825	148,995
Venezuela	773,580	1,160,265	1,872,545	2,050,165
Portugal and possessions	606,430	770,945	267,545	259,350
Argentine Republic	941,890	980,335	555,875	423,070
Mexico	767,830	691,425	1,607,375	1,683,305
Hayti	943,313	759,705	596,760	323,150
Sweden and Norway	380,025	519,400	379,025	440,975
Japan	408,125	372,810	1,199,370	1,070,285
Chili	252,135	318,765	303,375	329,585
San Domingo	331,623	195,515	285,020	270,150
Uruguay	228,089	218,690	478,020	393,060
Austria	7,370	37,520	1,568,165	1,701,420
Russia	76,055	104,960	496,100	535,165
Peru	147,700	133,405	59,420	48,935
Switzerland	1,565	7,680	2,409,385	2,597,985
Other countries	536,630	165,584	1,336,020	1,377,651
Total	71,016,930	68,582,364	97,327,210	104,262,981

NEW YORK.

The Specie included in the Tables was Exported to and Imported from the following Countries during the Years 1888 and 1887.

Country.	Exported to. 1888.	Exported to. 1887.	Imported from. 1888.	Imported from. 1887.
	£	£	£	£
Great Britain	4,863,655	2,232,849	13,420	1,199,455
British possessions	164,625	158,018	42,215	240,700
Germany	2,448,625	254,467	235,145	3,688,484
France and possessions	106,485	202,481	608,300	1,769,475
Spain „ „	1,005,565	435,500	329,055	1,144,000
Netherlands and possessions	4,230	4,800	15,750	69,000
U.S. of Colombia	147,940	132,200	244,525	..
Central American States	60,960	28,500	10,645	21,400
Brazil	3,450	..	435	19,500
China	275	..	..	..
Denmark and possessions	4,610	6,000	515	13,100
Venezuela	138,840	527,050	35,500	20,100
Mexico	545	4,502	121,535	19,153
Hayti	136,945	..	19,430	29,200
San Domingo	141,165	..	5,570	7,500
Peru	6,285	2,188	..	1,200
Other countries	4,185	28,259	8,455	117,024
Total	9,238,385	4,016,814	1,690,495	8,359,291

PROVIDENCE, R.I.

General report on trade. In reviewing the business and commerce of this city and the State of Rhode Island for the year 1888, it may be stated that the people generally have been prosperous and contented, with labour and the product of labour in good demand, and with prices fairly remunerative, and there has been no serious falling out between labour and capital.

Cotton and cotton goods. The business of the year has increased, and been generally satisfactory. All classes of goods manufactured here have been in active demand, and their manufacture continues without interruption. The printing-cloth manufacturers report goods sold ahead of production three to four months. The stock on hand at the close of the year was unusually low, and has been so throughout the year, the largest being 44,000 pieces in November. Prices of print cloths, 64s.; lowest and highest for the year, $3\frac{1}{8}$ c. and 4 c. respectively. The price of cotton in Providence market, $10\frac{1}{2}$ c. to $11\frac{3}{8}$ c.

Wool and woollens. The market has been very dull and sales slow, and not altogether satisfactory. Uncertainty in regard to changes in the wool tariff has been a disturbing factor in all that pertains to wool, its manufacture, and the products thereof. Stocks of manufactured goods are reported to be largely in excess of the demand. At the beginning of the year the prices of Ohio XX wools was 32 c. to 35 c.; for Michigan 26 c. to 27 c.; for territories, 9 c. to 25 c. In July, Ohio, 29 c. to 32 c.; Michigan, 22 c. to 26 c.; territories, 8 c. to 23 c.; and in December, Ohio, 33 c. to 37 c.; Michigan, 28 c. to 37 c.; and territories, 13 c. to 31 c.

Iron and steel industries. Providence is well known as an important centre of the iron and steel manufacture and trade. Engines, both locomotive and stationary, are shipped to all countries. Machinery for all kinds of manufactures,

UNITED STATES.

even for the sugar refineries of Havana, the mills of the German Empire, and for various purposes throughout Europe, is made here. These industries have been taxed to the utmost during the year, many of them operating day and night to fill orders.

The labour market. Wages.

It is very difficult to obtain reliable statistics in regard to wages, but so far as can be ascertained there have been few changes, and the general average, compared with that of the previous year, has been maintained. I give below some of the prevailing rates:—

		Dol.	c.
Carders in cotton mills	Per week	8	35
Spinners ,, ,,	,,	8	91
Weavers ,, ,,	,,	7	84
Carders in woollen mills	,,	10	30
Spinners ,, ,,	,,	8	75
Weavers ,, ,,	,,	8	59
Carpenters	Per day	2	25
Masons, brick	,,	3	50
,, stone	,,	2	75
,, plasterers	,,	3	50
Painters	,,	2	50
Plumbers	,,	3	0
Gas-pipers	,,	3	0
Machinists	Per day 2 dol. 25 c. to	2	50
Helpers	Per day	1	50
Day labourers	,,	1	50
Pavers	,,	2	25

Any list of wages is after all deceptive to intending immigrants from the old country for the reason, first, that these latter do not take into account the higher cost of living; and, second, because the wages quoted may be paid only to skilled and experienced workmen.

Immigration.

During the year many applications have been made at this Vice-Consulate for assistance in returning to England. These applicants are not shiftless persons, and do not owe present misfortune to idleness or to dissipation. In most cases they are honest, industrious men, willing to work at anything at any price. The story is repeated again and again. Allured by the vision of sudden wealth, with their families they left comfortable homes and steady employment in England, Scotland, and Ireland, and hurried to this country. Men in health, skilled in their trades, have been reduced to poverty, and when overtaken by illness the result is worse, and help from home, or public charity, must be relied upon.

Liquor traffic.

The liquor traffic has been the most important social question in the city and State during the past year. The sale of liquors was prohibited by constitutional amendment accepted by the people on April 7, 1886. The result has been so unsatisfactory to all classes, except the liquor sellers, that re-submission to the people is proposed.

Voting.

Previous to 1888 the naturalized citizen could not vote for all officers unless he was in possession of 134 dol. worth of real estate. In April, 1888, the constitution was amended, and the foreign-born voter placed on an equality with the native-born.

City buildings.

During the year 416 buildings were erected in the city of Providence, and 146 improved at an estimated cost of 1,779,480 dol. No census of population has been made since the last report.

Foreign ship arrivals.

Arrivals of vessels from foreign countries:—

	Number.
British	72
Italian	2
American	20

NEW YORK.

Foreign vessels brought:—

Articles.		Quantity.
Lumber	Feet	3,818,704
Shingles	,,	6,139,750
Laths	,,	8,752,500
Pickets	Pieces	50,820
Piling	,,	2,788
Wood	Cords	2,674
Salt	Pounds	5,792,135
Log-wood	Tons	4,897
Brimstone	,,	1,256
Potatoes	Bushels	6,675
Starch	Casks	149
Lime	Barrels	525
Coffee	Pounds	4,970
Scrap-iron	Tons	15

Statistics of the Port of Providence.—Foreign merchandise originally imported into other ports and transported in bond to this port in accordance with Acts of Congress, July 14, 1870, and June 10, 1880, providing for bonded cars and boats to the value of 160,545*l*.

Indirect receipt of foreign merchandise.

	£
Duties collected	53,220
Tonnage dues	93
Storage fees	229
Customs fees	367
Fines and penalties	28

Tonnage of the port:—

Tonnage of port.

Description.	Number.	Tons.
Sailing vessels	77	10,793
Steam vessels	36	17,962
Total	113	28,755

Domestic receipts of principal articles of merchandise:—

Receipts of domestic merchandise.

Articles.		Quantity.
Cotton	Bales	203,726
Wool	,,	84,155
,,	Sacks	45,496
Coal	Tons	1,061,237
Iron and steel	,,	43,042
Lumber	1,000 feet	64,339
Oil	Barrels	163,622
Waste	Tons	6,425
Beef	,,	16,069
Flour	Barrels	259,564
Corn	Bushels	1,676,188
Meal	,,	38,580
Oats	,,	1,375,000
Bran	,,	227,672
Dry goods	Cases	70,000
Print cloths	Bales	15,456
Liquors	Barrels	8,584
Chemicals	Packages	114,548
Dye woods	Tons	6,183

Prices.

Price of flour in the Providence Market, January, 5 dol. 35 c. per barrel; in December, 7 dol. per barrel. Price of Coal, February, 6 dol. 75 c. to 8 dol. per ton. In August the prices advanced 50 c. per ton, and in December they were 6 dol. to 8 dol. 50 c. per ton.

Freights.

Coastwise freights from eastern lumber districts, 2 dol. 75 c. to 2 dol. 87 c. per 1,000 feet. Gulf freights, 6 dol. 75 c. to 8 dol. 75 c. Coal freights from Baltimore, 85 c. to 1 dol. per ton.

Annex A.—RETURN of all Vessels Entered from and Cleared for a Foreign Port.

ENTERED.

Nationality.	Sailing.		Steam.		Total.	
	Number of Vessels.	Tons.	Number of Vessels.	Tons.	Number of Vessels.	Tons.
British	72	8,621	...	...	72	8,621
American	20	4,965	...	...	20	4,965
Italian	2	1,212	...	...	2	1,212
Total	94	14,799	...	...	94	14,799
„ 1887	122	19,354	...	...	122	19,354

CLEARED.

Nationality.	Sailing.		Steam.		Total.	
	Number of Vessels.	Tons.	Number of Vessels.	Tons.	Number of Vessels.	Tons.
British	61	7,222	...	...	61	7,222
American	3	487	...	...	3	487
Total	64	7,709	...	...	64	7,709
„ 1887	85	11,186	...	...	85	11,186

Annex B.—RETURN of Principal Articles of Export from Providence, R.I., during the Years 1888 and 1887

Articles.		1888.		1887.	
		Quantity.	Value.	Quantity.	Value.
			£		£
Coke	Tons	...	...	450	283
Coal	„	25	28	70	78
Vessels	...	...	...	...	124
Oil	Gallons	268	5	...	...
Total		...	33	...	435

RETURN of Principal Articles of Import into Providence, R.I., during the Years 1888 and 1887.

Articles.	Value.	
	1888.	1887.
	£	£
Dry goods	87,439	45,410
Chemicals	36,011	26,775
Metals, manufactures of	19,108	16,969
All others	3,687	42,456
Total	146,245	131,610

Annex C.—TABLE showing the Total Value of all Articles Exported from Providence and Imported into Providence from and to Foreign Countries during the Years 1888 and 1887.

Country.	Exports.		Imports.	
	1888.	1887.	1888.	1887.
	£	£	£	£
England	..	..	63,384	60,165
Scotland	..	..	1,709	1,299
Ireland	..	..	..	91
Canada	33	202	8,931	14,528
British West Indies	..	..	16,789	6,504
France	..	..	12,741	11,185
Germany	..	..	14,051	13,982
Austria	..	..	2,737	3,693
Belgium	..	..	45	..
Spain	..	..	134	..
Cuba	..	233	8,424	2,347
Greece	..	..	..	1,435
Hayti	..	..	7,509	9,766
Italy	..	..	5,068	2,313
Japan	..	..	43	..
Netherlands	..	..	922	..
Switzerland	..	..	3,358	3,243
Venezuela	..	..	400	..
All others	..	..	..	1,059
Total	34	435	146,245	131,610

UNITED STATES.

RETURN of the Number of Seamen who have been Engaged, Discharged, Left Behind, reported Dead or Deserted, or who have been Relieved at the British Consulate-General, New York, and showing the Total Number of British and Foreign Sailors who were Engaged, Discharged, &c., from British Ships, with the amount of Wages Paid at the Consulate to Seamen on Discharge from their Ships and from Hospital or Gaol; and also showing the Number of New Agreements entered into during the Year 1888.

Seamen.											Nationality.		Total Number of Seamen.	Wages.			Agreements.
Engaged.	Discharged.	Left Behind.			Died.			Deserted.	Relieved.	British.	Foreign.		Paid on Discharge from Vessels.	Paid on Discharge from Hospital or Gaol.	Total Wages Paid.	Number Opened.
		In Gaol.	In Hospital.	Total.	At Sea.	On Shore.	Total.						Dol. c.	Dol. c.	Dol. c.	
12,441	8,782	16	152	168	65	29	94	4,201	210	15,533	10,363	25,896	379,883 71	4,144 72	384,028 43	304

(1250 6 | 89—H & S 671)

FOREIGN OFFICE.
1889.
ANNUAL SERIES.

No. 546.

DIPLOMATIC AND CONSULAR REPORTS ON TRADE AND FINANCE.

UNITED STATES.

REPORT FOR THE YEAR 1888
ON THE
AGRICULTURE OF THE CONSULAR DISTRICT OF SAN FRANCISCO.

REFERENCE TO PREVIOUS REPORT, Annual Series No. 356.

Presented to both Houses of Parliament by Command of Her Majesty,
JUNE, 1889.

LONDON:
PRINTED FOR HER MAJESTY'S STATIONERY OFFICE,
BY HARRISON AND SONS, ST. MARTIN'S LANE,
PRINTERS IN ORDINARY TO HER MAJESTY.

And to be purchased, either directly or through any Bookseller, from
EYRE AND SPOTTISWOODE, EAST HARDING STREET, FLEET STREET, E.C., and
32, ABINGDON STREET, WESTMINSTER, S.W.; or
ADAM AND CHARLES BLACK, 6, NORTH BRIDGE, EDINBURGH; or
HODGES, FIGGIS, & Co., 104, GRAFTON STREET, DUBLIN.

1889.

[C. 5618—99.]   *Price One Penny.*

New Series of Reports.

Reports of the Annual Series have been issued from Her Majesty's Diplomatic and Consular Officers at the following places, and may be obtained from the sources indicated on the title-page:—

No.		Price.	No.		Price.
420.	Sandakan	1d.	483.	Rome	1d.
421.	Barcelona	1d.	484.	Lisbon	1d.
422.	Königsberg	1d.	485.	Port Said	2d.
423.	Tabreez	1d.	486.	Havre	3d.
424.	Guayaquil	1d.	487.	Boulogne	1d.
425.	St. Petersburg	1d.	488.	Callao	1d
426.	Tokio	1d.	489.	Barcelona	2d.
427.	Charleston	1d.	490.	Boulogne	2d.
428.	Amsterdam	1d.	491.	Taganrog	2d.
429.	Hamburg	4d.	492.	Kiungchow	1d.
430.	Trieste	1d.	493.	Sandakan	1d.
431.	New York	2d.	494.	Manila	1d.
432.	Antwerp	1d.	495.	Swatow	1d.
433.	Munich	1d.	496.	Guayaquil	1d.
434.	Buenos Ayres	1d.	497.	Rome	1d.
435.	Warsaw	1d.	498.	Santos	1d.
436.	Porto Rico	1d.	499.	Boston	1d.
437.	Réunion	1d.	500.	Aleppo	1d.
438.	Lisbon	1d.	501.	Bordeaux	2d.
439.	Venice	1d.	502.	Valparaiso	1d.
440.	Christiania	5d.	503.	St. Petersburg	1d.
441.	Maranham	1d.	504.	Rio de Janeiro	4d.
442.	Sofia	1d.	505.	Brest	1d.
443.	Copenhagen	1d.	506.	Dunkirk	1d.
444.	Galatz	1d.	507.	Genoa	2d.
445.	Tabreez	1d.	508.	Beyrout	1d.
446.	Bogotá	2d.	509.	Colonia	1d.
447.	St. Petersburg	3d.	510.	Marseilles	1d.
448.	Nice	1d.	511.	Kiukiang	1d.
449.	Stettin	2d.	512.	Buda Pesth	2d.
450.	Fiume	1d.	513.	Wênchow	10d.
451.	Chinkiang	1d.	514.	Coquimbo	1d.
452.	The Hague	1d.	515.	Charleston	1d.
453.	Malaga	1d.	516.	Riga	1d.
454.	Taganrog	1d.	517.	Mollendo	1d.
455.	Mozambique	1d.	518.	Taiwan	1d.
456.	Bogotá	2d.	519.	Wuhu	1d.
457.	Patras	1d.	520.	Corunna	2d.
458.	Galveston	1d.	521.	Noumea	1d.
459.	Buda Pesth	1d.	522.	San José	1d.
460.	Madeira	1d.	523.	Ningpo	1d.
461.	Warsaw	1d.	524.	Gothenburg	2d.
462.	Paris	2d.	525.	Hankow	2d.
463.	Baltimore	1d.	526.	Foochow	1d.
464.	Philadelphia	2d.	527.	Erzeroum	2d.
465.	New Orleans	2d.	528.	Ciudad Bolivar	1d.
466.	New Orleans	2d.	529.	Jaffa	1d.
467.	Cherbourg	1d.	530.	Ancona	1d.
468.	Buenos Ayres	1d.	531.	Savannah	1d.
469.	Algiers	1d.	532.	Batavia	1d.
470.	Ichang	1d.	533.	Adrianople	1d.
471.	Copenhagen	1d.	534.	Nisch	11d.
472.	Athens	1d.	535.	Vienna	1d.
473.	Cherbourg	1d.	536.	Odessa	8d.
474.	The Piræus	1d.	537.	Constantinople	2d.
475.	Galatz	1d.	538.	Damascus	1d.
476.	Tripoli	1d.	539.	Tientsin	1d.
477.	Saigon	1d	540.	Amoy	1d.
478.	Serajevo	1d.	541.	Mogador	1d.
479.	Brussels	2d.	542.	Vienna	1d.
480.	Bengazi	1d.	543.	Antwerp	1d.
481.	Odessa	1d.	544.	Lisbon	2d.
482.	Santo Domingo	1d.	545.	New York	1½d.

No. 546.

Reference to previous Report, Annual Series No. 350.

UNITED STATES.

SAN FRANCISCO.

Consul Donohoe to the Marquis of Salisbury.

My Lord,   *San Francisco, April* 17, 1889.

I HAVE the honour to enclose herewith Reports on Agricultural Matters from this Consulate, and from the Vice-Consulates of Portland, Astoria, Los Angeles, and Consular Agency at Eureka, for the year 1888.

I have, &c.
(Signed)   DENIS DONOHOE.

Report on Agriculture in the State of California.

There has been a fair crop, though not as large as was expected. In the middle section of the State the crop has been poor, whilst south of San Francisco the crops have been much larger than expected. San Luis, Obispo county, San Diego and Los Angeles counties have had the largest crops ever known. Prices have been remunerative throughout the year. *Wheat.*

The crop of barley throughout the State has been the largest ever known, and as there was a good demand for export to both England and Australia, with rather low prices, it was soon nearly all shipped. Late in the year there was a heavy advance in price, with but a small stock on hand. *Barley.*

Fruit production is steadily on the increase in California. It is stated that the number of fruit trees planted in 1888 cannot be less than 2,000,000, and the total value of the fruit produced in the State is given as 16,000,000 dol. *Fruit production.*

The following table gives the lbs. of fruit shipped East in 1887 and 1888 respectively:— *Fruit shipments.*

	1887.	1888.
	Lbs.	Lbs.
Ripe fruit	26,801,632	52,897,560
Dried fruit	14,704,910	20,059,690
Canned goods	42,616,820	38,264,750
Raisins	12,237,670	13,916,070
Total	96,361,032	125,138,070

Fruit growers complain of the high rates of freight charged by the railways for carriage of their goods to the Eastern States. The total quantity of green fruit shipped represents gross sales to the amount of 773,117 dol. 42 c., from which deduct 345,156 dol. 28 c. for freight, 2,430 dol. 2 c. for cartage, and 77,298 dol. 06 c. for commission, which makes a gross charge of 424,884 dol. 36 c., which would leave 348,233 dol. 06 c. to be returned to shippers, or about $2\frac{92}{100}$ c. per lb. These figures do not show the net returns, as expenses of picking, packing, &c., do not enter into the account sales as rendered. These expenses may be estimated at about 85 c. per 100 lbs.; so that taking these expenses into the calculation, the actual money return to the grower averages about $1\frac{91}{100}$ c. per lb.

Canned fruit and vegetables.

An estimate of the canned goods pack of 1888 is as follows:—

	Cases.
Apples	6,000
Apricots	180,000
Asparagus	5,000
Blackberries	5,000
Cherries (white)	50,000
,, (black)	30,000
Currants	5,000
Gooseberries	15,000
Grapes	40,000
Nectarines	5,000
Pears	125,000
Peas	25,000
Peaches	185,000
Plums	50,000
Quinces	6,500
Raspberries	3,000
Strawberries	20,000
Total	755,500
Miscellaneous—	
Pie fruits	25,000
Tomatoes	200,000
Jams and jellies	30,000
Grand total	1,010,500

Dried and evaporated fruits and vegetables.

There is a steady increase in dried and evaporated fruits and vegetables. A leading house in this trade gives the following statement:

SAN FRANCISCO.

The following represents the dried fruit products of 1888 :—

Articles.		Quantity.
Raisins	20 lb. boxes.	915,000
Honey, extracted	Lbs.	3,000,000
Honey, comb	,,	300,000
Beeswax	,,	20,000
French prunes	,,	3,000,000
German prunes	,,	100,000
Apples, sun dried	,,	100,000
Peaches ,,	,,	2,000,000
Plums ,,	,,	200,000
Pears ,,	,,	25,000
Grapes ,,	,,	2,000,000
Apricots ,,	,,	100,000
Nectarines ,,	,,	100,000
Figs ,,	,,	75,000
Apples, evaporated	,,	250,000
Apricots, bleached	,,	2,500,000
Peaches, bleached, peeled	,,	400,000
Peaches, bleached, unpeeled	,,	2,200,000
Nectarines	,,	60,000
Walnuts	,,	1,000,000
Almonds	,,	450,000
Plums, bleached	,,	40,000

Raisins. The year has been a favourable one to both producers and packers, and there has been a decided improvement in the quality. Some of the best brands have fetched equal prices in New York with the imported fruit. The county of Fresno produces the largest quantity in the State, the climate of that county being eminently suitable for the growth of grapes, and the absence of rain and fogs in the summer rendering the picking and manipulation an easy matter. A small quantity was shipped to London this year as an experiment.

Wine. The wine production of 1888 is estimated at about 17,000,000 gallons, about 4,000,000 gallons over that of 1887. The estimate made early in the year was much larger, but production was lessened by the hot weather, and many growers dried their grapes instead of using them in the wine press. The product of 1887–8 vintage was mostly, where sold, disposed of at from 11 to 16 c. a gallon. Many grape-growers not having wine houses on their vineyards dispose of their grapes to neighbouring presses, and the following prices may be quoted for the different varieties :—

Class.	Per Ton. Dols.	
Cabernet	25 to	30
Petit Pinet	25	30
Black Burgundy	18	20
Meunier	18	20
Riesling	18	20
Mataro	16	18
Zuifaudel	14	19
Carbono	14	18
Malvoise	8	9
Mission	7	9

Prices of farm produce. The following are the San Francisco prices of market produce ruling on March 7, 1889 :—

UNITED STATES.

Articles.		Value.	
		Dol. c.	Dol. c.
Wheat, No. 1	Per cental..	1 42½ to	1 45
Barley, choice	,,	0 97½	1 00
Oats, ,,	,,	1 10	1 12½
Corn, large yellow	,,	1 07½	1 12½
Rye	,,	1 50	1 65½
Hay, Alfalfa	Per ton	9 00	10 00
Butter	Per lb.	0 17	0 19
Cheese	,,	0 12	0 12½
Eggs	Per dozen..	0 16	0 18
Poultry	,,	6 00	7 50
Ducks	,,	8 00	10 00
Geese	Per pair	1 75	2 50
Turkeys, live	Per lb.	0 16	0 18
Honeycomb	,,	0 8	0 12½
Oranges, California, common	Per box	1 00	1 50
,, Los Angeles Navel	,,	2 00	2 50
,, Riverside Navel	,,	3 25	4 00
Lemons, Los Angeles	,,	1 25	2 00
Limes, California	,,	0 75	1 50
Apples	,,	1 00	2 25
Dried fruits—			
Pears, sliced	Per lb.	0 4½	0 5½
,, machine dried	,,	0 5½	0 8
Peaches, peeled, sun dried	,,	0 10	0 12
Apricots, bleached	,,	0 10	0 14
,, sun dried	,,	0 7	0 9
Plums, pitted	,,	0 5	0 7
,, unpitted	,,	0 2½	0 4
Prunes	,,	0 4½	0 6½
Blackberries	,,	0 12	0 14
Apples, sliced and quartered	,,	0 3	0 5½
Figs	,,	0 5	0 6
Nectarines	,,	0 25	0 9
Raisins, California, London layers	Per box	1 65	2 15
Vegetables—			
Cabbage	Per cental..	0 40	0 60
Carrots	Per sack	0 35	0 55
Beets	Per cental..	0 50	0 70
Turnips	,,	0 50	0 75
Cauliflower	Per dozen..	0 30	0 75
Artichokes	,,	0 25	0 50
Celery	,,	0 40	0 65
Okra, dried	Per lb.	0 10	0 12½
Peppers, dried	,,	0 7	0 9
Cucumbers	Per dozen..	1 00	2 00
Potatoes, new	Per lb.	0 1¼	0 2
Egg plant	,,	0 12½	0 15
Asparagus	,,	0 15	0 20
Wool—			
Northern fall clip	Per lb.	0 14	0 16
Middle counties clip	,,	0 12	0 14
San Joachim ,,	,,	0 10	0 12
Southern ,,	,,	0 8	0 10

SAN FRANCISCO.

PORTLAND, OREGON.

Mr. Vice-Consul Laidlaw reports as follows:—

There is no State in the Union which offers more or better inducements to the farmer and stockraiser than Oregon, and although my district is limited to the port of Portland, it seems proper that I should report upon the districts tributary to this port. *Agriculture.*

The area of Oregon is 96,000 square miles, but there is a very large section of Washington territory, east of the Cascade Mountains, the products of which are marketed here, and the business controlled by the merchants of Portland. Regarding this territory, I collate from information furnished by the State Board of Immigration. *Area of State.*

There are four large divisions of land, the arable qualities of which have already been proved by an experience now far beyond the experimental stage, viz.:— *Agricultural lands.*

1. The section situate between the Cascade and Coast Mountains, and extending from the divide between the Columbia river and Puget Sound watersheds on the north, to the Siskiyou Mountains on the southern boundary of Oregon on the south. This embraces the Willamette, Umpqua, and Rogue river valleys on Oregon, the lower lands along the Columbia, both in Oregon and Washington territory, and the Lewis and Cowlitz river in Washington territory. In this section there are from 12,000 to 13,000 square miles of land suited for general farming and fruit culture, and it is a magnificent body of rich agricultural land, though heavily timbered in some sections. The farming is often poor, but the average yield of wheat is 23 bushels per acre, well-tilled fields often reaching 35 to 50 bushels. There is an abundant rainfall in this section. *First division. Area. Quality. Rainfall.*

2. The section situated just west of the Cascade Mountains, watered by the John Day and Deschutes rivers and their tributaries, and bounded on the north by the Colombia river, on the south by the high plateau which forms the southern boundary of the watershed of the Deschutes river and its tributaries, on the west by the Cascade Mountains, and on the east by the limits of the watershed of the John Day river. The general character of this division is rolling, open land, free from timber, and what is known as "bunch grass lands." Up to a few years ago it was supposed that the larger part of this section was only suitable for grazing, but experience has proved it to be well adapted to general farming and fruit culture. The average crop of wheat under good cultivation is 30 bushels per acre. It contains about 13,000 square miles of territory, and that which is not arable is generally excellent grazing. The rainfall in this division is very light, yet there has been no failure of crops from drought. *Second division. General character. Quality. Area. Rainfall.*

3. All of North-eastern Oregon east of the watershed of the John Day river, and all of South-eastern Washington territory south of and situate in the bend of the Snake river, with a portion of the western part of Central Idaho. In its general limits it contains about 10,000 square miles of arable land, though, including mountain spurs and waste lands, it has a much greater superficial area. It is generally open and free from timber. The soil is usually easily cultivated, and will produce an average crop of 35 bushels of wheat per acre. There is a more abundant rainfall in this than in the preceding division of country. *Third division. Area. Quality. Rainfall.*

4. That section of country situate just north of the Snake river, and for the most part in Washington territory, watered by the Palouse river and its tributaries, and known as the Palouse country. It contains over 2,000 square miles of territory, by far the largest part of which is arable. The yield of wheat in this section is very large, on well-cultivated land averaging 35 to 40 bushels per acre. Oats, rye, *Fourth division. Area. Quality.*

barley, and Indian corn yield large crops, and fruit is grown with great success.

Grazing lands — The lands at present devoted to grazing are the southern part of Oregon east of the Cascade Mountains, the northern portion of that part of Washington territory east of the Cascades, and the valley and plateau lands of Idaho and Western Montana. These lands have been devoted to stock and used as grazing lands for years, are abundantly watered, and abound in nutritious grasses.

Climate. — The mild temperature of this region, so northerly situated, is due to the warm Japan Gulf current, which flows down the coast, and to the Rocky and Cascade Mountains, standing as a barrier to ward off the cold Arctic winds. Generally speaking, the range of temperature from summer to winter is small, and Oregon has really six distinct climates, viz.:—

1. The immediate coast climate, warm and mild, which varies little summer or winter, having a sea-breeze during the day, fog in summer, and excessive rains in winter.

2. The Willamette Valley, foggy in the mornings of spring and autumn, warm and smoky in summer, and with very heavy rains in winter.

3. The Umpqua Valley has a delightful climate, occasional fogs in the mornings of spring and autumn, mild summer and winter temperature, occasional showers in summer and occasional snows in winter, with very light winds the whole year.

4. The Rogue river valley is also noted for its climate, has fogs similar to the Umpqua, with warmer weather in summer and colder in winter, dry in summer, with snow and rain in winter. About one-half as much rain falls at Ashland annually as at Portland.

5. The climate of the lake region in the south-eastern part of the State, situated among the mountains, is very cold in winter, light rainfall, considerable snow, and a pleasant summer temperature.

6. That of Eastern Oregon, a plateau, warm in summer, cold in winter, light rainfall, and considerable snow.

General characteristics.
Rainy season.
Dry season.
The rainy season begins about October 15th, and ends about May 1st. During December, January, February, and March the rains are generally copious at the beginning and towards the close of the rainy season; the rain falls rather in showers than continually, with many intervals of warm, pleasant weather, lasting for days together. In the southern part of the States the rains occur more in showers during the wet season than continuously. During the dry season occasional showers, fog, and dews tend to keep the earth fresh. The frosts of spring and autumn are generally followed by dense fogs, so that the humidity of these dissolve the frost before the heat of the sun can strike the vegetation. Within the area of these fogs the late frosts do no harm to vegetation.

Snow. Snow rarely falls in the interior valleys or along the coast, and when it does it is never in quantities, and remains but a short time. Severe thunderstorms and other violent atmospheric disturbances are rarely, if ever, experienced.

Winds. The winds are scarcely ever strong; along the coast brisk winds occur during the summer months from noon to sundown. A sea breeze is felt in the interior valleys in the summer, but severe gales are unknown.

East of cascades. The Cascade Mountains dividing Oregon give to that portion to the east of them a climate very different to that of the west. In Eastern Oregon the temperature is much higher in summer and lower in winter. The winters are usually short and sometimes severe. Snow will remain on the ground at times for from four to six weeks. The summers are absolutely dry, and the annual rainfall is about 15 inches.

Good improved farms may be bought in Western Oregon for from 10 dol. to 50 dol. per acre, and in Eastern Oregon and Washington territory from 5 dol. to 50 dol., according to location. Farms can be rented at about 1 dol. 75 c. per acre, or one-third of crop. *Farms.*

Farm hands get about 25 dol. per month; harvest hands 1 dol. 75 c. to 2 dol. per day. *Wages.*

Good farm horses sell at from 200 dol. to 300 dol. per span; mules 50 dol. to 300 dol. per span; fine-blooded horses 300 dol. to 1,000 dol. each; milch cows 30 dol. to 50 dol.; sheep 1 dol. to 5 dol. per head; ordinary hogs 2 dol. to 6 dol. *Prices of animals.*

During 1888 the crops generally were very good. Wheat is the staple crop, but oats, barley, and flax seed yield very heavily, and corn is also grown in some sections east of the mountains. More attention has been paid of late years to fruit culture, and the orchards have yielded good returns. The wheat crop is harvested in July and August, and the receipts at this port were as under during the cereal year ending 31st July:— *Crops generally. Wheat.*

Year.	Willamette Valley.		Eastern Oregon and Washington Territory.	
	Wheat.	Flour.	Wheat.	Flour.
	Quarters.	Sacks.	Quarters.	Sacks.
1887–88	121,808	140,968	1,014,212	131,471
1886–87	272,010	142,539	619,099	80,595
August to December, 1888..	110,084	64,155	407,308	31,642
,, ,, 1887..	43,727	51,529	353,472	48,837

The receipts of oats here during the year were 202,802 centals Valley, and 2,597 centals Eastern Oregon, nearly three times greater than those of last year. *Oats.*

Barley is not largely grown, and the receipts here were much smaller than in 1887 from Eastern Oregon, while from the Valley a much larger quantity was received. *Barley.*

Potatoes and onions are largely grown and exported to California, but prices were low last year on account of large crops. *Potatoes and onions.*

A much larger quantity of green fruit came to market than hitherto, and it was all readily absorbed for home consumption and shipment to points in the Central and Western States at remunerative prices. *Fruit.*

An increased quantity of fruit was also dried, and sells readily in this form. The fruits grown to greatest perfection in Oregon are apples, pears, plums, and cherries. Peaches grow well in some localities, and although the climate is not very well adapted to the culture of the grape, yet it is grown successfully in Southern Oregon and in some sections of Oregon and Washington. *Dried. Fruits generally grown. Viticulture.*

Fruit canning has not hitherto been carried on to any great extent, because the production of fruits has been so uncertain until within the last few years, but this industry is increasing yearly. The product of two factories here was 30,000 cases during the year. *Canning of fruit.*

Flax seed is generally grown east of the mountains. Receipts this year would tend to show a lessened crop. *Flax seed.*

Although hops are subject to very violent fluctuations, in some years not realising sufficient to pay the cost of picking, yet, on the whole, they are a profitable crop. Picking during the year began in *Hops.*

UNITED STATES.

Sheep and wool.

Western Oregon or Valley wool.

Sheep now generally kept only as aids to farming.

Wool decreasing.

Eastern Oregon. Increasing product.

Wool clip.

September, and the average yield per acre was about 1,200 lbs. Acreage in cultivation increased a little during the year.

Oregon as a whole is one of the best portions of the United States for sheep and wool production, and those engaged in the business realise a quick and certain profit. The sheep usually kept are graded merinos. Oregon Valley wool, grown west of the Cascades, stands at the head of wool values of Pacific Coast production. Up to about 15 years ago sheep were kept largely in Western Oregon, for their wool as the first object, the increase finding a ready and profitable market to stock the larger ranges east of the Cascades. Since then wheat farming has received the most general attention, and sheep have been kept on wheat farms mostly as aids to clean husbandry: in consequence there is a decreasing return of wool from this section. East of the Cascade Mountains, on the contrary, sheep are increasing rapidly in numbers, and have driven cattle from the ranges in many sections of the country. The entire wool-clip of the Pacific North-West was as follows during the year:—

	Lbs.	Lbs.
Western Washington	500,000	
Willamette Valley	1,000,000	
Southern Oregon	500,000	
Total west of Cascades		2,000,000
The Dalles	4,500,000	
Grant's	500,000	
Arlington	2,500,000	
Echo	1,000,000	
Pendleton	2,000,000	
La Grande	1,000,000	
Baker City	750,000	
Total of Eastern Oregon		12,250,000
South of Snake River		2,000,000
North of Snake River		1,000,000
North of Columbia River		1,000,000
Total of Columbia region		18,250,000

These figures show that the sheep and wool industry is in a healthy condition, and represent the wool product of nearly 3,000,000 sheep.

Cattle.

There is hardly a trace left of the old Spanish cattle, and the ranges are now stocked with better grades of cattle. As the work of settlement pushes into the wilds, of course the great herds recede, and are replaced by smaller herds kept with more care by actual settlers. Last year there were few losses on the ranges, and there has been a good demand for beef cattle at fairly remunerative prices.

Horses.

Original stock much improved.

Fine stock.

The original stock of range herds was in many instances the Indian or Cayuse horse, with an infusion of the California mustang. Gradually there has been an improvement by careful and systematic breeding, and the herds of horses now represent in many instances a very good class of animals. Horses from the great range herds supply stock for the light work of cities and for street car lines in the Mississippi Valley. Much fine stock is bred in the Willamette Valley and in some portions of Eastern Oregon. I understand that horse breeding is quite a profitable business.

ASTORIA, OREGON.

Mr. Vice-Consul Cherry reports as follows:—

I have but little to add to my report of last year.

From inquiries I find that more tide land is being improved all for grasses for stock-raising and supplying the lumber camp teams. *Improved lands.*

Hay still leads the productions of this district. I understand that the crop was a good one, but late, owing to rains in June and July: it commanded from 4*l.* to 2*l.* 10*s.* per ton, averaging 3*l.* 5*s.*, and was all used in the district. *Hay.*

A limited quantity of oats is raised, but of superior quality, being all used by the farmers or their immediate neighbours. *Oats.*

Wheat and barley are not grown, the climate being too cool during the summer months. *Wheat and barley.*

Apples are the only fruit that are grown in sufficient quantity to more than supply the local demand, and are shipped to San Francisco, where I understand that they command a ready sale, as being a good keeping apple. *Fruits.*

There are no large orchards, but each settler grows a small orchard around his homestead, which in the aggregate makes a good showing.

The climate is very favourable to the growth of this and other fruits of the north of Europe.

Potatoes are the only vegetables that are grown in sufficient quantity for shipment, and that to San Francisco, where I am informed the market is glutted. *Vegetables.*

WILMINGTON AND LOS ANGELES.

Mr. Vice-Consul Mortimer reports as follows:—

In my last special report on agriculture I pointed out that, owing to the fact that the cultivation of semi-tropical fruits is the specialty of this district, little can be said as to the cultivation of the soil likely to be of any practical value to farmers in England. The large grain farms are being sold in small parcels (10 to 20 acres) for fruit farms, and the acreage in orange trees, vines, and other fruits is increasing yearly at a rapid rate. The orange trees are dying in large numbers in various parts of this district from the attacks of the red and white scale bugs, and, although no cheap effective remedy has been discovered, extensive orchards are constantly being planted in places but a few miles removed from infected groves.

The grape vines also are dying in all parts of this district from the effects of a new disease, for which no remedy has as yet been discovered. Oranges and lemons bear transport to the Eastern States, where they sell at high prices. Figs, olives, peaches, apricots, pears, prunes, grapes, &c., are canned and exported to the Eastern States and Europe. The product of grain will not probably increase, fruit farming being more profitable. In my last special report I stated that on large ranches (20,000 to 40,000 acres) the cost of ploughing the land and sowing and harvesting the grain averaged 2*s.* 5*d.* per acre. These figures are accurate, it being understood that the farmer has all necessary horses, mules, and agricultural implements, and that the cost of feeding and caring for the live stock is not included in this estimate. Farm labourers on the large grain ranches are not employed here by the year. They are engaged for a few months at seed time and harvest at 6*l.* to 8*l.* per month and board. The majority of them are unmarried, and many of them squander their earnings in a few days and become "tramps" until their services are again required on the ranches. The rainfall is so uncertain that the business of a grain farmer is more or less speculative. From present appearances the crop, which was in jeopardy three weeks ago from drought, will be abundant.

EUREKA.

Mr. Consular-Agent Hodgson reports as follows:—

Area of Humboldt county. Area of agricultural land. Of the 3,590 square miles, or 2,297,600 acres of land which Humboldt county, in the State of California, contains, about 450,000 acres are adapted to agriculture. The principal part of the farming is done on the coast-side of our timber belt, while on the landward side thereof lies the major part of the open or grazing land, and which is mostly hilly, Eel river and Mad river districts affording the greater part of the rich bottom land, which consists of a black sandy loam principally, though there is a slight presence of clay.

Soil. This soil is of a sedimentary composition and somewhat argillaceous. On the interior hills the soil is composed of disintegrated rock, mixed with organic matter and decayed vegetation.

Area of cultivated land. Product per acre. The Assessment Roll of the county shows only about 141,552 acres of cultivated lands. These lands produce as follows: 35 to 90 bushels of oats to the acre, 30 to 85 bushels of barley to the acre, 30 to 60 bushels of wheat to the acre, seven to eight tons of potatoes to the acre.

Fruit lands. The sections lying 10 miles inland from the coast produce the finest fruit that goes into market. The Klamath and Trinity river sections, and the Upper Eel river in particular, have the character of being among the finest fruit sections in the world. The climate, quality of soil, and lay of the land on the Klamath and Trinity rivers are pronounced by experts to make that section unexcelled as a grape and wine-producing country, though that interest is at present almost wholly undeveloped.

Grazing lands, &c. Prices per acre. Grazing land is rated at from 1 dol. 25 c., the Government price to 15 dol. per acre, and improved farms from 15 dol. to 200 dol. per acre.

Dairy farming. Exports of butter and cheese. We have the very best land for dairy farming in the world. Our production of butter during 1888 was 105,000 lbs., and of cheese 5,046 lbs. The Eel River Valley lands are A 1. Around the town of Ferndale, five miles from the coast, situated at the Foot hills on the south, the land produces more clover and keeps more stock to the acre than the best acre in Ireland or anywhere else.

Price of dairy farms. It has advanced this season in value from 100 dol. two years ago to 500 dol., and ever to 1,000 dol. per acre, and it is worth all that is asked.

Acreage in grain, &c. The following table shows the acreage sown in grain, taken from the Assessment Roll of 1888:—

Cereals, &c.		Quantity Sown.
Wheat	Acres	22,463
Barley	,,	23,846
Hay	,,	31,756
Oats	,,	24,972
Corn	,,	1,503
Fruit trees	Number	45,829

Horses, Cattle, &c.

	Number.
Calves	8,677
Beef cattle	986
Stock cattle	14,066
Cows (thoroughbred)	20
Cows (American)	10,480
Oxen	315
Colts	1,319
Horses (thoroughbred)	12
„ (American)	1,039
„ (Spanish)	3,723
Jacks	15
Mules	775
Goats (common)	263
„ (Angora)	6
Hogs	4,492
Poultry (dozen)	2,197
Sheep (graded)	463
„ (common)	151,973
Lambs	3,100

Humboldt is one of the favoured sections, so far as weather is concerned. For evenness of temperature, abundance of rainfall, and consequent assurance of good crops and general good health there is nothing wanting.

For the following statements showing the temperature and rainfall as recorded at the signal station here I have to thank Mr. Connell, the officer in charge:—

Mean Temperature by Months.

Month.	1887.	1888.
	Mean temp.	Mean temp.
January	47·0	44·6
February	41·4	48·1
March	49·3	47·7
April	48·5	50·9
May	51·5	53·0
June	52·7	58·8
July	52·5	56·5
August	54·5	56·0
September	53·4	56·5
October	52·3	53·0
November	50·6	50·2
December	47·5	53·0
Yearly mean	50·1	52·5

Before the United States signal station was established here the theory prevailed that there was no rainfall in Humboldt county during the summer months, but the following figures show the contrary. However, the rainfall of mid-summer is not rainfall according to the common use of the term, but rather the precipitation from dense fog, which, while it answers the demands of growing crops, does not interfere with the pleasures of out-door life. The figures given relate to this city, and probably to the entire coast of the county. The valley and hill sections of the county have their own climate, more rainfall, and a higher summer temperature.

UNITED STATES.

Comparative Statement for the past Two Years.

Month.	1887.	1888.
	Inches.	Inches.
January	8·86	12·95
February	9·07	1·98
March	2·28	4·09
April	5·55	1·05
May	3·51	0·76
June	1·92	4·66
July	0·06	0·44
August	0·07	..
September	0·21	0·06
October	0·55	1·15
November	2·66	3·41
December	4·93	5·93
Total	39·67	36·56

LONDON:
Printed for Her Majesty's Stationery Office,
By HARRISON AND SONS,
Printers in Ordinary to Her Majesty.
(1250 6 | 89---H & S   672)

FOREIGN OFFICE.
1889.
ANNUAL SERIES.

No. 555.

DIPLOMATIC AND CONSULAR REPORTS ON TRADE AND FINANCE.

UNITED STATES.

REPORT FOR THE YEAR 1888
ON THE
TRADE OF THE CONSULAR DISTRICT OF SAN FRANCISCO.

REFERENCE TO PREVIOUS REPORTS, Annual Series Nos. 313, 375, and 392.

Presented to both Houses of Parliament by Command of Her Majesty,
JUNE, 1889.

LONDON:
PRINTED FOR HER MAJESTY'S STATIONERY OFFICE,
BY HARRISON AND SONS, ST. MARTIN'S LANE,
PRINTERS IN ORDINARY TO HER MAJESTY.

And to be purchased, either directly or through any Bookseller, from
EYRE AND SPOTTISWOODE, EAST HARDING STREET, FLEET STREET, E.C., and
32, ABINGDON STREET, WESTMINSTER, S.W.; or
ADAM AND CHARLES BLACK, 6, NORTH BRIDGE, EDINBURGH; or
HODGES, FIGGIS, & Co., 104, GRAFTON STREET, DUBLIN.

1889.

[C. 5618—108.] *Price Twopence Halfpenny.*

New Series of Reports.

Reports of the Annual Series have been issued from Her Majesty's Diplomatic and Consular Officers at the following places, and may be obtained from the sources indicated on the title-page:—

No.		Price.	No.		Price.
429.	Hamburg	4d.	492.	Kiungchow	1d.
430.	Trieste	1d.	493.	Sandakan	1d.
431.	New York	2d.	494.	Manila	1d.
432.	Antwerp	1d.	495.	Swatow	1d.
433.	Munich	1d.	496.	Guayaquil	1d.
434.	Buenos Ayres	1d.	497.	Rome	1d.
435.	Warsaw	1d.	498.	Santos	1d.
436.	Porto Rico	1d.	499.	Boston	1d.
437.	Réunion	1d.	500.	Aleppo	1d.
438.	Lisbon	1d.	501.	Bordeaux	2d.
439.	Venice	1d.	502.	Valparaiso	1d.
440.	Christiania	5d.	503.	St. Petersburg	1d.
441.	Maranham	1d.	504.	Rio de Janeiro	4d.
442.	Sofia	1d.	505.	Brest	1d.
443.	Copenhagen	1d.	506.	Dunkirk	1d.
444.	Galatz	1d.	507.	Genoa	2d.
445.	Tabreez	1d.	508.	Beyrout	1d.
446.	Bogotá	2d.	509.	Colonia	1d.
447.	St. Petersburg	3d.	510.	Marseilles	1d.
448.	Nice	1d.	511.	Kiukiang	1d.
449.	Stettin	2d	512.	Buda-Pesth	2d.
450.	Fiume	1d.	513.	Wênchow	10d.
451.	Chinkiang	1d.	514.	Coquimbo	1d.
452.	The Hague	1d.	515.	Charleston	1d.
453.	Malaga	1d.	516.	Riga	1d.
454.	Taganrog	1d.	517.	Mollendo	1d.
455.	Mozambique	1d.	518.	Taiwan	1d.
456.	Bogotá	2d.	519.	Wuhu	1d.
457.	Patras	1d.	520.	Corunna	2d.
458.	Galveston	1d.	521.	Noumea	1d.
459.	Buda Pesth	1d.	522.	San José	1d.
460.	Madeira	1d.	523.	Ningpo	1d.
461.	Warsaw	1d.	524.	Gothenburg	2d.
462.	Paris	2d.	525.	Hankow	2d.
463.	Baltimore	1d.	526.	Foochow	1d.
464.	Philadelphia	2d.	527.	Erzeroum	2d.
465.	New Orleans	2d.	528.	Ciudad Bolivar	1d.
466.	New Orleans	2d.	529.	Jaffa	1d.
467.	Cherbourg	1d.	530.	Ancona	1d.
468.	Buenos Ayres	1d.	531.	Savannah	1d.
469.	Algiers	1d.	532.	Batavia	1d.
470.	Ichang	1d.	533.	Adrianople	1d.
471.	Copenhagen	2d.	534.	Nisch	1½d.
472.	Athens	1d.	535.	Vienna	1d.
473.	Cherbourg	1d.	536.	Odessa	8d.
474.	The Piræus	1d.	537.	Constantinople	2d.
475.	Galatz	1d.	538.	Demascus	1d.
476.	Tripoli	1d.	539.	Tienstin	1d.
477.	Saigon	1d.	540.	Amoy	1d.
478.	Serajevo	1d.	541.	Mogador	1d.
479.	Brussels	2d.	542.	Vienna	1d.
480.	Bengazi	1d.	543.	Antwerp	1d.
481.	Odessa	1d.	544.	Lisbon	2d.
482.	Santo Domingo	1d.	545.	New York	1½d.
483.	Rome	1d.	546.	San Francisco	1d.
484.	Lisbon	1d.	547.	Stettin	1½d.
485.	Port Said	2d.	548.	San Salvador	½d.
486.	Havre	3d.	549.	Trebizond	1d.
487.	Boulogne	1d.	550.	Nice	1d.
488.	Callao	1d.	551.	Baghdad	½d.
489.	Barcelona	2d.	552.	Fiume	1d.
490.	Boulogne	2d.	553.	Mogador	2d.
491.	Taganrog	2d.	554.	Buenos Ayres	1½d.

No. 555.

Reference to previous Report, Annual Series Nos. 313, 375, *and* 392.

UNITED STATES.

SAN FRANCISCO.

Consul Donohoe to the Marquis of Salisbury.

My Lord,   San Francisco, *April* 16, 1889.

I HAVE the honour to enclose herewith Annual Reports on the Trade and Commerce of San Francisco, Portland, Astoria, Port Townsend, Los Angeles, San Diego, and Eureka for the year 1888.

I have, &c.

(Signed)   DENIS DONOHOE.

Report on the Trade and Commerce of San Francisco for the Year 1888.

There has been a steady increase in the trade of this port during the past year, both as regards imports and exports, as will be seen by the tables annexed. **Trade increasing.**

In the exports the receipts of wheat in this market have been greater by about 42,000 tons than in 1887, and the exports have been larger. France has taken 1,809,381 centals during the year. **Wheat.**

The export of flour does not show much increase, and is given at 827,425 barrels. **Flour.**

The average price of best shipping wheat for the year has been as follows:— **Price of wheat.**

	Dol. c.		Dol. c.	
January	1 37½	to	1 40	per cental.
February	1 30		1 37½	,,
March	1 27½		1 33¾	,,
April	1 27½		1 45	,,
May	1 32½		1 45	,,
June	1 30		1 32½	,,
July	1 30		1 42½	,,
August	1 37½		1 60	,,
September	1 60		1 45	,,
October	1 57½		1 65	,,
November	1 65		1 55	,,
December	1 50		1 40	,,

The crop of barley in 1888 has been the largest known in California. The export to England and Australia has been considerable, and the crop has been pretty nearly all cleared out; probably not over 160,000 tons being left at the end of the year. **Barley.**

The range of prices for "Chevalier" was, from January to June, 1 dol. 20 c. to 1 dol. 35 c. An advance has since occurred, and it may now be quoted at about 1 dol. 50 c. per bushel.

(681)

Salmon. Catch of Columbia river decreasing. Alaska as a new fishing ground.

The principal part of the salmon pack of this coast is shipped to Great Britain and Australia, and the total receipts for 1888 are given as 529,362 cases, of which Alaska furnished 392,975 cases. The catch of fish in the Columbia river is steadily falling-off from year to year, and Alaska will probably make an even better show for next year, as many vessels are now leaving for there fully fitted out for the establishment of canneries on that coast, where, it is said, the fish are very numerous.

Canned fruit and vegetables.

In canned fruit and vegetables the tables do not show a very large export, though the quantity tinned last year was far larger than ever. Altogether about 700,000 cases have been sent away from this market, there having been a large demand for this class of goods in the Eastern States. This branch of trade may be said to have been extremely prosperous in 1888.

Timber.

The lumber receipts for the year are far the largest ever received at this port:—

	Feet.
Pine	267,253,700
Red wood	139,105,250
Total	406,358,950

Much of this is used for home consumption, and the shipments to the Eastern States by rail are considerable. Our Australian colonies take a large quantity, but chiefly from the Puget Sound ports.

Quicksilver.

As to quicksilver, the production in California shows a total of 33,250 flasks for the year, which is a slight falling-off from 1887. The average price for the year is the same, viz., 42 dol. 50 c. per flask.

Wine product of California short.

The wine product of California for 1888 has not by any means come up to expectations; it probably will reach from 16,000,000 to 17,000,000 gallons. The very great heat of last summer has had much to do with the short crop, and many owners of vineyards have found it more profitable to dry their grapes than to make wine of them.

Borax.

I have dropped borax from the table of exports, as I find that very little was exported, as the price ruling abroad was lower than prices here, which have increased.

Increased sugar imports.

In imports the principal one is sugar, and the receipts from the Sandwich Islands reached 99,564 tons and those from Manila 27,578 tons, which is a large increase on former years. There has been a falling-off in the receipts from Central America.

Increased coal imports.

The receipts of coal at this port are made up as follows:—

	Tons.
From British Columbia	298,515
„ Great Britain	117,000
„ Australia	280,903
„ Japan	10,408
Total	706,826

This is a very considerable increase from all parts.

As to the other imports, the tables speak for themselves.

Metal product.

From the circular of Messrs. Wells, Fargo, and Co., the net product of metals in the States and territories west of the Missouri river, excluding British Columbia and Mexico, for the last two years are given as follows:—

Year.	Gold.	Silver.	Copper.	Lead.	Total.
	£	£	£	£	£
1888	5,997,540	10,630,550	3,652,298	2,252,726	22,533,114
1887	6,500,013	10,166,777	2,072,549	1,926,215	20,665,554

SAN FRANCISCO.

The exports of silver during the past year to Japan, China, the Straits, &c., from San Francisco have been as follows—2,924,286*l*.

Railways.
There has been a steady progress in railway building during the year, principally by the Southern Pacific Company, who have added about 230 miles in branch roads to their system. Other lines have been built, besides, to the extent of about 130 miles.

Freights.
The following table gives the rates for freights current during each month in the year:—

	Cork for Orders.		Liverpool.	
	£ s. d.	£ s. d.	£ s. d.	£ s. d.
January	1 7 6 to	1 1 3	1 5 0 to	1 1 0
February	1 6 3	1 3 9	..	1 3 9
March	1 3 9	1 2 6	..	1 1 0
April	1 6 3	1 3 9	..	1 0 6
May	1 5 0	1 1 3	..	1 2 6
June	1 5 0	1 2 6	..	1 0 6
July	1 12 6	1 2 6	1 10 0	1 0 0
August	1 17 6	1 7 6	1 15 0	1 5 0
September	2 1 3	1 17 6	1 18 9	1 15 0
October	2 1 3	1 15 0	1 17 9	1 12 6
November	2 1 3	1 17 6	1 18 9	1 15 0
December	2 2 6	1 15 0	2 0 0	1 12 6

NOTE.—All values in this report are reduced to sterling at the rate of 5 dol. to the £.

Annex A.—RETURN of all Shipping at the Port of San Francisco in the Year 1888.

ENTERED.

Nationality.	Sailing.		Steam.		Total.	
	Number of Vessels.	Tons.	Number of Vessels.	Tons.	Number of Vessels.	Tons.
British	274	415,208	72	118,611	346	533,819
American, from foreign countries	233	195,898	154	236,158	387	432,056
American, from Atlantic ports of Union	51	79,130	1	1,200	52	80,330
Hawaiian	10	4,214	26	41,691	36	45,905
German	30	34,777	...	...	30	34,777
Bolivian	8	6,731	...	...	8	6,731
Italian	4	4,252	...	...	4	4,252
Others	12	8,057	6	5,306	18	13,363
Total	622	748,267	259	402,966	881	1,151,233
,, for the year preceding	547	607,665	233	330,981	780	938,646

UNITED STATES.

Cleared.

Nationality.	Sailing. Number of Vessels.	Sailing. Tons.	Steam. Number of Vessels.	Steam. Tons.	Total. Number of Vessels.	Total. Tons.
British	308	473,138	70	114,649	378	587,787
American, to foreign countries	272	238,654	153	231,155	425	469,809
American, to Atlantic ports of Union	20	34,740	...	...	20	34,740
Hawaiian	11	5,019	25	39,335	36	44,354
German	23	26,506	...	...	23	26,506
Bolivian	6	5,082	...	...	6	5,082
Italian	3	3,277	...	...	3	3,277
Others	15	8,277	7	5,240	22	13,517
Total	658	794,693	255	390,379	913	1,185,072
„ for the year preceding	480	535,574	238	336,667	718	872,241

The entries and clearances of American ships do not include the coasting trade or whaling and fishing voyages.

Annex B.—RETURN of Principal Articles of Export from San Francisco during the Years 1887–88.

Articles.		1888. Quantity.	1888. Value. £	1887. Quantity.	1887. Value. £
Wheat and flour	Tons	636,054	3,960,198	511,809	3,621,241
Tinned salmon	Cases	454,916	464,014	196,724	198,424
Barley	Centals	1,707,502	455,845	452,528	108,264
Tinned fruit and vegetables	Cases	173,036	147,081	148,749	109,449
Timber	Feet	21,069,359	118,713	17,135,868	65,202
Quicksilver	Flasks	11,921	94,774	9,545	79,812
Wine	Gallons	333,157	43,738	274,063	44,175
Other articles	...	...	2,878,669	...	3,091,581
Total	...	...	8,163,032	...	7,318,148

RETURN of Principal Articles of Import to San Francisco during the Years 1887–88.

Articles.		1888. Quantity.	1888. Value. £	1887. Quantity.	1887. Value. £
Sugar	Tons	132,703	2,475,341	99,612	1,831,807
Raw silk	Lbs.	3,469,736	2,313,170	3,286,450	2,461,855
Coffee	„	22,237,236	567,672	18,080,837	458,069
Coals	Tons	706,826	498,308	512,646	324,478
Rice	„	26,771	241,594	19,456	220,628
Tin plates	Boxes	354,306	240,000	211,205	138,800
Tea	Lbs.	7,613,287	199,216	8,028,068	222,956
Cement	Barrels	355,899	88,975	329,926	82,481
Scrap-iron	Tons	26,505	64,262	30,429	68,875
Pig-iron	„	20,971	52,427	14,410	34,650
Bullion and coin	Value	...	1,357,828	...	1,749,689
Other articles	...	...	1,623,047	...	727,049
Total	...	...	9,721,840	...	8,321,337

SAN FRANCISCO.

Annex C.—TABLE showing the Total Value of all Articles Exported from San Francisco and Imported to San Francisco from and to Foreign Countries during the Years 1887–8.

Country.	Exports. 1888.	Exports. 1887.	Imports. 1888.	Imports. 1887.
	£	£	£	£
Great Britain	3,682,200	3,311,481	1,169,826	888,325
Hawaiian Islands	567,410	524,585	2,241,617	1,881,056
France	557,677	30,652	334,271	308,194
China	495,289	614,053	1,267,554	1,278,435
Australia	365,011	204,904	276,032	290,707
Mexico	277,532	297,235	141,976	91,401
Central America	274,334	216,043	559,195	563,595
Canada	156,916	160,167	334,642	262,102
Japan	132,440	152,391	1,943,401	1,933,993
Belgium	50,362	40	184,455	98,026
Germany	22,608	13,905	201,709	191,157
Spanish possessions	16,888	4,040	521,641	153,291
India	2,851	347	414,176	224,443
Domestic ports and other countries	1,561,514	1,788,305	131,345	156,612
Total	8,163,032	7,318,148	9,721,840	8,321,337

PORTLAND, OREGON.

Mr. Vice-Consul Laidlaw reports as follows:—

Trade generally. The year of 1888 has been one of unexampled prosperity, and in nearly all branches of trade a larger business has been done than during any former year. The value as well of exports as of imports shows a large increase over last year, and although the exports do not reach those of 1886, this is due to the shipment at Tacoma of a large proportion of the wheat surplus from districts hitherto tributary to this port. **Increase in imports and exports** **Harvest.** The harvest of wheat, oats, and other grains has been large in all sections, and prices were better than for years past for nearly all farm produce. Of the tonnage employed in the foreign trade 90 per cent. was British—the same proportion as last year. **British tonnage.**

Imports. As usual the largest proportion of the import trade was done viâ San Francisco, or by sail and rail from the Eastern States. A small steamer has been running regularly from Vancouver, British Columbia, in connection with the Canadian Pacific Railway, and doing a good business.

Tinplates. Imports of tin plates were somewhat larger than last year, and prices averaged about 21s. 6d. for B.V. grades of coke. Direct imports of salt and rice were considerably less, while those of cement and pig-iron were much greater. One cargo was imported from Belgium consisting almost entirely of cement and glass, and the cement is well spoken of. From present appearances there will be a good demand for cement next year. 339 tons of foundry coke were imported from the United Kingdom, and 315 tons from Belgium. Of the coal imports 2,311 tons were received from Great Britain, 6,515 tons from British Columbia, and 4,794 tons from Australia. In addition 51,498 tons were received from coast mines. The market price of foreign coal averaged about 32s. during the year. The Oregon Iron and Steel Company has started its works with a much enlarged capacity, and it is likely that imports of pig-iron will be less in future. **Salt and rice. Cement and pig-iron. Coke. Coal.**

| | | UNITED STATES. |

Grain bags. I cannot give any correct statistics of imports of grain bags and wool packs which come from Calcutta viâ San Francisco. Prices averaged about 4d. for 22 by 36 standard grain bags. It will be seen by reference to Annex B that there has been a large import of steel rails and railway iron. This comes from Maryport for use on the Oregon Railway and Navigation Company's extensions.

Steel rails.

The increase in value of imports during the year was 115 per cent.

Exports— increase.
Coastwise and rail.
Influence of Tacoma felt.
Flour to China, &c.
Breadstuffs.

The total value of exports to foreign countries and by rail to the Eastern States was 17 per cent. more than in 1887. Shipments of produce by rail to the Eastern States and exports coastwise are valued at 1,860,280l., against 1,799,100l. last year. It must also be borne in mind that these figures do not include shipments by the Oregon Pacific Railway viâ Yaquina Bay to San Francisco, and also that 25 per cent. of the wheat exported hitherto through this port was last year shipped viâ Tacoma on Puget Sound. Shipments of flour to China and Japan were more than doubled, 61,502 sacks having been exported. The total shipments of breadstuffs, both foreign and coastwise, were 909,958 quarters of wheat, valued at 1,186,720l., and 505,844 sacks of flour, valued at 535,200l. Average values about 1l. 7s. 6d. per quarter f.o.b. for Oregon Valley wheat, and 1l. 5s. 6d. f.o.b. for Walla Walla or Eastern Oregon.

Wool. For years past the wool clip has steadily increased, as will be noted in the receipts and shipments of the last three years as given below, but the increase is entirely in the section east of the Cascades. The average market price of wool during the year was about 18 c., or 9d. per lb., for Valley, and 13 c., or 6½d. per lb., for Eastern, which are considerably lower than last year. The consumption of Oregon woollen mills varies very little from year to year.

Receipts and shipments at this port were as under:—

Year.	Receipts.		Shipments.	
	Valley.	Eastern.	Viâ San Francisco.	By Rail.
	Lbs.	Lbs.	Lbs.	Lbs.
During 1888	1,132,837	13,230,602	8,716,238	5,201,081
,, 1887	852,445	11,682,040	7,824,907	4,581,359
,, 1886	1,785,560	11,755,566	5,347,407	7,879,698

Hops. Receipts of hops were 3,669,291 lbs., and shipments were 2,196,096 lbs., which is a large increase. Before picking began, large contracts were made for future delivery at 6d. to 7d. (12 c. to 14 c.), and during August and September prices advanced to from 8d. to 10½d. (16 c. to 21½ c.) per lb. for average to extra choice, dropping afterwards to 7d. (14 c.) for best grade.

Timber. A largely increased coastwise trade has been done in timber, and about 20,000,000 feet has been shipped to Denver, Salt Lake, Ogden, and other interior towns. The business has been fairly profitable.

Fisheries.
Product.
Salmon, sturgeon, and halibut have been sent east in refrigeration cars, fresh, but, as usual, by far the greater proportion of the salmon catch has been canned. The product of the packing establishments of the Columbia river was about 368,000 cases of spring catch, including about 35,000 cases of second quality. Formerly Great Britain was the largest purchaser, but now by far the greater proportion is consumed

in the Eastern States. Astoria is the headquarters of this business, but 297,930 cases were shipped from this by rail eastward. The average price paid for Columbia river salmon was 6s. 6d., or 1 dol. 62½ c. per dozen 1 lb. tins, free on board ship here.

Money has been sufficiently plentiful during the year. Sixty days' bills on London fluctuated between 4 dol. 82 c. and 4 dol. 87 c. per £ sterling for bank, and from 4 dol. 81½ c. to 4 dol. 86½ c. for mercantile.

The engagements of tonnage during the last three years, exclusive of coasting voyages, have been as under:—

	Registered Tons.		
	1888.	1887.	1886.
Grain and flour cargoes	122,338	89,856	146,824
Salmon and assorted cargoes	4,189	3,227	5,873
Timber cargoes	8,268	6,020	3,136
Miscellaneous cargoes	1,655	850	2,961
Total	136,450	99,953	158,794

Of the foregoing 99 were British vessels, registering 118,215 tons, while last year 75 ships, registering 88,931 tons, entered here.

Rates of freight were higher than last year, the average rates for the year being 40s. 6d. for iron vessels and 37s. for wooden vessels to a port in the United Kingdom. Most of the wooden and many iron vessels now give the option of continental ports at same rates as to the United Kingdom. The highest rates paid during the year were 52s. 6d. and 48s., and the lowest 27s. 6d. and 30s., for iron and wood respectively.

There has only been a slight increase in the steam tonnage employed in the coasting trade. The Canadian Pacific Railway now runs a British steamer regularly between Vancouver, British Columbia, and this port.

Seamen's wages have been the same out of this port as last year (6l. per month for able seamen), and, in spite of statutes to the contrary, a bonus has been exacted from masters requiring crews amounting usually to about 9l. 10s. per man. I regret to report that the crimps in these ports, and particularly in Astoria, are even more exacting than hitherto, so that a seaman can hardly secure employment without the sanction of these rascally boarding-house keepers. It is expected that the Legislature, which meets in January, will exact some stringent measures to protect both seamen and masters.

The number and changes in crews of British ships entering this port during the year have been as under:—

Total Number of Crews.	Deserted.	Discharged.	Engaged.	Reported Dead.	Percentage of Desertion.	Hospital Permits.
1,872	241	58	87	5	12·87	15

From the above table it will be seen that the engagements at this port are very small. This is on account of the high-handed proceedings of Astoria crimps mentioned in my last year's report.

Improvement of Rivers and Harbours.

River, bars, and channels. — Last Congress made large appropriations for the improvement of the rivers and harbours of this State, the result of which will not generally be apparent till next year. Swan Island bar, in the Willamette river below Portland, was dredged to 20 feet at low water. St. Helen's bar, in the Columbia river, was sluiced by the propeller of a steamer, and during the closing months of the year over 1,000 feet was added to the dyke in course of construction by the United States engineers. It is expected that when completed the dyke will give at all times at least 20 feet at low water across the bar. At Martin's Island bar dams were constructed across the sloughs at Martin's and Burke's Islands in the Columbia river, which will have the effect of keeping this bar clear of silt, and give at all times at least 20 feet at low water. Some work was done clearing out the upper reaches of the Columbia river, and also of the Willamette river, navigable for light draught river steamers.

Mouth of the Columbia. — The appropriation for the great work of building the jetty at the mouth of the Columbia river was this year 500,000 dols., and the work is under charge of Major T. H. Handbury, United States Engineer corps. The work now in progress is the building of a low tide jetty, starting from Fort Stevens on South Cape, and extending in a westerly direction, with a slight curve to the south, across Clatsop Spit for a distance of about $4\frac{1}{2}$ miles to a point about 3 miles south of Cape Hancock. It will be of stone, resting upon a mattress foundation about 40 feet wide and from $2\frac{1}{2}$ to 5 feet thick. The stone extends to the level of mean low water. As the work proceeds a tramway is built, supported on piles driven along the line of the jetty about 24 feet above the level of low tide, and across this the material is transported. The jetty is now under construction for a little more than a mile, and at the close of the year 5,336 feet had been constructed partially, including jetty tramway. When the project is completed, it is expected that the result will be a wide, direct, and stable channel across the bar of the Columbia, carrying fully 30 feet at low water.

Yaquina Bay. — At Yaquina Bay very little was done except to repair breaches in the jetty already constructed, and commence operations on the north side jetty. *Steamers lost.* — Two fine steamers were lost entering this bay during the year.

Coos Bay. — At Coos Bay no work was done during the year, but there is now a good depth of water at the entrance consequent upon the work done there in previous years.

Coquille. — At Coquille there has been no extension of the work mentioned in my last report.

Pilotage and towage. — The expenses of pilotage and towage have been much reduced during the year, and it is expected that such further reductions will be made after the session of the Legislature that these expenses will be reduced to a very low figure.

Agriculture. — The past year has been a profitable one for the farmers who had good crops of wheat, oats, and other grain, and prices were much higher than for some time back. *Hops.* — The hop growers, however, found only a fair *Fruits.* — market for their produce, though much better than during 1887. Fruit growing was profitable, and the yield was generally good; there is, *Codlin moth.* — however, much complaint of late years of the ravages of the codlin moth.

Sheep and cattle. — The sheep and cattle business has been fairly good and has increased considerably. Profitable prices have been realised throughout the *Wool.* — year. Wool sold lower than during 1887, leaving only small returns to the grower.

There has been a continually increasing immigration into Oregon and Washington territory, and the Board of Immigration here estimates that the population of Oregon alone has been increased by about 60,000. During 1888 over 5,000 persons were employed in various manufacturing enterprises, and the estimated value of the product is 2,776,990*l.* In 1887 3,380 persons were employed, and the value was 1,560,800*l.* The Oregon Iron and Steel Company has increased its capacity, and completed its cast iron pipe foundry with a capacity of 25 tons daily. The works were started again (October 17), and the product to end of the year was 3,000 tons pig-iron, part of which was cast into 1,250 tons water pipe. The company's mine is about 2½ miles from the works, and is connected by a narrow gauge railway. It is a fissure vein of brown hematite, averaging 10 feet thick, and yielding 40 per cent. of metallic iron.

Population and industries.
Manufactures.
Oregon Iron and Steel Co.

A large amount of development work has been done on mines during the year both in Oregon and Washington territory and Northern Idaho. The yield of Oregon mines is probably no more than during 1887, but I have been unable to procure any reliable statistics. In the Cœur d'Alene districts of Northern Idaho there are now opened up and operated about nine different mines of lead and silver ore, the average produce of which, during the year, amounted to about 200 tons of concentrates per day, averaging about 70 per cent. of lead and 300 ounces of silver per ton. During 1889 five or six other mines will be opened up ready to produce. A group of gold properties have been worked on Elk Creek, near the lead and silver producing mines, yielding with a 20 stamp mill about 25,000 dol. bullion per month. In the Okanagon district of Washington territory some very rich claims are reported in process of development.

Mining.

The United States engineers have prosecuted the work of excavation on the canal basin and locks at the Cascades of the Columbia river, but it will be several years before this important work can be completed. Congress appropriated 300,000 dol. for the continuation of this work.

Public works. Canals.

The steel railroad drawbridge, mentioned in my last report, connecting Portland and East Portland, has been completed, and is in operation. Another bridge is projected.

Bridges.

A Union passenger station has been commenced, and will be completed as rapidly as possible.

Terminal works.

The only construction in my district during the year has been the Portland and Vancouver railroad, a narrow gauge line of about twelve miles, but throughout Oregon and Washington territory there has been considerable activity in building branches and feeders to the trunk lines.

Railways.

A cable railway is partially constructed leading to the heights behind the city, and there has also been considerable extension of horse car lines in the city. There are six miles of double track and four-and-a-half miles of single track now in operation. In East Portland there have been built about three miles of street car and motor lines.

Street railways.

The bonded debt of this city is limited to 100,000 dol., or 20,000*l.*, and the bonds bear 6 per cent. interest. Besides these there are water bonds outstanding to the extent of 120,000*l.*, bearing interest at 5 per cent. The receipts from the waterworks were equivalent to 24,561*l.*, and the disbursements 11,400*l.*, in addition to which the interest on coupons amounted to 50,000*l.* The total revenue of the city, exclusive of waterworks, which are managed by a commission specially created by the Legislature, was 272,854 dol., or 54,570*l.*, and the expenditures were equivalent to 47,524*l.* The cost of street improvements is paid by the owners of adjacent property, and was as

City finances.

UNITED STATES.

follows:—Street improvements 14,320*l.*, street extensions 972*l.*, sewers 11,269*l.* The city is well lighted by electricity.

Taxation. The State, county, city, and school taxes aggregated 3·10 per cent., estimated on a valuation of 40 per cent. of actual value.

Remarks.
City property.
Real estate transactions. Property in the city and suburbs has advanced very much during the year, and the transfers and sales have been much larger than last year. Real estate transactions recorded in the county of Multnomah amounted to 7,035,866 dol., while in 1887 they were 5,864,081 dol.

Hotel. A local company was organised with a capital of 100,000*l.* to construct a large and handsome brick and stone hotel, and it is now several stories high, but will take at least a year to complete.

Exhibition building. Another company, the North Pacific Industrial Association, with a capital stock of 30,000*l.*, has finished a fine exhibition building, divided into three pavilions, and having a frontage of 400 feet on one street and 200 feet on another. Many other fine buildings have been built during the year, and the estimated cost of dwellings built or under construction is 110,600*l.* Business buildings, inclusive of the hotel and exhibition, have been built or contracted for at a cost of 212,670*l.*, and the estimated expenditure on churches, schools, and hospitals is 36,700*l.*

Buildings.

Suburban. In the various suburbs, including East Portland and Albina, the estimated expenditure on buildings and improvements is 82,700*l.*

Labour. Skilled labour has been in good demand, and labourers and men willing to work have had no difficulty in procuring employment during the year.

NOTE.—The values given in this report are reduced to sterling, at the average rate of 5 dol. to the £.

Annex A.—RETURN of all Shipping at the Port of Portland, Oregon, in the Year 1888.

ENTERED.

Nationality.	Sailing. Number of Vessels.	Sailing. Tons.	Steam. Number of Vessels.	Steam. Tons.	Total. Number of Vessels.	Total. Tons.
British	96	114,938	9	5,805	105	120,743
United States—						
Foreign	2	2,750	...	...	2	2,750
Atlantic	4	5,651	...	...	4	5,651
Coasting	18	11,943	176	302,798	194	314,741
Norwegian	2	1,744	...	...	2	1,744
Total	122	137,026	185	308,603	307	445,629
„ for the preceding year...	...	...	...	...	222	363,245

CLEARED.

Nationality.	Sailing. Number of Vessels.	Sailing. Tons.	Steam. Number of Vessels.	Steam. Tons.	Total. Number of Vessels.	Total. Tons.
British	102	122,129	9	5,805	111	127,934
United States—						
Foreign	10	13,816	...	...	10	13,816
Coasting	18	7,742	173	294,891	191	302,633
German	1	1,726	...	...	1	1,726
Norwegian	2	1,744	...	...	2	1,744
Total	133	147,157	182	300,696	315	447,853
„ for the preceding year...	...	...	...	...	205	356,127

SAN FRANCISCO.

Annex B.—RETURN of Principal Articles of Export from Portland, Oregon, during the Years 1888 and 1887.

Articles.		1888.		1887.	
		Quantity.	Value.	Quantity.	Value.
			£		£
Wheat	Quarters	573,550	752,576	495,596	610,796
Wheat flour	Sacks	388,871	361,502	226,700	235,423
Timber	Million feet	2,093	3,905	150	500
Fish oil	...	...	...	...	2,600
Other articles	...	...	1,027	...	15,578
Total foreign exports	...	...	1,119,010	...	864,897

RETURN of Principal Articles of Import to Portland, Oregon, during the Years 1888 and 1887.

Articles.		1888.		1887.	
		Quantity.	Value.	Quantity.	Value.
			£		£
Coals	Tons	13,620	8,634	19,479	12,628
Tin and terne plates	Lbs.	2,522,755	15,496	2,237,806	12,921
Rice	,,	2,096,645	6,595	3,114,439	11,389
Earthenware and glassware	...	...	12,313	...	9,020
Salt	Lbs.	4,782,310	2,979	14,105,047	8,769
Cement	Barrels	37,637	6,757	26,427	5,586
Cigars and tobacco	...	...	8,238	...	5,463
Wines and liquors	...	...	3,231	...	3,136
Beer, porter, and ale	Gallons	36,742	5,026	12,382	2,143
Soda and chemicals	...	...	1,236	...	1,992
Oils	Gallons	21,477	1,567	24,816	1,441
Pig iron	Tons	1,900	4,097	463	1,401
Rails, bar iron, and manufactures of iron and steel	,,	20,533	92,577	...	...
Fire bricks	Number	706,960	1,344	135,000	255
Tea	Lbs.	128,356	1,636	52,054	1,865
Hemp	Tons	110	3,280	...	...
Glass	Lbs.	1,431,169	4,622	...	...
All other articles	...	...	24,662	...	16,963
Total foreign imports	...	...	204,290	...	94,972

NOTE.—The above returns do not include exports or imports coastwise or by rail, with the exception of articles transported in bond.

Annex C.—TABLE showing the Total Value of all Articles Exported from Portland and Imported to Portland, Oregon, from and to Foreign Countries during the Years 1888 and 1887.

Country.	Exports.		Imports.	
	1888.	1887.	1888.	1887.
	£	£	£	£
Great Britain	998,377	640,973	157,332	51,106
Belgium	..	124,099	3,898	..
British Columbia	516	17,253	7,498	3,010
China and Japan	40,009	30,170	22,578	21,999
Australia	..	..	2,518	10,250
Peru and Chile	2,200	13,322	..	..
France	77,908	39,080	752	626
Germany	..	..	1,779	1,907
Cuba	..	..	7,935	5,044
All other countries	..	..	..	1,030
Total	1,119,010	864,897	204,290	94,972

ASTORIA, OREGON.

Mr. Vice-Consul Cherry reports as follows:—

General business for 1888. Improvement is to be noticed, but more in the district than in the port of Astoria.

Imports. Imports show a falling-off, nearly all of which are tin plates from the United Kingdom.

Tin plates. The retail price of plates in jobbing lots was, on the average, 1*l.* 3*s.* per box for B.V. grade, varying from 1*l.*, sold prior to arrival to 1*l.* 6*s.* at the close of the season.

Salt. But little difference in price of salt is noted for Liverpool F.F.—3*l.* 10*s.* per ton.

Coals. A still decreasing import of coal is shown owing to the strike in the New Castle N.S.W. collieries, and partly to the enhanced cost of domestic coals from Puget Sound being used to a greater extent, Wallsend coals are selling from about 1*l.* 10*s.* to 1*l.* 13*s.* per ton.

Block tin. Block tin still arrives by San Francisco from Australia, the average price being high, 1*s.* 6*d.* per lb.

Exports. Exports show an increase in the quantities of wheat and flour, but a falling-off in the direct export of salmon, and an increased value in all exports, which makes a gross increase of 18 per cent.

Canned salmon. The total number of cases of canned salmon exported directly, all of which went to the United Kingdom, was 74,090 cases, containing on an average 48 lbs. per case, and was of a still higher value than for 1887, but shows a great falling-off in quantity, accounted for by an increased proportion of shipments going by way of San Francisco, owing to the lower freights offered at that port, and the increased demand in the United States.

Wheat and flour. A greatly increased export of wheat and flour from this port, together with better prices, is to be noted—caused, first, by the use of a larger class of vessels unable to load up the river; secondly, by the better price in the home market.

Lumber. Lumber shows a small falling-off, owing to the fact that increased rates of freight for foreign business takes away any chance of profit to the mills, the domestic markets taking the bulk of the output of this district.

Manufacturing and other industries. Lumbering shows a steady advance on the Columbia river, as well as in places north and south in this district.

The greatest thing to be noted is the way that "syndicates of lumber men" are securing large tracts of land covered by forest, by means of the so-called lumber entries, as a reserve to fall back upon when the lumber lands further east are exhausted; but how long it will be held it will be hard to tell.

Salmon fishing. The total fishing in the Columbia river in this district shows a marked falling-off in the spring catch of Chinook salmon, made up in part by the catching and using during the past season of other species of salmon, viz., "blue-backs" and "steel-heads," not heretofore used: the fishermen receive on an average 5*s.* per fish.

Salmon packing. The prices received for salmon packing ranged markedly higher in 1888 than in 1887, but owing to the increased price of raw fish, amounting to 3*s.* per case, the profits have been divided; but the closing out of a number of the co-operative packing establishments has no doubt made it better for those who remain in the business than it otherwise would have been.

The pack of this district is for—

	Cases.
The Columbia river, spring catch	300,000
" " inferior fish	70,000
" " full catch	3,000
Total	373,000

as compared with a total of 377,000 last year.

	Cases.
On the coast north of the Columbia	50,000
" " south " "	80,000

I am glad to report the packing of objectionable fall fish has almost altogether ceased, and I have no doubt that no more will be attempted to be put up after this.

A fact to be noted in the drift of business is that out of 12 co-operative canneries, worked on the plan of having only fishermen and workmen connected with the cannery as stock owners, only two are now being worked on that plan, all the others having had to close out of business.

Extensive preparations are being made for the coming season.

Alaska, however, is claiming the attention of a great number in this vicinity, who are caught by the promise of the low price of fish, irrespective of other considerations.

A new industry, which may perhaps develop itself, and may be of interest to florists and horticulturists, is the gathering and shipment of forest mosses for orchid cultivation, decoration, and plant transportation. *A small industry.*

The vessels coming to this river show an increase in tonnage over any other year, and in numbers over last year: the proportion of tonnage of vessels under the British flag still shows its usual very large proportion. Rates of freight increased at the latter part of the year to 1l. 12s. 6d. for orders to the United Kingdom, but declined at the end of the year. *Shipping.*

The jetty at the mouth of the Columbia river is still slowly progressing, a comparatively large appropriation from Congress allowing the work to be continued. It is claimed that the increased length of the jetty, though short as yet, has shown its usefulness in a better depth on the bar. *Government improvement.*

The largest number of immigrants are attracted here from the older lumber-producing States east of the Missouri river to engage in lumber manufacturing, but I notice that a good proportion of natives of Great Britain are settling here. *Immigration.*

The health of the district still remains very good. No contagious diseases have made their appearance. *Health.*

Annex A.—RETURN of all Shipping at the Port of Astoria, Oregon, U.S., during the Year 1888.

ENTERED.

Nationality.	Sailing.		Steam.		Total.	
	Number of Vessels.	Tons.	Number of Vessels.	Tons.	Number of Vessels.	Tons.
British	100	113,439	8	4,932	108	118,371
American	9	12,415	6	4,383	15	16,798
Norwegian	2	1,745	...	...	2	1,745
Total	111	127,699	14	9,315	125	137,014
" for the year preceding	...	...	...	...	97	109,409

UNITED STATES.

CLEARED.

Nationality.	Sailing. Number of Vessels.	Sailing. Tons.	Steam. Number of Vessels.	Steam. Tons.	Total. Number of Vessels.	Total. Tons.
British	105	126,202	8	4,932	113	131,134
American	11	12,399	10	10,596	21	22,995
German	1	1,726	...	...	1	1,726
Norwegian	2	1,745	...	...	2	1,745
Total	119	142,072	18	15,528	137	157,600
„ for the year preceding	...	...	...	...	109	124,082

Annex B.—RETURN of Principal Articles of Export from Astoria, Oregon, U.S., during the Year 1888.

Articles.		1888. Quantity.	1888. Value.	1887. Quantity.	1887. Value.
			£		£
Preserved salmon	Cases	74,095	109,761	142,482	146,800
Wheat	Bushels	864,382	149,729	543,940	80,000
Flour	Barrels	38,357	28,657	18,781	14,600
Lumber	M. feet	2,723	7,030	3,297	7,800
Sundries	...	...	80	...	891
Total	...	...	295,257	...	250,091

RETURN of Principal Articles of Import for 1888.

Articles.		1888. Quantity.	1888. Value.	1887. Quantity.	1887. Value.
			£		£
Tin plates	Boxes	33,405	33,405	69,704	44,744
Salt	Tons	180	223	75	89
Coal	„	2,347	1,733	3,381	2,222
Sundries	...	...	135	...	...
Total	...	...	35,496	...	47,055

Annex C.—TABLE showing the Total Value of all Articles Exported from Astoria, Oregon, and Imported to Astoria, Oregon, from and to Foreign Countries during the Years 1888 and 1887.

Country.	Exports. 1888.	Exports. 1887.	Imports. 1888.	Imports. 1887.
	£	£	£	£
Great Britain	263,000	240,000	22,037	44,750
British colonies	1,511	73	1,729	2,274
Other countries	30,341	9,095	1	..
Total	294,852	249,168	23,767	47,024

Port Townsend, Washington Territory.

Mr. Vice-Consul Alexander reports as follows :—

I have endeavoured to make this report as complete and interesting as possible, and I have been materially assisted in doing so through the kindness of Leslie Cullom, Esq., the collector of customs at this port, who has given me every facility for procuring the desired information in regard to commerce and shipping, and to whom I am very much indebted; and also to Eugene Sample, Esq., the Governor of the territory.

This territory is naturally divided by the Cascade mountains into two great parts, commonly known as eastern and western Washington. These in turn are subdivided into lesser parts, known as countries; they include the Puget Sound country, the Chehalis country, the Lower Columbia country, the Walla Walla country, the Palouse country, the Big Band country, the Yakima country, the Okanogan country, the Spokana and Colville countries.

Of these countries the chief is the Puget Sound. This includes all the countries bordering upon the body of water from which it takes its name. These countries vary somewhat in soil, climate, resources, and interest; they are all timbered, all have fisheries, all have minerals, and all have common highways to and from the east, and to and from the ocean. The waters of the sound are deep, and wide and safe, and the world possesses no finer harbour or group of harbours than Puget Sound; surrounded by a country possessing great resources, which requires a large population to develop, with railways and shipping for transportation. Business is still in its infancy, and yet, upwards of 1,000 ships, averaging 2,000 tons each, sailed out of these waters in 1888 with timber and coal alone. The shipment of wheat is being entered upon in earnest. One railroad is only enough to commence the business; the completion of the second and third roads will secure for Puget Sound a monopoly of the wheat transportation of Eastern Washington and northern Idaho at least. This country is not lacking in agricultural resources, oats are grown to the extent of 1,000,000 bushels per annum, the average yield per acre is at least 60 bushels, varying from 3*l*. 15*s*. to 6*l*. per ton. This is the great hop country of the territory, as well as the great fruit region; apples, pears, plums, quinces, prunes, cherries, strawberries, currants, and all small fruits grow in great quantities, and are of excellent quality. The climate, by providing green pastures the greater part of the year, and an enormous production of hay, adapts the Puget Sound country to the interests of the dairyman. *The Puget Sound country.*

Under this head are included the countries of Chehalis and Lewis, extending from the Pacific Ocean in the west to the summits of the Cascade mountains on the east, an area of 4,200 miles; it has one harbour, into which empties the Chehalis river after passing through fine agricultural lands still undeveloped. This country produces wheat, oats, hay, vegetables, hops, fruit, butter, and pigs; it is also heavily wooded in parts with fir, spruce, hemlock, cedar, ash and maple, and the getting of this timber into market has commenced a great industry. *The Chehalis country.*

In this are included all the countries fronting on the Columbia river from Pacific ocean to the Cascade mountains. It is timbered, well watered, and the valleys are exceedingly fertile. The leading industries are farming, lumbering and fishing. *The Lower Columbia country.*

This country is a triangular tract of land of almost 11,000 square miles, bounded by the Cascade mountains, Columbia, and Wenatchee rivers, and through the heart of which runs the Yakima river. This *The Yakima country.*

country compared with that of Puget Sound, is lightly timbered, and the timber inferior. There is some fir, pine and other woods chiefly on the mountain slopes, a number of small saw-mills being engaged in its preparation for the market. The great resource of the country is agriculture, it has done more to induce settlement and bring in capital than all else. The Wenatchee, Kittitas, and other valleys grow immense crops of grain, stock thrive in them, and to them for twenty years past have the Puget Sound towns looked for their supply of meat. In the mountains, and on the hills and wide plateaux adjacent to these valleys, are the finest bunch-grass stock-ranges of the north-west. Hops, vegetables, and fruit of the very finest kind are grown. Irrigation is in common use, and by means of the water so obtained vast tracts of land, otherwise dry and sterile, are brought into a high state of cultivation. In the Natchess and Tietan valleys, at the head waters of the Ahtanum, are inexhaustable coal-fields; besides gold, silver, iron and limestone. The only railroad yet is the northern Pacific's Cascade branch, but among others leading into this country are the Washington Central and the Seattle, Lake Shore, and Eastern.

Wenatchee. Kittitas.

Ahtanum.]

The Spokana country. This occupies the north-east portion of the territory, it is watered by the Spokana river and Clarke's Fork of the Columbia, with a number of small lakes. In the north are a continuance of the Okanogan hills and mountains, containing rich deposits of gold and silver. The timber is light, and wheat and stock are the chief products.

The Big Band country. The "Big Band" is a term applied to a great area of country in Central Washington, bounded on three sides by the Columbia river. This river flows in a rocky bed far below the level of the surrounding country, and, making a long detour, travels 200 miles to reach a point half that distance from the beginning of the "Band." Water is obtained by digging wells, the springs being all taken by the first settlers. This is strictly an agricultural country, the soil is ready for the crop, and attracts the settler at once. A large number of immigrants have gone into this country during the past year.

The Palouse country. The Palouse river has given its name to this section. The soil is very rich and productive, enormous crops of wheat being raised; farming is the chief occupation.

The Okanogan country. This country includes a region of about 9,000 square miles, bounded on the north by British Columbia, on the east by the Columbia river, on the south by the Columbia and Wenatchee rivers, and on the west by the Cascade mountains. In the south-western quarter the country is mostly low and open, to the north and east it is hilly, all through these hills are to be found rivers, lakes, and valleys, making charming places for farms; now cattle are raised in great quantities. This country is very rich in precious metals. The quartz on the Methow river is of a very rich character, and there is every reason to believe that, in the Okanogan country, Washington will have a mining region to be compared with anything in Colorado, Montana, Idaho, or Nevada.

The Walla Walla country. This country occupies the south-eastern portion of the territory. The first farming in eastern Washington was done here. The soil is extremely fertile, and for 30 years enormous crops have been grown on the same land without enrichment or irrigation. The surplus wheat of this country will amount to 250,000 tons annually. Great quantities of grapes, peaches, melons, prunes, berries and other fruits are grown and exported. From the Blue mountains, wood is obtained; the whole country is well watered by numerous streams.

Foreign commerce. In foreign commerce a great advance was made this year. Four ships loaded with general merchandise, arrived in Puget Sound from

Liverpool. Five ships came in from Japan with full cargoes of tea, and a large number of vessels, more than in all previous years combined, sailed for Europe freighted with the wheat of Washington territory. Timber exports to South America, Australia, Asia, and the islands of the Pacific, aggregated 150,000,000 feet, requiring 200 ships for transportation. Trade with British Columbia kept several large and magnificent steamers constantly employed, averaging 10 trips a week, their registered tonnage aggregating weekly upwards of 1,600.

The great resource of Western Washington in earlier days was timber, this for a long time exceeded in value all other products combined; this is now no longer the case, as coal and other resources are produced in large quantities, still the making and marketing of timber was never so great as in 1888. Many new mills were built, old mills enlarged, logging railroads were constructed, and a product 25 per cent. greater than ever before was put upon the market. The sawmills of Washington territory have a present daily capacity of 4,000,000 feet. The total cut of timber for the year was 706,985,000 feet, valued, in the rough, at about 1,556,000*l*. Estimating that 15 per cent. of the timber was dressed, and allowing each mill the usual amount of laths, pickets, and wood-slats, the value of the output in round numbers was 1,800,000*l*. During the same time these mills shipped 1,500,000 lineal feet of piles. Probably 400,000,000 feet were sent by rail and ship out of the territory; the large remainder being required for local consumption. At no time during the year was timber a drag on the market, prices were remunerative, rough timber being steady at 2*l*. to 2*l*. 2*s*. per 1,000 feet. Last September, Melbourne alone took 15,000,000 feet of Puget Sound fir, more than was formerly taken in a year.

Timber.

The year has been one of marked prosperity to the coal industry of Washington territory; it commanded exorbitant prices during the year, and the profits of its production were enormous; the output for the year was 1,100,000 tons, valued at about 800,000*l*. The prices realised show a marked increase over the total of last year, which great increase is mainly due to the strike amongst the coal-miners of Australia, and to the prevailing high over-sea freights. The principal market for Puget Sound coal is San Francisco.

Coal.

This territory is exceedingly rich in minerals, but owing to lack of capital to develop these resources a very limited idea can be formed of its value. Very little has been done with iron, but it is known that there are large deposits of this mineral in many parts of the territory; in some places there are large ledges of almost pure ironstone; in other parts deposits of a bog ore are met with, particularly in Jefferson County; on Port Townsend Bay a smelting furnace has been in operation from time to time for some years, from which 5,000 or 6,000 tons of pig-iron are now produced annually, its quality is excellent, and commands the highest rates in the San Francisco market. A magnetic ore has been discovered at Snoqualmie, in King County, and Cle-elum, in Kittitas County, also in the Skagit country, and preparations are being made to operate it.

Mineral deposits.

The recent discoveries in the new country of Okanogan of precious metals have caused great excitement, 1,500 quartz (chiefly gold) claims have been recorded; these mines will be thoroughly tested during the coming year.

Almost every mineral is found in this territory in greater or less quantities, among the principal are galena and copper, in addition to gold and silver.

Sandstone, of excellent quality for building purposes, is fairly dis-

(681)

Agriculture.

tributed throughout the country. There are also reports of marble-stone having been discovered, but it is impossible to develop many of these resources until transportation facilities are made.

As the country settles up, and immigration increases, so will the agricultural resources of the territory; large areas of land are being reclaimed, and made ready for the plough; river bottom-lands are being cleared, exposing a soil of remarkable productiveness. The farmer is well repaid for all his labour, everything that he can produce has been in great demand, and sold at prices leaving him a large profit; the great obstacle to the farmer was the means of transportation. The lack of railroad communication with the eastern portion of Washington Territory has hitherto prevented the Puget Sound waters from getting its share of the great wheat trade. The completion of the Cascade branch of the main line of the Northern Pacific Railway is the principal factor in the increased shipments.

Prior to the year 1877, the immense output of the Walla Walla district was shipped viâ Portland, Oregon, and not through its natural outlet, the Puget Sound. The wheat product of the entire territory is estimated at 15,000,000 bushels, equivalent to cargoes for 300 large ships; the yield per acre of eastern Washington exceeded that of Oregon, California, Dakota, and all other parts of the American Union, according to the Government reports; wheat can be grown in this section for 1s. 8d. per bushel, and sold at an average of 3s. per bushel. From the increased average of eastern Washington, with the preparations for handling and shipping wheat, it is estimated that the shipments of 1889 will be over 150,000 tons.

Oats are grown principally in the Puget Sound country, averaging 60 bushels to the acre, the principal market is San Francisco; this is also the great hay country.

Fruits and vegetables are grown successfully and profitably in any portion of the territory, varying, of course, according to the climate.

Western Washington, particularly the Puget Sound country, has obtained a world-wide reputation for its hops, upwards of 3,200 acres are planted in hops, the production being 1,600 lbs. per acre, against 600 lbs. per acre in the eastern States; 800 lbs. per acre in Europe; 1,000 lbs. per acre in Oregon; and 1,200 lbs. per acre in California. No such thing as a pest, blight, or failure was ever known here, and the only thing that limits the production is the want of pickers. In the early years the Indians were the sole reliance of the farmers for help to secure the crop; the large increase, though of the average, the gradual decrease of the supply of Indian help from their more fixed habits, together with the inclination of the white people to participate in the hop harvest has led up to a gradual change, and fully 10,000 persons are required about a month each year to gather the crop. Prices varied during the year from 7½d. to 1s. per lb., or an average, say, of 10d. per lb.

Fisheries.

The salmon catch on the Columbia river during the year was 360,000 cases. Giving this territory credit for one-half, we have 180,000 cases; 25,000 cases were put up on Puget Sound, doubling that of the best previous year's record; about 20,000 cases were put up at Gray's Harbour and other places; these figures aggregate 225,000 cases. The trade employs about 3,000 persons several months in the year, the capital invested being 200,000l., and the marketable value exceeded the investment. A few thousand barrels of salted salmon are usually put up each year, and during the past year the business was inaugurated of sending to eastern markets salmon in refrigerator railway carriages. The fisheries were also further extended last year. Three large fishing schooners came from the coast of Massachusetts, on the Atlantic, round Cape Horn, which were employed in catching halibut, and preparing it for market, their fishing grounds extending from the mouth of the Columbia river to Alaska; they met with very encouraging success; the bulk of the catch was sent, viâ rail, to the eastern States. The fur-seal fishery remained about as usual. The United States Government, through the fish commissioner, sent out during the winter over 100 lobsters and many thousands of eggs, which were planted in the Puget Sound waters. It is expected that they will thrive and multiply; it is an experiment. The whole consignment came across the continent in a railway carriage constructed especially for this purpose, and a commissioner to attend to them.

The waters of Puget Sound are noted for their freedom from obstructions to navigation. The Straits of Juan de Fuca, bounded on the south side by Washington territory, on the north by Vancouver Island, run east and west for a distance of 90 miles, varying in width from 11 to 20 miles. The prevailing winds in winter are easterly, and during summer months westerly. Vessels during westerly winds sail into Port Townsend (the port of entry with the custom house for the Puget Sound district), and when winds are unfavourable can engage the services of one of the numerous tow-boats found cruising off Cape Flattery, the entrance to the Straits. *Navigation.*

From Port Townsend vessels tow to port of loading, if for timber to one of the mills at, say, Port Discovery, eight miles distant, or to Hadlock, three miles; or to Ludlow, 12 miles; or to Gamble, 19; or to Blakelay, 33; or to Seattla, 34; or to Utsaladdy, 60; or to Gig Harbour, 62; or to Jacoma, 62; for coal to Seattla or Jacoma; if for wheat to Jacoma; all these several ports have facilities for loading ships of the largest tonnage. When loaded these vessels return to Port Townsend for final clearance from the custom house, thence proceeding to sea.

Washington territory is acquiring a railroad system of great magnitude and of national importance. Owing to its remoteness from the great centres of population and wealth, and to the consequent slowness of its earlier development, but little progress was made in railroad building until within the last few years. During the last year many new companies have been organised, and operations commenced. In 1885 the railroads of the territory aggregated 866 miles in length; and in 1888, 1,410 miles. The impulse that has been given to the population and business of this territory by the construction of 300 or 400 miles of railroad has been great. The most important railroad is the Northern Pacific Cascade branch, giving a main line from St. Paul to Jacoma, and direct communication between eastern and western Washington territory, and the great factor in the increased wheat exportation. The Seattla, Lake Shore, and Eastern is being built eastward from the Puget Sound to the grain fields of Eastern Washington territory, and with the ultimate view of connecting with some eastern road. Perhaps the most important of the roads now under construction is the line to connect with the Canadian Pacific, the completion of which will give all rail communication with eastern Canada to the principal towns of Puget Sound. *Railways.*

The population of this territory is growing marvellously, and the immigration has been very large, particularly during the year. The first census, that of 1860, gave evidence of 11,590 inhabitants; the second census, that of 1870, of 23,450; the third census, that of 1880, *Population.*

of 75,000. The gain of the number of inhabitants of the first decade was about 100 per cent.; the gain of the second decade was about 200 per cent. It is estimated that the population at the end of last year numbered 250,000, although many are inclined to put it at 300,000.

Territorial wealth.

The taxable property of the people of the territory in the year 1874 was assessed at about 2,500,000*l.*; in 1880, about 4,500,000*l.*; in 1884, 10,000,000*l.*; and last year 17,000,000*l.* The legal rate of interest is 10 per cent.

Weather.

The climate of Western Washington is governed entirely by the equatorial trade winds and the Japanese gulf-stream. In the winter season, from October to March, the warm equatorial trade-winds, laden with moisture blows steadily against the northern coast, keeping the temperature between 36° and 56°. In the spring, summer and autumn the trade winds blow south-easterly against the Alaska coast, veer round to the north-west, and come down the coast line, tempering the sun's heat. During June, July, August and September there are gentle breezes from the ocean every afternoon, and an exceedingly hot day is seldom known. The highest temperature in June was 76°, lowest 43°, average $61\frac{1}{2}°$; July, highest 87°, lowest 45°, average $62\frac{1}{2}°$; August, highest 88°, lowest 46°, average $62\frac{1}{4}°$. The coldest weather was in last January when the thermometer indicated 3° above zero, and lasted three days; the average temperature for the month was $33\frac{1}{2}°$. The eastern part of the territory is very much colder in winter, and correspondingly warmer in summer.

The country has been generally free from epidemics and diseases, although there were last winter some cases of small-pox, but they were strictly quarantined. There has been no contagious or infectious diseases, as far as I have been able to ascertain, among the cattle and horses; the whole country has been really in a very healthy condition, considering the great tide of immigration from all countries which has taken place.

I have appended to this report three annexes, marked respectively A., B. and C., from which it will be seen that there has been a marked improvement in commerce, particularly with Great Britain and the colonies; I have every reason to believe that next year will show a still greater increase. Trade during the past year has been one of great activity and prosperity, and the coming year, with the new mills and other industries projected, and with the increased railroad services, has an exceedingly bright outlook.

Annex A.—RETURN of all Shipping at the Port of Port Townsend in the Year 1888.

ENTERED.

Nationality.	Sailing. Number of Vessels.	Sailing. Tonnage.	Steam. Number of Vessels.	Steam. Tonnage.	Total. Number of Vessels.	Total. Tonnage.
British	68	76,404	20	2,706	88	79,110
American	162	164,162	767	685,377	927	849,539
Norway and Sweden	21	17,698	...	...	21	17,698
German	3	3,027	...	...	3	3,027
Chilian	4	3,371	...	...	4	3,371
Hawaiian	5	2,822	...	...	5	2,822
Italian	1	974	...	...	1	974
Russian	1	968	...	...	1	968
Nicaraguan	1	728	...	...	1	728
Total	266	270,154	787	688,083	1,053	958,237
,, for the year preceding	143	118,426	704	351,636	847	470,062

RETURN of all Shipping at the Port of Port Townsend in the Year 1888

CLEARED.

Nationality.	Sailing.		Steam.		Total.	
	Number of Vessels.	Tonnage.	Number of Vessels.	Tonnage.	Number of Vessels.	Tonnage.
British	73	85,059	21	2,814	94	87,873
American	173	182,712	767	658,353	910	841,065
Norway and Sweden	19	15,499	...	...	19	15,499
German	4	4,043	...	...	4	4,043
Chilian	4	3,374	...	...	4	3,374
Hawaiian	5	2,822	...	...	5	2,822
Italian	1	974	...	...	1	974
Russian	1	968	...	...	1	968
Total	280	295,451	788	661,167	1,068	956,618
,, for the year preceding	148	121,702	688	322,997	826	414,699

Annex B.—RETURN of Principal Articles of Export from Port Townsend during the Years 1887 and 1888.

Articles.		1888.		1887.	
		Quantity.	Value.	Quantity.	Value.
			£		£
Cattle	Heads	615	3,925	1,193	7,610
Hogs	,,	3,186	2,279	4,043	2,870
Horses	,,	131	2,672	100	2,613
Sheep	,,	23,732	10,512	22,802	10,806
Other animals	...	...	406	...	762
Wheat	Bushels	2,629,794	449,715	76,835	10,472
Flour	Barrels.	54,814	44,404	33,784	25,951
Other breadstuffs	...	...	11,161	...	4,948
Butter, eggs, &c.	...	...	3,811	...	3,792
Fish	...	...	509	...	680
Furs	...	...	11,400	...	3,361
Iron manufactures	...	...	13,507	...	10,263
Liquors	...	...	1,241	...	1,262
Oils	Gallons	...	8,141	232,767	918
Provisions—					
Bacon, ham, &c.	Lbs.	880,892	21,644	939,531	12,336
Timber	Met. feet	373,014,951	761,507	79,722	141,696
Agricultural implements	...	...	2,245	...	...
Books, maps, stationery	...	...	3,019	...	...
Fruit, fresh and canned	...	...	3,894	...	...
Hops	...	...	6,879	...	...
India rubber manufactures	...	...	2,981	...	...
Leather manufactures	...	...	2,167	...	...
Musical instruments	...	...	1,751	...	...
Tobacco, cigars, &c.	...	...	2,239	...	...
Vegetables, fresh and canned	...	...	763	...	...
Wool and woollen manufactrs.	...	...	1,319	...	...
Other articles	...	...	39,814	...	68,992
Total	...	...	1,413,958	...	309,382

UNITED STATES.

RETURN of Principal Articles of Import from Port Townsend during the Years 1887 and 1888.

Articles.				1888. Quantity.	1888. Value.	1887. Quantity.	1887. Value.
Free—					£		£
Raw furs and skins			...	...	33,720	...	25,507
Household furniture and personal effects			...	...	7,249	...	...
Tea			...	...	2,034	...	...
Other articles			...	...	576	...	...
Dutiable—							
Liquors			Gallons	...	1,654	4,513	808
Steel rails			Tons	...	13,988	4,359	21,471
Rice			Lbs.	...	2,346	364,905	1,504
Salt			...	...	700	...	...
Chinese goods			...	...	757	...	...
Cement			Barrels	...	605	2,056	469
Pig iron			Tons	...	1,030	1,020	2,248
Iron ore			,,	...	2,839	...	...
Coal			...	...	3,012	365	392
Wool			...	...	460	...	88
Other articles			...	...	6,844	...	12,582
Total			...	...	77,814	...	65,069

Annex C.—TABLE showing the Total Value of all Articles Exported from Port Townsend and Imported to Port Townsend from and to Foreign Countries during the Years 1888 and 1887.

Country.	Exports. 1888.	Exports. 1887.	Imports. 1888.	Imports. 1887.
	£	£	£	£
Great Britain	289,405	10,643	26,685	24,644
British Columbia	183,180	136,999	556,559	40,134
British Possessions, Australia	169,719	86,244	20	6
France	121,091	..	..	..
Chile	32,315	27,625	..	..
Hawaiian Islands	27,649	28,448	..	62
Peru	13,705	6,544	10	..
Mexico	12,299	3,840	..	..
Belgium	12,176	..	..	..
China	5,543	4,127	..	17
Argentine Republic	5,307	3,333	..	..
British East Indies	1,644	..	..	..
Uruguay	1,644	1,152	..	..
Japan	..	..	1,432	191
Germany	..	..	1	..
Other countries	..	877	..	15
Total	875,677	309,332	584,707	65,069

LOS ANGELES AND WILMINGTON.

Mr. Vice-Consul Mortimer reports as follows:—

For the past five years I have annually chronicled a remarkable growth in population, wealth, and industries in this district. The prosperity of the past has at last received a check, the extent of which it is as yet difficult to determine. Over speculation in real estate has produced its inevitable results; undoubtedly, however, the lesson now being taught will tend in future towards more permanent prosperity, though the growth may not be as heretofore phenomenal.

The cessation of speculation in real estate throughout this district has reacted on every branch of business, a large number of tradesmen have had to close their establishments in this city, and there are now hundreds of houses and shops to let, where formerly exorbitant rents were readily paid. Business generally is much more inactive and depressed than the following statements indicate. The principal architects of this city report the construction of buildings in the past three years as follows:— *Introductory remarks.*

		£
1886.	Buildings of the value of	800,000
1887.	,, ,, ,,	1,500,000
1888.	,, ,, ,,	2,000,000

For purposes of taxation property is assessed at about one-third of its value. The assessed value of the city and county of Los Angeles (the chief county of this district) for the past three years has been as follows:—

	£
1886..	8,000,000
1887..	19,000,000
1888..	21,500,000

Official records show that the aggregate considerations named in all conveyances of real estate, filed for record in the past three years, has been as follows:—

	£
1886..	5,600,000
1887..	19,000,000
1888..	12,500,000

The actual transactions for 1888 constitute, probably, not more than a third of the total for that year, the balance representing the completion of sales negotiated during the "boom" of 1887. Owing to the large amount of English capital invested here, I give elsewhere in this report further particulars about the "Boom in Real Estate." The Southern Pacific Company handled upwards of 500,000 tons of freight in Los Angeles in 1887, and upwards of 600,000 tons in 1888. I have not received particulars of the amount of freight handled by the rival company, The Atchison Topeka and Santa Fé Railway. A Bill is now before Congress to constitute the counties of this district (Los Angeles, San Bernardino, Ventura, Santa Barbara, San Luis Obispo, and Kern, 40,000 square miles) with San Diego (14,000 square miles) a new state, "Southern California."

The present population of the proposed state is but little over 300,000, of which more than half live in the city and county of Los Angeles. The fact that within above limits a population of several millions can be maintained in greater comfort than in any other portion of the United States, justifies the conclusion that the present depressed state of business is temporary, and will, I think, give place to an era of great prosperity in the near future.

Trade and Commerce.

The principal exports are grain, wine, and fruits of all descriptions.

The grain crop showed a most remarkable decrease on the product of the previous year, due, as stated elsewhere, to the purchase by *Grain.*

speculators of large tracts of land, who held for a rise in price, and did not cultivate the soil. The crop was so light that the surplus for export was nominal.

Canned fruits. I have no accurate statistics of the quantity of fruit canned in this city and vicinity. The Southern California Packing Company inform me that they have canned 700 tons of fruits, and 800 tons of tomatos. A dozen other packing companies have done a like amount of business. The fruit costs ½d. per lb., is packed in 2½ lb. cans, and sells here for 8s. to 11s. per dozen.

Honey. Large quantities of honey are shipped to Liverpool by way of New Orleans, value here 2d. per lb.

Raisins. It is stated in the press here that "4,000 boxes of California raisins, sent recently to London, realised better prices than the famous Malaga layers, and, in consequence, orders have come to this State from Amsterdam, Vienna, and Australia." The product of raisins has increased from 20,000 boxes in 1880 to 300,000 in 1888.

Oranges. The crop of oranges for 1887 amounted to 1,400 car-loads (14,000 tons), the present crop is estimated at 2,000 car-loads. This industry continues to be profitable in the districts where the trees have not been attacked by the "white scale."

Imports.

Los Angeles to be a port of delivery. The statistics in Annex B. convey no idea of the trade of Los Angeles, most of the imports being entered at San Diego, San Francisco, and New Orleans, and brought here by rail. A Bill is now before Congress to make Los Angeles a port of entry for the delivery of foreign goods brought here by rail.

Coals. The bulk of the coals consumed here continue to be imported from Australia. The average freight for the year has been 24s. per ton. For years previously the average freight was 14s. per ton, and I am informed that ships are again offering at 14s. and 15s. per ton. I am at a loss to understand why ships come here at these rates, in view of the facts— (1) that there is no coal here to compete with Australian coal; (2) that there is practically nothing for export, and ships have to pay 7s. per ton for sand ballast to get away; and (3) that ships have to lie in the outer harbour, and discharge into lighters, and in winter are in constant danger of being driven ashore by gales from the south-east. From 3 to 4 per cent. of the coals imported are lost in discharging from ship to lighter. Wholesale price of coals here is 2l. per ton.

Paints. Glass. Portland cement. Whitier, Fuller, and Co. inform me that they have received four cargoes in the past year, of 2,000 tons each, of dry paints, glass, and Portland cement. The average price of imported paints here is 8l. per ton (of 2,000 lbs.). Portland cement sells for 4l. to 4l. 10s. per ton. Upwards of 30 miles of cement side-walk has been laid in this city alone in the past year.

Crockery. A large amount of English crockery is sold here. Boote's 8-inch semi-porcelain dinner-plate sells for 6s. per dozen. Ironstone china, 4s. 5d. per dozen.

Hardware. Harness, &c. Haydn, Lewis, and Co. inform me that the demand for "fine goods" is increasing; in the past year cheap goods sold better than the finer qualities.

Tea. W. H. Murray, formerly a tea planter in Ceylon, has opened a store here for the sale of pure Ceylon teas, and is meeting with fair success. Green teas are so universally used here, however, that it will be some time before the superior quality of the wholesome Ceylon teas, sold by the new firm, will be thoroughly appreciated.

In addition to the imports noted in Annex B., upwards of 150,000,000 Lumber. feet of lumber was received from domestic ports, worth here over 5*l.* per 1,000 feet; also 500,000 railway ties, value 50,000*l.*

Shipping and Navigation.

In my report for 1887, I stated that the Government Engineer Breakwater advocated the construction of a breakwater from Point Firmin (see to protect map accompanying my report for the year 1886) in an easterly direc- outer harbour. tion, at an estimated cost of 800,000*l.* The Southern Pacific Company recently built a line from San Pedro to Point Firmin, 2½ miles, and commenced the construction of a pier designed to be 3,000 feet long and 100 feet wide. Work on this pier was suspended after a few hundred feet had been constructed, the Company having doubtless discovered that foreign-going ships could not safely discharge cargo alongside it until the breakwater is completed.

The Southern Pacific Company has been credited in the past with a desire to retard the improvement of Wilmington Harbour, on the ground that it was more profitable to haul freight from San Francisco to Los Angeles (482 miles), than from Wilmington to Los Angeles (21 miles).

In the past year, a number of ships with general cargoes for Los Angeles entered at San Diego, and their cargoes were shipped thence to Los Angeles, over the Atchison, Topeka, and Santa Fé Railway (110 miles). This railway is competing with the Southern Pacific Company for the business of Southern California, and the fact that ships with general cargoes for Los Angeles are now being sent to San Diego, explains the efforts of the Southern Pacific Company to bring ship and rail together at Wilmington (San Pedro).

The first appropriation by Congress for the improvement of Wilmington Harbour was for 40,000*l.* in 1871; 10 appropriations have been made since that date, amounting in the aggregate to 156,000*l.* The last appropriations were 10,000*l.* in 1884 and 15,000*l.* in 1886. In 1884 the Government Engineer reported that 45,000*l.* was necessary to deepen the channel sufficiently to admit foreign-going ships to the inner harbour. Efforts were made at the recent session of Congress to Appropria- secure an appropriation of 100,000*l.*, as a first appropriation for the tions for breakwater. The Bill passed the House, but was not signed by the improvement President. I am informed that the appropriation will probably be of Wilming- made at the next session of Congress. If my information is correct, ton Harbour. it would appear that the project of deepening the channel has been abandoned in favour of a breakwater in the outer harbour.

There is no competition in the business of discharging and loading Stevedoring. ships, the whole concern being in the hands of the Wilmington Transportation Company; their charges at present are as follows:—for discharging coals, 2*s.* 5*d.* per ton (60 c.), for this sum they supply donkey engines and water for same, men, tubs, &c., and, if the crew assist, the master is allowed 12*s.* per day for each sailor employed. Vessels discharging with their own crews can hire engines, &c., at Charges for the following rates:—donkey engine and driver per day, 2*l.* 12*s.*; water discharging for same, about 1*l.* 12*s.* per day; towing engine to ship and back, cargo. 6*l.* per day; tubs and trucks, 2*d.* per ton. The Company supply ballast (sand) and water at following rates:—ballast in lighter alongside ship, 5*s.* per ton; putting same on board, 2*s.* per ton; water, 1*d.* per gallon. In the past year, the "Plymouth" and one other British ship did not employ their crews to work coals, in consequence, they got quicker dispatch—the longshore men doing the work much more

UNITED STATES.

rapidly—and the crews did not desert. As deserters have to be replaced with coasting seamen, at 6*l.* per month, owners should consider whether it would not pay not to work the crews; sailors engaged in England at 2*l.* 10*s.* per month naturally object to do work here, for which longshore men receive 12*s.* to 15*s.* per day.

Pilotage. The Wilmington pilot claims pilotage fees, at the rate of 16*s.* per foot draught, from ships anchoring outside the outer-harbour line, where all foreign-going ships anchor, whether the master accepts his services or not, when payment is refused he libels the ship; and to save detention and expense, the masters pay his demands which average 16*l.* per ship.

Pilotage not compulsory. The question whether pilotage is compulsory in this open roadstead unprotected by the land, has not yet been judicially determined, two cases commenced about 18 months ago are, however, pending in the United States District Court in Los Angeles, as the statutes of California providing for the remuneration of pilots contemplate the piloting of a vessel into a port or harbour, and this service is certainly not performed at Wilmington, I am of opinion that pilotage cannot be held to be compulsory. Representations were made to the Governor about two years ago which resulted in the dismissal of the pilot. He was subsequently re-appointed, and the present Governor declines to interfere, leaving the matter to the decision of the courts.

The masters of several American ships have informed me that the pilot does not attempt to collect fees from them. The superintendent at Washington of the United States Coast and Geodetic Survey, writes that he is unable to define the harbour of Wilmington, but inclines to the opinion that the harbour is contained within a line drawn from Point Firmin to a point a little south of the mouth of the New San Gabriel river. This would leave the anchorage about half-a-mile outside the harbour-line.

Casualty. The British ship "Respigadera," from Australia, with a cargo of 2,500 tons of coals, struck a reef off Point Firmin when approaching the anchorage, sank, and became a total loss. The reef on which she struck was but 520 yards from the land, and although its existence was know it was not buoyed, nor was it marked on the master's chart.

AGRICULTURE.

Profits in agriculture. I am satisfied that the profits in fruit and general farming, on lands purchased at a reasonable figure, are remunerative here, though by no means as large as represented in the pamphlets issued by the railways, the Los Angeles Board of Trade and the Los Angeles Chamber of Commerce. These latter associations by the way are not departments of the Government, as many of my English correspondents suppose, but are simply associations of the principal business men designed to further the interests of the city and district. The Chamber of Commerce recently issued a pamphlet in which I find the following statement:— "The bearing grape vines in Los Angeles county aggregate 17,500 acres, which yield over 100,000 tons per annum. The vintage for this season is estimated at 3,500,000 gallons, and the production of brandy 1,000,000 gallons." I am advised that the average yield of vines in full bearing, per acre, is less than 4 tons; from the foregoing statement it would appear to be 5·71 tons per acre. In view of the fact that the disease now attacking the vines in this district is seriously menacing that industry, a statement that the product is 5·71 tons per acre is, to say the least, misleading. In the same pamphlet I find returns of profits made in various branches of agriculture, which, although each example may be true, are misleading in so far as they convey the idea that such profits are normal, especially with regard to orange culture, which industry owing to the ravages of the "white scale" is in a most deplorable condition in many places in this district. The Board of Trade also issue an annual report descriptive of the resources of this district. In their last report the President makes the following statement:—"I learn from authentic sources that over 75 per cent. of our land of all descriptions has been ploughed up, new orchards set out, and grain sown in enormous quantities." This statement was made last year when it was well known that the acreage in grain was less than usual, and as the highest estimate I can get of the land in cultivation is only 30 per cent. instead of 75, it will be seen that the statements referred to are not literally correct.

In my report for 1887 I directed attention to a new disease attacking the vines in this district, the ravages of which are steadily increasing, a number of vineyards having died in the past year. M. Pierre Viala, Professor of Viticulture in the National School of Agriculture at Montpellier, France, after careful examination of diseased vines, was unable to name the disease, or determine its character. Professor Dowlen, an expert employed by the State Board of Viticulture, reported recently, after examination of diseased vines sent to him from the north, that the disease has appeared in the vineyards in the northern part of the State. The presence of this disease is characterised by the leaves of the vines turning yellow and dropping off in the spring after the young branches have acquired a growth of 1 to 3 feet. Unless a remedy be discovered the extinction of the industry is but a question of time. *Disease attacking the vines.*

A large number of orange orchards have been cut down owing to the ravages of the cottony cushion scale, commonly called the "white scale." Several orchards, of 200 to 300 acres each, are now so badly attacked that the trees have ceased bearing, and will certainly die. A consignment of Australian parasites has been received here, which it is hoped will exterminate the "scale." It is stated that these parasites have proved effective in destroying the "scale" in Australia. In my report for 1885 I stated that the presence of this pest was ascribed by many to the fact that fertilizers not having been used the soil was becoming impoverished; and I cited Mr. Chapman's 250 acre orchard at San Gabriel which had been fertilized and was free of "white scale" and other pests. The fact that the trees in this grove are now dying, would indicate that good husbandry alone is not sufficient to conquer the pest. Mr. Chapman recently resigned his position as State Horticultural Commissioner, stating that losses by ravages of the "white scale" compelled him to retire from Horticultural pursuits. In my report for 1886 I stated that it was proposed to kill all scale bugs by constructing a tent over each tree and generating hydrocyanic acid gas in the tent. This process has been successfully applied, the only objection to it being the expense, the lowest estimate of the cost per acre being 15*l*. *"White scale." Orange trees dying. Remedy for disease attacking orange trees.*

D. W. Coquillett, agent of the United States Department of Agriculture, in his report to the department says:—"The apparatus patented by John P. Culver of Los Angeles, Cal., for applying the gas treatment, not only kills the bug, but effectually destroys the egg and germ. I find this treatment more satisfactory and much superior to the different washes and sprays that are found to be injurious to the body of the tree."

Notwithstanding the ravages of the "white scale," new orchards are *New orange orchards.*

28   UNITED STATES.

constantly being planted. The "scale" has not yet appeared at Pomona, a settlement about 30 miles east of Los Angeles; an orchard of 35,000 trees (500 acres) is now being planted there.

Government land.

The records of the government land office in this city show the acreage of public lands disposed of in the past three years as follows:—

1886	242,467 acres.
1887	363,827 ,,
1888	462,197 ,,

POPULATION AND INDUSTRIES.

Population.

The population of this city has increased from 75,000 to 80,000 in the past year. In my last report I am credited with the statement that "it is not improbable that the population of this city will reach 250,000 within four years," is a clerical error for "a few years."

Factories.

The following list of factories is taken from the Chamber of Commerce Pamphlet:—

"Following is a list of the number and character of the manufacturing establishments now in operation in this city, the aggregate value of which exceeds 10,000 000 dol.

"Bricks and tiles, 13; book-binding, 7; breweries, 2; brooms and brushes, 2; cement and artificial stone, 18; cigars, 10; clothing, 53; confectionery, 30; chemicals, 2; contractors and builders, 150; canneries and fruit crystallizing, 2; car-builders (not including the railroad shops), 2; copper foundries and brass works, 3; flour and feed mills, 4; foundries, machinery and boilers, 19; furniture, 9; harness saddlery, 28; ice (artificial), 3; jewelry, 6; marble and stone cutting, 7; paper mill, 1; photography and photo-lithography, 15; painting and glazing, 45; planing mills, sash, door and box factories, 19; printing and publishing, 26; pottery and sewer pipe, 6; terra cotta and pressed brick, 2; water-pipe (iron), 7; wagons and carriages, 31; wood mantel manufactories, 3; wineries (many more outside the city), 6; miscellaneous, 51; total, 582. Miscellaneous includes wire works, soap, vinegar and pickles, perfumery, cane goods, electrical apparatus, fire works, cooperage, distillery, spice mills, shoddy mills, seal engraving, show cases, stencil and rubber stamp works, stair builders, mattress factories, straw goods, tents and awnings, trunks, taxidermy, wood engraving, compressed yeast, crackers and tin cans. A large number of small concerns, employing but a few hands, are not included in the above list."

Newspapers.

Six daily, 20 weekly, and 5 monthly newspapers are published in this city. One daily paper is published in the German language, two weekly in Spanish, and one weekly in French.

Rate of wages.

For several years past mechanics have received from 16s. to 24s. per day. In the past year wages have been reduced from 40 to 50 per cent., and thousands of good workmen are now out of employment.

Oil.

It is stated that the output of oil from the wells of Los Angeles and Venture counties have increased about 20 per cent. in the past year. Value of last year's product, 200,000l.

The following minerals are found in this district, most of them are undeveloped:—

"Alabaster, asbestos, asphaltum, bituminous rock, borax, cement (pozzolana stone), chalk, copper, cinnabar, fire clay, fire sand, gas (natural), gold, granite, graphite. gypsum, iron, limestone, lithographic stone, lead, marble, mica, nickel, onyx, petroleum, potash, potter's clay, rock soap, soap-stone, soda, salt (rock), silver, sandstone, sulphur, tin, talc, hydraulic lime."

To the forgoing may be added a very inferior quality of bituminous coal, not worth mining. As long as coal has to be imported from Australia, and sells here wholesale for 2l. per ton the average current price, the foregoing raw materials add little to the wealth of the country.

Public companies.

The aggregate capital stock of the public companies incorporated here in the year 1888 exceeds 13,500,000l.

The Southern Pacific Company has constructed 127 miles of railroad in this district in the past year, and the Atchison, Topeka and Santa Fé Railway has constructed 69 miles. Railway construction.

Work has been suspended for some months on the Southern Pacific branch line to connect Los Angeles and San Diego. The Atchison Coast line has been completed, giving that company control of the two railroads between Los Angeles and San Diego. Two railways to San Diego.

In my report for 1887 I stated that there was a reasonable probability of the construction of a line from Los Angeles to Salt Lake City, 641 miles. It is now asserted by the press here, that the Union Pacific Railway is interested in the proposed line. A franchise has been granted the company for a 60 foot right of way through this city, and some work has been done. The completion of the line is of the utmost importance to this city and district, as it will form the third competing line between Los Angeles and the eastern States, and also because it will pass through extensive coal fields which will insure to Los Angeles fuel at a price sufficiently low to admit of the establishment of various manufacturing industries. Railway to Salt Lake city.
Importance to Los Angeles of Salt Lake Railway.

The system of cable roads referred to in my last report as being in course of construction is now nearly completed, cost 300,000*l*. The aggregate length of the cable, electric, and horse car lines in the streets of this city is about 60 miles. Tramways.

The city is lighted by 114 electric lamps of 342,000 candle power. Electric lights.

Murders, suicides, and deaths by accident numbered nearly 200 in the year; divorces to the number of 115 were granted by the courts in this county alone.

Many of the foregoing particulars are apparently of local interest only. I give them, however, on account of the very considerable number of English immigrants, arriving and to arrive here.

General Remarks.

The rate of interest on the best first mortgage security continues to be 12 per cent. to 13 per cent. on sums of 1,000*l*. and under, and 2 per cent. to 3 per cent. less on larger sums. The taxes payable by the mortgagee vary from year to year, but have never exceeded 3 per cent. in this city. The amendment to the constitution providing for the taxation of mortgagees was intended to lighten the burden of the borrower at the expense of the capitalist; it has had the reverse effect, and is retarding the development of the country in various ways. Capitalists at a distance being apprehensive of an increase in taxation hesitate to send their money here for investment, and local capitalists, who expect to get 10 per cent. net, invariably reserve in their mortgages a rate more than sufficient to cover taxes. Rate of interest on mortgage.

Several English companies here have not proved as successful as they would have done had they been managed by competent Americans, or Englishmen conversant with American business methods. I hear of several others projected, some of which will probably be floated in London, and all of which, if my information is correct, will prove more profitable to the promoters than to the shareholders. English companies.

The business of raising thoroughbred race horses here is proving very remunerative; a year old colt raised here has just been sold in New York for 5,200*l*. Thoroughbred horses.

The average number of cloudy days per annum for the past ten years has been 49, and of rainy days, that is days on which more than one hundredth part of an inch fell, 41. The death rate is the lowest of any city in the United States, if we deduct from the total deaths from Climate.

consumption contracted elsewhere; making this deduction the rate is less than 9 per 1,000 per annum. I have made several quotations in this report from the Chamber of Commerce pamphlet, the following, in this connection is so exhaustive that it really leaves nothing for me to add:—"The foregoing is a mere outline of the vast and diversified resources of Southern California. The health-giving, invigorating and ever-enjoyable climate is the crowning glory of this wondrously endowed and beautiful land, where hope is extended to all sufferers who come in time from the life-destroying and malarial sections of the country in the east, and a haven of rest is offered to all who are weary and afflicted."

Immigrants. For the past four years I have made constant use of a circular letter I printed in 1885 as an answer to the numerous letters I receive from all parts of the world inquiring about this district. The following extract from it is still the best advice I can give intending immigrants, with this additional caution, that the cultivation of the grape has become hazardous in this district owing to the new disease referred to in this report:—"I would advise you, before finally deciding to come here, to subscribe for the weekly edition of one or more of the papers published here ('Herald,' 'Times,' and 'Express,' price, each, 8s. per annum). I would also advise you to correspond with the secretary of the Los Angeles Board of Trade, Los Angeles; the secretary of the California Immigration Association, San Francisco, and the secretary of the Chamber of Commerce, Los Angeles. The profits in fruit culture are greatly exaggerated in the immigration pamphlets issued in London by railway agents, and in the pamphlets issued by the Los Angeles Board of Trade. Persons having sufficient capital to engage in the cultivation of the grape on a large scale can make money here. I am not at present advising anyone to come here, except persons in delicate health who have means of support. You will find full information about the climate of this district in my consular report for 1884. No rain falls here in the summer, consequently the country is seen at its worst in autumn, which is, therefore, the best time for intending settlers to see it; defects that at other times are latent—such as the presence of alkali, want of water, &c.—are then apparent to the most casual observer."

The "Boom" in real estate. The area of the city of Los Angeles (40 square miles) was not sufficiently extensive for the speculators in city lots, suburbs were laid out on every side, and upwards of 100 "cities" were projected within 40 miles of this city, many of these "cities" have no inhabitants as yet, and never have had any. It is no exaggeration to say that city lots (50 by 150 feet) were surveyed, and staked out in the county of Los Angeles sufficient for a population of several millions. In the period of the "Boom," lands were sold and resold at intervals of a few weeks, the price being considerably advanced on every sale. The small profits from the cultivation of the soil were despised, and many fine orange orchards and vineyards were neglected, the owners having *The "Boom."* purchased with a view only to reselling at a higher figure. Many of the new "Boom" cities have reverted to farming lands; and, in others, where some improvements were made, and so many lots sold that they could not be converted into farms, the value of the sub-divisions is merely nominal. I am informed that lots in Monrovia, which were sold during the boom from 3,000l. to 4,000l., cannot now be sold for 100l. The value of good agricultural land has not been affected by the fall in prices, and, in the city of Los Angeles, there has been some increase in the value of central property since the collapse of the boom. The great depreciation has been in the small

SAN FRANCISCO.

towns, notably, Pasadena and Monrovia, and in the "Boom cities." In these places it is difficult to say what property is worth.

NOTE.—In this report dollars have been converted into £ at the rate of 5 dol. per £.

I am indebted to Mr. Hinds, collector of customs, San Pedro, for the statistics in Annexes A, B, and C.

Annex A.—RETURN of all Shipping at the Port of Wilmington (San Pedro), California, in the Year 1888.

ENTERED.

| Nationality. | Sailing. || Steam. || Total. ||
	Number of Vessels.	Tons.	Number of Vessels.	Tons.	Number of Vessels.	Tons.
British	47	66,996	6	7,980	53	74,976
American	17	27,641	...	...	17	27,641
Other countries	28	21,972	...	...	28	21,972
Total	92	116,609	6	7,980	98	124,589
" for the year preceding	64	89,904	3	3,990	67	93,894

NOTE.—This return does not include 917 sailing and steam coasting vessels; aggregate tonnage, 543,475. The coasters for 1887 numbered 784; tonnage, 343,074.

CLEARED.

| Nationality. | Sailing. || Steam. || Total. ||
	Number of Vessels.	Tons.	Number of Vessels.	Tons.	Number of Vessels.	Tons.
British	48	68,051	6	7,980	54	76,031
American	18	27,688	...	...	18	27,688
Other countries	23	20,787	...	...	23	20,787
Total	89	116,526	6	7,980	95	124,506
" for the year preceding	63	87,805	3	3,990	66	91,795

Annex B.—RETURN of the Principal Articles of Export from Wilmington and Los Angeles, California, during the Years 1887–88.

| Articles. | | 1887. || 1888. ||
		Value.	Quantity.	Value.	Quantity.
		£		£	
Wheat and other grains	Tons	6,800	1,190	...	3,100
Canned fruits	Cases	...	...	...	...
Other articles	...	...	...	...	6,000
Total	...	6,800	1,190	...	9,100

RETURN of the Principal Articles of Import to Wilmington and Los Angeles, California, during the Years 1887–88.

Articles.		1887.		1888.	
		Value.	Quantity.	Value.	Quantity.
		£		£	
Coal	Tons	262,000	131,000	340,130	170,065*
Pig iron	,,	1,800	405	...	...
Cement	,,	...	...	14,644	3,661†
Railway iron		...	...	8,000	1,500
Other articles		2,400	567	910	554
Total		266,200	131,972	363,684	175,780

* The value of coals, taken at 2*l.* per ton, the average wholesale price here.
† Value taken at wholesale price here 4*l.* per ton.

Annex C.—TABLE showing the Total Value of all Articles Exported from Wilmington and Los Angeles and Imported to Wilmington and Los Angeles from and to Foreign Countries during the Years 1887–88.

Country.	Exports.		Imports.	
	1887.	1888.	1887.	1888.
	£	£	£	£
Great Britain	6,800	..	266,200	363,684
Total	6,800	..	266,200	363,684

SAN DIEGO.

Mr. Vice-Consul Allen reports as follows:—

During 1888 there has been a considerable falling-off in the amount of business consequent on a general depression in trade, which has been felt more or less all over the United States, also on the inevitable reaction after the feverish excitement of the "Boom" of 1887.

But already there are signs of recovering activity. Large sums of money have been raised on the security of real estate, and this money is being invested in the improvement of property of all kinds.

Large buildings are in course of construction in the town of San Diego, and in the country farmers are actively engaged in sowing barley and wheat on new land, and the acreage in fruit is being largely added to this season.

Water supply. Water in abundant quantity, and of the best quality, is now supplied to San Diego by means of an aqueduct, or "flume," some 35 miles long. Reservoirs are made in the mountains by damming the outlets of valleys, and the water is conveyed to the lands to be irrigated and to the town by means of open conduits and pipes.

There are two enterprises of this nature in the immediate vicinity of San Diego already completed, and several others are projected in the county—the San Luis Rey water system, Mount Tecorte system, and that of the Hewet Land Company, in the San Jacinto Valley, being the principal ones.

Railroads. The railroad to Los Angeles, known as the "Short Line," was opened in June last.

Another road, of more importance to San Diego (the Cayumaca and Eastern railroad), is now in course of construction. This line will connect with three transcontinental roads—the Southern Pacific, the Atlantic and Pacific, and the Union Pacific.

When this line is completed, San Diego will be the Pacific outlet for a vast country, and vessels will no longer be compelled to go to San Francisco, and ports to the northward of it, to look for outward cargoes.

The fact that the harbour of San Diego is the only one south of San Francisco—500 miles distant—makes it a certainty that this will, in the not distant future, become an important shipping point. Harbour.

The harbour is a very fine one. Captain Cook, of the United States surveying ship "Ranger," as reported in the San Francisco "Evening Bulletin" of June 23, 1888, "regards the San Diego harbour as one of the best in the world."

The absence of fogs makes the approach easy at all times. There is no swell on the bar, and there are no currents of any consequence inside. Shipping lying at the wharves is thoroughly protected, the harbour being completely landlocked.

San Diego is nearer to New York than San Francisco is by between 400 and 500 miles. It is also nearer to Australia, and as near to Japan and China.

Length of San Diego Bay	13	miles.
Available anchorage	6	square miles.
Average width of channel	800	yards.
Total area of bay	22	square miles.
Area at depth of 18 feet	3·75	,,
,, ,, 24 ,,	2·83	,,
,, ,, 30 ,,	1·97	,,
,, ,, 36 ,,	1·36	,,
Rise and fall of tide	5	feet.
Depth of water over bar	23	,,

These figures apply to lowest low tide.

Imports by sea are chiefly lumber, coal, pig-iron, and Portland cement. Imports.

Exports by sea are chiefly to Lower California, and consist of live stock, lumber, provisions, farm machinery, &c. Exports.

Forty-three British ships entered at this port during 1888, as against 29 in 1887. Shipping.

A return of from 8 to 10 per cent., clear of taxes and expenses, can be realised here by lending money on the security of first mortgages, the amount lent being from one-third to the half the value of the property mortgaged. This is a safe method of investing money. Loans.

No change has been made since 1887 in the Port Charges Towage and other rates, which will be found in Consular report for that year. Port charges.

UNITED STATES.

Annex A.—RETURN of all Shipping at the Port of San Diego, California, in the Year 1888.

ENTERED.

Nationality.	Sailing. Number of Vessels.	Sailing. Tons.	Steam. Number of Vessels.	Steam. Tons.	Total. Number of Vessels.	Total. Tons.
British	43	47,438	...	...	43	47,438
American, United States	33	12,248	129	29,094	162	41,342
Other countries	26	22,429	25	21,597	51	44,206
Total	102	82,115	154	50,691	256	133,806
„ for the year preceding	41	47,844	4	3,200	45	51,044

CLEARED.

Nationality.	Sailing. Number of Vessels.	Sailing. Tons.	Steam. Number of Vessels.	Steam. Tons.	Total. Number of Vessels.	Total. Tons.
British	51	56,497	...	...	51	56,497
American, United States	22	4,946	128	29,398	150	34,344
Other countries	11	10,179	25	10,950	36	21,129
Total	84	71,622	153	40,348	237	111,970
„ for the year preceding	24	28,639	2	1,604	26	30,243

Annex B.—RETURN of the Principal Articles of Export from San Diego, California, during the Years 1887–88.

Articles.		1888. Value.	1888. Quantity.	1887. Value.	1887. Quantity.
		£		£	
Wheat	Tons	7,952	1,202	...	...
Canned fruits	Cases	...	...	...	...
Baled hay	Tons	700	350	...	...
Oranges	Boxes	...	...	...	...
Wine	Gallons	...	...	...	...
Other articles	...	57,940	...	67,299	...
To Mexico—Live stock, lumber, provisions, farm machinery, &c., not classified	...	...	...	...	...
Total		66,592	...	67,299	...

RETURN of the Principal Articles of Import to San Diego, California, during the Years 1887–88.

Articles.		1888. Value.	1888. Quantity.	1887. Value.	1887. Quantity.
		£		£	
Coal and coke	Tons	59,017	100,228	34,517	51,575
Pig-iron	„	3,009	1,292	...	...
Cement	Barrels	17,233	92,871	5,119	28,045
Other articles	...	48,141	...	61,278	...
Total		127,400	...	100,914	...

Annex C.—TABLE showing the Total Value of all Articles Exported from San Diego and Imported to San Diego from and to Foreign Countries during the Years 1887–88.

Country.	Exports. 1888.	Exports. 1887.	Imports. 1888.	Imports. 1887.
	£	£	£	£
Great Britain	..	..	24,550	46,907
British possessions	..	..	52,841	32,915
Other countries	700	..	1,868	2,507
Lower California, Mexico	57,640	67,299	48,141	18,585
Total	58,340	67,299	127,400	100,914

EUREKA.

Mr. Consular Agent J. H. Hodgson reports as follows:—

In my first annual commercial report (1887), I gave rather a full description of this flourishing and rapidly-growing county, and purpose, in this report, confining my remarks simply to a review of those commercial items which from year to year are subject to change.

Second annual commercial report.

The year just closed has been a satisfactory one to bankers, merchants, farmers, builders, and mechanics. The lumber industry, however, the present main dependence of this country, has not realised, perhaps, all that was expected of it, notwithstanding the extraordinary demand which existed for our redwood lumber, especially from the southern portions of this State, in the early part of the year.

Commerce and trade.

Lumber industry.

The total tonnage of British and foreign vessels which entered and cleared at this port to and from foreign countries during 1888 is shown in Annex A appended hereto, and from which table it will be seen that the numbers for 1888, as compared with those of 1887, show, during the year, an increase in entrances of seven in the number of vessels and of 3,599 tons in the tonnage, and, as regards clearances, an increase of six in the number of vessels and of 3,257 tons in the tonnage. Only four British vessels entered and two cleared at the United States customs during 1887, as against nine entrances and 11 clearances of British vessels during 1888.

Shipping. Annex A. British and foreign.

Tonnage.

Entrances.

Clearances.

For the value of our imports and exports of articles of commerce of this port for the past year, reference is also asked to the shipments tabulated in Annexes B and C hereto, and from which an increase in both items over those of 1887 will be noticed.

Imports and exports. Annexes B and C.

The number of steam vessels arriving during the year was 210, and of sailing vessels 466. The departures were—steam vessels 210, sailing vessels 438. Among the steamers is included 52 trips of the Pacific Coast Steamship Company's steamers, the lost "City of Chester," "Los Angeles," and "Pomona"; and 46 trips of the Humboldt Steamship Company's steamer "Humboldt." The lumber vessels were often out of business during the year, some of them being "tied up" for weeks at a time, or trading elsewhere.

Shipping, coastwise included.

Two sailing schooners, two bay steamers, and one steam schooner have been built on Humboldt Bay during the year just closed.

Shipbuilding.

It has been estimated that the cut of redwood in the mills of Mendocino county, joining our county on the south, compiled from the best sources, was 110,000,000 superficial feet, as against the total cut

Capacity of redwood mills.

of the redwood mills of Humboldt county, both for the year 1887, of 159,703,000 feet, the operations of 13 mills, which have been running a portion only of the past year.

Price of redwood lumber.

It has occurred to me that perhaps the ups and downs of the prices of our redwood lumber, for, say, the past 20 years, may be considered matters of interest, and be also considered by our Government at home as useful information. To that end I am indebted to Messrs. Flannigan, Brosnan, and Co., one of the largest redwood millowners here, for the following carefully kept record, viz. :—During the first seven months of 1863, when the record begins, surface lumber sold at 26 dol. per thousand in San Francisco. In September it rose to 30 dol., and held that figure until the following August, when it dropped 2 dol., and in January, 1865, was again selling at 26 dol. In February it went up to 28 dol., and remained at that figure until December, 1866, when it reached 30 dol. From April, 1868, to February, 1869, it sold for 32 dol., when it went up to 35 dol., holding at that point until October, when it dropped to 26 dol. Another drop of 2 dol. occurred in December, and the following September the price went down to 22 dol., the lowest point then ever reached. From that point it crept up, until in September, 1872, it was selling for 32 dol. In June, 1873, another break occurred, and in June, 1874, it sold for 24 dol., having fallen steadily through the year. In December the price rallied to 30 dol., which held to August, 1876, when a break occurred which carried redwood to the lowest point ever reached, 18 dol. per thousand feet, during July, August, September, and October, 1879. At this time the market price for rough lumber was 12 dol., the lowest point reached. The recovery was very slow, and not until May, 1882, did the market assume anything like permanency. From that time until October, 1884, the ruling price was 30 dol., but a break was made, and it dropped to 22 dol. in 1885. From that time the tendency was upward again, and from June to the close of December, 1887, redwood sold for 30 dol. At the beginning of 1888 a dollar rise occurred, and for five months surfaced lumber brought 31 dol. In June it dropped to 26 dol., and the first of August to 24 dol., the present price. Rough clear has followed the general ups and downs of the redwood market, ranging from 12 dol. to 20 dol., while surfaced has ranged from 18 dol. to 35 dol.

Harbour improvements.

The contract has been let, and preliminary work commenced by the United States Government towards making our magnificent and landlocked harbour, available for deep-water ships of the largest draught, by the building of a sea-wall and other improvements to deepen the channel at the entrance.

Railways.

It is very probable that my next annual commercial report will chronicle the news that our connection with San Francisco and the Northern and Eastern States by railroad transportation is soon to be realised.

Annex A.—RETURN of all Shipping at the Port of Eureka, California, in the Year 1888, omitting Coasting Vessels, which do not enter or clear at Customs.

ENTERED.

Nationality.	Sailing. Number of Vessels.	Sailing. Tons.	Steam. Number of Vessels.	Steam. Tons.	Total. Number of Vessels.	Total. Tons.
British	9	4,537	...	...	9	4,537
United States of America	8	2,539	...	...	8	2,539
Norwegian	2	877	...	...	2	877
Italian	1	218	...	...	1	218
Danish	1	193	...	...	1	193
Total	21	8,364	...	...	21	8,364
,, for the year preceding	14	4,765	...	...	14	4,765

CLEARED.

Nationality.	Sailing. Number of Vessels.	Sailing. Tons.	Steam. Number of Vessels.	Steam. Tons.	Total. Number of Vessels.	Total. Tons.
British	11	5,423	...	...	11	5,423
United States of America	8	2,539	...	...	8	2,539
Norwegian	2	877	...	...	2	877
Italian	1	218	...	...	1	218
Danish	1	193	...	...	1	193
Total	23	9,250	...	...	23	9,250
,, for the year preceding	17	5,993	...	...	17	5,993

Annex B.—RETURN of Principal Articles of Export from Eureka, California, during the Year 1888 (Foreign and Domestic).

Articles.		1888. Quantity.	1888. Value. £	1887. Quantity.	1887. Value. £
Lumber, including 1,629 m. ft., value 6,520l., exported to Great Britain viâ San Francisco for India and Don Quixote	M. ft., nos. and bdls.	109,903,600	520,900	...	...
Farm produce	Sacks, lbs., boxes, bdls. &c.	...	30,100	...	...
Wool	Lbs.	1,754,417	63,158	...	...
Fish	Lbs., &c.	480,000	500	...	...
Furs, hides, leather	Bdls.	620	Value not ascertained.	...	...
Cattle and other live stock	Head	2,060	750	...	...
Tan bark	Cords	2,300	7,600	...	...
Total		...	623,008	...	581,343

UNITED STATES.

RETURN of Principal Articles of Import to Eureka, California, during the Year 1888 (from Foreign Ports only).

Articles.	1888. Quantity.	1888. Value.	1887. Quantity.	1887. Value.
	Tons.	£	Tons.	£
Coal	1,518	873	768	393
Total	1,518	873	768	393

The rate of exchange is calculated at 4·86 dol. to the 1l. sterling.

Annex C.—TABLE showing the Total Value of all Articles Exported from Eureka, California, and Imported to Eureka, California, during the Year 1888.

Country.	Imports 1888.	Imports 1887.	Exports 1888.	Exports 1887.
	£	£	£	£
Great Britain	6,520	..	873	393
British possessions—Australia ..	17,780	..	..	..
Hawaiian Islands..	3,098	..	..	..
Chile	1,550	..	..	..
Peru	862	..	..	..
Mexico	1,417	..	..	..
American (or domestic) ports ..	591,781	..	..	..
Total	623,008	581,343	873	393

LONDON:
Printed for Her Majesty's Stationery Office,
BY HARRISON AND SONS,
Printers in Ordinary to Her Majesty.

(1250 6 | 89—H & S 681)

FOREIGN OFFICE.
1889.
ANNUAL SERIES.

No. 570.

DIPLOMATIC AND CONSULAR REPORTS ON TRADE AND FINANCE.

UNITED STATES.

REPORT FOR THE YEAR 1888
ON THE
TRADE OF THE CONSULAR DISTRICT OF CHICAGO.

REFERENCE TO PREVIOUS REPORTS, Annual Series Nos. 330 and 362.

Presented to both Houses of Parliament by Command of Her Majesty,
JULY, 1889.

LONDON:
PRINTED FOR HER MAJESTY'S STATIONERY OFFICE.
BY HARRISON AND SONS, ST. MARTIN'S LANE,
PRINTERS IN ORDINARY TO HER MAJESTY.

And to be purchased, either directly or through any Bookseller, from
EYRE AND SPOTTISWOODE, EAST HARDING STREET, FLEET STREET, E.C., and
32, ABINGDON STREET, WESTMINSTER, S.W.; or
ADAM AND CHARLES BLACK, 6, NORTH BRIDGE, EDINBURGH; or
HODGES, FIGGIS, & Co., 104, GRAFTON STREET, DUBLIN.

1889.

[C. 5618—123.] *Price Three Halfpence.*

New Series of Reports.

Reports of the Annual Series have been issued from Her Majesty's Diplomatic and Consular Officers at the following places, and may be obtained from the sources indicated on the title-page:—

No.		Price.	No.		Price.
442.	Sofia	1d.	506.	Dunkirk	1d.
443.	Copenhagen	1d.	507.	Genoa	2d.
444.	Galatz	1d.	508.	Beyrout	1d.
445.	Tabreez	1d.	509.	Colonia	1d.
446.	Bogotá	2d.	510.	Marseilles	1d.
447.	St. Petersburg	3d.	511.	Kiukiang	1d.
448.	Nice	1d.	512.	Buda-Pesth	2d.
449.	Stettin	2d.	513.	Wênchow	10d.
450.	Fiume	1d.	514.	Coquimbo	1d.
451.	Chinkiang	1d.	515.	Charleston	1d.
452.	The Hague	1d.	516.	Riga	1d.
453.	Malaga	1d.	517.	Mollendo	1d.
454.	Taganrog	1d.	518.	Taiwan	1d.
455.	Mozambique	1d.	519.	Wuhu	1d.
456.	Bogotá	2d.	520.	Corunna	2d.
457.	Patras	1d.	521.	Noumea	1d.
458.	Galveston	1d.	522.	San José	1d.
459.	Buda Pesth	1d.	523.	Ningpo	1d.
460.	Madeira	1d.	524.	Gothenburg	2d.
461.	Warsaw	1d.	525.	Hankow	2d.
462.	Paris	2d.	526.	Foochow	1d.
463.	Baltimore	1d.	527.	Erzeroum	2d.
464.	Philadelphia	2d.	528.	Ciudad Bolivar	1d.
465.	New Orleans	2d.	529.	Jaffa	1d.
466.	New Orleans	2d.	530.	Ancona	1d.
467.	Cherbourg	1d.	531.	Savannah	1d.
468.	Buenos Ayres	1d.	532.	Batavia	1d.
469.	Algiers	1d.	533.	Adrianople	1d.
470.	Ichang	1d.	534.	Nisch	11d.
471.	Copenhagen	1d.	535.	Vienna	1d.
472.	Athens	1d.	536.	Odessa	8d.
473.	Cherbourg	1d.	537.	Constantinople	2d.
474.	The Piræus	1d.	538.	Damascus	1d.
475.	Galatz	1d.	539.	Tientsin	1d.
476.	Tripoli	1d.	540.	Amoy	1d.
477.	Saigon	1d.	541.	Mogador	1d.
478.	Serajevo	1d.	542.	Vienna	1d.
479.	Brussels	2d.	543.	Antwerp	1d.
480.	Bengazi	1d.	544.	Lisbon	2d.
481.	Odessa	1d.	545.	New York	1½d.
482.	Santo Domingo	1d.	546.	San Francisco	1d.
483.	Rome	1d.	547.	Stettin	1½d.
484.	Lisbon	1d.	548.	San Salvador	½d.
485.	Port Said	2d.	549.	Trebizond	1d.
486.	Havre	3d.	550.	Nice	1d.
487.	Boulogne	1d.	551.	Baghdad	½d.
488.	Callao	1d.	552.	Fiume	1d.
489.	Barcelona	2d.	553.	Mogador	2d.
490.	Boulogne	2d.	554.	Buenos Ayres	1½d.
491.	Taganrog	2d.	555.	San Francisco	2½d.
492.	Kiungchow	1d.	556.	Carthagena	½d.
493.	Sandakan	1d.	557.	Syra	1d.
494.	Manila	1d.	558.	Varna and Bourgas	1d.
495.	Swatow	1d.	559.	Thessaly	½d.
496.	Guayaquil	1d.	560.	Yokohama	1d.
497.	Rome	1d.	561.	Nantes	1½d.
498.	Santos	1d.	562.	Suakin	½d.
499.	Boston	1d.	563.	Algiers	1d.
500.	Aleppo	1d.	564.	St. Petersburg	2½d.
501.	Bordeaux	2d.	565.	Söul	1d.
502.	Valparaiso	1d.	566.	Newchwang	1d.
503.	St. Petersburg	1d.	567.	Roustchouk and Philippopolis	1d.
504.	Rio de Janeiro	4d.	568.	Stockholm	1½d.
505.	Brest	1d.	569.	Tonga	1d.

No. 570.

Reference to previous Reports, Annual Series Nos. 330 and 362.

UNITED STATES.

CHICAGO.

Acting-Consul Harriss-Gastrell to the Marquis of Salisbury.

My Lord,   *Chicago, May 25, 1889.*

I HAVE the honour to state that, as I have only begun to take charge of this Consulate, and as Mr. Sadler, the Vice-Consul, had already collected some statistics for use in the usual commercial report, I begged him to draw up that report for this Consular District; and I have now the honour to forward it together with the reports, annexed thereto, which I have received from Mr. Vice-Consul Bascome, of St. Louis; Mr. Vice-Consul Morphy, of St. Paul; and Mr. Vice-Consul Pearce, of Denver.

I have, &c.
(Signed)   J. P. H. GASTRELL.

Report on the Trade and Commerce of the Consular District of Chicago during the Year 1888.

Trade in general. The commercial history of Chicago for the year 1888 shows a fair measure of activity, despite the fear that the crops of the most important cereals would be poor, and the fact of this year being that of the election of a President of the United States. The wheat crop proved less than a normal one, but still allowed a moderate surplus for export. Comparatively high prices brought the bulk of corn (maize) to Chicago, and vast quantities were handled in this city. In the distribution of merchandise the merchants have fully held their own, and there is a tendency on the part of Eastern firms to establish branch houses for the purpose of sharing in the wealth of this city.

Trusts. Trusts have flourished, but now the field seems exhausted, and the popular feeling is adverse to monopolies.

Finance. The local money market has been satisfactory to money lenders, though much has been placed at as low a rate as 4½ per cent. on good security. The National banks of this city show a surplus and profit balance of 7,645,674 dol., as against 6,320,559 dol. of the preceding year, an average gain of about 10 per cent.

UNITED STATES.

Receipts and Shipmemts.

Flour. The flour market has been generally dull but steady, except at one time when a corner in wheat was effected, and much flour was bought up at higher rates for the purpose of being held over to command better market prices. The receipts of flour amounted to 6,034,006 barrels as against 6,250,000 barrels in 1887. The barrel of flour costs more now as compared with the bushel of wheat, on account of a decided reduction in the flouring value of the grain of last crop.

Wheat. The wheat market has been uncertain, and prices fluctuating, the average having been 3s. 1½d. per bushel for the first six months of the year. Later in the season a corner in wheat was successfully carried out by Mr. B. P. Hutchinson, who managed to possess himself of all the contract wheat in store. It was soon evident that there was a big " short interest in the market " who could not settle, and that Mr. B. P. Hutchinson held the control. On September 25 wheat was at 4s. 6d. per bushel, on the 27th inst. at 5s. 1½d., the next day at 6s. 3d., and finally at 8s. 4d. per bushel. At one time it is said that this successful operator controlled the handling of 10,000,000 bushels of wheat. The profits on this deal were enormous, and some smaller houses were so seriously crippled as to be obliged to close their business transactions.

Corn and other grain. The market for corn (maize) has been a general surprise. The prices have averaged 15 per cent. higher, and the receipts 30 per cent. more than last year; showing receipts of 70,150,302 bushels and shipment of 69,590,022 bushels, as against receipts of 51,500,000 bushels and shipments of 40,500,000 bushels for last year.

The receipts of oats amounted to 52,083,771 bushels, as against 40,500,000 bushels of last year. Prices fluctuated, the average in the year proving to be 28·60 c. per bushel.

Cattle. The receipts of cattle still continue good, and there is a marked increase in the dressed meat business. Prices have been fair, and no diseases reported.

Horses. The movement in horses exhibits a considerable increase over that of last year; arrivals totalling up to 55,333 head. Of this number 52,886 head have been shipped direct to Eastern States.

Sheep. An increase in sheep is also reported at fair rates. Choice Texans sold at 26s. in the early summer, and natives at 10s. 5d., there was also a fair demand for stock sheep.

Hogs. The receipt of hogs shows a decided falling off from that of the preceding years. The receipts amounted to 4,938,520, as against 5,470,850 in 1887, which again was a shortage of 1,250,000 of the preceding year.

The heavy reduction has chiefly been caused by the outbreak of hog cholera among the western herds.

The Provision Trade.

Hog packing. The work of hog packing shows a still further decrease. The decadence in activity was principally due to a want of material, the supply during the year never having got up to the demand, despite reduced railway rates, discriminated from the west in return, higher prices ruled for the animals and their products. The following table will show the number of hogs packed in this city and their value during the last two years:—

		1888.	1887.
No. of hogs		3,157,500	3,712,000
Value of hogs	£	8,210,000	8,200,000
Value of product	£	8,900,000	9,300,000

The butter trade has been in a healthy condition, and good prices realized. Butterine has been in fair demand, chiefly when the higher prices were ruling for butter. A decrease of about 25 per cent. is reported in the lard, lard oil, and stearine business. *Butter, butterine, lard.*

The business of beef canning shows a marked increase, and promises good in the future. As compared with hog packing, it seems that a much smaller capital is invested, to make a more valuable product. The three leading firms report a slaughter of 1,204,697 head, as against 1,026,147 head slaughtered in 1887, showing an increase of 278,550 head of cattle handled. *Beef canning.*

The Post-office shows an increase in receipts of 13·22 per cent., an increase in expenses of 7·46 per cent., an increase in net income of 16·53 per cent., an increase of 68,407,803 pieces handled (or 28 per cent.), and an increase of 35·64 per cent. in local postage, over the returns of last year. *The Post-office.*

Progress in the West.

Last year Dakota raised 38,036,000 bushels of wheat, Minnesota 27,881,000 bushels, and Iowa 24,196,000 bushels, on a total of a little more than 7,000,000 acres; total 90,113,000 bushels. These are the three great spring wheat areas. For 1887 the totals were:—Dakota, 52,406,000 bushels; Minnesota, 36,299,000 bushels; Iowa, 26,837,000 bushels; total 115,542,000 bushels. This falling-off of more than 20 per cent. in production is on the basis of measured bushels. The crop generally averaged very light, presumably on account of severe heat in the summer, followed by unusually early frosts at the close of August. Much wheat was frosted, and great distress consequently followed among the farmers of that section, and many farms were abandoned. At one time over 1,000,000 bushels of wheat stood on the railway track at Minneapolis last winter, which the elevators would not take in as it was so poor. But, later on, much of this was taken by mills outside and ground into flour, which, though of low grade quality, was better than at first expected. *Wheat in the west.*

The difficulties experienced this year have been much greater than ever before, in consequence of increased competition among the carriers, the railroad building in the West having been carried much further than the increase of population and settlement. *Railroad problem in the West.*

The Canadian railroads, skirting the United States borders,

(701)

have recently exercised a much more important influence on rates south of the border than heretofore. The Interstate Commerce Law of the United States forbids the charging of a higher rate for a short distance than for a longer one, thus the American railroads are obliged to keep up their through rates or reduce their local rates below a point hitherto considered as a paying one; the Canadian lines, not being hampered by this restriction, are consequently able to bid successfully for the through commerce between the west and the seabord. The operation, therefore, of the Interstate Commerce Law favours the increase of business on Canadian railroads, and, as thought by some, will also restore a part of the American export trade down the St. Lawrence, which used to be a much more important feature than at present.

The four principal "Grainger" railroads, *i.e.*, the Chicago, Milwaukee, and St. Paul; the Chicago and North Western; the Chicago, Burlington, and Quincy; the Chicago, St. Paul, and Omaha, show gross earnings of 80,904,295 dol., with an expenditure of 56,989,221 dol. this year, as against 87,023,800 dol., with an expenditure of 51,283,451 dol. in 1887; exhibiting in 1888, net earnings of 23,915,074 dol., as against 35,740,349 dol. in 1887, a decrease of about 1s. 3d. in net earnings.

These four railroads have a mileage of nearly 16,000 miles of track, which is not far from 11 per cent. of the total track mileage in the United States.

Iron ore.

The year 1888 has eclipsed all records of annual production during the 32 years of iron-ore producing in the Lake Superior region. The production exceeded that of 1887, known as the big year, by 5 per cent., and the sales by nearly 60 per cent. The total sale for Lake delivery this year amounted to 4,366,000 tons, an increase of 1,600,000 tons over last year. The total shipments from Lake Superior ports, during 1888, aggregated 5,000,000 gross tons, all of which, with the exception of 634,000 tons, was delivered at lower Lake ports.

An analysis of the returns of the year shows that the Gogebic mines produced an increase of 125,000 tons, the Menominee Range a decrease of 32,000 tons, the Marguette Range an increase of 34,151 tons, and the Vermilion Range an increase of 59,608 tons, as compared with the returns of last year.

Tin mines in the black hills of Dakota.

The tin mines, reported to be nearly equal to those in Cornwall, are only in the very first stages of development, sufficient capital not having yet been invested to determine true importance.

The mines are situated in the Harney Peak Hills, about 20 miles north of Rapid City, on a branch of the north-western road. Up to lately there were no concentrating apparatus, smelting furnaces, or mining machinery worth notice, but impulse has been given by the operations of an English syndicate. The Harney Peak Mining and Smelting Company has been organised, with 10,000,000 dol. stock, and has bought 300 miners' claims, about 3,100 acres, and 1,000 acres of placer claims. Over 100 men are now employed on the works, and the ore is reckoned to be concentrated to about 60 per cent. of tin at the mines. It is also proposed to erect smelting works at Rapid City.

The report of the coal mines for this year shows an improved state of affairs, the output of coal having been 10,278,890 tons, 1,000,000 tons in excess of the preceding year. The miners also realised an improved price for their labour, about 5 cents a ton above the prices of last year. Still, the average prices of the coal at the mines have continued to decrease slightly, being 1·085 dol. a ton, as against 1·111 dol. of last year. The number of producing mines has steadily increased since 1883, when it was 639 to 817 now. Of first class mines, *i.e.*, mines producing 50,000 tons or more, there are only 64. The Consolidated Coal Company of St. Louis owns 71 mines in this State, and this year produced 2,008,341 tons. The total output of Illinois mines during the last seven years has been 64,680,225 tons. The average price of mining is now 66 per cent. of the average value at the mines, five years ago it was only 54 per cent. Therefore, though the miner benefits by a slight increase in wages, the coal depreciates in value to a certain degree. *(Coal mines in Illinois.)*

There are now three oil wells on the Wyoming oil belt, all included in the district between the Wind River and Rattlesnake Mountains, in the southern portion of the territory. The combined production would be about 800 barrels per day, but this flow has to be checked on account of the lack of means of transport. The wells, which are only down 300 feet, produce a lubricating fluid of excellent quality, possessing but 41 per cent. of illuminating oil, which has been used on the Union Pacific Railroad, and proved to be very valuable. The Omaha Petroleum Company controls these interests, and intends to build a pipe line from the wells into Omaha, Nebraska, whence it can be shipped east and west. The capital of the Company amounts to 2,000,000 dol., and numerous further claims are being taken up all over the southern part of Wyoming. There seems reason to believe that the field will prove a large petroleum producing district in the near future, and that the wells will be satisfactorily worked, as vast coal fields are being discovered in the vicinity. *(Petroleum in Wyoming.)*

Annex B.—RETURN of Principal Articles of direct Export by Lake from Chicago during the Years 1888 and 1887.

Articles.		1888. Quantity.	1888. Value. £	1887 Quantity.	1887 Value. £
Wheat	Bushel	269,279	45,799	1,166,526	174,497
Corn	,,	2,667,576	261,331	1,529,512	134,389
Oats	,,	9,437	492	25,895	1,319
Flour	Barrels	4,565	3,362	1,014	736
Corn meal	,,	902	...	625	460
Pork	,,	2,414	7,035	4,979	13,828
Lard	Pounds	112,120	2,141	40,788	548
Cured meats	,,	43,294	737	7,530	163
Other articles	,,	623	1,004	34,329	1,599
Total		...	...	...	327,449

UNITED STATES.

Return of Principal Articles of Import to Chicago during the Years 1888 and 1887.

Articles.	Value 1888. (£)	Value 1887. (£)
Free goods	512,132	636,604
China and glassware	90,440	82,166
Caustic soda	28,142	49,430
Cigars, tobacco, and manufacture of	126,688	125,546
Dry goods	888,060	959,724
Iron, pig, manufacture of, and wire, &c.	20,593	37,564
Leather manufactures	51,683	46,531
Metal "	27,040	27,470
Musical instruments	47,343	46,531
Steel bars, bloom, &c.	6,100	13,870
Tin plate	319,332	289,656
Wines and liquors	62,774	69,423
Other articles	498,739	325,643
Total	2,678,222	2,710,425

Exchange is calculated at the rate of 4.85 dol. = £1 sterling.

Annex A.—Return of all Shipping at the Port of Chicago in the Year 1888.

Entered.

Nationality.	Sailing. Number of Vessels.	Sailing. Tons.	Steam. Number of Vessels.	Steam. Tons.	Total. Number of Vessels.	Total. Tons.
British	46	16,770	44	21,133	90	37,903
American	5,350	1,340,218	5,549	3,015,647	10,899	4,355,865
Total	5,396	1,356,988	5,593	3,036,780	10,989	4,393,768
" for the preceding year	6,248	1,521,783	4,580	2,346,682	10,826	3,868,465

Cleared.

Nationality.	Sailing. Number of Vessels.	Sailing. Tons.	Steam. Number of Vessels.	Steam. Tons.	Total. Number of Vessels.	Total. Tons.
British	48	17,372	44	21,189	92	38,561
American	5,474	1,381,144	5,540	3,067,193	11,014	4,448,337
Total	5,522	1,398,516	5,584	3,088,382	11,106	4,486,898
" for the preceding year	6,282	1,621,024	4,638	2,368,591	10,920	3,989,615

St. Louis.

Mr. Vice-Consul Bascome reports as follows:—

The state of the trade and commerce of St. Louis for 1888 has been generally satisfactory to the business men. The commercial growth has been steady, as indicated by the amount of business transacted through the clearing house of the banks, through the post-office and the business exchanges of the city. The discussion of the tariff and the pending Bill in Congress to reduce the tariff revenue about 14,000,000*l.*, had a tendency to unsettle some lines of trade and to curtail them.

In commodities handled on the exchanges, the business in nearly all lines largely exceeded that of the previous year, 1887.

In flour and grain, the receipts reduced to bushels were 51,195,121 bushels, against 48,748,562 bushels in 1887.

The amount of flour manufactured was 2,016,619 barrels, the second largest output in the United States, and an increase over that of 1887 of 30,902 barrels.

The business in provisions shows an increase of 61,054,966 lbs. in receipts and shipments, being 396,237,164 lbs. in 1888, and 335,182,198 lbs. in 1887.

In livestock, the total number handled was 1,991,232 head.

In cotton, the gross receipts reached 521,156 bales, of which 226,852 bales were sold in this market. The shipments were 519,103 bales, of which 158,409 bales were for export, the larger proportion for England.

In wool and hides, the business largely exceeded that of any any previous year.

For the sale of hardware, woodenware, and drugs, and for the manufacture of beer, tobacco, saddlery, and stationery, this city claims to have the largest establishments in the United States.

St. Louis flour is shipped to all European centres of importance and its beer to San Francisco, Australia, Mexico, and central America.

The tonnage receipts by railways and river have declined (903,299 tons in the past year) from 14,359,059 tons in 1887 to 13,455,760 tons in 1888. The loss being in wheat, 1,500,205 bushels, attributable to the short crop in the territory from which this city draws its supply.

There has been a falling off in lumber and logs of 47,917,081 feet, in shingles 11,003,235 pieces, and lathes 28,684,388 pieces, attributable to the increase in the number of saw mills in the territory which St. Louis heretofore supplied. With these exceptions the business in other products shows an increase.

There was a falling off in the river tonnage for 1888 or 264,180 tons, mainly in the lower Mississippi, and is accounted for by the fact that the foreign grain movement was largely curtailed on account of the short crop of corn of 1887, and the high price of the wheat crop of 1888; the latter the result partly of a short crop, and a corner in wheat last September which forced the price up to a point leaving no margin for shipment to Liverpool or other foreign ports. During the month of November 200,000 bushels of wheat shipped to New Orleans and intended for export to fill a French order was ordered to be returned from New Orleans to St. Louis, meantime the consignees and owners, having bought up their contracts on the other side. After purchase of contracts, and the payment of double river freights, the sale and delivery at the point of original shipment is said to have resulted in a net profit ranging from 10 c. to 15 c. per bushel.

The shipment of flour and bulk grain to New Orleans for foreign shipment in 1888 was, wheat 1,354,415 bushels, corn 6,418,233 bushels, oats 1,981,794 bushels, flour 313,327 barrels.

Foreign Shipments of Flour from St. Louis viâ Atlantic Seaports.

Destination.	1888.	1887.
	Barrels.	Barrels.
England	65,631	115,235
Scotland	59,705	93,529
Ireland	2,422	17,585
Holland	137	525
Belgium	..	8,278
South America	405	1,397
Portugal	2,745	..
Canada	110,335	65,225
Cuba	12,147	13,542

Nearly all the above was shipped in sacks of various weights, and is reduced to barrels for convenience in calculation.

The export trade of the past year shows a slight falling off in the amount shipped by Atlantic seaports, and considerable decrease in the exportation viâ New Orleans. The decrease in the movement of wheat was not confined to the jetty route, as the total amount exported from the United States was but a little more than half as much as for the previous year.

The movement of corn decreased somewhat owing to the short crop of 1887, and consequent increase in value, especially during the first half of the year, but shipments by the jetty route were liberal, being only exceeded by New York. At the close of the year the export demand was steady, every tow for New Orleans taking its full quota of corn, and as the corn crop of 1888 was a large one and the river transportation favourable, doubtless, the movement of corn will be very large during the coming year. The movement viâ the Atlantic ports shows an increase in cotton and some other articles, but a falling off in flour, the result of the same conditions that governed wheat.

Shipments of Bulk Grain to New Orleans for Export.

Article.	1887.	1888.
	Bushels.	Bushels.
Wheat	3,973,737	1,247,952
Corn	7,365,340	5,844,042

CHICAGO.

DIRECT Shipments from St. Louis to Foreign Countries in Tons.

	1887.	1888.
	Tons.	Tons.
By rail, eastward	128,522	121,657
,, river to New Orleans	325,412	201,072
Total ..	453,934	322,729

STATEMENT of Bulk Grain Exported from New Orleans to England in 1887 and 1888 was as follows.

Article.	1887.	1888.
	Bushels.	Bushels.
Wheat	1,962,817	450,911
Corn	4,091,961	3,762,450

AVERAGE Rates of Freight for 1887 and 1888 in Cents Per Bushel by Steamer from St. Louis to Liverpool viâ New Orleans.

Month.	1887.	1888.
	Cents.	Cents.
January	$19\frac{3}{4}$	$14\frac{1}{2}$
February	$19\frac{1}{2}$	$13\frac{1}{2}$
March	18	12
April	$14\frac{1}{10}$	$12\frac{1}{2}$
May	$11\frac{1}{4}$	$12\frac{3}{4}$
June	12	$12\frac{1}{4}$
July	$12\frac{1}{2}$	$11\frac{1}{4}$
August	$14\frac{1}{4}$	$13\frac{1}{4}$
September	$13\frac{1}{2}$	$19\frac{1}{2}$
October	$13\frac{1}{2}$	$20\frac{1}{4}$
November	$14\frac{1}{2}$	$20\frac{1}{4}$
December	15	$19\frac{1}{4}$

COMPARATIVE Business in Leading Articles Handled in the Exchanges at St. Louis for 1887 and 1888.

Articles.		1887.	1888.
Flour, amount manufactured ..	Barrels ..	1,985,717	2,016,619
,, ,, handled	,, ..	3,633,194	3,973,155
Wheat, total receipts	Bushels ..	14,510,313	13,010,108
Corn ,, ,, ...	,, ..	16,576,386	20,269,499
Oats ,, ,, ...	,, ..	9,768,545	10,456,760
Rye ,, ,, ...	,, ..	236,726	421,514
Barley ,, ,, ...	,, ..	2,932,192	3,044,961
All grain received (including flour reduced to wheat) ..	,, ..	48,748,562	51,195,121
Cotton, receipts	Bales ..	520,063	521,156
Bagging, manufactured	Yards ..	15,000,000	12,000,000
Hay, receipts	Tons ..	85,394	107,884
Tobacco ,, ...	Hogsheads	37,592	27,149
Lead, receipts in pigs 80 lbs. ..	Pigs ..	1,432,054	1,853,781
Hog product, total shipments ..	Lbs. ..	220,613,987	246,238,457
Cattle, receipts	Head ..	464,828	546,875
Sheep ,, ...	,, ..	417,425	456,669
Hogs ,, ...	,, ..	1,052,240	929,230
Horses and mules, receipts ..	,, ..	57,048	58,458
Lumber and logs ,, ...	Feet ..	675,144,047	627,226,966
Shingles, receipts	Pieces ..	77,288,735	66,285,500
Lath ,, ...	,, ..	43,334,705	14,650,317
Wool, total receipts	Lbs. ..	17,347,186	19,626,629
Hides ,, ...	,, ..	26,175,972	31,814,049
Sugar, received	,, ..	105,670,926	138,561,200
Molasses, shipped	Gallons ..	1,952,265	3,807,070
Coffee, received	Bags ..	184,312	192,940
Rice, receipts	Packages ..	79,604	74,181
Coal ,, ...	Bushels ..	66,524,925	67,676,875
Nails ,, ...	Kegs ..	706,472	596,579
Potatoes ,, ...	Bushels ..	1,301,636	1,219,893
Salt ,, ...	Barrels ..	394,676	330,110
,, ,, ...	Sacks ..	32,060	24,649
,, ,, ...	Bush. in bulk	320,490	254,700
Butter	Lbs. ..	9,234,043	11,109,733
Tons of freight of all kinds received and shipped	..	14,359,059	13,455,760

Financial.

The aggregate clearings of the St. Louis Banks in 1888 was 180,094,975*l.*, and in 1887 178,905,546*l.*, showing an increase of 1,189,429*l.*, or 6·5 per cent.

The banking capital has not been increased much, and the rate of interest charged has been lower, except during the moving of the crops, when 8 per cent has been the ruling rate.

The improvement of the finances of the city for the past three years has been great.

The Bonded Debt on April 13, 1885, was 4,403,200*l.*, and was reduced up to December 15, 1888, to 4,386,420*l.* During the period mentioned 1,468,820*l.* Bonds, bearing 6, 7, and 8 per cent. interest, were refunded at 3·65 and 4 per cent.; 397,000*l.*, 4 per cent., Bonds selling at a premium of 2·68 per cent.

The extension of the city appears to be gradual and healthy, and in the past year the Corporation undertook the sprinkling of 270½ miles of thoroughfare, and it is expected in the current year to sprinkle the whole 327 miles of streets; Corporation sprinkling being proved to be much more economical than by private owners of property.

The business of the post office has increased largely during the past two years; the carriers required to collect and deliver the city's mails being 123 in 1886, and 214 in 1888, an increase of 75 per cent. The appended figures show the increase in mail matter handled :— {Post-office statistics.}

	1888.	1886.
Delivered—		
Registered letters	199,251	183,994
Mail letters	36,768,477	26,027,857
Mail postal cards	7,546,159	4,455,983
Drop letters	13,200,197	6,004,009
Drop postal cards	6,998,502	3,819,038
Papers, circulars, &c.	17,672,890	10,092,909
Collected—		
Letters	31,956,495	17,558,137
Postal cards	10,623,286	5,677,836
Papers, circulars, &c.	7,856,983	3,648,244

The increase in two years is as high as 100 per cent. on drop letters, drop postal cards delivered, and postal cards and papers collected.

The area of the city is still 62½ square miles. The population is estimated to have increased about 25,000, but as no census has been taken the actual population cannot be stated until the census to be taken in 1890 has been completed.

The increase in assessed value of real estate the past year has been 2,232,538*l*.

The notable buildings finished the past year were :—the Odd Fellows Hall, of Missouri granite, at a cost of 90,000*l*.; the Mercantile Library, of granite and brick, 80,000*l*.; the Fagin Building, 50,000*l*.; the Bank of Commerce, 60,000*l*.; the Laclede Building, 80,000*l*.; the Lionberger Building, 70,000*l*.; and the Liggett and Myers Stores, of granite, to cost 180,000*l*. Total improvements for year 1,605,900*l*.

The manufactories comprise flour, candies, clay products, glass, furniture, carriages, saddlery, tobacco, agricultural implements, railway supplies, street railway cars, stoves, boilers, electrical apparatus, boots and shoes, beer, white lead, linseed oil, cotton-seed oil, and pig lead.

The traffic across the Mississippi river by the Eads Bridge in 1888, from east to west, was 140,110 cars, carrying 2,129,687 tons of freight, and from west to east 75,788 cars, equal to 909,456 tons.

The Merchants' Bridge and Terminal Co. are building a new bridge in the northern portion of the city, about three miles north of the Eads Bridge, which will largely increase the transfer and terminal facilities.

The new bridge is to have two channel spans not less than 500 feet clear, and one span 300 feet clear width of channel way, and shall be not less than 50 feet high above high-water mark.

It will be a double-track steel structure, consisting of three spans entirely of steel, each $518\frac{1}{2}$ ft. long, and two approach structures 425 ft. long, making a total length of bridge 2,425 ft.; and proportioned to carry a moving load of three tons per lineal foot.

Foreign imports. There was a slight increase in the value of commodities imported into St. Louis during 1888 over the previous year, amounting to 2,874*l*. 4*s*., the value of imports in 1888 being 715,222*l*. 4*s*., against 712,348*l*. in 1887, as will appear by the following table:—

COMPARATIVE Condensed Statement of Goods Imported into St. Louis in 1887 and 1888 showing the Foreign Values and Duties Collected.

Commodities.	1888. Value. £ s. d.	1888. Duties. £ s. d.	1887. Value. £ s. d.	1887. Duties. £ s. d.
Ale and beer	4,091 16 0	1,147 10 6	1,639 8 0	449 10 9
Anvils	3,056 4 0	968 13 6	4,678 4 0	1,503 0 10
Barley	69,346 0 0	9,112 17 4	48,216 15 0	6,806 17 0
Chemicals	13,572 16 0	5,594 0 7	20,266 0 0	6,515 3 2
China and earthenware	24,716 4 0	13,923 5 0	28,989 8 0	16,215 18 2
Cutlery	19,765 12 0	9,295 8 0	18,919 0 0	9,062 16 0
Free goods of all kinds	53,445 16 0	...	74,348 0 0	...
Glass and glassware	19,845 16 0	10,587 2 7	25,006 4 0	15,727 2 1
Guns and firearms	17,533 4 0	5,323 17 3	19,349 12 0	6,198 11 3
Hops	19,537 0 0	5,786 5 10	20,963 0 0	6,540 1 8
Manufactures of cotton	36,454 12 0	15,354 3 10	43,619 8 0	17,720 9 1
" iron and steel	139,474 4 0	53,586 0 0	198,526 0 0	76,885 17 1
" wool	30,289 8 0	20,888 9 10	37,743 16 0	25,593 10 2
Rice granulated	45,153 8 0	9,030 13 10	19,389 16 0	3,877 19 2
Sugar	62,944 0 0	45,425 1 10	8,717 12 0	6,116 16 8
Tobacco, cigars, and cigarettes	24,769 16 0	31,496 14 6	24,137 4 0	29,963 9 3
Wines and liquors	16,084 16 0	10,571 10 2	14,276 4 0	9,345 8 8
Liquors reimported	13,510 12 0	12,012 10 6	16,396 0 0	14,945 3 10
Miscellaneous	101,631 0 0	30,981 13 7	87,166 9 0	32,806 18 2
Total	715,222 4 0	291,085 18 8	712,348 0 0	286,274 13 0

The duties on foreign imports received at the St. Louis custom house were 291,085*l*. 18*s*. 8*d*. in 1888, and 286,274*l*. 13*s*. in 1887, showing an increase of 4,811*l*. 5*s*. 8*d*. in 1888.

GENERAL Exhibit of Imported Merchandise through the various Ports of Entry showing Foreign Values and Duties Collected.

Custom-house transactions, 1888.— Port of St. Louis.

Ports.	Foreign Value.	Duty.
	£ s. d.	£ s. d.
Baltimore	22,179 4 0	9,842 5 9
Boston	2,478 16 0	683 17 2
Detroit	4,503 0 0	763 17 6
New Orleans	160,384 0 0	51,784 3 6
New York	318,864 0 0	145,884 4 9
Philadelphia	102,184 16 0	42,784 2 8
Port Huron	95,142 16 0	39,219 2 4
Portland	62 16 0	38 11 6
San Francisco	204 0 0	62 16 9
Galveston	173 16 0	22 16 9
Total	706,182 4 0	291,085 18 8

Note.—Currency estimated at 5 dol. to the £ for convenience.

INTERNAL Revenue Collections.

Designation.	1887.	1888.
	£ s. d.	£ s. d.
Lists (chiefly banks)	884 19 1	740 1 1
Spirit stamps*	369,533 3 4	267,082 0 5
Tobacco ,,	644,554 16 0	640,148 17 1
Cigar ,,	28,039 15 10	28,376 12 8
Snuff ,,	755 10 4	809 0 8
Beer ,,	258,789 2 2	275,885 15 1
Special tax stamps..	24,636 16 3	28,286 6 2
Total	1,327,194 3 0	1,241,328 13 2

SAINT PAUL.

Mr. Vice-Consul Morphy reports as follows:—

The unprecedented tide of prosperity which has set in upon this part of the United States, and especially the cities of St. Paul and Minneapolis, is not, as has now been proven, the result of any spasmodic effort, having for its object to produce a sudden and unsound expansion without due regard to future stability, but is the outcome of persistent effort, and the unstinted expenditure of money at a geographical point which nature indicated as possessing all that could be desired for the centralisation of men and commerce. It is impossible for the present generation to estimate the capabilities of these two cities: as the further development of the vast country to the north and west will, no doubt, tempt them to extend their boundaries to limits yet untried.

* One distillery was closed during the year under arrangement of the Whisky Trust.

UNITED STATES.

The erection of Dakota into separate States of the Union will give an impetus to trade and general development, which will, doubtless, give birth to other new cities such as St. Paul and Minneapolis, or inspire men of calibre to lay hold of locations already selected, and push them into prominence.

Confining myself more particularly to this city, I find it difficult in a brief report to give even a faint picture of its present, or to present its future.

Improvements and enterprises which a few years ago would have startled the community by their audacity, are now matters of every day occurrence, and receive but a passing notice.

A salient view of the various departments of industry and finance, will convey better than any other means the true condition of this city.

The population, which in 1887 was reported at 155,577, has risen to 180,585.

The number of permits for building in 1888 was 4,455.

The value of the buildings erected was 12,939,314 dol., and it may be here remarked that many of the buildings are absolutely fire-proof, and if extended in one continuous line would occupy a frontage of 20 miles. This places St. Paul in the fourth rank as compared with other cities of the United States with regard to the value of building improvements done last year, while the city of Minneapolis stands sixth, there having been expended there in buildings, 9,731,068 dol.

Besides the above amount expended on buildings by individuals and private corporations, it is relevent to add that the sum of 2,290,000 dol. has been expended on public improvements, distributed thuswise :—

Grading	67	miles of streets.
Paving	7	„ „
Constructing	17	„ of sewers.
„	41	„ of wooden sidewalks.
Constructing	8	„ of stone and cement sidewalks.

The sum of 67,000 dol. has been expended on city bridges, besides which the City Council has given a final order for grading 17 additional miles of street, for paving $2\frac{1}{2}$ miles of street, for constructing $2\frac{1}{2}$ miles of sewer, and laying 46 miles of wooden sidewalks.

The activity of the money market is another strong indication of the healthy commercial condition of the city. During the year loans and discounts have reached the sum of 20,000,000 dol.

The capital paid in on stock has reached the sum of 7,000,000 dol.; individual and other deposits, 13,791,152 dol. 55 c. The St. Paul Clearing House records for the past year, 194,913,011 dol. 43 c.

The amount of duties collected at the port of St. Paul, from January 12, 1888, to January 12, 1889, amount to the sum of 177,686 dol. 89 c.

Every attention is paid to intellectual and physical culture.

The St. Paul Library supplies abundant and choice reading matter for all classes, and the Historical Society holds a high place with the "literati," as furnishing a class of reading not generally to be found in either public or private collections.

The public parks are numerous in the central part of the city and furnish delightful places of rendezvous; their value is further enhanced by ever flowing fountains whose delights are increased by musical matinées during the summer evenings.

The educational interests of the city have attained a very high status; they have been carefully guarded, and no department indicates more clearly than this the progress which is sure to win and secure the future stability of this city.

From the business reports it is sure that the past year has been at least one of the most successful on record; more territory has been occupied, and more sales made than ever before. The wholesale business shows an aggregate of 101,000,000 dol. as against 84,000,000 dol. in 1887; a large part of the difference being made up of goods going into consumption by farmers whose expenditure for the comforts, and even the luxuries of life seems to indicate an increase of wealth and good taste.

The increased volume of trade has brought into existence 40 new wholesale houses, and from present appearances that increase will be considerably exceeded this year. The enlargement of another branch of business deserves special mention as indicating the pushing character of the people, and the almost unlimited capacity to absorb production. I refer to the manufacturing interests. Encouraged by the exceptional facilities presented by the various railways, and by the seductive offers made by the owners of suburban towns abutting on St. Paul, and resting on these railways, manufacturers have been induced to invest large sums for the establishment of their various businesses.

It is found that during the past year 35 manufactories have been built, representing a capital of nearly 8,000,000 dol. with a capacity to employ 6,000 workmen.

Another significant fact going to show the healthy condition of the money market in this city and State, a Bill is now pending before the Legislature now in session, to reduce the legal rate of interest from 10 per cent. to 8 per cent. A Bill is also before the Legislature to repeal the Alien Act.

Since the last annual report from this Vice-Consulate, a cable railway of $2\frac{1}{2}$ miles in length has been constructed in this city. It affords rapid service to those residing in the western part of the city, and during the present summer another similar line will be projected eastward. These two will furnish ample facility for local travel in these two directions.

DENVER.

Mr. Vice-Consul Pearce reports as follows:—

The business growth of Denver during 1888 has greatly exceeded that of any previous year.

It has been estimated that the value of new buildings erected during the year amounts to the large sum of 1,500,000*l.* sterling. This is mainly due to the rapid increase in population.

The transactions in real estate alone amounted to 8,000,000*l.*

The records of the clearing house show a total of nearly 20,000,000*l.*, an increase over the previous year amounting to nearly 3,500,000*l.*

This prosperity may be said to extend throughout the whole of the State of Colorado, as the returns of the value of taxable property in the State show a gain over 1887 of nearly 5,500,000*l.*

Denver's position, as a large railroad centre, has been further strengthened during the year by direct connection (through the Denver, Texas, and Forworth railroad) with the port of Galveston, in Texas, and a large import and export trade may be expected through this new link with the Gulf of Mexico. The Missouri, Pacific, and Rock Island railroads, two very extensive systems east of the Missouri river, have extended their roads west to Colorado, and now make their own separate connections with Denver.

Industries. — Mining, the chief industry of the State, shows, during 1888, a very marked increase in the value of the metal product over 1887, the difference being about 500,000*l.*; the value of the entire product for the year is estimated as follows:—

	£
Silver	3,424,395
Gold	825,787
Lead	1,158,080
Copper	31,169
Total	5,439,431

During the past year, railroad connections have been made with Aspen (a large silver mining district about 300 miles west of Denver). From the increased facilities now afforded for the transportation of the silver ore to the various smelting establishments in the State, Aspen will help in future to increase, very materially, the total output of silver in Colorado.

Coal. — Ten years ago the coal production of Colorado was only 200,000 tons per annum, but the returns for 1888 show a product for the year of 2,185,477 tons (2,000 lbs. each), of this quantity 700,574 tons have been sent to points in Kansas, Nebraska and Texas. From this it may be seen that a very large percentage of the entire product is marketed in neighbouring States.

The average value of the coal, on the cars at the mine, is said to be 9*s.* 2*d.* per ton; this represents a total value of nearly 1,000,000*l.*

Almost every variety of coal is to be found in the State, from the lower grades of lignite, up to a good quality of anthracite.

The area of discovered coal in the State is said to be enormous, and we have it, on the evidence of good authorities, that there is every prospect of Colorado being the largest and most important coal State in the Union.

A remarkable increase in the oil product of the State is shown in 1888.   *Petroleum.*

In 1887 the product was hardly 300 barrels of crude oil per day; while the total yield for 1888 is reported to be 300,000 barrels, representing a money value of about 60,000*l*. The only developed oil region in the State is the district around the town of Florence, in Fremont County. The wells vary in depth, from 1,200 ft. to 2,000 ft., and are sunk entirely in shale, no sand rock as yet having been encountered in drilling. The average product from each well is 40 barrels per day.

At the present time the output of these wells is sufficient to supply the demand for illuminating oil of Colorado, Wyoming, Utah, Montana, and New Mexico.

Colorado railroads have been increased in mileage during the year to the extent of 268 miles, making a total mileage of 4,302·44; this is represented by the various roads as follows:—   *Railroad building.*

	Miles.
Denver and Rio Grande	1,478·84
Union Pacific	1,076·60
Denver, Texas, and Forworth	240·00
Burlington and Missouri	350·00
Denver, Utah, and Pacific	44·00
Colorado Midland	428·00
Atchison, Topeka, and Santa Fé	390·00
Missouri Pacific	120·00
Silverton and Red Mountain	15·00
Rio Grande and Western	40·00
Total	4,302·44

The climate of Colorado has been so extensively described that it is scarcely necessary to do more than refer, briefly, to the preparations that are being made in the interests of invalids, and people generally who suffer from pulmonary affections, and who find relief from the dry climate and pure air of the mountains. It is proposed to establish in certain favoured localities in the mountain districts, health resorts, where people may live surrounded by comforts and conveniences, and still be within easy distance of a large city.   *Climate.*

The rapid increase in the population of Denver, and the extension of its manufacturing interests, make it almost imperative that such sanitariums should be established in localities most favoured by natural scenery and shelter from winds.

The year 1888 has been an eventful one in many ways, so far as Colorado interests are concerned.

The subject of irrigation has received a large share of public attention, and it has been proposed to adopt a system of storage reservoirs for the purpose of reclaiming the arid lands of the State, and bring them into extensive cultivation.   *Construction of reservoirs for irrigation.*

An appeal has been made to the Government, which has been favourably received, and already an expenditure of 20,000*l*. has been sanctioned for the preliminary surveys in regard to the scheme. It is difficult to estimate the value of such an enterprise as this, as lands are increasing in value every year and nearly all

UNITED STATES.

Imports.

the desirable portions, covered by the present system of irrigation, have been taken up.

The object of this storage system is to provide very extensive reservoirs at certain points where they can be filled from various streams, at seasons when there is a large excess of water which, at present, is allowed to waste.

These reservoirs can then be tapped when the water is required for agricultural purposes.

There has been an increase in the value of British goods imported through the Denver custom house, during 1888, of over 3,000*l*. The following is a record of the past three years:—

	1886.	1887.	1888.
	£	£ s.	£ s.
Total value ..	3,201	5,043 12	8,109 12

It must be understood that the above figures only represent a value of the British goods which have passed the Denver custom house, and not the actual value of goods received in Denver, the bulk of which having, in all probability, been cleared at other ports of entry.

Return of the Principal Articles of Import to Denver during the Year 1888.

	£	s.	d.
Earthenware, brown	264	4	0
China ware	131	12	0
Manufactured silk lace	125	8	0
,, cotton lace	250	8	0
,, linen	80	0	0
,, wool, cloths	2,887	12	0
,, ,, clothing	36	16	0
,, ,, carpets	786	16	0
Personal effects	523	4	0
Books	19	8	0
Varnish	74	8	0
Fur and felt hats	65	0	0
Wines and spirits	227	16	0
Mining machinery	1,215	4	0
Terne plate	539	12	0
Assayers balances	66	0	0
Guns	224	0	0
Bicycles	221	0	0
Caustic soda	311	16	0
Miscellaneous articles	59	8	0
Total	8,109	12	0

(1250 7 | 89—H & S 701)

COMMERCIAL. No. 13 (1890).
(UNITED STATES.)

FURTHER REPORTS

ON THE

STATUS OF ALIENS AND FOREIGN COMPANIES

IN THE

UNITED STATES.

[In continuation of "Commercial No. 14 (1888):" C. 5579.]

Presented to both Houses of Parliament by Command of Her Majesty.
March 1890.

LONDON:
PRINTED FOR HER MAJESTY'S STATIONERY OFFICE
BY HARRISON AND SONS, ST. MARTIN'S LANE,
PRINTERS IN ORDINARY TO HER MAJESTY.

And to be purchased, either directly or through any Bookseller, from
EYRE AND SPOTTISWOODE, EAST HARDING STREET, FLEET STREET, E.C., AND
32, ABINGDON STREET, WESTMINSTER, S.W.; OR
ADAM AND CHARLES BLACK, 6, NORTH BRIDGE, EDINBURGH; OR
HODGES, FIGGIS, & CO., 104, GRAFTON STREET, DUBLIN.

[C.—5969.] *Price* 1d.

Further Reports on the Status of Aliens and Foreign Companies in the United States.

[In continuation of "Commercial No. 14 (1888):" C. 5579.]

Sir J. Pauncefote to the Marquis of Salisbury.—(*Received March 5.*)

My Lord,   *Washington, February* 21, 1890.

WITH reference to your Lordship's despatch of the 25th November last, I have the honour to forward herewith despatches which I have received from Her Majesty's Consuls in the United States, reporting on the changes which have occurred in the States and Territories within their Consular jurisdiction in the Laws affecting the status of aliens and alien Corporations since the last Report on the subject was written.

There appear to have been very few changes made since 1886.

I have, &c.
(Signed)   JULIAN PAUNCEFOTE.

Inclosure 1.

Consul-General Booker to Sir J. Pauncefote.

Sir,   *New York, January* 7, 1890.

I HAVE the honour to acknowledge the receipt of your Circular of the 20th December last, and to report, in response to the request contained therein, that there have been no changes in the Laws of the States within my Consular jurisdiction, comprising the States of New York, New Jersey, Delaware, Connecticut, and Rhode Island, affecting the status of aliens and alien Corporations since my Report to Sir Lionel West on the 27th October, 1886.

I have, &c.
(Signed)   WM. LANE BOOKER.

Inclosure 2.

Consul Henderson to Sir J. Pauncefote.

Sir,   *Boston, December* 28, 1889.

IN compliance with the instructions in your Circular despatch of the 20th instant I have the honour to report that the following Laws, having reference to the status of alien Corporations (none having been enacted in regard to individual aliens), have been added to the Statutes of the States of Massachusetts, New Hampshire, and Maine, subsequently to the year 1886.

In Massachusetts, an Act (chap. 321 of the 10th May, 1888), entitled, "An Act authorizing foreign Manufacturing Corporations to hold Real Estate in this Commonwealth," which provides that manufacturing Corporations established under the Laws of other States may purchase and hold such real estate in the Commonwealth as may be necessary for conducting their business.

In New Hampshire, an Act (approved the 7th June, 1889) which provides that all manufacturing Corporations not established under the Laws of the State, doing or which may hereafter do business therein, may acquire, purchase, hold, or convey real estate and other property.

In Maine, an Act (chap. 166 of 1889) which provides that foreign Corporations doing business continuously in the State, and having constantly an officer or agent resident therein, shall be entitled to all provisions of law relating to limitation of actions, the same as domestic Corporations.

In Vermont, whose Supreme Court has held that the right to interfere with aliens holding real estate in the country belongs to the National and not to the State sovereignty, no Laws affecting aliens have been passed since 1886, but it may not be out of place here to cite a Resolution (No. 123 of 1886) agreed to by the State Legislature, to the effect that the State Senators and Representatives in Congress be requested to give their early attention to the fact of the acquirement and possession by aliens of vast tracts of public lands in the country, and to labour for such legislation as may arrest the evil.

I have, &c.
(Signed) C. A. HENDERSON.

Inclosure 3.

Consul Segrave to Sir J. Pauncefote.

Sir, Baltimore, January 4, 1890.
IN reply to your Circular despatch of the 20th ultimo, I have the honour to report to you that, within my knowledge, no alterations have taken place in the Laws affecting the status of aliens within this Consular district since the date of my last Report on this subject.

I have, &c.
(Signed) W. F. SEGRAVE.

Inclosure 4.

Acting Consul Harriss-Gastrell to Sir J Pauncefote.

Sir, Chicago, February 10, 1890.
IN reply to your despatch of the 20th December last, I have the honour to inform you, after due inquiry, that, as far as I can ascertain, no change has taken place in the Laws affecting aliens within this Consular district.

I have, &c.
(Signed) J. P. HARRISS-GASTRELL.

Inclosure 5.

Consul Donohoe to Sir J. Pauncefote.

Sir, San Francisco, February 5, 1890.
I HAVE the honour to acknowledge the receipt of your Circular of the 20th December last, instructing me to make a Report as to what, if any, changes have been made in the Laws of the States within my Consular jurisdiction as to the status of aliens and alien Corporations since the Report from this Consulate made on the 25th October, 1886

I have the honour to annex a Report on the subject for the States of California, Nevada, and Washington, and territories of Idaho and Utah. The Governor of Arizona informs me that there are no legal discriminations against aliens in that territory.

I inclose a copy of a despatch from Vice-Consul Laidlaw, of Portland, as to a change in the insurance Laws as affecting alien Corporations.

I have, &c.
(Signed) DENIS DONOHOE.

Inclosure 6.

Laws relating to Aliens and Alien Corporations.

California.—No changes since October 1886.

Nevada.—Any non-resident alien, person, or Corporation may take, hold, and enjoy any real property or any interest in lands upon the same conditions as any resident citizen.

N.B.—No restrictions, except that aliens who have not declared their intention to become citizens cannot obtain mines, &c., by patent from the State.

Idaho.—The Revised Statutes of this territory contain no Statute as to the rights of aliens to convey real property. The "Alien Land Act" of Congress of the 3rd March, 1887 (which see), obtains in this territory, and prescribes and defines the rights of aliens.

Utah.—Aliens take by descent as if citizens, and may be inherited from as if citizens; but if a non-resident alien shall fail to appear and claim succession within five years after the death of the person to whom he claims succession, the Probate Court may cause the property to be reduced to the possession of the territory, or cause the same to be sold and the proceeds deposited in the territorial Treasury for the benefit of such non-resident alien or his legal representative, to be paid to him whenever, within five years after such deposit, proof to the satisfaction of the Probate Court is produced to the County Clerk that he is entitled to succeed thereto. If no one succeeds to the estate or the proceeds, it or they escheat to the territory for benefit of Public School Fund.

Aliens are prohibited from acquiring, holding, or owning real estate in Utah, or any interest therein, except such as may be acquired by inheritance or in good faith in the ordinary course of justice in the collection of debts created prior to the 3rd March, 1887. See "Alien Land Act" of Congress of the 3rd March, 1887, for further provisions and restrictions. This Act obtains in Utah.

Washington.—Washington has just been admitted to the Union as a State. As a territory the "Alien Land Act" obtained.

The Legislature at its coming Session will probably pass some legislation on the subject.

The Code of Washington (passed when it was a territory) provided that:—

"Any alien" (except Chinamen) "may acquire or hold lands, &c., by purchase, devise, or descent, may mortgage, convey, or devise the same, and if he dies intestate the same descends to his heirs.

"Any alien (except as above), whether a resident of this territory or not, may construct, lease, use, sell, or purchase any railroad or bridge within the territory, and enjoy the same powers and privileges that resident citizens now have or may hereafter acquire." (Code, §§ 19, 24, 2420.)

Of course, these provisions were modified by the passage of the "Alien Land Act" by Congress. Now that Washington is a State the "Alien Land Act" ceases to apply, and, until further legislation, the sections of the Code cited above would obtain.

Inclosure 7.

Vice-Consul Laidlaw to Consul Donohoe.

Sir, *Portland, January 8, 1890.*

WITH reference to your inquiry as to the status of aliens and alien Corporations resident or carrying on business within the State of Oregon, I have to report that there has been no change made in the Laws as to the status of aliens since my Report of the 7th October, 1886.

There have been some changes made in the insurance Laws, and I inclose a pamphlet published by the Secretary of State embracing these changes.*

The Acts of 1887 and 1889 provide that a certificate must be obtained from the Secretary of State, who is *ex officio* Insurance Commissioner, before any Company, alien or otherwise, can transact an insurance business. Also that the deposit of 50,000 dollars heretofore required may be made in "interest-bearing bonds of the United States, or in bonds of the State of Oregon, or any municipal, school, district, or county bonds issued by authority of law in the State of Oregon, the market value of which is at or above par, or bonds or notes secured by first mortgage upon

* Not printed.

unencumbered real estate within the State of Oregon of double the amount loaned thereon, or money of the United States. It is also provided that in lieu of such deposit, any foreign Corporation may make an investment in real estate within the State of Oregon of the value of not less than 65,000 dollars, provided such investment shall be approved by the Insurance Commissioner. The title to such real estate to be vested in the State Treasurer as Trustee for the Corporation making such investment."

No Insurance Company organized outside of the State of Oregon can do business unless it proves to the Insurance Commissioner that it has an unimpaired cash capital of at least 200,000 dollars, and must file with him a power of attorney authorizing a citizen and resident of the State to make and accept service in any Court. No Company not incorporated in the United States can transact an insurance business in this State (except marine insurance) unless it has deposited or invested for the benefit of its policy-holders in the United States in at least one State a sum equal to 200,000 dollars in excess of its liabilities in the United States. This is in addition to the 50,000 dollars deposited with the State Treasurer.

So far as I can ascertain, there have been no further changes in the Laws affecting alien Corporations.

I have, &c.
(Signed) JAMES LAIDLAW.

Inclosure 8.

Consul Clipperton to Sir J. Pauncefote.

Sir, Philadelphia, February 4, 1890.

I BEG to acknowledge the receipt of your Circular despatch of the 20th December last, requesting that further report be made with regard to the Laws in force in the various States and territories of the United States, so far as they respectively affect the status of aliens and alien Corporations resident or carrying on business within their limits.

It would appear, so far as this Consular district is concerned, that since the last Report from this Consulate, in 1886, there have been no changes in the Laws upon this subject in the States of Pennsylvania, Ohio, Indiana, and Michigan.

I have, &c.
(Signed) ROBT. CHAS. CLIPPERTON.

Inclosure 9.

Consul Cridland to Sir J. Pauncefote.

Sir, Charleston, January 11, 1890.

WITH reference to your Circular despatch of the 20th ultimo, requesting me to furnish you with a Report as to what, if any, changes have been made in the Laws within the States of this Consular district affecting the status of aliens and alien Corporations since the Report furnished in 1887, I have the honour to state that after due inquiry in the four States, I find that the only additional Law passed on the subject has been in Georgia, a copy of which I beg to inclose herewith.

I have, &c.
(Signed) FREDERICK J. CRIDLAND.

Inclosure 10.

BONDS OF CORPORATIONS.

Record by Secretary of State of Georgia.

(No. 1679.)

ALL public and private Corporations must have a record made by the Secretary of State of every issue or indorsement of bonds for circulation. The circulation of unrecorded bonds is forbidden under a penalty of 500 dollars for each bond.

Inclosure 11.

Consul Lyall to Sir J. Pauncefote.

Sir, Galveston, *December* 28, 1889.

I HAVE the honour to acknowledge the receipt of your inclosure, dated the 20th December, containing a Circular and Reports respecting "Alien Laws" in force in (United States) States and territories. With reference to "further information" on this subject being demanded, I would respectfully submit that no changes have been made in the Laws of the States within my Consular jurisdiction since my last Report was written, and that no disabilities are, in consequence, at present inflicted on aliens and alien Corporations in Texas and New Mexico.

I have, &c.
(Signed) WALTER T. LYALL.

Inclosure 12.

Consul de Fonblanque to Sir J. Pauncefote.

Sir, New Orleans, *January* 6, 1890.

REFERRING to your Circular of the 20th December, 1889, I do not find that any Laws have been passed in the States comprising this Consular district affecting the status of aliens or of alien Corporations since my last Report on this subject.

I have, &c.
(Signed) A. DE J. DE FONBLANQUE.

COMMERCIAL. No. 13 (1890).
(UNITED STATES.)

Further Reports on the Status of Aliens and Foreign Companies in the United States.

[In continuation of "Commercial No. 14 (1888);"
C. 5579.]

Presented to both Houses of Parliament by Command of Her Majesty. March 1890.

LONDON:
PRINTED BY HARRISON AND SONS

FOREIGN OFFICE.
1890.
ANNUAL SERIES.

No. 643.

DIPLOMATIC AND CONSULAR REPORTS ON TRADE AND FINANCE.

UNITED STATES.

REPORT FOR THE YEAR 1889
ON THE
AGRICULTURE OF THE CONSULAR DISTRICT OF NEW YORK.

REFERENCE TO PREVIOUS REPORT, Annual Series No. 431.

Presented to both Houses of Parliament by Command of Her Majesty,
FEBRUARY, 1890.

LONDON:
PRINTED FOR HER MAJESTY'S STATIONERY OFFICE,
BY HARRISON AND SONS, ST. MARTIN'S LANE,
PRINTERS IN ORDINARY TO HER MAJESTY.

And to be purchased, either directly or through any Bookseller, from
EYRE AND SPOTTISWOODE, EAST HARDING STREET, FLEET STREET, E.C., and
32, ABINGDON STREET, WESTMINSTER, S.W.; or
ADAM AND CHARLES BLACK, 6, NORTH BRIDGE, EDINBURGH; or
HODGES, FIGGIS, & Co., 104, GRAFTON STREET, DUBLIN.

1890.

[C. 5895—46.] *Price One Penny.*

New Series of Reports.

Reports of the Annual Series have been issued from Her Majesty's Diplomatic and Consular Officers at the following places, and may be obtained from the sources indicated on the title-page:—

No.		Price.
517.	Mollendo	1d.
518.	Taiwan	1d.
519.	Wuhu	1d.
520.	Corunna	2d.
521.	Noumea	1d.
522.	San José	1d.
523.	Ningpo	1d.
524.	Gothenburg	2d.
525.	Hankow	2d.
526.	Foochow	1d.
527.	Erzeroum	2d.
528.	Ciudad Bolivar	1d.
529.	Jaffa	1d.
530.	Ancona	1d.
531.	Savannah	1d.
532.	Batavia	1d.
533.	Adrianople	1d.
534.	Nisch	11d.
535.	Vienna	1d.
536.	Odessa	8d.
537.	Constantinople	2d.
538.	Damascus	1d.
539.	Tientsin	1d.
540.	Amoy	1d.
541.	Mogador	1d.
542.	Vienna	1d.
543.	Antwerp	1d.
544.	Lisbon	2d.
545.	New York	1½d.
546.	San Francisco	1d.
547.	Stettin	1½d.
548.	San Salvador	½d.
549.	Trebizond	1d.
550.	Nice	1d.
551.	Baghdad	½d.
552.	Fiume	1d.
553.	Mogador	2d.
554.	Buenos Ayres	1½d.
555.	San Francisco	2½d.
556.	Carthagena	½d.
557.	Syra	1d.
558.	Varna and Bourgas	1d.
559.	Thessaly	½d.
560.	Yokohama	1d.
561.	Nantes	1½d.
562.	Suakin	½d.
563.	Algiers	1d.
564.	St. Petersburg	2½d.
565.	Söul	1d.
566.	Newchwang	1d.
567.	Roustchouk and Philippopolis	1d.
568.	Stockholm	1½d.
569.	Tonga	1d.
570.	Chicago	1½d.
571.	Adana	½d.
572.	Buenos Ayres	3d.
573.	Frankfort	1½d.
574.	Canton	1½d.
575.	Tamsui	5½d.
576.	Palermo	3d.
577.	Amsterdam	1d.
578.	Ajaccio	½d.
579.	Shanghai	1½d.

No.		Price.
580.	Warsaw	½d.
581.	Teneriffe	1d.
582.	Tangier	2d.
583.	Surinam	½d.
584.	Loanda	1d.
585.	Alexandria	1d.
586.	Cagliari	1d.
587.	Smyrna	½d.
588.	Mannheim	1d.
589.	Nagasaki	1d.
590.	Hakodate	1d.
591.	Bushire	1d.
592.	Chinkiang	½d.
593.	Pakhoi	1d.
594.	Hiogo	1½d.
595.	Bangkok	1d.
596.	Serajevo	1d.
597.	Copenhagen	1½d.
598.	Cephalonia	½d.
599.	Chefoo	½d.
600.	Guatemala	1½d.
601.	Tonga	½d.
602.	Tahiti	1d.
603.	Stettin	2d.
604.	Vera Cruz	1½d.
605.	Christiania	4d.
606.	Pernambuco	1½d.
607.	Trieste	1½d.
608.	Tunis	½d.
609.	Havana	2d.
610.	Frankfort	½d.
611.	Tabreez	½d.
612.	Bilbao	1d.
613.	Barcelona	½d.
614.	Tokio	1d.
615.	Naples	2½d.
616.	Batoum	½d.
617.	Odessa	1d.
618.	La Rochelle	1d.
619.	Rome	1d.
620.	Nice	1d.
621.	Kiukiang	½d.
622.	Paris	1d.
623.	Salonica	1½d.
624.	Réunion	1d.
625.	Ichang	1d.
626.	Bogatá	1d.
627.	Malaga	2d.
628.	Porto Rico	1d.
629.	Bushire	2½d.
630.	The Hague	½d.
631.	Berlin	1d.
632.	Adrianople	1½d.
633.	Rome	1½d.
634.	Santiago	½d.
635.	Tahiti	½d.
636.	Maranham	½d.
637.	Mexico	2d.
638.	Christiania	1d.
639.	Copenhagen	1d.
640.	Paris	1d.
641.	Venice	1d.
642.	Cherbourg	½d.

No. 643.

Reference to previous Report, Annual Series No. 431.

UNITED STATES.

NEW YORK.

Consul-General Booker to the Marquis of Salisbury.

My Lord, New York, December 16, 1889.

I HAVE the honour to transmit herewith a Report upon the Agriculture of the States of New York, New Jersey, Connecticut, Rhode Island, and Delaware.

I have, &c.
(Signed) WM. LANE BOOKER.

Report upon the Agriculture of the States of New York, New Jersey, Connecticut, Rhode Island, and Delaware, for the Year 1889.

The United States' Bureau of Agriculture was, in March last, elevated to an Executive Department of the Government, and the result will be more valuable general and statistical information in regard to the agriculture of the whole country than the Bureau has been able to afford. It will necessarily take some time for the department to perfect its organisation, and to get into working order the changes and innovations proposed by the secretary. In reference to this the secretary in his first report, just published, states:—"It is not necessary for me to dwell at this time upon the past growth of this institution; how there have been assigned to it from time to time additional duties and power until now, when it comes forward as a completed wing of the executive branch of the Government, entitled to its full share of attention and protection, and needing at this time careful and intelligent effort in order that the foundation now ready to be laid shall be the commencement of a great and lasting department, well fitted to extend its usefulness over a great agricultural domain. I deemed it my first duty, therefore, to give particular attention to such a re-adjustment of the current affairs of the department as should make it better conform to its new relations under the law, and then to give careful thought to the formulation of plans for a thorough and complete re-organisation of the new department. I am not unmindful of the difficulties of the duties which have fallen to me in this regard, nor do I think that I shall overstate those to which I shall here refer.

[Marginal note: Bureau of Agriculture made a Government Department. Its duties.]

"At the very beginning I was disappointed to find that the appropriations made for the operations of the department for the current fiscal year were those based upon the old organisation of the department, and that no provision had been made for a single anticipated want of the department in its new field of duty. Therefore, my first efforts had to be restricted to the study and formulation of plans for re-organisation; to the systematising of the records of the department; to the consolidation, so far as possible, under one head, of work of one character, but being conducted in different divisions of the department; to a formulation of a better system for the faithful accounting of public property, and in general the application of business-like principles throughout the department. I have performed this duty while awaiting the meeting of Congress, when its attention might be called to the condition of affairs to which I have alluded, and to the urgent need of immediate attention."

Agricultural experiment stations.

With reference to agricultural experiment stations, a most important branch of the department, the secretary states: "As a central agency for the agricultural experiment stations of the country established by Act of Congress, it is the duty of the department, through the office of experiment stations, to indicate lines of inquiry for the stations, to promote the co-ordination of their work, to furnish them needed advice and assistance, and to collate and publish the results of their experiments. To this end it conducts a large and increasing correspondence relating to the scientific, administrative, and general interests of the individual stations and the enterprise as a whole. Its representatives visit stations, agricultural colleges, and kindred institutions. It collects statistics and other information regarding agricultural science; compiles results of inquiry past and present in this country and in Europe, which are greatly needed, and earnestly called for by the station workers and others interested in agricultural science; and puts the results of station work in practical form for general distribution in farmers' bulletins.

"For the ensuing year this office needs means proportionate to the pressing demand for the enlargement of its work in all the lines named, including especially the collating of fruits of experience and making them available to the stations and the agriculture of the country, and the promotion of inquiries of general importance in connection with the stations in different sections of the land. With other lines of inquiry, the study of the far-reaching problems relating to the food and nutrition of domestic animals and of man, and the systematic investigation of our soils, already begun in accordance with special provision by Act of Congress, should be undertaken on a broad and scientific basis.

"The development of the experiment station enterprise in this country is a noteworthy illustration of the readiness of the American people to grasp and to utilise new and valuable ideas. Beginning only 14 years ago, it has grown out to the furthest limits of the land, enlisted the best colleges and universities and the ablest investigators, and secured both state and national resources for its maintenance. It now employs nearly 400 workers to promote agriculture by scientific investigation and experiment, and to diffuse as well as increase the knowledge which improves farm practice and elevates farm life. It has the favour of a great army of practical farmers, to whom it has already brought substantial benefits. The experience thus far gained evinces the wisdom of Congress in distributing the work throughout the country where it may be adapted to the wants of the various sections, and placing it in connection with institutions of learning which are, in general, labouring faithfully to fulfil the trust imposed upon them.

" Crudity and mistakes are here and there apparent. But the general effort of the stations toward the greatest usefulness, the wise action of the Association of American Agricultural Colleges and Experiment Stations, the cordial support of the people, State Legislatures and Congress, and the practical results already obtained, imply that the National Government has made no mistake in undertaking this enterprise on a larger scale than has been attempted elsewhere in the world. At the same time we should remember that quality more than magnitude decides the value of every enterprise, and that this one can attain its highest success only in proportion as the laws which underlie the practice of agriculture are discovered and made available to the practical toilers of the farm."

NEW YORK.

The product of the cereals, &c., of the State of New York in 1887–88 is given in the following table:—

		1887.			1888.		
		No. of Acres in each crop.	Quantity produced.	Average yield per Acre.	No. of Acres in each crop.	Quantity produced.	Average yield per Acre.
Wheat	Bushels	666,883	10,137,000	15·2	660,214	9,309,000	14·1
Indian corn	,,	709,406	23,410,000	33·0	705,859	22,870,000	32·4
Barley	,,	340,028	6,733,000	19·8	No statistics available.		
Oats	,,	1,413,088	33,208,000	23·5	1,398,957	40,570,000	29·0
Rye	,,	234,506	2,533,000	10·8			
Buckwheat	,,	317,663	4,130,000	13·0	No statistics available.		
Potatoes	,,	353,433	23,327,000	66·0			
Hay	Tons	5,059,913	5,818,000	1·15			

The values of the various crops were estimated by the United States Department of Agriculture at:—

Crops.	Year.	Value.
		£
Wheat	1888	2,109,380
Indian corn	,,	2,732,500
Oats	,,	3,092,250
Rye	1887	318,300
Barley	,,	943,150
Buckwheat	,,	450,900
Potatoes	,,	2,979,300
Hay	,,	12,897,900

UNITED STATES.

Cheese factories and creameries.

The following, tabulated from the Report of the State Dairy Commissioner, gives a good deal of useful information in regard to the cheese factories and creameries of this State, and the business of the dairy farmer, embracing, as the table does, statistics in connection with all the counties in which dairy farming is carried on to any extent.

STATISTICAL Table, tabulated from the Report of the State Dairy Commissioner in regard to Cheese Factories and Creameries.

Counties.	Number of Factories and Creameries Visited.	Amount of Milk in lbs. delivered at Factories and Creameries during entire season.	Number of Cows from which supply came.	Average Number of Cows per Factory or Creamery.	Average Amount of Milk in lbs. per Cow during season.	Average Number of lbs. Milk to make 1 lb. Cheese.	Average Number of lbs. Milk to make 1 lb. Butter.
Alleghany	85	84,215,985	26,935	316	3,142	$10\frac{1}{20}$	...
Broome	16	12,240,800	6,168	385	1,984	$10\frac{7}{10}$	$38\frac{3}{15}$
Callerangus	115	150,771,096	36,432	317	4,133	9·76	$24\frac{1}{2}$
Cayuga	11	7,621,200	3,200	291	2,380	$9\frac{5}{9}$	$47\frac{1}{4}$
Chatauqua	93	75,227,481	30,236	326	2,484	10	$22\frac{2}{3}$
Chenning	16	23,015,960	5,620	351	4,095	$13\frac{1}{2}$	$25\frac{12}{25}$
Chenango	42	46,518,192	15,742	375	2,955	$12\frac{1}{20}$	38
Cortland	33	28,837,185	9,475	285	3,043	$11\frac{1}{12}$	29
Delaware	16	17,006,250	4,830	371	3,520	$13\frac{8}{11}$	$28\frac{2}{3}$
Erie	65	41,107,632	18,420	284	2,231	$10\frac{8}{10}$	$39\frac{3}{5}$
Fulton	2	877,500	235	117	3,724	10	...
Genessee	10	4,953,999	2,786	279	1,419	$10\frac{1}{9}$	26
Herkimer	99	159,125,256	35,661	362	4,462	9·98	43
Jefferson	41	59,192,826	17,030	416	3,475	10·17	46
Lewis	65	89,027,541	26,922	448	3,306	10	$25\frac{1}{2}$
Livingston	2	2,028,000	780	390	2,600	10	...
Montgomery	35	33,422,760	9,370	302	3,567	10·18	33
Madison	60	102,416,540	18,429	307	2,854	10·97	$43\frac{5}{100}$
Monroe	2	2,626,500	550	275	3,910	10	...
Niagara	2	2,145,000	650	325	3,900	10	...
Oneida	69	94,550,402	32,169	466	2,949	10·24	35
Onandaga	11	8,425,800	2,536	254	3,322	$10\frac{8}{11}$	34
Ontario	5	...	1,640	328	...	10	...
Orleans	2	1,644,300	366	183	4,492	10	25
Oswego	37	69,731,280	17,230	466	4,047	10	40
Otsego	45	25,576,604	14,063	335	1,818	$11\frac{1}{13}$	$33\frac{1}{3}$
St. Lawrence	80	94,901,559	39,766	497	2,383	$10\frac{38}{100}$	$24\frac{7}{50}$
Schenectady	1	270,000	90	90	3,000	$10\frac{1}{4}$	...
Schuyler	4	838,680	345	86	2,430	12	27
Seneca	1	720,000	100	100	3,200	10	25
Stenben	19	6,781,002	4,749	264	1,427	$9\frac{13}{15}$	...
Tioga	9	5,544,000	3,190	355	1,737	$11\frac{2}{3}$	23
Tompkins	5	6,552,000	1,725	345	3,218	$10\frac{3}{5}$	24
Wayne	4	1,101,600	1,085	271	1,015	10	...
Wyoming	57	55,115,334	19,215	337	2,868	$10\frac{20}{100}$	42
Yates	2	120,000	70	35	1,714	$9\frac{3}{4}$	...

There are within the State of New York more than 10 per cent. of the milch cows of the United States. The Report of the United States Commissioner of Agriculture, on January 1, 1889, states that there were then in the United States 15,298,625 cows, valued at 75,442,600*l*., and in this State 1,552,373 milch cows, of the value of 9,465,750*l*.

The State Dairy Commissioner estimates that there are 82,400,000*l*. invested in the dairy business within this State, and the gross value of the dairy product in 1888 I estimate at 24,256,000*l*. This estimate is based upon information furnished in various shapes by the Commissioner.

NEW YORK.

In the year ending October 1, 1888, there were received in New York, 5,747,558 cans, 40 gallons each, milk; 119,194 cans of cream, 40 gallons each; and 75,183 cans of condensed milk, 40 gallons each. I have no statistics available to show exactly what of the above is the product of this State; but it is safe to say, by the statistics, as far as they go, of the railroads bringing it, that more than three-fourths can fairly be claimed for it.

Oleomargarine. The Dairy Commissioner reports that no oleomargarine, or imitation butter, is now made in the State so far as he has been able to ascertain, and it is confidently believed none is made. Compared with the amount which has been sold in previous years, not very much is being sold within the State; some made in other States is being shipped into this State; and occasionally clandestinely sold in small quantities by dealers bold enough to make such sales, and take the chance of being found out and prosecuted.

Horse breeding. Horse breeding is a progressive business in this State, and the number of horses on farms is constantly increasing. At the end of 1887 there were 674,018, and at the close of 1888, 680,758. The value has varied but little in the past few years; but prices are 25 per cent. higher than they were ten years ago. The average price is given by the United States Agricultural Department at 7*l.* for horses under one year; 12*l.* 6*s.* between one and two years; 17*l.* 2*s.* between two and three years; 21*l.* 15*s.* over three years; and 18*l.* 10*s.* the average of all ages.

NEW JERSEY.

The product of the cereals, &c., of New Jersey in 1887 and 1888 is given in the following table:—

		1887.			1888.		
		Number of Acres in each Crop.	Quantity Produced.	Average Yield per Acre.	Number of Acres in each Crop	Quantity Produced.	Average Yield per Acre.
Wheat	Bushels	143,083	1,459,000	10·2	141,652	1,785,000	12·60
Indian corn	,,	346,866	10,406,000	30·0	350,335	11,351,000	32·40
Rye	,,	103,518	994,000	9·6	No statistics available.		
Oats	,,	138,830	3,221,000	23·2	140,218	3,688,000	26·30
Buckwheat	,,	36,084	426,000	11·8			
Potatoes	,,	41,301	2,767,000	67·0	No statistics available.		
Hay	Tons	493,591	616,990	1·25			

The values of the different crops were estimated by the United States Department of Agriculture at—

Crops.	Year.	Value.
		£
Wheat	1888	404,480
Indian corn	,,	1,239,300
Oats	,,	273,500
Rye	1887	108,460
Buckwheat	,,	51,775
Potatoes	,,	416,400
Hay	,,	1,604,530

On January 1 of last year there were in the State 181,676 milch cows, which is a steadily increasing number. 7*l.* is given as the average value. Graded Jerseys, Alderneys, and Holsteins, are the favourite breeds for dairy purposes. Cows average about 3,500 lbs. milk, and give from 15*l.* to 18*l.* per cow. There are about 50 creameries in the State. Fattening cattle was at one time an important feature in the farming of the State, but competition from the West has almost entirely put an end to it.

Indian corn and oats are grown to advantage, and in some localities, where the demand for the straw is good, rye. In the counties near Philadelphia and this city, garden crops and small fruits are largely cultivated. In one county near to Philadelphia 20,000 out of 57,000 acres improved land are devoted to vegetables. Farmers complain greatly of the railroad charges for the carriage of fruit and milk; for the latter, 40 c. (1*s.* 9*d.*) per can of 40 quarts is charged whether the distance be 50 miles or 250 miles; this will probably be changed under the Inter-State Law.

The experiment station is of great use to the farmers of New Jersey. The farm connected with the station, and the laboratory built last year at a cost of 6,000*l.*, are both under able management, and furnish the information needed by the agriculturist.

CONNECTICUT.

The product of cereals, etc., of Connecticut for the years 1887 and 1888 is given in the following table:—

		1887.			1888.		
		No. of acres in each crop.	Quantity produced.	Average yield per acre.	No. of acres in each crop.	Quantity produced.	Average yield per acre.
Wheat	Bushels	2,171	37,000	17·0	2,149	32,000	14·9
Indian corn	,,	58,140	1,977,000	34·0	56,977	1,778,000	31·2
Barley	,,	638	14,000	21·9	No statistics available.		
Oats	,,	39,417	1,088,000	23·3	39,811	1,055,000	26·4
Rye	,,	29,381	353,000	12·0			
Buckwheat	,,	10,974	117,000	10·7			
Tobacco	Lbs.	6,198	9,173,000	1480·0	No statistics available.		
Potatoes	Bushels	32,172	2,349,000	73·0			
Hay	Tons	574,649	632,114	1·1			

The values of the different crops were estimated by the United States Department of Agriculture at—

Crops.	Year.	Value.
		£
Wheat	1888	7,910
Indian corn	,,	238,073
Oats	,,	93,452
Barley	1887	1,961
Rye	,,	50,175
Buckwheat	,,	15,426
Tobacco	,,	270,220
Potatoes	,,	435,505
Hay	,,	1,914,167

There is a great deal of land in this State unoccupied. Farms with all requisite buildings and ready for occupancy, can be bought in many instances at much below the cost of the improvements; this is the result of the exodus from the north-eastern States to the west, where farming appears to offer greater attractions. Indian corn, oats, potatoes, tobacco, fruit and garden crops can be grown to advantage, but wheat and barley are not profitable crops. Dairy farming is on the increase, and will probably be in the future a much more important feature than it now is in the husbandry of the State. There are at present about 140,000 milch cows.

The State agricultural experiment station is in active operation and doing important work in giving practical information to the agriculturists.

DELAWARE.

The product of the cereals, &c., of Delaware for the years 1887 and 1888 is given in the following table:—

		1887. Number of Acres in each Crop.	1887. Quantity produced.	1887. Average yield per Acre.	1888. Number of Acres in each Crop.	1888. Quantity produced.	1888. Average yield per Acre.
Wheat	Bushels	94,790	929,000	9·8	94,790	1,194,000	12·6
Indian corn	,,	216,595	4,332,000	20·0	220,927	3,844,000	17·4
Oats	,,	21,623	458,000	21·2	21,839	450,000	20·6
Rye	,,	857	6,000	7·0	} No statistics available.		
Potatoes	,,	4,224	283,000	67·0			
Hay	Tons	55,683	66,829	1·2			

The values of the different crops are estimated by the United States Department of Agriculture at—

Crops.	Year.	Value.
		£
Wheat	1888	245,695
Indian corn	,,	348,420
Oats	,,	32,445
Rye	1887	692
Potatoes	,,	30,800
Hay	,,	165,180

UNITED STATES.

RHODE ISLAND.

The product of the cereals, &c., of Rhode Island for the years 1887 and 1888 is given in the following table:—

		1887. Number of Acres in each Crop.	1887. Quantity produced.	1887. Average yield per Acre.	1888. Number of Acres in each Crop.	1888. Quantity produced.	1888. Average yield per Acre.
Indian corn	Bushels	12,946	414,000	32·0	12,558	382,000	30·4
Oats	,,	6,353	165,000	26·0	6,353	174,000	27·4
Rye	,,	1,345	14,000	10·4	\		
Barley	,,	840	19,000	22·6	} No statistics available.		
Potatoes	,,	6,688	522,000	78·0	/		
Hay	Tons	105,356	115,892	1·1			

The values of the different crops were estimated by the United States Department of Agriculture at—

Crops.	Year.	Value.
		£
Indian corn	1888	55,085
Oats	,,	15,771
Rye	1887	2,220
Barley	,,	2,818
Potatoes	,,	96,770
Hay	,,	399,905

LONDON:
Printed for Her Majesty's Stationery Office,
By HARRISON AND SONS,
Printers in Ordinary to Her Majesty.
(1250 2 | 90—H & S 799)

FOREIGN OFFICE.
1890.
ANNUAL SERIES.

No. 648.

DIPLOMATIC AND CONSULAR REPORTS ON TRADE AND FINANCE.

UNITED STATES.

REPORT FOR THE YEAR 1889
ON THE
TRADE OF THE CONSULAR DISTRICT OF BALTIMORE.

REFERENCE TO PREVIOUS REPORT, Annual Series No. 463.

Presented to both Houses of Parliament by Command of Her Majesty,
MARCH, 1890.

LONDON:
PRINTED FOR HER MAJESTY'S STATIONERY OFFICE,
BY HARRISON AND SONS, ST. MARTIN'S LANE,
PRINTERS IN ORDINARY TO HER MAJESTY.

And to be purchased, either directly or through any Bookseller, from
EYRE & SPOTTISWOODE, EAST HARDING STREET, FLEET STREET, E.C., and
32, ABINGDON STREET, WESTMINSTER, S.W.; or
ADAM AND CHARLES BLACK, 6, NORTH BRIDGE, EDINBURGH; or
HODGES, FIGGIS, & Co., 104, GRAFTON STREET, DUBLIN.

1890.

[C. 5895—51.] *Price Three Halfpence.*

New Series of Reports.

REPORTS of the Annual Series have been issued from Her Majesty's Diplomatic and Consular Officers at the following places, and may be obtained from the sources indicated on the title-page:—

No.		Price.	No.		Price.
522. San José		1d.	585. Alexandria		1d.
523. Ningpo		1d.	586. Cagliari		1d.
524. Gothenburg		2d.	587. Smyrna		½d.
525. Hankow		2d.	588. Mannheim		1d.
526. Foochow		1d.	589. Nagasaki		1d.
527. Erzeroum		2d.	590. Hakodate		1d.
528. Ciudad Bolivar		1d.	591. Bushire		1d.
529. Jaffa		1d.	592. Chinkiang		½d.
530. Ancona		1d.	593. Pakhoi		1d.
531. Savannah		1d.	594. Hiogo		1½d.
532. Batavia		1d.	595. Bangkok		1d.
533. Adrianople		1d.	596. Serajevo		1d.
534. Nisch		1½d.	597. Copenhagen		1½d.
535. Vienna		1d.	598. Cephalonia		½d.
536. Odessa		8d.	599. Chefoo		½d.
537. Constantinople		2d.	600. Guatemala		1½d.
538. Damascus		1d.	601. Tonga		½d.
539. Tientsin		1d.	602. Tahiti		1d.
540. Amoy		1d.	603. Stettin		2d.
541. Mogador		1d.	604. Vera Cruz		1½d.
542. Vienna		1d.	605. Christiania		4d.
543. Antwerp		1d.	606. Pernambuco		1½d.
544. Lisbon		2d.	607. Trieste		1½d.
545. New York		1½d.	608. Tunis		½d.
546. San Francisco		1d.	609. Havana		2d.
547. Stettin		1½d.	610. Frankfort		½d.
548. San Salvador		½d.	611. Tabreez		½d.
549. Trebizond		1d.	612. Bilbao		1d.
550. Nice		1d.	613. Barcelona		½d.
551. Baghdad		½d.	614. Tokio		1d.
552. Fiume		1d.	615. Naples		2½d.
553. Mogador		2d.	616. Batoum		½d.
554. Buenos Ayres		1½d.	617. Odessa		1d.
555. San Francisco		2½d.	618. La Rochelle		1d.
556. Carthagena		½d.	619. Rome		1d.
557. Syra		1d.	620. Nice		1d.
558. Varna and Bourgas		1d.	621. Kiukiang		½d.
559. Thessaly		½d.	622. Paris		1d.
560. Yokohama		1d.	623. Salonica		1½d.
561. Nantes		1½d.	624. Réunion		1d.
562. Suakin		½d.	625. Ichang		1d.
563. Algiers		1d.	626. Bogatá		1d.
564. St. Petersburg		2½d.	627. Malaga		2d.
565. Söul		1d.	628. Porto Rico		1d.
566. Newchwang		1d.	629. Bushire		2½d.
567. Roustchouk and Philippopolis		1d.	630. The Hague		½d.
568. Stockholm		1½d.	631. Berlin		1d.
569. Tonga		1d.	632. Adrianople		1½d.
570. Chicago		1½d.	633. Rome		1½d.
571. Adana		½d.	634. Santiago		½d.
572. Buenos Ayres		3d.	635. Tahiti		½d.
573. Frankfort		1½d.	636. Maranham		½d.
574. Canton		1½d.	637. Mexico		2d.
575. Tamsui		5½d.	638. Christiania		1d.
576. Palermo		3d.	639. Copenhagen		1d.
577. Amsterdam		1d.	640. Paris		1d.
578. Ajaccio		½d.	641. Venice		1d.
579. Shanghai		1½d.	642. Cherbourg		½d.
580. Warsaw		½d.	643. New York		1d.
581. Teneriffe		1d.	644. Patras		1d.
582. Tangier		2d.	645. Bourgas		½d.
583. Surinam		½d.	646. St. Petersburg		3d.
584. Loanda		1d.	647. Taganrog		½d.

No. 648.

Reference to previous Report, Annual Series No. 463.

UNITED STATES.

BALTIMORE.

Consul Segrave to the Marquis of Salisbury.

My Lord,   *Baltimore, January* 29, 1889.

I HAVE the honour herewith to transmit to your Lordship Reports on the Trade and Commerce of Baltimore, Norfolk, and Richmond, for the year 1889.

I have, &c.
(Signed)   W. F. SEGRAVE.

Report on the Trade and Commerce of Baltimore for the Year 1889.

The trade and commerce of Baltimore for 1889 have been more extensive and sound than might have been expected from the experience of the past year, though the improvement in business came almost entirely in the concluding six months. [Trade.]

There has been a general increase of business, which is the more gratifying, as the season has been marked by singular climatic disturbances, resulting in unexampled calamities from floods.

The augmented Bank clearances, amounting to nearly 30,000,000 dol., are the best evidence of this prosperity. [Bank clearances.]

Exports were larger during 1889 than in any year since 1880, and show an excess of over 17,000,000 dol. over those of the previous year, whilst the imports exceeded those of 1888 by over 3,000,000 dol. [General trade.]

The most notable feature of the year's trade has been the heavy increase in the movement of corn (maize) through this port, due in a great measure to the reduction, by the railways, of freight charges to an average basis of 5 c. per 100 lbs. below that of wheat. [Movement of corn.]

West of the Mississippi this difference has been in operation for years, but, in consequence of the preponderating influence of New York, holding direct communication by water with the West, it had never been imposed on the trunk lines from the Mississippi, eastwards.

The Baltimore and Ohio Railway having taken the initiative, the principle was forced upon the other lines, to the great advantage, first, of the railways, and, secondly, to the Port of Baltimore itself.

Baltimore draws as naturally from the corn belt, as Duluth and New York do from the wheat fields of Dakota, and any system of transport which will cheapen the cost of bringing corn from Kansas and Nebraska to the seaboard, will prove of great advantage to the railways and to the seabord market.

Corn which costs from 12 c. to 15 c. a bushel at the place of production, requires from 22 c. to 25 c. per bushel to bring it to the sea. Should the difference in its favour, which is now maintained, be ultimately abolished, there is no doubt that the grain will be held back until the cheaper water carriage to Canada or New York will be open, and so allow of its being moved in that direction.

Trade capacity of Baltimore. The tonnage of Baltimore exceeds that of any port in the United States, with the exception of New York and, perhaps, Philadelphia.

It is first in the trade of canned goods, fruit, vegetables, oysters, &c., which amounts in value to over 16,000,000 dol., and it manufactures, on an average, from 80,000,000 to 100,000,000 cans annually.

It possesses one of the largest leaf tobacco markets in the country, as well as an extensive business in manufactured tobacco.

Its imports of tin plate, coffee, and chemicals, are second only to those of New York.

Its commission business is to the value of from 250,000,000 dol. to 300,000,000 dol. annually, and the produce of its factories is estimated at the value of 140,000,000 dol. a year.

Harbour approaches. Pressure is being put on the Federal authorities to improve the harbour approaches. Ocean freight is now almost exclusively carried in large steamships requiring a considerable depth of water, and the tendency is to increase their carrying capacity by building them still larger.

Only a year or two back, the greatest draught of any vessel then loading at Baltimore was 25 feet 8 inches. A new steamship of 6,000 tons capacity, and with a draught of 27 feet, has been recently added to one of the regular lines trading with this port, and others of like dimensions will shortly be added.

The opinion is strongly expressed that the commercial interests of Baltimore require that, in the near future, a depth of at least 28 feet, with a breadth of over 400 feet, should be secured for the channel which forms the approach to the harbour.

Disintegration of the grain trade. On examining the statistics of the Department of Agriculture for the past year, it would appear that the export of flour from the four great Atlantic ports had exceeded the shipments of wheat by nearly 125 per cent., that is, assuming a barrel of the former to be equivalent to $4\frac{1}{2}$ bushels of the latter. This substitution of flour for wheat is the result of economical causes. Of course, in the condition of flour, wheat can be conveyed over long distances by sea and land much more cheaply, and, moreover, divested of bran, screenings and dirt.

Under the new system, the necessities of the market have produced means suitable for the occasion.

The granting of bills of lading at the mill door establishes a title to the flour, which accompanies it upon its travels, and identifies it on arrival at its destination.

The brand of the miller guarantees its quality, and the carrier ensures its delivery. Thus the miller is master of the situation, and his flour finds its way into every village in England, and will continue to do so, so long as he treats his customers with common honesty, and they can depend on the quality of his stuff.

The beef and pork packers were at one time in possession of the English market, but lost it through their dishonest greed. At this moment their productions are absolutely excluded from many countries, and the American packer is supplanted by foreigners, who now control the business which was at one time almost exclusively American.

The large increase in wheat production all over the world has deprived the farmer of profitable markets.

The price of wheat has declined never again to be restored, and what competition there may be is only such as the miller creates.

The farmer's main grievance is, however, against the railways, which exact rates of freight that deprive him of his legitimate profit, and make it perfectly indifferent to him, where his grain is marketed. *Railway rates.*

Sooner or later the State must either acquire or construct one grand trunk-line with a view to regulate the entire system. If such a line were substantially built and worked upon equitable rates, the relief would be speedy.

Its by-laws, regulations, and example would, as a matter of expediency, be imitated by the independent lines.

It would equalise prices and conditions of transport, and from the experience obtained in the management, the State would become closer in touch and sympathy with the vast agricultural interests of the nation.

It would put an end to "cutting," "rebates," and "discriminations," and secure permanent and undisturbed rates of freight.

A system is now under consideration by which the present method of storing grain will be completely revolutionised. Should it prove a success, the elevators now in general use will become obsolete, and every farmer will be supplied with a substitute by which he will be able to store his grain for years at little cost and no risk. *Tanks for storage of food products.*

The inventor maintains that he can manufacture steel tanks of any required capacity, and at a cost averaging from 4 c. to 5 c., say 2d. to 2½d., for each bushel of capacity, as against 40 c. to 50 c. now expended on wooden elevators. The steel tanks will be filled with grain by a simple process. When the tank is full, a percentage of air is exhausted and a quantity of carbonic acid gas admitted.

The valves are then closed and the grain will keep sound for

(806)

years. Having exhausted the oxygen there is no chance of fermentation, and, as a consequence, no decay or rot. At the same time, all animal life perishes and the grain is secure against the ravages of weevils, which are so destructive. With a tank costing 500 dol., the farmer has storage for 10,000 bushels, and can hold his crop against low prices until the market improves.

Fire cannot burn it, nor damp nor rain injure it.

The process by which the grain is manipulated is as simple as it is effective. It consists in an airtight receiver, leading from which is a large pipe so arranged as to be held over the grain in the receiver it is desired to unload. By means of a suction fan the air is exhausted in the receiver, and rushing to fill the vacuum is sufficient, it is said, to draw the grain into the pipe, through which it passes to the tank.

Should the process prove a success, it will most effectually put an end to the proceedings of those persons whose business appears to be the making of fictitious valuations of bread stuffs.

I subjoin Annex A, return of all shipping at the port of Baltimore; Annex B, return of exports and imports; Annex C, table showing value of all exports and imports.

Shipping: incompetent seamen.

The system under which seamen and firemen are now engaged and shipped on board foreign-going vessels requires the urgent consideration, not only of the administration, but of the shipowners and underwriters as well.

As at present carried out, the latter have no security that seamen are physically competent to undertake the duties they contract to perform.

The halt and the lame, men suffering from loathsome diseases, as well as frequently those recently discharged from hospital in a condition of debility, are constantly being shipped as able seamen and firemen, with the result that a few days at sea completely knocks them up, and the ship has to be worked practically short-handed.

This, of course, entails expense on owners, and is too often a source of danger to the vessel itself.

No sooner does the ship arrive at the port of destination than these men are sent to hospital at the cost of the English taxpayer, and substitutes have to be engaged by the ship at often enhanced rates of wages.

To give some idea of the cost entailed upon the Imperial Exchequer, it may be stated that in this port the hospital expenses of these so-called seamen for the past quarter amounted to over 60*l.*, and this may be taken as a fair average expenditure.

The remedy for this unfortunate state of things appears to lie in some form of medical supervision.

Seamen proposing to engage in foreign-going ships should be compelled to submit to medical examination, and no seaman should be permitted to ship who was not provided with a medical certificate of soundness. In the greater ports, as London, Liverpool, Glasgow, a trifling fee would cover all the expense, and in minor ports means might be easily devised to meet the expenditure. Even if the medical officer were appointed and paid by Government, there is no doubt that, in the long run, the arrangement would be found to be profitable and economical, as well to shipowners as to Government.

The increase in exports for 1889 over 1888 amounts to 17,239,262 dol., or about 3,000,000*l.*, and that of imports for the same period to 3,573,113 dol., or about 715,000*l.*

Flour. The receipts of flour at Baltimore during the past year are unparalleled, and the fact that the export is not in proportion shows, not only, the result of a short crop of fruit and vegetables, but also increased home consumption consequent on low prices.

Wheat. Receipts of wheat have been lower that in any year since 1876; this is, in the main, to be attributed to the failure of the crop east of the Alleghanies, and the short demand for export. The shipments, however, show in favourable contrast to the receipts, but all the same, the wheat trade has been disappointing.

Corn, maize. Receipts of corn have been larger than in any of the ten preceding years. The foreign shipments are proportionally high, and show where a market is to be found so soon as, through greater transportation facilities from the Southern States, the supply will be enormously increased.

The stock in the elevators at the close of the year was—

	Bushels.
Wheat	1,184,449
Corn	1,386,505
Oats	141,295

Cotton. The year's business in cotton has been, on the whole, satisfactory. It opened with cotton at $9\frac{1}{4}$ c. and $9\frac{7}{8}$ c.

These prices ruled until March, when there was an advance which continued until May, at which time the price was $11\frac{3}{8}$ c. There was a further advance of $\frac{1}{4}$ c. in August, which brought cotton up to $11\frac{5}{8}$ c., the highest price during the year.

The present year will show a further increase in the acreage under cotton, and which increase has been going on for the past seven or eight years. The average yield last season was $35\frac{1}{3}$ bales per acre, and it is anticipated that it will be still larger next season.

Lumber. The lumber trade has been doing well in the past year, and is at present in a very healthy condition, with better prices prevailing.

Good staves and walnut logs continue in demand, and at remunerative prices.

Tobacco. Low prices and unfavourable weather during the summer, caused the tobacco crop to be the smallest raised for the past 30 years. It was some 6,000 hogsheads less than the crop of 1888, and there was much which was deficient in colour. Owing, however, to the usual demand from France, and the indifferent prospects of the coming crop, the great proportion was disposed of, though at low prices. The better descriptions are now in good demand, with prices improving in consequence of their scarcity.

Canned goods. Prices for canned goods are much depressed, averaging 25 per cent. below previous years. To this, however, must be excepted peaches and oysters—the former in consequence of a short crop, and the latter as the take has been one-sixth less than in the previous year.

Oysters. Each succeeding year oysters are gathered of smaller size, and yielding less meat. They are as plentiful as ever, but are not permitted to mature. About 47,000,000 cans of fruit, vegetables, and oysters were filled during the year.

Cattle. The export of live stock shows a very large increase over that of former years, in a great measure owing to the facilities afforded by the growing capacity of the steam vessels engaged in the trade, many of which are now large enough to transport from 800 head to 1,200 head per trip.

The increase in the number of cattle exported from Baltimore in 1889 amounts to 35,000 head, considerably over the total export for 1888, which was only 23,400 head, and more than double that for 1887, which was only 16,527, showing that this business has increased over 350 per cent. during the past two years.

Evaporated apples. Attention was drawn in a former report to the process of preserving apples by evaporation, which, it is maintained, is the most successful manner of preserving the flavour and freshness of the fruit.

The very large extension in the export trade in this article, chiefly to the Continent, shows the success which has attended the business, and how much the fruit is appreciated by the foreign consumers.

In addition to the numerous articles enumerated in Annex B, may be mentioned, as exemplifying the diversified and varied nature of the trade of Baltimore, the following as examples:—Clothes' pins, organs and pianos, rubber coats, churns, sewing machines, washboards, buggies, clay pigeons, and safes.

Customs receipts. The total receipts of the customs from all sources during 1889 amounted to 3,049,113 dol., showing an increase over 1888 of 211,404 dol.

Emigration. During the past year 171 steamships brought 29,429 immigrants to this port.

The following foreign nationalities were represented:—

BALTIMORE.

England	480
Scotland	11
Ireland	210
British possessions	22
	723
Austria	2,272
Belgium	14
Bohemia	753
Bulgaria	1
Denmark	391
France	2
Germany	20,157
Hungary	538
Italy	2
Netherlands	5
Poland	12
Roumania	23
Russia	3,090
Sweden and Norway	365
Switzerland	19
	28,367

The balance was made up by American subjects.

Annex A.—RETURN of all Shipping at the Port of Baltimore in the Year 1889.

ENTERED.

Nationality.	Sailing. Number of Vessels.	Sailing. Tons.	Steam. Number of Vessels.	Steam. Tons.	Total. Number of Vessels.	Total. Tons.
British	20	6,808	483	698,389	503	705,197
American (Foreign Trade only)	142	62,625	...	...	142	62,635
German	2	2,473	68	125,736	70	128,209
Italian	12	7,274	...	...	12	7,274
Swedish and Norwegian	3	1,392	7	3,573	10	4,965
Spanish	...	...	9	20,152	9	20,152
French	...	...	6	10,817	6	10,817
Austrian	1	793	...	...	1	793
Total for 1889	180	81,365	573	858,667	753	940,032
,, 1888	195	80,676	390	585,644	585	666,320
Increase in 1889	...	...	183	273,023	168	273,712

CLEARED.

Nationality.	Sailing. Number of Vessels.	Sailing. Tons.	Steam. Number of Vessels.	Steam. Tons.	Total. Number of Vessels.	Total. Tons.
British	21	7,779	484	697,043	505	704,822
American (Foreign Trade only)	135	41,885	1	228	136	42,113
German	2	2,473	68	125,736	70	128,209
Italian	13	7,742	...	...	13	7,742
Swedish and Norwegian	3	1,392	7	3,573	10	4,965
Spanish	...	...	9	20,152	9	20,152
French	...	...	5	9,459	5	9,459
Austrian	1	793	...	...	1	793
Total for 1889	175	62,064	574	856,191	749	918,255
,, 1888	217	86,791	387	579,724	604	666,515
Increase in 1889	...	...	187	276,467	145	251,740

Annex B.—Return of Principal Articles of Export from Baltimore for 1889.

		1889.		1888.	
Articles.		Quantity.	Value.	Quantity.	Value.
Bread Stuffs—					
Wheat	Bushels...	4,507,165		4,161,129	
Flour	Barrels...	2,332,805		2,417,874	
Corn (maize)	Bushels...	16,617,177		4,419,977	
Cornmeal	Barrels...	6,332		1,395	
Oats	Bushels...	131,999		5,670	
Oatmeal	Pounds...	3,729,599		394,200	
Provisions—					
Beef, canned and salt	,,	32,038,944		15,874,000	
Bacon	,,	4,809,319		1,530,105	
Hams	,,	1,592,388		818,942	
Pork	,,	3,186,624		1,886,406	
Cheese	,,	435,086	Total Value of Exports for 1889, 61,131,509 dol.	9,261	Total Value of Exports for 1888, 44,892,247 dol.
Lard	,,	34,868,112		20,335,791	
Canned goods	Cases...	404,277		164,888	
Oils—					
Petroleum	Gallons...	8,633,508		7,224,751	
Lubricating	,,	483,432		334,761	
Cotton seed	,,	169,707		20,600	
Lard oil	,,	141,861		...	
Lumber	Feet ...	25,427,000		11,883,000	
Staves	Number	3,354,000		2,065,000	
Cotton	Bales	170,110		175,884	
Cloths	Square yards	147,933		132,085	
Apples, dried and evaporated	Pounds...	6,683,790		1,496,874	
Tobacco—					
Leaf	,,	57,194,668		40,150,142	
Stems	,,	6,152,012		5,142,590	
Cigars	Number	501,000		40,000	
Tallow	Pounds..	13,237,823		6,611,807	
Seeds	Bushels...	7,712,777		9,238,365	
Starch	Pounds...	4,833,900		2,184,860	
Oil cake	,,	51,097,665		32,847,106	
Rosin	Barrels...	57,858		32,847	
Leather	Pounds...	363,491		131,606	
Copper matte	Tons	27,790		16,600	
Cattle	Head ...	59,357		23,286	

BALTIMORE.

RETURN of Principal Articles of Import into Baltimore for 1889.

		1889.		1888.	
Articles.		Quantity.	Value.	Quantity.	Value.
Metals—					
Iron ore	Tons	273,250		119,573	
Pig iron	,,	20,589		10,007	
Bar iron	,,	900		271,331	
Steel hoops	Pounds	114,275		345,352	
,, ingots	,,	10,640,102		10,851,475	
Tin plate	,,	116,223,306		108,916,294	
Chemicals—					
Lime, chlorate of	,,	2,219,211		3,555,091	
Potash, muriate	,,	11,132,726		10,950,985	
Soda, nitrate	,,	12,563,176	Total Value of Imports for 1889, 15,435,375 dol.	10,697,491	Total Value of Imports for 1888, 11,862,262 dol.
Sulphur	Tons	17,711		15,827	
Guano	,,	6,290		3,791	
Soda, ash	Pounds	67,862,281		57,547,915	
Soda, caustic	,,	1,540,960		2,300,000	
,, all others	,,	13,211,553		16,454,977	
Fruit—					
Cocoa nuts	Number	1,979,000		2,013,000	
Bananas	Bunches	386,615		313,743	
Pine apples	Dozen	286,271		337,630	
Oranges	Boxes	22,490		19,026	
Lemons	,,	11,836		10,288	
Coffee	Pounds	40,728,243		27,665,484	
Rice	,,	96,120		1,189,570	
,, granulated	,,	6,489,350		8,438,660	
Salt	,,	35,275,461		58,786,909	
Cement	Barrels	51,637		16,193	
Textiles—					
Cotton cloth	Square yards	62,395		75,418	
Woollen ,,	,,	104,001		125,943	
,, dress goods	,,	525,080		410,184	
Asphalt	Pounds	4,193,280		3,528,000	
Licorice	,,	2,219,211		3,555,094	
Whiskey	Barrels	13,908		22,119	
Linseed	Bags	147,287		...	
Fire bricks	Casks	4,743		...	
,, ,,	Number	717,000		...	

Annex C.—TABLE showing the Total Value of all Articles Exported from and Imported into Baltimore, U.S.A., to and from Foreign Countries during the Years 1888–89.

Country.	Exports.		Imports.	
	1889.	1888.	1889.	1888.
	£	£	£	£
Great Britain	8,400,000	6,100,000	1,800,000	1,850,000
Germany	1,000,000	1,500,000	250,000	80,000
Brazil	500,000	300,000	600,000	325,000
Holland	600,000	250,000	..	..
France	1,000,000	550,000	..	..
Belgium	500,000	300,000	40,000	20,000
Cuba	20,000	30,000	100,000	50,000
Italy	50,000	100,000	100,000	55,000
Spain	..	..	115,000	50,000
Algeria	..	..	50,000	..
Denmark	40,000	..	..	..
Sweden	20,000	..	..	..
Argentine Republic	75,000	..	..	..
Other countries	21,302	145,257	32,075	20,880
Total	12,226,302	9,275,257	3,087,075	2,450,880

NORFOLK.

Harbour of Norfolk. The favourable location and natural advantages of this port are attracting general attention. The harbour is within 30 miles of the Atlantic Ocean, always open and free from ice, with 26 to 28 feet of water in its approaches.

Railway connection. There is a concentration of six great lines of railways, which in the last few years have made this their deep-water terminus. Two of these railways have, within the last year, extended their rails to this port, while the others have been building extensions and perfecting through connections, until they cover the country north-west to Chicago and St. Louis, west to Memphis and Kansas city, and south to Mobile and New Orleans, and all intermediate points, making the railway transportation of this port second to none in the country.

Steamship lines. Coastwise the port is connected with Boston, New York, Philadelphia, Baltimore, Washington and Richmond, by lines of first-class passenger and freight steamers.

These railway and steamship lines, in connection with the natural advantages of this port, and the soil and climate of the adjacent country, promise to make it one of the most important ports on the Atlantic seaboard.

The comparative statements submitted herewith show the marked increase in shipping and general business.

Shipping. The total number of vessels entered in 1889 has been 317, with an aggregate of 401,404 tons, against, in 1888, a total of 244 vessels, aggregating 283,506 tons, showing increase in favour of 1889: 73 vessels, 117,898 tons.

General business. A comparative statement shows increase in nearly all staple commodities handled; especial attention is called to cotton, during
Cotton. season ending August 31, 1888, 500,308 bales; season ending August 31, 1889, 506,171 bales.

Logs and lumber. Logs and lumber in 1888, 244,262,817 feet; in 1889, 309,093,594 feet; increase in 1889, 64,380,777 feet.

Meat. Meats, in 1888, 4,720,100 lbs.; against, in 1889, 9,158,120 lbs.; increase, 5,438,020 lbs.

Coal. Attention is called to the statement of development of the coal trade, as of special interest to British steamship owners, because it has been only four years since it was opened by the extension of the Norfolk and Western Railway Company, to the coal mines of south-west Virginia. Since that time it has been demonstrated that the Pocahontas coal is a first-class steaming coal, and inexhaustible in quantity, and it has made this one of the most important and popular coaling stations in this country. The quantity
Coaling port. shipped from here has been in—

Years.	Tons.
1886	504,153
1887	661,522
1888	883,759
1889	1,013,214

BALTIMORE.

Population. The census for 1880 shows within the city limits 22,000; a census just completed shows 33,000 within the city limits, while with Portsmouth on the opposite side of the Elizabeth river, and the villages adjacent to Norfolk, there is concentrated here a population of 60,000, which is increasing in about the same ratio as shown above between 1880 and 1889 within the city.

TABLE showing the movement of Shipping at this port, without including the coasting trade in American vessels; and the return as to these vessels represents the entries and clearances to and from foreign ports only:—

ENTERED.

Nationality.	Sailing. Number of Vessels.	Tons.	Steam. Number of Vessels.	Tons.	Total. Number of Vessels.	Tons.
British	4	1,547	289	378,450	293	379,999
American	7	3,284	...	...	7	3,284
German	3	1,552	2	3,059	5	4,611
Spanish	...	...	7	10,453	7	10,453
Italian	3	1,695	...	...	3	1,695
Norwegian	...	...	1	450	1	450
Portuguese	...	...	1	914	1	914
Total	17	8,078	300	393,326	317	401,404

CLEARED.

Nationality.	Sailing. Number of Vessels.	Tons.	Steam. Number of Vessels.	Tons.	Total. Number of Vessels.	Tons.
British	6	3,046	285	360,654	291	363,700
American	34	13,690	1	392	35	14,082
German	3	1,552	2	3,059	5	4,611
Spanish	...	...	7	10,453	7	10,453
Italian	3	1,695	...	...	3	1,695
Norwegian	...	...	1	450	1	450
Portuguese	...	...	1	914	1	914
Total	46	19,983	297	375,922	343	395,905

Trade and commerce.

TABLE showing the Principal Articles of Export and Import at this Port during the past Year, value calculated at 5 dol. to the 1*l*.

EXPORTS.

Articles.		Quantity.	Value.
Cotton	Bales	244,182	
Coal	Tons	84,390	
Bark	Bags	13,637	
Grain	Bushels	30,795	
Staves and heading	Pieces	5,253,241	
„ „	Cars	15	
Factory sweepings	Bales	200	
Cattle	Head	607	
Rosin	Barrels	1,820	
Bridge iron	Pieces	92	
Flour	Sacks	2,200	
Tobacco	Shapes	3	
„	Packages	1	
„	Hogsheads	1,140	
„	Tierces	96	
Turpentine	Barrels	1,000	
Silver-plated ware	Boxes	1	
Furniture	Pieces	26	
Dry goods	„	23	
Coffee	Bags	12	
Shuttle blocks	Crates	217	
Treenails	Pieces	19,537	
Persimmon and dogwood	„	49,334	
	Tons	791	
Logs, oak, walnut, &c.		3,272	
„ „ „ „	Tons	101	
Plank, oak, poplar, &c.	Pieces	267,322	
„ „ „ „	Tons	1,746	
Spokes, hickory, &c.		61,107	
Walnut blocks		2,395	
Hoops	Bundles	1,900	
Hornbean	Pieces	380	
Miscellaneous lumber		9	

Total Value of Exports, 2,561,171*l*. 2*s*.

IMPORTS.

Articles.		Quantity.	Value.
Guano	Tons	1,946	
Salt	Sacks	52,772	
„	Tons	2,253	
Kainit	„	2,500	
Manure salt	„	1,496	
Phosphate earth	„	400	
Cotton ties	Bundles	17,600	
Whale oil	Casks	18	
Wine	Octaves	37	
„	Casks	15	
„	Barrels	15	
Olives	Casks	4	
Bisque ware			
Personal effects			

Total Value of Imports, 36,178*l*.

BALTIMORE.

COMPARATIVE Statement of Coal delivered at Lambert's Point Pier and Local at Norfolk during the Years 1886–89.

Year.	Nationality.	Steamers.	Bunkers.	Cargo and Bunkers.	Total Steamers.	Ships, Barks, &c.	Ocean Tugs and Barges.	Schooners.	Total Vessels.	Foreign.	Coast-wise.	Steamers.	Ocean Tugs.	Local.	Total.
										Tons.	Tons.	Tons.	Tons.	Tons.	Tons.
1886	British	80	84	1	85	33	..	564	682	15,983	409,089	21,158	..	57,923	504,153
	Spanish	4													
	Norwegian	1													
1887	British	125	157	..	157	28	..	741	926	14,779	552,598	27,982	..	56,163	661,522
	Spanish	12													
	American	8													
	Norwegian	6													
	German	6													
1888	British	142	146	13	159	20	126	761	1,066	32,271	742,950	42,051	3,506	62,981	883,759
	Spanish	10													
	American	3													
	German	3													
	Italian	1													
1889	British	231	228	29	257	9	375	506	1,147	23,932	841,378	70,015	7,203	70,686	1,013,214
	Spanish	5													
	American	17													
	German	3													
	Norwegian	1													

UNITED STATES.

COMPARATIVE Statement of the Receipts of Merchandise at this Port for 1888–89.

Articles.		1888.	1889.
Cotton (season ending August 31)	Bales	500,308	506,171
Lumber	Feet	138,625,263	205,727,463
Logs	,,	105,637,554	103,366,131
Staves	M	5,843,966	9,076,153
Shingles	M	30,914,540	52,690,985
R. R. Ties	M	185,173	243,687
Hay	Tons	7,709	12,648
Corn	Bushels	736,858	519,401
Oats	,,	247,970	272,397
Meal	,,	183,924	239,915
Rice	,,	6,168	19,370
Bran	,,	103,442	153,158
Rye	,,	1,181	6,248
Wheat	,,	138,338	20,029
Peanuts	Bags	289,162	175,964
Coffee	,,	10,248	9,671
Sugar	Barrels	30,154	28,565
Molasses, &c.	,,	5,995	6,588
Cheese	Boxes	14,168	14,184
Butter	Tubs	20,185	20,081
Flour	Barrels	181,798	191,400
,,	Bags	2,300	59,893
Pork	Barrels	11,080	13,587
Beef	,,	900	1,049
Fish	,,	17,121	19,533
,,	Boxes	6,818	6,829
Meat	Pounds	4,720,100	9,158,120
,,	Tierces	1,071	618
,,	Barrels	4,703	7,702
,,	Boxes	14,036	14,496
Lard	Tierces	6,391	4,998
,,	Cases	20,197	17,470
,,	Tubs	565	551
Oil, coal	Barrels	40,853	28,977
Oil, cotton seed	,,	5,799	29,970
Cotton seed meal	Bushels	61,530	8,330
Fertilizers	Tons	3,411	4,780
Hides	Packages	20,657	23,574
Horses and mules	Head	922	1,501
Hogs and sheep	,,	21,230	6,811
Cattle	,,	2,949	7,343
Naval stores	Barrels	14,198	22,375
Potatoes	,,	75,949	65,894
Truck	,,	17,069	51,888
,,	Boxes	2,193	56,147
Eggs	Barrels	25,664	12,464
,,	Crates	5,555	5,954
Salt	Sacks	141,083	105,459
Coal, Pocahontas	Tons	938,369	1,020,508
Pig iron	,,	38,545	89,265
Iron ore	,,	727	1,266
Coke	,,	168	966
Tobacco leaf	Hhds.	13,119	21,003
,,	Tierces	1,191	2,681
,,	Cases	601	1,694
,, manufactured	Packages	229,538	112,431

RICHMOND.

There has been a great increase in the number of British steamers at this port during the year, coming here to load with cotton in ballast from United States ports, having landed their cargoes there, and are included as entered foreign.

The following table shows the movement of shipping at this port, without including the coasting trade in American vessels, and the return as to these vessels represents the entries and clearances to and from foreign ports only.

RETURN of all Shipping at the Port of Richmond in the Year 1889.

ENTERED.

Nationality.	Sailing. Number of Vessels.	Sailing. Tons.	Steam. Number of Vessels.	Steam. Tons.	Total. Number of Vessels.	Total. Tons.
British	7	1,379	39	61,973	46	63,352
American	9	4,701	...	...	9	4,701
Swedish	3	695	...	...	3	695
German	5	969	...	...	5	969
Portuguese	1	224	...	...	1	224
Brazilian	1	200	...	...	1	200
Spanish	...	...	2	2,587	2	2,587
Total	26	8,168	41	64,560	67	72,728
,, for the preceding year	25	8,638	24	36,980	49	45,618

CLEARED.

Nationality.	Sailing. Number of Vessels.	Sailing. Tons.	Steam. Number of Vessels.	Steam. Tons.	Total. Number of Vessels.	Total. Tons.
British	7	1,379	38	60,354	45	61,733
American	9	4,701	...	...	9	4,701
Swedish	3	695	...	...	3	695
German	5	969	...	...	5	969
Portuguese	1	224	...	...	1	224
Brazilian	1	200	...	...	1	200
Spanish	...	...	2	2,587	2	2,587
Total	26	8,168	40	62,941	66	71,109
,, for the preceding year	29	10,432	29	45,834	58	55,766

RETURN of the Principal Articles of Export from Richmond during the Years 1888 and 1889, calculated at 5 dol. per 1*l*.

EXPORTS.

Articles.		1889. Quantity.	1889. Value.	1888. Quantity.	1888. Value.
Cotton	Bales	204,975		176,807	
Flour	Barrels	89,607		76,701	
Lard	Pounds	1,500		10,450	
Cattle	Heads	992	Total Value of Exports, 2,023,456*l*.	...	Total Value of Exports, 1,786,246*l*.
Staves	Pieces	1,500		...	
Machinery	Boxes	4		...	
Sundries		...		...	
Tobacco	Pounds	2,806		61,231	

(806)

UNITED STATES.

IMPORTS.

Articles.		1889. Quantity.	Value.	1888. Quantity.	Value.
Salt	Tons	300		...	
,,	Sacks	6,761		16,531	
Guano	Tons	786		2,000	
Plaster	,,	21	Total Value of Imports, 7,396*l*.	1,796	Total Value of Imports, 9,241*l*.
Wine	Gallons	1,033		...	
Woollens	Cases	4		...	
Fish	Barrels or Boxes	237		1,692	
Seeds	Packages	200		...	

Stock of grain in elevator, December 31, 1889, was 47,072 bushels of wheat, 3,433 maize, 9,646 bushels oats, 2,047 bushels rye. No wheat or maize was exported during the year. Exports of flour were almost entirely to South America.

Population and industries. General business. The year opened with a bright prospect for all branches of trade and industries, but the long continued rains and floods contributed much to diminish the expectations then entertained of increasing prosperity. However, the result of the year's business has been on the whole satisfactory.

Iron industries. There are in this city 24 establishments engaged in the manufacture of iron in every way; in the manufacture of locomotive engines and railroad supplies, &c., employing 3,438 hands, with a capital of 2,348,500 dol.

Tobacco. There are about 120 factories engaged in the manufacture of tobacco, for chewing and smoking as cigars and cigarettes, one concern alone turning out 2,000,000 cigarettes per day.

The tobacco trade employs 7,409 hands; capital engaged in the tobacco business estimated at 3,367,000 dol.

Flour. Three large flour mills employ 224 hands; have not been working to full capacity this year.

The estimated number of manufactories of all kinds in Richmond is 724, employing about 21,000 hands, and a capital engaged of 13,429,000 dol.

Building. Building has been active during the year, especially of small houses in the suburbs; probably 500 new houses have been erected in the city and beyond the corporate line.

Population. The population of Richmond is estimated with the suburbs at 100,000 inhabitants, of which probably 40,000 are coloured.

Vital statistics. Mortality. The deaths, reported by the President of the Board of Health, were 1,869, of which 838 were white, and 1,031 coloured. Average mortality of whole population 18·69 per 1,000. Average mortality of white population 13·17 per 1,000. Average mortality of coloured population 23·43 per thousand.

FOREIGN OFFICE.
1890.
ANNUAL SERIES.

N°. 649.

DIPLOMATIC AND CONSULAR REPORTS ON TRADE AND FINANCE.

UNITED STATES.

REPORT FOR THE YEAR 1889
ON THE
TRADE OF THE CONSULAR DISTRICT OF NEW ORLEANS.

REFERENCE TO PREVIOUS REPORT, Annual Series No. 465.

Presented to both Houses of Parliament by Command of Her Majesty,
MARCH, 1890.

LONDON:
PRINTED FOR HER MAJESTY'S STATIONERY OFFICE,
BY HARRISON AND SONS, ST. MARTIN'S LANE,
PRINTERS IN ORDINARY TO HER MAJESTY.

And to be purchased, either directly or through any Bookseller, from
EYRE AND SPOTTISWOODE, EAST HARDING STREET, FLEET STREET, E.C., and
32, ABINGDON STREET, WESTMINSTER, S.W.; or
ADAM AND CHARLES BLACK, 6, NORTH BRIDGE, EDINBURGH; or
HODGES, FIGGIS, & Co., 104, GRAFTON STREET, DUBLIN.

1890.

[C. 5895—52.] *Price Twopence.*

New Series of Reports.

Reports of the Annual Series have been issued from Her Majesty's Diplomatic and Consular Officers at the following places, and may be obtained from the sources indicated on the title-page:—

No.		Price.	No.		Price.
527.	Erzeroum	2d.	588.	Mannheim	1d.
528.	Ciudad Bolivar	1d.	589.	Nagasaki	1d.
529.	Jaffa	1d.	590.	Hakodate	1d.
530.	Ancona	1d.	591.	Bushire	1d.
531.	Savannah	1d.	592.	Chinkiang	½d.
532.	Batavia	1d.	593.	Pakhoi	½d.
533.	Adrianople	1d.	594.	Hiogo	1½d.
534.	Nisch	1½d.	595.	Bangkok	1d.
535.	Vienna	1d.	596.	Serajevo	1d.
536.	Odessa	8d.	597.	Copenhagen	1½d.
537.	Constantinople	2d.	598.	Cephalonia	½d.
538.	Damascus	1d.	599.	Chefoo	½d.
539.	Tientsin	1d.	600.	Guatemala	1½d.
540.	Amoy	1d.	601.	Tonga	½d.
541.	Mogador	1d.	602.	Tahiti	1d.
542.	Vienna	1d.	603.	Stettin	2d.
543.	Antwerp	1d.	604.	Vera Cruz	1½d.
544.	Lisbon	2d.	605.	Christiania	4d.
545.	New York	1½d.	606.	Pernambuco	1½d.
546.	San Francisco	1d.	607.	Trieste	1½d.
547.	Stettin	1½d.	608.	Tunis	½d.
548.	San Salvador	½d.	609.	Havana	2d.
549.	Trebizond	1d.	610.	Frankfort	½d.
550.	Nice	1d.	611.	Tabreez	½d.
551.	Baghdad	½d.	612.	Bilbao	1d.
552.	Fiume	1d.	613.	Barcelona	½d.
553.	Mogador	2d.	614.	Tokio	1d.
554.	Buenos Ayres	1½d.	615.	Naples	2½d.
555.	San Francisco	2½d.	616.	Batoum	½d.
556.	Carthagena	½d.	617.	Odessa	1d.
557.	Syra	1d.	618.	La Rochelle	1d.
558.	Varna and Bourgas	1d.	619.	Rome	1d.
559.	Thessaly	½d.	620.	Nice	1d.
560.	Yokohama	1d.	621.	Kiukiang	½d.
561.	Nantes	1½d.	622.	Paris	1d.
562.	Suakin	½d.	623.	Salonica	1½d.
563.	Algiers	1d.	624.	Réunion	1d.
564.	St. Petersburg	2½d.	625.	Ichang	1d.
565.	Söul	1d.	626.	Bogota	1d.
566.	Newchwang	1d.	627.	Malaga	2d.
567.	Roustchouk and Philippopolis	1d.	628.	Porto Rico	1d.
568.	Stockholm	1½d.	629.	Bushire	2½d.
569.	Tonga	1d.	630.	The Hague	½d.
570.	Chicago	1½d.	631.	Berlin	1d.
571.	Adana	½d.	632.	Adrianople	1½d.
572.	Buenos Ayres	3d.	633.	Rome	1½d.
573.	Frankfort	1½d.	634.	Santiago	½d.
574.	Canton	1½d.	635.	Tahiti	½d.
575.	Tamsui	5½d.	636.	Maranham	½d.
576.	Palermo	3d.	637.	Mexico	2d.
577.	Amsterdam	1d.	638.	Christiania	1d.
578.	Ajaccio	½d.	639.	Copenhagen	1d.
579.	Shanghai	1½d.	640.	Paris	1d.
580.	Warsaw	½d.	641.	Venice	1d.
581.	Teneriffe	1d.	642.	Cherbourg	½d.
582.	Tangier	2d.	643.	New York	1d.
583.	Surinam	½d.	644.	Patras	1d.
584.	Loanda	1d.	645.	Bourgas	½d.
585.	Alexandria	1d.	646.	St. Petersburg	3d.
586.	Cagliari	1d.	647.	Taganrog	½d.
587.	Smyrna	½d.	648.	Baltimore	1½d.

No. 649.

Reference to previous Report, Annual Series No. 465.

UNITED STATES.

NEW ORLEANS.

Consul De Fonblanque to the Marquis of Salisbury.

My Lord,   February 1, 1890.

I HAVE the honour to enclose herewith my Annual Trade Reports for this Consular District for the year 1889.

I have, &c.

(Signed)   A. DE G. DE FONBLANQUE.

Trade Report, 1889.

During the past commercial year, the great industrial development throughout the States forming this Consular district has continued to show an ever-increasing activity, especially in the territory directly tributary, in a commercial sense, to New Orleans. A great deal of new southern territory has been opened up; the furnaces of Alabama are selling every ton of iron that they can make; the consumption of crude and finished iron, of cheap dry goods, and of shop and mill products, generally, is growing with amazing rapidity. The case recently of a southern town, of a few thousand inhabitants, which raised 500,000 dol. towards the erection of a cotton mill in its midst, is an evidence that the south is growing wealthy, and needs only the co-operation of northern and foreign capital to develop its great latent powers. The most rapid strides of progress in the south are in the territory directly tributary, in a commercial way, to New Orleans, which is the most accessible of all the Gulf ports, and the one offering the best conveniences for the trade. She is the principal American shipping point for cotton, and the chief staples of husbandry in the States, where her influence predominates. The sugar production in Louisiana and in the contiguous districts of Texas, and the rice crop of the State—an average annually increasing—give her a trade with every leading domestic market.

The manufactures of New Orleans, which, when I took charge of its Consulate in 1872, were hardly worth comment, are now said to employ 24,000 male and female hands, and to produce goods valued at 40,000,000 dol.

General remarks.

Iron.

Progress in the south.

Manufactures in New Orleans.

UNITED STATES.

If the purchase of non-necessaries be a token of prosperity—and it is generally understood to be so—then never in my memory has this city been so prosperous, for the purchase of Christmas and New Year's gifts exceeds that of former years in a very marked degree.

Defalcation of State treasurer.

The only serious drawback has been the defalcation of the State treasurer—an official so honoured and trusted that, when the Constitution was amended in a manner to oust the Governor, the treasurer was retained in office by a special enactment. The character and amount of bonds fraudulently issued is as follows:—

Fraudulent issue of bonds.

	Dollars.
Mechanical and Agricultural College bonds	196,200
Seminary bonds	82,200
Consolidated bonds exchanged, and not destroyed	25,200
Constitutional bonds illegally issued	70,000
Baby bonds illegally issued	420,000
Total	793,600

It is probable that this is a correct statement, and that the worst is known respecting all the securities named, chiefly the "Baby bonds;" but, as the absconder has the plates of these in his possession, it is possible that he has used them abroad, and that further illicit issues have been made, and are to be accounted for.

Liability of the State.

The question whether the State can be held responsible by innocent holders for value of the stolen bonds, or whether the former can demand their return and repayment of the interest paid on coupons, is *sub judice*.

The fraud.

The history of this fraud is a simple one. The ex-treasurer had absolute control of his department for nearly 10 years, and at the end of this prolonged term a committee of experts certified that his accounts were in exceptionally perfect order. But in the meantime the political section of the Democratic party, to which the ex-treasurer belonged, had been defeated. The treasury passed into new, and perhaps hostile, hands. Suspicions were aroused, and an inquiry by a grand jury elicited the fact that bonds, which under an Act of the Legislature were to have been converted into others and destroyed, had been preserved after such conversion and re-issued. As to the "Baby bonds," they appeared to have been disposed of by their custodian as though they were his own property. These disclosures paralysed for a time all dealings in State securities. No one knew whether the bonds he held were good or not. No bank was certain as to the value of the security it held, but when the numbers and designations of the illegal issues were published confidence was restored, and the regular State bonds are now quoted at better than normal rates.

Confidence restored.

Report of Stock Exchange.

The following is from the annual report of the Stock Exchange. There has been a marked advance in the bidding prices of nearly all the securities on the list from December 10, 1888, to December 9, 1889, as follows:—

Louisiana 4s., from $90\frac{1}{4}$ to 94, $3\frac{3}{4}$ points; premium bonds, from $139\frac{1}{2}$ to $145\frac{1}{4}$, $5\frac{3}{4}$ points; City 5s., from $98\frac{1}{4}$ to 102, $3\frac{3}{4}$ points. Other city bonds have varied but little. Bank, insurance, and

NEW ORLEANS.

street railroads stocks, by the last official quotations prior to the annual meetings of December 1888 and December 1889, have advanced as follows: Bank of Commerce, from 8⅝ to 10⅞, 2 dol. 25 c. per share; Canal Bank, from 147 dol. 75 c. to 167 dol. 50 c., 19 dol. 75 c. per share; Germania National Bank, from 185 dol. to 202 dol. 50 c., 17 dol. 50 c. per share; Germania Savings Bank, from 165 dol. to 170 dol., 5 dol. per share; Hibernia National Bank, from 157 dol. to 168 dol., 11 dol. per share; Louisiana National Bank, from 157 dol. to 186 dol., 29 dol. per share; Metropolitan Bank, from 123 dol. 75 c. to 151 dol., 27 dol. 25 c. per share; Mutual National Bank, from 131 dol. to 138 dol., 7 dol. per share; New Orleans National Bank, from 560 dol. to 608 dol., 48 dol. per share; People's National Bank, from 74 dol. 50 c. to 88 dol. 25 c., 13 dol. 75 c. per share; State National Bank, from 109 dol. to 131 dol., 22 dol. per share; Union National Bank, from 126 dol. to 143 dol. 75 c., 17 dol. 75 c. per share; Whitney National Bank, from 210 dol. to 245 dol., 35 dol. per share: an average advance for 12 months of 18 dol. 66 c. per share. *Market price of stocks. Bank.*

Insurance stocks have not appreciated to the same extent. New Orleans Insurance Company and Lafayette Company remain the same, while Hibernia has decreased 24 dol. per share; but still the average increase has been 3 dol. 68 c. per share, including these:—Crescent, from 48 dol. to 50 dol. 50 c., 2 dol. 50 c. per share; Firemen's, from 53 dol. to 63 dol., 10 dol. per share; Germania, from 118 dol. to 119 dol. 50 c., 1 dol. 50 c. per share; Home, from 90 dol. to 96 dol., 6 dol. per share; Merchants', from 57 dol. to 65 dol. 50 c., 8 dol. 50 c. per share; Merchants and Traders', from 115 dol. to 123 dol., 8 dol. per share; New Orleans Insurance Association, from 18 dol. 50 c. to 27 dol. 37½ c., 8 dol. 87½ c. per share; Sun, from 123 dol. to 127 dol. 50 c., 4 dol. 50 c. per share; Southern, from 84 dol. to 99 dol. 50 c., 15 dol. 50 c. per share; Teutonia, from 123 dol. 50 c. to 130 dol., 6 dol. 50 c. per share. *Insurance stocks.*

Street railroads have all advanced: Carrollton, from 88 dol. to 111 dol. 75 c., 23 dol. 75 c. per share; Crescent City, from 68 dol. 75 c. to 92 dol. 25 c., 23 dol. 50 c. per share; Canal and Claiborne, from 18 dol. 75 c. to 23 dol. 50 c., 4 dol. 75 c. per share; New Orleans City and Lake, from 108 dol. 50 c. to 115 dol. 75 c., 7 dol. 25 c. per share; Orleans, from 63 dol. 50 c. to 68 dol. 75 c., 5 dol. 25 c. per share; St. Charles Street, from 67 dol. 75 c. to 80 dol. 75 c., 13 dol. per share: averaging 14 dol. 58 c. per share. *Street railway stocks.*

The following stocks have also advanced: Slaughter House, from 40 dol. 62½ c. to 52 dol. 37½ c., 11 dol. 75 c. per share; New Orleans Gas Light, from 94 dol. 87½ c. to 102 dol. 62½ c., 7 dol. 75 c. per share; New Orleans Waterworks, from 63 dol. to 87 dol., 24 dol. per share; Standard Guano, from 127 dol. 50 c. to 185 dol. 57 c., 50 dol. per share.

This also seems to show confidence and prosperity.

The question of "bagging" for covering cotton bales has been *Cotton.*

(807)

Cotton bagging.

fully discussed during the last 12 months, but without result. The New Orleans Cotton Exchange, and some other exchanges in the south, voted to adopt the Odenheimer cotton bagging, weighing 12 ozs. to the yard, as a substitute for jute, but the Liverpool Exchange declined to adopt the proposition. It seems difficult to induce all parties interested to agree upon an universal tare in weighing the bales.

Tare.

I believe that some time last year Liverpool agreed to make the tare on cotton, like that on sugar and other articles, actual tare, and that a resolution to this effect was posted, but became a dead letter. This inconvenience of making a separate calculation on every bale of a 6,000,000 crop is obvious, but then it is equally clear that neither farmer nor factor can reasonably be expected to make the spinner a present of 12 lbs. of cotton in every 500, which is about what he would do if he accepted jute tare for the lighter covered bale.

The Jute Bagging Trust.

The Jute Bagging Trust, whose dissolution was expected in January, survives, and has lowered its prices, but not improved the quality of its goods. I have seen more half-exposed, ragged, and torn bales this year than ever before. To this imperfect protection I attribute in some degree the fires in cotton ships, and in cargoes discharged from them, which have again become unpleasantly frequent.

Fires in cotton ships.

The maritime journal called "Fairplay" is responsible for a correspondent who writes on this subject:—" Speaking to a gentleman who had lived in an American port for some years, he expressed his opinion that most of these fires were incendiary, or that if the cotton was not actually set on fire, some substance was placed with it in the hope that a fire might break out whilst the ship was loading, in order that the cotton would have to be picked and repacked at the port. This seems a miserable state of things, but my informant is a firm believer that it exists. He has seen hundreds of times cigarettes smoked on quay, on deck, and even in holds, whilst the last few bales were being stowed."

Levee dangers.

The American port, of which this is written, cannot be New Orleans, for here smoking is strictly prohibited in or about a cotton-loaded ship; but, as I have before observed in these reports, the unprotected state in which bales are left on the levees, subject to sparks from passing tug boats, steamers, locomotive engines, and disordered electric lights with broken glasses, makes it a matter of wonder to me that any ship lands a cotton cargo in safety. These dangers would in my judgment be materially diminished if the bales were packed in a more closely-woven fabric, and less carelessly compressed. With regard to the insinuation of incendiarism, it is a curious coincidence that almost all the fires break out in the forehold. In one case (the s.s. "Ayrshire") I found a defective coal shoot leading down the forehold into the stoke hole, and through which sparks might have found their way into the cotton stowed in the former; but with this exception I know of no reason why the fore part of a ship should be more liable to accident, or crime, than the after portion, but many which tend to a contrary conclusion. I have held naval courts to investigate the cause of these fires. I do not find that any serious attempts are made by underwriters to get at the facts of the case, at a time when they might betray the origin of the catastrophe. I think that if, immediately after the fire is put out, the holds were sealed and no one permitted to touch their remaining contents, until a thorough examination by competent persons was held, we should know more than we do at present. This is done with house fires, and frequently with useful results; but a ship must be got ready for sea again in hot haste, and if a Consular inquiry be held there is nothing but oral evidence available at the time when it can be commenced. *No sufficient investigation.*

Owing to causes which I need not here inquire into, the negroes are leaving some districts of the South in large numbers; and, as I write, a report comes from Charleston that 4,000 have left the state of South Carolina in one week, and that this emigration is said to be going on at the rate of 1,000 a day. *Negro exodus.*

From its political point of view this subject can have no place in a commercial report, but it has its economical side, and from this the question comes: Can the South do without negro labour? I venture to think, after careful consideration of all that has been advanced to the contrary, that the States which form this Consular district cannot. I know that a large portion of Texas is settled and cultivated by white labour, and that a number of persons whose opinion is entitled to respect consider that Louisiana, Mississippi, Florida, and Alabama might be colonised in like manner, but I am afraid that due consideration has not been given to differences of climate, of soil, and especially of race in those amongst whom the new comers would have to make their homes and fortunes. The German immigrants who have been successful in Texas found not only a virgin soil, but an unclouded political and social atmosphere. They disturbed no vested interests, they had no prejudices to encounter, or hostile organisations to defeat. The older States, now in question, though sparsely populated, contain a number of persons whose watchword appears to be rule or ruin. These, linked together by family ties, a common prejudice, and love of ease, are not likely to look on approvingly at a movement which might impair their influence, and impel them to unaccustomed personal exertion. *The race question.* *Prospects of white labour.*

A foretaste of what might happen to successful foreign farmers has lately been felt by successful Hebrew trades in Delhi and East Carrol (Louisiana), where an organisation has taken action against what they deem obnoxious storekeepers. Finding that they are stronger than the law (for nothing beyond resolutions have been passed against them), their next movement might be against foreign farmers who were too thrifty, or foreign labourers who worked too well; so that, as matters stand, I do not think there is encouragement for white immigrants either from other States or abroad. *Outrages on Hebrews.*

Annex A contains a return of shipping—British and foreign—at this port during the year 1889. As compared with that for 1888 it shows an increase of 87 in the number of British ships *Shipping.*

(entered), and of 138,563 in tonnage, and an increase of 61 ships (cleared), and of 107,817 in tonnage. The grand totals for the two years are:—

ENTERED.

	Ships.	Tonnage.
1888	974	1,194,678
1889	1,149	1,329,150

CLEARED.

	Ships.	Tonnage.
1888	969	1,109,164
1889	1,069	1,289,346

Seamen. Of late years I have observed, with regret, a spirit of antagonism growing up between masters and their crews. It would seem as though either side started with a preconcerted intention of being as disagreeable as possible. For this I find (at least) two reasons: the manner in which seamen are robbed and maltreated by the crimps, and the isolation of masters owing to the introduction of steam. In former times the master was constantly brought into touch with his men. He saw them at their work, distinguished smart seamen from skulkers, and was in turn appreciated; so that Captain A. could always have his pick and choice of good men, whilst Captain B. would be obliged to put up with a mob of "branch combers." On regular lines, where a bonus is given for continuous service, something of the old spirit prevails, but in the general ship—or, as it is called, the "Tramp" —whose crew are hustled on board at the last moment by the crimps (often under circumstances which would justify prosecution by the Society for the Prevention of Cruelty to Animals, if hogs were being laden), the sailors start with a grievance, and not sufficient logic to place it where it belongs. Deep down amidships throbs the power which sends the ship on her way. Shut in his cabin or enthroned on the bridge, the captain becomes an abstraction. Little seamanship is required for the light sails and straight courses of his ship. His firemen and trimmers are far from him. His sailors have become mere washers of decks and scrubbers of paint. The interest and mutual respect which arise out of work done in common does not exist, and the antagonism which, I regret, has gradually crept in—so also has the strike.

Causes of discontent. As it is now clear that sailors and firemen can combine, it would be well if owners and their masters were to look around for the causes of discontent and misconduct, and set a good example by removing them.

NEW ORLEANS.

Pay of sailors. Whether the pay of sailors and firemen is fair, as compared with that of other equally skilled labourers, is a question into which I do not propose to enter; but my experience in this port teaches me that the better they are paid the better they behave, and the less they cost the ship in the long-run. When wages out of Liverpool were raised desertions diminished. The man had made something, and desired to keep it. The higher rate of pay which ruled here would not compensate him for the loss. The extra 1*l*. 10*s*. for, say, two months, was more than saved to the owners, because the expense of replacing a deserter (from first to last) for one month is at least 4*l*.

Low pay—high rate of desertions.

Rations. There is a wide field of improvement in the stores put on board a British ship for the use of the crew, and in the manner of their preparation for food. The truth of the old proverb, which defines the directions from which victuals and cooks, respectively, come, is strongly proved on many a sea. From time immemorial the "sea-cook" has been a word of scorn to sailors, even to the second generation; but more, I think, on account of his ignorance of nautical matters, than the deficiencies that might be found in his culinary methods. There were good sea-cooks once, excluding, of course, the "chefs" who rule the roast in great liners, and the competent men engaged on regular ships; the representative sea-cook of the period is dirty, wasteful, helpless, and unaccommodating.

Cooking.

When a captain complains to me of rows and general depravity amongst his men, I always ask, "What sort of a cook have you?"

The improvement I have suggested in stores does not refer to quality or cost, but to device and variety.

Intolerable contracts. It often happens that the contract made between the ship and the seaman becomes intolerable to one side or the other, and there is no way to dissolve it abroad, except by sentence of a Naval Court. But such cases often arise where no offence within the jurisdiction of such a tribunal has been committed. Any Consul can cite dozens of cases in which the continuance of a man in his ship threatens subversion of her discipline, or in which the safety or comfort of the man require his discharge for no fault of his own. The discharge, by mutual consent, is all one-sided. The master is glad to get rid of the bad man, even at the risk of the ship's liability for him afterwards; but he stands by the second mate or boatswain, who may have been "down upon" the good one—refuses him his discharge, and leaves him to his only remedy, desertion. I would respectfully suggest that Consuls be given jurisdiction to inquire into such cases, and if it be proved to their satisfaction that the contract has become intolerable to either side, to discharge that side, making such an order as to payment or forfeiture of wages as may seem just. I am sure that some provision of this kind would give great satisfaction to honest seamen, and only inconvenience bad officers. The Consul might be required to take depositions on oath, and forward them, with the reasons of his decision, to the Board of Trade.

Suggestion for mutual release.

UNITED STATES.

Crimping in American ports.

Masters complain bitterly of the trouble and annoyance they have with their crews in American ports, but here I have yet to find one who will take advantage of the laws passed for his protection. The rule is to give the crimp and his runners full swing, and to accept the loss of the whole or a portion of the crew as a matter of course.

Shipment of sick men.

Men physically incompetent to do seamen's work are frequently shipped without examination. They lay up when the ship has been a few days at sea, and are discharged into hospital at the first foreign port. Having received an advance, the wages left in the hands of the Consul are hardly ever sufficient to pay expenses, and the man has frequently to be sent home at the public expense. In this way men in an advanced state of consumption, crippled with rheumatism, affected with disease of the heart, ruptured, &c., have been allowed to engage, and become a burden on the fund voted by Parliament.

I would respectfully suggest that the hospital expenses of a seaman so left behind abroad should fall on the ship, unless it can be shown that he was apparently in good health at the time he commenced the voyage.

Public works.

The question of draining, &c., tax.

The project for draining and paving New Orleans by means of a tax on landed property, to be passed upon by public vote, was defeated. The measure was affected by all the objections which unhappily attach to public works in all American municipalities, but it had hardly been defeated before its adversaries repented of their work—the deliberate resolution of a city of 250,000 inhabitants to protect dirt and preserve disease having subjected it not only to unfavourable comment, but actual loss. Nature, as though angry at this disregard of her laws, has withheld the frosts, which help to destroy the germs of disease, and the rain-storms, which supplement the scavengers incomplete labour, and our streets, gutters, and canals are in a condition which threatens disaster when summer sets in.

Naval yard at New Orleans.

A commission appointed to select the site for a new United States Navy-yard has reported in favour of Algiers (which is to New Orleans, topographically, what Southwark is to London).

If this project be carried out it would entail the construction of military works for the protection of the Mississippi river.

Bridge at New Orleans.

There is also some talk about a bridge, but I think that many years will have to pass before one can be deemed a commercial possibility.

Intestate estates of aliens.

In my report upon the status of aliens in this country, published on page 35 of the general report on the subject (Commercial No. 17, 1887, United States), I pointed out that British subjects are at a disadvantage with other foreigners, whose Governments have Consular conventions with the United States, because (inter alia) the property of those dying intestate is taken possession of by the State, and not by the Consul, who has the best means of discovering and communicating with absent heirs.

In a very recent case, in which I had been instrumental in

obtaining for the intestate (under his father's will) the property which was in his possession at the time of his death, and consequently knew all about the matter, I respectfully requested the probate judge to allow me, under the above circumstances, to suggest the name of an attorney for absent heirs, with whom I would act. His Honour was good enough to reply that he would not take any suggestion from the British Consul; and he appointed a stranger to me. Numerous and expensive advertisements will now be formally issued for persons whom I could reach for a five cent. stamp, a door is left wide open for claims which I might be in a position to question, and although this estate (consisting entirely of money in bank) can be easily realised, I shall be surprised if the next-of-kin get 15 per cent. of it.

Annex A.—RETURN of all Shipping at the Port of New Orleans in the Year 1889.

ENTERED.

Nationality.	Sailing. Number of Vessels.	Sailing. Tons.	Steam. Number of Vessels.	Steam. Tons.	Total. Number of Vessels.	Total. Tons.
American	65	21,455	394	462,082	459	483,537
British	23	11,672	448	578,223	471	589,895
Austrian	6	3,975	...	...	6	3,975
French	1	375	17	43,975	18	44,350
German	...	...	...	...	18	24,456
Italian	24	9,894	23	13,485	47	23,379
Mexican	10	1,728	7	4,261	17	5,989
Norwegian and Swedish	5	5,243	11	6,427	16	11,670
Spanish	20	11,472	77	130,427	97	141,899
Total	154	65,814	977	1,238,880	1,149	1,329,150

CLEARED.

Nationality.	Sailing. Number of Vessels.	Sailing. Tons.	Steam. Number of Vessels.	Steam. Tons.	Total. Number of Vessels.	Total. Tons.
American	53	16,885	362	448,253	415	465,138
British	20	5,612	422	567,581	442	573,193
Austrian	3	1,872	...	...	3	1,872
French	1	379	17	43,975	18	44,354
German	...	...	...	...	17	22,662
Italian	20	7,631	23	13,485	43	21,116
Mexican	13	2,336	5	3,093	18	5,429
Norwegian and Swedish	5	5,243	11	6,427	16	11,670
Spanish	20	11,532	77	132,380	97	143,912
Total	135	51,490	917	1,215,194	1,069	1,289,346

Annex B.—PRINCIPAL Cargoes carried in British Ships during 1889.

Articles.	Package.	Quantity.
Cotton..	Bales ..	1,174,909
Cotton products —		
Oil ..	Barrels	37,706
Seed ..	Sacks ..	4,728
Meal ..	,, ..	512,906
Cake ..	,, ..	361,717
Soap stock ..	Barrels	15,867
Grain –		
Corn ..	Bushels	11,291,870
,, ..	Sacks ..	108,910
Wheat..	Bushels	739,185
,, ..	Sacks ..	14,855
Timber—		
Staves ..	Pieces ..	570,748
Lumber	,, ..	136,409
,, ..	Feet ..	2,968,366
Flour ..	Sacks ..	7,770
Tobacco ..	Hogsheads ..	3,935
Lead bullion ..	Pigs and bars..	68,317
Tallow ..	Tierces..	1,497

MOBILE (ALABAMA.)

Mr. Vice-Consul Barnewall reports as follows :—

Commercial year commencing September 1st, 1888, and ending August 31st, 1889.

Cotton receipts. Prices. Receipts 229,184 bales, valued at 10,329,322 dol. 88 c., against 207,377 bales, valued at 9,613,997 dol. 77 c., receipts of the year preceding. Average price per bale, 45 dol. 7 c.; average price per lb., $8\frac{83}{100}$ c., against $9\frac{28}{100}$ c. per lb. the year preceding.

Exports—cotton. There has been a falling-off this year in the direct exports to Liverpool of 11,990 bales, and an increase to other points of 18,391 bales, showing a net increase in exports of 6,401 bales.

Timber. The favourable outlook at the close of last season has followed this important part of the pitch-pine trade through the past year, and there has been a decided improvement on previous ones.

Shipments. Shipments of timber were larger than in any year except 1883–84 and 1884–85, and the total value of exports from this port is over 100,000 dol. larger than last year. This is in part due to the improvement in prices. The shipments direct from Mobile do not represent the amount of timber sold in this market, as large amounts of timber were towed during the year from this place to Ship Island from vessels loading there—about 1,159,689 cubic feet— which is added to the exports, and would no doubt make the timber trade of the past year the largest in the history of Mobile.

The total shipments (foreign) for the past year are about 500,000 cubic feet larger than last year, and hewn shows a decrease, while sawn an increase over last year; but this is in part owing to the change in trade. Previous to 1883-84 very little sawn timber was shipped to Europe, but since then sawn has gradually taken the place of hewn, and the shipments of sawn this year from this port are about 700,000 cubic feet larger than last year, and the largest on record.

Prices. The value of foreign shipments shows the average value of hewn to be $14\frac{1}{2}$ c. per cubic foot, against $12\frac{1}{8}$ c. last year; sawn shows an average of $13\frac{7}{16}$ c. per cubic foot against $12\frac{1}{2}$ c. last year.

Prospects coming season. The present outlook for next season is very encouraging, as there are indications of a fair demand from Europe and South America, and unless ocean freights rise to a prohibitory point the trade of the coming year will no doubt be good and increasing.

Lumber. In this important branch of business the trade of the past year has been good and satisfactory, and the largest in the history of Mobile. About 55,000,000 feet were shipped from Mobile by vessels and railroads; but if we add the lumber to the sawn and hewn timber shipments we will have a trade of over 100,000,000 feet for the past 12 months.

This large increase in the pitch-pine trade would have been much larger but for the scarcity of tonnage. The trade by rail with the west and north-west was restricted by the low prices in the west, and high rates of freight from the south. Notwithstanding this, about 5,000,000 feet were shipped from Mobile by rail.

Exports. The total exports, foreign and coastwise, is 48,000,000 feet against 29,000,000 feet last year, and 32,000,000 feet in 1881-82 (the largest year previous to the past one), and represents a trade of over 600,000 dol., showing also nearly 100 per cent. increase in value over last year. The export foreign is 8,000,000 feet larger than last year, and the largest on record. The export coastwise is 11,000,000 feet larger than last year, and also the largest on record. Compared with last year, the exports show an increase of 1,728,000 feet to the United Kingdom, 1,987,000 feet to France, 420,000 feet to Holland, 1,205,000 feet to Germany, 700,000 feet to Africa, 10,000,000 feet to New York, 1,300,000 feet to Boston, and 100,000 feet to Providence. The principal decrease was 700,000 feet to Cuba, 300,000 feet to Philadelphia, and 600,000 feet to Baltimore.

Naval stores. The trade of the past year has been devoid of any special change.

Rosin and turpentine. Receipts: rosin, 106,129 barrels; turpentine, 23,927 barrels; total value, 550,650 dol.; against rosin, 132,055 barrels; turpentine, 28,725 barrels; total value, 635,643 dol. the year preceding.

Vegetables, shipments, value, &c. The vegetable trade continues to increase year by year, adding greatly to the wealth of this county. Shipments are made to nearly all the leading places, including Chicago, Cincinnati, St. Louis, Kansas City, Pittsburg, Philadelphia, Buffalo, and New York.

The value of the crop in this county is estimated at 371,113 dol., against 393,000 dol. last year, showing a decrease of 22,113 dol., but exhibits an increase of 62,000 dol. over the crop of 1887.

Staves. — In this branch of business there has been a decided improvement in the past year, and the foreign shipments of pipe staves are the largest on record. There are a number of buyers in this market, and large shipments have been made to Liverpool, Spain, and Portugal. There has been a marked improvement in the quality of the staves coming to this market, and a steady demand prevailed during the year.

Prices. — Prices ruled higher than last year, and the average price of shipments (foreign) is 135 dol. per 1,000 of 1,200 pieces, against 121 dol. last year, and 117 dol. the year before.

Shipments. — The shipments of pipe staves (foreign) the past year amount to 350,963 staves, valued at 38,972 dol., against 51,291 staves, valued at 5,202 dol. the year preceding.

New railroads. — *Mobile, Jackson, and Kansas City Railroad.*—The line of this road has been finally located from Mobile (Ala.), as far as Jackson, (Miss.). The profile and maps are completed, and the report of the chief engineer printed. It seems that the line can be constructed at a small cost, and that it will add immensely to the commerce of Mobile. It penetrates the finest pitch-pine forests in the south, and at the same time the country is well adapted to agricultural pursuits.

Harbour company. — *Mobile and Dauphin Island Railroad and Harbour Company.*—This long-talked-of scheme, after passing through many vicissitudes and overcoming much opposition, is at last about to be carried out by an English company. The new company is convinced that Mobile Bay, on account of its geographical position, depth of water, and ample ship room, should be the great port of the gulf. The company will build ample docks at deep water at the terminus of the railroad, with all modern facilities for handling coal, iron, grain, fruits, and all ocean freights.

Mobile Bay is the nearest gulf port to St. Louis, Cincinnati, Memphis, Chicago, and Kansas City, and a large part of the imports and exports of those cities will no doubt pass through Mobile Bay when such terminal facilities are made.

NEW ORLEANS.

Annex A.—RETURN of all Shipping at the Port of Mobile in the Year 1889.

ENTERED.

Nationality.	Sailing. Number of Vessels.	Sailing. Tons.	Steam. Number of Vessels.	Steam. Tons.	Total. Number of Vessels.	Total. Tons.
British	45	26,355	23	28,536	68	54,891
American	70	23,042	...	...	70	23,042
Austrian	4	2,074	...	...	4	2,074
Portuguese	2	868	...	...	2	868
German	...	...	1	1,170	1	1,170
Spanish	4	1,243	1	1,167	5	2,410
Finland	1	1,018	...	...	1	1,018
Russian	5	2,834	...	...	5	2,834
Danish	1	302	...	...	1	302
Italian	3	2,180	...	...	3	2,180
Dutch	9	4,830	...	...	9	4,830
Swedish	6	3,775	...	...	6	3,775
Netherlands	1	499	...	...	1	499
Hondurian	7	424	...	...	7	424
Norwegian	17	12,667	...	...	17	12,667
Coastwise	49	21,822	9	7,590	58	29,412
Total	224	103,933	34	38,463	258	142,396
„ for the year preceding	...	...	...	...	203	111,217

CLEARED.

Nationality.	Sailing. Number of Vessels.	Sailing. Tons.	Steam. Number of Vessels.	Steam. Tons.	Total. Number of Vessels.	Total. Tons.
British	48	28,509	24	29,493	72	58,002
American	56	15,590	...	...	56	15,590
French	2	676	...	...	2	676
German	2	1,963	1	1,170	3	3,133
Spanish	4	1,395	1	1,167	5	2,562
Portuguese	3	1,458	...	...	3	1,458
Norwegian	16	10,536	...	...	16	10,536
Russian	4	2,247	...	...	4	2,247
Swedish	8	4,750	...	...	8	4,750
Dutch	8	3,781	...	...	8	3,781
Austrian	5	2,816	...	...	5	2,816
Danish	1	302	...	...	1	302
Hondurian	9	552	...	...	9	552
Italian	2	1,591	...	...	2	1,591
Finland	1	1,018	...	...	1	1,018
Coastwise	66	29,251	4	4,067	70	33,318
Total	235	106,435	30	35,897	265	142,332
„ for the preceding year	...	...	...	...	207	109,492

Shipping.

Annex B.—RETURN of Principal Articles of Import to Mobile during the Years 1888-89—1887-88.

		1888.		1887.	
Articles.		Quantity.	Value.	Quantity.	Value.
			£ s. d.		£ s. d.
Bagging	Pieces	25,306	...	18,415	...
Iron ties	Bundles	56,355	...	36,836	...
Bacon	Hogsheads	12,736	...	13,777	...
Cotton	Bales	229,003	2,150,242 14 2	207,377	2,002,916 3 10
Coffee	Sacks	15,135	...	15,572	...
Corn	,,	472,253	...	325,556	...
Flour	Barrels	133,049	...	135,141	...
Fertilisers	Sacks	200,817	...	165,430	...
Hay	Bales	80,960	...	63,071	...
Lard	Tierces	5,332	...	3,490	...
Molasses	Barrels	2,858	...	3,560	...
Oats	Sacks	130,741	...	105,076	...
Potatoes	Barrels	16,024	...	17,460	...
Pork	,,	1,196	...	965	...
Rice	,,	5,535	...	4,831	...
Salt	Sacks	46,416	...	23,540	...
Soap	Boxes	22,090	...	19,767	...
Sugar	Barrels	14,289	...	16,569	...
Tobacco	Boxes	29,030	...	25,055	...
Whiskey	Barrels	5,862	...	6,090	...
Coal	Tons	45,074	...	39,433	...
Wool	Lbs.	857,500	45,554 13 9	652,800	29,952 1 8

Value £ sterling, 4 dol. 80 c.

I cannot enumerate articles imported from foreign countries, nor give the value of above enumerated articles, with exception of cotton and wool.

Annex C.—TABLE showing the Total Value of all Articles Exported from Mobile and Imported to Mobile from and to Foreign Countries during the Years 1887-88—1888-89.

EXPORTS.

	£	s.	d.
1887-88	717,727	6	4
1888-89	638,884	14	0

IMPORTS TO 30TH JUNE, 1889.

	£	s.	d.
1887-88	15,924	7	6
1888-89	32,056	0	10

I have no means of dividing the above exports as to countries, except as regards cotton included in above.

	£	s.	d.
Great Britain, 1887-88	603,529	18	8
,, ,, 1888-89	474,155	3	7

NEW ORLEANS.

RETURN of Principal Articles of Export from Mobile during the Years 1888-89—1887-88.

Articles.		1888 and 1889.		1887 and 1888.	
		Quantity.	Value.	Quantity.	Value.
			£ s. d.		£ s. d.
Cotton	Bales	229,184	2,151,942 5 4	222,783	2,151,712 9 6
Timber	Cubic ft.	3,122,943	92,171 9 5	2,575,784	64,955 12 8
Lumber	Feet	48,284,162	124,451 12 5	29,257,844	72,446 0 4
Rosin	Barrels	4,830	1,304 11 8	25,435	7,930 17 0
Staves	Mill.	350,963	8,119 3 4	51,291	1,083 15 6
Shingles	1,000	520,510	380 11 5	655,950	444 2 8
Merchandise	...	...	2,094 3 8	...	1,040 6 0
Vegetables	...	...	77,315 4 2	...	81,936 9 2
Cotton-seed meal	Sacks	6,720	1,437 10 0	...	...
Total	...	...	2,459,216 11 5	...	2,381,549 12 10

£ sterling valued at 4 dol. 8 c.

CONDITION of Dredged Channel, Mobile Harbour, July and August, 1889.

Locality.	Dredged 1881-1889, Examination July and August, 1889.				
	From the Initial Point, Miles.	Width, Feet.	Depth, Feet.	Minimum Top Width, Feet.	Maximum Central Depth, Feet.
Initial point in Mobile River to upper gap obstructions	0·64	145	18 to 20	200	19 to 20
Upper gap of obstructions to Cluster No. 2	1·07	245	18 19	300	22
Cluster No. 2 to lower gap of obstructions	1·48	155	18 19	200	20
Lower gap of obstructions to Cluster No. 27	13·91	145	19 20	200	19 to 20
Cluster No. 27 to Cluster No. 33	16·17	105	18 19	200	15 16
Cluster No. 33 to Cluster No. 46	23·35	145	19 20	200	18 20
Cluster No. 46 to Cluster No. 51	25·91	185	18 19	200	14 18

PENSACOLA.

Mr. Vice-Consul Howe reports as follows on the trade of Pensacola:—

The business of the port during the year was almost without intermission, and the export of Florida's great staple—pitch-pine wood—shipped mostly from and through Pensacola, was, as will be seen by the tables annexed, beyond the average trade of the port for some years past. Pitch-pine advanced in price during the early part of the year in leading timber-dealing centres of the United Kingdom—the bulk of the Pensacola exports go there yearly—and shipments continued quite active for some time.

Exports.

Pitch-pine advanced in price.

UNITED STATES.

Imports. The chief articles of import to Pensacola are principally from the large markets of the United States, north and west, and these yearly supplies include a liberal portion of things of British growth and manufacture. The largest portion of this import trade amounts in value to over 2,000,000 dol. yearly, the Pensacola market supplying some of the smaller places around it. Some other articles of import—salt, particularly—come direct from the United Kingdom and other foreign countries.

Direct trade. Referring to the remarks in my last yearly report relating to direct trade between the United Kingdom and this port, and other places near by, I adhere to what I then suggested; and, as regards the way that this trade is conducted in these southern cities, I here **Questions from England.** repeat my answer to questions put to me by large manufacturers in England, that there are not any distinct wholesale establishments at Pensacola, but the houses here supply from their well-stocked retail and wholesale stores many of the surrounding places in the State of Florida. In my last report I alluded to other Southern States in some of the larger cities, of which there are large wholesale houses that deal immensely in goods like the manufactures of **Bradford manufactures.** Bradford (I had inquiry from Bradford) and other manufacturing places, referred to in my report. Houses in this description of trade make their purchases in the large northern markets, New **Time of purchasing.** York particularly, in the spring and autumn, for summer and winter business. The houses which stand highest have open credits in New York and the other large northern markets, buying **Financial arrangements.** at stated periods and remitting continually. Other arrangements for smaller houses are, that as much money as can be paid down at once is credited against purchases, and notes given for balances at about four months.

I do not know that manufactures and shippers in the United Kingdom could deal financially with customers in these places in the way above described. This business, I think, should be con- **Agency.** ducted as before suggested, that is, through an agency or bureau of similar utility. The agency, I think, should work directly with those in the United Kingdom who may be induced to sell goods through it. No doubt a small beginning should be made which would lead to development or not, just as the trade would appear. I have given hints and made suggestions. I must leave them to be worked out if found practicable. As remarked by a trade publication in England (the "Ironmongery"), referring to my report, "The prime question is—Is there not a distinct advantage to be gained by working the markets of the Southern States directly, and not through the medium of northern buyers alone? That general attention has been called to the matter should be sufficient to lead our manufacturers to investigate it thoroughly."

Purchase of extensive mills and timber-land by English company. A very notable transaction at Pensacola during the year—reference to which will, I think, be interesting to many persons in the United Kingdom—was the formation of what may be termed an English company, which bought up several large milling establishments, with their immense tracts of pitch-pine timber-land, within easy shipping distance of the port of Pensacola.

The saw-mills referred to were previously owned by local companies and individual owners; and under their former management were successfully operated, and produced a very large proportion of the immense yearly exports of manufactured pitch-pine timber and lumber from Pensacola. It is thought that under the present undivided control and management of these mills, their former extensive business will be fully kept up, if not materially increased, in output and shipments abroad. *Former large proportion of exports.*

In reporting upon this company I am able to state, with much pleasure, that the carrying through of the scheme in its various details to its final consummation by purchase and possession was mostly, if not entirely, due to a business gentleman of the United Kingdom, who has for a long time been practically intimate with the Pensacola timber trade.

The chief directory of the company is, I am informed, composed of prominent bankers and other men of business in London and other parts of the United Kingdom. Some of the members are of the United States. The general managing director of the concern, who resides in London, is the gentleman above alluded to as forming the company. The chief office is in London, and a local board of directors look after the affairs of the company at Pensacola. The company is now fairly launched, and is doing a very active business in shipments of cargoes. The purchase-money amounted to a large sum. *Chief directory in London.*

It will, I think, interest British underwriters and all those concerned to know that during the year the Legislature of the State of Florida passed an Act providing for the appointment in every port in the State (to which has come during the past five years an average of not less than 50 vessels per year, of not less than 200 tons burthen each), of a custodian of lost timber and lumber. These bonded officers are to keep a careful watch over the waters of their respective ports, and to recover all timber and lumber found, and safely keep such property until disposed of. The disposition of the timber and lumber recovered is to be by delivery to the duly proved owner of the property, on the payment of the prescribed fee of 50 c. for each piece of timber recovered, and delivered at the custodian's boom, and for lumber the sum of 1 dol. per 1,000 feet superficial measurement. And it is made unlawful for any person, other than the legally-appointed custodians and their respective agents, to pick up, recover, or in any manner interfere with any timber or lumber found adrift in the waters of the places designated in the Act, and persons violating this provision of the Act are to be held guilty of a misdemeanour, and, upon conviction, punished by a fine of not more than 100 dol., or by imprisonment in the county jail for a period not exceeding three months, or by both fine and imprisonment, as the court shall adjudge. *Act passed for the appointment of a custodian of lost timber.* *Penalty for obstructing the Act.*

I had for years written and spoken on the subject, pointing out the nefarious doings that were connected with the timber that drifted from vessels loading cargoes in these waters to the loss of underwriters. *Former unscrupulous practices in connection*

(807)

UNITED STATES.

With drifted timber.

In laying the subject before the mayor of this city, just before the passing of the Act, when endeavouring through him to secure by city ordinance or State legislation protection at this port for British underwriters, I gave several facts in relation to drifted timber. I stated that from the years 1877 to 1888 inclusive, the average number of casualties per year, whereby timber went adrift from British vessels in the harbour of Pensacola, was 14. I especially pointed out that during the year 1888 there were 22 occasions when large quantities of timber drifted from British vessels in the harbour of Pensacola, amounting to about 4,000 pieces, an average of about 180 pieces from each vessel; that there were saved of such drifted timber 1,480 pieces (their recovery paid for by the masters at high rates), leaving an apparent average loss from each vessel of about 67 pieces of timber. Thus it appeared that during the year 1888 the number of pieces of timber counted as lost and paid for by underwriters amounted actually to about 2,520, at an average of not less than 7 dol. each piece, an apparent total amount of 17,640 dol. To this amount could have been added the salvage at high rates (ranging from 1 to 2 dol. each piece) demanded for the release of the timber picked up, and paid by the masters of the vessels from which it had drifted in order to secure its repossession. The self-appointed salvors, or rather persons who were professionally engaged in the obstruction of the recovery of the property, by the masters pleasing themselves whether they would return to the ship the timber picked up, or dispose of it otherwise. That the latter course was often adopted is apparent, because much of the drifted timber was never returned to the ship, although certainly picked up, as this is almost a land-locked harbour, in which timber could never be entirely lost.

Average loss per year.

Total loss of timber during the year 1888.

Drifted timber disposed of to highest bidder.

Record.

In giving these particulars I had, in substantiation of my statements, a record in extended protests at this office. During the year 1888 there were 22 protests entered by me for lost timber from British vessels in the harbour of Pensacola.

Taking the above as a basis, the loss from ships other than British loaded at Pensacola, in which British underwriters were largely concerned, can be estimated.

Successful operation of the act.

Very soon after my communication to the mayor of Pensacola the Act was passed, and since it has come in force hardly any timber or lumber has been lost in the harbour of Pensacola (although the average casualties continue to occur), the legal custodian in nearly every case securing all the timber that has drifted from vessels in the harbour, and restoring the same to the respective masters on proving property (all timber is now distinguished by a brand put on by masters when commencing to load) and paying the prescribed fee. The enactment is a most admirable one, and works well in the interests of all concerned. Since the coming in operation of the Act, no report of lost timber to be covered by protest has been received at this office from British masters, nor have protests by local notaries for vessels other than British been presented at this office, as they formerly frequently were, for my attestation for use in the United Kingdom.

I have reason to believe that British shipowners dealing with Pensacola should be better informed on the question of quarantine at this port than they now appear to be.

The quarantine system at Pensacola.

Within the past year an Act was passed by the Legislature of the State of Florida creating a State board of health. This enactment was the outcome, I think, of the late yellow fever epidemic at Jacksonville, Florida. County boards of health are authorised by the Act, but are subordinate to the State board; hence the Pensacola board of health is subject to the supervision of the State board in its regulations and proceedings as regards quarantine matters. About May 1 the county board of health issues a proclamation which lays down the minimum period (seven months last year) of quarantine, and then gives the rules and regulations governing quarantine.

Creation of a State board of health.

Among the quarantine rules and regulations to be especially regarded by British shipowners in chartering their vessels for this port, during the quarantine period, is the almost stereotyped regulation that no vessel arriving at the port of Pensacola, between the first and last days of quarantine, from any port or place where yellow fever or other malignant disease prevails, shall be permitted to discharge ballast or cargo, or load cargo in the port of Pensacola.

Vessels from infected ports not allowed to enter.

The next regulations to be observed are, that all vessels arriving in the bay of Pensacola during the quarantine term shall proceed to the quarantine station to be inspected, and, if deemed necessary by the quarantine physician, shall discharge ballast or cargo, and be submitted to cleansing and disinfectant process; that the master of each vessel cleansed or fumigated at the quarantine station shall pay for such cleansing and fumigation—steamships, 75 dol.; ships, 50 dol.; barques and other vessels, other than brigs and two-masted schooners, 40 dol.; brigs, 20 dol.; two-masted schooners, 15 dol.

Regulations concerning cleansing and fumigation.

It is further laid down by the board of health that no person from any vessel arriving between the dates of quarantine shall be permitted to leave such vessel until she shall have performed quarantine in accordance with the rules and regulations of the board of health.

Many British vessels arrived off the port of Pensacola, during the last quarantine term, under charter to load at Pensacola, but were prevented from entering, being from infected ports, as alleged by the board of health here. Fortunately, during the quarantine term some owners applied to me for information, and were enabled by my advice to alter the course of their vessels. The rules and regulations do not say that vessels from infected or suspected ports shall not enter, but such is virtually the meaning, as pilots will not bring them in under certain stipulations of the board, which would quarantine the pilots; and these vessels, if even in, would not be allowed to load. The vessels referred to as having arrived off the port, and been prevented from entering, had to seek other ports and fresh business. The loss to owners, in these cases, must have been very heavy, but there was no help for it; and though there are many things apparently quite inconsistent, I think, with even-

Vessels from infected ports refused entry.

a rigid quarantine, in the conduct of quarantine affairs at this port, still I must say that the regulations respecting the entry of vessels from infected ports are not, in my opinion, out of place. Those abroad interested in this subject are only to imagine the terrible results of the introduction of a single case of yellow fever here (which would also place many other towns in jeopardy), and they will be ready to allow that no chances can be taken in admitting vessels from an infected or even suspicious port. Only those who have passed through an epidemic of yellow fever can realise the misery and anguish that arise from and follow this much-dreaded disease. In fact, the people of this city would rather see the business of the place suspended for months than allow the entry of one vessel from an infected or even a suspected port.

Loss of time to vessels owing to lack of proper facilities at quarantine stations.

The very great fear of the introduction of yellow fever in Pensacola causes protective measures, in my opinion, beyond reason.

Sailing vessels to discharge ballast, and to be cleansed and fumigated, take many days and weeks before they are ready to proceed to the harbour to take in their cargoes. The facilities for discharging ballast at the quarantine station are so few, owing to deficiency of wharves, that the vessels in taking their turn lose a great deal of time.

Discharge of ballast at quarantine.

With reference to the discharge of ballast at the quarantine station, one firm here, which had been accustomed to discharge the ballast of the vessels chartered by them, and had made this a charter stipulation at a certain rate, have from time to time demanded from masters the estimated amount of such discharge, although masters had been already compelled to pay for the discharge at quarantine before they could secure permits of release to proceed to Pensacola harbour.

Suit entered by British masters for recovery of amount paid for discharge of ballast as being unconstitutionally exacted.

A distinguished solicitor of this city advised several British masters, who had been compelled by the regulations of the board of health to discharge their ballast at the quarantine station, to enter suit for the amount demanded in such compulsory manner as being unconstitutionally exacted, but the result was not in favour of the masters in the lower court. An appeal has been taken to the Supreme Court of the State.

Scale of charges unfairly proportioned.

The scale of charges for vessels cleansed and fumigated at the quarantine station appears unfair. 75 dol. would be a large amount to take for a steamship of 88 tons, when the same amount is taken for a similar vessel of 1,700 tons. The same objection will stand, I think, as regards other vessels taken by their rig instead of their tonnage; many barques, for instance, going far beyond ship-rigged vessels, while small schooners, not over 100 tons each, pay the same as those hundreds of tons larger.

Large amount of money collected during quarantine.
Apparently unnecessary

An immense amount of money appears to be taken for the fumigation and cleansing of vessels during the quarantine season.

Having lately been instructed to report on the apparently unnecessary detention and fumigation of a British steamer that arrived at the quarantine station from Cape Verd, I addressed a communication to the president of the board of health of Pensacola respecting her.

Detention of a steamer from Cape Verd.

It was contended by the Steamship Owners' Association of the North of England that this steamer was not only from a very healthy port, but was clean in every particular, but that in spite of her perfect sanitary condition she was detained for five days, and had to undergo the regular process of fumigation, &c.

Complaint by Steamship Association of England.

The reply was to the effect that the quarantine physician thought it necessary to detain her, and subject her to the usual process of fumigation, &c.

As regards my remarks respecting other cases, it was stated that it was the policy of the board not to subject any vessel to any greater detention or hardships in quarantine than in their opinion was absolutely necessary for the health of the port. I was also informed that, at a recent meeting of the board, it was resolved that a committee of the board should proceed to the New Orleans quarantine station in order to inspect the plan and methods in force there, and report on the advisability of their being adopted here; and that it was contemplated to thoroughly equip the Pensacola quarantine station for fumigation, &c., and that the board of health hoped that, by the next season, shipowners would have no reason to complain about the quarantine.

Proposed improvement in facilities for fumigation, &c.

I have observed that much dissatisfaction has been expressed about the libelling and seizure of British vessels in ports of the United States, and inter alia at Pensacola, hence I think it proper to touch upon this subject.

Libelling of British vessels.

Some of the cases above referred to were outrageously unfair, but I have been powerless in the matter.

Seizures often unfair.

A dispute arises between the master of a vessel and the charterer. The charterer argues that the terms of the charter have not been adhered to, that certain spaces of the ship have not been given for cargo, that sufficient deck cargo has not been taken, and points of like disagreement. Disputes of this kind arise particularly with steamers, when the lump sum charter is in force. The master, in some cases, endeavours to meet the demands of the charterer; the latter yields in his turn; and in these instances, as I am aware, conciliatory means and tone are adopted, and the disagreement ended.

Nature of suits arising from lump sum charter.

But there are also other cases in which the charterer has insisted on his views alone being right, making no concession whatever; and the master, naturally stung by what he considers as beyond fair play demanded, has resisted, and the result has been the libelling of the ship by charterers and disastrous consequences, even when the case may have been partly or entirely gained by the shipowner. The ship is at a great disadvantage in these suits, which sometimes are held over the ship, only to force the demand conceded to save the libel arrest.

In the last two cases decided upon in Admiralty at this port, in which British steamers were concerned, the points at variance were in one case as follows:—The steamer was chartered under

Nature of last cases decided.

the lump sum charter to load timber and deals. The vessel proceeded in her loading and was ready for sea, when the charterer libelled her on the following grounds—1st, that the terms of the charter, as regards her tonnage, had been broken, her tonnage not being the same as represented at the time of chartering; 2nd, that the master took on coal at this port, instead of coaling at a between port, and thus, as was alleged, cargo was shut out which should have been carried under the lump sum charter; 3rd, that there was kept in the vessel ballast that excluded cargo, to which space, it was said, the charterers were entitled.

Decision of the court. The decision of the court in this case was as follows:—That the vessel had been represented as being 1,557 tons; that she was really only 1,386: this was admitted by ship. The court allowed a proportionate reduction from the amount of freight—175*l*. off 2.550*l*. The coal claim was disallowed by the court, as the charter-party did not specify that the vessel was to coal at an intermediate port. The ballast claim was disallowed, the court ruling that the master could use his own judgment about keeping in ballast.

The next case was that of a steamer which had been chartered at New Orleans on a lump sum charter to load pitch-pine wood at Pensacola. The charterers were entitled, as was alleged, to the entire carrying capacity of the vessel, including all spaces in which cargo may have previously been carried. The vessel took in at New Orleans a quantity of coal which occupied a large space of the deck-room, and the charterers contended that they were entitled to the deck space, and sued for damages equivalent to estimated loss by reason of being shut out. The decision by the court in this second of the two cases referred to above was as follows:—That it appeared that the master had part of the ship's deck covered with coal, and stated that he did not intend to take a deck load; that he also had water in one of the ballast tanks which gave the ship a list to starboard, and caused her to appear overloaded on deck; and that the master's conduct thus was not satisfactory. The court found by the evidence submitted in the cause that the vessel might have taken 205 loads more than she did, and that her failure to do so under the terms of the charter caused a damage to libellant of nearly 1,600 dol., and the court ordered a decree to be entered for the amount allowed in favour of the libellant.

As regards the case first above related, both sides, I think, should have come together by arbitration. In the second case the charterer, as I thought and advised at the time, should have been met with some compromise. The master, as he told me, gave the particulars of dispute by cable to his owners, and took their instructions, in connection with the advice of his counsel here. Still, I was of opinion that the case should be compromised. Owners at home can hardly form a proper opinion, and advise accordingly. In some of these civil suits it would be better, I think, for the owners to leave the master and Consular officer to work through the complications. In the case last given, I approached the charterers for a compromise in equity, which they would readily have accepted, but overtures were refused by the master acting for the owners.

While on this subject I will refer to something new in the libelling of ships at this port. A vessel is chartered, and according to the terms of charter the master, sided with by his owner, demands demurrage for detention in loading. The charterer, on the other hand, refuses to pay, and puts forward this, that, and the other as releasing him from the liability and demand. The master then simply notes a protest—an old-standing custom in maritime affairs—in order to make good his claim, if he is right in the demand, at the termination of the voyage. The charterer then libels the vessel, on the alleged ground that his interests will be impaired with a note of protest hanging over the shipment. In a recent case here a British ship was libelled and detained by the charterer for 30 days, the owners refusing to bond their ship. This was a case in which demurrage was due and demanded, and on refusal of payment a note of protest was entered in this office, as in protection of claim hereafter.

Something new in the libelling of ships.

Libelling vessels for noting protests.

In this last case the ship was bonded by the owners, and now lawsuits are pending both in this country and in the United Kingdom, and the issues at stake involve a large expenditure. It appears monstrous that because a master notes a protest, simply in protection of his supposed rights, such proceedings should be allowable. The vague terms of charter parties often lead in the end to much of this trouble. Shipowners should be more careful, I think, in the freight agreements accepted by signature.

Bonded.

For the purpose of illustrating the increase in this class of vessels at this port, I add to the regular yearly tables required for this report a comparative statement of British steam tonnage at Pensacola for the past 12 years inclusive—the only years, to my knowledge, in which foreign steam carriers have entered the port. In my report for the year 1887 I gave it as my opinion that steamers, and British steamers particularly, would in future be employed in larger proportion than formerly in each succeeding yearly business of this port, and I think I was and am still correct in such belief. During the year 1888 the largest number of steamers (nearly all British) that ever loaded at Pensacola during one year cleared from the port. In the year just closed nearly double the number and tonnage of this class of vessel, compared with the year before, loaded and cleared from Pensacola.

Steam tonnage at Pensacola.

There is a decrease in sailing vessels. Many of the old sailing vessels of the United Kingdom continue to arrive yearly at Pensacola under foreign flags, those of Norway and Sweden particularly. Of the tonnage given in this report under the head of Sweden and Norway about one-third was formerly under the British flag.

Decrease of sailing vessels of the United Kingdom entered at Pensacola. Large proportion of vessels of Sweden and Norway formerly British.

In my last yearly report I mentioned that the city government of Pensacola had passed an ordinance appointing a shipping master for the port of Pensacola. This worked admirably for some months, when the crimps, who had at first obstructed the

Shipping master, late ordinance. Ordinance overthrown as being unconstitutional.

law and often fought it, at last managed to have it overthrown. One of the class was convicted when counsel, trying the issue for the fraternity of crimps, appealed the case, and a State judge ruled that the ordinance was unconstitutional, dealing, as it did, with things connected with foreign commerce, with which, it was argued, the general government alone was qualified to deal. The ordinance thereupon ceased to be in operation, and the old system —engagement of seamen through the crimps direct, with all of its attendant evils—is again in full play.

Case of the "Paragon."

I was called upon to investigate a death that had occurred of one of the crew last engaged on the "Paragon." It appeared that a young American seaman, who had duly signed the agreement but was not willing to join the vessel, or, at any rate, not ready to join her at the moment, was surreptitiously induced to go on board to visit her. He was taken there by two employés of the sailor-boarding-house keeper, who had him under control. The seaman went aboard without his effects, and the men who took him there left him on board against his will, promising that they would soon return for him. Finding that it was not intended that he should leave the vessel again, as after waiting some time he was not called for, he jumped overboard, and in endeavouring to swim to the shore, or to some vessel in the harbour, was drowned. My investigation of the case by examination of the master, officers, and others of the crew of the "Paragon" supported the facts as stated above, and it was further elucidated that the young seaman had, in his protestations against being left on board by the persons taking him to the vessel, made remarks pointing to his not having been settled with as regards his accounts with the crimps ashore.

"Paragon" case one of several. Investigation by city authorities.

This is one of several deaths that have happened at this port on British vessels under similar circumstances.

In the case above given, I appealed to the city authorities requesting investigation and action against the persons on shore who contributed to the seaman's death. The investigation was held, but nothing came of it.

Shipment of coal to Cuba.

In my last yearly report I mentioned that shipments of coal were being made from Pensacola to ports in the island of Cuba, and stated that I had been informed that extensive operations thus would follow. I am now able to state that it appears that this business has been permanently gone into by a company organised for a regular business between this port and Cuba by the shipment of coal and other things. Extensive preparations, by building of wharves, &c., have been made for the receipt of coal by railroad from the coal mines of Alabama, and shipments are regularly now going forward. The mode of transportation of the coal to Cuba is by barges, which are towed by a steam-tug from this harbour to Cuba, and are towed back. The British steam-tug "Scythian" has been, so far, engaged in the towage of the barges. The exact value of the coal delivered at Cuba is about $5\frac{1}{2}$ dol. per ton. The coal is of a bituminous nature, and is of very good quality, I am told. I am not aware that any other quality of coal is mined at the Alabama coal-fields; there may be, however, a coal of harder substance than the coal now shipped hence.

A Chamber of Commerce has lately been incorporated at Pensacola. The objects of the association are, as given by the bye-laws, "to advance the trade, business, and commerce of Pensacola, and to promote the general prosperity and material interests of this city and its vicinity, and to produce harmony and good feeling among the business community; to acquire and disseminate valuable commercial and economic information; and generally to secure to its merchants the benefits of co-operation in the furtherance of their legitimate pursuits." {Incorporation of a Chamber of Commerce at Pensacola.}

The executive officers of the corporation are among the leading business men of Pensacola, and I have no doubt it will be of good effect in the trade of the port, which is being developed year by year.

The marine railway, remarked upon in my last yearly report, has been delayed in its construction, but is now about nearly ready to be put in operation. I repeat my former remarks on this subject, as regards the benefit that will arise from this construction, and will be glad to see it ready for taking out vessels that may require repairs, or to be looked after, before proceeding hence with cargoes of timber. {Marine railway nearly completed.}

The health of Pensacola for the year has been very good; no unusual sickness or epidemics of any kind having appeared here. The average yearly mortality of Pensacola in its regular course, without appearance of epidemic, is about 26 per 1,000, on a population ranging from 13,000 to 15,000. All things in keeping with prosperity here still continue. Buildings as residences and for business purposes continue to be built, and, altogether, again I must say to the well-wishers of Pensacola in the United Kingdom, and those particularly that do business with this port, that there is every indication of a continuance of its present prosperity. The difference, now, for the better in this place, in comparison with its condition when I took charge of the post 13 years ago, is immense, the population now being more than double what it was then, and most of the buildings in the principal part of the town being of late and improved construction. {Health of Pensacola.}

UNITED STATES.

Return of all Shipping at the Port of Pensacola in the Year 1889.

Entered.

Nationality.	Sailing. Number of Vessels.	Sailing. Tons.	Steam. Number of Vessels.	Steam. Tons.	Total. Number of Vessels.	Total. Tons.
British	82	56,944	45	54,561	127	111,505
American	103	37,669	1	864	104	38,533
Swedish and Norwegian	160	126,120	...	...	160	126,120
Italian	143	88,297	...	...	143	88,297
Austrian	41	26,596	...	...	41	26,596
German	21	19,747	...	...	21	19,747
Russian	22	14,616	...	...	22	14,616
Dutch	18	12,136	1	956	19	13,092
French	11	6,297	...	...	11	6,297
Spanish	1	348	3	4,019	4	4,367
Other countries	4	3,408	...	...	4	3,408
Total	606	392,178	50	60,400	656	452,578
,, for the year preceding	454	311,881	27	34,392	481	346,273

Cleared.

Nationality.	Sailing. Number of Vessels.	Sailing. Tons.	Steam. Number of Vessels.	Steam. Tons.	Total. Number of Vessels.	Total. Tons.
British	81	59,558	44	53,499	125	112,967
American	91	34,956	1	864	92	35,820
Swedish and Norwegian	159	121,426	...	...	159	121,426
Italian	150	91,347	...	...	150	91,347
Austrian	39	25,659	...	...	39	25,659
German	17	14,690	...	...	17	14,690
Russian	19	12,042	...	...	19	12,042
Dutch	17	10,641	1	956	18	11,597
French	10	6,115	...	...	10	6,115
Spanish	2	691	3	4,019	5	4,710
Other countries	2	1,445	...	...	2	1,445
Total	587	378,510	49	59,248	636	437,818
,, for the year preceding	449	312,484	27	34,392	476	346,876

NEW ORLEANS.

TABLE showing the Total Value of all Articles Exported from Pensacola and Imported to Pensacola from and to Foreign Countries during the Years 1888–89.

Country.	Exports. 1889. £ s. d.	Exports. 1888. £ s. d.	Imports. 1889. £ s. d.	Imports. 1888. £ s. d.
United Kingdom	331,456 16 9	221,741 6 9	...	...
Argentine Republic	93,151 7 7	56,116 7 9	...	...
Italy	60,741 14 0	67,517 18 11	...	...
Netherlands	48,483 5 6	32,390 7 1	...	...
France	38,629 4 7	35,568 11 1	...	...
Uruguay	29,395 0 0	19,459 12 8	...	...
Germany	23,014 9 0	20,347 0 0	...	...
Spain and colonies	20,570 6 9	17,462 13 3	...	...
Belgium	19,678 9 7	14,558 5 8	...	...
Brazil	9,020 0 0	7,910 17 6	...	...
Austria	3,899 17 2	2,213 10 4	...	...
Portugal	3,873 17 3	9,983 10 3	...	...
Norway	2,417 7 9	...	...	...
United States of Colombia	902 10 0	6,260 0 0	...	...
Other countries	...	3,331 3 9	...	...
Total foreign countries	685,234 5 11	514,861 5 0	*...	*...
„ ports in the United States	44,707 10 0	51,740 13 6	*...	*...
Total	729,941 15 11	566,601 18 6	...	...

* See note elsewhere in this report about value of imports.

RETURN of Principal Articles of Export from Pensacola during the Years 1888–89.

Articles.	1889. Quantity.	1889. Value. £ s. d.	1888. Quantity.	1888. Value. £ s. d.
Sawn pitch-pine timber	14,609,244	380,449 1 3	10,256,650	267,100 5 3
Pitch-pine lumber	126,131,000	315,327 10 0	104,744,226	261,935 11 3
Hewn pitch-pine lumber	1,347,717	30,885 3 8	1,499,198	34,367 12 5
Cedar	4,655	339 8 6	27,222	1,984 18 9
Coal	4,205	2,628 2 6	615	384 7 6
Other articles	...	312 10 0	...	829 3 4
Total	...	729,941 15 11	...	566,601 18 6

In the above table lumber is in superficial thousand feet, valued at 12 dol. (2*l.* 10*s.*); sawn timber, at average of 12½ c. (6¼*d.*) per cubic foot—basis, 40 feet average; hewn timber, at average of 11 c. (5½*d.*) per cubic foot—basis, 100 cubic feet average; coal in tons, at 3 dol. (12*s.* 6*d.*); cedar, at 35 c. (1*s.* 5½*d.*) per cubic foot.

UNITED STATES.

RETURN of Principal Articles of Import to Pensacola during the Years 1889–1888.

Articles.	Value.	
	1889.	1888.
	£ s. d.	£ s. d.
Chief articles	*	*
Other „	*	*

COMPARATIVE Statement of British Steamers arriving at Pensacola for the past 12 Years inclusive.

Year.	Number.	Tonnage.
1878	..	..
1879	..	..
1880	..	..
1881	4	3,872
1882	13	16,260
1883	11	14,139
1884	3	3,396
1885	8	9,477
1886	4	4,326
1887	5	6,225
1888	22	28,333
1889	45	54,561
	115	140,589

* On first page of this report remarks will be seen descriptive of articles, and approximative in value of imports, to Pensacola during the years given above. A positive statement cannot be obtained of imports, except shipments on British vessels. During the year 1889 the value of cargoes brought here on British vessels amounted to £1,430.

LONDON:
Printed for Her Majesty's Stationery Office,
By HARRISON AND SONS,
Printers in Ordinary to Her Majesty.

(1250   3 | 90—H & S   807)

FOREIGN OFFICE.
1890.
ANNUAL SERIES.

No. 650.

DIPLOMATIC AND CONSULAR REPORTS ON TRADE AND FINANCE.

UNITED STATES.

REPORT FOR THE YEAR 1889
ON THE
AGRICULTURE OF THE CONSULAR DISTRICT OF NEW ORLEANS.

REFERENCE TO PREVIOUS REPORT, Annual Series No. 466.

Presented to both Houses of Parliament by Command of Her Majesty,
MARCH, 1890.

LONDON:
PRINTED FOR HER MAJESTY'S STATIONERY OFFICE,
BY HARRISON AND SONS, ST. MARTIN'S LANE,
PRINTERS IN ORDINARY TO HER MAJESTY.

And to be purchased, either directly or through any Bookseller, from
EYRE & SPOTTISWOODE, EAST HARDING STREET, FLEET STREET, E.C., and
32, ABINGDON STREET, WESTMINSTER, S.W.; or
ADAM AND CHARLES BLACK, 6, NORTH BRIDGE, EDINBURGH; or
HODGES, FIGGIS, & Co., 104, GRAFTON STREET, DUBLIN.

1890.

[C. 5895—53.] *Price One Penny.*

New Series of Reports.

Reports of the Annual Series have been issued from Her Majesty's Diplomatic and Consular Officers at the following places, and may be obtained from the sources indicated on the title-page:—

No.		Price.	No.		Price.
528. Ciudad Bolivar		1d.	589. Nagasaki		1d.
529. Jaffa		1d.	590. Hakodate		1d.
530. Ancona		1d.	591. Bushire		1d.
531. Savannah		1d.	592. Chinkiang		½d.
532. Batavia		1d.	593. Pakhoi		1d.
533. Adrianople		1d.	594. Hiogo		1½d.
534. Nisch		11d.	595. Bangkok		1d.
535. Vienna		1d.	596. Serajevo		1d.
536. Odessa		8d.	597. Copenhagen		1½d.
537. Constantinople		2d.	598. Cephalonia		½d.
538. Damascus		1d.	599. Chefoo		½d.
539. Tientsin		1d.	600. Guatemala		1½d.
540. Amoy		1d.	601. Tonga		½d.
541. Mogador		1d.	602. Tahiti		1d.
542. Vienna		1d.	603. Stettin		2d.
543. Antwerp		1d.	604. Vera Cruz		1½d.
544. Lisbon		2d.	605. Christiania		4d.
545. New York		1½d.	606. Pernambuco		1½d.
546. San Francisco		1d.	607. Trieste		1½d.
547. Stettin		1½d.	608. Tunis		½d.
548. San Salvador		½d.	609. Havana		2d.
549. Trebizond		1d.	610. Frankfort		½d.
550. Nice		1d.	611. Tabreez		½d.
551. Baghdad		½d.	612. Bilbao		1d.
552. Fiume		1d.	613. Barcelona		½d.
553. Mogador		2d.	614. Tokio		1d.
554. Buenos Ayres		1½d.	615. Naples		2½d.
555. San Francisco		2½d.	616. Batoum		½d.
556. Carthagena		½d.	617. Odessa		1d.
557. Syra		1d.	618. La Rochelle		1d.
558. Varna and Bourgas		1d.	619. Rome		1d.
559. Thessaly		½d.	620. Nice		1d.
560. Yokohama		1d.	621. Kiukiang		½d.
561. Nantes		1½d.	622. Paris		1d.
562. Suakin		½d.	623. Salonica		1½d.
563. Algiers		1d.	624. Réunion		1d.
564. St. Petersburg		2½d.	625. Ichang		1d.
565. Söul		1d.	626. Bogotá		1d.
566. Newchwang		1d.	627. Malaga		2d.
567. Roustchouk and Philippopolis		1d.	628. Porto Rico		1d.
568. Stockholm		1½d.	629. Bushire		2½d.
569. Tonga		1d.	630. The Hague		½d.
570. Chicago		1½d.	631. Berlin		1d.
571. Adana		½d.	632. Adrianople		1½d.
572. Buenos Ayres		3d.	633. Rome		1½d.
573. Frankfort		1½d.	634. Santiago		½d.
574. Canton		1½d.	635. Tahiti		½d.
575. Tamsui		5½d.	636. Maranham		½d.
576. Palermo		3d.	637. Mexico		2d.
577. Amsterdam		1d.	638. Christiania		1d.
578. Ajaccio		½d.	639. Copenhagen		1d.
579. Shanghai		1½d.	640. Paris		1d.
580. Warsaw		½d.	641. Venice		1d.
581. Teneriffe		1d.	642. Cherbourg		½d.
582. Tangier		2d.	643. New York		1d.
583. Surinam		½d.	644. Patras		1d.
584. Loanda		1d.	645. Bourgas		½d.
585. Alexandria		1d.	646. St. Petersburg		3d.
586. Cagliari		1d.	647. Taganrog		½d.
587. Smyrna		½d.	648. Baltimore		1½d.
588. Mannheim		1d.	649. New Orleans		2d.

No. 650.

Reference to previous Report, Annual Series No. 466.

UNITED STATES.

NEW ORLEANS.

Consul De Fonblanque to the Marquis of Salisbury.

My Lord,   New Orleans, February 1, 1889.

I HAVE the honour to enclose herewith my Annual Report on Agriculture for this Consular District for the year 1889.

The Vice-Consul at Mobile informs me that he has nothing to say on this subject but what would be a repetition of his report for the year 1888.

I have, &c.
(Signed)   A. DE G. DE FONBLANQUE.

Report on Agriculture, 1889.

The past year has been one of almost unprecedented drought. The rainfall for its last three months and for the whole twelve at selected stations of the Louisiana weather service, and the normals for the north and south of the State, is shown as follows:— *The drought.*

NORTH LOUISIANA STATIONS.

	October.	November.	December.	Year.
Farmerville	0·75	6·05	0·75	34·29
Minden	0·07	4·24	1·03	27·73
Shreveport	1·06	9·10	0·64	46·17
Monroe	0·44	6·58	1·56	43·43
Vicksburg, Mississippi	0·16	4·59	0·99	46·30
Liberty Hill	0·46	7·18	1·71	44·86
Grand Cane	0·80	8·10	0·60	45·56
Vidalia	1·18	3·36	1·00	33·01
Alexandria	0·17	4·84	0·92	37·84
Marksville	0·17	3·43	1·08	17·52
Means	0·43	5·75	1·03	37·67
Normals	3·46	5·12	5·33	54·77

Rainfall.

UNITED STATES.

South Louisiana Stations.

	October.	November.	December.	Year.
Clinton	..	3·29	1·69	38·22
Amite	3·21	2·72	1·20	48·01
Melville	0·46	1·78	2·71	36·70
Hammond	..	4·44	0·84	43·60
Baton Rouge	0·11	2·80	..	..
Grand Coteau	T	2·85	3·75	45·31
Maudeville	..	2·98	0·39	34·62
Maurepas	..	3·17	1·30	38·86
Plaquemine	0·30	2·37	1·44	40·35
Crowley	..	3·62	1·74	41·70
Lake Charles	0·10	3·50	1·85	36·37
Donaldsonville	0·15	3·30	1·45	38·92
Shell Beach	..	4·80	1·95	34 80
Mount Airy	T	3·57	0 50	35·26
New Iberia	..	1·20	1·59	36·99
Abbeville	0·02	3·19	1·63	39·53
New Orleans	0·26	2·18	0·67	48·45
Cameron	0·15	4·36	2·52	42·00
Thibadoux	0·17	2·28	0·88	41·34
Homna	0·28	3·25	1·62	54·27
Port Eads	0·02	2·05	1·50	40·92
Means	0·25	3·08	1 50	40·92
Normals	2·80	4·21	4·91	60·29

Its effects. This has, of course, seriously affected the rice crop, where the planter, relying upon natural irrigation, had not or could not provide pumps. I append copy of a bulletin* of the Louisiana Agricultural Experimental Station upon rice and its by-products, embodying a chemical investigation of this cereal by Professor B. B. Ross.

Annex A. Rice.

Annex B. Sugar. Also a further bulletin, No. 23,* upon the diffusion process as applied to sugar cane.

General L. Sewell has favoured me with the following upon the subject of ramie culture:—

Ramie. "Oakbourne plantation, in the parish of Lafayette, Louisiana, was considered a spot with good promise for the successful planting of the ramie. It is a plantation well watered by natural and artificial means, and, after sufficient grain was planted for the support of the live stock, about 100 acres of land was prepared for the cultivation of the ramie. The cultivation by seed was not adopted, being of slow growth and at best uncertain. Sufficient roots were obtained with considerable difficulty, so much so that only 85 acres were put under cultivation. The method pursued

Planting. was to plough and prepare the land, taking care that the earth was well pulverised. Then ridges were formed in the way usual for sowing cotton. The ridges were 4 feet apart, and each root or

Manure. piece of root from 3 to 4 inches long, and less than 1 inch broad, was placed in the furrow previously prepared of about 5 to 6 inches deep, and from 12 to 18 inches apart. The ridges or rows were slightly enriched with stable manure, and before a week the sprouting was distinctly seen, and before 48 hours the

* Sent to Royal Gardens, Kew.—Ed.

lines were well marked. Four months afterwards, when the growth had become rapid and the crop was 7 to 9 feet high, and well matured for cutting, there was a severe drought of several weeks, followed by hailstorms and heavy rain, all of which the plant withstood with little or no injury.

Roots planted in June (the worst time of the year for planting) were ready for cropping in October. June planting was imposed upon me from the fact of difficulty in obtaining roots in time for the next month for planting, *i.e.*, February. The crop, as we had it, although a first yield, proved abundant, and was cut and gathered in less than 24 hours. The new growth commenced, and in November I had a stand of nearly 4 feet, when there came a severe freeze and cut it to the ground. The dried or injured stalks were shaved down, and now, in the month of January, the growth is fully 4 feet high. The unprecedented warmth of the late season must be taken into consideration, and as it is only reasonable to suppose that during the month of February there will be a freeze, it will again retard its growth towards the maturity usually looked for in the latter part of February. Three crops a year in a tropical climate is a certainty, and two may reasonably be expected in Louisiana with considerable profit. After the first planting, the roots being perennial, it is simply a continual successive growth requiring little or no cultivation. *Growth.*

Effect of frost.

I have decorticated and obtained, so far, several bales of 500 pounds each of fibre, and as yet there are no market reports as to price.

It is intended to put in cultivation 250 acres of plant, the planting to commence during the month of February, for which purpose there is an abundance of roots, sufficient to plant 500 acres or more. *Decortication.*

This enterprise of ramie culture in Louisiana may be said to be in its incipiency, although for a long time it has been considered desirable to cultivate a product more certain and free from the common enemies to which cotton and sugar is subjected; yet no one would do more than plant small patches of no earthly use, except to gaze at and talk about. I have made this essay boldly, and that it is a success even in a climate only semi-tropical I have made evident. *Previous operations.*

There is an opinion prevailing that there has not yet been produced a decorticator that can perform its work effectually. This was true years ago when decorticators were sadly inefficient, and now the unbelief aids the natural inertness of these southern people.

I give you here the results obtained from the Schiefier decorticator, over the signature of an engineer whose assistance I called in to aid me. *The "Schiefier" decorticator.*

One hundred pounds of fibre an hour is a magnificent work, and I am satisfied that it will be found difficult to construct a machine that will yield more, although this is an age of progress, and no doubt improvements will be made.

UNITED STATES.

Bad effect of wet soil.

The "Schiefner" was worked by an eight-horse power engine. One machine is sufficient to take off a crop of 100 acres, or more in profitable time.

Contrary to all ideas that ramie would grow healthily in wet and undrained lands, I found that the plant perished if water remained sluggishly on the ground between the roots. My crop was taken off with a mowing machine, and under some difficulty, in consequence of my planting in ridges.

Future plans.

My future planting will be on a dead level—in rows only two feet apart—in beds of 20 feet, 40 feet, or 60 feet wide, and as long as the field allows: each bed to be apart sufficient to allow mowing machine and mules attached thereto to enter on their work, moving round each plot or bed comfortably. When planted in the way I shall take in future, the ramie will at last grow thickly together, thus preventing branching out of arms, and forcing the stalk to grow straight and high, and I am satisfied we shall have the stalks fully 12 feet tall.

Value of the fibre.

The fibre in its rough state is worth about 10 c. a pound; when degummed and bleached, it will bring from 60 c. to a dollar a pound, according to quality.

During the process of degumming and bleaching there is a loss of at least from 30 to 40 per cent. of fibre; but even if a loss of 50 per cent. is sustained, the difference of price is more than compensatory.

There is a movement in Mexico to pursue the cultivation of ramie and other fibres with which that country abounds, and I am invited by the highest authorities to aid in establishing the plant.

The certificate mentioned in the above is as follows:—

"New Orleans, January 9, 1890.

Certificate of results in decorticating.

"This is to certify, that at a trial made about the 19th day of November, 1889, of the decorticator on Oakbourne Plantation, near the town of Lafayette, Louisiana, the result was 19 lbs. or 19½ lbs. in 15 minutes. This was done with ramie only partially dried on the boiler, and was fed to the machine more or less tangled, and some of it had branches, all of which was a disadvantage to the decorticator. In regard to its capacity, I am of the opinion that with ramie properly dried and straight (without branches), and fed straight to the machine, the lowest possible capacity would be 100 lbs. per hour.

(Signed)   "P. W. DIEUDORF."

Another report on a kindred subject, furnished me by Dr. Chambers, reads thus:—

Power of decorticator.

"The decorticating and degumming fibre machine, to which I called your attention, produces from 3,500 lbs. to 4,000 lbs. per two-horse power, with four men to feed the vegetable stalks to the mashers per day. The machine that has been built and erected on Metarie ridge, on the property of Mr. Fred. W. Eichbolz, was invented by and patent granted to Charles Johnson, by Patent

Department, U.S.A., June, 1888; but the sole right and use now transferred to Mr. Eichbolz and Dr. M. Chambers.

"This decorticator breaks thoroughly all the woody matter and separates it from the fibrous plants without the least injury to the fibre. The gum-washing machine attached removes all the gummy residue entirely from jute, ochre, and other fibrous plants, containing long and silk like staple. There is no necessity to strip the leaves from jute or ochre or break off the end. When the plant has passed through the breakers there is not a particle of woody matter left. It is then put into a box containing only pure water, permitted to rot, and then passed into the gum-washing machine. This done it is washed, dried, and baled for market. Process of decortication.

"Jute has been cultivated in India for centuries, but only lately has it attracted the attention of the planters of the Southern States of America. In the cultivation of jute a warm humid climate is essential to success. It will grow upon comparatively dry lands or in flooded valleys. The land intended for a jute crop must be thoroughly broken up. The time of sowing the seed varies with the condition of soil and climate; March and April are the best months for sowing. The seed is sown broadcast from 15 to 20 lbs. to the acre. It matures in 12 weeks, and grows to the height of from 12 to 18 feet. The yield is from 3,000 to 4,000 lbs. of fibre to the acre. It is cut while the plant is in flower, because then the fibre is glossy. It ripens about five weeks after it flowers, and then it loses much of its commercial value, as the fibre becomes woody. Jute.
Sowing jute.
Cutting.

"The okra plant has been worked with great success. It is easier cultivated, will grow on any southern soil, requires but very little attention, and when passed through same process as jute in the decorticating and degumming results in a long silky fibre, glossy, and superb in length. Okra will produce same amount of fibre as jute and much easier to work, as it will rot sooner than jute, and for cordage, twine, bagging, matting, upholstery work, mattrasses, pillows, &c., for all of which the okra fibre has been fully tested, it is equal to any vegetable fibre. With this machine, herein described, have worked sisal, henniquin, ramie, bear grass, and all with success, as the mashers are so arranged as can change to work any fibre needed." Okra.

Dr. D. L. Phares, who occupies an important position in the Mississippi College and Experimental Station, and is a practical farmer, has written an article on dishorning cattle which may be summarised thus:— Dishorning cattle.

"There is no danger and not much pain in dishorning cattle, if the work is skilfully and quickly performed at the proper season of the year, and properly attended to until the healing process is complete. The cattle should be in good order and well fed.

"Several strong reasons are given why cattle should be dishorned:—

"First—Cattle hook and torment each other, the stronger

UNITED STATES.

Reasons for dishorning. constantly persecuting the weak; horns are used as tormentors, not usually as a protection. Strong cattle with sharp horns are the tyrants and persecutors of weak and helpless cattle in the herd, and dishorning makes them peaceable and harmless.

"Second—A great many more cattle can be made comfortable in the same area of pens or yards without horns than with them. Hornless beeves suffer less in railroad cars than horned cattle.

"Third—Dr. Phares says that beeves fatten better without horns than with them, and milch cows are benefited by dishorning. After the healing process is complete, the cows give more and richer milk after being dishorned.

"Fourth—To prevent the necessity of dishorning, the miniature horns on calves should be removed with a sharp knife, removing the hair and button with one quick cut. The pain is not severe, not so much as a single stab by a sharp horn might give, and then the pain is over; the hooking propensity of the animal and the horn are both nipped in the bud, and you have a peaceable Galloway or Muley, home-made and disarmed for life."

Operation on calves.

PENSACOLA (FLORIDA).

Mr. Vice-Consul Howe reports as follows:—

Agriculture. I endeavoured in my last yearly report on agriculture at and around this post, and, to some extent, in the State of Florida, to give a few points of interest to agriculturists in the United Kingdom; but particularly did I think that the report might be of service to tillers of the soil in the tropical and semi-tropical portions of the British possessions abroad, where the climates are more like the climate of this portion of the United States. This is not a topic of much scope from this quarter; I shall, however, again try to give some further points of interest in connection with the subject.

Kitchen gardening. As simple as the cultivation of vegetables appears to be, still it requires a little skill, which must be acquired by experience. A good garden, properly cultivated, should supply the table with a succession of crops throughout the growing season, and many families here are supplied altogether from their own gardens. In selecting a spot for the garden the situation most suitable would be towards the south-east, that it may have the morning sun. Planting near trees should be avoided, as their roots would exhaust the soil, and the shade injure the crops. A garden should be laid out in a convenient and attractive manner: "a garden containing half an acre well cultivated will produce sufficient vegetables to supply a moderate-sized family throughout the year."

Market gardening. This is a business very much followed at and around Pensacola, and throughout the State of Florida; and much success, apparently, attends those at Pensacola and its vicinity following this gardening business for a living. It is said that 10 acres in vegetables, well cultivated and properly managed, will prove more profitable than a 50-acre farm producing the ordinary farm crops. I have been informed that a few heads of cabbage will, in frequent seasons, sell for as much as a bushel of corn; and a few bunches of early asparagus for as much as a bushel of wheat. Good vegetables will always sell at a good profit, and hungry cities can rarely be overstocked with them.

In my last yearly report on agriculture I enumerated most of the vegetables grown here, and especially made mention of some of them as regards their cultivation, &c. I shall now bring in some vegetables not written upon directly in my last report. *Last report gave most of the vegetables. Refer to more in this.*

I have before me a paragraph, in a recent issue of the "Times," from which I see that Lord Dartmouth, when lately expressing his approval of the "Fruiterers' Company" for the encouragement of fruit culture in the United Kingdom, remarked that, in addition to his thorough approval of the object, he would be very glad if it shall be found possible to establish in different localities local orchards and fruit gardens, so as to prove to the neighbourhoods what kinds of fruit trees and plants best suited particular soils. His lordship also remarked that he particularly hoped that the culture of the tomato—though, as he said, "not strictly speaking a fruit," and which was imported from foreign countries in large quantities—would not be lost sight of in connection with the movement. His lordship could hardly, I think, have picked out a vegetable article (I certainly think it is more vegetable than fruit) of greater value in domestic life to refer to than the tomato. I learn from a publication on agriculture that "35 years ago this vegetable was considered unfit for the table, and now there are none more popular." Numbers of acres of the tomato are annually grown at Pensacola and in its vicinity, and quantities of them are daily sold throughout their season in these markets. *Tomato.*

The tomato will grow almost anywhere, I believe, with but very little trouble, and the various ways in which it can be used adds to its value. The tomato can be presented in several ways, and serves as a nice sweet to fall back on at any time. It is delicious in soups and in so many other dishes, and is canned in large quantities throughout the United States for home consumption, as well as for shipment abroad. *The tomato easy of cultivation.*

It is said to be a point of good gardening to have this dish (the tomato) early, to accomplish which "sow in a spent hot-bed early in spring, and air freely in fine weather. For a late crop sow the seeds in a very warm spot of the garden, and cover them up at night or during cold weather with boards. When the weather becomes mild and pleasant, transplant them in a sheltered part of the garden facing south or south-east; as the plants advance support them with a few branches or tie them up to stakes. The earliest plants should have their tops pinched off as soon as they have set their fruit, which will cause them to ripen earlier. It is also a very good plan to plant a few plants in flower pots or boxes very early in the season, and place them near the glass in a green-house, or even on a window-sill. Keep them well watered to encourage their growth until the weather becomes settled, then *Point of good gardening.*

transplant them to the garden, this will greatly increase their earliness. Most cultivators allow their tomato vines to grow wild and support themselves: they, perhaps, have never given it a thought that by training and properly pruning them they will not only increase their productiveness, but the fruit will ripen better, and be of a much finer quality. This is really the case: besides, it looks more orderly and much prettier to train or support them. There has been no vegetable so highly improved as the tomato. The old varieties are to-day valueless in comparison with those of recent introduction."

Favourite varieties. A few of the favourite varieties of the tomato grown here are the "Acme," which is "perfection in its beauty, solidity, and earliness;" the "Paragon," a "very popular variety, colour bright crimson, smooth, solid, of excellent flavour, bears transportation well, very productive, an excellent market variety;" the "Yellow Plum," used for preserving; and the "Red Pear or Plum-shaped" varieties, for producing their fruit in clusters, desirable for preserving or pickling purposes.

The tomato is said to have a special tonic effect upon weak eyes.

Lettuce. Several varieties of the lettuce are planted here from early spring to early summer. When up, they are trimmed out to eight inches apart, but to have good heads they must have rich soil. Among the favourite varieties here are the early Dutch butter, which is a celebrated and entirely distinct variety, and is very popular; it produces white solid heads about equal to a cabbage. The improved royal cabbage stands the heat, and is remarkably adapted to warm climates, or for planting to succeed early varieties. The drumhead cabbage variety is said to be quite hardy, and an excellent summer variety.

Okra. The okra is a highly esteemed little vegetable; it is used particularly in soups. A separate dish of boiled okra at table is very nice, served with its appropriate dressing. The okra is the chief component in the dish called gumbo—okra, or gumbo, the vegetable is sometimes termed—which is a highly-flavoured stew, made principally of fowl, fish, or oysters; and this dish is very nice, and very often introduced at table in these parts. The okra grows extensively in the British West Indies, and is of superior quality there. The seed is sown here, late in spring, in rich soil. It is said that the grown pods of the okra may be preserved for winter use by cutting them in halves, and stringing them to dry; also that the seeds can be ripened, which, when roasted, make a very excellent substitute for coffee.

Onion. The onion is, I think, one of the most nutritious vegetables grown. To grow the onion successfully the soil cannot be too rich, and, however good it may be, it requires manure for every crop. I do not think that the onion is much grown, or that it attains much of a size around here; at least, I do not hear of or see many that are grown at Pensacola. Quantities are brought here from other places—the western markets particularly. The onion is extensively grown in the island of Bermuda, and is, I think, quite an article of commerce there for shipment abroad; but it is not, I believe, grown to any extent in the other British islands of the West Indies. I think the climate in most of the other islands is hardly suited—too much continued warmth, or not, at times at least, enough cold. Among the several varieties the improved Bermuda is highly recommended to southern cultivators in these parts by the large seed suppliers of the north.

Cabbages are not, as a rule, successfully cultivated at and around Pensacola. Those grown by the gardeners here do not, I think, come up to such head and size as the cabbages grown in the northern and western portions of the United States, and of which a large quantity are brought to the Pensacola market during the season. {Cabbage.}

I see that to destroy the cabbage-worm—a great pest in the cultivation of this vegetable—the plants should be syringed with strong tobacco water. A few applications will destroy the worms entirely. A mixture of paris green and plaster is still more effective, but should not be used after the heads are forming. {Cabbage-worm.}

Peas of many varieties are grown here. It is very essential to a well-cultivated garden to have a full supply of this indispensable vegetable throughout its season. The planting of peas begins in spring in the southern climate. The market gardener is advised that the pea is one of his most important and profitable crops, and that he cannot bestow too much care in the seed selected for sowing. The pigeon-pea of the British West Indies I have never seen here, still I think it could be easily cultivated in these parts. It is a delicious pea, and may be served in several ways. At Barbados it is dried, and may be had in quantities thus, at any time I believe. {Peas.}

As I remarked in my last report on agriculture, Irish potatoes are grown here very extensively, but they do not attain a large size as a rule; still, they are very nice in flavour, and are sown and reaped in large quantities; they are sown in the early spring and reaped in early summer. It is said that this potato requires a rich sandy loam, with very liberal and clean culture, and that thoroughly decomposed manure is the best to apply, and that when that is not abundant bone dust or guano should be added. {Irish potatoes.}

In the island of Bermuda the Irish potato is successfully grown, and as well as the onion, as above mentioned, is there, I believe, quite an item in the trade of that island.

I see in an American publication of the Northern States on agriculture that "it is a matter of no small importance to the farmer to be able to keep his crop of potatoes in good condition through our long winters, and to offer them for sale free from blemish or mildew in the spring. A well-kept potato generally brings three or four times its value in market in early spring than the same stock will if sold in the fall, paying an extra profit over and above the cost of storing, handling, and care required; of the three methods of storing in general use, each has its champions. They are: storing in barrels, bins, heaps or pits. The advantage of placing in barrels is, they can be easily handled, do not suffer {Preservation of potatoes.}

from abrasion, can be readily looked over, and, if disease presents itself, it can be checked or removed. When thousands of bushels are raised on one farm, this method cannot be followed, on account of the time and expense involved. Bins are largely used by our large farmers, especially those near large cities, as the roots can at any time be reached and made ready for market. A dry, cool, well ventilated cellar, with the light excluded, is the best place for storing them. It has been found very advantageous in preventing decay to sprinkle lime in the barrels or bin at the rate, say, of 1 lb. to each barrel. It acts as an absorbent, and neutralises the earthy odours, thus directly acting as a preventive of decay to the roots. The importance of excluding light from potatoes, and keeping them as cool as possible, cannot be over-estimated as a means of preserving the crop."

Sweet potatoes. Remarks about the sweet potato are, I think, only of interest to those in the tropical parts of the British possessions. As stated in my last report on agriculture, the sweet potato is, in the British West Indies, a leading article of food, particularly amongst the negroes. For the benefit of cultivators of the sweet potato in the places above alluded to, I give, as follows, some extracts from a Pensacola paper about the sweet potato, whereby an idea appears to be put forward as regards its presentation, and its being thereby made a constant commercial commodity. The paper, obtained from a practical and extensive agriculturist at Pensacola, gave his views to the effect that "the sweet potato could be desiccated. It may be evaporated in the manner in which you would proceed with pears or other fruit. You would just slice it up as you would for stock feed and exhaust it of its moisture. Like dried fruit, it will retain its saccharine, and as well its nutritious, properties. One of these days the business of drying sweet potatoes for the export trade will be a profitable industry." The worthy and well-informed gardener who gave his views, as above shown, also added that "the dried vegetable might be sent to various points in Europe, and to different points in South America also. It is peculiarly a product of the temperate zones." He further stated that he "lived in Mexico for a while, and it does not thrive in that country. The latter is too near the equator. Besides, the soil there is not adapted to the sweet potato production. The vegetable thrives best in our sandy lands. It may be grown so easily, cheaply, and abundantly in the southern parts of the United States, more so than in any other part of the globe, that the ramifications of an export trade in the article might be extended to embrace the uttermost parts of the earth, it being one of the cheapest of cheap and good food products." The gentleman is a practical and well-to-do farmer, and expresses "his intention of operating an evaporator on his surplusage of fruit next season, and incidentally he will try his hand on the desiccation of the sweet potato — merely in a tentative way." It is his "conviction that some day such an industry will be of profitable prosecution in the south."

Now, there certainly appears to be food for the reflection of scientists in agriculture in the ideas above given. And if the desiccation of the sweet potato can be brought about for commercial purposes, will not our own colonies of the tropics be able to do a large, a very large, portion of the suggested trade?" What an industry might be worked up in the British West India islands if it be found practicable to preserve the sweet potato, as suggested.

The beet is extensively grown in and around Pensacola, and the cultivation of it is very successfully carried on here, and it attains very large size and is of excellent quality. It appears that the variety of the beet termed "mangel" is held in high repute. I learn that the cultivation of mangels has long been one of the most extensive root crops grown in Great Britain, and is becoming a very popular crop with the farmers of this country, who are gradually learning by experience that it is not only the best and cheapest food for their stock during long winter months, but one that is greatly enjoyed and eagerly devoured. Their cultivation is simple, and after sowing and thinning out the young plants, they will require no more care than a crop of potatoes: cultivating and keeping clear of weeds is all that is necessary. On good, rich sub-soiled ground, from 600 to 1,000 bushels can be grown to the acre. In feeding them they should be sliced, and if steamed and mixed with a little bran so much the better. Five lbs. of seed is required to sow an acre. {Beet.}

Turning now to the cultivation of fruit in Pensacola, and throughout the State of Florida, I must point to the remarks in my last agricultural report as regards the leading kinds so successfully grown hereabout—pears, peaches, figs, grapes, strawberries, and (to be written upon separately) the orange. Most of the first above-named fruits—the orange is not successfully cultivated at and around Pensacola, but in the suitable parts of Florida—form quite a large revenue to the gardeners. {Fruit.}

The orange I must especially refer to again in this report. I wrote upon it at length in my last, and then endeavoured to impress upon our people in climates like this—particularly those of the British West Indies—that they ought to do a large proportion of the trade that is done in this country, as well as in other places by the growth (the increased growth) and export of oranges. I pointed out that I believed, with energy and push and the attention given there, the same as here, on business principles, that they would to a large measure be successful. I was much pleased to see lately that a movement had been made in some of the islands to export oranges and bananas thence to the United States. The island of Jamaica (distinct from the Windward and Leeward group, however, which I mostly refer to) now brings her fruit trade up to or beyond her (formerly considered) chief staple, sugar and molasses, &c. I see by "Whitaker's Almanack" for 1890 that "the chief articles of export in order of importance from Jamaica are:—Sugar, 288,402*l.*; rum, 202,420*l.*; tropical fruits, 337,652*l.*; coffee, 321,440*l.*; dye woods, 360,750*l.*; pimento, 44,728*l.*" This statement is for the year 1888, and it will be {Oranges.}

seen that fruits, principally oranges and bananas, were beyond all other exports, except dye-woods. The island of Montserrat also is successful in the growth of the lime, 100,000 gallons of lime-juice being exported from that island yearly, according to "Whitaker's Almanack."

I see by "Cassell's Concise Cyclopædia" that during a year, some time past (1880), the oranges and lemons imported into Great Britain amounted to 3,658,799 bushels. It may be that the yearly importations of these fruits have much increased in the United Kingdom since the year given.

LONDON
Printed for Her Majesty's Stationery Office,
By HARRISON AND SONS,
Printers in Ordinary to Her Majesty.
(1250 3 | 90—H & S 808)

FOREIGN OFFICE.
1890.
ANNUAL SERIES.

No. 661.

DIPLOMATIC AND CONSULAR REPORTS ON TRADE AND FINANCE.

UNITED STATES.

REPORT FOR THE YEAR 1889

ON THE

TRADE, &c., OF TEXAS.

REFERENCE TO PREVIOUS REPORT, Annual Series No. 458.

Presented to both Houses of Parliament by Command of Her Majesty,
MARCH, 1890.

LONDON:
PRINTED FOR HER MAJESTY'S STATIONERY OFFICE,
BY HARRISON AND SONS, ST. MARTIN'S LANE,
PRINTERS IN ORDINARY TO HER MAJESTY.

And to be purchased, either directly or through any Bookseller, from
EYRE & SPOTTISWOODE, East Harding Street, Fleet Street, E.C., and
32, Abingdon Street, Westminster, S.W; or
ADAM AND CHARLES BLACK, 6, North Bridge, Edinburgh; or
HODGES, FIGGIS, & Co., 104, Grafton Street, Dublin.

1890.

[C. 5895.—64.]   *Price One Penny*

New Series of Reports.

Reports of the Annual Series have been issued from Her Majesty's Diplomatic and Consular Officers at the following places, and may be obtained from the sources indicated on the title-page:—

No.		Price.	No.		Price.
545.	New York	1½d.	603.	Stettin	2d
546.	San Francisco	1d.	604.	Vera Cruz	1½d.
547.	Stettin	1½d.	605.	Christiania	4d.
548.	San Salvador	½d.	606.	Pernambuco	1½d.
549.	Trebizond	1d.	607.	Trieste	1½d.
550.	Nice	1d.	608.	Tunis	½d.
551.	Baghdad	½d.	609.	Havana	2d.
552.	Fiume	1d.	610.	Frankfort	½d.
553.	Mogador	2d.	611.	Tabreez	½d.
554.	Buenos Ayres	1½d.	612.	Bilbao	1d.
555.	San Francisco	2½d.	613.	Barcelona	½d.
556.	Carthagena	½d.	614.	Tokio	1d.
557.	Syra	1d.	615.	Naples	2½d.
558.	Varna and Bourgas	1d.	616.	Batoum	½d.
559.	Thessaly	½d.	617.	Odessa	1d.
560.	Yokohama	1d.	618.	La Rochelle	1d.
561.	Nantes	1½d.	619.	Rome	1d.
562.	Suakin	½d.	620.	Nice	1d.
563.	Algiers	1d.	621.	Kiukiang	½d.
564.	St. Petersburg	2½d.	622.	Paris	1d.
565.	Söul	1d.	623.	Salonica	1½d.
566.	Newchwang	1d.	624.	Réunion	1d.
567.	Roustchouk and Philippopolis	1d.	625.	Ichang	1d.
568.	Stockholm	1½d.	626.	Bogatá	1d.
569.	Tonga	1d.	627.	Malaga	2d.
570.	Chicago	1½d.	628.	Porto Rico	1d.
571.	Adana	½d.	629.	Bushire	2½d.
572.	Buenos Ayres	3d.	630.	The Hague	½d.
573.	Frankfort	1½d.	631.	Berlin	1d.
574.	Canton	1½d.	632.	Adrianople	1½d.
575.	Tamsui	5½d.	633.	Rome	1½d.
576.	Palermo	3d.	634.	Santiago	½d.
577.	Amsterdam	1d.	635.	Tahiti	½d.
578.	Ajaccio	½d.	636.	Maranhan	½d.
579.	Shanghai	1½d.	637.	Mexico	2d.
580.	Warsaw	½d.	638.	Christiania	1d.
581.	Teneriffe	1d.	639.	Copenhagen	1d.
582.	Tangier	2d.	640.	Paris	1d.
583.	Surinam	½d.	641.	Venice	1d.
584.	Loanda	1d.	642.	Cherbourg	½d.
585.	Alexandria	1d.	643.	New York	1d.
586.	Cagliari	1d.	644.	Patras	1d.
587.	Smyrna	½d.	645.	Bourgas	½d.
588.	Mannheim	1d.	646.	St. Petersburg	3d.
589.	Nagasaki	1d.	647.	Taganrog	½d.
590.	Hakodate	1d.	648.	Baltimore	1½d.
591.	Bushire	1d.	649.	New Orleans	2d.
592.	Chinkiang	½d.	650.	New Orleans	1d.
593.	Pakhoi	1d.	651.	Samos	½d.
594.	Hiogo	1½d.	652.	Buda-Pesth	1½d.
595.	Bangkok	1d.	653.	Tripoli	½d.
596.	Serajevo	1d.	654.	Buenos Ayres	½d.
597.	Copenhagen	1½d.	655.	Paris	1d.
598.	Cephalonia	½d.	656.	Cherbourg	1d.
599.	Chefoo	½d.	657.	Warsaw	½d.
600.	Guatemala	1½d.	658.	Rome	1½d.
601.	Tonga	½d.	659.	Saigon	½d.
602.	Tahiti	1d.	660.	Buenos Ayres	½d.

No. 661.

Reference to previous Report, Annual Series No. 458.

UNITED STATES.

GALVESTON.

Consul Lyall to the Marquis of Salisbury.

My Lord,   *Galveston, February* 19, 1890.

I HAVE the honour to enclose Consular Report (Commercial) for 1889.

I have, &c.
(Signed)   WALTER T. LYALL.

Report on the Trade and Commerce of Galveston for the Year 1889.

The great bulk of foreign export from Galveston is cotton and cotton-seed oilcake.

Imports and exports, foreign trade, shipping, &c.

COTTON.

	Quantity.	Value. Currency.	Value. Sterling.
	Bales.	Dol.	£
Exported to England	305,095	15,207,671	3,160,000
Other countries	150,501	7,527,583	1,567,000

OILCAKE.

	Quantity.	Value. Currency.	Value. Sterling.
	Lbs.	Dol.	£
Exported to England	51,015,854	482,981	106,000
,, Germany and Netherlands	43,378,145	399,433	83,100

UNITED STATES.

The total value of foreign imports during the year 1889 is 507,957 dol. (105,750*l*.), of which 238,503 dol. (49,670*l*.) was from Great Britain.

The number of British steam and sailing vessels entering Galveston during 1889 was as follows:—

	Vessels.	Tonnage.
With cargo	31	129,272
Without cargo	81	90,618
Number of British vessels cleared with cargo	121	129,272
Number of U.S. vessels entering with cargo	28	10,166
Number of U.S. vessels cleared with cargo	26	10,883

Texas as a field for emigration.

Texas has a brilliant commercial future, and, being comparatively close to Europe, will always attract its share of transatlantic emigration. Its advantages are a fertile soil, and, for the most part, healthy climate and immense undeveloped commercial, agricultural, and mineral resources. Its progress is, however, checked by the high customs tariff and by the prevailing spirit of lawlessness.

Trusts.

I have already, in my Consular reports for 1887 and 1888, fully described the action of the tariff and the disastrous effects on the commonwealth of the commercial corners, rings, trusts, &c., which are its offspring; it is therefore hardly necessary to go over the ground again. I may remark, however, that the Hon. Joseph Abbott has (January 19) entered the lists in Congress, with a Bill directed against these abuses.

This Bill, after clearly defining the action of rings, trusts, and combinations to raise prices of necessaries, and the evil therefrom resulting, proposes the following remedial measures:—

Section 2. That the formation or organisation of a trust in any State or States for the purpose of controlling or limiting the price of any product, merchandise, or commodity, or forestalling the market value of any such product, merchandise, or commodity in any other State or territory of the United States or the district of Columbia, is hereby declared to be against public policy and unlawful.

Section 3. That the formation or organisation of a trust within the territories of the United States or the district of Columbia is hereby declared to be against public policy and unlawful.

Section 4. That any person acting in his own behalf, or as the agent, attorney, or representative of any firm, copartnership, corporation, or any association whatever, who shall aid, directly or indirectly, in the organisation of a trust, or be in any manner interested therein, or who shall, after the passage of this Act, knowingly aid in the business of a trust heretofore organised, or be in any way interested therein, shall be deemed guilty of a misdemeanour, and upon conviction thereof shall be fined in any sum not less than 500 dol. and not more than 10,000 dol., or by imprisonment for any period of time not less than three months, and not more than two years, or by both such fine and imprisonment, in the discretion of the court.

Section 5. That all contracts or agreements made by a trust, or by any person, firm, or association of persons, or corporation acting for a trust in furtherance of the object of such trust, are hereby declared to be against public policy and unlawful, and the district and circuit courts of the United States shall not take jurisdiction or cognisance of any controversy arising out of any such contract or agreement.

Section 6. That whenever it shall be made to appear to the satisfaction of the President of the United States that a trust has been or is about to be organised for either of the purposes named in the first section of this Act, and that the merchandise, product, or commodity, or the like thereof, covered or proposed to be covered or handled by such trusts, when produced out of the United States is subject to import duty when imported to the United States, he shall be and is hereby authorised, if in his opinion the public welfare require, to suspend in whole or part the collection of the duty or duties now fixed by law upon such merchandise, product, or commodity for such time as he may deem proper.

Section 7. That all laws in conflict herewith are hereby repealed.

It is unlikely, however, that the Bill will pass.

Of lawlessness there continue to be many sad instances. Some acts of violence are connected with racial quarrels; others are in encounters with firearms, or in interference with the course of justice.

The statistics (agricultural) for 1889 are not yet printed, those for 1888 containing over 400 pages, lately published by the Agricultural Commission. Mr. Foster shows very considerable agricultural progress to have taken place. They may be summarised as follows:— *Agriculture in Texas.*

Number of counties in Texas	245
Number of counties organised	200
Area of state—square miles	252,696
Population, 1880	1,591,749
Estimated increase to January 1, 1890	604,696
Population (estimated) January 1, 1890	2,196,439
Summaries of agricultural products—	
Cotton, acres planted	3,483,181
,, bales produced	1,243,908
,, value	48,466,412 dol.
Corn, acres planted	3,224,104
,, bushels produced	76,607,312
,, value	26,211,177 dol.
Wheat, acres planted	386,120
,, bushels produced	4,850,002
,, value	3,440,984 dol.
Oats, acres planted	567,468
,, bushels produced	17,845,666
,, value	4,774,429 dol.
Barley, acres planted	6,559
,, bushels produced	195,996
,, value	89,227 dol.
Rye, acres planted	7,549
,, bushels produced	87,051
,, value	63,071 dol.

Millet, acres planted	66,997
,, tons produced	117,893
,, value	822,403 dol.
Sweet potatoes, acres planted	45,685
,, ,, bushels produced	5,127,729
,, ,, value	2,264,890 dol.
Irish potatoes, acres planted	9,768
,, ,, bushels produced	1,134,152
,, ,, value	641,957 dol.
Hay, cultivated, acres in	40,295
,, ,, tons produced	94,225
,, ,, value	666,061 dol.
,, prairie acres cut	182,240
,, tons produced	226,163
,, value	1,223,174 dol.
Sugar cane, acres planted	15,456
,, ,, barrels sugar produced	41,237
,, ,, value syrup	717,016 dol.
,, ,, barrels sugar produced	36,484
,, ,, value sugar	746,210 dol.
Sorghum cane, acres planted	36,476
,, ,, barrels, syrup	63,484
,, ,, value syrup	1,049,139 dol.
,, ,, cut for hay, acres	58,988
,, ,, tons hay cut	197,456
,, ,, value hay cut	1,117,807 dol.
Cotton seed, tons produced	621,954
,, ,, value	4,353,678 dol.
Melons, acres in	10,137
,, value	384,350 dol.
Vegetables, acres in	24,181
,, value	2,176,726 dol.
Peaches, acres in	60,578
,, value	1,515,756 dol.
Apples, acres in	10,724
,, value	319,115 dol.
Pears, acres in	878
,, value	34,583 dol.
Plums, acres in	2,729
,, value	59,549 dol.
Grapes, value	148,975 dol.
Total acres planted	8,236,598
Total value produced	100,543,479 dol.
Number tenant farmers	90,521
Number hired farm labourers	52,399

The above shows an increase in cotton and corn acreage over 1887, but a reduced price.

The acreage of wheat, barley, millet, &c., is reduced, caused by the abandonment of many farms in the dry western and northern districts ("faute d'irrigation"). Some of these, however, have since been reoccupied, and it is probable that the statistics for 1889–1890 will show considerably increased productiveness.

The large amount realised from cotton, the staple export, given at 48,466,412 dol., joined to 4,353,678 dol. from cotton-seed oil and oilcake, though apparently enormous, actually only averages 15 dol. 16 c., or about 3l. value of yield per acre, while the value of the sweet potatoes or yam crop averaged 49 dol. 55 c., or nearly 10l. per acre; and of the sugar-cane, in consequence of the prohibitive import duty on sugar, to 94 dol. 66 c., or nearly 20l. per acre.

In fact, the statistics show that more money is likely to be made in Texas by cultivating sugar cane, potatoes, vegetables, and fruits than by cotton and corn, the two staple industries of the Southern States.

This bears out the experience of many Anglo-Indian planters, who discovered later on that they could have realised more money by such products than by tea, coffee, and indigo, the prices of which are in a manner under control by brokers and syndicates, and which have to pass through many hands.

Mr. Forster, the agricultural commissioner, states that there is, in Texas, one tenant farmer to every five adults of the rural population, which he places at 452,605.

Tenant farmers and farm labourers comprise a third of the entire adult population of Texas; another third is composed of shopkeepers, mechanics, and townspeople generally; and the remainder of landowners, cattlemen, cowboys, the local officials, fishermen, hunters, gaolbirds, outlaws, people of no occupation, and negroes, of whom alone there are said to be half a million* in Texas.

An agricultural population of under 500,000 in a country as large as France and Belgium shows that there is an immense area of land still awaiting cultivation.

Irrigation. The great *sine qua non* of Texas is irrigation. The soil, from east to west, north to south, only requires water properly laid on to be a paradise and garden of productive enterprise.

The water is to hand in the great unfailing rivers the Trinity, Brozos, and the Rio Grande, which intersect the country, to say nothing of the innumerable magnificent reservoirs and artificial lakes, which could be cheaply constructed in the hilly districts, which are admirably adapted by nature for the purpose. Next comes the road question. The richest lands in Texas are the black, cotton soil counties, a precisely similar formation to that of the Central Indian Provinces, Goojerat, the Deccan, &c., in India.

This soil, which cracks and crumbles during dry weather, becomes during rainy weather a gluey sludge, over which all transport—unless regular macadamised roads are constructed—becomes impossible, wagons, carts, &c., sinking at once to the axle.

Export trade. Hence the export trade is often at a standstill for weeks at a time, simply because it is impossible to feed the lines of railway which convey produce to the seaports. It has frequently been proposed to utilise the abundant convict labour of Texas in roadmaking, but this commonsense idea is negatived on the score of expense, which would be incurred for guards to watch the convicts and prevent their escape *en masse*, so that the question is still pending; and we have a vast and fertile country, with railroads, it is true, but without ordinary roads, *i.e.*, none in rainy weather, no farther advanced, in fact, in that respect than Turkey, Persia, or India before British occupation; worse, indeed, if anything.

* At the present rate of increase of the negro population, there will be a million negroes in Texas by the end of this century.

Climate.

Another requisite is acclimatisation. The climate of Texas and New Mexico is very much that of sub-tropical Asia, only moister. We find great heat to prevail in summer, and the winter season is warm throughout, but interspersed with streaks of cold weather, whenever the wind happens to be from the north-east, north, or north-west. Consequently, the cereals, domestic animals, fruits and vegetables, which would succeed best, are not those of northern countries.

Cattle.

For Asiatic cattle, especially Indian, for Asiatic buffaloes, fat-tailed Arabian or Syrian sheep, Indian and Persian goats, *et hoc genus omne*, the climate and soil is excellently adapted, and their introduction would, I am convinced, be most profitable.

Arab, Persian, and Syrian breeds of horses and ponies would also improve matters, while the fruits and vegetables of China and Northern India, the oranges of the Himalayas, mountain bananas, mountain sugar-cane, and certain cereals, which resist alternatives of heat and cold, would succeed admirably.

None of these improvements have yet been taken in hand, the fact being that there being no State acclimatisation, or other society for the purpose, private landowners, farmers, &c., are individually unable or unwilling to incur the expense. Most Texans also have been educated into a notion that they are ahead of the rest of the world in arts, arms, science, and civilisation, that what Texas does not know is not worth knowing, and consequently turn a deaf ear to suggestions, especially if made by the outside European.

If driven to confess shortcomings, the excuse made is invariably that Texas is "a new country," "that we shall have everything in time" and put everything to rights, "Rome was not built in a day," &c.

But Australia, Tasmania, and New Zealand are younger colonies than Texas, which was annexed from Mexico as long ago as 1836; and the Texans, when they took possession, found ranches and cattle runs ready stocked, horses, &c., all ready to hand, whereas in Australia we found nothing but a desert. Australia, again, is at the antipodes, whereas Texas was at the door of the United States. Besides the natural resources of Australia are, with the exception of climate, far inferior to those of Texas, especially as to its rivers.

Yet the Australian colonies have developed since 1850:—

1st. A magnificent breed of horses, largely and profitably exported to India for army and other purposes.

2nd. The finest draught cattle in the world.

3rd. Excellent breeds of sheep, exporting millions of dollars worth of wool annually to England, Europe, and even to the United States.

4th. An extensive mercantile marine trading with China, India, the Archipelego, the Pacific Islands, and Japan, and even to Western America.

5th. They have developed extensive coal, copper, and other mining industries, railways, roads, a thoroughly efficient police, and a respectable volunteer army.

6th. Numerous manufacturing enterprises of all descriptions.

None of the above industries and inprovements are possessed by Texas, with the exception of railways, constructed and owned by northern capitalists and run to suit their views.

Australia has also imported and acclimatised vines, melons, and all sorts of fruits suitable to the climate, and she produces wines which rival the best European vintages; and all this progress has been quietly acheived, without one quarter of the fuss and flourish of trumpets which in the Western States herald the tracing-out of a bogus town in a desert, or the opening of a single line of bad railway leading nowhere.

The littoral of Texas is a peculiar one, the water deepening outwards from the shore, very gradually, at the rate, roughly speaking, of not more than one fathom or six feet to the mile, along the whole seaboard from New Orleans to the Rio Grande. The bottom is composed of hard, smooth, but shifting sand. *The deep water question.*

Thus at one mile from the shore the depth is one fathom, at two miles two fathoms, and so on, consequently vessels of heavy draught anchoring in the roads off any particular port or harbour have to ride at a distance of five or six miles from land.

The extensive inland bays, which line the northern coast of the gulf for hundreds of miles, are for the most part lagoons of an average depth of nine or ten feet only, and bars of sand accumulate both at the mouths of these bays and of the great rivers. The question is to secure permanent deep channels over or rather through these bars, at the most advantageous commercial points, and thus to attract foreign shipping, and develop outlets for the enormous and ever-increasing produce of the Southern and Western States, which, principally in consequence of the difficulties experienced in loading seagoing vessels on the gulf, is now either conveyed expensively by railroad to Atlantic ports,* or not conveyed at all. In 1888 the States west of the Mississippi river produced more than 500,000,000 bushels of Indian corn and maize in excess of the local demand. The total tonnage of this surplus product was 16,065,000 tons. In that year (1888) the surplus breadstuffs of the Western States, most of which was exported, amounted to over 20,000,000 tons.

The harvest of 1889 is expected to far exceed this estimate, *i.e.*, the statistics of Kansas alone showing a surplus of 150,000,000 bushels of corn.

In fact, the Great West not only supplies the European import demand for bread and beef, but for cotton also; and the difference in distance of railway transport in favour of the Galveston and Gulf route from as many as twenty different western States and territories averages 651 miles from each.

It is also shown that if these 20 States could forward their produce to Europe by way of the Gulf of Mexico instead of, as

---

* The Arkansa and Missouri farmers are said to be largely using Indian corn as fuel at the present writing.

at present, by the Atlantic ports, a saving of at least 120,000,000 dol. per annum would be effected.

The plans for opening out all these ports, or passes as they are called, are similar, being copied from those in use for many years in Europe, consisting of confining the tides and river currents between jetties, and thereby causing a "scour" at ebb tides, at the same time preventing the lateral currents along the shore from depositing fresh sand in the channel.

Harbours. Operations have been going on at Galveston for the last two years, and three miles of solid jetty, composed of hugh blocks of stone quarried in the interior, has been constructed.

This three miles of jetty has, it is asserted, already deepened the water on the bar, but the jetty will require prolonging for another four miles before the proper effect is produced. The corresponding northern jetty, commencing from Bolivar point, which will be five miles in length, has not yet been commenced. The total estimate is 7,000,000 dol.

Work is also being carried on at the mouth of the Brazos river, 60 miles, and at Aransas pass, 200 miles, to W.S.W. of Galveston, at both which points it is estimated that from 20 to 30 feet permanent deep water is obtainable, and for far less cost than at Galveston.

The Aransas pass plan would open out a fine harbour (perfectly sheltered behind St. Joseph's island), of an average depth of 12 to 30 feet. The Aransas pass is indeed altogether the cheapest available point on the gulf as regards first cost, but all other requisites—docks, warehouses, wharves, railways, and city—would have also to be constructed, whereas Galveston is a ready-made seaport, only requiring a deep-water channel of communication to make her the great export mart of the Western States.

LONDON:
Printed for Her Majesty's Stationery Office,
By HARRISON AND SONS,
Printers in Ordinary to Her Majesty.
(1250 3 | 90—H & S 819)

FOREIGN OFFICE.
1890.
ANNUAL SERIES.

N⁰. 664.
DIPLOMATIC AND CONSULAR REPORTS ON TRADE AND FINANCE.

UNITED STATES.

REPORT FOR THE YEAR 1889
ON THE
TRADE OF THE CONSULAR DISTRICT OF BOSTON.

REFERENCE TO PREVIOUS REPORT, Annual Series No. 499.

Presented to both Houses of Parliament by Command of Her Majesty,
APRIL, 1890.

LONDON:
PRINTED FOR HER MAJESTY'S STATIONERY OFFICE,
BY HARRISON AND SONS, ST. MARTIN'S LANE,
PRINTERS IN ORDINARY TO HER MAJESTY.

And to be purchased, either directly or through any Bookseller, from
EYRE & SPOTTISWOODE, EAST HARDING STREET, FLEET STREET, E.C., and
32, ABINGDON STREET, WESTMINSTER, S.W; or
ADAM AND CHARLES BLACK, 6, NORTH BRIDGE, EDINBURGH; or
HODGES, FIGGIS, & Co., 104, GRAFTON STREET, DUBLIN.

1890.

[C. 5895—67.] *Price One Penny.*

New Series of Reports.

Reports of the Annual Series have been issued from Her Majesty's Diplomatic and Consular Officers at the following places, and may be obtained from the sources indicated on the title-page:—

No.		Price.	No.		Price.
542.	Vienna	1d.	603.	Stettin	2d.
543.	Antwerp	1d.	604.	Vera Cruz	1¼d.
544.	Lisbon	2d.	605.	Christiania	4d.
545.	New York	1½d.	606.	Pernambuco	1½d.
546.	San Francisco	1d.	607.	Trieste	1½d.
547.	Stettin	1½d.	608.	Tunis	½d.
548.	San Salvador	½d.	609.	Havana	2d.
549.	Trebizond	1d.	610.	Frankfort	½d.
550.	Nice	1d.	611.	Tabreez	½d.
551.	Baghdad	½d.	612.	Bilbao	1d.
552.	Fiume	1d.	613.	Barcelona	½d.
553.	Mogador	2d.	614.	Tokio	1d.
554.	Buenos Ayres	1½d.	615.	Naples	2½d.
555.	San Francisco	2¼d.	616.	Batoum	½d.
556.	Carthagena	½d.	617.	Odessa	1d.
557.	Syra	1d.	618.	La Rochelle	1d.
558.	Varna and Bourgas	1d.	619.	Rome	1d.
559.	Thessaly	½d.	620.	Nice	1d.
560.	Yokohama	1d.	621.	Kiukiang	½d.
561.	Nantes	1½d.	622.	Paris	1d.
562.	Suakin	½d.	623.	Salonica	1½d.
563.	Algiers	1d.	624.	Réunion	1d.
564.	St. Petersburg	2¼d.	625.	Ichang	1d.
565.	Söul	1d.	626.	Bogotá	1d.
566.	Newchwang	1d.	627.	Malaga	2d.
567.	Roustchouk and Philippopolis	1d.	628.	Porto Rico	1d.
568.	Stockholm	1½d.	629.	Bushire	2¼d.
569.	Tonga	1d.	630.	The Hague	½d.
570.	Chicago	1¼d.	631.	Berlin	1d.
571.	Adana	½d.	632.	Adrianople	1½d.
572.	Buenos Ayres	3d.	633.	Rome	1½d.
573.	Frankfort	1½d.	634.	Santiago	½d.
574.	Canton	1½d.	635.	Tahiti	½d.
575.	Tamsui	5½d.	636.	Maranham	½d.
576.	Palermo	3d.	637.	Mexico	2d.
577.	Amsterdam	1d.	638.	Christiania	1d.
578.	Ajaccio	½d.	639.	Copenhagen	1d.
579.	Shanghai	1½d.	640.	Paris	1d.
580.	Warsaw	½d.	641.	Venice	1d.
581.	Teneriffe	1d.	642.	Cherbourg	½d.
582.	Tangier	2d.	643.	New York	1d.
583.	Surinam	½d.	644.	Patras	1d.
584.	Loanda	1d.	645.	Bourgas	½d.
585.	Alexandria	1d.	646.	St. Petersburg	3d.
586.	Cagliari	1d.	647.	Taganrog	½d.
587.	Smyrna	½d.	648.	Baltimore	1½d.
588.	Mannheim	1d.	649.	New Orleans	2d.
589.	Nagasaki	1d.	650.	New Orleans	1d.
590.	Hakodate	1d.	651.	Samos	½d.
591.	Bushire	1d.	652.	Buda-Pesth	1¼d.
592.	Chinkiang	½d.	653.	Tripoli	½d.
593.	Pakhoi	1d.	654.	Buenos Ayres	½d.
594.	Hiogo	1½d.	655.	Paris	1d.
595.	Bangkok	1d.	656.	Cherbourg	1d.
596.	Serajevo	1d.	657.	Warsaw	½d.
597.	Copenhagen	1½d.	658.	Rome	1½d.
598.	Cephalonia	½d.	659.	Saigon	½d.
599.	Chefoo	½d.	660.	Buenos Ayres	½d.
600.	Guatemala	1½d.	661.	Galveston	1d.
601.	Tonga	½d.	662.	Galatz	1½d.
602.	Tahiti	1d.	663.	Antwerp	1d.

No. 664.

Reference to previous Report, Annual Series No. 499.

UNITED STATES.

BOSTON.

Consul Henderson to the Marquis of Salisbury.

My Lord,   Boston, February 27, 1890.

I HAVE the honour to enclose a Report on the Trade and Commerce of Boston and the Boston Consular District for the year 1889.

I have, &c.
(Signed)   A. HENDERSON.

Report on the Trade and Commerce of Boston and the Boston Consular District for the Year 1889.

General condition of trade and industry.

The year 1889 was marked by many vicissitudes, and much variation in the result as affecting different branches of trade. As a rule profits were small, due rather to over-supply and close competition than to strikes, which were neither numerous or of long duration. A fire in Boston destroyed several large business buildings and a considerable amount of merchandise, principally dry goods, causing a loss estimated at about 800,000$l.$; and a fire in Lynn, 10 miles from Boston, and the principal seat of boot and shoe factories, swept away half the business portion of the town, the loss being estimated also at about 800,000$l.$, and temporarily crippled trade, which was moreover injuriously affected by many heavy failures in the leather trade. Business in general was depressed during the first half of the year, but revived and became very active during the latter six months, excepting in the woollen goods trade, which continued to suffer from foreign competition and the high duty on wool.

Cotton and cotton goods.

The cotton market was fairly active throughout the year, prices running up from $4\frac{7}{8}d.$ to $5\frac{3}{4}d.$ ($9\frac{7}{8}$ c. to $11\frac{1}{2}$ c.), in August, then gradually declining to $5\frac{1}{8}d.$ ($10\frac{1}{4}$ c.) in December, whilst cotton goods continued in steady demand at prices leaving a fair profit to manufacturers, and the year closed with a firm market.

UNITED STATES.

Wool and woollen goods. The volume of business in wool showed a large falling-off from that of 1888. The year opened with small stocks in the hands of dealers, but with a sluggish demand by manufacturers who had purchased largely in the previous autumn, and who, owing to a mild winter and reduced consumption of wearing apparel, were not willing to buy more than they required for immediate use. This circumstance and the failure of several woollen mill corporations not only kept prices from rising, but, notwithstanding a sharp advance in foreign markets, produced a gradual fall of from 3 c. to 4 c. per lb. between August and November, followed by a subsequent rise of ½ c. to 1 c., at which the market remained firm, with stocks amounting to 26,500,000*l.* of native, and 5,500,000*l.* of foreign wool on hand.

The year was a very unfavourable one for woollen manufacturers. Mild weather and foreign competition kept down both consumption and prices, and mills were neither busy or returning much profit on their limited production.

Clothing trade. The winter trade at the beginning and end of the year was very slack, but a fair amount of business was done in light apparel during the summer, and the result of the year's work was not altogether unsatisfactory.

Hides and leather. The hide and leather markets, which had shown signs of improvement in the autumn of 1888, but which was not long maintained, continued dull throughout the whole year, causing a considerable fall in prices, numerous failures amongst dealers and speculators, a serious check to credit and borrowing power, affecting all engaged in the trade, and a consequent falling-off in production. This last circumstance, however, without leading to any immediate advance, reduced the supply to a point below the demand for consumption, and restored a firmer tone and a more hopeful feeling.

Boots and shoes. The manufacture of boots and shoes, which has steadily increased for many years past, amounted in 1889 to 3,425,000 cases, or 125,000 cases more than in 1888, notwithstanding the sharp competition and low prices that prevailed, a fair profit was realised by manufacturers.

Indiarubber and rubber goods. The open winter of 1888–89 caused a large falling-off in the demand for rubber goods, and the price for the raw material declined to a very low point. This reduced importations, which, being followed by improved consumption, and the fear that the Brazilian Revolution might affect future supplies, produced a reaction, and prices went up considerably, fine para, which had ranged from 2*s.* 10½*d.* to 3*s.* 1*d.* (69 c. to 74 c.), being quoted at 3*s.* to 3*s.* 5*d.* (72 c. to 84 c.).

Iron, steel, and other metals. The depressed condition of the iron market in 1888 was succeeded by a sharp advance early in 1889, due to the gradual curtailment of production which had ceased to be profitable, and to a general revival of demand for iron products. Pig iron No. 1 (which, with other grades, was almost entirely of native manufacture) rose from 3*l.* 12*s.* to 4*l.* (18 dol. to 20 dol.); bar iron, from 7s. 5d. to 10s. (1 dol. 85 c. to 2 dol.); steel rails, from 5l. 12s. to 7l. (28 dol. to 35 dol.); at which latter figure all in stock was taken up, and large orders given for further supplies to meet extensions and repairs of roads throughout the country. With the collapse of the French Copper Syndicate, Lake copper went down from 8½d. (17 c.) to 6½d. (13 c.), and casting brands to 5d. (10 c.), but with increased consumption rallied by ¾d. (1½ c.) to 1d. (2 c.). In pig tin and pig lead the demand was moderate but steady, with occasional slight fluctuation in price not exceeding 1d. to 1½d. (2 c. to 3 c.).

Lumber. Building operations were extensively carried on throughout the year, and the lumber trade was brisk at well maintained prices.

Paper. The manufacture of paper, though not very profitable, owing to the competition of the increasing number of factories, has been brought to such a high state of development, and reduced so much in cost of production, by improved machinery and the successful use of wood pulp under a special process, that it has become possible to establish a large export trade not only in rivalry with, but directly to, the United Kingdom, as well as to Australia and other countries.

Fish trade. The stock of mackerel was very small at the end of 1888, whilst very little was then obtainable either from Canada or Ireland, and the market was bare in June when the catch commenced. The New England Fishing Fleet had very poor success, but supplies were received from Canada and Ireland, where the catch was large, and also from Sweden. These supplies somewhat overstocked the market, and prices, which had been high, declined sharply, but subsequently assumed a stronger tone, with, however, a slack trade.

The actual catch of the New England Fleet, which had continuously fallen since 1885, when it was 330,000 barrels, was in 1889 under 18,000 barrels, whilst imports were 39,000 barrels against 31,000 barrels in 1888. It may be observed that the scarcity of mackerel for the last few years, causing an increase in price, has also led to the substitution of other food products to take its place, and consequently to a considerable falling-off in the demand.

The codfish catch was, as in the case of mackerel, lighter than for many years, and wet weather was in addition injurious to the process of curing. Owing to the short supply the market continued firm and prices steady.

Flour and grain. The "corner" started in November, 1888, in the flour and wheat market was short-lived, and the year opened with falling prices, which continued during the spring under the influence of excellent crops both as to quantity and quality. A good demand for exportation then gave the market a firmer tone, and prices were steady, though somewhat lower than 1888, up to the end of the year. Flour ranged from 14s. to 22s. (3 dol. 50 c. to 5 dol. 50 c.) per barrel, according to quality. Indian corn, 1s. 9d. to 1s. 9¾d.

UNITED STATES.

(42 c. and 43½ c.) per barrel. Oats, 1s. 3½d. to 1s. 4¼d. (31 c. and 32½ c.) per bushel.

Provisions. The low cost of grain and mill-feed, affording cheap food for cattle and swine, induced a considerable decline in the price of provisions, and a brisk demand for exportation, and pork, lard, and beef packers were kept busy all the year. Fresh meats were in good supply, but generally of inferior quality, and prices were low except for choice lots.

Produce. The manufacture of butter and cheese was much in excess of the demand for consumption and exportation, and prices were consequently low. The potato crop in the Eastern States was seriously affected by rot, but supplies were received from the West, from Canada, and, later, from Scotland, and the market became well stocked, but remained steady. A large quantity of hay was cut, but was very generally damaged by rain at the time of harvesting, and, with the exception of sound lots, sold cheap. The apple crop was short, but of good quality, and prices were well maintained.

Sugar. The sugar market was for a time controlled by a powerful trust company operating in New York, and the price was run up to 4⅝d. (9¼c.) per pound, but subsequent competition on the part of individual refiners who had not joined the trust, caused it to decline to 3¼d. (6½ c.) in spite of the fact that consumption exceeded receipts of raw sugar, and the quantity refined.

Mercantile failures. With a decrease of 719 firms in business in this consular district, the number of failures, as compared with those in 1888, increased from 922 to 1,097, and the amount of liabilities from 2,288,000l. to 4,535,000l.

Foreign commerce. The foreign commerce of Boston, which constitutes about nine-tenths of the foreign trade of the district, shows a satisfactory increase. Exports, of which 237,000l. represented foreign imports re-exported, amounted during the year to 14,168,450l. against 11,656,300l. in 1888; and foreign imports were 13,049,402l. against 12,880,000l.

Foreign maritime trade. The custom-house returns give the total number of arrivals of vessels at Boston in the foreign trade as 2,364 vessels of 1,424,246 tons, viz., 1,772 British vessels of 1,104,671 tons, an increase of 126,386 tons from 1888; 156 other foreign vessels of 99,691 tons, a decrease of 12,416 tons, and 436 American vessels of 219,884 tons, an increase of 11,711 tons, the total increase being thus, 125,681 tons.

The consulate record, which includes all British vessels arriving at Boston, whilst the custom-house returns exclude those arriving from foreign ports viâ a port in the United States, shows the arrival of 1,812 British vessels of 1,115,451 net register tons, of which 510 vessels of 922,051 tons, being an increase of 124,771 tons, were steamers, and 1,301 vessels of 193,400 tons, or an increase of 4,965 tons were sailing vessels.

Ocean freights. Outward freights, from the United Kingdom to Boston, which are mostly charged under long time contracts, did not differ materially from those of 1888, as shown in the consular report for that year.

Homeward freights, from Boston to the United Kingdom, were as follows:—

Articles.		Date.	Price.
			s. d. s. d.
Grain	{ Per Bushel	January 1 to August 1 ..	0 1¾ to 0 4
	„	August 1 to December 31	0 4 0 5
Cattle	Per Head ..	January to December ..	60 0 90 0
Flour ..	{ Per Ton ..	„ June	14 0 9 0
	„ ..	June to September ..	9 0 15 0
	„ ..	September to December ..	15 0 18 9
Provisions ..	{ „ ..	January to May	25 0 10 0
	„ ..	May to December ..	10 0 25 0
Leather ..	{ „ ..	January to July	40 0 30 0
	„ ..	July to December ..	30 0 45 0
Apples.. ..	{ Per Barrel ..	January to December ..	2 6 3 0
	„ Pound	„ August ..	0 13/64 0 7/64
	„	August to December ..	0 7/64 0 ¼

Bankers sight bills remained steady at 4 dol. 89¼ c. per 1*l*. Exchange. from January to June, when it rose to 4 dol. 89½ c.; in July it declined to 4 dol. 88½ c., and in August to 4 dol. 87½ c.; in September it rallied to 4 dol. 88½ c., was 4 dol. 88¼ c. in October, fell to 4 dol. 85½ c. in November, and closed in December at 4 dol. 85.

In the Boston consular report, No. 312 of 1888, it was stated that the decennial census of the State of Massachusetts for 1885 was to be published in three volumes, and an abstract was given of Part I. of Vol. 1, relating to "Population," and in the consular report on agriculture, No. 398 of 1888, an abstract was given of Vol. 3, which had reference to "Agriculture and Mines." Part II. of Vol. 1 and Vol. 2 have now been published in completion of the various subjects embraced in the census.

Part II. in continuation of Part I., of Vol. 1 (which applied to the entire population as regards increase, sex, age, number of voters, size of families, colour and race, nativity, and conjugal condition), comprises social statistics as to occupations, labour of children, school attendance, school property, libraries and reading rooms, illiteracy, procreation, prisoners and convicts, homeless children and paupers, and general physical condition of the population, whilst Vol. 2 gives statistics in regard to manufactures, fisheries, and maritime commerce.

An abstract of Part II. of Vol 1 and of Vol. 2 is given herewith as follows:—

Abstract of Part II., Vol. 1.

1.—OCCUPATIONS by Sex, Age, and Nativity.

UNITED STATES.

Occupations.	Sex. Male.	Sex. Female.	Age. Under 10 Years.	Age. 10 to 13 Years.	Age. 14 to 19 Years.	Age. 20 to 29 Years.	Age. 30 to 39 Years.	Age. 40 to 49 Years.	Age. 50 to 59 Years.	Age. 60 to 79 Years.	Age. 80 Years and over.	Age. Years Unknown.	Nativity. Native Corn.	Nativity. Foreign Corn.
Government	9,621	1,311	...	...	316	2,352	2,874	2,665	1,592	1,101	31	1	8,765	2,167
Professional	16,555	14,250	...	...	1,508	11,460	7,743	5,051	2,862	2,115	62	4	26,997	3,808
Domestic service	11,573	522,583	...	393	34,563	132,309	122,153	101,042	73,705	65,661	4,288	37	328,657	205,499
Personal ditto	14,282	9,788	...	...	1,579	6,655	5,907	4,680	3,238	1,984	22	5	13,467	10,603
Trade	94,936	11,837	...	...	16,264	33,769	23,796	16,322	9,802	6,673	143	4	85,158	21,615
Transportation	48,675	143	...	...	3,452	17,075	13,031	8,442	4,547	2,250	20	1	33,043	15,775
Agriculture	77,257	404	...	...	9,548	15,796	11,415	11,546	11,829	16,588	926	13	59,476	18,185
Fisheries	7,973	7	...	...	583	2,853	1,921	1,387	762	466	8	...	4,146	3,834
Manufacturers	231,822	112,762	...	...	67,958	131,910	82,788	57,619	34,419	19,497	365	28	238,076	156,508
Mining	1,562	...	...	...	147	518	387	268	163	78	...	...	521	1,041
Labourers	32,905	31	...	...	2,333	8,083	6,466	6,464	5,096	4,383	105	6	10,980	21,956
Apprentices	5,183	495	...	...	4,644	1,018	12	4	...	...	...	...	4,450	1,228
Children at work	1,907	1,133	11	3,029	...	...	...	...	...	...	...	...	1,955	1,085
Scholars	164,469	162,115	130,475	135,662	63,897	1,493	49	5	3	1	...	...	303,413	28,171
Students	4,561	2,581	18	72	2,658	4,178	174	38	3	...	...	1	6,758	384
Retired	18,168	7,494	...	...	4	122	411	1,070	2,994	15,959	5,101	...	19,782	5,880
Not gainful	108	102	...	...	18	52	26	19	19	63	13	...	143	67
Not productive	13,945	10,267	2,463	733	1,736	4,008	3,331	3,161	2,667	4,889	1,206	18	16,500	7,712
Unemployed 12 months	753	69	...	...	55	191	103	92	139	222	20	1	453	369
Dependents	2,836	3,550	227,213	...	38	80	87	156	552	3,709	1,763	...	2,961	3,425
At home	113,770	113,443	...	...	...	...	...	...	...	...	...	...	216,111	11,102
Not given	10,023	29,892	...	1,175	11,428	10,828	4,545	2,889	2,368	5,215	1,442	25	33,462	6,453
	932,884	1,009,257	360,180	141,064	222,734	384,750	287,219	222,920	156,760	150,854	15,516	144	1,415,274	526,867
	1,942,141					1,942,141							1,942,141	

BOSTON.

2.—LABOUR of Children.

Occupations.	At Work. Only.	At Work. And at School.	Total Children at Work. Male.	Total Children at Work. Female.	Total Children at Work. Total.
Government service..	..	1	1	..	1
Professional ..	1	2	3	..	3
Domestic service	162	103	32	233	265
Personal service	45	79	79	45	124
Trade	237	180	332	83	417
Transportation	9	5	14	..	14
Agriculture ..	133	153	286	..	286
Fisheries ..	9	3	11	1	12
Manufactures	747	1,091	1,081	757	1,838
Mining	1	1	1	..	1
Labourers ..	17	14	31	..	31
Apprentices..	38	10	36	12	48
Total..	1,399	1,641	1,907	1,133	3,040
Native born..	543	1,112	1,264	691	1,955
Foreign born	556	529	643	442	1,085

3.—SCHOOL Attendance.

Ages of Scholars.	In Schools. Public.	In Schools. Private.	Students.	Aggregates. Male.	Aggregates. Female.	Aggregates. Total.
Under 5 years	366	144	1	258	253	511
5 to 9 ,,	120,661	9,315	17	65,753	64,240	129,993
10 to 13 ,,	126,993	10,299	72	68,724	68,640	137,364
14 to 19 ,,	56,971	6,926	2,658	31,876	34,679	66,555
20 years and over	701	849	4,394	3,484	2,460	5,944
Total	305,692	27,533	7,142	170,095	170,272	340,367
Native born	281,057	23,468	6,758	155,400	155,883	311,283
Foreign born	24,635	4,065	384	14,695	14,389	29,084

4.—SCHOOL Property.

Number of public schools, 3,439; value of buildings and other public school property, 4,853,050*l.*

Number of private schools, 541; value of buildings and other private school property, 2,273,967*l.*

5.—LIBRARIES and Reading Rooms.

Number of libraries (the first of which was opened in the year 1638), 2,371; number of books, manuscripts, and pamphlets in 2,368 libraries from which returns were received, 5,876,856; value of books in 2,353 libraries, 1,177,790*l.*; circulation in 2,021 libraries, 9,342,924.

Number of reading rooms (the first opened in 1807), 194; number of persons using 119 reading rooms, 2,107,260.

UNITED STATES.

6.—ILLITERACY.

Sex.	Population 10 Years of Age and over.			Number of Illiterates.		
	Native Born.	Foreign Born.	Total.	Native Born.	Foreign Born.	Total.
Male	518,511	233,236	751,747	6,735	38,815	45,550
Female	559,357	270,857	830,214	7,163	69,550	76,713
Total	1,077,868	504,093	1,581,961	13,898	108,365	122,263

7.—PROCREATION.

Nativity of Married Women.	Married Women.		Total.	Children.		Total Children.
	Having no Children.	Having Children.	Married Women.	Not Living.	Living.	
Native born	58,850	232,704	291,554	223,609	560,890	784,499
Foreign born	23,711	154,941	178,652	272,518	537,030	809,548
Total	82,561	387,645	470,206	496,127	1,097,920	1,594,047

8.—PRISONERS and Convicts.

Sex.	Able-bodied.	Infirm.	Native Born.	Foreign Born.	Single.	Married.	Total.
Male	3,327	67	2,234	1,160	2,258	1,136	3,394
Female	647	50	324	373	312	385	697
Total	3,974	117	2,558	1,533	2,570	1,521	4,091

YEARS OF AGE.

Sex.	14 to 19.	20 to 29.	30 to 39.	40 to 49.	50 to 59.	60 and over.	Total.
Male	344	1,388	804	532	219	107	3,394
Female	79	256	194	110	36	22	697
Total	423	1,644	998	642	255	129	4,091

9.—HOMELESS Children and Paupers.

(a) HOMELESS CHILDREN.

Sex.	Able-bodied.	Infirm.	Native Born.	Foreign Born.	Single.	Married.	Total.
Male	2,704	301	2,800	205	3,005	...	3,005
Female	2,001	226	2,079	148	2,219	8	2,227
Total	4,705	527	4,879	353	5,224	8	5,232

YEARS OF AGE.

Sex.	Under 1.	1 to 4.	5 to 9.	10 to 13.	14 to 20.	Unknown.	Total.
Male	99	342	899	989	666	10	3,005
Female	117	286	784	607	414	19	2,227
Total	216	628	1,683	1,596	1,080	29	5,232

BOSTON.

(b) PAUPERS.

Sex.	Able-bodied.	Infirm.	Native Born.	Foreign Born.	Single.	Married.	Total.
Male	1,108	3,021	2,575	1,554	2,121	2,008	4,129
Female	1,282	2,983	2,123	2,142	1,800	2,465	4,265
Total	2,390	6,004	4,698	3,696	3,921	4,473	8,394

YEARS OF AGE.

Sex.	21 to 29.	30 to 39.	40 to 49.	50 to 59.	60 and over.	Unknown.	Total.
Male	513	684	738	644	1,532	18	4,129
Female	468	758	840	693	1,495	11	4,265
Total	981	1,442	1,578	1,337	3,027	29	8,394

10.—Physical Condition of the Population.

Nature of Infirmity.	Male.	Female.	Native Born.	Foreign Born.	Total.
Acute disease	575	609	873	311	1,184
Chronic disease	7,519	6,845	10,820	3,544	14,364
Blind	2,086	1,496	2,525	1,057	3,582
Deaf	1,255	1,718	2,546	427	2,973
Dumb	74	60	112	22	134
Deaf and dumb	438	390	687	141	828
Insane	2,344	2,919	3,317	1,946	5,263
Idiotic	987	651	1,467	171	1,638
Maimed	2,205	177	1,719	663	2,382
Lame	3,454	1,682	3,825	1,311	5,136
Bedridden	135	298	334	99	433
Paralytic	1,437	1,103	1,994	546	2,540
Deformed	399	281	582	98	680
Total	22,908	18,229	30,801	10,336	41,137

Cases of persons suffering from more than one infirmity are given under two or more heads, the actual number of infirm individuals in the total population of 1,942,141 being 39,213.

UNITED STATES.

Abstract of Volume 2.

1.—MANUFACTURES.

The number of manufacturing establishments in Massachusetts in the year 1885 was 23,431, viz. :—

Private firms	22,482
Corporations	920
Associations	23
Societies	3
Institutions	3

The number of general partners was 28,177; that of special partners, 117; and the number of stockholders, 42,731.

The amount of capital invested in manufactories was 100,124,872*l.*, viz. :—

	£
In land	6,888,500
Buildings and fixtures	16,894,825
Machinery	20,191,124
Implements and tools	2,859,742
Cash capital	34,688,190
Credit capital	18,602,491

The value of stock used was 77,951,492*l.*
The value of goods made was 134,926,850*l.*, viz. :—

	£
Boots and shoes	23,815,915
Building materials and stone	9,633,628
Clothing and straw goods	9,012,213
Findings and trimmings	324,041
Food preparations	17,253,461
Iron goods	6,135,587
Other metallic goods	7,448,467
Leather	5,720,299
Paints, oils, and chemicals	1,263,108
Paper and paper goods	4,456,151
Printing and publishing	3,262,063
Textiles	28,035,071
Wooden goods	4,865,249
Wood and metal goods	4,117,238
All other goods	9,584,359

The number of manufactories employing salaried persons was 2,144; the number of salaried persons employed, 9,590; and the amount of salaries paid, 2,169,273*l.*, or an average of 226*l.* 4*s.* each.

The number of manufactories employing wage earners was 17,125; the number of wage earners employed, 419,966; and the amount of wages paid, 29,483,063*l.*

The number of persons employed on June 30, 1885, in manufacturing and mechanical work, was 379,328, viz. :—

	Males.	Females.
Under 10 years of age	6	18
10 to 13 ,,	2,057	1,427
14 to 20 ,,	35,360	33,996
21 and over ,,	226,401	80,063
Total of each sex	263,824	115,504

2.—Fisheries.

Fishery operations are carried on in 67 towns in the State of Massachusetts.

The number of firms engaged in fisheries in 1885 was 809; the number of persons employed as fishermen, shore labourers, factory hands, and other curers and packers, 15,435; the number of vessels employed 866 of 68,211 tons, and the original cost of vessels and outfit, 1,395,257*l.*; whilst the capital invested in work, apparatus, and supplies, was 1,732,116*l.*

The amount of returns of food-fish, food-fish products, shell-fish, whale, seal, and other products, was 1,292,540*l.*

The percentage of value of fish caught, was:—

In American waters	49·47
In British waters	1·87
On the High Seas	48·86

3.—Maritime Commerce.

The number of mercantile vessels owned in Massachusetts in the year 1885, was:—

	Vessels.	Tons.
Coastwise	461	171,660
Ocean	259	323,865
Coastwise and Ocean	77	30,675
Total	797	526,200

The value of vessels was 5,582,121*l.*; the amount received for freight, 2,146,327*l.*; the amount received for passengers, 436,867*l.*; and the average gross earnings per vessel, 3,241*l.*

A summary of population, products, valuation, and taxation, is printed at the end of Volume 3, of which the following are the totals for the State in the year 1885—

		£	s.	d.
Population		1,942,141		
Products of Manufactures, Agriculture, and Fisheries		145,770,599	0	0
Valuation of real and personal estate		356,469,829	0	0
Taxes for State, County and Town purposes		5,170,063	0	0
Average product per capital		75	1	2
,, valuation ,,		183	11	0
,, taxation ,,		2	13	3

UNITED STATES.

In addition to the census of Massachusetts for the year 1885 taken and compiled by the State Bureau of Statistics of Labour, the Bureau has recently published its nineteenth annual report.

The report is divided into two parts, the first giving statistics of strikes and lock-outs from the year 1825 to 1886 inclusive, and the second embodying certain information derived from the census returns in regard to citizens, aliens, polls, and voters in 1885.

The following is an abstract of the report:

1.—STRIKES AND LOCK-OUTS.

The number of strikes and lock-outs in Massachusetts from 1825 to 1880 inclusive, not distinguished from each other in former records, was 184, 25 of which occurred in 1880.

The number of establishments in which strikes occurred from 1881 to 1886 inclusive was:—

In 1881	35
1882	78
1883	33
1884	46
1885	97
1886	706
Total	995

Aggregate days duration of strikes	30,506
Average ,, ,, ,,	30·7
Number of strikes successful	351
,, ,, partially successful	457
,, ,, unsuccessful	187

	£
Loss of wages by employés	840,098
Contributions received by employés	53,340
Loss incurred by employers	394,176

Number of employés engaged in and affected by strikes, 54,889 males, 26,165 females; total 81,054.

No lock-outs are recorded for 1881 and 1882. The number of establishments in which lock-outs occurred was:—

In 1883	12
1884	2
1885	12
1886	121
Total	147

Aggregate days duration of lock-outs	11,254
Average ,, ,, ,,	76·6
Number of lock-outs successful	88
,, ,, partially successful	1
,, ,, unsuccessful	58

	£
Loss of wages by employés	190,662
Contributions received by employés	27,325
Loss incurred by employers	110,135

Number of employés locked out, males 10,844, females 3,484; total 14,328.

BOSTON.

2.—CITIZENS, ALIENS, POLLS, AND VOTERS.

Number of citizens being legal voters, viz. :—Native born, 343,886; naturalized, 98,730; total 442,616.

Non-voting citizens of legal age to vote	26·212
Aliens of voting age	99·131
Total rateable polls	567·959
Males of voting age not polls	4·767
Total males of voting age	572·726
Alien percentage of total polls	17·45
Voters percentage of population	22·79
Voters percentage of males of voting age	77·00

Of foreign born males of voting age, 35 per cent. of English Canadians, 18 per cent. of French Canadians, 39 per cent. of persons born in other British possessions, 51 per cent. of those born in England, 60 per cent. of those born in Ireland, 50 per cent. of those born in Newfoundland, 31 per cent. born in Nova Scotia, 33 per cent. born in Prince Edward's Island, 47 per cent. born in Scotland, and 54 per cent. of those born in Wales, had become citizens and legal voters.

69 per cent. of total legal voters voted for Presidential electors in 1884, and 47 per cent. for Governor of the State in 1885.

N.B.—Sterling amounts in this report are given at 4s. to the dol.

LONDON:
Printed for Her Majesty's Stationery Office,
By HARRISON AND SONS,
Printers in Ordinary to Her Majesty.
(1250 4 | 90—H & S 822)

FOREIGN OFFICE.
1890.
ANNUAL SERIES.

No. 668.

DIPLOMATIC AND CONSULAR REPORTS ON TRADE AND FINANCE.

UNITED STATES.

REPORT FOR THE YEAR 1889
ON THE
TRADE OF THE CONSULAR DISTRICT OF CHARLESTON.

REFERENCE TO PREVIOUS REPORT, Annual Series No. 515.

Presented to both Houses of Parliament by Command of Her Majesty,
APRIL, 1890.

LONDON:
PRINTED FOR HER MAJESTY'S STATIONERY OFFICE,
BY HARRISON AND SONS, ST. MARTIN'S LANE,
PRINTERS IN ORDINARY TO HER MAJESTY.

And to be purchased, either directly or through any Bookseller, from
EYRE & SPOTTISWOODE, EAST HARDING STREET, FLEET STREET, E.C., and
32, ABINGDON STREET, WESTMINSTER, S.W; or
ADAM AND CHARLES BLACK, 6, NORTH BRIDGE, EDINBURGH; or
HODGES, FIGGIS, & Co., 104, GRAFTON STREET, DUBLIN.

1890.

[C. 5895—71.]   *Price One Penny.*

New Series of Reports.

Reports of the Annual Series have been issued from Her Majesty's Diplomatic and Consular Officers at the following places, and may be obtained from the sources indicated on the title-page:—

No.		Price.	No.		Price.
542.	Vienna	1d.	605.	Christiania	4d.
543.	Antwerp	1d.	606.	Pernambuco	1½d.
544.	Lisbon	2d.	607.	Trieste	1½d.
545.	New York	1½d.	608.	Tunis	½d.
546.	San Francisco	1d.	609.	Havana	2d.
547.	Stettin	1½d.	610.	Frankfort	½d.
548.	San Salvador	½d.	611.	Tabreez	½d.
549.	Trebizond	1d.	612.	Bilbao	1d.
550.	Nice	1d.	613.	Barcelona	½d.
551.	Baghdad	½d.	614.	Tokio	1d.
552.	Fiume	1d.	615.	Naples	2½d.
553.	Mogador	2d.	616.	Batoum	½d.
554.	Buenos Ayres	1½d.	617.	Odessa	1d.
555.	San Francisco	2½d.	618.	La Rochelle	1d.
556.	Carthagena	½d.	619.	Rome	1d.
557.	Syra	1d.	620.	Nice	1d.
558.	Varna and Bourgas	1d.	621.	Kiukiang	½d.
559.	Thessaly	½d.	622.	Paris	1d.
560.	Yokohama	1d.	623.	Salonica	1½d.
561.	Nantes	1½d.	624.	Réunion	1d.
562.	Suakin	½d.	625.	Ichang	1d.
563.	Algiers	1d.	626.	Bogotá	1d.
564.	St. Petersburg	2½d.	627.	Malaga	2d.
565.	Soul	1d.	628.	Porto Rico	1d.
566.	Newchwang	1d.	629.	Bushire	2½d.
567.	Roustchouk and Philippopolis	1d.	630.	The Hague	½d.
568.	Stockholm	1½d.	631.	Berlin	1d.
569.	Tonga	1d.	632.	Adrianople	1½d.
570.	Chicago	1½d.	633.	Rome	1½d.
571.	Adana	½d.	634.	Santiago	½d.
572.	Buenos Ayres	3d.	635.	Tahiti	½d.
573.	Frankfort	1½d.	636.	Maranham	½d.
574.	Canton	1½d.	637.	Mexico	2d.
575.	Tamsui	5½d.	638.	Christiania	1d.
576.	Palermo	3d.	639.	Copenhagen	1d.
577.	Amsterdam	1d.	640.	Paris	1d.
578.	Ajaccio	½d.	641.	Venice	1d.
579.	Shanghai	1½d.	642.	Cherbourg	½d.
580.	Warsaw	½d.	643.	New York	1d.
581.	Teneriffe	1d.	644.	Patras	1d.
582.	Tangier	2d.	645.	Bourgas	½d.
583.	Surinam	½d.	646.	St. Petersburg	3d.
584.	Loanda	1d.	647.	Taganrog	½d.
585.	Alexandria	1d.	648.	Baltimore	1½d.
586.	Cagliari	1d.	649.	New Orleans	2d.
587.	Smyrna	½d.	650.	New Orleans	1d.
588.	Mannheim	1d.	651.	Samos	½d.
589.	Nagasaki	1d.	652.	Buda-Pesth	1½d.
590.	Hakodate	1d.	653.	Tripoli	½d.
591.	Bushire	1d.	654.	Buenos Ayres	½d.
592.	Chinkiang	½d.	655.	Paris	1d.
593.	Pakhoi	1d.	656.	Cherbourg	1d.
594.	Hiogo	1½d.	657.	Warsaw	½d.
595.	Bangkok	1d.	658.	Rome	1½d.
596.	Serajevo	1d.	659.	Saigon	½d.
597.	Copenhagen	1½d.	660.	Buenos Ayres	½d.
598.	Cephalonia	½d.	661.	Galveston	1d.
599.	Chefoo	½d.	662.	Galatz	1½d.
600.	Guatemala	1½d.	663.	Antwerp	1d.
601.	Tonga	½d.	664.	Boston	1d.
602.	Tahiti	1d.	665.	Madeira	½d.
603.	Stettin	2d.	666.	New Hebrides	½d.
604.	Vera Cruz	1½d.	667.	Riga	1d.

No. 668.

Reference to previous Report, Annual Series No. 515.

UNITED STATES.

CHARLESTON.

Consul Cridland to the Marquis of Salisbury.

My Lord,   Charleston, S.C., February 20, 1890.

I HAVE the honour to enclose herewith a Report of the Trade and Commerce of the Port of Charleston for the past year, showing also some of the principal productions and resources of the State of South Carolina during the same period.

I have, &c.
(Signed)   FREDERICK J. CRIDLAND.

Report of the Trade and Commerce of Charleston, South Carolina, for the Year 1889.

An examination of the tables of British shipping at this port for the past year will exhibit quite an increase in the total tonnage and values of cargoes, inward and outward, over the previous year, and considering the strong efforts made in the neighbouring ports to gain the largest share of the exports from the Atlantic seaboard by every possible means, Charleston seems to hold its own trade, especially in the mining and export of phosphate rock. Undoubtedly its cotton exports would also increase if the enterprising capitalists of the port would purchase or obtain control over the railroads in the State, and especially the South Carolina railroad, which is now in the hands of a receiver, and which will before long be sold. If this road could be controlled in this city, by means of reasonable freights and enlarged transportation facilities, a large amount of trade now diverted to other ports could be centred here. The public journals are constantly reminding their readers of these facts, and showing the necessity of more enterprise by those whose means are large. Time will show whether this good advice will be taken or not. A sight of the beautiful harbour of Charleston, large enough for 10 times the number of ships now visiting the port yearly, would convince anyone of what capital and enterprise could do for its benefit. If the inhabitants of its shores would endeavour to emulate what Nature has done,

[Side notes: Increase of British shipping at Charleston. Benefit to the trade of the port by the purchase of the South Carolina railroad to be sold. What could be done by the inhabitants to increase the commerce of the port.]

(826)

UNITED STATES.

Efforts to deepen the entrance to the port. Efforts of very little use without a much larger outlay. Cotton receipts for two years, 1888-89. Average weight of bale 450 lbs. English. Receipts falling off, uncertainties. Damage to crop by rains.

their action would never be regretted in the future. It is also to be hoped that the efforts of the United States engineers and contractors to deepen the entrance to the port will meet with successs. It is a great misfortune that the United States Government does not appropriate a sum of money large enough, and which would cause the work now undertaken outside the bar to be completed within a given period.

The receipts of cotton, the principal article of export from this port during the season commencing September 1, 1888, and ending August 31 last, amounted to 416,490 bales, against 450,068 bales during the preceding year. The falling-off in the receipts illustrates the uncertainty and accidents to which the staple is liable. At the close of the summer of 1888 the prospect for a large crop was most favourable. The season had been all that could be desired, and the fruit pickings gave promise of a better crop in all respects than had been gathered and marketed for many years; but in September came the most unfavourable weather and continuous and excessive rains, lasting till the end of October, the abundant moisture rotting the cotton bolls, and the crop, when picked, was found to be in a most deteriorated condition, also in quantity, and in value from 30 to 40 per cent., which proved a most serious loss to the planters in this State. Had the crop turned out as expected, in all probability the receipts and exports from Charleston would have been much larger.

Exports of cotton to Europe.

Exports of Cotton from Charleston.

	1889.	1888.
	Bales.	Bales.
To Liverpool	54,545	69,110
Bremen	78,337	76,510
Barcelona	51,515	64,571
Russia	41,109	36,473
France	25,742	25,843
Italy	10,155	6,060
Belgium	..	6,475
Total to ports in Europe	261,403	285,042

Export of cotton to the United States ports.

	1889.	1888.
	Bales.	Bales.
To New York	144,521	142,797
Philadelphia	..	4,404
Boston	1,236	1,000
Other United States ports	..	..
Total to United States ports	145,986	148,201
Total to foreign and U.S. ports	407,389	433,243

CHARLESTON.

RECEIPTS OF NATIVE AND FOREIGN RICE AT CHARLESTON FOR THE PAST TWO YEARS.

As before stated, during the months of September and October, 1888, the excessive rains materially damaged the cotton crop, and the same cause affected the rice crop and came very nearly ruining many planters, their crops having been short for several seasons past. The excessive rain prevented the gathering of the rice then ripe, consequently a vast quantity was lost, and much of what was finally gathered was damaged or of a poor quality, and a good deal of rice had to be imported for consumption, it being one of the principal articles of daily food in this State for the native population, both white and black.

Receipts of rice.
Damage to crop.
Necessity for importing rice.

Year.	Barrels.	Average Weight of Barrels. English Weight.
		Lbs.
1889	72,565	325
1888	81,290	300

Amount of rice received from planters.

The foreign rice imported consisted of 110,000 bushels in an unfinished state, and was milled in the city. The crop of the past season, grown in the rice-growing sections of the State, is now being brought to this port, and it looks as if the last rice harvested will show a favourable result and remuneration to the planter. It is probable that this year no foreign rice will be imported for home consumption. The native grain being of a very superior quality, and the foreign article being considered the reverse, it does not meet with much favour by consumers.

Imported rice.
Prospect of rice crop of 1889-90.
Foreign rice not in favour.

Notwithstanding the limited rice crop harvested in 1888-89, much native rice was exported to New York and to the interior of the United States.

EXPORTS.

	1888-89.	1887-88.
	Barrels, of 325 lbs.	Barrels of 325 lbs.
To New York	19,733	25,626
Philadelphia	..	3,755
Interior towns	37,832	31,909
Total	57,565	61,290

Rice exports.

Phosphate Mining and Fertilisers.

During the past year the trade in phosphate rock and fertilisers was full of activity. There was no depression at any period of the year, but, on the contrary, there was an increased demand for the products of both the mines and the mills. The South Carolina phosphate rock seems to be most widely known,

South Carolina phosphates and fertilisers.

(826)

UNITED STATES.

Trade increasing yearly.

is of a regular grade, uniform, and trustworthy, and there is, and must continue to be, a steady growth of this trade year after year. The mining companies are keeping pace with the demands upon their resources. If any doubt exists as to the correctness of this statement, a stranger has only to observe the number of large three-masted schooners arriving at Charleston and departing for northern ports loaded with phosphate rock, and this goes on all the year round, proving of vast benefit to this port and, of course, increasing its commerce. Last year 251 vessels were cleared at this port with rock for home and foreign markets.

Number of vessels carrying the phosphate rock to the northern ports.

In 1880 210,000 tons of phosphate rock was mined in this portion of the State. Last year the total output of the mines was 510,000 tons, the local manufacturing companies using 80,000 tons in the making of fertilisers. The demand for the crude rock comes from the United Kingdom, France, Germany, and even from Japan, where fertiliser works have been established, obtaining their supplies from this State. Phosphate land rock has not only been in demand during the past year, but many large and valuable places have changed hands, there being much inquiry from England for phosphate lands, and probably before long some of the valuable mines will be owned by English capitalists. The deposits being near water transportation, and the ease with which the mining operations are conducted and the great improvements which have been made in the preparation of the material for market, have attracted the attention of those persons who are looking for profitable investments.

Rock mined. A ton of rock weighs 2,240 lbs. English weight. Amount of phosphate rock used in Charleston factories. Foreign demand. Demand for phosphate lands.

Advantage of situation.

Price of rock.

The price for crude rock last year was 1*l*. 5*s*. per ton of 2,240 lbs.; for dried rock 1*l*. 9*s*. 2*d*. per ton, same weight. Very great care is taken in the preparation of both river and land deposits.

EXPORTS.

Exports of phosphate rock for two years, 1888-9.

	1889.	1888.
	Tons.	Tons.
To foreign ports	5,876	2,927
Coast ports	181,961	172,541
Carried to the interior	41,559	36,733
Local consumption	80,000	70,000
	309,396	282,201

Articles imported for mixing with the ground rock to increase its value.

In order to increase the value of the South Carolina phosphate rock for fertilising purposes, the manufacturers thereof import from Europe and South America the following named articles in large quantities annually, and, by mixing them with the ground rock, find a much larger demand for the fertiliser.

CHARLESTON.

QUANTITY and Value of Chemicals and Fertilisers Imported into Charleston during the last Two Years.

Articles.	1889. Quantity.	1889. Value.	1888. Quantity.	1888. Value.
	Tons.	£	Tons.	£
Kanit from Germany	16,423	20,553	7,122	9,154
Brimstone from Sicily	20,810	66,770	15,532	53,918
Nitrate of soda from Chile	2,424	15,251	1,309	8,545
Muriate of potash from Chile	2,476	15,364	851	6,028
Other fertilisers	1,625	2,038	1,003	1,903
Total	43,758	119,976	25,817	79,549

Quantities and value.

The timber and lumber trade of the last year shows an increase both in the exports to foreign as well as to home markets. The stock was large, and the mills in this country were kept constantly at work the whole year. The prices ranged upward, and are likely to continue so this year.

Timber and lumber, or deals.

The exports for the past two years were as follows:—

	In 1889.	In 1888.
	Feet.	Feet.
To foreign ports	4,574,279	3,455,551
United States ports	45,958,401	41,813,860
Total	50,532,680	45,269,411

This shows that the timber and lumber (deals) trade has quadrupled itself in 10 years, the total exported in 1879 being 12,931,179 feet.

Increase of trade.

The naval store trade shows an increase in the receipts of turpentine and a decrease in that of rosin compared with 1888, but the prices during the past year having been very remunerative made the outcome of the crop most profitable and satisfactory to all parties interested in this State. As the stocks of naval stores at all points have been greatly reduced, owing to limited production, it will probably give an impetus to the business this year.

Naval stores. Turpentine and rosin.

Stock reduced.

UNITED STATES.

COMPARATIVE Statement showing the Receipts and Exports of Naval Stores at Charleston for the past Two Years.

RECEIPTS.

Receipts and exports of naval stores.

	In 1889.		In 1888.	
	Turpentine in Casks.	Rosin in Barrels.	Turpentine in Casks.	Rosin in Barrels.
Stock on hand	2,394	17,866	1,440	33,816
Receipts	42,558	148,188	41,776	167,096
Total	44,952	166,054	43,216	200,912

EXPORTS.

Exports to Europe.

	In 1889.		In 1888.	
	Turpentine in Casks.	Rosin in Barrels.	Turpentine in Casks.	Rosin in Barrels.
To Great Britain	10,242	16,271	5,856	40,233
Germany	6,805	54,989	12,519	25,151
Holland	9,450	10,669	11,740	35,497
Austria	..	9,570	950	26,300
Italy	802	16,693	..	18,955
Russia	..	8,934	..	7,502
Belgium	1,769	..	..	..
Other countries	..	450	..	7,031
Total	29,068	117,576	31,065	160,669

Measure and weight of naval stores in casks or barrels. Exports to coast ports.

Casks of turpentine average 51 gallons English measure, and the average weight of a barrel of rosin is 415 lbs. English measure. Both articles are made in the extensive pine forests of South Carolina, and brought to this market for sale or shipment.

The coastwise exports of naval stores from Charleston for the past two years was a follows:—

	1889.		1888.	
	Turpentine in Casks.	Rosin in Barrels.	Turpentine in Casks.	Rosin in Barrels.
To New York	9,941	30,716	5,286	20,548
Other ports	4,118	1,056	3,902	669
Total	14,059	31,772	9,188	21,217

Price of turpentine and rosin.

The price of turpentine in 1888 varied from 1s. 2½d. to 1s. 7d. per gallon. In 1889 the price ranged from 1s. 5½d. to 2s. 1d. per

CHARLESTON.

gallon. The price of rosin is regulated according to its quality or grade. In 1888 the price ranged from 3s. 4d. to 7s. 1d. It 1889 it ranged from 3s. 1½d. to 7s. 3d. per barrel.

PRODUCTIONS of the Soil in South Carolina in 1889.

Articles.	Measure.	Quantity.	Acres.	Value.
				£
Cotton	Bale of 450 lbs.	639,998	1,561,280	5,999,982
Rice	Lb. of 16 ozs.	93,134,508	77,996	388,061
Indian corn	Bushel of 62 lbs.	20,751,133	1,586,829	2,766,818
Peas	,, 60 ,,	1,051,500	158,831	190,585
Potatoes	,, 60 ,,	428,354	6,628	78,531
Potatoes (sweet)	,, 50 ,,	3,437,579	39,147	366,388
Hay	Ton of 2,000 lbs.	35,100	...	93,600
Fodder	,, ,,	177,724	...	570,198
Sugar cane syrup	Gallon	485,740	3,055	52,621
Sorgum cane syrup	,,	806,483	10,721	67,206
Tobacco	Lb. of 16 ozs.	377,897	168,782	14,172
Wheat	Bushel of 62 lbs.	1,175,595	303,948	262,060
Oats	,, 48 ,,	3,571,952	...	501,845
Apples	Barrel	...	...	14,414
Peaches	Box	...	...	31,198
Pears	,,	...	8,000	3,217
Melons	...	3,000,000	...	83,334
Pea vine hay	Ton	145,000	...	392,709
Grapes	Baskets	...	...	18,384
Phosphate rock (river)	Ton of 2,240 lbs.	212,101	...	234,616
,, ,, (mine)	,, ,,	310,000	...	387,500
Total		...	...	12,487,439

The estimated value of the principal crops in South Carolina for 1889 is 11,710,718l., an increase of 2,420,000l. over 1888.

Annex A.—RETURN of all Shipping at the Port of Charleston for 1889.

ENTERED.

Nationality.	Sailing. Number of Vessels.	Sailing. Tons.	Steam. Number of Vessels.	Steam. Tons.	Total. Number of Vessels.	Total. Tons.
British	8	3,492	54	61,321	62	64,813
American	552	192,313	216	477,217	768	669,530
Norwegian and Swedish	36	15,722	1	1,409	37	17,131
Italian	28	11,371	...	...	28	11,371
Spanish	17	5,984	1	1,605	18	7,589
German	12	5,705	3	3,610	15	9,315
Other countries	2	790	...	...	2	790
Total	655	235,377	275	545,162	930	780,539
,, for the year preceding	485	220,675	257	216,610	742	437,285

UNITED STATES.

CLEARED.

Nationality.	Sailing. Number of Vessels.	Sailing. Tons.	Steam. Number of Vessels.	Steam. Tons.	Total. Number of Vessels.	Total. Tons.
British	11	4,831	58	66,210	69	71,041
American	538	200,027	220	480,780	757	680,807
Norwegian and Swedish	36	15,771	1	1,409	37	17,180
Italian	29	11,873	...	...	29	11,873
Spanish	17	5,984	2	2,382	19	8,366
German	14	6,539	3	3,610	17	10,149
Other countries	3	1,216	1	1,249	4	2,465
Total	648	246,241	285	555,640	933	801,881
,, for the year preceding	477	218,454	261	225,339	738	443,793

Annex B.—RETURN of the Principal Articles of Export from the Port of Charleston, South Carolina, to the United States and Foreign Markets during the Years 1889–88.

Articles.		1889. Quantity.	1889. Value. £	1888. Quantity.	1888. Value. £
Cotton, Upland	Bales	408,701	3,831,572	442,720	4,150,500
,, Sea Island	Bags	7,789	154,157	7,348	145,429
Rice	Barrels	72,565	226,766	81,290	254,031
Turpentine	Casks	42,558	177,325	41,776	147,957
Rosin	Barrels	148,188	54,026	167,096	60,920
Phosphate rock, crude	Tons	304,396	380,495	267,830	282,939
,, ,, ground	,,	7,650	15,117	14,371	22,455
Lumber and crop ties	Feet	55,532,680	127,261	50,269,411	104,728
Fertilisers	Tons	172,050	742,719	181,192	796,215
Cotton goods manufactured in Charleston	Bales	58,194	666,806	54,247	619,713
Fruits and vegetables	Packages	81,822	328,750	211,000	412,500
Potatoes of both kinds*	Barrels	77,609	125,000	130,558	187,500
Jute bagging manufactured in Charleston	Bales	...	135,417	...	62,500
Total		...	6,965,411	...	7,247,38

* In the United States the common potato is called "Irish potato," to distinguish it from the "sweet potato," so much cultivated and used as an article of food in the Southern and Northern States, and also in the west of the United States. It will not grow in a cold climate.

RETURN of the Principal Articles of Import from Foreign Countries into Charleston during the Years 1889–88, and Value.

	Total Value of Imports in 1889. £	Total Value of Imports in 1888. £
From Great Britain—Salt, iron ties, beer, spirits, and wine		
Germany—Kanit*		
Sicily—Sulphur	135,820	119,952
Chile—Nitrate of soda and potash		
British West Indies—Fruit		

* Kanit, an inferior kind of salt used as a fertiliser.

CHARLESTON.

Annex C.—RETURN showing the Total Value of Exports from Charleston to Foreign Countries during 1889-88.

	1889.	1888.
	£	£
To Great Britain, Spain, Germany, France, Italy, and Belgium—		
Cotton	2,450,653	2,630,602
Turpentine	121,117	110,022
To Great Britain—		
Rosin	42,866	58,577
Phosphate rock	8,360	3,659
Total	2,622,996	2,802,860

The separate values for each country could not be obtained from any local report of trade of Charleston.

In consequence of the adoption by this city of the Holt system for the disinfection of vessels arriving at the quarantine station of this port from infected places, and now in operation, vessels, which heretofore were detained for 10, 15, 30, or 60 days before obtaining permission to come up to the port, will be disinfected by the new process so thoroughly that all danger will be removed in a few days—probably five days being the limit. No alteration has taken place in the depth of water at the entrance to the bay of Charleston since the last report, and vessels, when drawing over 16½ feet, meet with difficulty in crossing the bar. At high tides vessels do cross drawing 17 feet. *(New system for disinfecting infected vessels arriving at Charleston for cargoes. No change in depth of water at entrance to port.)*

There is a strong movement throughout the Southern States in reference to manufacturing, in order to prevent the everlasting drain of money sent to the North to purchase what can just as well be made in the South, and every year now shows a decided improvement in the manufacturing of cotton and many other articles. *(Manufacturing on the increase, especially cotton.)*

With reference to the amount of cotton grown and used in this Consular district by its cotton factories it appears that— *(Amount of raw cotton used in the four States forming the Consular district of Charleston.)*

	Bales.
North Carolina consumed in 1888	76,360
South Carolina " "	111,003
Georgia " "	133,877
Tennessee " "	36,437
Total	357,677

(Cotton mills in South Carolina increasing yearly.)

	Mills.	Spindles.	Looms.
In the year 1880 South Carolina had	14	82,334	1,676
" " 1882 " " "	26	181,743	3,418
" " 1889 " " "	44	417,730	10,687

UNITED STATES.

Profits and dividends.

It will be seen by this rapid increase of mills that manufacturers and capitalists are evidently becoming convinced of the advantage in bringing the raw material into closer relation, without the invention of long lines of transportation; and this advantage is more clearly made manifest by the dividends upon investments in the past, which have lately ranged from 8 to 20 per cent. per annum.

State prosperity. Credit, bonds, banks. Surplus in State treasury. Resources being developed. Climate, summer and winter.

It may be safely stated that the State of South Carolina is in a prosperous condition. The State's credit is good—its bonds are in demand—the interest is paid regularly. The national banks and the savings banks are all doing well, and their credit is excellent. There is a surplus in the State Treasury of over 60,000 dol. (12,500l.); the resources of the State are being every year more developed; new railroads are about to be built, others are being finished. Its climate is all that could be desired during the winter months, and the highlands and mountains in the upper part of the State and in North Carolina afford healthy and cool retreats during the summer and autumn.

Sterling exchange. Freights.

Sterling exchange ranged high in 1889 (4 dol. 80 c. to 4 dol. 86 c. per £ sterling), and shipowners were well satisfied with the cotton, timber, and phosphate freights obtained by their ships.

LONDON:
Printed for Her Majesty's Stationery Office,
By HARRISON AND SONS,
Printers in Ordinary to Her Majesty.
(1250 4 | 90—H & S 826)

FOREIGN OFFICE.
1890.
ANNUAL SERIES.

No. 691.

DIPLOMATIC AND CONSULAR REPORTS ON TRADE AND FINANCE.

UNITED STATES.

REPORT FOR THE YEAR 1889

ON THE

TRADE OF SAVANNAH (GEORGIA).

REFERENCE TO PREVIOUS REPORT, Annual Series No. 531

Presented to both Houses of Parliament by Command of Her Majesty,
MAY, 1890.

LONDON:
PRINTED FOR HER MAJESTY'S STATIONERY OFFICE,
BY HARRISON AND SONS, ST. MARTIN'S LANE,
PRINTERS IN ORDINARY TO HER MAJESTY.

And to be purchased, either directly or through any Bookseller, from
EYRE & SPOTTISWOODE, EAST HARDING STREET, FLEET STREET, E.C., and
32, ABINGDON STREET, WESTMINSTER, S.W.: or
ADAM AND CHARLES BLACK, 6, NORTH BRIDGE, EDINBURGH; or
HODGES, FIGGIS, & Co., 104, GRAFTON STREET, DUBLIN.

1890.

[C. 5895.- 91.] *Price One Penny.*

New Series of Reports.

Reports of the Annual Series have been issued from Her Majesty's Diplomatic and Consular Officers at the following places, and may be obtained from the sources indicated on the title-page:—

No.		Price.	No.		Price.
565.	Söul	1d.	628.	Porto Rico	1d.
566.	Newchwang	1d.	629.	Bushire	2½d.
567.	Roustchouk and Philippopolis	1d.	630.	The Hague	½d.
568.	Stockholm	1½d.	631.	Berlin	1d.
569.	Tonga	1d.	632.	Adrianople	1½d.
570.	Chicago	1½d.	633.	Rome	1½d.
571.	Adana	½d.	634.	Santiago	½d.
572.	Buenos Ayres	3d.	635.	Tahiti	½d.
573.	Frankfort	1½d.	636.	Maranham	½d.
574.	Canton	1½d.	637.	Mexico	2d.
575.	Tamsui	5½d.	638.	Christiania	1d.
576.	Palermo	3d.	639.	Copenhagen	1d.
577.	Amsterdam	1d.	640.	Paris	1d.
578.	Ajaccio	½d.	641.	Venice	1d.
579.	Shanghai	1½d.	642.	Cherbourg	½d.
580.	Warsaw	½d.	643.	New York	1d.
581.	Teneriffe	1d.	644.	Patras	1d.
582.	Tangier	2d.	645.	Bourgas	½d.
583.	Surinam	½d.	646.	St. Petersburg	3d.
584.	Loanda	1d.	647.	Taganrog	½d.
585.	Alexandria	1d.	648.	Baltimore	1½d.
586.	Cagliari	1d.	649.	New Orleans	2d.
587.	Smyrna	½d.	650.	New Orleans	1d.
588.	Mannheim	1d.	651.	Samos	½d.
589.	Nagasaki	1d.	652.	Buda-Pesth	1½d.
590.	Hakodate	1d.	653.	Tripoli	½d.
591.	Bushire	1d.	654.	Buenos Ayres	½d.
592.	Chinkiang	½d.	655.	Paris	1d.
593.	Pakhoi	1d.	656.	Cherbourg	1d.
594.	Hiogo	1½d.	657.	Warsaw	½d.
595.	Bangkok	1d.	658.	Rome	1½d.
596.	Serajevo	1d.	659.	Saigon	½d.
597.	Copenhagen	1½d.	660.	Buenos Ayres	½d.
598.	Cephalonia	½d.	661.	Galveston	1d.
599.	Chefoo	½d.	662.	Galatz	1½d.
600.	Guatemala	1½d.	663.	Antwerp	1d.
601.	Tonga	½d.	664.	Boston	1d.
602.	Tahiti	1d.	665.	Madeira	½d.
603.	Stettin	2d.	666.	New Hebrides	½d.
604.	Vera Cruz	1½d.	667.	Riga	1d.
605.	Christiania	4d.	668.	Charleston	1d.
606.	Pernambuco	1½d.	669.	Algiers	2d.
607.	Trieste	1½d.	670.	Stuttgart	1d.
608.	Tunis	½d.	671.	Havre	3d.
609.	Havana	2d.	672.	The Piræus	1d.
610.	Frankfort	½d.	673.	Syra	1d.
611.	Tabreez	½d.	674.	Boulogne	1d.
612.	Bilbao	1d.	675.	Taganrog	2d.
613.	Barcelona	½d.	676.	Wuhu	½d.
614.	Tokio	1d.	677.	Batoum	1d.
615.	Naples	2½d.	678.	Manila	1d.
616.	Batoum	½d.	679.	Tamsui	1d.
617.	Odessa	1d.	680.	Kiungchow	1d.
618.	La Rochelle	1d.	681.	Swatow	1d.
619.	Rome	1d.	682.	Stettin	6d.
620.	Nice	1d.	683.	Bordeaux	2½d.
621.	Kiukiang	½d.	684.	Port Said	1d.
622.	Paris	1d.	685.	Coquimbo	½d.
623.	Salonica	1½d.	686.	Warsaw	1d.
624.	Réunion	1d.	687.	Ichang	1d.
625.	Ichang	1d.	688.	Wênchow	1d.
626.	Bogotá	1d.	689.	Trebizond	1d.
627.	Malaga	2d.	690.	Damascus	½d.

No. 691.

Reference to previous Report, Annual Series No. 531.

UNITED STATES.

SAVANNAH.

Consul Cridland to the Marquis of Salisbury.

My Lord,   *Charleston, S.C., March* 10, 1890.

I HAVE the honour to enclose to your Lordship a Report of the Trade and Commerce of the Port of Savannah, Georgia, for the past year, received this day from Mr. Vice-Consul Robertson.

I have, &c.
(Signed)   FREDERICK J. CRIDLAND.

Report on the Trade and Commerce of Savannah for the Year 1889.

The trade and commerce of Savannah during the year 1889 has been most satisfactory.

A cursory glance at the rapid growth of Savannah during the past decade cannot be other than interesting and valuable, showing as it does the extraordinary progress the city is making.

Population. The census of 1880 gave the population of Savannah as 30,078. At the present time, or nine years after, it has reached, if not passed, 60,000, or, in other words, the city has doubled its population in the past ten years.

Real estate. Consequent on the vast increase in the population, the value of all real estate has risen enormously. Ten years ago building lots—then on the outskirts of the city—were sold from 18*l.* 10*s.* (90 dol.) to 41*l.* (200 dol.) each. Since then, owing to the extension of the city limits, the same lots have changed hands at 410*l.* (2,000 dol.) to 1,025*l.* (5,000 dol.) each. Beyond the city limits, the increase has been even more wonderful. Land there in 1880 sold for 41*l.* (200 dol.) per acre, now it cannot be bought under 1,025*l.* (5,000 dol.) an acre. This great and rapid increase represents the actual value of the land, the prices not having been forced by speculation. It is the natural and necessary result of the vast increase in the population and growth of the city.

Banks. Ten years ago Savannah had but four banks; at the present time she has eight. The fact that this additional capital has

UNITED STATES.

Wealth of the city.

found employment at remunerative rates clearly indicates enlarged business.

The wealth of the city during the past ten years has kept pace with the other marvellous strides of prosperity, and is now nearly four times as great as in 1880.

There are few cities, if any, that can show a better record than the above; and the greatest cause of satisfaction is, that this vast increase is purely the result of legitimate business.

Railroads.

The Columbus and Western extension—mentioned in my last report—was, early in 1889, opened for traffic, thereby giving to Savannah immense commercial advantages, as well as a convenient line to Birmingham and the great West.

The principal lines now under construction and in contemplation are the Savannah, Americus and Montgomery, and the South Bound. The latter road is already in operation from Blackville to Barnwell, and the prospect for its construction to Savannah are excellent. This road if carried through would open up to the trade and market of Savannah the richest cotton belt of South Carolina.

Crops.

The returns for the season 1888–89, which ended about April,—and to which allusion was made in my last report,—show a large falling-off in the receipts of cotton at this port in comparison with the previous year. The shortage being 69,000 bales. This large decrease caused no alarm, however, because the cause of it was well understood, and in fact the shortage was looked for.

The season for 1889–90 will conclusively show that Savannah is in no danger of losing her position as the second cotton port of importance in the United States. Up to the end of the year the receipts at Savannah were within 40,000 bales of the total receipts for the season 1888–89, and it is confidently expected that by the close of the season, when all the available cotton has been marketed, that the receipts will be larger than ever before handled at this port.

The following table shows the total cotton crops of the United States, with the relative receipts at Savannah from 1884–90:—

Year.	Estimated Crop.	Estimated Receipts at Savannah.
	Bales.	
1884–85	5,706,165	728,087
1885–86	6,575,695	803,359
1886–87	6,505,087	804,412
1887–88	7,046,833	892,388
1888–89	6,938,290	828,168
1889–90	7,500,000	925,000

The increase in the receipts at Savannah for 1889–90, as shown by the above table, is attributed to three things. Increased acreage of land planted. The splendid season for growing and picking of the cotton, and the extension of the railroads into territories which have marketed their cotton at this port.

The area planted in rice was materially reduced. Planters had suffered so severely for several seasons past, from the heavy floods, that many plantations were left uncultivated in 1889.

The season was, however, a very successful one for those who planted. The yield per acre was far above the average, and prices —owing to the limited planting—were particularly good.

The year's business in naval stores was very gratifying. There was an immense increase in the amount of spirits of turpentine handled at this port, and though there was a slight decrease in the total number of barrels of resin brought to Savannah, yet the prices were so good, particularly for spirits, that the year proved a prosperous one to the factors engaged in the business. *Naval stores.*

I regret to report that several fires on ship-board have taken place during the year. The fires at this port generally occur during October, or the busiest month of the season. During this time cotton is rushed so rapidly to market, that thousands of bales are left lying awaiting transportation, entirely unprotected by covering, at the many wayside stations along the different railroads, exposed to the sparks from passing trains, &c., and, in my opinion, the cause of the casualties at this port, are, to a great extent, due to this fact. *Fires.*

During the early part of the year Savannah suffered considerable loss from fires generally. The destruction of two of the presses of the Cotton Press Association in the midst of the season threatened at one time to seriously interfere with the loading of vessels. An old press of the Association was, however, put in order, and by working night and day all the cotton offered was pressed with scarcely any appreciable delay to the vessels in port.

Savannah lays no claim as yet to be classed among the manufacturing cities of America. There is, however, every indication that this will soon be otherwise. The capitalists of the city are rapidly realising the fact that money invested in home enterprises will return to them better interests than they can obtain elsewhere. *Enterprises.*

To this end, early in the year a brewery was established under the title of the Savannah Brewery Company, with a capital of about 20,560*l.*, in 1,000 shares of about 20*l.* 10*s.* per share.

The enterprise has proved a most wonderful success; after only six months' actual work—the beer was put on the market July 1—a dividend equal to 18 per cent. was declared on December 31, that is to say, 5 per cent. was paid to the shareholders, and 15 per cent. put into a reserve fund. The shares cannot be bought for anything less than double their par value.

The Savannah Cotton Mill Company, with a capital of about 20,560*l.*, in 1,000 shares of about 20*l.* 10*s.* per share, was also incorporated early in the year. A portion of the shares of this company were issued on the instalment plan, than is, 10 monthly payments of 2*l.* 1*s.* per share, thereby giving to small investors a better, or easier, opportunity of investment than is usually offered. The building is now under construction, and will be ready for occupation by the opening of the next season. When finished the mill will have a capacity of 10,000 spindles, and it is confidently expected to pay a handsome dividend to the shareholders.

For years the city of Savannah had felt the need of increased and more commodious hotel accommodation, consequent on her growing trade and popularity as a resort for travellers. To meet this want a company was formed, and a palatial hotel, "The De Soto," was erected, and opened to the public on the last day of the year 1889. The building stands on an area of 1½ acres, and is the largest and best appointed hotel in the south, with the possible exception of the "Pouce de Acou" at St. Augustine, Florida.

Harbour improvements. — The improvements in the river and harbour have been steadily and successfully carried on throughout the year, with the result that the harbour is in a better condition now than ever before. The growing commerce of the port requires a still further deepening of the channel to a depth of at least 26 feet; and it is confidently expected that Congress, at its approaching session, will appropriate sufficient money to enable this important work to be commenced.

Quarantine. — Notwithstanding the great improvements made at the quarantine station, mentioned in my last report, they have been found insufficient for the requirements of the port. To remedy this an eligible site on Cockspur Island has been secured from the General Government, and assurance is given by the municipal authorities that ample provision will be made to make the station what the commerce of the port requires it to be before the opening of another season.

Health. — One of the most important factors in the rapid growth and prosperity of Savannah is her superb health record. Malarial, typhoid, and bilious fevers have, within the past few years, been reduced to a minimum, and by comparison with other cities of the same size she has one of the best ratings in the United States.

Some few years ago it was considered unsafe to remain in the city during the summer months, and a general exodus used to take place. Now but few families think of leaving; in fact the population is greater during the summer months than it is in the winter. Thousands of people come from all parts of Georgia and neighbouring States to enjoy the sea breezes afforded by the islands around Savannah.

Tonnage. — There was a large increase in the number of British vessels entering and clearing at this port, and the tonnage was considerably in excess of any previous year. During the month of October alone 33 British steamships, with a tonnage of 43,138 tons, arrived at Savannah for cargo.

Imports and exports generally. — The imports and exports for the year have been very satisfactory.

Imports. — The annexed tables A and B show a small increase in the imports for the present year over 1888.

SAVANNAH.

Fertilisers. This article of importation shows a considerable increase over last year.

Cotton ties. The importation of cotton ties shows a large increase over last year, and is accounted for by the good crop.

Other articles. With the exception of the two articles abovementioned, the imports vary but little year after year.

Exports. Nearly all articles of export have very materially increased for the year 1889, as will be seen by reference to the annexed returns.

Cotton. I attribute the large increase in the exportation of cotton for the year 1889 to three things: first, the exceptionally fine weather throughout the whole cotton belt for the growing and making of the staple; second, the increased acreage planted in cotton; and thirdly, the additional territory available to the Savannah market by the increased railroad extension.

Cotton seed. The exportation of cotton seed continues to increase.

Lumber and timber. There was a considerable decrease in the lumber exported from here during 1889. This is accounted for by the fact that vessels secured cotton and other cargoes, offering more remunerative freights.

Spirits of turpentine. The exportation of spirits of turpentine forms a large portion of the export business of Savannah. Year by year a large increase is noticeable, and the trade is in every way satisfactory to all concerned.

Resin. A large increase is shown in the exportation of this article of commerce. The trade is continually growing, and there is every indication of it assuming very much larger proportions.

All other articles. The value of the exportations under this heading is nearly double that of 1888.

Annex A.—RETURN of Principal Articles of Export from Savannah during the Years 1889–88.

Articles.		1889. Quantity.	1889. Value.	1888. Quantity.	1888. Value.
			£		£
Cotton	Lbs.	232,687,650	4,923,312	159,183,557	3,117,426
,, seed	,,	1,336,680	2,452	1,008,260	1,653
Lumber and timber	Feet	15,011,786	27,083	30,128,000	46,226
Spirits of turpentine	Gallons	5,013,830	398,185	4,143,854	299,112
Resin	Lbs.	627,289	152,959	428,058	96,998
All other articles	...	...	16,952	...	8,568
Total		...	5,520,943	...	3,569,983

UNITED STATES.

RETURN of Principal Articles of Import from Savannah during the Years 1889–88.

Articles.		1889. Quantity.	1889. Value.	1888. Quantity.	1888. Value.
			£		£
Fertilizers	Tons	17,815	40,162	10,362	16,768
Cotton ties	Bundles	80,885	11,747	42,980	5,413
Salt	Lbs.	12,880,379	3,068	11,864,714	2,097
Rice	,,	...	...	4,959,639	14,423
Molasses	Gallons	61,100	1,937	77,923	2,885
Brimstone	Tons	3,200	11,913	1,245	3,865
Fruit and nuts	...	...	7,895	...	...
All other articles	...	...	20,963	...	25,289
Total	...	...	97,685	...	70,740

Annex B.—TABLE Showing the Total Value of all Articles Exported from Savannah and Imported to Savannah from and to Foreign Countries during the Years 1889–88.

Country.	Exports. 1889.	Exports. 1888.	Imports. 1889.	Imports. 1888.
	£	£	£	£
Britain	1,696,406	1,391,217	48,205	24,110
Germany	1,423,415	651,328	15,093	21,499
Spain	649,281	342,210	29	65
Russia	598,041	307,858	..	..
Netherlands	135,040	185,328	60	..
Belgium	242,170	134,298	1,685	401
Brazil	4,580	2,402	..	10
Italy	358,023	..	11,913	..
France	267,487	..	460	..
Other countries	146,500	555,342	20,240	24,655
Total	5,520,943	3,569,983	97,685	70,740

Annex C.—RETURN of all Shipping at the Port of Savannah in the Year 1889.

ENTERED.

Nationality.	Sailing. Number of Vessels.	Sailing. Tons.	Steam. Number of Vessels.	Steam. Tons.	Total. Number of Vessels.	Total. Tons.
British	27	15,580	96	120,762	123	136,342
American	51	24,867	386	323,695	437	348,562
Norwegian	109	56,278	8	3,862	117	60,140
German	35	18,261	3	4,426	38	22,687
Others	62	34,169	2	2,584	64	36,753
Total	284	149,155	495	455,329	779	604,484

SAVANNAH.

CLEARED.

Nationality.	Sailing. Number of Vessels.	Tons.	Steam. Number of Vessels.	Tons.	Total. Number of Vessels.	Tons.
British	26	13,584	89	110,140	115	123,724
American	46	21,238	371	307,090	417	328,328
Norwegian	99	50,484	8	3,862	107	54,346
German	36	18,201	4	5,627	40	23,828
Others	54	29,871	2	2,584	56	32,455
Total	261	133,378	474	429,303	735	562,681

LONDON:
Printed for Her Majesty's Stationery Office,
By HARRISON AND SONS,
Printers in Ordinary to Her Majesty.
(1250 5 | 90—H & S 853)

FOREIGN OFFICE.
1890.
ANNUAL SERIES.

N°. 718.

DIPLOMATIC AND CONSULAR REPORTS ON TRADE AND FINANCE.

UNITED STATES.

REPORT FOR THE YEAR 1889
ON THE
TRADE OF THE CONSULAR DISTRICT OF SAN FRANCISCO.

REFERENCE TO PREVIOUS REPORTS, Annual Series No. 555.

Presented to both Houses of Parliament by Command of Her Majesty,
JUNE, 1890.

LONDON:
PRINTED FOR HER MAJESTY'S STATIONERY OFFICE,
BY HARRISON AND SONS, ST. MARTIN'S LANE,
PRINTERS IN ORDINARY TO HER MAJESTY.

And to be purchased, either directly or through any Bookseller, from
EYRE & SPOTTISWOODE, EAST HARDING STREET, FLEET STREET, E.C., and
32, ABINGDON STREET, WESTMINSTER, S.W.; or
ADAM AND CHARLES BLACK, 6, NORTH BRIDGE, EDINBURGH; or
HODGES, FIGGIS, & Co., 104, GRAFTON STREET, DUBLIN.

1890.

Price Sixpence.

[C. 5895—121.]

New Series of Reports.

Reports of the Annual Series have been issued from Her Majesty's Diplomatic and Consular Officers at the following places, and may be obtained from the sources indicated on the title-page:—

No.		Price.	No.		Price.
596.	Serajevo	1d.	657.	Warsaw	½d.
597.	Copenhagen	1½d.	658.	Rome	1½d.
598.	Cephalonia	½d.	659.	Saigon	½d.
599.	Chefoo	½d.	660.	Buenos Ayres	½d.
600.	Guatemala	1½d.	661.	Galveston	1d.
601.	Tonga	½d.	662.	Galatz	1½d.
602.	Tahiti	1d.	663.	Antwerp	1d.
603.	Stettin	2d.	664.	Boston	1d.
604.	Vera Cruz	1½d.	665.	Madeira	½d.
605.	Christiania	4d.	666.	New Hebrides	½d.
606.	Pernambuco	1½d.	667.	Riga	1d.
607.	Trieste	1½d.	668.	Charleston	1d.
608.	Tunis	½d.	669.	Algiers	2d.
609.	Havana	2d.	670.	Stuttgart	1d.
610.	Frankfort	½d.	671.	Havre	3d.
611.	Tabreez	½d.	672.	The Piræus	1d.
612.	Bilbao	1d.	673.	Syra	1d.
613.	Barcelona	½d.	674.	Boulogne	1d.
614.	Tokio	1d.	675.	Taganrog	2d.
615.	Naples	2½d.	676.	Wuhu	½d.
616.	Batoum	½d.	677.	Batoum	1d.
617.	Odessa	1d.	678.	Manila	1d.
618.	La Rochelle	1d.	679.	Tamsui	1d.
619.	Rome	1d.	680.	Kiungchow	1d.
620.	Nice	1d.	681.	Swatow	1d.
621.	Kiukiang	½d.	682.	Stettin	6d.
622.	Paris	1d.	683.	Bordeaux	2½d.
623.	Salonica	1½d.	684.	Port Said	1d.
624.	Réunion	1d.	685.	Coquimbo	½d.
625.	Ichang	1d.	686.	Warsaw	1d.
626.	Bogotá	1d.	687.	Ichang	1d.
627.	Malaga	2d.	688.	Wênchow	1d.
628.	Porto Rico	1d.	689.	Trebizond	1d.
629.	Bushire	2½d.	690.	Damascus	½d.
630.	The Hague	½d.	691.	Savannah (Georgia)	1d.
631.	Berlin	1d.	692.	Barcelona	2½d.
632.	Adrianople	1½d.	693.	Santos	1d.
633.	Rome	1½d.	694.	San José	1d.
634.	Santiago	½d.	695.	Batavia	1d.
635.	Tahiti	½d.	696.	Genoa	1½d.
636.	Maranham	½d.	697.	Calais	2d.
637.	Mexico	2d.	698.	Marseilles	1d.
638.	Christiania	1d.	699.	Brest	1d.
639.	Copenhagen	1d.	700.	Lisbon	2½d.
640.	Paris	1d.	701.	Leghorn	2d.
641.	Venice	1d.	702.	Rio Grande do Sul	1d.
642.	Cherbourg	½d.	703.	Tainan	1d.
643.	New York	1d.	704.	Kewkiang	4d.
644.	Patras	1d.	705.	Fiume	1d.
645.	Bourgas	½d.	706.	Odessa	2d.
646.	St. Petersburg	3d.	707.	Suakin	½d.
647.	Taganrog	½d.	708.	Hankow	½d.
648.	Baltimore	1½d.	709.	Amoy	1d.
649.	New Orleans	2d.	710.	Buda-Pesth	1½d.
650.	New Orleans	1d.	711.	Corunna	2d.
651.	Samos	½d.	712.	Mogador	2d.
652.	Buda-Pesth	1½d.	713.	Cadiz	½d.
653.	Tripoli	½d.	714.	Cadiz	1d.
654.	Buenos Ayres	½d.	715.	Rio de Janeiro	2½d.
655.	Paris	1d.	716.	Newchwang	½d.
656.	Cherbourg	1d.	717.	Chinkiang	½d.

No. 718.

Reference to previous Report, Annual Series No. 555.

UNITED STATES.

SAN FRANCISCO.

Consul Donohoe to the Marquis of Salisbury.

My Lord, San Francisco, *April* 10, 1890.

I HAVE the honour to enclose herewith Annual Reports on the Trade and Commerce of San Francisco, Portland, Astoria, Port Townsend, Los Angeles, San Diego and Eureka, for the year 1889.

I have, &c.
(Signed) DENIS DONOHOE.

Report on the Trade and Commerce of San Francisco for the Year 1889.

There has been a fair increase in the trade of this port during the year 1889; this increase has been steady, and promises well for the future prosperity of San Francisco. — Trade increasing.

The crop of wheat has been one of the largest in this State ever known, and the area set out in wheat is estimated at 3,104,088 acres, and the yield at 30,196,509 centals. The farmers complain of low prices; for which, however, they are compensated by the increased yield of their land. The crop remaining on hand on December 1 is estimated at 15,300,360 centals. — Wheat.

The exports of flour show a large increase over 1888, in which year 827,425 barrels were exported, whilst this year 1,333,539 barrels were shipped. Great Britain received 425,529 barrels, and China and Japan 386,346 barrels. The market ruled low during the year. — Flour.

The crop of barley has been smaller, and prices lower than last year. There is a very great falling-off in the shipment; the quantity shipped to Great Britain is given as 352,962 centals. — Barley.

As I said in my report last year, the principal supply of salmon might be expected from the Alaska Canneries. The receipts in San Francisco in 1889 were as follows:— — Salmon.

UNITED STATES.

	Cases.
Alaska	646,801
Oregon	130,264
British Columbia	47,354
Puget Sound	8,206
Port Kenyon	1,800
Eureka	671
Crescent City	371
Fort Bragg	20
Sacramento	52,048
Total	887,535
Exports by sea	484,680
„ transit	44,699
By rail (11 months)	103,014
Total	632,393

There is thus, making liberal allowance for local consumption, at least 180,000 cases of this season's on hand on January 1, 1890.

Salmon pack. The entire pack of last season for the Pacific coast is as follows:—

	Cases.
Columbia river	426,300
Streams in Washington	85,000
California streams	70,500
Alaska streams	680,000
Total for United States	1,261,800
British Columbia total	422,000
Grand total	1,693,800

Value of pack. The value of the entire pack is given as 1,812,800*l.*

Dried fruits. It is difficult to estimate the dried fruit product of California, as no statistics are kept in the different producing counties, and every year fruit trees are being planted throughout the State in large numbers. A mercantile house largely engaged in this business gives the following estimate for the year:—

	Lbs.
Raisins, 20 lb. boxes, 900,000, or	18,000,000
„ in bags	1,000,000
Grapes „	2,000,000
French prunes	15,000,000
German and Hungarian prunes	200,000
Bleached and evaporated apricots	2,000,000
„ unpeeled peaches	2,500,000
„ peeled „	200,000
Sun-dried peaches	500,000
Bleached and evaporated nectarines	200,000
Pitted plums	200,000
Pears	50,000
Evaporated apples	400,000
Sun-dried „	100,000
Figs, black and white	100,000
Walnuts	1,500,000
Almonds	500,000
Extracted honey	2,000,000
Honey, in the comb	200,000
Bees-wax	30,000

SAN FRANCISCO.

The raisin crop did not come up to expectations as regards quantity, as the second crop of grapes was mostly destroyed by the heavy rains of the month of October. The quantity put on the market has, however, shown considerable improvement in quality, and the steady demand from the Eastern States has put up the price considerably. The demand for California dried fruits is steadily increasing, and though the export is small to foreign countries, the home demand at the Eastern and Central States is steady and constant.

Raisins, crop less than expected.

The actual shipment of canned fruits was as follows:—

Canned fruits.

	Cases.
By rail	529,760
„ sea	264,832
Total	794,592

A part of this shipment was of old stock.

Of that by sea the principal part went to Great Britain, Australia, and New York, and the rest was scattered everywhere.

The following is the estimated pack of the season:—

Description of canned fruit.

	Cases.
Apples	6,000
Apricots	40,000
Asparagus	5,000
Blackberries	5,000
Cherries, white	50,000
„ black	30,000
Currants	5,000
Gooseberries	15,000
Grapes	40,000
Nectarines	5,000
Pears	100,000
Peas	25,000
Peaches	150,000
Plums	50,000
Quinces	6,000
Raspberries	3,000
Strawberries	20,000
	555,000

MISCELLANEOUS.

	Cases.
Pie fruits	25,000
Tomatoes	150,000
Jams and jellies	30,000
Total	205,000
Grand total	760,000

The lumber receipts for the year were 476,506,931 feet as compared with 406,358,950 feet in 1888. The total export from the Pacific coast ports of the United States for the year have been 142,111,740 feet. Besides this 61,385 cubic feet of redwood has been exported to England.

Timber, increased receipts.

Redwood.

The estimated quantity made in California during the year is

Wine.

(886)

Small product.

14,500,000 gallons as compared with 17,000,000 gallons for 1888. The average in vines is said to be 180,000 acres against 150,000 in 1888. The great falling-off in the wine product is to be accounted for by the very low prices which have prevailed, and the large quantity of poor low-class wines which were only fit for distilling, and were disposed of in that way. Many of the vineyard owners dried their grapes, being induced to do this by low prices of wine, and a better return for their product under that form. The wine market rather rallied towards the end of the season, and new wines of 1889 vintage, for which only about 4d. to 5d. a gallon could be got in October, fetched at the end of the year 9d. to 10d.

Sugar.

The receipts of sugar at this port have increased, the principal supply coming from the Hawaiian Islands, and amounting to 111,302 tons. The receipts from Manila show a small falling-off as compared with 1888, and amounted during the year to 26,564 tons.

Coal.

The receipts of coal at this port were as follows:—

	Tons.
From British Columbia	381,460
„ Great Britain	43,678
„ Australia	303,285
„ Japan	4,540
Total	732,963

This is an increase of about 26,000 tons from 1888.

Quicksilver.

The total production of quicksilver in California in 1889 amounted to 25,650 flasks, as against 33,250 flasks in 1888. The average price for the year is 9l. per flask.

Metal product.

From the annual statement of Messrs. Wells, Fargo & Co., the net product of metals in the States and territories west of the Missouri river, excluding British Columbia and Mexico, for the last two years is given as follows:—

Year.	Gold.	Silver.	Copper.	Lead.	Total.
	£	£	£	£	£
1889	6,505,532	12,961,727	2,958,752	2,918,664	25,344,675
1888	5,997,540	10,630,550	3,652,298	2,252,726	22,533,114

The exports of silver during the past year to Japan, China, The Straits, &c., from San Francisco have been as follows—3,684,480l.

Freights.

The following table gives the rates for freights current during each month of the year:—

	Cork for Orders.	Liverpool.
	£ s. d. £ s. d.	£ s. d. £ s. d.
January	2 2 6 to 1 16 3	1 16 3 to 1 15 6
February	2 2 6 1 17 6	1 18 9 1 13 9
March	2 2 6 1 10 0	1 12 6 1 7 6
April	2 1 3 1 5 0	1 10 0
May	1 18 9 1 7 3	1 15 0 1 7 3
June	1 12 6 1 11 3	1 5 0 1 3 9
July	1 17 6 1 8 0	1 17 6 1 10 6
August	1 18 9 1 12 6	1 18 0 1 10 6
September	1 16 6 1 15 0	1 16 6 1 11 3
October	1 18 9 1 14 6	1 15 0 1 10 0
November	1 17 6 1 10 0	1 15 9 1 15 0
December	1 17 6 1 12 6	1 13 9 1 15 0

Manufacturing interests in California have always suffered from two causes, the first of which is the higher price of skilled labour as compared with the Eastern States. Of unskilled labour there is always a superabundance, owing to the number of Chinese, as well as the peculiar floating population which has drifted out to the Pacific coast, and has to take employment at any price that offers. The second difficulty which manufacturers encounter here is the high price of coal; the deposits of coal in this State may be said to be valueless and barely worth the expense of transportation, hence all supplies are drawn from the State of Washington, British Columbia, England, or Australia. I saw a statement made that to produce one horse-power an average steam-engine consumes three pounds of coal, and an engine of 200 horse-power will cost nearly 6l. a day more for fuel in this State than it would cost in any of the eastern manufacturing centres. It adds a good deal to the price of fuel to have to bring it from a distance of 1,000 miles or more and pay freight for its carriage: thus the price of coal in New York is about one-third of what it is in San Francisco. These causes have seriously affected the prosperity of many manufacturing concerns of various kinds that have been tried on the Pacific coast.

Manufacturing interests.

The very efficient Labour Commissioner of this State in an able report which he has just made states that a few years ago there were 12 woollen mills in California running 76 carding machines. At present only half that number are running with a capacity of only 28 carding machines. The principal mill on this coast, the Pioneer of San Francisco, has been obliged to close; this mill had 37 sets of carding machines and about 700 employés. The Commissioner in stating the collapse of the woollen manufacturing industry of California says:—

Woollen mills.

"Our manufacturers in California have not only been unable to sell goods to eastern buyers, but eastern manufacturers have shipped goods to this market and undersold manufacturers here. The Pioneer mills of San Francisco, erected especially for the purpose of woollen manufacture, and splendidly equipped with all the latest appliances for turning out a superior quality of goods, has lost money year after year, and the original shareholders could realise little more than 10 per cent. on their investment. The question of over-production affects all manufacturers alike, eastern as well as middle or western. One of the managers stated, however, that when eastern manufacturers have a large surplus of stock on hand, and are driven to the necessity of raising money, they generally send their goods to distant markets. In that way California has become a favourite dumping ground for overstocked eastern manufacturers, and our local mill-owners have suffered the consequences."

"Aside from this there are several valid reasons why Californian manufacturers are placed at a decided disadvantage in the effort to compete with those of the States east of the Rockies. These reasons, outside of some minor ones, may be summed up as follows:—Higher rate of interest on loans, higher wages paid to employés, higher prices paid for fuel, higher water rates, higher taxes, higher rates for insurance.

Real estate. The sales of real estate in this city for the year amounted to 6,753,814*l*., as against 4,948,896*l*. in 1888. The number of
Building. building improvements were 1,363, of a net value of 1,531,182*l*.
Railroads. About 130 miles of new roads have been opened to traffic during the year in California.
Business failures. The failures during the year are stated by the principal mercantile agency to be as follows:—San Francisco 193 failures, assets 85,153*l*., liabilities 212,100*l*., and for the balance of the State 520 failures, assets 395,990*l*., liabilities 647,793*l*.

Note.—All values in this report are reduced to sterling at the rate of 5 dol. to the 1*l*.

Annex A.—RETURN of all Shipping at the Port of San Francisco in the Year 1889.

ENTERED.

Nationality.	Sailing. Number of Vessels.	Sailing. Tons.	Steam. Number of Vessels.	Steam. Tons.	Total. Number of Vessels.	Total. Tons.
British	220	341,265	54	92,717	274	433,982
American, from foreign countries...	288	218,034	184	289,625	472	507,659
American, from Atlantic ports of Union ...	40	70,840	1	780	41	71,620
Hawaiian	20	10,110	33	55,582	53	65,692
German	17	20,302	...	...	17	20,302
Bolivian	9	7,845	2	1,698	11	9,543
Italian	5	5,316	...	...	5	5,316
Others	13	9,327	7	2,815	20	12,142
Total	612	683,039	281	443,217	893	1,126,256
,, for the year preceding	622	748,267	259	402,966	881	1,151,233

SAN FRANCISCO.

CLEARED.

Nationality.	Sailing.		Steam.		Total.	
	Number of Vessels.	Tons.	Number of Vessels.	Tons.	Number of Vessels.	Tons.
British	202	307,494	56	95,258	258	402,752
American, to foreign countries	285	240,001	171	279,774	456	519,775
American to Atlantic ports of Union	17	28,505	...	...	17	28,505
Hawaiian	18	8,725	36	58,183	54	66,908
German	24	28,257	...	...	24	28,257
Bolivian	8	7,100	3	2,547	11	9,647
Italian	4	4,336	...	...	4	4,336
Others	9	6,343	10	3,968	19	10,311
Total	567	630,761	276	439,730	843	1,070,491
„ for the year preceding	658	794,693	255	390,379	913	1,185,072

N.B.—The entries and clearances of American ships do not include the coasting trade, or whaling and fishing voyages.

Annex B.—RETURN of Principal Articles of Export from San Francisco during the Years 1888-89.

Articles.		1889.		1888.	
		Quantity.	Value.	Quantity.	Value.
			£		£
Wheat and flour	Tons	692,544	4,305,545	636,054	3,960,198
Tinned salmon	Cases	484,680	512,869	454,916	464,014
Wine	Gallons	3,649,441	307,063	333,157	43,738
Tinned fruits and vegetables	Cases	225,793	187,019	173,036	147,081
Barley	Centals	811,904	177,901	1,707,502	455,845
Timber	Feet	17,671,425	81,796	21,069,359	118,713
Quicksilver	Flasks	5,386	47,115	11,921	94,774
Brandy	Gallons	185,568	39,917	...	...
Other articles	...	...	3,795,594	...	2,878,669
Total	...	...	9,454,819	...	8,163,032

RETURN of Principal Articles of Import to San Francisco during the Years 1888-89.

Articles.		1889.		1888.	
		Quantity.	Value.	Quantity.	Value.
			£		£
Sugar	Tons	141,758	3,035,229	132,703	2,475,341
Raw silk	Lbs.	3,689,133	2,633,575	3,469,736	2,313,170
Coffee	„	20,272,586	584,760	22,237,226	567,672
Coals	Tons	732,963	515,861	706,826	498,308
Tin plates	Boxes	435,118	435,118	354,306	240,000
Rice	Tons	20,802	217,207	26,771	241,594
Tea	Lbs.	7,489,216	187,144	7,613,287	199,216
Cement	Barrels	251,406	50,030	355,899	88,975
Scrap-iron	Tons	18,105	58,836	26,505	64,262
Pig-iron	„	12,478	54,314	20,971	52,427
Bullion and coin	...	...	1,511,640	...	1,357,828
Other articles	...	...	993,947	...	1,623,047
Total	...	...	10,257,661	...	9,721,840

Annex C.—TABLE showing the Total Value of all Articles Exported from San Francisco and Imported to San Francisco from and to Foreign Countries during the Years 1888-89.

Country.	Exports. 1889.	Exports. 1888.	Imports. 1889.	Imports. 1888.
	£	£	£	£
Great Britain	3,845,683	3,682,200	926,916	1,169,826
Hawaiian Islands	690,551	567,410	2,814,830	2,241,617
China	535,534	495,289	1,070,473	1,267,554
Australia	450,762	365,011	324,386	276,032
Mexico	360,736	277,532	163,210	141,976
Central America	279,532	274,334	562,002	559,195
Canada	186,508	156,916	382,295	334,642
Japan	165,672	132,440	2,287,766	1,943,401
France	115,629	557,677	351,069	334,271
Pacific Islands	106,933	..	46,951	..
Belgium	41,234	50,362	118,531	184,455
Germany	13,799	22,608	235,953	201,709
Spanish Possessions	10,998	16,888	522,835	521,641
India	5,974	2,851	297,867	414,176
Domestic ports and other countries	2,645,274	1,561,514	152,577	131,345
Total	9,454,819	8,163,032	10,257,661	9,721,840

PORTLAND, OREGON.

Mr. Vice-Consul Laidlaw reports as follows:—

General trade. The general trade of this district was very much larger during the year 1889 than in any year past, and, although exports have decreased, import values are greater, and the value of manufactured produce show a gratifying increase. The shipments, viâ Tacoma, have decreased in a much greater proportion. The *Harvest.* harvest of wheat in the Willamette Valley was heavier, but, on account of the dryness of the season, that of Eastern Oregon was far below an average, both in quantity and quality. Oats were an exceptionally good crop. Prices of produce were generally *British tonnage.* lower than last year. As usual, the tonnage employed in the foreign trade was mostly British, the proportion to the whole having been 85 per cent.

Imports. A large proportion of the import trade is done by sail and rail from the Eastern States and San Francisco. There was a diminished import of rails, iron, steel, and cement, but a large increase in tin plates, salt, rice, tea, and hemp. The receipts of bags from India, cigars and tobacco from Cuba, upon which duties were paid here, were very much greater.

The British trade, as well in imports as in exports, was much smaller.

All of the window glass came from Belgium. About 600 tons of foundry coke were imported from England, and, of the coal imports, 2,929 tons were received from the United Kingdom,

7,408 tons from British Columbia, 14,698 tons from Australia. From coast mines, about 44,200 tons were brought to this market. The market laboured all the year under an overstock and unsatisfactory prices.

The total value of exports to foreign countries and by rail to the Eastern States was 16 per cent. less than during 1888. Estimated value of all produce shipped to the Eastern States and coastwise is 1,666,000*l*., last year's estimate being 1,860,280*l*. These figures are exclusive of shipments, viâ Yaquina Bay, to San Francisco. Trade in flour to China and Japan decreased, 49,684 sacks having been shipped, while last year's shipments were 61,502 sacks. One cargo of wheat was exported to Chile, and, owing to the increased facilities for shipment to British Columbia, the tables show a much larger export to that market. The total shipments of breadstuffs, both foreign and coastwise, were 440,490 quarters of wheat, of an estimated value of 570,700*l*., and 437,855 sacks of flour, valued at 492,667*l*. Average values during the year, about 25*s*. 6*d*. f.o.b. per quarter for Oregon Valley wheat, and 24*s*. 6*d*. for Eastern Oregon, better known as Walla Walla. Home consumption of breadstuffs has largely increased with the rapid increase of population. A new and important factor in the grain business is the establishment of terminal grain elevators both here and at Tacoma, with smaller feeders at interior points. These rival companies created much competition in Eastern Oregon and Washington, to the no small benefit of the farmers. Their tendency is to hold wheat rather than export it, and the prices here must, in the future, be largely dependent upon the action taken by these large companies. On the other hand, this method greatly simplifies the export business, rendering it easy to purchase an entire cargo or more when required, leaving the elevators to collect the small parcels together by their well organised system. The terminal elevator here is a huge building of wood, cased with galvanised iron, and, inclusive of machinery, costs over 40,000*l*. It is crowned with a three-story cupola, and its dimensions are 325 feet long, 134 feet high, and 68 feet wide, and is lighted by electricity. The lower story has a railroad track through it, and a number of cars can be unloaded at the same moment. The grain is hauled out of the cars by steam shovels into steam tanks, from which it is elevated to the top floor, where it may either be weighed or allowed to pass through cleaners, and then taken by lift to the scale floor, where there are 16 scales, each capable of weighing a car load. It is then spouted into the bins, of which there are 130, with a capacity of 1,000,000 bushels. By this method grain can be handled very cheaply and expeditiously, and can be shipped either in bulk or bags.

There has been a considerable decrease in receipts of wool from the Willamette Valley, but a large increase in those from Eastern Oregon and Washington. The average market value during the year was about 19 c., or 9½*d*. per lb. for Valley, and 17 c., or 7½*d*. per lb., for Eastern. These prices are higher than

Marginal notes: Exports, decrease. Coastwise and rail. Flour trade to China, &c. Wheat to Chile. Increased flour trade to British Columbia. Breadstuffs, total export. Increased home consumption. Elevator systems create a change in grain trade. Wool.

those of last year, and 1889 has, on the whole, been a satisfactory year to growers. In both sections, the quality was superior to that of 1888 wools. The following are the receipts and shipments during the past two years:—

| Year. | Receipts. || Shipments. ||
	Valley.	Eastern.	Viâ San Francisco.	By rail.
	Lbs.	Lbs.	Lbs.	Lbs.
During 1889	702,790	15,305,095	8,313,849	6,061,473
„ 1888	1,132,837	13,230,602	8,716,238	5,201,081

Hops—poor business last year. The consumption of the Oregon woollen mills reached about 1,750,000 lbs. Receipts of hops were smaller than last year, being only 2,074,058 lbs. The yield per acre was not as great as during 1888, and the quality was only fair. Prices were very poor and unremunerative to the grower, averaging about 8 c. (4d.) per lb. Some were contracted before picking as high as 12½ c. or 6¼d. per lb.

Timber. The lumber mills have been running throughout the year to their full capacity, and, although the foreign trade is small, a large coasting and interior trade has been done, and the total exports increased 5,845,000 feet.

Fisheries. Salmon product. Rail shipments. Canning not profitable now. The product of the salmon-packing establishments of the Columbia river was about 330,000 cases. By far the largest proportion is now shipped to the Eastern States, and the overland shipments from this were 212,911 cases. The average market price was about the same as last year, 6s. 6d. per dozen 1 lb. tins, f.o.b. here. The business is not profitable now, as cost of the raw fish is too high. Although the quality is much superior to any other fish, the Alaska and British Columbia product being cheaper, is now the most important factor in this business. Some quantity of fresh fish, salmon, sturgeon, and halibut, is annually sent east in refrigerator cars. There is a steam schooner now steadily employed fishing off the coasts of Oregon and Washington, she is owned by the Deep Sea Fishing Company of this place. A clearing house was opened here July 15. and its weekly clearings have averaged 246,566l. The money market has been more stringent during the past year, but accommodation has been obtainable for most legitimate business purposes. Exchange has been low the entire year, and at the close is lower than it has been for years past. Sixty days bills on London fluctuated between 4 dol. 77½ c. and 4 dol. 87 c. per 1l. sterling for bank, and from 4 dol. 77 c. to 4 dol. 86½ c. for mercantile.

Fishing Company.

Money market.

Clearing house.

Exchanges.

Shipping. The engagements of tonnage during the last two years, exclusive of coasting voyages, have been as under:—

Articles.	Register Tons.	
	1889.	1888.
Grain and flour cargoes	76,014	122,338
Salmon and assorted cargoes	5,334	4,189
Timber cargoes	5,129	8,268
Miscellaneous cargoes	1,152	1,655
Total	87,629	136,450

58 of these were British vessels, registering 74,274 tons. Last year 99 British ships, registering 118,215 tons, entered here.

Rates of freight averaged higher than last year, 2*l*. 12*s*. 6*d*. and 2*l*. 7*s*. 6*d*. being the highest, and 1*l*. 13*s*. and 1*l*. 10*s*. being the lowest for iron and wood respectively. The average was 2*l*. 3*s*. for iron and 1*l*. 16*s*. 8*d*. for wooden ships to a port in the United Kingdom, a large proportion giving option of Havre and Antwerp at the same rate as to the United Kingdom. There has been some increase in the number of steamers employed in the coasting trade, in the smaller craft only. The British ss. "Danube" continued to run regularly between this port and Vancouver, British Columbia. *Freights.* *Steam tonnage.*

Seamen's wages have been rather lower than last year, men having been often obtained at 5*l*. per month for able-bodied seamen. An Act passed by the legislature of Oregon, February 21, 1889, has done much to check the crimping business, and has lowered the percentage of desertion perceptibly. The boarding houses have been practically driven from this port, and the authorities have done everything possible to render the law effective. At Astoria, which is now the very paradise of the crimps, the local authorities have thrown every difficulty in the way of those interested in carrying out the provisions of the Act, but even there they have been afraid to carry on their nefarious business with the same open violence and contempt of law and decency as heretofore. A copy of the Act is given in annex D. *Sailors.* *Working of the new Act against crimps.*

The number and changes in crews of British ships entering this port during the year have been as under:—

Total Number of Crews.	Deserted.	Discharged.	Engaged.	Reported Dead.	Percentage of Desertions.	Hospital Permits.
1,628	157	81	140	5	9·65	11

With the exception of a few minor casualties the only damage done to any British ship was the sinking of the "Clan Mackenzie" while laying at anchor on her way up the river. She was run into and sunk by the steamer "Oregon," whose pilot mistook the ship's riding light for a range light. Two of the ship's crew were killed in their bunks, as the accident happened during the night. *Casualty.*

UNITED STATES.

River bars and channels. During the year the United States engineers continued the work of improving the rivers, and some dredging was done at Swan Island bar. A propeller steamer was used to sluice the bar at Skamokawa. The jetty at St. Helen's bar was extended, and considerable improvements made in the upper reaches of the Columbia and Willamette rivers.

Mouth of Columbia. The great jetty at the mouth of the Columbia was extended very considerably, and a marked improvement, as the work progresses, is showing itself in the main channels.

Minor harbours. The jetties at Yaquina, Coos Bay, and Coquille, have been extended more or less during the year.

Pilotage. Several amendments to the Acts relative to pilotage were passed by the last legislature. Rates of pilotage on the Columbia river bar, formerly 8 dol. per foot draft under 12 feet, and 10 dol. per foot over that draft, were reduced to 4 dol. per foot draft, and 2 c. per ton for each ton over 1,000 tons register; and river pilotage, formerly 4 dol. per foot draft, was reduced to 2 dol. per foot draft, and 2 c. per ton for each ton over 1,000 tons register. The provisions of this Act will be found in the Annex E. The State of Washington has concurrent jurisdiction over the Columbia river and rates of pilotage chargeable by pilots licensed by that State have not been reduced, which shipmasters should bear in mind.

Towage schedule. On May 21, 1889, the Oregon Railway and Navigation Company, which practically controls the business of bar and river pilotage and towage, guaranteed the following schedule of rates for two years as total charges for pilotage and towage from the sea, or from Astoria to Portland, and return by tugboats owned by the company and pilots in its employ:—

	Dol.
Vessels not exceeding 800 tons register	450
Over 800 tons register to 1,200 tons register	500
„ 1,200 „ 1,600 „	550
„ 1,600 „ 2,100 „	600
„ 2,100 „ (special agreement)	0
Use of tug's hawser	20 each way
Moving a vessel in port	10

Lighterage on grain and its products between Portland and Astoria, 50 c. per 2,000 lbs.

Lighterage on other freight 1 dol. per ton weight or measurement, at the Company's option.

Agriculture. Wheat. The past year has not been a profitable one for farmers, the wheat harvest in the Willamette Valley was large and fine, but prices were low. In Eastern Oregon the crop was a partial failure, caused by a dry season. Oats, barley, potatoes, and other farm produce did not bring remunerative prices; and hops were a drug in the market. The fruit crops generally were poor, but prices were high. The codlin moth caused much damage in the orchards.

Oats, &c.

Fruit.

Codlin moth.

Sheep and cattle. Profitable prices were realised for wool, and growers have had no reason to complain; but prices of cattle have been lower, and I am informed that this branch of husbandry has not been profitable, and that the large herds of cattle are being gradually driven off the ranges by sheep.

The immigration into Oregon and Washington continues large, and the increase of manufacturing enterprises in Portland has been very great. The following is a comparison of the last three years:— *Population and industries. Manufactures.*

Year.	Persons Employed.	Estimated Value of Product.
		£
1887..	3,380	1,560,880
1888..	5,000	2,776,990
1889..	7,500	3,951,600

The Oregon Iron and Steel Company at Oswego ran full blast nearly all the year, and produced about 10,000 tons of charcoal pig-iron. Its pipe works also run to their full capacity, using up a large proportion of this product. The company is putting in a Davis and Colby roasting furnace to increase capacity and utilise the waste gases from the furnace. More mines are being developed annually in Oregon, Washington, and Northern Idaho. It is impossible to procure reliable statistics of the gold product of Oregon mines, which are mostly to be found in Baker, Grant, Jackson, and Josephine counties. There are now opened up and operating over 12 mines in the Cœur d'Alene district of Northern Idaho, the average produce of which during the year was about 350 tons of concentrates daily, averaging about 70 per cent. lead, and 40 oz. silver per ton. *Oregon Iron and Steel Company. Mining.*

The appropriations by Congress for prosecution of the important work on the canal and locks at the cascades of the Columbia river have been so fitful and inadequate, that much money is wasted in protecting work already done, during enforced periods of idleness, for want of funds. Progress is, therefore, slow. The United States engineers continued the prosecution of this work, so often referred to in my previous reports. *Public works.*

There has been no construction in my district, but in some parts of Oregon and Washington there has been some addition made to branch lines of the roads terminating here. The Oregon Railway and Navigation Company has now become, by lease, practically a part of the Union Pacific system, and its 1,019 miles of road have been operated by the latter. The Oregon and California (475 miles) is leased and operated by the Southern Pacific Railroad Company, and the Oregonian Railway Company, a Dundee Corporation, with a narrow gauge system of 153 miles, connecting with the Portland and Willamette Valley Railroad, also narrow gauge, running to Portland, a distance of 30 miles, have both come under the control of the Southern Pacific Company. The Oregon Pacific Railroad, terminating at Yaquina Bay, has extended its road eastward during the past year. After crossing the Cascade Mountains, it will be continued to Boise City, Idaho. *Railways.*

Some little improvement has been made, but present terminal *Terminal facilities.*

facilities are a disgrace to the railroads interested. It is believed that some agreement will be arrived at and a fine passenger station be built or begun in 1890.

Street railways. The cable railway mentioned in my last report has been practically completed. During the year several miles of new electric lines have been built leading to suburban districts, and some of the horse-car lines are being changed into electric roads. These work very smoothly and satisfactorily, using an overhead wire and seeming to be under perfect control. The posts used are not ornamental to the streets.

City finances. Water bonds. Waterworks receipts, &c. The water commission sold the equivalent of 10,000*l.* more 5 per cent. bonds during the year, realising 9 per cent. premium. Receipts from the waterworks were equivalent to 26,640*l.*, and the disbursements to 16,281*l.*, in addition to the interest on 120,000*l.* outstanding bonds equal to 6,000*l.* Preparations are being made to increase the supply, and new pipes are being laid continuously.

Revenue. The total revenue of the city, exclusive of waterworks, but including balances carried over from 1888, was equivalent to 62,935*l.*, and the expenditures were 49,662*l.* Cost of improvements paid by owners of contiguous property were: street improvements 7,067*l.*, street extensions 2,677*l.*, and sewers 13,116*l.*

Payments by property owners.

Taxation. The State, county, city and school taxes aggregated 3·20 per cent. This city has never been what is called on this coast a "boom" town, but has steadily grown in wealth and importance. The following are the values of transfers and sales of real estate recorded in this county of Multnomah, over two-thirds being of city and suburban property, during the last three years:—

Remarks.

Real estate transactions.

	Dollars.	£
in 1887	5,864,081 =	1,172,816
1888	7,035,866 =	1,407,173
1889	14,140,352 =	2,828,070

Buildings. The magnificent hotel referred to in my last has been completed, also a beautiful opera house and the exhibition building was opened with great success during the year. There has been great activity in the building trade, and many fine brick business buildings have been completed, or are in course of construction.

Dwellings scarce. Dwellings are very scarce, and rents high, though a vast number have been built both in Portland and suburbs.

Labour. Skilled labour and labourers generally have been in demand throughout the year, and there is little excuse for any man willing to work going idle.

Health. There was some small-pox in this district early in the year, but it was speedily stamped out, and although malarious fevers are rather prevalent, the general health has been good.

NOTE.—The values given in this report are reduced to sterling at the average rate of 5 dol. per 1*l.* sterling.

Annex A.—Return of all Shipping at the Port of Portland, Oregon, in the Year 1889.

Entered.

Nationality.	Sailing. Number of Vessels.	Sailing. Tons.	Steam. Number of Vessels.	Steam. Tons.	Total. Number of Vessels.	Total. Tons.
British	57	72,120	19	10,663	76	82,783
American	...	...	...	...	...	...
Foreign	1	853	3	4,285	4	5,138
Atlantic	5	7,739	...	...	5	7,739
Coasting	18	4,630	249	300,197	267	304,827
German	3	3,151	...	...	3	3,151
Total	84	88,493	271	315,145	355	403,638
,, for the preceding year...	...	...	...	...	307	445,629

Cleared.

Nationality.	Sailing. Number of Vessels.	Sailing. Tons.	Steam. Number of Vessels.	Steam. Tons.	Total. Number of Vessels.	Total. Tons.
British	58	72,245	18	10,102	76	82,347
American	...	...	...	...	...	...
Foreign	5	7,015	3	5,085	8	12,100
Coasting	8	2,277	249	297,605	257	299,882
German	3	3,151	...	...	3	3,151
Total	74	84,688	270	312,792	344	397,480
,, for the preceding year...	...	...	...	...	315	447,853

Annex B.—Return of Principal Articles of Export from Portland, Oregon, during the Years 1889–88.

Articles.		1889. Quantity.	1889. Value.	1888. Quantity.	1888. Value.
			£		£
Wheat	Quarters ...	293,855	393,085	573,550	752,576
Wheat flour	Sacks ...	297,287	328,460	388,871	361,502
Timber	Thous. feet	1,713	3,828	2,093	3,905
Canned salmon	Pounds ...	48,000	1,300	...	...
Other articles	...	...	...	...	1,027
Total foreign exports	...	...	726,673	...	1,119,010

UNITED STATES.

Return of Principal Articles of Import to Portland, Oregon, during the Years 1889–88.

Articles.		1889. Quantity.	1889. Value.	1888. Quantity.	1888. Value.
			£		£
Coals	Tons	25,035	17,760	13,620	8,634
Tin and terne plates	Pounds	3,524,299	21,570	2,522,755	15,496
Rice	,,	2,818,305	10,171	2,096,645	6,595
Earthenware and glassware	...	...	16,633	...	12,313
Salt	Pounds	5,361,632	3,745	4,782,310	2,979
Cement	Barrels	24,579	4,981	37,637	6,757
Cigars and tobacco	,,	40,147	17,289	...	8,238
Wines and liquors	...	...	2,659	...	3,231
Beer, porter, and ale	Gallons	13,033	1,779	36,742	5,026
Soda and chemicals	Pounds	639,334	1,116	...	1,236
Oils	Gallons	15,437	492	21,477	1,567
Pig iron	Tons	1,054	2,923	1,900	4,097
Rails, bar iron, and manufactures of iron and steel	,,	4,759	27,653	20,533	92,577
Firebricks	Number	399,725	432	706,960	1,344
Tea	Pounds	193,741	4,537	128,356	1,636
Hemp	Tons	506	21,161	110	3,280
Glass	Pounds	1,253,138	4,491	1,431,169	4,622
Bags and bagging	...	...	30,194	...	...
Manufactures of silk	...	...	5,230	...	...
Pickles and sauces	...	...	1,350	...	...
All other articles	...	...	10,748	...	24,662
Total foreign imports	...	...	206,914	...	204,290

N.B.—The above returns do not include exports or imports coastwise or by rail, with the exception of articles transported in bond.

Annex C.—Table showing the Total Value of all Articles Exported from Portland and Imported to Portland, Oregon, from and to Foreign Countries during the Years 1889–88.

Country.	Exports 1889.	Exports 1888.	Imports 1889.	Imports 1888.
	£	£	£	£
Great Britain	640,619	998,377	100,396	157,332
Belgium	..	..	5,061	3,898
British Columbia	21,636	516	1,276	7,498
China and Japan	55,170	40,009	31,521	22,578
Australia	..	..	9,368	2,518
Peru and Chile	8,820	2,200	..	..
France	..	77,908	739	752
Germany	..	..	..	1,779
Cuba	..	..	17,632	7,935
Philippine Islands	..	..	22,348	..
India	..	..	18,769	..
All other countries	428	..	404	..
Total	726,673	1,119,010	206,914	204,290

Annex D.—An Act passed February 21, 1889, for the Prevention of, and Punishment for Enticing and Harbouring Seamen from Ships, Steamers and other Vessels at the Ports of Portland and Astoria, Oregon, U.S.A.

Be it enacted by the Legislative Assembly of the State of Oregon:—

Sec. 1. That Sec. 1952, of the general laws of Oregon, as annotated by William Lair Hill, be amended to read as follows:—

Sec. 1952. That if any person or persons shall entice, persuade, or by any means attempt to persuade any seaman to desert from, or without permission of the officer then in command thereof, to leave or depart from, either temporarily or otherwise, any ship or steamer or other vessel, while such ship, steamer or other vessel is within the waters under the jurisdiction of this State, or within the waters of concurrent jurisdiction of this State and the Territory of Washington, such person or persons shall, upon conviction thereof before any justice of the peace, or before a circuit court of this State, be punished by imprisonment in a county jail for not less than 1 nor more than 6 months, or by a fine not less than 50 dol. nor more than 200 dol., or by both such fine and imprisonment.

Sec. 2. That Sec. 1953, of the general laws of the State of Oregon, as annotated by William Lair Hill, be amended to read as follows:—

Sec. 1953. If any person shall knowingly, and with manifest intention to deprive the owner or master of any ship or vessel, of the service of any seaman, harbour or secrete, or by any means aid in harbouring or secreting, with the intention aforesaid, any seaman mentioned in this Act, such person or persons shall, upon conviction thereof before a justice of the peace or circuit court, be punished by imprisonment in the county jail not less than 60 days nor more than 6 months, or by a fine of not less than 50 dol. nor more than 250 dol.

Sec. 3. If any person or persons shall demand or receive, either directly or indirectly, from any seaman or apprentice, or from any person seeking employment as a seaman or apprentice, or from any person on his behalf, any remuneration whatever for providing him with employment on board a sea-going vessel, he shall for every such offence, on conviction thereof before any justice of the peace or circuit court of this State, be punished by imprisonment in a county jail for a period not less than 10 nor more than 100 days, or by a fine not less than 20 dol. nor more than 200 dol.

Sec. 4. If any person or persons shall demand or receive, either directly or indirectly, from any owner or master, or agent of owner or master of a sea-going vessel, any remuneration whatever, other than a fee of 10 dol. per man, for supplying any seaman or apprentice to be entered on board such sea-going vessel, he shall for every offence, on conviction thereof before a justice of the peace or circuit court, be punished by imprisonment in a county jail for a period not less than 10 nor more than 100 days, or by a fine not less than 20 dol. nor more than 200 dol.

Sec. 5. If any person, not acting in an official capacity, shall board or attempt to board any ship or vessel on the Willamette or Columbia river, not engaged in the carrying of passengers for hire, without the consent first obtained of the captain, master or other officer in command thereof at the time, such person, on conviction thereof before any justice of the peace or circuit court, shall be fined not less than 20 dol. nor more than 100 dol., or be imprisoned in a county jail not less than 10 nor more than 100 days, or both.

Sec. 6. No officer or seaman of a sea-going vessel or ship shall be arrested or imprisoned for debt; and any officer executing a process of arrest for debt upon such officer or seaman shall, upon conviction thereof before any justice of the peace or circuit court, be fined in a sum not less than 20 dol. nor more than 100 dol.

Sec. 7. It is hereby made the duty of the mayor and common council of the cities of Portland and Astoria, in this State, severally to appoint or designate a person or officer, whose duty it shall be to see that this Act is not violated and that the provisions thereof are enforced; and such person or officer, so appointed or designated, shall have all the authority and powers of a peace officer, and may make arrests for violations of the provisions of this Act, and shall perform such other duties as to the enforcement of this Act as may be enjoined upon him by the common council of said cities respectively, and shall receive such compensation for his services as said common council may by ordinance provide.

Annex E.—A BILL for an Act to Amend Title 1 of Chapter 66 of Hill's Annotated Laws of Oregon, relating to Pilotage at the Columbia River Bar, and on the Columbia and Willamettte Rivers.

Be it enacted by the Legislative Assembly of the State of Oregon:—

Sec. 1. That Sec. 3894 of Hill's Annotated Laws of Oregon be, and the same is hereby amended so as to read as follows:—Sec. 3894. Each of said commissioners shall be commissioned by the Governor, and before entering upon the duties of his office, shall take and subscribe an oath of office, and file the same with the Secretary of State, to the effect that he will support the Constitution of the United States and of this State, and faithfully discharge the duties of the office of pilot commissioner according to law and the best of his ability. A person to be eligible to the office of pilot commissioner under this Act shall be over 21 years of age, must be a citizen of the United States and of this State, and two of said commissioners must have been engaged as master or mate of sea-going vessels or steamers, and to have at least two years' experience as such master or mate, prior to their election as such commissioners.

Sec. 2. That Sec. 3904 of Hill's Annotated Laws of Oregon

be, and the same is hereby amended so as to read as follows:—
Sec. 3904. The board has the power, and it is its duty, under this Act, to maintain a sufficient number of capable pilots upon the bar and river pilot grounds, and to exercise a general supervision over the subject of pilotage upon said grounds, and to that end may do and provide as follows:—

1. Examine and license pilots for said pilot grounds.
2. Hear and determine all complaints against any of said pilots.
3. Make and alter rules for the government of such pilots, and the maintenance of an efficient pilot service on the pilot grounds aforesaid not inconsistent with the laws of this State or of the United States; and to enforce the same by any lawful and convenient means, including the suspension or removal of any such pilot, and the imposition on him of a penalty not exceeding 250 dol. for any violation thereof.

Sec. 3. That Sec. 3906 of Hill's Annotated Laws of Oregon be, and the same is hereby amended so as to read as follows:—
Sec. 3906. An application for a pilot's license must be made in writing to the board, stating briefly the applicant's name, place of birth, age and experience as a navigator and pilot; and if, upon examination, such applicant is found worthy and qualified as herein provided, he shall be licensed for the term of one year.

Sec. 4. That Sec. 3908 of Hill's Annotated Laws of Oregon be, and the same is hereby amended so as to read as follows:—
Sec. 3908. No person shall be licensed as a pilot by the board unless he is an American citizen of the age of 21 years, of temperate habits, and good moral character; nor unless he possesses the requisite skill and experience as a navigator and pilot, together with practical knowledge of the currents, tides, soundings, and bearings, and distances of the several shoals, rocks, bars, points of land, lights, and fog signals, of or pertaining to the navigation of the pilot ground, for which he applies for a license to act as pilot; nor in case of the bar pilot ground, unless it satisfactorily appears that the applicant is provided with, or is attached to, a pilot boat or tug boat.

Sec. 5. That Sec. 3910 of Hill's Annotated Laws of Oregon be, and the same is hereby amended so as to read as follows:—
Sec. 3910. A person whose application for a pilot license has been refused may apply again after the expiration of six months, but not sooner; and a person whose license has been revoked or withheld for negligently, ignorantly, or wilfully running a vessel aground or on shore, or otherwise putting her in danger of serious injury, is thereafter ineligible to receive a license as pilot.

Sec. 6. That Sec. 3912 of Hill's Annotated Laws of Oregon be, and the same is hereby amended so as to read as follows:—
Sec. 3912. The pilot schooner belonging to the State of Oregon shall be under the direction and control of the Board of Pilot Commissioners, who shall establish rules and regulations for the use thereof; and said board shall be, and is hereby empowered to insure said schooner for the full amount of the value of the

same, and to equip and maintain said schooner in good seaworthy condition. And there is hereby appropriated out of the moneys in the Treasury, not otherwise appropriated, the sum of 1,500 dol. annually for such insurance and maintenance. The president of the board shall act as agent, husband, and managing owner of said pilot schooner on behalf of the State of Oregon; and in the event of such schooner being lost or disabled, it shall be the duty of said board to provide the pilots with an adequate vessel in which to ply their vocation as bar pilots until said board can conveniently purchase or construct a suitable pilot schooner to take the place of the schooner so lost or disabled, the amount of money so expended not to exceed the amount received on the policy of insurance, and a sum, together with the insurance, that shall not exceed 10,000 dol. Said schooner shall be kept cruising at all times outside the Columbia river bar, with bar pilots on board, unless prevented by tempestuous weather; and said schooner shall at all times, and at the expense of the pilots, carry such sufficient supply of provisions and water as may be necessary for the relief of vessels in distress, and such pilots must at all times extend aid to all vessels in stress of weather or in case of disaster; and if any such pilot or pilots fail to comply with any of the provisions of this section, it shall be good cause for suspension or removal; provided that this section shall not affect any claim for salvage arising out of services involving extraordinary danger or risk.

Sec. 7. That Section 3918 of Hill's Annotated Laws of Oregon be, and the same is hereby amended so as to read as follows:—Sec. 3918. The compensation allowed for piloting a vessel upon or over the bar pilot grounds per foot draft of said vessel is as follows: For piloting an inward or outward bound vessel to or from Astoria over the bar, or from within the bar to the open sea, 4 dol. per foot draft of said vessel, and 2 c. a ton for each ton over 1,000 tons, registered tonnage of said vessel; from or within the bar, and below Sand Island, one-half that rate; and from or above Sand Island, one-quarter of the same.

Sec. 8. That Sec 3919 of Hill's Annotated Laws of Oregon be, and the same is hereby amended so as to read as follows:— Sec. 3919. The compensation for piloting a vessel upon the river pilot ground per foot draft of such vessel between Astoria and Portland, whether ascending or descending, is 2 dol. per foot draft, and 2 c. for each ton over and above 1,000 tons registered tonnage of said vessel, which sum shall include services of said pilot for taking said vessel to and from the dock to and from which said vessel is destined; and the board is authorised to prescribe a proportionate compensation for pilot service between other points on said ground, and for moving a ship in port from one dock to another, or for one part of the dock to another of the same dock; the charge therefor shall be a sum not exceeding 5 dol., and the pilot shall, on being thereunto requested by the master of a ship, be required to do such work, and for such compensation. Every river pilot appointed and qualified under the provisions of this Act is required to render his services promptly for the compensation provided by law in piloting any vessel up or down the Columbia or Willamette rivers when requested by the master of such vessel. If a river pilot shall speak a vessel as herein provided, and the services of such pilot or some other river pilot licensed under this Act, selected by the master of such vessel, shall be rejected by such master, the pilot first speaking said vessel shall be entitled to half pilotage, to be recovered of said master or vessel.

Sec. 9. That Sec. 3920 of Hill's Annotated Laws of Oregon be, and the same is hereby amended so as to read as follows:—
Sec. 3920. The pilot who first speaks a vessel not exempt from compulsory pilotage, as provided in Sec. 3917, or duly offers his services thereto, as a pilot, on or without the bar pilot ground, is entitled to pilot such vessel over the same. The master may decline to accept the services of any pilot and may navigate his vessel over said pilot grounds without a pilot, but, nevertheless, he shall, if inward bound, pay to the pilot who first speaks his vessel, one-half of the amount of pilotage to which said pilot would have been entitled if his offer had been accepted and the services performed accordingly, and if outward bound the master may contract with any bar pilot licensed under this Act.

Sec. 10. That Sec. 3927 of Hill's Annotated Laws of Oregon be, and the same is hereby amended so as to read as follows:—
Sec. 3927. A pilot who receives a license under this Act, must pay therefor to the secretary a fee of 10 dol., and for each yearly renewal thereof a fee of 5 dol., and must once a month make to the board a statement in writing of all moneys received by him during the month last past for pilotage, together with the date of such receipt, the name, tonnage, draft, nationality, and class of the vessel, and the name of the master thereof, from which the same was received.

Sec. 11. That Sec. 3933 of Hill's Annotated Laws of Oregon be, and the same is hereby amended so as to read as follows:—
Sec. 3933. The fees and compensation of the pilot commissioners and of the secretary shall be as follows: For the granting and execution of a branch or warrant, 10 dol. to be paid by the applicant; for hearing and determining any complaint, 5 dol. per day each, to be paid out of the State Treasury on the warrants of the Secretary of State; for making semi-annual tours of inspection, and their report to the legislative assembly, 200 dol. each per annum, to be paid semi-annually out of the State Treasury on the warrants of the Secretary of State, who is authorised and required to audit and allow the same; provided, that if any member of the board shall fail to make such tour of inspection, in such case no warrant shall be issued to such member. The secretary shall receive a salary of 600 dol. per annum, out of the State Treasury on the warrants of Secretary of State, who is authorised and required to audit and allow the same.

Sec. 12. That Secs. 3923 and 3924 of Hill's Annotated Laws of Oregon be, and the same are hereby repealed.

ASTORIA.

Mr. Vice-Consul Cherry reports as follows:—

General business. Has steadily improved during the past year, the whole district showing a large increase in wealth and population.

Imports. Show an increase mostly in tin plates from the United Kingdom.

Tin plates. The retail price of tin plates in jobbing lots was from 1*l.* to 1*l.* 2*s.* per box of 10 coke steel plates B.V. grades.

Salt. But little difference is to be noted, the price for F.F. Liverpool being 3*l.* 10*s.* per ton.

Coal. An increase on the previous year is to be noted, but the price is somewhat lower 1*l.* 8*s.* to 1*l.* 10*s.* per ton for Newcastle, N.S.W., Wallsend coal.

Exports. Show a large increase in all articles excepting wheat, and a total higher value than last year.

Canned Salmon. Shows a large increase both in amounts and values, besides an invoice cleared through by San Francisco to the United Kingdom.

Wheat. As stated shows a falling-off in amount and a decline in value from the preceding year.

Flour. Shows increased values as well as volume.

Lumber. Shows a large increase which would have been larger if the freight rate had been lower, and vessels for the trade were more easily to be had.

Manufacturing industries, lumber. Shows a steady increase, but as heretofore the bulk of the output is taken by California by coasting craft. The foreign trade suffering for want of suitable vessels, four coasters being pressed into service for the Australian trade. The lumber trade will reach large proportions in the very near future.

Salmon fishing. The total salmon fishing of the Columbia river shows a small increase in the amount packed, the fishermen received 5*s.* per fish, but certain allowances brought the price up to 5*s.* 6*d.* and 6*s.* received for each fish.

The catch—owing to the low summer rise in the Columbia river, which left the fish wheels out of water—was confined almost altogether to the lower Columbia from the sea to 50 miles up.

Seives and traps are slowly pushing out the gill net fishing, the latter being very much more expensive to the cannerymen as they have to bear the frequent losses occasioned by careless fishermen. The business is steadily by force of circumstances falling into fewer hands. The number of canneries are diminishing, and consequently the competition among the cannerymen will not be so great.

Preparations for fishing. At the present no preparations are being made for the coming fishing season as heretofore has been the custom.

Salmon packing. The prices received for canned salmon was better than that of the year before, going up to from 1*l.* 6*s.* 6*d.* to 1*l.* 8*s.* per case of 48 1 lb. tins, but a higher price paid for raw fish took the extra profits. The latter part of the season the price fell rapidly, owing to the reported large pack in Alaska and British Columbia.

I understand that a number of the new canneries started in Alaska, in 1889, met with losses on account of the great expenses incident to starting, and the cost of freight and keep up there.

The pack of this district:—

	Cases.
The Columbia river spring catch	3[illegible]1,000
" " inferior fish	42,000
" " fall fish	1,000
Total	364,400

as compared with a total of 373,000 cases in 1888, showing a slow but steady decline.

	Cases.
On the coast north of the Columbia	54,000
" south "	84,500
Total	128,500

Sturgeon fishing.

This is becoming an industry of growing importance; the consumption, however, is confined entirely to the domestic market of the United States. The fishermen received 1*d.* per pound gross weight; the raw fish are taken to the nearest railway, and there it is cut into convenient pieces, packed in ice, and sent to New York by rail, part of which is retailed fresh, and the bulk is reported to be smoked, and some canned, the market price there being 5*d.* per lb.

The catch at different points of the Columbia river amounts to from 20 tons to 25 tons per day, and is practically an all the year fishery, and consequently giving steadier employment to the fishermen than the salmon one, which lasts but 100 days in the year.

Fisheries of the Columbia river.

The fisheries of this river will, in a few years, when transportation is cheaper and easier, and population is larger, be enormous, and I believe, although the salmon pack is diminishing, it is yet only in its infancy.

Shipping.

There is a marked falling-off in the arrivals of vessels for the year, those under the British flag showing the largest amount.

This is occasioned by the low-price offered for grain, and the comparatively high freight rates. Part of this freight rate is chargeable to the fact that all vessels in the grain trade have to go up the river for over 100 miles to Portland, and as the river is at its lowest during the grain shipping season, it has become the custom to detain vessels till the spring tides to enable them to come down at their best draught, and over this all lighterage is charged to the vessel, and when laden the master has to return to Portland to settle accounts. These delays I have found average from eight to ten days more than if the vessel had taken on her cargo at this port. This detention, together with the fluctuating lighterage charges, is charged for by owners at the maximum, much to the detriment of the commerce of the Columbia river.

Government improvements.

A great deal of work has been done during the past year on the jetty of the mouth of the Columbia river. This jetty has been extended for a distance of over two miles, with the most satisfactory result of deepening the entrance on the shoalest place by three feet, besides washing away a large extent of sands known as the "outer middle sands," thereby increasing the width of the entrance, and making it more accessible.

Internal improvements.

The citizens of this town and the county subscribed a sufficient sum to commence the construction of a railroad to a junction with a transcontinental line in the interior, the distance being about 85 miles. This road is now under construction, and will doubtless be finished within the contract time, October, 1891.

Besides this railroad two other transcontinental lines are preparing surveys, &c., for a connection with their lines to this port.

Results.

The result of this is already shown in the enhanced value of property in this town and neighbourhood, and it will no doubt be the means of keeping a fair proportion of the grain shipping at this port, as well as to develop the lumber export trade, and the opening out of some extensive coal beds to the south of this, and now quite inaccessible.

Law protecting seamen.

A law enacted by the last legislature for the punishment of men engaged in enticing seamen to desert, and then reshipping them at a heavy expense to owners, came into operation, and was effectually carried. It has the effect of reducing the number of desertions at this port to a small figure, but I notice that the desertions in Portland, Oregon, have increased during the same period.

Health.

Health has remained uniformly good for the past year.

Annex A.—RETURN of all Shipping at the Port of Astoria, Oregon, United States, during the Year 1889.

ENTERED.

Nationality.	Sailing. Number of Vessels.	Sailing. Tons.	Steam. Number of Vessels.	Steam. Tons.	Total. Number of Vessels.	Total. Tons.
British	60	75,663	...	...	60	75,663
American	6	5,798	5	2,176	11	7,974
German	3	2,938	...	...	3	2,938
Equadorian	1	778	...	...	1	778
Total	70	85,177	5	2,176	75	87,357
,, for preceding year	...	...	...	...	125	137,014

CLEARED.

Nationality.	Sailing. Number of Vessels.	Sailing. Tons.	Steam. Number of Vessels.	Steam. Tons.	Total. Number of Vessels.	Total. Tons.
British	55	86,211	...	...	55	86,211
American	8	2,026	7	7,628	15	9,654
German	3	3,125	...	...	3	3,125
Equadorian	1	778	...	...	1	778
Total	67	92,140	7	7,628	74	99,768
,, for preceding year	...	...	...	...	137	157,600

Annex B.—RETURN of Principal Articles of Export from Astoria, Oregon, United States, during the Years 1889-88.

Articles.		1889.		1888	
		Quantity.	Value.	Quantity.	Value.
			£		£
Preserved salmon	Cases	135,614	189,900	74,095	109,761
Wheat	Bushels	559,090	91,800	864,382	149,729
Flour	Barrels	54,210	44,450	38,357	28,657
Sawn lumber	M. feet	5,239	10,353	2,723	7,030
Sundries	...	...	520	...	891
Total		...	337,023	...	293,068

RETURN of Principal Articles of Import.

Articles.		1889.		1888.	
		Quantity.	Value.	Quantity.	Value.
			£		£
Tin plates	Boxes	35,300	35,650	33,405	33,405
Salt	Tons	103	120	180	223
Coal	,,	3,343	2,344	2,347	1,723
Sundries	...	...	285	...	80
Total		...	38,399	...	35,441

Annex C.—TABLE showing the Total Value of all Articles Exported from Astoria, Oregon, and Imported to Astoria, Oregon, from and to Foreign Countries during the Years 1889-88.

Country.	Exports.		Imports.	
	1889.	1888.	1889.	1888.
	£	£	£	£
Great Britain	300,000	263,000	23,000	22,037
British colonies	7,400	1,511	2,360	1,729
Other countries	3,450	30,341	..	1
Total	310,850	294,852	25,360	23,767

PORT TOWNSEND.

Mr. Vice-Consul Alexander reports as follows:—

I have the honour to submit to you most respectfully my sixth annual report for the year ending December 31, 1889, giving you briefly a summary of the commerce and trade of the State of Washington during this period.

In procuring the data for the statistical portion of this report, and the several annexes, I have been materially assisted by C. M. Bradshaw, Esq., collector of customs at this port, who has courteously given me free access to the records in the customhouse.

UNITED STATES.

Geographical delimitations of Washington State.

For the benefit of those who may desire to know the character and general condition of this new State, Washington is the extreme northwest State of the Union; it lies between parallels of latitude 45 degrees 30 minutes and 49 degrees north, and of longitude 117 degrees and 124 degrees 45 minutes west. Its greatest length is 340 miles east and west, and its greatest breadth 240 miles. It embraces an area of 64,944 square miles. It is bounded on the north by the straits of San Juan du Fuca and British Columbia, on the east by Idaho, on the south by Oregon and the Columbia river, and on the west by the Pacific Ocean. The territory was organised by Act of Congress of March 2, 1853, when it was separated from Oregon. The Act enabling Washington to come into the Union as a State was passed February 22, 1889, and the presidential proclamation was issued November 11, 1889. It has, therefore, been a State only since that time. Its politics are republican. The advantage of the new condition over the old cannot well be appreciated by persons who have not lived in a territory. It amounts practically to the difference between dependent government and self government. The territorial officers were appointed by the president, generally of foreigners to the needs of the territory. Money for the territorial administration was provided, often too sparingly, by Congress.

Legislation.

The laws governing the territory were complex, often harmful. Now conditions are changed. Public affairs are administered at home, and the various cities and towns of the new State are unhampered by unreasonable limitations upon public enterprise. Indebtedness can be incurred by cities aggregating for all purposes 10 per cent. of the assessable property, and the State can create a funded debt of 80,000*l*. The new constitution just adopted is generally considered a wise and conservative document. It contains no burdensome and unusual restrictions either upon corporations or individuals, capital or labour. Railroads will be governed by a railroad commission, and reasonable maximum rate laws. Money is subject to no usury laws, and the rate of interest is therefore governed entirely by the laws of supply and demand. The average is 8 to 10 per cent. Wages are good, the labourer earning from 8*s*. to 10*s*. per day; skilled labour secures very much better pay, say, average of 16*s*. The cost of living is reasonable, rents are high, but the advantages to the homeseeker much more than counterbalance this drawback, which can at the most be only temporary.

Taxation.

Taxation for all purposes except city, state, county, school, and road, averages about 18 mills. The only heavy tax in cities is the road tax, incurred in the extension of streets, but it is invariably assessed to the abutting property, and is therefore not general.

The burden of taxation will undoubtedly be lightened within a very few years by vast state or county funds that will accrue from the sale of what is known as "tide," or "shore," lands on Puget Sound, and on the sea coast. These are "mud flats" between high and low water mark, and exposed at low water.

They cover a great area in the harbours of Puget Sound, and being adjacent to the business portions of cities, are very valuable. The tide lands of Puget Sound are at a rough estimate worth about 2,000,000*l*. These lands are now the State's, and are to be disposed of by sale. It is estimated that the interest from the accruing fund will within a very few years bear all the expenses of the State government. The general government has likewise given the State nearly 3,000,000 acres of land for school purposes. This land cannot be sold for less than 2*l*. per acre. When disposed of there will be realised in the aggregate a school fund of 6,000,000*l*. at the lowest possible estimate. Over 600,000 acres of land were donated by Congress for public buildings, scientific schools, State university, normal schools, and agricultural college, &c.

The State is divided into two great parts by the Cascade Mountains, known as Eastern and Western Washington. The general characteristics of the West are its nearly unbroken covering of timber, and its great deposits of coal and iron ; and of the East, its wide and almost uninterrupted range of tillable land. There is a further separation of Western Washington into the Puget Sound country, consisting of the counties bordering upon the Sound, and the coast and river region, comprising those counties adjacent to the Columbia river, and on the Pacific Ocean. Eastern Washington is divided into districts or counties. The distinction between these districts arises through a difference of natural products, or because of some natural barrier or stream separating one from another. Their products are so rich and varied as to make the new State one of the most diversified and infinite in resources; it is the gradual recognition of this fact which has stimulated the growth of the State beyond all expectation, and caused an inflow of immigration, within the past three years, almost unprecedented in the history of Western States. *State division.*

As an agricultural and fruit-producing State Washington possesses the elements which promise a great future. Commerce, mining, and manufacture will always furnish employment to a large portion of the population, but agriculture and fruit raising will be the leading industries. That part of Eastern Washington known as the Columbia river basin is devoted almost exclusively to grain and stock production. This famous " wheat belt " of the inland empire has an average width of about 25 miles, and extends about 300 miles in the State of Washington. The soil is uniformly rich, a dark loam. The average yield per acre is about 20 or 25 bushels of wheat. The climate, permitting nine months of farm work, with few interrupting rains in the spring, and none in harvest time, enables the farmer to overcome obstacles of transportation, &c., incident to a new country, and undersell almost any country in the world's market. The price averages about 2*s*. 6*d*. per bushel. Failures are practically unknown in the wheat crop. Not one-tenth of this land is at present cultivated. The lands are yet quite cheap; railroads are being built, and a strong stream of immigrants is pouring into the country. The *Agriculture.*

Fruit.

immigrant need only turn over the virgin soil and harvest a good crop the second year.

The varieties of fruit most commonly produced are apples, pears, peaches, prunes, plums, cherries, quinces, and grapes; also strawberries, raspberries, gooseberries, cranberries, huckleberries, and currants. These are grown with great success in all parts of the western division, and on the agricultural lands and in the timber of the eastern division. Almost every farmer now plants an orchard. Any kind of vegetable can be grown to perfection in this State, with the exception of corn, maize, and Indian corn. The production of hay is one of the common and most profitable industries of Western Washington, and, I may say, when near a market, the most profitable; it can be grown at 28s. per ton, and sells readily from 40s. to 60s., according to the season, sometimes going up to 120s. Hop growing is carried on principally along the eastern shore of Puget Sound. The crop in 1889 was about 35,600 bales. The acreage is about 4,500, and the yield about 1,600 lbs. to the acre. The cost of production is not over 4d. per lb. The quality is first grade; average price, say 6d. per lb., very low this year.

Timber and lumber.

Besides the peculiar adaptability of a great portion of this State to farming and fruit growing there is another fact of great importance to those interested in these pursuits: it is the ready market at home for their products. The commerce and shipping on the Sound and on the Columbia river, the working of the mines, coal, iron, and other metals, the lumber industry at the mills and various logging camps will employ many thousands of persons, who, for their daily supply of provisions, will be dependent upon the farmer. A large proportion of the farm products, such as flour, beef, pork, mutton, poultry, butter, cheese, vegetables, and fruit will be used for home consumption, while Idaho, Montana, and British Columbia will also demand a good share.

While the production of lumber presented no new feature during the year, the marketing of the product varied in essential particulars from the year before. Lumber manufactured in 1889 amounted to 684,182,851 feet; in 1888 it amounted to 454,985,146 feet, showing an increase of 229,197,706 feet. There was a falling-off in foreign shipments, and an extraordinary increase in the local demand; "local" means Eastern Washington as well as Puget Sound. Foreign cargoes show a great decrease, due to the scarcity of tonnage. Any other freight is better than lumber for first-class ships. The demand has been as great, but the orders have been declined for the lack of transportation facilities. This scarcity of tonnage has been partially met by the mill companies, who have sent to foreign ports such coasting vessels as they could spare from their respective fleets. Until last year only two cargoes had been shipped from Puget Sound to London, but last year nine cargoes were carried, a large part of the orders consisting of sticks from 16 by 16 to 24 by 24, and from 61 to 90 feet long. Trees from which this lumber is obtained are lofty, straight-grained and free from knots, from 24 to 60 inches in diameter. During the year a large number of local mills were established, and one large mill for exporting lumber by rail into the interior of Eastern Washington and the timberless States west of the Mississippi river. One cargo was shipped across the continent to Boston, Massachusetts.

In regard to the fishing industry I will simply say that it is making progress and developing. *Fishing.*

Mining for precious metals has been carried on in the Cascade Mountains, and on the Suake, Columbia, and other rivers for some years, and about 40,000*l.* per annum has been produced, but it is expected that when the railway taps the Okanogan and the Colville districts marvellously rich deposits will be discovered and brought down to the shipping places. At present there are no means of transportation. *Mining.*

Deposits of granite and marble have been found in both Eastern and Western Washington, and a number of quarries have been established, and many are in full operation.

The output of coal in the State of Washington for 1889 was 911,529 tons, valued at 911,500*l.*; except for the interruption to the King County mines by the great fire at Seattle, which destroyed shipping facilities, the year's industry was steady; "local" sales were four times as large as last year, and are constantly increasing; fresh facilities at Seattle are now made for receiving and discharging 2,000,000 tons a year outside of the "local" demand. San Francisco takes the bulk of the coal output, a large quantity going to Portland, Oregon. *Coal.*

Three transcontinental railroads now compete for the traffic of Washington. The Northern, the Union, and the Canadian Pacific. The Northern has its three terminals at Seattle, Jacoma, and Portland, Oregon, and by its trunk line and feeders drain the larger part of the State. The Union Pacific having leased the Oregon short line, running from Granger, Utah, to Portland, Oregon, reaches Eastern Washington by the network of roads leased from the Oregon Railway and Navigation Company, having a northern terminus at Spokane Falls. The trade of Puget Sound is reached through a new line of steamships plying between the Sound and Portland, and by a traffic arrangement with the Northern Pacific, the Canadian Pacific is now extended to Seattle and Puget Sound from Vancouver, British Columbia, by a line of steamships, but it is expected that all rail connection with Seattle will be secured during the coming spring over the Seattle, Lake, Shore and Eastern by an extension from Luohornish to the boundary line, and junction there with a span of the Canadian built down from Mission, a point about 40 miles east of Vancouver. During the past year more miles of railroad have been built in this State than in any other year of its history. At the beginning of 1889 there were 1,268 miles of road in operation, and there are 312 miles of new road upon which rails have actually been laid and trains operated, making a total of 1,580 miles. *Railroads.*

The increase of steamboat traffic has not been less notable. So heavy is the trade on Puget Sound that the present equip- *Shipping.*

UNITED STATES.

Agriculture.

ment is inadequate. Several new companies have been constructed. The number of steamboats now number about 125.

An estimate of the agricultural growth of the State of Washington may be obtained from the reports obtained from the United States district land offices; the business transacted in these offices for the year ending November 31, 1889, shows that 13,597 entries were made, representing 2,344,214 acres, brought or to be brought under the plough, seeder, and harvester, and an outlay of 800,000*l*. to secure title to the land from the Government; add to this the amount spent by settlers to improve and reclaim their lands, say an expenditure of 400,000*l*., which, added to the price paid, makes a total of 1,200,000*l*., expanded in the preliminary acts of reclaiming heretofore wild lands; of these great expenditures Eastern Washington expended about 280,000*l*., while Western Washington expended nearly 520,000*l*. The acreage in Eastern Washington is, in round numbers, 908,782 acres; while the western portion of the State has a total of 1,435,432 acres. This shows that the vacant lands of Eastern Washington are being gradually tilled, and the timber lands are being taken up in the west.

The several annexes which I append will show more particularly the commerce and trade of this new State with foreign countries; portions of the year have been unusually dull, which may account for the marked decrease in the returns for the preceding year. It is, however, confidently expected that prosperity and success will attend the future development of Washington.

Annex A.—RETURN of all Shipping at the Port of Port Townsend in the Year 1889.

ENTERED.

Country.	Sailing. Number of Vessels.	Sailing. Tons.	Steam. Number of Vessels.	Steam. Tons.	Total. Number of Vessels.	Total. Tons.
British	52	51,412	18	4,425	70	55,837
U.S. (America)	52	38,116	841	617,430	893	655,546
Norway	14	10,986	...	...	14	10,986
Sweden	12	10,574	...	...	12	10,574
Chile	9	7,856	...	...	9	7,856
Germany	4	4,382	...	...	4	4,382
Hawaiian Islands	4	1,839	...	...	4	1,839
Nicaragua	2	1,553	...	...	2	1,553
Italy	1	980	...	...	1	980
Ecuador	1	778	...	...	1	778
Total	151	128,476	859	621,855	1,010	750,331
„ for 1888	266	270,154	787	688,083	1,083	958,237

SAN FRANCISCO.

CLEARED.

Country.	Sailing. Number of Vessels.	Sailing. Tons.	Steam. Number of Vessels.	Steam. Tons.	Total. Number of Vessels.	Total. Tons.
Britain	49	49,651	24	7,781	73	57,432
U.S. (America)	123	102,429	813	549,346	936	651,775
Norway	16	13,515	...	...	16	13,515
Sweden	14	8,814	...	...	14	8,814
Chile	9	7,870	...	...	9	7,870
Germany	3	2,763	...	...	3	2,763
Hawaiian Islands	3	1,839	...	...	3	1,839
Nicaragua	3	2,389	...	...	3	2,389
Italy	1	980	...	...	1	980
Ecuador	1	778	...	...	1	778
Total	222	191,028	837	557,127	1,059	748,155
,, for Year 1888	280	295,451	788	661,167	1,063	956,618

Annex B.—RETURN of Principal Articles of Export from Port Townsend during the Years 1888 and 1889.

Articles.		1889. Quantity.	1889. Value. £	1888. Quantity.	1888. Value. £
Cattle	Head	589	4,266	615	3,925
Hogs	,,	2,406	3,160	3,186	2,279
Horses	,,	273	13,799	131	2,672
Sheep	,,	30,513	14,384	23,732	10,512
Other animals	...	...	391	...	406
Wheat	Bushels	1,134,803	196,364	2,629,794	449,715
Flour	Lbs.	13,884	11,240	54,814	44,404
Other breadstuffs	...	...	4,517	...	11,161
Butter, eggs, &c.	...	...	4,662	...	3,811
Fish	...	...	1,357	...	509
Furs	...	...	6,762	...	11,400
Iron manufactures	...	...	16,229	...	13,507
Liquors and spirits	...	...	1,560	...	1,241
Oils	...	...	8,003	...	8,141
Provision, bacon, &c.	...	...	18,475	...	21,644
Vegetables, fresh, canned	...	...	327	...	763
Fruits, fresh, canned	...	...	2,844	...	3,894
Hops	...	...	821	...	6,879
Books, stationery, &c.	...	...	2,916	...	3,019
Agricultural implements, &c.	...	...	302	...	2,245
Timber	M. feet	109,765	235,773	373,014,951	761,507
Manufactures of wood	...	...	6,350	...	...
Wool, woollen manufactures	...	...	4,489	...	1,319
Tobacco, cigars	...	...	1,822	...	2,289
Other articles	...	...	86,452	...	39,814
Total	...	...	627,256	...	1,413,958

Return of Principal Articles of Import to Port Townsend during the Years 1888 and 1889.

Articles.		1889. Quantity.	1889. Value. £	1888. Quantity.	1888. Value. £
Free—					
Tea	...	...	995	...	2,034
Raw furs and skins	...	...	30	...	33,720
Brimstone	...	...	100	...	...
Coffee	...	...	45	...	8,625
Other articles	...	...	362	...	...
			1,532		
Dutiable—					
Liquors, spirits	...	...	2,175	...	1,654
Rice	...	...	3,178	...	2,346
Salt	...	...	1,172	...	700
Cement	...	...	6,472	...	605
Steel rails	Tons	1,500	6,918	...	13,988
Pig iron	,,	2,468	5,267	...	1,030
Iron ore	,,	13,642	5,614	...	2,839
Coal	,,	5,364	3,867	...	3,012
Firebrick	...	...	1,181	...	...
Granite, rough	Tons	1,071	684	...	...
Steel tin plate	...	...	681	...	...
Cattle	...	...	224	...	...
Fish	...	...	117	...	...
Furs, deeped	...	...	355	...	...
Tobacco	...	...	65	...	...
All other articles	...	...	10,677	...	8,061
			48,640		
In Bond—					
Tea	...	...	135,129	...	...
Furs and seal skins	...	...	6,729	...	...
Skins and hides	...	...	2,086	...	...
Liquors	...	...	381	...	...
All other articles	...	...	1,344	...	...
In Bond	...	...	145,669		
Free	...	...	1,532		
Dutiable	...	...	48,640		
Grand total	...	...	195,841	...	77,814

Note.—In the import table the total of free and dutiable goods together amount to 50,172*l.* Those in bond were shipped to other places in the United States and Canada. The pound sterling has been reckoned at 48,665 dol., the custom-house standard at this port.

Annex C.—TABLE showing the Total Value of all Articles Exported from Port Townsend and Imported to Port Townsend from and to Foreign Countries during the Years 1888 and 1889.

Country.	Exports. 1889.	Exports. 1888.	Imports. 1889.	Imports. 1888.
	£	£	£	£
Great Britain	228,203	289,405	21,589	26,685
British Columbia	149,316	183,180	27,267	556,599
British Possessions, Australasia	104,316	169,719	675	20
Chile	57,520	32,315	..	..
Hawaiian Islands	29,587	27,649	52	..
Argentine Republic	23,085	5,307	..	..
Peru	18,432	13,705	..	100
Uruguay	4,519	1,644	..	..
Mexico	3,904	12,299	330	..
China	2,941	5,543	..	..
French Possessions, Australasia	2,128	..	..	..
Japan	1,220	..	279	1,432
Ecuador	1,104	..	..	..
Other countries	981	135,511	..	1
Total	627,256	875,677	50,172	584,837

LOS ANGELES AND WILMINGTON.

Mr. Vice-Consul Mortimer reports as follows :—

Introductory remarks.

In my last report I stated that the great prosperity and rapid development of this district had at last received a check, the extent of which it was then difficult to determine. The inactivity and depression in business still continues, and there are many indications that the period of depression will continue for two or three years. The completion of a third trans-continental railway, connecting Los Angeles with the Eastern States, which will, I think, be accomplished within three years, will be the signal for an era of prosperity, and business activity, greater and more permanent than that which in the past six years has attracted so much attention to Los Angeles and its vicinity. The following comparative statements fairly indicate the extent of the present depression in business. In 1888, new buildings were constructed in the city of Los Angeles to the value of 2,000,000l., and in 1889 to the value of 900,000l. The considerations named in the conveyances of realty filed for record in the year 1889, aggregated in value 7,100,000l., a decrease of upwards of 40 per cent. on the operations of 1888, and 12,000,000l. less than in 1887. The Los Angeles clearing-house reports clearings as follows :—

	£
1888	12,600,000
1889	7,400,000

(886)

These figures represent all the city banks, except four small institutions organised during the year 1889. Making a liberal allowance for these new banks, the decrease is over 35 per cent. In view of the fact that clearing-house returns fairly gauge the condition of business in this country, this marked decrease is the best test of the extent of the general depression in business. 172 divorces were granted by the Superior Court in Los Angeles county during 1889, an increase of 59 on the number granted in 1888. Although the activity of the divorce court is a sign of depression in business, I cannot say that it is an infallible one, as I see in the lists for 1889 that one lady (aged 27) obtained her third divorce in March, was remarried in April, and obtained her fourth divorce in November last. I do not wish to express an opinion on the subject of free trade and protection, I may say, however, that the great distress here among the labouring classes shows, that during the period of unexampled prosperity from 1883 to 1888, they either neglected to save, or, owing to the protective tariff, they were unable to save much out of their wages. The tariff increases the cost of necessaries to the consumer about 50 per cent.; as, however, the wages of the working classes here are, on an average, more than 100 per cent. in excess of the wages paid in the north of Europe, distress, in times of depression, must to some extent be ascribed to lack of thrift. The receipt of an apparently high wage, magnifies the importance of the labourer in his own eyes, he does not confine his expenditure to necessaries, and the high tariff on luxuries soon exhausts his resources. If the working classes lived as economically here as they do in Europe, distress, during periods of depression, would be unknown. All property, real and personal, is taxed annually, and for this purpose an annual valuation or assessment is made; the assessed value of all property in the six counties—40,000 square miles—composing this district, was, exclusive of railways:—

	£
In 1880	7,300,000
„ 1889	33,700,000

The assessed value of the city and county of Los Angeles was:—

	£
In 1888	21,500,000
„ 1889	18,700,000

British interests.

In so far as British interests are concerned, the most important matters in this report will be found under the following headings: Railway to Salt Lake City, Unsuccessful English Companies, Advice to British Capitalists, Advice to Emigrants, Treatment of Vagrants, Sewer Bonds, and Non-resident Purchasers of California Lands.

Trade and commerce.

The chief exports are grain, wine, oranges, and other fruits. I have no accurate statistics of the amount of grain produced in this district; the surplus for export was not large, and was shipped, chiefly in coasting vessels, from Hueneme, a port of delivery within the collection district of Wilmington.

Wine. The depression in the wine trade continues. I am informed that large quantities of wine from this district were sold in New York below cost of production. The trade suffers greatly from the manufacture and sale of an adulterated article in the Eastern States. A Bill is now before Congress providing for a tax of 5*d.* per pint " on all beverages containing alcohol designated or sold as wine, or as a substitute for wine, not made from grape juice and prepared in accordance with methods recognised as legitimate in standard published works on the subject." Whether this Bill will be passed, or if passed will be effectual, is at least problematical.

Oranges. In my last report I estimated the orange crop for 1889, then being harvested, at 2,000 car loads; it proved to be 2,700 car loads (27,000 tons). The manager of the Earl Fruit Company estimates the crop now being harvested at 2,400 car loads, other estimates place it as high as 3,500 car loads. The fruit is packed in boxes averaging in weight 70 lbs., and containing about 125 oranges, 300 boxes (21,000 lbs.) make a car load. The following figures for 1889 show the relative importance of the California crop:—

	Boxes.
Florida..	2,000,000
Importations from Mediterranean	1,500,000
Southern California	810,000

Many people think that the crop of this district will soon eclipse the importations from Europe and the Southern States, believing that the California orange is the best. Estimates showing the profit in orange culture will be found elsewhere in this report. A committee of Congress has just recommended that the duty on oranges be increased from 1*s.* 3*d.* to 2*s* 6*d.* per box. This increase is no doubt designed to protect the California orange from the Mexican product, which, owing to cheap land, and cheap labour, is produced for about 60 per cent. less. The California orange sells here at from 8*s.* to 12*s.* per box, and in the Eastern States at 16*s.* to 24*s.* per box.

Canned fruit. The manager of the Southern California Packing Company reports that his company packed 30,000 cases of fruit in 1889. Each case contains 2 dozen cans of $2\frac{1}{2}$ lbs. each, and sells here for 10*s.* to 16*s.* per case. He estimates the total fruit pack of Southern California at 70,000 cases, and adds, " The outlook for 1890 is better than it has been for two years, while high prices will not be received we think there will be a good demand, and that leads to prosperity,"

Raisins. The product of raisins in this district has risen from 20,000 boxes in 1880 to 300,000 in 1889. The duty on raisins will probably be increased from $\frac{3}{4}d.$ to $1\frac{1}{4}d.$ per pound.

Imports.

Coals. The importation of coals from Australia in British ships in the last three years has exceeded 30,000 tons, principally for the Southern Pacific Railway. It was stated recently in the local press that this company had arranged to obtain its supply from

British Columbia, and, as only two cargoes have arrived from Australia in the last seven months, I wrote to the general manager for such information as he was at liberty to give me. In reply he writes me : " Our company owns large coal deposits which we are working in British Columbia. It is also true that our people are owners, and are operating very extensive coal mines in Washington, with negotiations now pending for additional coal-fields in that State, on account of the 75 c. (3s.) per ton duty against all coal from Vancouver. We may have to build a short line of railroad from the contemplated coal lands to tide-water on the Puget Sound, but this will not take very long when the matter is fully determined." Since the opening of the Southern Pacific Railway from New Orleans to Los Angeles in 1883, that company has unsuccessfully competed for the shipment of the surplus grain from this district to Europe, viâ New Orleans, and this notwithstanding the fact that from time to time to time cars are returned empty from here to New Orleans. Should the company procure all its coals from British Columbia and Washington, however, the number of ships coming to this coast will be materially lessened, and rates of freight may advance sufficiently to admit of the company obtaining a share of the business. In my report for 1883, I stated that the railway rate on grain to Liverpool viâ New Orleans was 1l. 16s. per ton, and that that rate would not pay. In 1884 the rate was advanced to 2l. 5s. per ton. This is probably the lowest rate the company can profitably charge.

Owing partly to lack of harbour facilities, and partly to the fact that there is as yet nothing here for export by sea, the imports for Los Angeles are entered at San Diego, San Francisco, New Orleans, and New York, and brought here by rail.

The Ceylon teas introduced here by W. H. Murray and Co. are finding favour. Joseph Tetley and Co., of London, established an agency here recently, and sell a good black tea at 2s. 10d. per lb. Heretofore black teas, worth in London about 1s. 6d. per lb., have sold here for 4s. to 5s. As there is no duty on tea this is only to be accounted for by the fact that most of the people here drink green tea or coffee.

In 1888 153,000,000 feet of lumber was landed at Wilmington from domestic ports. In 1889 the import decreased to 46,000,000 feet.

Shipping and Navigation.

The annexed map (for which I am indebted to Mr. George B. King, C.E.) shows the trans-continental and local lines of railway, the port of Wilmington, and the new port of Redondo. It will be seen that the Bay of San Pedro, where foreign-going vessels anchor, is wholly unprotected from the south-east gales. Occasionally vessels at anchor in the bay are driven ashore and wrecked. The anchorage is so exposed that vessels frequently lose 10 or 12 days owing to the bay being too rough to admit of lighters being brought alongside. The government has expended

131,000*l*. in improving the inner harbour and the entrance thereto, and there is now sufficient water on the bar to admit the largest coasting vessels at high tide. The president of the Chamber of Commerce here writes me that the last two appropriations (10,000*l*. in 1884, and 15,000*l*. in 1886) remain unexpended, " the whole amount being but a little more than sufficient to purchase the appliances for the prosecution of the work." In 1884 the government engineer estimated that an expenditure of 45,000*l*. would deepen the channel sufficiently to admit foreign-going ships to the inner harbour, and the above appropriations were made pursuant to his recommendation. In 1886, as stated in my report for 1887, the same engineer recommended the construction of a breakwater enclosing the bay of San Pedro, at a cost of 800,000*l*. basing his recommendation on the fact that Wilmington possesses advantages over San Francisco for the overland transportation of Asiatic and Australian commerce, the chief advantage being that the railroad haul from the Eastern States is 500 miles less than to San Francisco, and is equivalent to 800 miles, owing to the comparatively easy grades on the southern route. The Member of Congress for this district wrote to the president of the Chamber of Commerce under date January 9, 1890, as follows: "No recommendation has been made for an appropriation by the engineer office, and consequently no estimate has been submitted to Congress for any sum to be expended in making an improvement. . . . . No plan of improvement of the San Pedro harbour has yet been adopted; at least no plan of inclosing a deep-sea harbour by a breakwater has been adopted by Congress."

It appears from the foregoing that there is little prospect at present of any improvement of the inner or outer harbour. General cargoes for Los Angeles, and coals for the Los Angeles Gas Company, and others, formerly shipped direct to Wilmington, are now shipped viâ San Diego, on account of the delay and loss in discharging into lighters at San Pedro. Private parties have expended large sums of money in efforts to make harbours at Ballona, 16 miles west, and Redondo, 21 miles south-west of Los Angeles. The former is admittedly a failure; the latter is protected only from the south-east gales (see map accompanying this report). If the money used at these places had been expended at Wilmington, in conjunction with the government funds, Los Angeles would now have the best port south of San Francisco, ensuring to this district a greater degree of prosperity than can be expected from any other public improvement. *No prospect of a harbour for Los Angeles.*

In my report for 1888 I gave the charges at the port of Wilmington for loading and unloading vessels. The charge for towing donkey-engines to ships and back is 6*l*., not 6*l*. per day as it has been incorrectly printed. *Stevedoring charges.*

In my report I stated that the Wilmington pilot claimed pilotage fees, averaging 16*l*. per vessel, from vessels anchoring in San Pedro Bay outside the outer harbour line. Two suits were then pending in the United States district court here, and, as seafaring men are agreed that pilotage is unnecessary in the open roadstead *Pilotage. Pilotage compulsory.*

it was hoped that the decision of the court would end the matter. The question was finally settled in March last by an Act of the Legislature of California, of which the following is the portion affecting foreign-going ships. "The following shall be the rates of pilotage into and out of the bay of San Pedro *at the outer anchorage*. All vessels under 500 tons 5 dol. per foot draught. All vessels over 500 tons 10 c. (5d.) per ton for each and every ton gross registered tonnage. When a vessel is spoken, and the services of a pilot are declined, the pilot shall be entitled to one-half pilotage." The Act further provides that vessels engaged in the coasting trade between ports of the United States on the Pacific coast shall be exempted from pilotage charges unless a pilot be actually employed. Under this Act the pilot's fees on a vessel of 2,000 tons would be 40*l*. inwards, and 40*l*. outwards if the pilot was employed. This is considerably in excess of the fees levied in San Francisco. I understand that this is the only open roadstead in the world where pilotage fees are compulsory.

Casualty.

The British ship "Old Kensington" arrived from Newcastle, New South Wales, April 4, 1889, with a cargo of 2,640 tons of coals. The cargo ignited spontaneously some time prior to her arrival, and the fire had gained such headway that it was found necessary to beach her. Messrs. Lloyd's agents in San Francisco inform me that they do not recollect any case of spontaneous combustion of Newcastle coals.

Agriculture.

"White scale" exterminated.

For the past five years I have annually drawn attention to the ravages of the Icerya, or "white scale," in the orange groves of this district. A year ago many of the principal orange-growers in the vicinity of Los Angeles had abandoned their efforts to exterminate this pest, concluding that their trees must die. Fortunately, it was learned that an Australian parasite, the Vedolia Cardinalis, had exterminated the white scale in Australia; a colony of the bugs was imported and placed on the trees in the Wolfskill orchard in this city; they multiplied so rapidly that in a few months the scale was entirely exterminated in this district; many trees, which a year ago were nearly dead, have revived and borne half a crop this season.

Other scale bugs.

The red scale is doing a great deal of damage to the orange trees. It is as destructive as the white scale was a year ago, the only difference being that it does not multiply as rapidly. Spraying and washing the trees has little effect other than to retard the fatal work of the insect. The purple scale, which proved very destructive to the orange trees in Florida, recently appeared here, and the San Jose scale has also appeared and done much damage. The extermination of the white scale has taught orchardists to look to nature for relief, and every effort is being made to discover parasites which will attack the pests I have named.

In my report for 1884 I gave the then generally accepted

figures of the cost of planting a 10 acre orange grove, and caring for it for five years. These figures represent the total cost, including land which is placed at 200*l*., to be 860*l*.; receipts in same period 1,000*l*. I stated that the price of 10 acres of land suitable for orange culture should be placed at 400*l*., and that the receipts were much exaggerated.

<small>Profits in orange culture.</small>

The following figures are now quoted, the price of land being placed at the highest price for unimproved orange land:—

	£
10 acres of land	1,200
Planting and cultivating trees for five years, loss of interest, taxes, &c.	1,482
Total cost for first five years	2,682
Receipts from sale of oranges	682
Loss on first five years	2,000
Expenses from 5th to 8th year	1,080
Receipts from 5th to 8th year	3,572

It would appear from these figures that in eight years a 10 acre orange grove will pay for itself, and leave the owner a profit of 492*l*., and thereafter will pay not less than 1,000*l*. per annum. I submitted these figures to an Irish gentleman who purchased a small orange grove about four years ago, and who is now planting a large one. He says, "good land suitable for orange culture, with a good water right, can be purchased for 60*l*. to 70*l*. per acre. The expenses are fairly stated, and the estimate of receipts, as far as my experience extends, is a fair one." He adds, "If I did not consider it pretty certain to be profitable you may be sure I would not go into it on a larger scale as I am about to do, for I am preparing to plant 40 acres more. I fully expect to net at least 10 per cent. on the money invested. If there were no drawbacks, the profits on orange growing would be, I think, enormous; but in California they seem to lose sight of the drawbacks. The chief one I consider are storms, which destroy at least half your crop some years, and injure the trees, so that you may have no crop, or only half a crop, the next year. This I hope, in a great measure, to obviate by planting plenty of windbreaks. Then some years the crop, even on high mess lands, will be injured by frost. The scale bugs, too, are to be dreaded. I consider also that part of the profits will have to be spent on manures when the trees are in full bearing. I would not take a present of an orange grove near Los Angeles, or anywhere in the vicinity of the sea, or where there is much fog, if the gift was coupled with a condition that I should work it. I will be a sadder and much disappointed man this day six years, if I find that I cannot make orange growing pay a better and safer interest on money than anything else I know." The writer of the foregoing is a successful business man, in whose judgment and integrity I place implicit confidence. As he is withdrawing money, invested on the best first mortgage security at 10 per cent. net, to put it into an orange grove it must be admitted that he has the courage of his opinions. In explanation of some of his remarks, I may say that ravages of the scale bugs have been confined to the vicinity of Los Angeles, where, however, but little loss has been sustained from windstorms and frost. On the other hand, Riverside, Ontaria, and Pomona (see map accompanying this report) have escaped the bugs, but have suffered great loss from both windstorms and frosts. The eucalyptus tree grows to a height of 40 to 50 feet in four years, and when closely planted, in double rows, around an orange grove, forms a good protection from windstorms.

Vine disease. The vine disease, described in my last two reports, is still unchecked, and now seriously menaces the existence of the viticultural industry in this immediate vicinity. At first it attacked chiefly the mission vines; now other varieties of red vines are dying, and the white varieties are also suffering. The disease first appeared in its present dangerous form in the southern part of this country, and destroyed many vineyards. Professor Dowlen, an expert employed by the Viticultural Commission to ascertain its cause, and, if possible, discover a remedy, inclines to the opinion that it is due to a fungus. On the other hand, Mr. Wheeler, Chief Executive Officer of the Viticultural Commission, reports that he is fully convinced that the fungus found on the dead vines is not the prime cause of the decadence of the vines, and that it attacks them only when they have been weakened from other causes. Professor Dowlen, who is, I understand, a graduate of an English University, writes me as follows:—" The cause of the disease has not yet been proved, nor would I like to say that a sure remedy has been found. In an experimental hot-house I have succeeded in keeping vines free from disease, but I have not met with the same amount of success out of doors. . . . The disease is present in the Riverside vineyards, but has not done the mischief there that it has around Los Angeles. It appears to have been known at Riverside for years past, but has never done serious harm there. A similar state of things obtains at Napa Valley, where the disease has been known for many years, but has never caused any trouble. With respect to the likeness between the 'mal nero' of the Italian vineyards and the disease here, though there is a great similarity between the two diseases their identity has not been proved. This question is under investigation."

The phylloxera, which is still doing great damage to the vineyards about 400 miles north of this district, has not yet appeared here.

Population and Industries.

Population. The population of this city, which, a year ago, I estimated at 80,000, remains about the same; thousands of real estate dealers, "boomsters," and others have gone away in the past two years, and their places have been filled by new comers from the Eastern States and elsewhere.

A complete list of the factories in this city will be found in my report for 1888. The following paragraph in my last report is still correct:— *Factories.*

"For several years past mechanics have received from 16s. to 24s. per day. In the past year wages have been reduced from 40 to 50 per cent., and thousands of good workmen are now out of employment." *Wages.*

The aggregate capital stock of the public companies incorporated here in the year 1888 exceeded 13,500,000l. In 1889 the total was a little over 45,500,000l. *Public companies.*

In my last two reports I commented on a projected railway from Salt Lake City, in the territory of Utah, to Los Angeles, a distance of 640 miles. The construction of this line is of the utmost importance to this city and district, both because it will be the third competing trans-continental line from this city to the Eastern States, and also because it will pass through a rich mining and agricultural country, which will become tributary to Los Angeles. I am assured by the president of the Chamber of Commerce, and other gentlemen here in whom I have confidence, that the line will pass through vast deposits of good coal within 260 miles of Los Angeles, which can then be sold here at about 1l. per ton, a reduction of 50 per cent. on the present price. This will entirely cut off shipments from England and Australia, and will admit of the establishment of manufactures here, the raw materials for which are now practically valueless, owing to the high price of fuel. The Union Pacific and the Denver and Rio Grande Railways have had surveying parties in the field; the general manager of the latter road writes me, under date March 17, 1890, that no definite action has been taken by the board of directors of his company. It is generally believed that the line will be constructed by the Union Pacific. This company has constructed from Salt Lake to Milford, in Southern Utah, and is now constructing to Pioche, in Nevada, which latter point is within 400 miles of Los Angeles. The vice-president of the Union Pacific wrote me March 14, 1889: "Our engineer is looking the line up, but we have not reached a point where any decision can be made;" and, under date March 3, 1890, "we are in very much the same situation as we were on March 14, 1889, when we addressed you last. We shall construct this year from Milford to Pioche, but that is all that is under consideration for the present." *Railway to Salt Lake City.*

The line will, no doubt, be constructed from Pioche to Barstow or Mojave—stations in this district on the Santa Fé route—within the next five years, possibly within two or three; its completion will affect British interests as follows: first, it will put an end to the importation of coals from England, Australia, and British Columbia to Southern California; second, it will be of great value to this district, and so favourably affect the very large amount of British capital invested here; third, apart from these and other considerations, it will present opportunities for the investment of money in mining industries—gold, silver, copper, iron and coal.

Carson and Colorado Railway.

It is constantly stated in the press here that the Carson and Colorado Railroad, connecting Carson City, Nevada, with Inyo county, California, will be extended to Los Angeles. In reply to an enquiry from me, the president of that railway writes me as follows: "Our company has no idea of extending its line to Los Angeles. Our aim is to try and connect with the Utah Southern (Union Pacific) whenever it is extended from Pioche to Barstow or Mojave, and how soon that can be accomplished is more than I can say. We hope, however, that it may be effected during the next two years, and doubt if anything more than that can be expected in the meantime." I quote this letter in confirmation of my opinion, that the Union Pacific will reach Los Angeles within three to five years' time.

New railway to Pasadena.

A new railway has just been completed between this city and Pasadena, a distance of 10 miles, and trains are now run hourly, at reduced rates.

Railway losses from "washouts."

In my report for 1885 I drew attention to the loss of several million dollars sustained by the Southern Pacific Company, owing to "washouts," on its line from Los Angeles to San Francisco, and added: "As the mountains at the points where the damage occurred are very precipitous, and the soil friable, it would appear that the damage and consequent loss is liable to be repeated whenever the rainfall is exceptionally heavy." In December last, owing to an exceptionally heavy rainfall, this line was so badly "washed out" that there was no communication by rail between Los Angeles and San Francisco for 11 days. The aggregate loss of the trans-continental and local railways in December, in this district alone, from "washouts," must have exceeded 400,000*l.*

Temescal tin district.

In my report for 1884 I directed attention to some valuable tin mines in this district, and stated that they were not being worked, owing to litigation. A telegram has just been published here announcing the sale to an English syndicate of the mines I referred to for 300,000*l.* Colonel Baker, the reputed owner, informs me that he is not a party to the sale, and that his claim has not been settled.

Oil. New English company.

For some years I have annually commented on the increase in this district in the output of oil, and its increasing use for manufacturing purposes. The flowing wells at Puente, the discovery of which I referred to in my report for 1886, have been purchased (March, 1890) by an English syndicate, the Anglo-Californian Petroleum Company, Limited, for 180,000*l.* Mr. Lacey, one of the vendors, informs me that the present output, 150 barrels (6,000 gallons) per day, sells readily in this city. That the working capital of the company, 75,000*l.*, will be largely used in increasing the output, and that, at present prices, 8*s.* per barrel, oil is cheaper for manufacturing purposes than coals at 1*l.* per ton. The present consumption in this city is about 400 barrels per day. If the supply of oil can be increased indefinitely, as stated by the owners of oil lands, the question of cheap fuel supply for manufacturing purposes can be solved without the Utah coal. It is proposed to pipe the oil from Puente to Los Angeles, 16 miles. (See map annexed.)

General Remarks.

For the past six years I have annually pointed out the remarkably good opening existing here for the investment of money on mortgage. In the past three years the German Savings and Loan Society, of San Francisco, has invested 800,000*l*. at 9 and 10 per cent. gross, and I learn from their agent here, that all the mortgages are proving satisfactory. An English mortgage company, the Northern Counties Investment Trust, Limited, commenced business here a few months ago; as it is well managed I am satisfied it will be successful. English companies—paper, land, wine, and mining companies—organised to do business here in the past five years, have been unprofitable owing to such causes as (1) being too heavily handicapped with promotion money, (2) bad management, (3) errors in management arising from ignorance of American methods of business, (4) misfortunes that could not have been foreseen, and (5), in the case of mining companies, attempting to extract ore from non-ore-bearing rock. The local press has just reported one of these cases; it appears from the report that nearly 40,000*l*. has been expended on the faith of the representations of an English expert, that the ore was worth from 80*l*. to 120*l*. per ton, it now proves to be not worth mining. Two of the companies I allude to will eventually be profitable, as they own large tracts of land which are constantly increasing in value.

Mortgage companies rate of interest.

Unsuccessful English companies.

A local paper commenting recently on the sale, to an English syndicate, of an island a few miles from the coast, on which low grade ore is found, points out that the mines can be worked with English coals brought here as "ballast;" and, at the conclusion of the article, states that the ore can be shipped to England for reduction as "ballast." The editor informs me that the article was "inspired" by the promoter, probably for republication in England. The island, which is about nine miles long, and one-third to one mile wide was sold for 80,000*l*., and may be worth that much apart from the ore. Another local paper commenting on the sale, regards it as "serious" that this island should pass into the control of a foreign corporation, because "we understand that one of the parties is a British officer of high rank.' It "passed into the control" of a local capitalist, for 20,000*l*., three years ago, who was the vendor to the English syndicate.

An English firm cabled me some months ago, requesting me to cable them my opinion of a mining property in this vicinity. I replied that I knew nothing of the mine in question, and asked authority to employ an expert. Some months later one of the firm called on me, and I gathered from conversations with him that he was interested only in making a sale to an English company, and would not be affected if the working of the mine proved unremunerative. I am informed by a miner who has known the property for the past 20 years that it is practically valueless.

The local press has reported several times the sale, to an English syndicate, of 7,000 or 8,000 acres in this district, known as the Beaumont colony. An English expert sent out to examine the water right of the colony called on me a few days ago, and informed me that the sale would be carried out. In reply to my inquiry as to the price, he stated that "he believed" it was 30*l*. per acre. I trust he was mistaken in his belief, as the best valuation I can get of these lands is 6*l*. per acre, an adjoining proprietor offers his lands at 4*l*. per acre.

The sale to an English syndicate of 200,000 acres about 30 miles south-west of this city is also reported to me. If this enterprise is not too heavily handicapped with promotion money it may be profitable. The agent for the owner tells me that the price is 3*l*. per acre.

25,000 acres near this city, which was offered to me in 1885 for 3*l*. 8*s*. per acre, was sold for 12*l*. per acre during the "boom" in 1887, and is now offered in London and Belgium at 30*l*. per acre. It will pay interest on 6*l*. per acre, and is worth that amount.

Dozens of schemes in this district, similar to the foregoing examples, are now being offered to the British investor. Those of them that are carried out will no doubt be further burdened with heavy promotion money in London. Apart from the promoters charges, however, it is certainly not wise to pay 100 per cent. more than was asked during the "boom" of 1887, especially when local capitalists can buy at 50 per cent. below "boom" prices. Such great dangers beset the British investor in Southern California, from promoters in London, from mismanagement by English managers unfamiliar with this country,—whose sole qualifications are possibly a reputation for honesty, and relationship to one of the directors,—and from impositions by vendors and their agents here, that I am reluctantly compelled to advise British capitalists not to invest in Southern California Companies. I give this advice unwillingly, as there are many openings here for the profitable investment of capital; for example, in the storage and sale of water. The following item in the "Los Angeles Daily Herald" of March 15, 1890, illustrates this:—

"A big English syndicate has bought the entire Gage real estate interest near San Bernardino. The purchase includes 6,000 acres of land, the Gage canal and the entire water rights attaching to these. The tract is to be colonised with intelligent farmers from England."

These lands were recently acquired from the United States Government for 10*s*. per acre, under the Desert Land Act; their whole value depends on the water supply, and the question whether the price paid by the syndicate, 200,000*l*., is a reasonable one, depends on the quantity of water available at the end of the dry season. Lands adjoining this 6,000 acre tract, now valued at 50*l*. to 60*l*. per acre, were assessed some years ago for 3*s*. per acre, the increased value being due wholly to an adequate supply of water. In Ontario and other places water has been obtained by tunnelling into the mountains, and in many places storage reservoirs have been constructed in the cañons. An inch of water, miner's measurement, will irrigate from 5 acres to 8 acres, according to the nature of the soil, and is worth from 100*l*. to 300*l*. There are probably 2,000,000 acres of good land in this district, worth, as dry lands, from 2*l*. to 3*l*. per acre, which, with water, would produce enough to pay interest on 40*l*. to 50*l*. per acre. The lands I refer to are on the south side of the mountains shown on map accompanying this report, and do not form a part of the Antelope Valley or Mojave Desert.

Of all the countries to which emigration is directed, it is most true of California that practical experience of the country is an essential element of success. As far as my experience extends, I can say positively that the most successful emigrants have been the ones who worked in subordinate positions until they had acquired sufficient experience to invest their capital profitably. One young Scotchman, after working for five years as a farm labourer at 6*l*. per month and board, saved enough to purchase a small farm, and is now fairly well off. As a general rule, I may say, that the men who do not succeed here would not succeed any better elsewhere. The training and good qualities which command success in the overcrowded labour markets of the Eastern States and Europe, will command a greater and quicker measure of success here, success being understood to mean the rapid acquisition of money; limiting the word in this way, I feel justified in saying that those of the industrious and energetic, the goal of whose ambition is to acquire a competence, have better opportunities here than in any other part of the United States of which I have any knowledge. Irishmen and Canadians succeed well here because they readily adapt themselves to the manners and customs of the people. Englishmen are more successful in thoroughly English colonies like British Columbia, and in view of the facts that the vast agricultural and mineral wealth of that colony is almost unexplored, that the opportunities to make money are fully as good there as here, that the surroundings are more in harmony with English ideas, and that Englishmen are likely to live happier and more useful lives there than here. I invariably advise my English correspondents to write to the Commissioner of Lands, Victoria, British Columbia, before deciding where they will settle.

Advice to emigrants.

People who are almost worthless from lack of industry, energy, and thrift, or from intemperance, are much more likely to lead an easy life in a highly civilised, than in a newly-settled country, hundreds of cases of men who had energy enough to conceive the idea of "bettering" themselves, but not energy enough to do it, have come to my notice. The most recent was that of a man who had an easy berth in a large firm in London, at a salary sufficient to enable him to live. He could not get exactly the same employment here, and could not adapt himself to anything else, the result being that when his slender means were exhausted he was reduced almost to starvation.

It has been stated in the press here that poor labourers seeking employment are sometimes arrested as vagrants by the

Treatment of vagrants.

constables solely to obtain the fees allowed for making the arrest, and are committed to the chain-gang. It was stated in the "Los Angeles Daily Times" a few weeks ago, that 22 of the chain-gang, refusing to work more than six hours a day, were put in dungeons, that they made a great deal of noise, and to quiet them the jailer turned the hose on them, and that "some of the worst continuing to howl, were taken out and hung up by the thumbs until they gave in, which was in a very short time." Since writing the foregoing, the following item was published in one of the local papers:—

"This thing of arresting an honest mechanic simply because he is out of work, and sending him to jail as a vagrant, and, because he refuses to go out in chains to work on the highways, 'trice him up' until his thumbs are pulled out of joint, must not only stop, but the atrocity committed must be atoned. Our people are worse than barbarians for tolerating such atrocities."

Exhibitions.

A number of the principal merchants and landowners in this city and district are subscribing 300*l*. per month to maintain permanent exhibitions of the products of Southern California in two or three of the large cities of the Eastern States, and it is not improbable that such an exhibition will be maintained in London for a couple of years. A railway train, fitted as a travelling exhibit, is now being hauled through the cities of the Eastern States, it attracts much attention, and passes under the name of "California on Wheels." The object in both cases is to attract a desirable class of settlers to this district; animated by the same object, the Chamber of Commerce of this city prepared a list of good lands for sale at reasonable prices, and distributed it throughout the country. The list covers about 500,000 acres, in subdivisions of 25 acres and upwards. The following is a specimen of the information contained in it:—"60 acres, 11 miles from Los Angeles, three miles from railway station, a rich, sandy loam, level land; grows alfalfa and deciduous fruits; 45 dol. an acre, small cash payment; water at 35 feet in any quantity; two crops of grain, two crops of vegetables, and seven crops of alfalfa annually." If this land is free of alkali it is certainly cheap at 9*l*. per acre. Persons who contemplate settling here should correspond with the secretary of this body.

Results of the "Boom."

The decrease in 1889 of nearly 3,000,000*l*. in the assessed value of all property in the city and county of Los Angeles, is due almost wholly to the shrinkage in value of the embryo cities described in my report for 1887. The following is taken from a newspaper report of the proceedings before the State Board of equalisation, at Sacramento, on an application by the supervisors of Los Angeles county for a reduction in the assessment of this county:—

"The figures of the assessment of Los Angeles for 1889 are about 14,000,000 dol. less than for 1888. Notwithstanding this, Supervisor Davis asserted that property in the county is assessed far beyond its value. Everything has been wrecked by the 'boom,' and financial men have gone down by the hundreds. He gave the location of large tracts of alkali lands which are assessed for 40 dol. and 60 dol. an acre which were suitable only for the home of horned-toads and jack-rabbits. Many of these tracts, however, have been subdivided into town lots, and sold at fabulous prices, but are now abandoned by the purchasers.

"One of the most curious things which came out was offered by Supervisor Davis. It was a document giving the history and present condition of 60 paper towns in all portions of the county. The 60 town sites comprised 79,350 town lots now listed by the assessor, and at present the whole 60 had but 2,351 inhabitants. The statistics were compiled by V. J. Rowan, a surveyor, on the 4th instant, and he took only towns laid out since January 1, 1887. The names included many that sound grotesquely. At many of the town sites vast sums of money have been expended in building hotels, churches, and schoolhouses, which are now abandoned or offered for sale at a fraction of their cost. One hotel was mentioned which cost 60,000 dol., which has since been given to a college society.

"Among the towns were Border City, having 1,920 lots platted and not a single inhabitant; Chicago Park, 2,286 lots and one inhabitant—the watchman who takes care of the 'leading' hotel; Carlton, 4,060 lots and no inhabitants; Manchester, 2,304 lots, with not a soul in it; West Glendale, 8,128 lots and no inhabitants; Sunset, 2,032 lots and one inhabitant, he being, as in the other case, the watchman of an expensive hotel."

Sewers are about to be constructed in this city at a cost of 100,000*l.*; to meet this expenditure sewer bonds, bearing interest at 5 per cent., will be issued by the city, and sold from time to time as the money is required. The local banks will probably purchase most of these bonds, and re-sell them at a small premium. I regard these bonds as an exceptionally good investment for people who are satisfied with 5 per cent. for their money.

Sewer bonds.

It is difficult to estimate the percentage of deaths in this city, owing to varying estimates of population. The rate is not over 12 per 1,000, however, and would be less if deaths from consumption, contracted elsewhere, were deducted. The mildness of the climate admits of sea-bathing in mid-winter, and on the seacoast the heat of summer is not excessive. In the editorial column of the Los Angeles "Daily Herald," I find the following description of a sea-bath on December 31:—

Climate.

"Arrived on the seashore we found that, maugre the late storm, nature was smiling and benignant. A sun of great brilliancy overspread the matchless configuration of this to be great international and transcontinental watering place. The expanse of the greatest of oceans was cerulean, as usual, with the exception of a narrow strip at the ocean's edge, which represented the late storm in a considerable contribution of murkey fresh water. The survey being satisfactory, the trio procured bathing suits and plunged into what Richard Swiveller has called, with great felicity, 'the briny.'"

I make this quotation because it conveys some idea of the climate, and is a fair specimen of editorial work here. For full information about this climate I beg to refer to my consular report for the year 1884.

The following item is taken from the Los Angeles "Evening Express" of March 6, 1890:—

Non-resident purchasers of Californian land.

"N. L. Rigby this morning received a letter from a gentleman in London, England. The party stated that during the past two months he had sold Californian land, located in Kern county, to 64 purchasers, all well-to-do, who intend to come to the United States and live. The gentleman stated that he intended to remain in the world's metropolis until April when he would come to California with the colonists to whom he had sold land. He expects to increase his sales to 100 between now and April 1.

"This would seem to indicate that the people of Great Britain know something about the value of land in this section, and are profiting by their knowledge."

Although I know nothing of the enterprise referred to in the foregoing cutting. I am absolutely certain that intending settlers are extremely unwise to purchase land in California without personally inspecting it. I always advise new comers to reside here for some months, and acquire some knowledge of the country and people before purchasing land here.

NOTE.—In this report dollars have been converted into 1*l.* sterling at the rate of 5 dol. per 1*l.* sterling.

I am indebted to Mr. Hinds, collector of customs, San Pedro for the statistics in Annexes A., B., and C.

Annex A.—RETURN of all Shipping at the Port of Wilmington (San Pedro), California, in the Year 1889.

ENTERED.

Nationality.	Sailing.		Steam.		Total.	
	Number of Vessels.	Tons.	Number of Vessels.	Tons.	Number of Vessels.	Tons.
British	16	22,461	6	7,980	22	30,441
American	7	10,824	...	...	7	10,824
Others	12	11,553	...	...	12	11,553
Total	35	44,838	6	7,980	41	52,818
,, for the year preceding	92	116,609	6	7,980	98	124,589

NOTE.—This return does not include 586 sailing and steam-coasting vessels; aggregate tonnage 489,500. The coasters for 1888 numbered 917; tonnage, 543,475.

CLEARED.

Nationality.	Sailing.		Steam.		Total.	
	Number of Vessels.	Tons.	Number of Vessels.	Tons.	Number of Vessels.	Tons.
British	16	23,047	6	7,980	22	31,027
American	7	10,824	...	...	7	10,824
Others	12	11,553	...	...	12	11,553
Total	35	45,424	6	7,980	41	53,404
,, for the year preceding	89	116,526	6	7,980	95	124,506

Annex B.—RETURN of the Principal Articles of Export from Wilmington, California, during the Years 1888-89.

Articles.	1888.		1889.	
	Quantity.	Value.	Quantity.	Value.
	Tons.	£	Tons.	£
Wheat	3,100	..	..	..
Other articles	6,000	..	7	120
Total	9,100	..	7	120

The following is a summary of imports in coasting vessels (domestic) trade :—

Articles.		Quantity.	Value.
			£
Lumber	Feet	46,333,999	123,600
Railway ties	Number	942,681	94,300
Other articles	Tons	25,804	260,000

RETURN of the Principal Articles of Import to Wilmington, California, during the Years 1888-89.

Articles.		1888.		1889.	
		Quantity.	Value.	Quantity.	Value.
			£		£
Coal	Tons	170,065	340,130	67,620*	135,240
Pig iron	,,	...	...	200	453
Cement	Barrels	3,661	14,644	...	...
Railway iron	Tons	1,500	8,000	...	...
Other articles	,,	554	910	209	154
Total		175,780	363,684	68,029	135,847

* The value of coals taken at 2l. per ton, the average wholesale price here.

Annex C.—TABLE showing the Total Value of all Articles Exported from Wilmington and Imported to Wilmington from and to Foreign Countries during the Years 1888-89.

Country.	Exports. 1888.	Exports. 1889.	Imports. 1888.	Imports. 1889.
	£	£	£	£
Great Britain	..	120	363,684	135,847
Total	..	120	363,684	135,847

SAN DIEGO.

Mr. Vice-Consul Allen reports as follows:—

General business. There is little to chronicle for the past year. Trade has been dull throughout the State, and there has been a consequent falling-off in the amount of shipping entering this port, but the number of vessels bound hither is now increasing.

Shipping. Annex A. shows that the falling-off is chiefly in British shipping, there having been only 11 entries during 1889 as against 43 in 1888. This is due to the decreased importation of coals from Australia, and cement from Great Britain. The totals for 1889, however, are still considerably in excess of those for 1887.

Exports. Gold discoveries in Lower California. Annex C. shows a large increase in the exports for 1889. This is due to the rush to the gold mines in Lower California, Mexico, which took place in March, 1889, the miners' stores and outfits having all been exported hence.

The excitement lasted a few weeks only, as the "placer" or surface diggings proved unproductive. The large majority of the people who went in search of gold were lightly equipped, and were entirely without experience. As soon, therefore, as they found that they could not make ordinary labourers wages at surface washing, they returned to San Diego complaining that the reported gold find was a fraud.

It is extremely difficult to obtain really trustworthy information regarding the Lower Californian mines, but I am inclined to think that there are "ledges" there that can be made to pay well if properly worked. As, however, no shaft has been sunk to a greater depth than 70 or 80 feet, the value of the mines is still very uncertain.

Trade with Mexico. Trade between San Diego and the coast of Mexico is improving, several cargoes of "prima vera" wood have lately been imported from Manzanillo, and have been sent by rail to the Eastern States, but I have been unable to ascertain with any certainty if any profit has been made in the business.

Cultivation of soil. The area under cultivation in San Diego county has been largely increased this season, but accurate statistics are not obtainable. In one district alone in the northern part of the county there are this year over 100,000 acres in grain, where three years ago there were not 10,000 acres.

There has also been a great demand for fruit trees, both citrus and deciduous, and nurserymen have made more profits. The country around San Diego Bay seems to be specially adapted to lemon growing. Some of the finest lemons I have ever seen are grown within 5 miles of the bay. This is a very profitable industry.

The captain of the United States steamer "Albatross" reported the existence of fishing banks within 100 miles of this port, and a company was formed to catch and to preserve the fish. Owing, however, to the lack of a good market, the enterprise came to nothing. *Fishing banks.*

A Bill has just been passed by Congress making San Diego a "port of immediate transportation," i.e., a port at which merchandise can be entered in bond for transportation to other points. *Customs regulations.*

An appropriation has been made for the erection of Government buildings, custom-house and post office. A quarantine hospital is also to be established here, and the military "post" will probably be greatly strengthened. *Government buildings.*

There are already two iron foundries here, and as there is abundance of iron found in this country there is a prospect of the further development of this industry when cheap fuel is brought hither from the Utah coal fields and from Mexico. *Manufactories.*

A watch factory is already in operation, and nail, wire, gauze, and match factories are about to begin work.

The "Cuzamaca and Eastern Railroad," which I mentioned in my last report, has not been built to a connection with the "Southern Pacific," and it is now extremely doubtful when, or if, the junction will be made. The city of San Diego has raised a subsidy, to be given, on certain conditions, to any railroad company that will build a connecting link with another transcontinental line. So far nothing has been settled, but it is very probable that, during the coming year, good progress will be made toward the attainment of this object, which is of such importance to the city. *Railroads.*

The United States census of 1880 gives San Diego county a population of 8,613. The population of the county is now estimated at 75,000, and that of the city at 31,000. *Population.*

		£	Dollars.	
Assessed valuation of real estate in city	..	5,860,246 =	28,480,798	Assessed values, &c.
,, ,, personal property	..	776,603 =	3,774,291	
,, ,, railroads ,,	..	626,993 =	3,047,190	

			Miles.
Number of miles of railroad in county is	.. .. ..	340
,, ,, telegraph ,,	.. .. ..	630
,, ,, telephone ,,	.. .. ..	60
,, ,, water flumes ,,	.. .. ..	35

			Number.
Number of cattle in the county of San Diego	.. ..	25,198
,, horses ,, ,,	.. ..	9,539
,, sheep ,, ,,	.. ..	41,779
,, hogs ,, ,,	.. ..	2,487
,, stands of bees ,,	.. ..	14,917

UNITED STATES.

Crops for past year.

ACREAGE cultivated and Yield for Past Year.

Articles.	Acres.	Yield.
Oranges	308	10,250 boxes
Raisins	8,034	167,000 ,,
Wine	} 2,264	{ 78,500 gallons
Brandy		1,768 ,,
Deciduous fruits	38,017	740,000 lbs.
Barley	17,384	6,563 tons = 147,000 centals
Oats	160	67 ,, = 1,500 ,,
Corn (maize)	400	538 ,, = 2,058 ,,
Other crops	15,000	..

Climate.

I give the following extracts from the report of Dr. Gochenauer, the health officer of San Diego, as they may be of interest to invalids:—

"The advantages we claim for this climate are its purity, equability and freedom from those extreme changes incident to less favoured countries; and we urge these as highly advantageous to all those who are endeavouring to maintain or regain their health, as well as to all pleasure seekers who desire the comforts of perfect climatic conditions."

"This city is so situated that the climate is almost unchanging. The meteorological table published elsewhere will show that the winter temperature is but a few degrees from that of the summer, and while our winds are never too cold nor too strong for the comfort and pleasure of the most nervous invalids, they are continuous. Our almost perpetual sunshine also plays an important part in the economy of our sanitary conditions, and the perfection of our climate for comfort and health."

"———— tables concerning the health of our schools, and the mortuary statistics of this city speak volumes, and clearly justify our claims for San Diego as the finest health resort in the world."

Loans.

Money is still worth from 8 per cent. to 10 per cent. clear of taxes and expenses.

Annex A.—RETURN of all Shipping at the Port of San Diego, California, in the Year 1889.

ENTERED.

Nationality.	Sailing. Number of Vessels.	Sailing. Tons.	Steam. Number of Vessels.	Steam. Tons.	Total. Number of Vessels.	Total. Tons.
British	11	14,179	...	...	11	14,179
American	42	19,840	121	35,067	163	54,907
Others	10	8,226	3	613	13	8,839
Total	63	42,245	124	35,680	187	77,925
,, for the year preceding	102	82,115	154	50,691	256	133,806

SAN FRANCISCO.

CLEARED.

Nationality.	Sailing.		Steam.		Total.	
	Number of Vessels.	Tons.	Number of Vessels.	Tons.	Number of Vessels.	Tons.
British	12	15,456	...	...	12	15,456
American	22	8,537	120	34,780	142	43,317
Others	3	1,843	3	1,153	6	2,996
Total	37	25,836	123	35,933	160	61,769
,, for the year preceding	84	71,622	153	40,348	237	111,970

Annex B.—RETURN of the Principal Articles of Export from San Diego, California, during the Years 1888-89.

Articles.	1888.		1889.	
	Quantity.	Value.	Quantity.	Value.
		£		£
Articles not classified	..	66,592	..	87,909

RETURN of the Principal Articles of Import to San Diego California, during the Years 1888-89.

Articles.		1888.		1889.	
		Quantity.	Value.	Quantity.	Value.
			£		£
Coal	Tons	100,228	59,017	56,527	33,949
Pig-iron	,,	...	...	...	...
Cement	Barrels	92,871	17,233	17,953	3,451
Other articles	Tons	...	48,141	...	11,319
Total		193,099	124,391	74,480	48,719

Annex C.—TABLE showing the Total Value of all Articles Exported from San Diego and Imported to San Diego from and to Foreign Countries during the Years 1888-89.

Country.	Exports.		Imports.	
	1888.	1889.	1888.	1889.
	£	£	£	£
Great Britain	..	..	24,550	3,451
British Possessions	..	..	52,841	33,949
Other countries	700	..	1,868	..
Mexico	57,640	..	48,141	10,319
Not classified	..	87,909	..	..
Total	58,340	87,909	127,400	47,719

UNITED STATES.

EUREKA.

Mr. Consular Agent J. H. Hodgson reports as follows:—

Depression in trade. The year 1889 will be remembered as a year of much general depression for the county of Humboldt, and especially so during the last six months of the year. Some interests have certainly prospered during the year, but in nearly all branches of trade a smaller business has been done than during former years. *Labour not in great demand.* Labour has not been in great demand, owing to our lumber mills having been run on an uncertain basis, the mill-owners being compelled to reduce the output of lumber, during the first half of the year, by closing for stated times first one and then another of the mills. *No market for butter.* The dairy farmers, for the early months of the year, had no market, and little butter was shipped. This cut off a considerable inflow of money. Wet weather in the spring months blighted the potato and oat crops, and even the fruit crops suffered considerably. *Feed good.* Sheep and cattle men fared well, however; feed has been good throughout the year, and wool and beef have brought good prices.

Building interest. Notwithstanding the general depression, various communities have pushed ahead. Building in and around our city has gone on with as much apparent energy as in better years, an indication of growth and progress not to be overlooked. *City improvements.* This is especially true of the city, where building operations have never ceased for a day. Handsome business blocks, a new bank structure, the central school building, and many beautiful and elegant private residences attest this fact. Streets have been greatly improved, a new system of waterworks put in, and our electric light system enlarged and perfected. *Breakwater.* The breakwater, or sea wall, referred to in my annual report of last year, has been commenced by the Government on the South Spit, at the entrance of our harbour, and work will be continued there during the summer months of the present year.

The usual Annexes A., B., and C. (the former giving a return of foreign shipping at this port, and the latter the exports and imports thereat) will be found attached to this report.

British shipping. Only one British ship entered and cleared here during the year.

British ship wrecked. On July 7, 1889, the British four-masted iron schooner, "Collary," 402 tons register, Captain Alfred Ball, with 500 tons of coal from Sydney, N.S.W., drifted ashore in a fog on the ocean beach, about 8 miles north of the entrance of Humboldt Bay, and became a total wreck; captain, officers, and crew took to the ship's boats, and were saved. The shipwrecked seamen were properly taken care of by the consular agent at this port. At the naval court held in San Francisco, Captain Ball was exonerated from all blame, and his certificates returned to him.

Shipping. The number of arrivals and departures for the year of vessels, coastwise and foreign, is considerably less than for 1888. In that year 210 steam and 466 sailing vessels arrived, and 210 steam and 438 sailing vessels departed. In 1889 the totals were:—

SAN FRANCISCO.

	Arrived.	Departed.
Steam	269	255
Sail	359	352
Total	628	607

There was a falling-off of 107 sail, and a gain of 59 steam arrivals, and a loss of 86 sail, and a gain of 45 steam departures.

As an indication of the growth of the county during the year, the three passenger steamers engaged in the business, viz., "Humboldt," "Pomona," and "North Fork," brought 9,024 incoming passengers, and took away 7,583 outgoing passengers; this would leave 1,441, showing that "our county is growing." *Passenger traffic.*

There have been a large number of homestead and pre-emption entries of land during the year, and there is still a large amount of the public domain awaiting settlement. *Government land homesteaded and pre-empted.*

Two handsome vessels were launched during the year—the "Charles E. Falk," from Bendixsen's ship yard, and the "Olga" from Matthew's yard. *Ship building.*

According to a careful calculation the lumber mills of the county have averaged only about nine months' work during the year; the total output of lumber probably not exceeding 12,000,000 feet, as against 159,703,000 feet cut during 1888. Prices, however, have remained steady during the entire year at from 14 dol. to 24 dol. *Lumber.*

The rainfall for 1889 has been excessive, fully 10 inches above the average. Mr. Connell, of the United States Signal Service, kindly furnishes the following comparative statement of rainfall in inches:—Mean temperature: 1887, 40·17; 1888, 36·48; 1889, 48·70. Annual mean temperature: 1887, 50·1; 1888, 52·5; 1889, 52·8. The extreme point for the year was about the freezing point, while the thermometer never got above 70 degrees in the warmest days. *Rainfall.*

In closing my third annual report on the trade and commerce of Eureka, Cal., I desire to express my thanks to Mr. W. G. Bonner, proprietor of the "Humboldt Mail," in this city, for the information embodied in this report.

Annex A.—RETURN of all Shipping at the Port of Eureka, California, in the Year 1889, omitting Coasting Vessels which do not Enter or Clear at Customs.

ENTERED.

Nationality.	Sailing. Number of Vessels.	Sailing. Tons.	Steam. Number of Vessels.	Steam. Tons.	Total. Number of Vessels.	Total. Tons.
British	1	498	...	...	1	498
United States of America	...	...	...	...	...	...
Total	1	498	...	...	1	498
,, for the year 1888	21	8,364	...	...	21	8,364

(886)

UNITED STATES.

Cleared.

Nationality.	Sailing. Number of Vessels.	Sailing. Tons.	Steam. Number of Vessels.	Steam. Tons.	Total. Number of Vessels.	Total. Tons.
British	1	498	...	...	1	498
United States of America	9	2,720	...	...	9	2,720
Total	10	3,218	...	...	10	3,218
,, for the year 1888	23	9,250	...	...	23	9,250

Annex B.—RETURN of Principal Articles of Export from Eureka, California, during the Years 1889–88.

FOREIGN AND DOMESTIC.

Articles.		1889. Quantity.	1889. Value. £	1889. Value. Dol.	1888. Quantity.	1888. Value. £	1888. Value. Dol.
Lumber	1,000 feet	85,000,000	304,761	1,523,805	...	520,900	2,604,500
Farm produce	Boxes, barrels, &c.	...	26,900	134,500	...	30,100	150,500
Wool	Bales, bags, &c.	4,547	69,840	349,200	...	63,158	315,790
Fish	Cases and barrels	2,902	1,110	5,550	...	500	2,500
Furs, hides, leather	Bundles, bales, &c.	1,031	2,750	13,750	...	Value not ascertained	...
Cattle and other live stock	Heads	...	562	2,810	...	750	3,750
Tan bark	Cords	...	2,000	10,000	...	7,600	38,000
Miscellaneous	...	...	10,000	50,000	...	...	...
Total	...	...	417,923	2,089,615	...	623,008	3,115,040

RETURN of Principal Articles of Import to Eureka, California, during the Years 1889–88.

FROM FOREIGN PORTS ONLY.

Articles.	1889. Quantity. Tons	1889. Value. £	1889. Value. Dol.	1888. Quantity. Tons	1888. Value. £	1888. Value. Dol.
Coal	..	..	..	1,518	873	4,365
Total	..	..	..	1,518	873	4,365

NOTE.—The rate of exchange above is calculated at 5 dol. to the 1*l.*

Annex C.—TABLE showing the Total Value of all Articles Exported from Eureka, California, and Imported thereto, during the Years 1889-88.

	Exports.				Imports.			
Country.	1889.		1888.		1889.		1888.	
	Sterling.	Currency.	Sterling.	Currency.	Sterling.	Currency.	Sterling.	Currency.
	£	Dol.	£	Dol.	£	Dol.	£	Dol.
Great Britain viâ San Francisco	7,762	38,812	6,520	32,600	...	...	...	...
British possessions, Australia	4,491	22,455	17,780	88,900	...	...	873	4,365
Hawaiian islands	8,094	40,470	3,098	15,490	...	...	...	...
Chile	...	...	1,550	7,750	...	...	...	...
Peru	1,483	7,417	862	4,310	...	...	...	...
Mexico	803	4,014	1,417	7,085	...	...	...	...
American (domestic) ports	394,520	1,972,597	591,781	2,958,905	...	...	...	...
Papeete, Tahiti	770	3,850	...	...	...	...	...	...
Total	417,923	2,089,615	623,008	3,115,040	...	...	873	4,365

NOTE.—The values in this table are reduced to sterling at the rate of 5 dol. to the 1l.

LONDON:
Printed for Her Majesty's Stationery Office,
By HARRISON AND SONS,
Printers in Ordinary to Her Majesty.
(1250   6 | 90   H & S   886)

FOREIGN OFFICE.
1890.
ANNUAL SERIES.

No. 730.

DIPLOMATIC AND CONSULAR REPORTS ON TRADE AND FINANCE.

UNITED STATES.

REPORT FOR THE YEAR 1889

ON THE

AGRICULTURE OF THE CONSULAR DISTRICT OF SAN FRANCISCO.

REFERENCE TO PREVIOUS REPORT, Annual Series No. 546.

Presented to both Houses of Parliament by Command of Her Majesty,
JUNE, 1890.

LONDON:
PRINTED FOR HER MAJESTY'S STATIONERY OFFICE,
BY HARRISON AND SONS, ST. MARTIN'S LANE,
PRINTERS IN ORDINARY TO HER MAJESTY.

And to be purchased, either directly or through any Bookseller, from
EYRE & SPOTTISWOODE, EAST HARDING STREET, FLEET STREET, E.C., and
32, ABINGDON STREET, WESTMINSTER, S.W; or
ADAM AND CHARLES BLACK, 6, NORTH BRIDGE, EDINBURGH; or
HODGES, FIGGIS, & Co., 104, GRAFTON STREET, DUBLIN.

1890.

[C. 5895–133.]   *Price One Penny.*

New Series of Reports.

Reports of the Annual Series have been issued from Her Majesty's Diplomatic and Consular Officers at the following places, and may be obtained from the sources indicated on the title-page:—

No.		Price.	No		Price.
616.	Batoum	½d.	673.	Syra	1d.
617.	Odessa	1d.	674.	Boulogne	1d.
618.	La Rochelle	1d.	675.	Taganrog	2d.
619.	Rome	1d.	676.	Wuhu	½d.
620.	Nice	1d.	677.	Batoum	1d.
621.	Kiukiang	½d.	678.	Manila	1d.
622.	Paris	1d.	679.	Tamsui	1d.
623.	Salonica	1½d.	680.	Kiungchow	1d.
624.	Réunion	1d.	681.	Swatow	1d.
625.	Ichang	1d.	682.	Stettin	6d.
626.	Bogotá	1d.	683.	Bordeaux	2½d.
627.	Malaga	2d.	684.	Port Said	1d.
628.	Porto Rico	1d.	685.	Coquimbo	½d.
629.	Bushire	2½d.	686.	Warsaw	1d.
630.	The Hague	½d.	687.	Ichang	1d.
631.	Berlin	1d.	688.	Wênchow	1d.
632.	Adrianople	1½d.	689.	Trebizond	1d.
633.	Rome	1½d.	690.	Damascus	½d.
634.	Santiago	½d.	691.	Savannah (Georgia)	1d.
635.	Tahiti	½d.	692.	Barcelona	2½d.
636.	Maranham	½d.	693.	Santos	1d.
637.	Mexico	2d.	694.	San José	1d.
638.	Christiania	1d.	695.	Batavia	1d.
639.	Copenhagen	1d.	696.	Genoa	1½d.
640.	Paris	1d.	697.	Calais	2d.
641.	Venice	1d.	698.	Marseilles	1d.
642.	Cherbourg	½d.	699.	Brest	1d.
643.	New York	1d.	700.	Lisbon	2½d.
644.	Patras	1d.	701.	Leghorn	2d.
645.	Bourgas	½d.	702.	Rio Grande do Sul	1d.
646.	St. Petersburg	3d.	703.	Tainan	1d.
647.	Taganrog	½d.	704.	Kewkiang	4d.
648.	Baltimore	1½d.	705.	Fiume	1d.
649.	New Orleans	2d.	706.	Odessa	2d.
650.	New Orleans	1d.	707.	Suakin	½d.
651.	Samos	½d.	708.	Hankow	½d.
652.	Buda-Pesth	1½d.	709.	Amoy	1d.
653.	Tripoli	½d.	710.	Buda-Pesth	1½d.
654.	Buenos Ayres	½d.	711.	Corunna	2d.
655.	Paris	1d.	712.	Mogador	2d.
656.	Cherbourg	1d.	713.	Cadiz	½d.
657.	Warsaw	½d.	714.	Cadiz	1d.
658.	Rome	1½d.	715.	Rio de Janeiro	2½d.
659.	Saigon	½d.	716.	Newchwang	½d.
660.	Buenos Ayres	½d.	717.	Chinkiang	½d.
661.	Galveston	1d.	718.	San Francisco	6d.
662.	Galatz	1½d.	719.	Bussorah	½d.
663.	Antwerp	1d.	720.	Beyrout	1d.
664.	Boston	1d.	721.	Adrianople	½d.
665.	Madeira	½d.	722.	Nantes	½d.
666.	New Hebrides	½d.	723.	Caracas	1d.
667.	Riga	1d.	724.	Mogador	½d.
668.	Charleston	1d.	725.	Tientsin	1d.
669.	Algiers	2d.	726.	Foochow	1d.
670.	Stuttgart	1d.	727.	Port au Prince	½d.
671.	Havre	3d.	728.	Callao	1d.
672.	The Piræus	1d.	729.	Puerto Plata	½d.

No. 730.

Reference to previous Report, Annual Series No. 546.

UNITED STATES.

SAN FRANCISCO.

Consul Donohoe to the Marquis of Salisbury.

My Lord, San Francisco, April 19, 1890.

I HAVE the honour to enclose, herewith, Reports on Agricultural Matters from this Consulate and from the Vice-Consulates of Portland, Astoria, Los Angeles, and Consular Agency at Eureka, for the year 1889.

No Reports will be furnished this Year by the Vice-Consuls at Port Townsend or San Diego.

I have, &c.
(Signed)   DENIS DONOHOE.

Report on Agriculture in the State of California.

The rains towards the close of 1888 encouraged the belief of still earlier rains in 1889, but there was little or none until well on in February. This of course gave more time for outdoor work on the farms, and consequently a larger acreage was seeded to grain.

Wheat. The crop of wheat of California, as stated by the county assessors, is given at 30,196,509 centals, and the area seeded as 3,104,088 acres. Prices ruled low, however, and there is some grumbling amongst the farmers. Colusa county had the largest production, and Tulare county comes next; the acreage in grain in the former being 403,008, and in the latter 349,000.

Barley. The acreage in barley for California is given as 1,166,218 acres, and the crop as 9,895,877 centals. Prices have been low and barely remunerative to the grower.

Green fruits. The crop of fruit in 1889 was, as usual, large of some varieties while that of others was light. The crop of strawberries and blackberries, particularly the latter, was very large, causing low prices to obtain during the time of the heaviest deliveries. The raspberry crop was about an average. In tree fruit the crop of apricots was about an average to the tree, although owing to more young trees coming into bearing, the aggregate outturn was above

(907)

an average. The peach and apple crops were short, but the quality averaged better. The prune crop was large and of generally good quality. The crop of nectarines showed an increase, but as this fruit is gaining in favour prices kept well up. The pear and plum crops were only slightly above an average, but that of figs was larger. The grape crop was very large, and low prices prevailed for both table and wine. The large and constantly increasing demand for Californian green fruits at the distributive points in the Central and Eastern States caused the markets to be largely relieved of their surplus. With better and lower overland railroad facilities the eastern shipments ought to increase in 1890. This is due to the general favour with which Californian fruits are being received by eastern consumers. Heavy shipments of apples were made in the autumn months to China, Japan, Australasia, and Mexican and Central American ports. Overland shipments the past year aggregate as follows—41,670,490 lbs.

Citrus fruits. The area planted in oranges for the State of California is given as 50,195 acres, and the product as 1,069,435 boxes.

Raisins. The crop of 1889 has been estimated at 24,750,000 lbs., a large proportion of which, after providing for local consumption, is shipped to the Eastern States. Some thousands of boxes have been shipped to Australia, and I understand this business is likely to increase, as the raisins packed in California have been found to keep well.

Canned fruits. It is difficult to obtain any reliable statistics as to canned fruits, but it is generally conceded that the pack of this coast has been about 25 per cent. below that of 1888. The apricot pack was probably fully as heavy; the peach pack not over 40 per cent.; that of Bartlett pears not over 60 per cent.; the plum pack probably equal, whilst that of the other varieties of fruit averaged about the same as in 1888.

Wool. The Californian wool clip of 1889 has been one of the best, as far as condition is concerned, that has been marketed for several years past; this was due to good pasturage and spring rains. The receipts of wool from this State at San Francisco have been 83,019 bales.

Hops. The estimated yield of hops within the State has been 34,200 bales with a total acreage of 4,735.

Wine. With an estimated yield of 14,500,000 gallons for the year, which is a considerable falling-off from the quantity produced in 1888, 17,000,000 gallons, the producers have been able to realise a larger price on the vintage than before. The improvement in quality is perceptible, as low class wines are now distilled for brandy, and there is a growing demand for this spirit, which answers well for fortifying purposes, and is now exported for that purpose. A very fair table wine, both red and white, is now produced, and a good trade is gradually springing up for it with an increased demand for both export and consumption in the Eastern and Central States. I can obtain a good table wine (red), in bottle, from a wine merchant here, produced on his own vineyard, at twelve shillings a dozen, returning the bottles. This is a perfectly pure red wine with a slight Burgundy flavour, and favourably compares with the table wines one drinks at a first class hotel in Paris.

Many of the large landed proprietors in California are dividing up their properties, and selling off in small lots to actual settlers. This plan will probably prove advantageous to both parties; but settlers are warned not to believe all statements made by those who have lands for sale, and particularly not to purchase without a thorough inspection made on the spot, and seeing how the farmers in the neighbourhood are getting on, and hearing their opinion as to crops, cost of irrigation, and market facilities. There are plenty of low priced farms to be had, but it will often be found that dearer land in a good neighbourhood, with better facilities for disposing of your produce, will prove the cheaper bargain of the two. Those who come to California for fruit farming had better understand, that until the fourth year after planting they will receive no return for their outlay, and unless they have enough means to carry them over this term they will make a dismal failure, and be probably stranded in a foreign country. *Farms in California.*

PORTLAND, OREGON.

Mr. Vice-Consul Laidlaw reports as follows:—

The year 1889 has been a profitable one for the agriculturist in some sections of the district tributary to this port, but quite the reverse in others. The Willamette Valley had good crops of wheat, oats, and potatoes as well in yield as in quality, and receipts of all agricultural produce were larger than last year. Prices of wheat, the staple produce, were lower, and oats and potatoes were the most profitable crops and brought good prices during the last half of the year, though I doubt if the average prices were remunerative. East of the Cascades Mountains a dry season reduced the crops very materially, and much of the wheat was thin and shrivelled. In this section the oats, barley, and flax seed were all light crops for the same reason. *Crops generally. Willamette Valley. Good crops. East Oregon crops a partial failure.*

The receipts of wheat at this port were as under during the cereal years ending July 31 each year:— *Wheat.*

	Willamette Valley.		Eastern Oregon.	
	Wheat.	Flour.	Wheat.	Flour.
	Qrs.	Sacks.	Qrs.	Sacks.
1888–89	199,095	251,614	571,403	81,425
1887–88	121,808	140,968	1,014,212	131,471
1886–87	272,010	142,539	619,099	80,595
Aug.–Dec. 1889	158,551	96,330	256,469	41,870
„ „ 1888	142,403	122,908	419,983	34,491
„ „ 1887	43,727	51,529	353,472	48,837

Oats. The oat crop in the Valley was large and fine. The following is a comparison of receipts in centals:—

Cereal years.		Calendar years.		Five months ending December 31.	
1888–89.	1887–88.	1889.	1888.	1889.	1888.
530,596	205,606	502,363	379,700	215,976	294,209

Barley. Barley is principally grown in Eastern Oregon, and the crop was almost a complete failure.

Flax seed. The crop of flax seed was much smaller than last year; some little quantity was received from the Valley, and the receipts from Eastern Oregon of new crop have only been about one-third of those of 1888.

Potatoes. The potato crop was good, and during the last six months of the year farmers realised excellent prices, also for onions and other garden produce.

Fruit. Receipts of green fruit were comparatively small. A large percentage of the apple crop in the Willamette Valley was unmerchantable, both from the dryness of the season and the ravages of the codlin moth. Very good prices were realised for all fruits.

Fruit canning. Fruit canning was carried on to a limited extent; one of the two factories working on peas, cherries, blackberries, and pears.

Hops. The average yield of hops per acre was 1,100 lbs., and the crop was about 12 per cent. less than last year though about 10 per cent. more land was planted. Receipts were 2,242,500 lbs., and prices were generally low, netting very little over the cost of picking.

Sheep and cattle.
Wool. The wool product, particularly in Eastern Oregon and Washington is increasing yearly. Receipts were in round numbers 18,000,000 lbs. Eastern Oregon and Washington; Willamette Valley, 1,500,000 lbs.; and Umpqua, 500,000 lbs. Profitable prices were realised.

Cattle. Cattle are becoming less numerous and not so profitable, as the ranges are eaten off and winter feeding has to be resorted to in many sections. The number of live stock slaughtered here during the year was:—cattle, 19,200; sheep, 60,000; and swine, 3,000. Prices did not fluctuate much, and at the close of the year quotations were as under:—

Prices of meat.

		Live.	Dressed.
		Cents.	Cents.
Beef	Lb...	2½ to 3	6
Mutton	,, ..	3 ,, 3¼	6 to 7½
Hogs	,, ..	4 ,, 4¼	5
Veal	,, ..	6 ,, 8	..

SAN FRANCISCO.

In order to give a general idea of the agricultural products of the different counties of the State I append a table collated from the assessors' returns; but these are notoriously under estimated, representing generally less than half of the actual number of animals.

Assessors' returns.

Counties.	Acres of improved Land.	Horses and Mules.	Cattle.	Sheep and Goats.	Swine.	Square Mile Area.
Willamette Valley—						
Multnomah	158,402	2,337	4,082	752	809	430
Benton	323,997	2,996	10,649	13,902	1,279	1,300
Clackamas	361,556	3,825	1,456	10,212	5,934	1,560
Lane	466,266	6,703	23,829	19,511	9,436	5,780
Linn	463,056	7,386	19,342	36,908	5,978	2,400
Marion	396,637	6,035	13,449	27,380	5,959	620
Polk	233,275	3,182	7,991	19,824	5,500	560
Washington	259,562	3,721	10,958	6,755	4,238	460
Yamhill	184,112	4,696	9,803	16,500	6,600	720
Total	2,846,863	40,881	101,559	151,744	45,733	13,830
Southern Oregon—						
Douglas	497,317	4,313	15,777	50,749	9,452	4,500
Jackson	192,374	...	10,119	12,576	7,866	2,500
Josephine	76,819	1,198	4,604	1,195	2,027	1,800
Klamath	341,437	6,909	15,562	1,150	1,183	6,000
Total	1,107,947	12,420	46,062	65,670	20,528	14,800
Eastern Oregon—						
Baker	101,816	6,045	27,491	14,987	1,101	2,500
Crook	81,799	11,232	20,090	222,137	399	7,500
Gilliam	81,988	8,206	12,710	109,266	693	2,000
Harney	154,520	10,890	47,028	85,494	122	12,000
Grant	114,716	12,196	18,189	240,201	882	6,000
Malheur	103,863	11,438	28,297	85,220	165	9,500
Lake	79,462	10,210	37,384	135,863	1,416	6,250
Morrow	126,279	8,239	8,618	146,560	1,365	1,900
Umatilla	380,209	14,702	16,584	146,353	4,497	3,500
Wasco	169,777	7,896	9,052	175,166	2,643	2,850
Union	275,414	13,227	21,406	58,259	5,970	3,150
Sherman	...	...	...	...	...	750
Wallowa	72,731	6,145	11,228	57,621	1,713	2,500
Total	1,742,574	120,426	258,077	1,477,127	20,966	60,400
Coast Counties—						
Columbia	219,567	1,169	5,976	2,748	1,366	780
Clatsop	123,967	548	3,821	876	522	780
Curry	93,350	831	5,045	17,628	639	1,170
Tillamook	99,011	635	4,910	1,529	392	1,600
Coos	291,903	1,950	12,080	7,280	3,067	1,560
Total	827,798	5,133	31,832	30,061	5,986	5,890
Recapitulation—						
Willamette Valley	2,846,863	40,881	101,559	151,744	45,733	13,830
Southern Oregon	1,107,947	12,420	46,062	65,670	20,528	14,800
Eastern Oregon	1,742,574	120,426	258,077	1,477,127	20,966	60,400
Coast Counties	827,798	5,133	31,832	30,061	5,986	5,890
Total	6,525,182	178,860	437,530	1,724,602	93,213	94,920

ASTORIA, OREGON.

Mr. Vice-Consul Cherry reports as follows:—

There is but little to add since my last report.

Hay is still the leading crop, and more tide-land is being reclaimed, all for this crop. The price of hay has gone up from 2*l*. 8*s*. to 5*l*. per ton.

Hay.

Of oats there is not sufficient grown to supply the wants of the district.

Oats.

Fruits.

Apples, on account of the codlin moth and worm, are very scarce, and are now three times the usual price—12*s.* per box of 45 lbs.

The total agriculture of the district is not sufficient for the demand, excepting potatoes, which are shipped to San Francisco.

WILMINGTON AND LOS ANGELES.

Mr. Vice-Consul Mortimer reports as follows:—

In former special reports on agriculture I pointed out, that owing to climatic differences there was little to be said about agriculture here likely to interest farmers in England.

Orange culture.

Orange culture has received an impetus, owing to the extermination of the "white scale," an insect pest which, a year ago, was rapidly killing the orange trees.

The acreage in grain is not likely to increase, owing to the fact that grain farming will not pay interest on the present value of land in this district. In a former report I stated that the cost per acre on a 25,000 acre ranch, of ploughing, seeding, and harvesting, was 2*s.* 5*d.*, and the net profit 7*s.* per acre. The particular ranch to which I referred was purchased about 15 years ago for 25,000*l.* (1*l.* per acre); it is worth now, and is saleable at, 6*l.* per acre, and efforts are now being made to sell it in London for 30*l.* per acre!

Profits in grain farming.

Market gardening.

Market gardening is exclusively in the hands of Chinamen. A great deal of land in the immediate vicinity of Los Angeles is rented to them at 3*l.* to 4*l.* per acre per annum, payable monthly in advance. They are very thrifty and industrious, and, it is stated, make good profits out of this industry. They furnish an ample supply of vegetables to householders in Los Angeles for the moderate charge of 1*s.* 6*d.* to 2*s.* 6*d.* per week, depending on the number of people in each house and variety of vegetables supplied.

Beet sugar.

A great deal of interest has been taken here in the past year in the manufacture of beet sugar. Some sugar manufacturers inspected this district, contemplating the establishment of extensive works. Nothing has been done however, and it is now stated in the local Press, that the establishment of a beet sugar factory here will depend on the action of the present Congress as to the duties on sugar, that is to say, if the present duty be not lowered, the factory will be started.

Race-horses.

The business of raising thoroughbred race-horses is increasing here, and proving very remunerative. Persons engaged in the business have recently sold a number of young horses at auction in New York for 1,000*l.* to 4,000*l.* apiece. In a former report I remarked that it was worthy of consideration whether horses for the British army could not be raised here, and shipped to England viâ New Orleans; the expense of raising them is small, as, owing to the mildness of the climate, live stock can feed in the fields all the year round. For information about orange culture, and viticulture, I beg to refer to my annual report for this year.

Eureka.

Mr. Consular Agent J. H. Hodgson reports as follows:—

I have very little to add to my special report on agriculture, dated February 22, 1889.

The Ninth District Agricultural Association held their tenth annual fair in the latter end of September, 1889, and handsome premiums were awarded. The general attendance from all over this extensive county shows a wide-spread interest in this district fair, which is held in the town of Rohneville, a town pleasantly situated near the Foothills, in the valley of Eel River, 22 miles south of Eureka, surrounded by very rich farming and timber land, and reached by the Eureka and Eel Railway. The recent fair came nearer to a model institution in many respects than any previous meeting. The races may be considered to have promoted the interest of horse breeders, and the fact that almost all the horses entered were Humboldt stock, gave that feature of the fair a more legitimate standing than usually obtains. The immense diversity of resources indicated by the displays was striking. While by no means large, there was yet enough to show the magnificent possibilites of this region.

2nd Annual Report on Agriculture. Annual district fair commented on.

The advancement that has been made in so short a time in the improvement of all kinds of stock in our country ought to make our people proud; but the magnitude of the stock raising interest in our midst, both present and prospective, is but little realised by the great mass of our citizens. They have reason also to be proud of what they have proved as to the wonderful adaptability and advantages this county has in raising stock of all kinds.

Stock-raising interest.

The climate of Humboldt county represents nearly the whole of the Pacific coast. We have the cool sea coast, where butter never melts; and the warmer sections further inland, with positively green grass all the year round. Our people have, by the introduction of different grasses, proved, on the coast, that they can make gilt edge butter the year round; and further, that they have the best grass-land on earth. The statements of some of our best citizens as to the number of cows, and stock of all kinds, kept to the acre, somewhat stagger the credulity of those not acquainted with the facts, but they are facts for all that.

Advantages of Humboldt county for stock raising, &c.

Considering all the drawbacks consequent upon the settlement of a new county, and the fact that our county is almost detached from the outside world by a lack of proper transportation facilities, she has made a splendid record in her stock business. We have to-day some very finely bred stock, allied in blood to the best in the world, and with the investment of some capital and energy I see no reason why we may not become as noted in this direction as we are for our wool and other products. We have cheap land, and with the improvements we have made in the last few years in cattle, sheep, horses, and swine, I see no reason why this county, for the purpose of raising fine stock, should not be the peer of any section of country in the world.

Humboldt county is not a large grain-producing section, owing

Grain.

Hay.
Oats.
Wheat.
Barley.

Average bushels to the acre

Potatoes.

Fruits.

to the formation of the land. More of its land, however, is adapted to that industry than is used at present. About 100,000 acres are sown to grain and hay. Oats are of a superior quality and are largely raised. Wheat is not extensively raised; only about 20,000 acres being sown. Last year 40,000 sacks of oats, 5,000 sacks of barley, and 6,000 sacks of peas were shipped from the county. The grains produce is as follows in Humboldt:—oats, 35 to 90 bushels to the acre; barley, 30 to 80; wheat, 30 to 60.

Potatoes we can raise, and good ones; they thrive well on our bottom lands, yielding 7 to 10 tons to the acre.

Of late years it has been demonstrated that Humboldt county is practically a fruit growing county, the only drawback to this industry being the lack of ample means of transportation: this drawback is being overcome, and will be completely removed by the advent of railroad connection with the rest of the State. This is promised us in the near future.

Peaches are equal to those raised anywhere in the State, in fact bring a higher price and sell quicker than those imported into the county.

Apples of all varieties do well in every portion of the county, and from the fact that they sell at 1 dol. 75 c. and 2 dol. per box wholesale, is evidence sufficient to prove that this county can produce apples of a superior quality.

The Bartlett pear thrives well here; apricots and nectarines also do well. Prunes of all varieties are now raised in every portion of the county; plums also. Cherries grow well all over the county, especially in Eel River valley.

Small fruits of all kinds grow luxuriantly.

LONDON:
Printed for Her Majesty's Stationery Office,
By HARRISON AND SONS,
Printers in Ordinary to Her Majesty.
(1250 6 | 90—H & S 907)

FOREIGN OFFICE.
1890.
ANNUAL SERIES.

No. 731.

DIPLOMATIC AND CONSULAR REPORTS ON TRADE AND FINANCE.

UNITED STATES.

REPORT FOR THE YEAR 1889
ON THE
TRADE OF THE CONSULAR DISTRICT OF PHILADELPHIA.

REFERENCE TO PREVIOUS REPORT, Annual Series No. 464.

Presented to both Houses of Parliament by Command of Her Majesty,
JUNE, 1890.

LONDON:
PRINTED FOR HER MAJESTY'S STATIONERY OFFICE,
BY HARRISON AND SONS, ST. MARTIN'S LANE,
PRINTERS IN ORDINARY TO HER MAJESTY.

And to be purchased, either directly or through any Bookseller, from
EYRE & SPOTTISWOODE, EAST HARDING STREET, FLEET STREET, E.C., and
32, ABINGDON STREET, WESTMINSTER, S.W.; or
ADAM AND CHARLES BLACK, 6, NORTH BRIDGE, EDINBURGH; or
HODGES, FIGGIS, & Co., 104, GRAFTON STREET, DUBLIN.

1890.
Price Twopence Halfpenny.

New Series of Reports.

Reports of the Annual Series have been issued from Her Majesty's Diplomatic and Consular Officers at the following places, and may be obtained from the sources indicated on the title-page:—

No.		Price.	No.		Price.
613.	Barcelona	½d.	672.	The Piræus	1d.
614.	Tokio	1d.	673.	Syra	1d.
615.	Naples	2½d.	674.	Boulogne	1d.
616.	Batoum	½d.	675.	Taganrog	2d.
617.	Odessa	1d.	676.	Wuhu	½d.
618.	La Rochelle	1d.	677.	Batoum	1d.
619.	Rome	1d.	678.	Manila	1d.
620.	Nice	1d.	679.	Tamsui	1d.
621.	Kiukiang	½d.	680.	Kiungchow	1d.
622.	Paris	1d.	681.	Swatow	1d.
623.	Salonica	1½d.	682.	Stettin	6d.
624.	Réunion	1d.	683.	Bordeaux	2½d.
625.	Ichang	1d.	684.	Port Said	1d.
626.	Bogotá	1d.	685.	Coquimbo	½d.
627.	Malaga	2d.	686.	Warsaw	1d.
628.	Porto Rico	1d.	687.	Ichang	1d.
629.	Bushire	2½d.	688.	Wênchow	1d.
630.	The Hague	½d.	689.	Trebizond	1d.
631.	Berlin	1d.	690.	Damascus	½d.
632.	Adrianople	1½d.	691.	Savannah (Georgia)	1d.
633.	Rome	1½d.	692.	Barcelona	2½d.
634.	Santiago	½d.	693.	Santos	1d.
635.	Tahiti	½d.	694.	San José	1d.
636.	Maranham	½d.	695.	Batavia	1d.
637.	Mexico	2d.	696.	Genoa	1½d.
638.	Christiania	1d.	697.	Calais	2d.
639.	Copenhagen	1d.	698.	Marseilles	1d.
640.	Paris	1d.	699.	Brest	1d.
641.	Venice	1d.	700.	Lisbon	2½d.
642.	Cherbourg	½d.	701.	Leghorn	2d.
643.	New York	1d.	702.	Rio Grande do Sul	1d.
644.	Patras	1d.	703.	Tainan	1d.
645.	Bourgas	½d.	704.	Kewkiang	4d.
646.	St. Petersburg	3d.	705.	Fiume	1d.
647.	Taganrog	½d.	706.	Odessa	2d.
648.	Baltimore	1½d.	707.	Suakin	½d.
649.	New Orleans	2d.	708.	Hankow	½d.
650.	New Orleans	1d.	709.	Amoy	1d.
651.	Samos	½d.	710.	Buda-Pesth	1½d.
652.	Buda-Pesth	1½d.	711.	Corunna	2d.
653.	Tripoli	½d.	712.	Mogador	2d.
654.	Buenos Ayres	½d.	713.	Cadiz	½d.
655.	Paris	1d.	714.	Cadiz	1d.
656.	Cherbourg	1d.	715.	Rio de Janeiro	2½d.
657.	Warsaw	½d.	716.	Newchwang	½d.
658.	Rome	1½d.	717.	Chinkiang	½d.
659.	Saigon	½d.	718.	San Francisco	6d.
660.	Buenos Ayres	½d.	719.	Bussorah	½d.
661.	Galveston	1d.	720.	Beyrout	1d.
662.	Galatz	1½d.	721.	Adrianople	½d.
663.	Antwerp	1d.	722.	Nantes	½d.
664.	Boston	1d.	723.	Caracas	1d.
665.	Madeira	½d.	724.	Mogador	½d.
666.	New Hebrides	½d.	725.	Tientsin	1d.
667.	Riga	1d.	726.	Foochow	1d.
668.	Charleston	1d.	727.	Port au Prince	½d.
669.	Algiers	2d.	728.	Callao	1d.
670.	Stuttgart	1d.	729.	Puerto Plata	½d.
671.	Havre	3d.	730.	San Francisco	1d.

No. 731.

Reference to previous Report, Annual Series No. 464.

UNITED STATES.

PHILADELPHIA.

Consul Clipperton to the Marquis of Salisbury.

My Lord,   *Philadelphia, April* 30, 1890.

I HAVE the honour to enclose herewith a Report on the Trade and Commerce of Philadelphia during the year 1889.

    I have, &c.
    (Signed)   ROBT. CHAS. CLIPPERTON.

Report on the Trade, Commerce and Manufactures of the Consular District of Pennsylvania, Ohio, Indiana and Michigan for the Year 1889.

The States of Pennsylvania, Ohio, Indiana and Michigan have encountered no obstacles to their continued growth since the report for the years 1887 and 1888, and the year 1890 is ushered in under auspicious circumstances. Financial, commercial, industrial and productive interests are in a healthy condition. It is to be remarked, however, that the anthracite coal trade and the manufacture of woollens during the past three months have suffered in consequence of the mild weather throughout the entire winter. Ice there has been none, while the American winters in this latitude as a rule furnish an ample supply at a thickness of from 5 to 10 inches. To these two industries, coal and woollens, the climate has been distressing, but to the consuming public at large it has been a great boon. Navigation, mining, masonry and all other occupations for the working classes have continued without interruption. Railway traffic, passenger and freight, has largely profited. Agricultural interests have held their own. Crops have been abundant, and the farmers have

(920)

survived notwithstanding the burdens of a high national tariff. Iron and steel are beyond all peradventure fully established, and the day is not far distant, it is said, when this gigantic industry—now so highly protected—will cry out for free trade.

Trusts. "Trusts," or combinations of manufacturers and producers, are extending over all sections of the country. By this novel method of alliance in the trades, competition is removed and prices fixed by the governers of the trusts. The system is baneful to the consuming public and destructive to all minor establishments refusing to "go in," millions are invested in the system and the various branches of trade are swallowed up by it. English capital has taken extraordinary leaps in the formation of trusts.

The eight hour movement. There are many indications in this country that tend strongly to the reduction of the hours of daily labour as an essential requisite of social progress. Members of the National Congress favour it and the public at large, without concerning themselves as to its results, favour it. If wages decline in proportion to the reduction in the hours of labour, employers would have no cause to complain. In this case the wage-earners would have to decide. If, however, the employers must pay the same for 8 hours as for 10, the hostility between the employed and employers will continue. For a quarter of a century there has been a reduction in the hours of labour in many branches of the trades, but a reduction in wages has followed to but a very slight extent. Employers strive for cheap labour and free raw material from abroad in order that the largest profits may be secured to meet all contingencies. Labour, however, whether of hand or brain, becomes wearied by excessive toil, and its capacity is diminished both in regard to quantity and quality of production. The question is a serious one and the difficulty is to bring about the change, which is inevitable, with as little friction as possible. The issue is likely to be this year (1890), the carpenters and joiners take the initiative, May 1, by order of the National Labour League.

While writing a report comes from Chicago that the plumbers, numbering 1,000, have "struck" for a general advance to 3 dol. 75 c. (15s. 7d.) per day for an eight hour, as a minimum, day's wages, and Saturdays' half-holidays. Doubtless this beginning will spread with more or less speed to all the skilled trades, and that the eight-hour day for mechanical labour will sooner or later extend throughout the entire country.

The labour market. Serious agitations in the labour market are predicted for the year 1890, and already strikes have commenced to crop up. In some of the Western States strikes for shorter hours and the same pay have occurred. In Chicago the carpenters have demoralised the building trade, while in Pittsburgh and vicinity a great railroad strike is imminent upon a claim for an advance of wages, and the redress of sundry alleged grievances. Should this strike be ordered—and it is daily looked for—it is quite probable to become contagious, and spread throughout the United States. Both the employers and employés are having daily conferences. The men have been very orderly, and fears of a repetition of the dreadful railway riots of 1877, when 1,200,000*l.* worth of property was destroyed and many lives sacrificed, are not apprehended.

In the mining districts of Pennsylvania the Huns are creating a great deal of dissatisfaction. They are engaged chiefly as labourers in the mines and iron works, and have taken the places of large numbers of Americans and Irish, who as a rule have families to support. They are very economical, and from month to month send their savings home to Hungary, following themselves after they have accumulated what they consider a competency for the rest of their lives. Their pay is from 4*s.* 2*d.* to 4*s.* 8*d.* per day, and it is questionable if they earn even that reduced pay. They do not strike. They generally work in gangs of four or five men each under American bosses, and go about their duties in a listless indifferent manner. They herd together in rows of houses or shanties, and live in a miserable manner. Their living does not cost them over 6*s.* 3*d.* per week. The rest of their earnings are hoarded, goes abroad, or is expended on vile liquor, to which they are addicted.

Canned goods.
An examination has been made of certain samples of vegetables preserved in glass jars having a loose plate of glass held in place by a metallic cap, over which is another ordinary stamped metallic cap. It is intended to use a metal for the inside cap not subject to the preservative fluid or by the juices of the vegetable, and tin has been selected by the packer. If pure tin were selected doubtless but little harm could ensue, but the tin employed contains lead, and this metal to a greater or less degree is dissolved by the action of the preserving fluids. Canned asparagus and peas, especially become contaminated with lead to an unwholesome degree. A single dose of this mineral poison taken into the system would not be fatal; yet a metallic poison, however small, taken at every meal must produce more fatal effects than are generally apprehended, as nearly all metallic poisons are cumulative, and in the end a point is reached where the system is so impregnated as to occasion injurious and even poisonous results. The matter has been taken in hand by the sanitary committee of the board of health.

Instances of metallic poisoning from using canned goods have occurred at different times throughout the country, and a notable case in this city is now under investigation where a family of six were seriously attacked, the result of eating canned peas purchased at a neighbouring grocery.

Increase of blindness.
Oculists state that defective sight is becoming more general in the United States, and blindness, particularly among the poor, shows a steady growth. Purulent ophthalmia of infancy is prevalent in charitable institutions, poor-houses, &c. The disease shows itself within a fortnight after birth. A recent investigation of the blind in the county almshouses and asylums of an adjoining State developed the fact that one out of every five cases of blindness

(920)

was due to ophthalmia, and that the cases could have been cured if they had been properly treated in time. The remedy is simple, but prompt treatment is essential. The disease is said to be contagious, and but few or no special precautions have been taken in any of the institutions to prevent its spreading. The increase of the blindness throughout the country has been so marked of late years—four times as great as the increase of population—that it has been made the subject of special investigation by the American Ophthalmological Society, the investigation including a study of the ophthalmia so prevalent in Egypt, to which the opthalmia of infancy is closely akin.

The liquor traffic.

The Philadelphia Liquor License Court is composed of four judges, who have by law plenary powers over the granting of licenses for the wholesale and retail trades in the city of Philadelphia. This court, since the enactment of the Brook's High License Law two years ago, have endeavoured to administer the Act of the Legislature so as to give the community the full benefit of its true intent and meaning, viz., to restrain and regulate the sale of intoxicating beverages with a view to check drunkenness and the vices and crimes resulting therefrom. This court in its administration one year ago acted with excessive stringency, so much so that the Supreme Court of the Commonwealth over-ruled some of its decisions and opened the door for a practically unlimited granting of wholesale licenses. Doubtless the higher court adjudicated upon the letter of the law and not its spirit. The result has neutralised materially the beneficial intent of the law, and has done a large amount of mischief in the city of Philadelphia, practically enlarging the scope of purchase and use of intoxicants by the quart, gallon, or cask. The applications for licenses arose at once in ponderous numbers, and a wholesale-retail system sprung up. This decision, so unexpected, held that the lower court must issue "wholesale" licenses as a matter of course, unless sufficiently strong remonstrances are filed against it. Hence two one-pint bottles, and four half-pint bottles, are sold as a wholesale quart to an enormous extent.

Another system has also loomed up, called "Speak-easies," for the illegal traffic in spirits in secret places. Doubtless in the course of time the liquor traffic, either by additional legislation or by prosecutions under the public nuisances law, will be brought to a satisfactory basis, and the "Speak-easies," "bottle shops," "bucket shops," and other nefarious means of spreading the evils of intoxication will be eliminated.

The License Court recently gave the ward constables a reprimand for their apparent apathy in ferreting out the illicit places for the sale of alcoholic stimulants. The constables are averse to an exacting performance of their duties in this respect, because when their time comes round for re-election by the residents of their respective wards, the chances of continuance in office would be very seriously interfered with. The police department of Philadelphia estimate the number of "Speak-easies" at

1,200, and it is believed that if a greater number of drinking places were licensed that the tendency towards less intoxication would prevail. Drunkenness in saloons has been almost wholly suppressed. In 1887 there were 34,037 persons arrested for drunkenness and disorderly conduct. In 1888 the number fell to 24,923, and in 1889 to 20,097. Of the 189 arrests made for selling liquor illegally 92 persons were convicted, 31 were acquitted, and 15 discharged by the magistrates for lack of evidence; two died before being tried, and 49 cases remain to be tried. There is an increasing opinion that more public-houses should be licensed and the fees higher, in order to restrict the applicants to a more law-abiding portion of the community.

The license judges have just finished their labours, and the licenses applied for and issued were:—

	1890.	1889.	1888.
Applications filed	2,921	3,214	3,431
Number issued	1,173	1,204	1,343

The licenses granted in the year 1887 were before the passage of the Brook's High License Bill. The applications for wholesale licenses increased from 475 in 1888 to 1,272 in 1890.

Two decisions of the Supreme Court of the United States have just been announced to the effect that State laws providing for the seizure of spirits brought into a State from other States is adverse to the constitutionality of the laws of prohibition States. It is held that such laws are interferences with the Inter-State Commerce Act of Congress, and therefore invalid. These decisions menace all laws passed by the different States of the Union, and permit the importation from State to State of original packages, large or small, of liquors, and legalise their sale in the State into which they were sent.

The constitutional principle involved in this case is that the movements of inter-State commerce cannot be obstructed by the police regulations of any State. The decision is also in harmony with the personal and property rights of the citizens. After the delivery, however, of the original packages in a State, the State's own legislature will have jurisdiction over its re-sale or actual prohibition of its sale. The original sale and delivery is exclusively an inter-State transaction of commerce, and no State can send a constable to intercept the transit or delivery of such original package, in order to ascertain its contents and confiscate it if contraband under a prohibitory liquor law.

The commonwealth of Pennsylvania has been prosperous throughout the years 1888 and 1889; her population has gradually increased; agriculture has yielded favourable returns, notwithstanding many failures among farmers in certain sections of the State, the result of carrying too heavy incumbrances on the lands. The out-put of the mines has steadily gained, and the products of iron and coal have held their own. Internal and inter-State commerce have shown an increased tonnage, and the numbers of persons employed enhanced. The growth of railways, although checked in some directions, has been vigorous in others. New territory for the production of mineral oils and natural gas has been discovered and opened up. The utilisation of the natural gas and of the vast accumulation of culm in the anthracite coal regions, and the development of new bituminous coalfields in several parts of the State, have proved of great advantage to the manufacturing industries in all sections, especially with reference to the manufacture of iron and the products thereof. There has been a vigorous and healthy development of the smaller cities indicated by the paving and lighting of streets, the construction of electric motors and horse tramways. Manufactures have been but slightly retarded by strikes and lock-outs, and the increasing tendency between the wage-earner and the wage-payer to consult before differences arise, and to arbitrate when they have arisen, show very satisfactory results. There has been a depression in prices of all manufactured goods, owing chiefly to an over-production.

Two amendments to the constitution, one abolishing the payment of a tax as a qualification for voting and reducing the minimum of required residence in the State by the voter to 30 days, and the other for the absolute prohibition of the manufacture, sale, or keeping for sale of any intoxicating liquors to be used as a beverage, were voted upon by the citizens of the State, and both defeated by a large majority. The prohibition vote was:—

Against	484,644
For	296,617
Majority	188,027

The suffrage vote was:—

Against	420,323
For	183,371
Majority	236,952

The finances of the State are in good condition:—

	£	s.	d.
The public debt amounts to	3,558,553	1	0
Assets in sinking fund	2,099,122	19	10
Amount of debt unprovided for	1,459,430	1	2

The interest on the State bonds ranges from $3\frac{1}{2}$ per cent. to 6 per cent.

The States of Ohio, Indiana, and Michigan continue to increase in population, agricultural products, and mining. The latest statistics of these States have not as yet been issued for public use.

PHILADELPHIA.

This county met this year with its most serious disaster, either by flood or fire, on Friday, May 31, 1889. In the Connemaugh Valley, Allegheny Mountains, the centre of the State of Pennsylvania, the city of Johnstown was swept away. The towns of Connemaugh, Cambria City, Mineral Point, and half a score of small villages were also annihilated. 3,500 lives were lost, and 15,000,000*l.* sterling of property was swept away in one day and night. Expansive grounds and a dam above, and contiguous to, Johnstown were used as fishing and hunting fields of a private club. There was a broad expanse of water of great depth. A magnificent club house and handsome private cottages were on the grounds. The artificial lake was 3½ miles long to 1¼ miles wide. The unprecedented rain storms caused this immense body of water to break away, and the terrible destruction came. The visitation was so appalling that some days elapsed before the public mind comprehended its horrors. The pulse of the civilised world, however, soon throbbed in sympathy with the sufferers, and money, surgical skill, nurses, and clothing flowed into the valley with a promptness and liberality as unprecedented as the calamity itself. Throughout the country 200,000*l.* was raised in 24 hours, and the subscriptions continued to pour in. Chaos has since succumbed to discipline and reconstruction throughout this "valley of death."

The Johnstown flood.

The city of Philadelphia as a manufacturing centre continues to grow and to become more populated. The street-paving is improving; the water supply increases; the lighting by coal gas and electricity is becoming more brilliant; the horse, cable, and electric tramways more numerous; the police force more effective; the licenses for public-houses more restricted; the erection of churches, gigantic buildings for offices, and the increase of dwellings for the working classes continue to an unprecedented extent. The figures tabulated for the last-named buildings loom up to proportions unheard of in any other city of the Union, and perhaps the world. In 1880, the number of permits issued for new buildings was 1,364; in 1885, 5,670; in 1887, 7,020, and in 1889, 11,965, making a total for ten years of 51,659 new dwellings erected. January 1, 1890, there were 200,073 dwellings, and one quarter of them built during the last 10 years. The progress has been steady and the houses were chiefly of small dwellings for the industrial classes, averaging 7 to 8 rooms, with hot and cold water, bath rooms, gas, heaters in cellars and ranges in the kitchens. They command a rent of from 40*s.* to 60*s.* per month; are neat, fairly built and comfortable. The rent quoted covers all charges except for gas and coal consumed.

City of Philadelphia.

The population of Philadelphia is now rated over 1,000,000, and the public baths were patronised by over 1,000,000 persons during the last year. The Department of Public Works (water and gas) aggregated receipts of 1,246,767*l.*, and expended 955,343*l.*, leaving a surplus of 291,424*l.*, which was expended for permanent improvements.

UNITED STATES.

Shipping and navigation.

The shipping at the port of Philadelphia, which fell off in 1888 from the previous year, has regained its former status British shipping was as follows:—

	1887.	1888.	1889.
Entrances	675	603	681
Tonnage	804,055	682,777	775,996

In 1889 of these figures 150 with a tonnage of 86,502 were sailing vessels, and 531 with 689,404 tons were steamers. There were 15 sail, and 20 steam entrances in ballast, chiefly from South American ports, where no return cargoes could be got. The American entrances in ballast were 9, with a tonnage of 13,631. The trade under all flags for 1889 is as follows:—

Entrances.	Sail. Number of Ships.	Sail. Tonnage.	Steam. Number of Ships.	Steam. Tonnage.
American	375	198,991	20	38,568
Argentine Republic	1	506	..	..
Austrian	1	479	..	..
Belgian	..	..	20	41,160
British	159	86,502	531	689,404
Danish	1	1,129	..	..
Dutch	5	6,467	..	..
French	4	3,003	2	2,587
German	29	28,888	36	66,225
Hawaian	1	989	..	..
Italian	69	40,245	..	..
Norwegian	65	45,362	2	3,000
Portuguese	4	1,565	..	..
Russian	1	619	..	..
Spanish	8	5,596	3	5,604
Swedish	1	842	..	..

Grand total for 1888—ships, 1,229; tonnage, 1,061,057; and for 1889—ships, 1,326; tonnage, 1,264,731; being an increase of 97 ships, with a tonnage of 203,674.

For the year 1890 all indications point to a large increase of British shipping at this port due to a rapidly growing West Indian sugar, fruit, and iron ore trade.

The steady advance of steam vessels over sail proceeds from year to year in deep sea voyages, and so far as British bottoms are concerned, it would seem that sailing ships are to be eventually swept from the waters.

Steamship lines increasing.

There are now running to and from this port the following ocean steamship lines:—American Steamship Company, with six steamers, Philadelphia to Liverpool; Atlantic Transportation Company, with six steamers, Philadelphia, Baltimore, London

PHILADELPHIA.

and Swansea; North Atlantic Steamship Company, five steamers, Philadelphia to London; Allan Line, with four steamers, Philadelphia and Glasgow; Hamburg-American Line, with four steamers, Philadelphia and Hamburg; Merchant Fruit Company, with five steamers, Philadelphia and Jamaica; Baltimore Fruit Company, with six steamers, Philadelphia and Central America; Howes Fruit Company, with three steamers, Philadelphia, Jamaica, and Bluefields; Mediterranean Fruit Line, five steamers, Philadelphia and Mediterranean Ports; Earn Line, with 18 steamers, Philadelphia, Cuba, and St. Thomas; Red Star Line, with two steamers, Philadelphia and Antwerp; Pollock's Belfast Line, with two chartered steamers, Philadelphia and Belfast.

The American trade is tabulated as follows:—Coastwise trade, 1889 (American flag only allowed), 2,263 schooners.

American trade.

	Brigs.	Steamers.	Ships.	Barks.	Schooners.	Total.
Entrances	8	1,443	11	21	2,269	3,752
Clearances	29	1,647	9	69	2,389	4,172

Messrs. William Cramp and Sons have turned out the following work:—

Iron shipbuilding at the port of Philadelphia.

United States cruiser "Philadelphia"—length, 335 feet; breadth, 48½ feet; main draught, $19\frac{5}{24}$ feet; displacement, 4,324 tons; maximum indicated horse-power, 105,000; twin screw, horizontal triple expansion, speed guaranteed at 19 knots; 12 6-inch breech-loading rifles; four 6-pounders, R.F.; four 3-pounders, R.F.; two 1-pounders, R.F.; three 37-mm. R.C.; four Gatlings. Contract price, 278,350*l*. 10*s*. 3*d*., with a premium of 10,309*l*. 5*s*. for each quarter knot over 19.

United States cruiser "Newark"—length, 320 feet; 49⅙ feet breadth; 18¾ feet main draught; displacement, 4,083 tons; guaranteed maximum indicated horse-power, 8,500; twin screw horizontal triple expansion; speed in knots, 18; batteries, 12 6-inch breech-loading rifles; four 6-pounders, R.F.; four 3-pounders, R.F.; two 1-pounders, R.F.; three 37-mm., R.C.; four Gatlings. Contract price, 257,319*l*. 11*s*. 9*d*., and 20*l*. 12*s*. 9*d*. for each unit of horse-power over 8,500.

United States protected cruiser "Baltimore." Length, 335 feet; 48½ feet breadth; 18½ feet main draught; displacement, 4,413 tons; guaranteed horse-power, 9,000; indicated horsepower on four hours' trial at sea, 10,064,418; twin screw horizontal triple expansion; speed in knots, 20·1; batteries, six 6-inch, four 8-inch breech-loading rifles; four 6-pounders, R.F.; two 3-pounders, R.F.; two 1-pounders, R.F.; four 37-mm., R.C.; two Gatlings. Contract price, 273,195*l*. 17*s*. 6*d*., and 21,946*l*. 15*s*. 2*d*. premium for excess in horse-power.

United States cruiser "Yorktown"—length, 230 feet; breadth, 36 feet; main draught, 14 feet; tons displacement,

1,700; guaranteed horse-power, 3,000; indicated horse-power on four hours trial at sea, 3,398·25; twin screw horizontal triple expansion; speed in knots, 16·7; batteries, six 6-inch breech-loading rifles; two 6-pounder R.F.; two 3-pounder R.F.; one 1-pounder R.F.; two 37 mm. R.C.; two Gatlings. Contract price, 93,814*l*. 8*s*. 8*d*., and 9,211*l*. 6*s*. 9*d*. premium for excess in horse-power.

United States pneumatic dynamite gun cruiser "Vesuvius"—length, 246¼ feet; breadth, 26 5/12 feet; main draught, 9 feet; 725 tons displacement; indicated horse-power, 4,216; twin screw vertical triple expansion; speed in knots, 21,646; speed guaranteed, 20 knots; batteries, three pneumatic dynamite guns, 15-inch calibre; and three 3-pounder R.F. Contract price, 721,164*l*. 18*s*. 1*d*.

In addition to the naval cruisers abovementioned, the Messrs. Cramp have turned out three iron merchant vessels, with an aggregate tonnage of 8,958, and ten engines of indicated horse-power 28,928; also at present under way four iron merchant ships of an aggregate tonnage of 12,450, and eight engines of an indicated horse-power 28,300. John H. Dialogue, steamship builder, has turned out eight vessels of lighter tonnage and horse-power, to be used chiefly for coast service.

Vessels built by the Pusey and Jones Company in the year 1889 were as follows:—

One propeller for the United States Marine, 145 feet by 3 feet by 12 feet 3 inches.

Three propellers for United States Marine Hospital Service, two 87 feet by 16½ feet by 6 feet 10 inches; one 103 feet 6 inches by 16½ feet by 6 feet 10 inches.

One twin screw boat for South America, 80 feet by 18 feet by 5 feet 6 inches.

One propeller for Pennsylvania Railroad Company, 82 feet by 19 feet by 8 feet 6 inches.

Propeller for service in North Carolina, 85 feet by 24 feet by 7 feet 6 inches.

Two steel hull stern paddle wheel boats for Florida, one 130 feet by 24 feet by 4 feet; and one 110 feet by 28 feet by 4 feet.

Two stern paddle wheel steamers for Trinidad, British West Indies (steel), one 125 feet by 25 feet by 4 feet 6 inches; and one 60 feet by 17 feet, by 4 feet.

One propeller steamer for the Sanitarium Association of Philadelphia, 130 feet by 24 feet by 9 feet.

The hulls are iron in all cases where not mentioned as steel.

The Delaware River Iron Ship Building and Engine Works, of Chester, have constructed six steamships, with an aggregate of 19,000 tons, and of a value of nearly 400,000*l*.

Other shipbuilders have not sent in any returns.

The Portuguese Government have invited a well-known American firm of shipbuilders to submit proposals for the construction of four new cruisers. On account of recent differences it is said that Portugal has not invited any English shipbuilders to tender bids. It is very doubtful that Americans will get these contracts on account of their inability to compete with the English yards in consequence of higher costs of material and labour, which it is said is from 30 per cent. to 40 per cent. greater than in the European yards.

This service is becoming of inestimable value, and yearly increasing in efficiency. The stations number 222, and are distributed on the sea and lake coasts. The coasts of New Jersey (41 stations), Rhode Island and Long Island (38 stations), and Cape Henry and Cape Fear River districts (28 stations), are the greatest in number, as those districts are the most dangerous. In the year 1888 there were 411 disasters to registered vessels, having on board 3,653 souls, of whom 12 only suffered death. The estimated value of the ships lost was 1,221,474*l*. 5*s*., and of cargoes 748,687*l*. 12*s*. 7*d*., being a total value of property involved of 1,970,161*l*. 17*s*. 7*d*.; of this amount 1,603,382*l*. 9*s*. 6*d*. was saved, and 366,779*l*. 8*s*. 1*d*. lost. Vessels totally lost, 71. The casualties to smaller craft, yachts, &c., 133, having 297 persons aboard, 5 of whom were lost, and the property involved amounting to 40,811*l*. 7*s*. 2*d*., of which 1,582*l*. 14*s*. 7*d*. was lost. Total casualties coming within the scope of the service, 544; property involved, 2,010,973*l*. 4*s*. 9*d*.; property saved, 1,642,611*l*. 2*s*. 1*d*; property lost, 368,362*l*. 2*s*. 8*d*.; persons involved, 3,950; persons lost, 17; shipwrecked persons succoured at stations, 743; total number of days succour, 1,898; ships totally lost, 71. In addition to these statistics, 37 other persons in danger of life, having fallen from docks, &c., were rescued. In the year's operations 492 vessels were worked off when stranded, repaired when damaged, piloted out of dangerous places, and miscellaneously assisted by station crews. In 229 instances vessels running into danger were warned off by the signals of the patrols. The surf boat was used 529 times, making 907 trips. The self-righting and self-bailing lifeboat was used 67 times, making 94 trips. Smaller boats were used 152 times, making 199 trips; the breeches buoy was used 19 times, making 175 passages. The wreck gun was employed 29 times, firing 63 shots. The heaving stick was used 17 times. 760 persons were landed by the surf boat; by the life-boat, 94; by the smaller boats, 130; by river life skiffs, 32; by the breeches buoy, 162; rescued by using a surf boat as an extemporised bridge from a sinking steamer to a pier, 73 lives; 4 persons were landed from a vessel drifting in the ice floes by a small boat drawn back and forth with the whip line which had been connected with the vessel by the wreck gun. A similar use of the whip line rescued 6 men from a stranded vessel, who came ashore hand over hand on the line. 14 were saved by means of lines thrown to them; 7 saved by the men jumping into the surf; 1 by a buoy thrown to him with a line attached; and 2 drifting in the ice in a small boat were drawn ashore by a line. The lives lost in proportion to the number of persons on board the vessels involved was 1 out of every 232. The saving of property is in proportion of 32*s*. saved to 4*s*. expended in the maintenance

Life-saving stations on the coast of the United States.

of the service. The result of the year's work is summarised as follows:—

Total number of disasters	4,396
„ value of vessels	11,695,804*l*. 2*s*. 6*d*.
„ „ „ cargoes	5,067,700*l*. 16*s*. 6*d*.
„ „ „ property saved	11,400,753*l*.
„ „ „ „ lost	5,362,751*l*. 19*s*.
„ number of persons involved	39,414
„ „ „ lives lost	561
„ „ „ persons succoured	7,116
„ „ „ days succour afforded	19,105

The details of General Superintendent Kimball's report to the United States Government is replete with incidents of skill, courage, and self-sacrifice on the part of members of the various station crews, and instance the value and humanity of a most interesting as well as most important branch of the United States Government service.

Nautical school ship. A nautical school ship has been established at this port under the auspices of a board of directors and its able and efficient president, Captain Charles Lawrence. The State Legislature has appropriated 2,000*l*., and the city of Philadelphia, 3,000*l*. per annum towards the support of the school. The United States sloop of war "Saratoga" was sent to this station by the General Government, and is now used as a school ship, with Commander Green in charge. The object is to educate American youth in effective navigation and seamanship. After graduation there is little doubt that most of the young men will become officers in the American merchant marine service.

Harbour wages of seamen, &c. The condition of the harbour, demurrage, lay-day scales, and pilotage at Philadelphia continue the same as in the trade reports for 1887 and 1888, Nos. 177 and 464, Annual Series.

The wages for seamen for the year 1890 have been scaled by the Seamen's Union as follows:—

	Monthly wages.	Advance.
	Dollars.	Dollars.
Northern part of Europe (steamers)	30	30
„ „ „ (sail)	30	40
Deep water	18	40
Europe, south of Bayonne	25	40
„ north „	25	30
Greenland	25	30
Mediterranean, west coast of Africa	20	30
South America	20	30
West Indies (steamers)	25	15
„ „ (sail)	25	25

Immigration. Immigration at the port of Philadelphia has fallen off in the aggregate. English immigrants dropped from 10,903 in 1888, to 5,337 in 1889. The Irish fell from 7,987 in 1888 to 6,163 last year. The total decrease being from 37,018 for 1888 to 24,128 in 1889. These figures do not include non-immigrants or persons belonging and returning to the United States after foreign travel, numbering 1,627. The tabulated figures are as follows:—

Country.	1889. Males.	1889. Females.	1889. Total.	1888. Total.
England	2,959	2,378	5,337	10,903
Wales	74	77	151	481
Scotland	861	679	1,540	3,378
Ireland	3,051	3,112	6,163	7,987
Norway	724	502	1,226	1,612
Sweden	962	624	1,586	2,992
Denmark	202	139	341	127
Netherlands	14	8	22	..
Belgium	101	59	160	345
France	120	85	205	293
Spain	25	2	27	4
Italy	61	20	81	87
Switzerland	22	16	38	32
Germany	2,420	1,782	4,202	5,955
Russia	522	289	811	674
Finland	14	11	25	..
Poland	857	460	1,317	1,448
Austria-Hungary	130	40	170	157
Hungary	139	43	182	80
Roumania	19	4	23	..
Turkey	28	9	37	..
Greece	71	8	79	29
Algeria	2	..	2	..
Egypt	13	1	14	..
Arabia	163	24	187	..
Armenia	92	23	115	..
Assyria	21	11	32	..
West Indies, British	19	17	36	..
,, ,, Danish	1	..	1	..
,, ,, Spanish	18	..	18	..
Total	13,705	10,423	24,128	..
Non immigrants, aliens, and United States citizens	1,144	483	1,627	..
Total arrivals	14,849	10,906	25,755	..

A study of the above table develops the existence of a gradual shifting of nationalities in the current of immigration. Italian, Polish, Hungarian, Turkish, Greek, Egyptian, Arabian, Assyrian, Armenian are on the increase, which is deplored by statisticians, and considered unfortunate for the welfare of the country, and a blow to the stability of the labour market. The destination of these nationalities is also an interesting study. The English do not colonise; they spread all over, wherever their skill, thrift, and energies are best remunerated. Nor do the Irish; they permeate all channels where labour is in demand. It is the same with the Germans. The Welsh, Scandinavians, the Slavaks, Poles and Hungarians colonise, chiefly in Pennsylvania, a state noted for its mines of coal and slate, petroleum and natural gas. In and around the picturesque town of Scranton, in Pennsylvania, the Welsh are thickly settled, and Welsh performances are given at a theatre. Many children born and raised in the district adhere to their vernacular, and do not acquire the English language. Temperate, industrious and happy, they are a boon to the State, and are referred to by Americans with pride. Far different is it with colonists of some other nationalities who settle in the State of Pennsylvania; reckless and cruel they become a threat and a hindrance to the moral growth of Christian communities.

The Scandinavians resort to the farming districts of the West, as but few of them are skilled labourers or artisans. Danes and Fins go to the enormous forests of the North-Western States, seemingly attracted by the bracing climate and the spirit of independence prevailing therein. The Italians are of three classes: common labourers, miners, farmers, and grape growers. The first are an inferior lot coming chiefly from around Naples and work on railroads, city, streets, &c., a large part of this class remain in the cities whence they are sent by their " padrones " to all sections as required, returning when a contract has been completed. The next class, or miners, come from Northern Italy; they are of much higher intelligence and moral standard than the labourers, and go chiefly to the coal mining districts of the Western States. The farmers and wine growers, also from Northern Italy, settle in the wine growing districts of the State of California. Many French and Swiss also resort to these districts. The French, however, as a rule settle in the large cities or go to New Orleans and French Canada. The Russian, Polish and Roumanian Hebrews settle in the large cities. Most of them are tailors and about a third pedlars. Of late years a great many German Russians, whose forefathers about 100 years ago emigrated from Wurtemburg to Russia, have come to this country. They retain their German language, traditions and customs, and are all farmers. Large, and powerful built men, they form a picturesque sight on landing, with their sheep-skin overcoats, all clad in the same way, and followed by a string of children. From the Austro-Hungarian monarchy come the Slavaks, Poles and Hungarians who are chiefly coal miners; the Bohemians, Tyrolese, Dalmatians, Kroatians, and Moravians, as a rule gravitate to the coal and iron districts of Pennsylvania. Hollanders and Belgians, peaceable and tractable, resort to the farming districts, glass manufactures and mines. The Armenians and Arabs become pedlars or tradesmen and remain in the larger cities, some are silk weavers, others miners and common labourers.

The Greeks are fruit and flower vendors and railroad labourers.

The receipts of cereals, provisions, &c., at Philadelphia, in 1888 and 1889 were:— *Trade and commerce.*

		1888.	1889.
Flour	Barrels	1,319,163	1,041,565
Wheat	Bushels	2,555,600	2,544,100
Corn	"	2,973,900	5,962,500
Oats	"	4,662,750	4,494,360
Barley	"	1,283,400	643,600
Wool	Bales	188,509	110,950
Cotton	"	84,941	83,074
Lard	Tierces	48,544	20,890
"	"		74,809
Pork	"		3,097
Petroleum, crude	Barrels	485,039	891,279
" refined	"	424,764	857,819
Butter	Packages	362,044	370,838
Cheese	"	243,876	217,565
Eggs	Barrels and crates	489,193	50,794
"	"		470,319
Tobacco leaf	Hogsheads	22,120	22,902
Tobacco, manufactured	Baskets	131,444	120,820
Whiskey	Barrels	37,959	59,853

The decline in the export trade is marked for the past few years. Between the years 1877 and 1888 there has been a steady decline in the percentage of Philadelphia exports (chiefly in grain) from 11·2 per cent. in the former year to 6·3 per cent. in the latter, as compared to the exports from the list of principal northern ports of the United States, viz:—Boston, New York, Baltimore, Philadelphia and Norfolk.

The imports, however, have increased. They were in 1877 5·1 per cent., and in 1888 7·1 per cent. In 1886 the receipts of wheat at Philadelphia as per consular report for that year were 6,289,611 bushels, while in 1889 they were but 2,544,100 bushels, showing a decrease of 3,745,511 bushels. The total value of exports of breadstuffs from Philadelphia for 1889 was 1,670,183 dol.

The trade during the first 2 months of 1890 has taken a fresh start, and charters at good rates are awaiting the arrival of steamers from all sources to load grain.

New York and Baltimore are overflowing with grain shipments.

The exports of the months of January and February were as follows:—1889, 4,619,577 dol.; 1890, 4,977,988 dol.

The present low price of corn has been the chief cause of this sudden activity in the exportation of breadstuffs.

The total consumption of sugar in the United States was during the years:— *Sugar and molasses.*

	Tons.
1881	993,532
1887	1,392,909
1888	1,457,267
1889	1,457,561

UNITED STATES.

The consumption per head is reported as 51·015 lbs. in 1889; 52·65 lbs. in 1888; 52 lbs. in 1887; and 51 lbs. in 1886.

The total receipts in the United States through the 4 ports of New York, Boston, Philadelphia, and Baltimore, were 1,008,810 tons for 1889, and 1,084,810 tons in the previous year.

Receipts of sugar at the ports of—

	1888.	1889.
	Tons.	Tons.
Philadelphia	220,044	248,330
New York	695,883	659,154
Boston	..	101,326

The distribution of sugar:—

	1888.	1889.
	Tons.	Tons.
Philadelphia	220,044	248,330
New York	709,925	676,879
Boston	169,764	104,686

The entire consumption in the United States, both foreign and domestic, was 1,457,561 tons. The State of Louisiana supplied 145,000 tons, or one-tenth. The rest of the United States supplied 31,500 tons, or one-forty-eighth. The remainder, 1,281,061 tons, came from foreign countries.

The raising beetroot and sorghum sugar made little progress in 1889, as regards the increased quantity produced, but experiments on a larger scale than heretofore met with fair success under discouraging circumstances. Better results are predicted for the year 1890, under enlarged expenditure of labour and capital.

The duties collected on sugars for the year ending June 1, 1889, averaged one penny per pound, which added to the value of the imports of foreign sugar for the year ending December 1, 1889, figures 9,896,907*l*. This total does not include the sugar from the Sandwich Islands, upon which there is no duty.

The average bond prices (fair refining) in the United States for 45 years was 4·67 c. (2½*d*.).

The lowest prices from 1848 to January, 1885, were—

	Cents.
1885	2·87
1887	2·60
1888	2·79
1889	2·79
January, 1890	3·17

PHILADELPHIA.

Molasses.

Total received from foreign countries—
200,494 hogsheads	18,127,218 tierces.
Total gallons	24,951,270
Add stock at all ports	86,950
Total supply in gallons	25,038,220
Deduct exports and shipments	802,988
	24,235,232
Deduct stock at all ports, December 31, 1889	765,051
Total consumption of foreign molasses in 1889	23,470,181
Estimated crop of Louisiana, Texas, and other Southern States	18,544,416

The averages for 1888 and 1889 were—

	Per Gallon.	
	1888.	1889.
	Cents.	Cents.
N.O. prime to choice	42·18	41
Porto Rico	33·17	36
Barbadoes	20·84	32
Barbadoes	25·66	..
English	..	..

Imports and exports.

The imports at all the United States ports in the fiscal year ending June 30, 1889, were—

	£
Free of duty	52,883,933
Subject to duty	100,751,456
Total	153,635,389

The exports were—

	£
Domestic goods	148,511,878
Foreign	2,519,436
Total	151,031,314

The imports at Philadelphia in 1889 were as follows—

	£
Free of duty	1,027,567
Subject to duty	9,487,237
Total	10,514,804

The exports at Philadelphia were—

	£
In American steam vessels	560,983
„ sailing „	648,338
In Foreign steam vessels	4,075,032
„ sailing vessels	1,190,639
Total	6,474,992

(920)

UNITED STATES.

Textiles.   The manufactures of the city of Philadelphia have not been tabulated by any statistician, and no serviceable approximations have been indulged in for all branches of trade-production. This is accounted for by the fact that in June, 1890, the United States census will be taken, when all returns will be official and exhaustive. The production of carpets has increased, though some styles have not held their own, notably Smyrna rugs, which have fallen off. Ingrains have increased, the out-put being estimated at 4,400,000*l.* Hand-loom ingrains have decreased, while art squares in hand-looms have increased. Brussells, Wiltons, tapestries and Venetian damasks have decreased, while Smyrna whole carpets in hand-looms have increased. Axminster velvets are practically not made in Philadelphia any longer. Bag, net and chain carpets, so named, hold their own in the manufacture.

Failures.   Failures have occurred in the trades and commercial enterprises of the United States and Canada during the year 1889 as follows:—

Classes.	Number.	Average.	Aggregate.
		£	£
Less than £1,000	8,834	412	3,642,886
£1,000 to £2,000	2,004	1,143	2,892,371
£2,000 to £5,000	1,491	3,092	4,611,340
£10,000 to £20,000	262	14,433	3,781,443
£20,000 to £100,000	150	41,237	6,185,567
£100,000 to £200,000	19	144,330	2,742,268
£200,000 or over	12	309,278	3,711,340
Total	12,772	..	27,567,215

There have been a few heavy failures in the city of Philadelphia, but on the whole the commercial mart has suffered less than other cities of equal class. The failures during the first quarters of 1889–90 were:—

	Number of Failures.		Actual Assets.		Liabilities.	
	1889.	1890.	1889.	1890.	1889.	1890.
			£	£	£	£
Eastern States	511	500	1,307,692	379,542	3,123,285	956,760
Middle States	757	907	912,503	1,025,186	1,829,963	2,466,483
Southern States	774	542	498,271	502,410	972,487	960,716
Western States	886	716	913,207	801,663	1,672,813	1,534,768
North-Western States	418	357	385,816	275,772	642,549	495,136
Pacific States	290	283	154,808	313,928	312,799	534,884
Territories	33	21	27,051	17,189	54,699	23,271
Total	3,369	3,326	4,199,348	3,315,780	8,608,595	6,972,018
New York City	163	196	165,291	336,171	4,515,424	907,957
Canada and Provinces	536	502	458,461	532,744	947,958	1,004,881

Petroleum.   The trade in petroleum has increased, and heavy shipments have been made to the east. The exports at Philadelphia for 1889 were 3,168,745 barrels of 50 gallons each, exceeding those of the previous year by 511,002 barrels.

The shipments from Philadelphia, Baltimore, and New York were:—

	1878.	1883.	1889.
	Barrels.	Barrels.	Barrels.
Philadelphia	1,503,883	1,561,732	3,168,745
Baltimore	753,106	216,192	173,210
New York	4,074,044	7,604,081	8,607,281
Total	6,330,983	9,382,003	11,949,236

The percentage of the whole export trade from the three ports of refined naptha, lubricating and residuum, was not so large for Philadelphia as in the years 1885, 1886 and 1887. The percentage of the trade in 1885 was 29·8; in 1886, 28·8; in 1887, 30·3; and in 1889, 26·5 per cent. In the first two months of 1890 the reduction of the shipments from Philadelphia is most marked, and follows closely upon the absorption by the Standard Oil Company of one of its most important rivals in pipe lines and refineries. This powerful "trust" is not furthering the interests of Philadelphia or of Pennsylvania, the chief oil-producing State of the Union.

Natural gas. The extraordinary product of the coal districts was first handled in paying quantities in 1885. In three years its annual displacement of coal was 12,906,000 tons, estimated in value at 4,000,000*l*., and that is said to be only about one-half the rate of the present displacement. There are now more than 9,000 miles of mains, exclusive of smaller conveying pipes. The cheapness of the gas and the enterprise of competing companies have been the principal stimulants of its introduction. New territory has been rapidly developed, and in many cases gas has been furnished free to consumers.

Not taking into consideration the many thousands of companies that have organised, bored wells, struck water and quit business, the total capitalisation in the name of "natural gas" in this country exceeds 20,000,000*l*.

Agriculture In certain sections of the country agriculturists complain of the shrinkage in prices of products. This is notably the case in the State of Pennsylvania, and is receiving considerable attention by the farmers. In 1865 wheat was 10*s*. per bushel; oats, 4*s*. per bushel; corn (maize), 5*s*. 10*d*. per bushel; potatoes, 6*s*. 3*d*. per bushel; butter, 2*s*. 6*d*. per lb. In 1889 the prices of wheat ranged from 3*s*. 4*d*. to 3*s*. 10*d*. per bushel; corn (maize), 1*s*. 8*d*.; and the other products named will not average over one-third the prices of 1865. In the face of this shrinkage in the values of farm products, the same tariff of taxes prevails now that were imposed in the prosperous times of the Civil War.

It is proposed to prepare a separate report on the subject of agriculture in the four States of this Consular district as soon as the statistics have been compiled by the proper authorities for public use.

UNITED STATES.

Coal, anthracite and bituminous.

The coal trade of 1889 felt the heavy out-put of hard coal, or anthracite, of the preceding year and the mild winter. The soft coal, or bituminous, trade also suffered from the mild winter, and from strikes among the miners, and short supply of transportation facilities. The past year was a dull one in the coal industry of the United States. The light winter of 1888-89 caused large stocks to be carried over by producers, dealers, and consumers. The out-put of anthracite coal of Pennsylvania was:—

Year.	Gross Tons.*
1886	32,136,362
1887	34,641,017
1888	38,145,718
1889	35,407,710

The smaller sizes of anthracite coal increased in shipments, and the quantity furnished the iron furnaces also increased. The use of anthracite is from year to year extended over a wider range in the United States and Canada. To the consumers in the Eastern, or New England, States a direct all-rail traffic increases as compared with the transportation by sea in coal barges towed around the coast by steamers. This departure from shipments by water will increase the sales of all sizes of anthracite in the New England markets. The average reduction of prices for hard coal in 1889 as compared with 1888 is 35 c. (1s. 5½d.) per ton on the free burning coals, and about 20 c. (10d.) on the hard white ash coals. Soft coals, or bituminous, continues to be sold at low figures. The last year's rates touched the lowest prices. The operators agreed upon a price, 2 dol. 60 c. (10s. 9d.) per ton, at loading ports, but a strict adherence thereto was not kept up. Central Pennsylvania did not mine so much as in the previous year. The floods of midsummer in the Allegheny valleys put an end to all operations for a time, and towards the close of the year there was a tendency to hold back the tonnage with the hope of realising more profitable prices. In part this strengthened the market, but it extended but a few weeks into the year 1890. In the Western districts of Pennsylvania the operators had a fair year though sadly hampered at times by a scarcity of cars. The increasing production of Virginia, Tennessee, and Alabama shows a keen competition with Pittsburgh in the southern markets.

The State of Ohio shows about as large an out-put as in the preceding year, and outside of this Consular district, in the States of Kentucky, Tennessee, and Alabama, the increase is well marked, and the development in these States was so great that the year 1890 is looked forward to with great encouragement. The far Western States did a larger business in anthracite in 1889 than in any previous year.

The employés in and about the mines throughout the coal producing districts of the United States number as follows:—

* Gross tons = 2,240 lbs.

PHILADELPHIA.

	Number.
Pennsylvania (anthracite)	117,000
,, (bituminous)	61,000
Ohio	25,000
Illinois	30,000
Iowa	12,000
Alabama	8,600
West Virginia	8,000
Indiana	7,000
Kentucky	6,500
Tennessee	6,000
Maryland	5,500
Colorado	5,500
Virginia	5,000
Kansas	4,500
Missouri	3,200
Wyoming	3,000
Total	307,800

The wages paid for mining coal to this army of miners and helpers range from 30 c. (1s. 3d.) to 1 dol. 25 c. (5s.) per net ton (2,000 lbs.) These wages vary according to the hardness or thickness of the coal, but for a general report it is not necessary to particularise. A change is looked for to date from May 1, 1890. The anthracite coal fields of Pennsylvania are of the greatest importance because of the out-put and the wide extent of country where the product is sold. 40,000,000 tons annually are mined. For the year 1888 the out-put was 41,638,426 gross tons (2,240 lbs.), and for 1889 it was (not including colliery consumption) 35,407,710 gross tons. From 1820 to 1889 the grand total figures 756,801,458 gross tons. The shipments by districts in 1889 were:—Schuylkill, 10,474,364 gross tons; Lehigh, 6,285,421; Wyoming, 18,647,925; total 35,407,710 gross tons.

The traffic of the coal railroads (8 in number), which are known as the initial interests or lines of transit, over which all the hard coal sent to market must pass when leaving the mines, are:—

	1887. Tons.	1888. Tons.	1889. Tons.
Philadelphia and Reading Railroad	7,555,252	7,175,095	7,272,592
Central Railroad of New Jersey	4,852,859	5,742,279	6,027,505
Lehigh Valley Railroad	5,784,450	6,592,715	7,444,163
Delaware, Lackawana, and Western	6,220,793	6,996,192	5,259,239
Delaware, and Hudson Canal Company	4,048,340	4,486,188	3,819,045
Pennsylvania Railroad	3,818,143	4,554,440	3,300,867
,, Coal Company	1,603,456	1,624,433	1,308,309
New York, Lake Erie, and Western	759,834	974,373	954,283
Total	34,641,017	38,145,718	35,385,401

All the figures for 1889 are not official. The percentages of the initial coal carrying roads are (for 1886-88) the Reading Company averaged 20·55 per cent.; the Delaware, Lackawana, and Western, 17·36 per cent.; the Delaware and Hudson, 11·29 per cent.; the Pennsylvania Railroad Company, 11·22 per cent.; the Pennsylvania Coal Company, 4·55 per cent.; the Erie, 2·27 per cent. Thus the ability to produce 40,000,000 tons annually or less, can readily be transported to the seaboard.

The distribution of this enormous mineral product is in the following named sections of the country. No one division grows disproportionately, and it is somewhat surprising that those sections of the country where the people have been longest known as consumers of hard coal should continue to show growth.

	1886.	1887.	1888.
	Tons.	Tons.	Tons.
To Pennsylvania, New York, and New Jersey	21,222,163	22,508,082	23,053,581
To New England	5,288,389	5,590,972	6,082,440
To Western States	3,157,272	3,707,118	5,039,568
To South	1,455,720	1,739,052	1,969,829
To Pacific Coast	5,615	6,820	6,930
To Dominion of Canada	970,306	1,057,737	1,956,405
To foreign ports	36,898	31,237	36,965
Total gross tons	32,136,363	34,641,017	38,145,718

The prices of anthracite coal in 1889 were lower than for some years previous thereto. At the mines, Lehigh and Schuylkill, coal brought:—Lump, 8s. 4d. per ton; grate and egg (large size), 9s. 9d.; stove and small stove, 10s. 9d.; chestnut, 10s.; pea, 5s. 2d.

These coals cost the steamships, for lump, 18s. 7d. per ton; factories, for lump and egg, at mines, 10s. 4d.; delivered, 18s. 10d. per ton; for housekeeper's stove and small stove, 1l. 1s. 8d. and 1l. 2s. 9d. per ton; pea coal (a very small brand of coal now becoming popular for domestic use), 14s. 6d. per ton.

The anthracite (hard coal) is almost exclusively a domestic fuel, the "steam trade" having gravitated to bituminous, and the "furnace trade" to coke. Philadelphia is the most important coal trade centre. The local consumption here is placed at 2,000,000 tons of hard coal, and 500,000 tons of soft (bituminous) coal per annum. The shipments from the port, of both hard and soft coals, will average annually 4,000,000 tons gross. Philadelphia has suffered, and continues to suffer, by railroad discrimination, caused by the lack of competition among the carriers. The Pennsylvania railroad and the Philadelphia and Reading railroad have the whole trade, and freights to Philadelphia—100 miles from the mines—are 2½d. per ton more than those to New York, 100 miles beyond. This is an injustice which the coal consumers and manufacturers do not appear to have the power to adjust.

PHILADELPHIA.

The temperature of the winters have a marked effect on the consumption of anthracite coal. Thus, five cold winters—1879, 1881, 1883, 1885 and 1887—the production averaged 27,789,488 tons per annum; while five warm winters—1876, 1878, 1880, 1882, and 1884—the average production was 23,876,380 tons.

It is a curious circumstance connected with this enormous out-put of the most valuable of minerals that there should be a dealer known as the "basket man." He is found in all cities of 30,000 or more population, and may be termed a pilferer of the poorer classes. He may be established in a small grocery with a grog-shop attached, together with second-hand furniture and a wood yard. Strolling through the streets in the poorer sections can be seen outside of hovel-like shops baskets of a small size of anthracite coal, containing anywhere from a bushel to a peck. That which cost the "basket man" 5 dol. a ton is dealt out in these small parcels at the rate of 10 dol. or 12 dol. per ton. The profit is made, a few cents. at a time, from poor wretches who must have the fuel or freeze. *The "basket man."*

The anthracite coal production has grown steadily notwithstanding the ups and downs of prices. Thus:— *Growth.*

	Tons.
Mined in 1870	16,182,000
" 1875	19,712,000
" 1880	23,437,000
" 1885	31,623,000
" 1889	35,500,000

The tariff on coal from 1824-43 was 3d. per bushel, or 7s. per gross ton; from 1843-46, 7s. 3½d. per ton; in 1846, 30 per cent. ad valorem; 1847-61, 24 per cent. ad valorem; 1862-64, 4s. 2d. per ton; 1865, 4s. 7d.; 1866-72, 5s. 2d.; and since August, 1872, 3s. 2d. per ton. In the period from June, 1854, to March, 1866, the reciprocity treaty was in force, and coal from the British North American Possessions was admitted free of duty. *Imports and exports of coal.*

| Year. | Exports. || Imports. |
	Anthracite.	Bituminous.	Bituminous.
	Tons.	Tons.	Tons.
1886	682,175	532,846	824,057
1887	680,138	643,563	906,634
1888	944,383	780,248	877,504
1889	943,304	841,798	1,155,329

The tabulated exports do not include the coal sent to Canada by rail.

The slack or "culm" made at the breakers is being utilised. It can be used in its crude state, or agglomerated into bricks after European methods. Both features are attracting a great deal of attention. As a steam-producing power it is effective and economical. The fuel cost for the same amount of work is estimated as follows:— *Anthracite, slack or culm.*

			s.	d.
26,086 cubic feet of gas at 5d. per 1,000 feet			10	11
3,131 lbs. of bituminous coal at 6s. 3d. per ton			8	9
3,166 „ coking bituminous at 6s. 3d. per ton			8	10
3,178 „ anthracite at 10s. 5d. per ton			14	7
4,300 „ pea size at 4s. 2d. per ton			8	1
4,283 „ of buckwheat at 3s. 1½d. per ton			6	0
4,762 „ culm at 5s. per ton			0	11

When to these figures are added the costs of handling the coal and ashes, the entire costs will stand :—Prepared anthracite, 19s. 10d.; coking bituminous, 14s. 1½d.; free bituminous, 14s.; pea coal, 13s. 6d.; buckwheat, 11s. 5d.; gas, 10s. 10d.; and culm, 6s. 4d.

The Philadelphia and Reading Railroad Company is interested in the making of culm bricks. For this purpose the waste is ground to powder in immense crushers, mixed with a composition of pitch, water, &c., and pressed in two machines, which compress the mixed fuel and pitch into bricks under a pressure of between 50 and 60 tons. The bricks are pushed out of the jaws of the press at the rate of 40 to the minute, or 80 for the two machines in operation. A speed can be run up to 50 bricks per minute, but it is not considered safe. As the bricks tumble out an automatic arm pushes them along a tumble-like shute, where they are caught by the paddles of an endless chain and carried out over a tressle to the stocking yard, or diverted from their course nearer the factory, and packed, smoking hot, into the railway cars ready for shipment to market. Each brick is about 10 × 7 × 6, and weighs from 17 to 18 lbs. They are said to be used with great success on the Reading Railway.

Coal mine casualties. The mine inspectors of Pennsylvania report 453 persons killed; 364 in the anthracite, and 89 in the bituminous mines. The number of widows made 217, and the number of orphans 653. A life was lost for each 119,013 tons in the anthracite collieries, and a life for each 443,821 tons mined in the bituminous collieries. The fatal casualties are attributed to the carelessness of those who suffered. Seldom was there more than one person injured at any one time. In all except a few of the gangways the working men use naked lights, and in nearly all cases where explosions occurred oversight or recklessness was the cause. Falls of roof and fall of coal are the most numerous causes, and these are the most difficult to deal with by supervision. The American, English, Welsh, and Irish are the most experienced miners, and yet the statistics go to prove that the casualties number as many to them as they do to those who are rated as inexperienced.

Miners' wages. Miners' wages are not clearly understood by the reading public, owing to the peculiar manner in which the miners are paid, contracts entering into the work so largely. Regarding those miners classed as "contract miners," the figures for 1888, the last year that can be fairly used as an estimate, show that the competent and industrious miner could have worked 246 days in the year. All miners do not have the same opportunity, although the term applies to all, whether engaged in breast, gangway, or airway, robbing pillars, or even if a section of a mine be included in a contract that employs a number of men. Those in gangways and airways have no limit to their work, while those in breasts can only mine a certain number of cars, seven being the usual number, at 3s. 7d. per car, for both mining and loading. The miner who worked 246 days earned a total of 306l. 15s., loading seven cars daily, mined an average of 24 cars to a keg of powder, escaped with a dockage of 5 per cent., and was paid 4s. 2d. each for two dozen props placed in position: his expenses for labour were 246 days at 8s. 9d., and for powder 44l. 4s. 2d., with enough other items to aggregate 154l. 17s. This would give the miner an average of 11s. per day. These figures may be accepted as an average, while there are men who earn more and a great many who realise less. Steady work is out of the question. About 10,000 men are now out of employment.

Changes and new enterprises in the iron trade of the United States during the past two years have been numerous. The low prices for many iron and steel products of 1888 and the first six months of 1889 did not affect the activity in the trade and the extension of facilities for the manufacture of iron and steel in all forms. The erection of blast furnaces in the Southern States, and of steel works in the Northern States, continued from month to month. In November 1889 there were 575 blast furnaces in active operation or in process of construction. The charcoal furnaces and the anthracite furnaces are gradually decreasing, while the bituminous and coke furnaces are on the increase. The annual capacity of the 575 completed furnaces in November, 1889, was 13,168,233 net tons, and the aggregate capacity of all the blast furnaces throughout the United States at the close of 1889 is not only much larger than it was two years ago, but the average capacity is also much larger. In November, 1889, the average capacity was 22,901 net tons per annum, or 440 net tons per week.

Iron and steel.

The rolling mills and steel works are enumerated at 445 completed rolling mills and steel works in the United States, November, 1889, with 11 building. In the two years 1888 and 1889, 39 new rolling mills and steel works were built and 27 abandoned, leaving a net gain of 12. Of the 39 new enterprises completed in the last two years many of them embraced works for the manufacture of steel by either the Bessemer or the open hearth process.

The rolling mill capacity numbered 4,914 in November, 1889; the heating furnaces numbered 2,733; the number of trains of rolls 1,510; the annual capacity of the rolling mills in finished iron and steel 9,215,000 tons; the number of rolling mills manufacturing cut nails and spikes was 75, with 6,066 nail machines.

The Standard Bessemer Steel Works in November, 1889, throughout the United States numbered 41, completed with 88 converters, with no new plants in course of erection. The annual ingot capacity of the completed and building standard Bessemer Steel Works was 5,600,000 tons, Clappe-Griffiths and Robert-Bessemer plants both being excluded.

The Clappe-Griffiths steel industry in this country has made no progress in the last two years; indeed, it has slightly retrograded. In November, 1889, there were only eight completed plants, containing in all 14 converters, with an annual ingot capacity of 200,000.

The Robert-Bessemer steel process was introduced into this country within the past two years from France. It is a modification of the Bessemer process, and in November, 1889, seven completed plants were in activity, containing 11 converters, with three in course of erection, and one plant in course of erection. All converters operated by this new method are of small capacity, used in making castings and for miscellaneous purposes.

The open-hearth steel industry continues in favourable progress. In November, 1889, the number of completed open-hearth furnaces were 116, with 23 furnaces building, and a number previously built were remodelled and enlarged. The annual capacity of the open-hearth furnaces completed in November, 1889, is estimated at 1,000,000 net tons of ingots, and of the 23 furnaces then in course of erection 200,000, showing a total capacity of 1,200,000 tons, against 815,000 tons in 1887.

The Crucible Steel Works has been practically stationary for a number of years, owing to competition of steel made by other methods. In November, 1889, there were 43 completed crucible steel works, containing 3,378 pots, and three plants building to contain 150 pots.

Bassic Bessemer steel has not so far been made in this country, except experimentally. In Pennsylvania two works are making very soft bassic open-hearth steel.

Pig-iron is now made in 24 States; rolling mills are found in 28 States and one territory; cut nails are made in 15 States; wire nails in 13; Bessemer steel in 11; Clappe-Griffiths steel in 3; Robert-Bessemer steel in five; open-hearth steel in 11; crucible steel in 11; iron ore forges in five; and pig iron-scrap bloomaries in five States. Natural gas as fuel is used in 104 rolling mills and steel works, but the annual increase has been very light. During the past year there has been much interruption to its use at many iron and steel works, caused by an inadequate supply, and some manufacturers are contemplating a return to the use of coal entirely. Whether this inadequate supply at some works is due to a diminished supply from nature's storehouse, or to a diversion of the popular fuel from manufacturing to domestic use, is not clear from the published explanations which have been made. Mr. Swank, the able editor of the Bulletin of the American Iron and Steel Association, asserts that the maximum consumption of natural gas in the manufacture of iron and steel has been reached, if not passed. Petroleum is a new fuel now used in 21 iron and steel works, either wholly or in part.

PHILADELPHIA.

The production of all kinds of pig-iron in the States of this Consular district in 1889 was:—

Blast Furnaces, December 31, 1889.				Production. Tons of 2,000 lbs. includes Spiegeleisen.
States.	In.	Out.	Total.	
Pennsylvania	151	77	228	4,181,242
Ohio	49	25	74	,1215,572
Michigan	10	16	26	214,356
Indiana	1	1	2	9,839
Total	211	119	330	5,621,009
„ for all the States	344	226	570	8,517,068

Production of charcoal pig-iron:—

Blast Furnaces, December 31, 1889.				Production. Tons of 2,000 lbs. includes Spiegeleisen.
States.	In.	Out.	Total.	
Pennsylvania	5	11	16	15,951
Ohio	8	4	12	22,467
Michigan	10	15	25	214,356
Indiana	..	..	..	..
Total	23	30	53	252,774
„ for all the States	63	80	143	644,300

Production of bituminous coal and coke pig-iron:—

Blast Furnaces, December 31, 1889.				Production. Tons of 2,000 lbs. includes Spiegeleisen.
States.	In.	Out.	Total.	
Pennsylvania	62	15	77	2,583,132
Ohio	41	21	62	1,193,105
Michigan	..	1	1	..
Indiana	1	1	2	9,839
Total	104	38	142	3,786,076
„ for all the States	177	68	245	5,952,414

UNITED STATES.

Production of anthracite and anthracite and coke pig-iron:—

States.	Blast Furnaces, December 31, 1889. In.	Out.	Total.	Production. Tons of 2,000 lbs. includes Spiegeleisen.
Pennsylvania	84	51	138	1,582,159
Ohio	..	..	..	..
Michigan	..	..	..	..
Indiana	..	..	..	..
Total	84	51	138	1,582,159
„ for all the States	105	84	189	1,925,729

Unsold stocks of all kinds of pig-iron held for sale by the markers or their agents:—

	Tons of 2,000 lbs.
Pennsylvania	67,005
Ohio	27,579
Michigan and Indiana	25,102
Total in Consular district	119,686
„ for all the States	277,401

The stock of unsold anthracite and anthracite and coke pig-iron in Pennsylvania amounted to 34,498 tons; charcoal pig-iron, 7,453 tons; bituminous coal and coke pig-iron, 25,054 tons.

The stock on hand, according to the fuel used, in the producing States:—

	Tons.
Bituminous	86,772
Anthracite	77,502
Charcoal	113,127
Total	277,401

Stocks of pig-iron in Pennsylvania and Ohio districts:—

	Dec. 31, 1887. Tons.	Dec. 31, 1888. Tons.	Dec. 31, 1889. Tons.
Lehigh Valley	31,519	4,788	2,255
Schuylkill	19,103	31,313	22,714
Upper Susquehanna	6,589	9,435	3,845
Lower „	7,023	10,602	5,694
Shenango Valley	29,955	17,857	6,272
Allegheny County	33,841	7,704	567
Miscellaneous coke	17,269	19,400	18,205
Charcoal	8,876	7,904	7,453
Hanging rock, bituminous	4,062	13,792	3,813
Mahoning Valley	12,365	2,531	12,149
Hocking Valley	2,301	9,557	4,909
Miscellaneous	9,869	6,743	3,678
Hanging rock, charcoal	3,610	4,480	3,030

PHILADELPHIA.

Production, according to fuel used in 1889 :—

Description.	Blast Furnaces. Dec. 31, 1889.	2,000 lbs. includes Spiegeleisen.
		Tons.
Anthracite	182	1,920,354
Charcoal	143	644,300
Bituminous	245	5,952,414
Total	570	8,517,068

Production of Bessemer pig-iron in 1889 :—

	Tons.
New York	76,947
New Jersey	24,004
Pennsylvania	2,216,948
Maryland	14,478
West Virginia	106,787
Ohio	452,646
Illinois	544,965
Missouri	73,845
Wisconsin	17,697
Colorado	1,267

The imports of iron and steel and iron ore into the United States during the 11 months of 1889 were :—

Imports of iron and steel.

Articles.	11 Months, 1889.	Value.
	Gross Tons.	Dollars.
Pig-iron	142,230	2,863,137
Scrap-iron	35,917	447,492
„ steel	2,241	33,964
Bar-iron	29,579	1,097,132
Iron rails	14	229
Steel rails	6,202	163,110
Cotton ties	20,815	630,950
Hoop and scroll iron	6	291
Steel plate, &c.	14,014	783,215
„ blooms, &c.	72,362	1,989,837
Sheet and iron plate iron	7,032	446,456
Tin plates	331,311	21,726,707
Wire rods	73,768	2,412,278
„ and wire rope	4,093	728,197
Anvils, forging, &c.	1,400	179,254
Chains	621	77,618
Total	741,596	33,567,867
Iron ore	784,231	1,852,392

The prices of pig-iron have been changeable, those of to-day being 6s. higher than those ruling a year ago, and 12s. higher than those ruling in May last, which was the lowest of the year, and almost the lowest on record. In January, 1889, No. 1

Prices.

Foundry was quoted at 18 dol. 50 c., and Gray Forge 16 dol.; in May the former at 17 dol., and the latter at 15 dol. 25 c.; in December the former at 19 dol. 25 c., and the latter at 17 dol. 25 c. Muck bars averaged from 26 dol. to 27 dol. per ton. In December the prices rose to 31 dol. at mill, as against 28 dol. 75 c. the year previous. Billets rose from 28 dol. 50 c. in January to 37 dol. in December. Manufactured iron was variable, in prices ranging 1·75 c. per pound to 2 c. for best refined, showing an advance of 30 c. per 100 lbs. from the lowest quotations. Skelp-iron ranged from 1 dol. 75 c. to 1 dol. 95 c. The present tendency is to higher prices. The plate trade has been quoted from 1 dol. 9 c. to 1 dol. 95 c. delivered. Iron plates were quoted from 1 dol. 85 c. in summer to 2 dol. 35 c. in December. The latest quotations were:—

Description.	Iron.		Steel.	
	Dol.	c.	Dol.	c.
Tank	2	35	2	75
Shell	2	65	3	0
Flange	3	25	3	25
Fire-box	3	75	3	75
Angles	2	80	2	75

Steel rails from 27 dol. to 35 dol. per ton early in December; old rails from 22 dol. 50 c. to 29 dol. per ton; scrap-iron from 21 dol. 50 c. to 26 dol.

Railways. — The railways in the United States continue to extend their possessions and to exercise their arbitrary powers. The whole number of railway corporations in the United States last year is reported to be 1,718, and the mileage approximated at 156,500 miles; the number of employés 689,912, the trainmen numbering 135,580, switchmen, flagmen, and watchmen 31,896, and other employés, 522,436. The wages paid these classes range at over 73 per cent. for the men, whose pay is from 4s. 2d. to 8s. 4d. per day. The average daily rate of all employés paid by specific time on 60 roads is 6s. 10d., yet nearly 61 per cent. of the whole number received less than the average rate of all, while only about 39 per cent. received the above average for all. Of the whole number of employés 101,905 earn less than 20l. per year, 32,621 earn from 20l. to 40l. per year, and 21,517 earn from 40l. to 60l. The average earnings on all the 60 roads per year is 48l. 12s., although less than 60 per cent. of all earn less than this average; 224,570 individual men were employed on an average 147 days each, and their pay 48l. 12s. for the year employed. These men were employed to fill 105,807 positions; that is to say, if 105,807 men had been employed on full time they would have accomplished the same results that were accomplished by the greater number working on an average of 147 days each during the year. It is not to be concluded that

118,763 men are out of employment, although it is a fact that this feature of the problem offers a field for investigation and discussion.

The Pennsylvania Railroad has been called to account by the commercial community of Philadelphia for an indirect cause of the decadence of the grain and export trade of the port. This road has been directly charged with having made discriminating allowances upon the export and import traffic viâ Baltimore, which had a material tendency to direct to that city trade which would otherwise naturally have sought shipment viâ Philadelphia. The trade over other railways coming to Philadelphia had begun largely to increase, so that the volume of that traffic passing through this port in November and December, 1889, was much larger than it had been for some time previously. The Pennsylvania Railroad officials have failed to give any satisfactory explanation of the charges made against them, and practically the port of Philadelphia must be content with the "leavings" of the enlarged export trade of New York and Baltimore.

Other complaints have been rife in the public mind against the Pennsylvania Railroad. A majority of the common stock of this company is reliably stated to be held in England, and it is not amiss that the expression of American opinion on the conduct of the company's present management should be reported for the information and guidance of English holders. The Northern Central Railroad, a company running through a country which is poor compared with that tributary to the Pennsylvania Railroad, has recently declared a dividend of 5 per cent. for six months, while the Pennsylvania Railroad has contented itself with a 5 per cent. dividend for 12 months. It is looked upon as an enigma that the former road can earn twice as much as the latter, with its splendid equipment and immense business. The southern terminus of the Northern Central is Baltimore, and its chief traffic is hauling grain to that city from Harrisburgh, where it is received from the Pennsylvania road. So far as the earnings of the Pennsylvania road are concerned, in respect to its traffic to Philadelphia, the road has become of less importance than either the Baltimore and Ohio road, the Lehigh Valley, or the Reading roads. While the Pennsylvania Company was shipping 3,200 cars of grain to this port, the Reading Company, including those brought to it by the Baltimore and Ohio and Lehigh Valley roads, sent in 4,700 cars, or 1,500 more. The Pennsylvania road is apparently wedded to a policy of increasing Baltimore's commerce, and thereby adding to the increasing dividends of its branch line, the Northern Central Railroad. This policy is of twofold injury—injury to the port of Philadelphia, and injury to the shareholders of the company. The managers appear to be content with doing one-tenth of the export trade of the port, and with its continued and uninterrupted opposition to all efforts for increasing terminal facilities for other railways. Baltimore has two railways—the Pennsylvania and the Baltimore and Ohio—consequently there is competition. Philadelphia has

(920)

nominally three—the Pennsylvania, Baltimore and Ohio, and the Reading; but the two latter have been so hampered and tied up that it is only of late that they have been able to force a competition with its great rival.

The status of the Northern Central Railroad Company and its terminal facilities—the Baltimore Elevator and Lighterage Company—to the Pennsylvania Railroad Company is a matter of severe public criticism. The market price of the Pennsylvania Railroad shares in Philadelphia is from 54 dol. to 54½ dol., and the Northern Central Railway is 67½ dol., having gone up from under 20 dol. per share.

LONDON:
Printed for Her Majesty's Stationery Office,
By HARRISON AND SONS,
Printers in Ordinary to Her Majesty.
(1250 6 | 90—H & S 920)

633

FOREIGN OFFICE.
1890.
ANNUAL SERIES.

No. 739.

DIPLOMATIC AND CONSULAR REPORTS ON TRADE AND FINANCE.

UNITED STATES.

REPORT FOR THE YEAR 1889

ON THE

TRADE OF THE CONSULAR DISTRICT OF CHICAGO.

REFERENCE TO PREVIOUS REPORT, Annual Series No. 570.

Presented to both Houses of Parliament by Command of Her Majesty,
JUNE, 1890.

LONDON:
PRINTED FOR HER MAJESTY'S STATIONERY OFFICE,
BY HARRISON AND SONS, ST. MARTIN'S LANE,
PRINTERS IN ORDINARY TO HER MAJESTY.

And to be purchased, either directly or through any Bookseller, from
EYRE & SPOTTISWOODE, EAST HARDING STREET, FLEET STREET, E.C., and
32, ABINGDON STREET, WESTMINSTER, S.W.; or
ADAM AND CHARLES BLACK, 6, NORTH BRIDGE, EDINBURGH; or
HODGES, FIGGIS, & Co., 104, GRAFTON STREET, DUBLIN.

1890.
Price Twopence.

[C. 5895—142.]

New Series of Reports.

Reports of the Annual Series have been issued from Her Majesty's Diplomatic and Consular Officers at the following places, and may be obtained from the sources indicated on the title-page:—

No.		Price.	No.		Price.
615.	Naples	2½d.	677.	Batoum	1d.
616.	Batoum	½d.	678.	Manila	1d.
617.	Odessa	1d.	679.	Tamsui	1d.
618.	La Rochelle	1d.	680.	Kiungchow	1d.
619.	Rome	1d.	681.	Swatow	1d.
620.	Nice	1d.	682.	Stettin	6d.
621.	Kiukiang	½d.	683.	Bordeaux	2½d.
622.	Paris	1d.	684.	Port Saïd	1d.
623.	Salonica	1½d.	685.	Coquimbo	½d.
624.	Réunion	1d.	686.	Warsaw	1d.
625.	Ichang	1d.	687.	Ichang	1d.
626.	Bogotá	1d.	688.	Wênchow	1d.
627.	Malaga	2d.	689.	Trebizond	1d.
628.	Porto Rico	1d.	690.	Damascus	½d.
629.	Bushire	2½d.	691.	Savannah (Georgia)	1d.
630.	The Hague	½d.	692.	Barcelona	2½d.
631.	Berlin	1d.	693.	Santos	1d.
632.	Adrianople	1½d.	694.	San José	1d.
633.	Rome	1½d.	695.	Batavia	1d.
634.	Santiago	½d.	696.	Genoa	1½d.
635.	Tahiti	½d.	697.	Calais	2d.
636.	Maranham	½d.	698.	Marseilles	1d.
637.	Mexico	2d.	699.	Brest	1d.
638.	Christiania	1d.	700.	Lisbon	2½d.
639.	Copenhagen	1d.	701.	Leghorn	2d.
640.	Paris	1d.	702.	Rio Grande do Sul	1d.
641.	Venice	1d.	703.	Tainan	1d.
642.	Cherbourg	½d.	704.	Kewkiang	4d.
643.	New York	1d.	705.	Fiume	1d.
644.	Patras	1d.	706.	Odessa	2d.
645.	Bourgas	½d.	707.	Suakin	½d.
646.	St. Petersburg	3d.	708.	Hankow	½d.
647.	Taganrog	½d.	709.	Amoy	1d.
648.	Baltimore	1½d.	710.	Buda-Pesth	1½d.
649.	New Orleans	2d.	711.	Corunna	2d.
650.	New Orleans	1d.	712.	Mogador	2d.
651.	Samos	½d.	713.	Cadiz	½d.
652.	Buda-Pesth	1½d.	714.	Cadiz	1d.
653.	Tripoli	½d.	715.	Rio de Janeiro	2½d.
654.	Buenos Ayres	½d.	716.	Newchwang	1d.
655.	Paris	1d.	717.	Chinkiang	½d.
656.	Cherbourg	1d.	718.	San Francisco	6d.
657.	Warsaw	½d.	719.	Bussorah	½d.
658.	Rome	1½d.	720.	Beyrout	1d.
659.	Saigon	½d.	721.	Adrianople	½d.
660.	Buenos Ayres	½d.	722.	Nantes	½d.
661.	Galveston	1d.	723.	Caracas	1d.
662.	Galatz	1½d.	724.	Mogador	½d.
663.	Antwerp	1d.	725.	Tientsin	1d.
664.	Boston	1d.	726.	Foochow	1d.
665.	Madeira	½d.	727.	Port au Prince	½d.
666.	New Hebrides	½d.	728.	Callao	1d.
667.	Riga	1d.	729.	Puerto Plata	½d.
668.	Charleston	1d.	730.	San Francisco	1d.
669.	Algiers	2d.	731.	Philadelphia	2½d.
670.	Stuttgart	1d.	732.	Pakhoi	1d.
671.	Havre	3d.	733.	Bilbao	1d.
672.	The Piræus	1d.	734.	Dunkirk	1d.
673.	Syra	1d.	735.	Vienna	1d.
674.	Boulogne	1d.	736.	Nantes	1½d.
675.	Taganrog	2d.	737.	Paramaribo	1d.
676.	Wuhu	½d.	738.	Honolulu	½d.

No. 739.

Reference to previous Report, Annual Series No. 570.

UNITED STATES.

CHICAGO.

Acting-Consul Hayes-Sadler to the Marquis of Salisbury.

My Lord,   Chicago, May 16, 1890.

I HAVE the honour to enclose to your Lordship my Annual Report on the Trade and Commerce of Chicago for the year 1889.

The Reports of Mr. Vice-Consul Bascome of St. Louis, Mr. Vice-Consul Morphy of St. Paul, and Mr. Vice-Consul Pearce of Denver are likewise transmitted.

I have, &c.
(Signed)   R. H. HAYES-SADLER.

Report on the Trade and Commerce of the Consular District of Chicago during the Year 1889.

Trade in general. The commercial record of this city during the year 1889 presents less of variety than those of the preceding years. Business was fairly active all through, but few new matters were presented, except those that involved changes in the mode of investing capital.

As has usually been the case, uneasiness as to the crop yield was entertained during the first part of the year, but the rains having set in early no material depression in prices was caused except in wheat. The inflow of farm produce has been steady, as also the distribution to the east and to Europe. Manufacturers have been busy, and in the packing line a fair increase has been shown. Wages have been well maintained despite a lower price for produce, hence no strikes of any magnitude took place during the year. Chicago manufacturers are extending their trade beyond seas, two shiploads of machinery having been recently sent to South Africa, the freight alone of which is stated to have amounted to 13,608*l*.

European influence has been markedly felt on the course of business in this Consular district. The influx of British capital invested in the purchase of grain elevators, breweries, and other properties in this and other cities, may cause an important influence on the grain trade of Chicago.

Trusts.

One important result of this proffered capital is the comparative easiness of the money market even at times when, beyond this district, general stringency appears to have been the case.

The so-called trusts have grown more and more in disfavour and their influence proportionately less. Corporate bodies have been formed with all the appearances of a trust, yet keeping well within the definition of the word "trust" as defined by the various legislatures in this district, citing the common law principle, "that whatever tends to create a monopoly is unlawful as contrary to public policy;" and showing that the taking of a corporate form will not prevent trusts being dealt with according to their true character.

Railroads.

Railroads have done a large carrying at fairly satisfactory rates. A closer economy in the management has been one feature, and a preference is shown to increase rolling-stock and re-metal the lines than to increase track mileage, though one hears of branch lines and extensions in course of construction.

City business.

Leaving out of the question all speculative transactions in produce, and all deals in real estate and buildings, the business of Chicago during the year 1889 can be summarised as amounting to 1,177,000,000 dol. as against 1,125,000,000 dol. of last year, an increase of 52,000,000 dol., or about 3½ per cent.

Financial.

This year has been a notably prosperous one for those engaged in Chicago banking houses. During the first three months call loans were easily obtained at 5 per cent., and private money has been loaned at 4 and 4½ per cent. The large reserves of banking capital caused lively competition among lenders to the benefit of borrowers. Up to June the market fluctuated considerably, then suddenly became firm. For the next two months the market was tight, but gradually became easier, then fairly firm till October, rates on call loans advanced from 5 per cent. to 6 per cent., and were maintained till the end of the year. Two new banks were organised under State Law, and have done their fair share of business.

The following table will show the condition of the 21 national banks in December 1889 and 1888:—

	December, 1889.	December, 1888.
	Dollars.	Dollars.
Capital	16,250,000	16,250,000
Surplus profits	8,826,415	7,645,000
Deposits	94,346,958	85,558,842
Loans and discounts	71,247,283	65,030,101

An increase within one year of about 14 per cent. in surplus, 10 per cent. in deposits, and 9 per cent. in loans.

Produce.

The markets were not so active, and averaged lower than last year. A larger movement in grain, seeds, and live stock was noticeable, but little excitement was shown, and quotations remained steady.

CHICAGO.

The greatest fallings-off were in flour and coal; in the first case other routes for through shipments to the east and European points had been chosen, and in the latter from a more general use of crude petroleum as fuel. This article had been introduced from Lima, Ohio, by means of pipes into South Chicago, and has already made headway in manufactories against coal, as being more reliable, less expensive, easier to handle, and with less trouble giving a quicker and steadier heat. Messrs. Gormally and Jeffery, of Chicago (bicycle manufacturers), being the first to employ, within the city limits, this article as fuel in a wholesale way, and the result has proved thoroughly satisfactory.

Hog packing has generally increased, owing to a larger supply from the west.

The cattle business has extended, owing to the demand encouraged by the lower prices quoted, and also on account of the removal of the restrictions placed on shipments of Chicago beef to other States.

Very little heavy speculation in produce has taken place this year, only four being noted, *i.e.*, the Fairbank wheat deal in the spring, the Milwaukee oat deal in the summer, a short boom in corn in November, and a corner in pork engineered by Messrs. Wallace and Sawyer in the latter part of the year. It is not considered that these deals proved of great financial success to the speculators.

Under the term of provisions, beef is no longer included on the Chicago Board of Trade, and the meaning is now confined to the hog and its products. The trade has been throughout active and steady, with almost an entire absence of speculative excitement; the commission brokers in this line have done little or no business, the orders for shipments to outside points being filled directly at the packing houses or at their city offices. Hogs were plentiful, and shipments were encouraged by a discrimination of rates; thus an influx of shipments from the west caused a decided lowering of prices, and met a ready demand. The foreign trade also showed a marked increase, various shipments from this city to Liverpool averaging 3,000 boxes of meat and 1,000 tierces of lard more per week than at similar times last year.

The market in pork fluctuated from 8 dol. 37½ c. to 13 dol. 37½ c. per barrel for October delivery, showing a general average of 11 dol. 2¼ c. per barrel, as against a general average in 1888 of 14 dol. 7½ c.

The agitation of two years ago in England in favour of pure lard has caused a greater demand for a pure article shipped from this city to the discrimination against all other classes of this article, prices fluctuating from 5 dol. 75 c. to 7 dol. 62½ c., an average of 6 dol. 43 c. per tierce as against a general average in 1888 of 8 dol. 39 c.

It will thus be noticed that there is a heavy falling-off in the selling price of these two articles.

The trade in flour shows a marked reduction. The partial failure of wheat crops in the north-west in the year 1887 caused a season of great dulness. The commission business in flour has received a severe blow from the fact that millers have begun to dispense with middlemen and ship direct to consumers, establishing their own agents in the various cities even across the Atlantic. Prices have generally ruled steady, with only a small margin of profits on sales.

The receipts for the year 1889 from other points were nearly one-third less than those of the year 1888. A great deal of poor flour from the partly-frozen 1888 crop of wheat in the north-west (mentioned in my last report) was placed on the market. This flour was not considered unsound, and met with a fair sale, though some of the millers found it took five bushels of wheat to make one barrel of flour.

There is still a fair export business here, but it has the appearance of veering round to the low grades which can be used for mixing by Transatlantic dealers. The volume of trade, though reduced as far as concerns outside dealers, has been fully compensated by an increased local demand, owing to increased population and surroundings.

Wheat. The wheat market, usually replete with excitement, has this year been notably tame and uninteresting. The receipts averaged higher than in 1888, owing to better and fuller crops. Local prices averaged lower on a large supply, the average being 3s. 7d. per bushel, with little variety in rise or fall. It has been stated that, after deducting an estimate for home consumption, there would be left a surplus sufficient to permit an export of 50 per cent. more of wheat and flour than was possible during the last year. Prices fluctuated from the lowest—3s. 1d. per bushel—to the highest—4s. 6d.—at a general average of 3s. 6½d. per bushel, as against a lowest of 2s. 11d., a highest of 8s. 4d., and a general average of 3s. 9½d. per bushel in 1888.

Wheat in the north-west. Towards the close of the year it was reckoned that there were in the north-west country elevators, in Minnesota, North and South Dakota an aggregate of 9,904,000 bushels of wheat in first class order and ready to ship. The shipments to Canada in 1889 amounted to 586,596 bushels, at a value of 97,955*l*. 10s.

Corn. The same remarks may be applied to the corn market, which was unusually tame and quiet. Most of the time the speculative part of the market was simply a local "scalp," even the selling by receivers for future delivery from the country being to the men who buy or sell from one day to another without any intention of carrying. The through shipments of corn were enormous and chiefly consigned to Canadian points. Prices varied from the lowest 1s. 2d. to the highest 2s. 6½d., at a general average of 1s. 5d. per bushel, against a lowest of 1s. 4d., a highest of 2s. 6d. and an average of 1s. 9d. in 1888. The shipments of corn to Canada in 1889 amounted to 5,540,524 bushels representing a value of 391,054*l*.

Live stock. Chicago can fully deserve its title as being the largest cattle market in the world, over 11,000,000 food animals having been received during the year 1889. This business has been undeniably

CHICAGO.

a good one both for producer and consumer, being based on a cash payment system, and with a rule closely adhered to, that each day's supply of hogs, sheep, and cattle (amounting to thousands) should be sold and paid for within a few hours of unloading. Prices were certainly low, but abundance of cheap food made up a good balance. Prices varied little, seldom exceeding 5d. to 10d., and though values were low a ready market was found. At first beeves were selling at 1l. 0s. 7½d. to 1l. 1s. 10d., but this price, owing to the enormous number on hand, soon decreased to 17s. 6d. and 17s. 11d. for the best offered, to 12s. 6d. and 14s. 7d. for ordinary native steers. Large numbers of Texas cattle arrived, and at a low average of 9s. 4½d. per head, met with a good sale. This class of cattle are carefully isolated at the stock yards, on account of the beeves being more or less affected with Texas fever, and to prevent contagion. Cattle.

The market was active and satisfactory throughout, despite certain districts having suffered, as commonly is the case, from hog cholera. The supply seemed unlimited, and prices fluctuated from 1l. 0s. 7½d. and 1l. 1s. 8d. in January, to 19s. 2d. and 18s. 6½d. in midsummer. The following table shows the number of hogs slaughtered in 1889 and 1888, and the value of the product:— Hogs.

1889.			1888.		
Number Slaughtered.	Value of Animals.	Value of Product.	Number Slaughtered.	Value of Animals.	Value of Product.
	£	£		£	£
4,060,000	9,055,680	10,319,588	3,157,500	8,443,300	9,587,630

The number of cattle killed in Chicago during 1889 was about 1,772,000 head. The following table will show the amount of capital invested and the value of product for the last two years:— Packing of cattle.

1889.			1888.		
Capital.	Wages Paid.	Value of Product.	Capital.	Wages Paid.	Value o Product.
£	£	£	£	£	£
2,886,600	2,742,270	23,092,780	2,886,600	2,577,320	22,165,000

This year has been a notable one in the iron and steel business. Up to the middle of the year steel rails were quoted at 5l. 7s. 8d., but soon rose to 7l. 8s. 5d., maintaining an average for the year of about 6l. 0s. 2d. per ton. Iron and steel.

In May last the North Chicago Rolling-mills, the Union, and the Joliet Steel Companies were amalgamated into one company known as the Illinois Steel Company.

This company produced as its output for the year 1889, 466,000 tons of pig-iron, 460,147 tons of steel rails, 43,488 tons of wire rods, 4,030 tons of beams and slabs, 18,031 tons of spiegel and ferromanganese, and 50,289 tons of billets.

Labour question. No labour troubles were experienced, and wages remained normal. It is reported that this company will expend some 800,000*l.* during the next 18 months in the construction of four additional blast furnaces at South Chicago, new buildings, and blast furnaces at Joliet, and other works.

Post-office. This year no official return has been published by the Post-office. It was found, when the new administration came into power, that the returns of the previous year were represented as entirely out of proportion, and in consequence no comparison could be made. A practical enquiry has proved that a considerable increase has taken place in the number of letters handled, consequent upon increased population and business prosperity. Little legislation has taken place.

Legislation. In November the territories of Montana and Dakota were admitted into the union; the territory of Dakota being divided into two States known as North and South Dakota.

In June a Bill was passed in Illinois, and came into force July 1, whereby "no person acting for the State, or any municipality in the State, nor any contractor under any such municipality can under this Act employ other than native-born United States citizens, or those who have declared their bonâ fide intention to become United States citizens, when such employés are to be paid, wholly or in part, directly or indirectly, out of funds raised by taxation, and any such employer finding such other person in his employment is at once to discharge him."

Annex A.—RETURN of Principal Articles of Direct Export by Lake from Chicago during the Years 1889–88.

Articles.		1889.		1888.	
		Quantity.	Value £	Quantity.	Value £
Wheat	Bushels	586,596	104,108	269,279	45,799
Corn	,,	5,540,524	415,617	2,667,576	261,331
Oats	,,	131,949	5,940	9,437	492
Flour	Barrels	15,962	16,032	4,565	3,362
Cornmeal	,,	1,925	835	902	...
Pork	Pounds	3,748,520	28,514	...	...
,,	Barrels	...	...	2,414	7,035
Lard	Pounds	12,560	191	112,120	2,141
Cured meats	,,	14,880	185	43,294	737
Other articles	Packages	2,651	1,579	623	1,004
Total	...	...	573,001	...	...

Exchange is calculated at the rate of 4 dol. 85 c. = 1*l.*

CHICAGO.

Annex B.—RETURN of Principal Articles of Import to Chicago during the Years 1889–88.

Articles.	Value. 1889.	Value. 1888.
	£	£
Free goods	496,257	512,132
China and glassware	106,836	90,440
Caustic soda	13,280	28,142
Cigars, tobacco, &c.	112,309	126,688
Dry goods	933,980	888,060
Iron, pig, manufacture of, and wire, &c.	22,656	20,593
Leather manufactures	61,285	51,683
Metal　　　,,	32,422	27,040
Musical instruments	39,704	47,343
Steel bars, bloom, &c.	310	6,100
Tin plate	296,925	319,332
Wines and liquors	67,381	62,774
Other articles (general)	601,673	498,739
Total	2,785,018	2,678,222

The amount of duty collected on the imports for the year 1889 amounted, in Chicago, to 1,040,984*l*. Exchange at the rate of 4 dol. 85 c. = 1*l*.

Annex C.—RETURN of all Shipping at the Port of Chicago during the Year 1889.

ENTERED.

Nationality.	Sailing. Number of Vessels.	Sailing. Tons.	Steam. Number of Vessels.	Steam. Tons.	Total. Number of Vessels.	Total. Tons.
British	171	51,170	79	53,301	250	104,471
American	4,403	1,174,240	5,149	3,243,175	9,552	4,417,415
Total	4,574	2,225,410	5,228	3,296,476	9,802	4,521,886
,, for the year preceding	5,396	1,356,988	5,593	3,036,780	10,989	4,393,768

CLEARED.

Nationality.	Sailing. Number of Vessels.	Sailing. Tons.	Steam. Number of Vessels.	Steam. Tons.	Total. Number of Vessels.	Total. Tons.
British	413	128,536	148	97,014	561	225,550
American	4,308	1,129,027	5,154	3,274,607	9,462	4,403,634
Total	4,721	1,257,563	5,302	3,371,621	10,023	4,629,184
,, for the year preceding	5,522	1,398,516	5,584	3,088,382	11,106	4,486,898

UNITED STATES.

St. Louis.

Mr. Vice-Consul Bascombe reports as follows:—

Trade growing. — The commercial growth of the city has been steady, and generally satisfactory.

The business transacted through the exchanges, custom-house, post-office, and bank clearings has shown a gratifying increase. The change in the political control of the Government under the present Administration inaugurated in March last gives assurance that no very marked modifications will be made in the tariff, although the matter is now before Congress.

The commodities handled on the exchanges show a gratifying increase over the previous year, attributable somewhat to the increased crops of wheat and corn in the territory from which St. Louis draws its supplies.

Grain receipts. — The grain and flour receipts, reduced to bushels, for the year 1889 were 68,466,596 bushels, against 51,195,121 bushels received in 1888, an increase of 17,271,475 bushels.

Flour manufactured in the city. — St. Louis is credited with the second largest output of flour manufactured in the United States, being for the year 1889 2,066,442 barrels, an increase over the previous year of 49,833 barrels, there being 2,016,619 barrels manufactured in 1888.

Flour including country mills. — The amount of flour manufactured and handled in the exchange, including that manufactured by members of the exchange in country mills, amounted to 3,181,591 barrels in 1889, against 3,046,055 barrels in 1888, and the total amount handled by millers and dealers was 4,249,264 barrels.

Cotton. — The receipts of cotton for the season of 1889 amounted to 544,189 bales, against 521,156 bales in 1888, an increase of 23,033 bales for the year.

Grain to Europe. — The shipments of grain to Europe, viâ the Mississippi river to New Orleans, were, with the exception of the year 1880, the largest since the export trade was inaugurated, the shipments of corn being by far the largest ever made. The amount forwarded for export during the year was 1,672,361 bushels of wheat, and 13,315,952 bushels of corn.

Provisions. — The business in provisions has also increased largely during the year. The total of hog product amounted to 314,810,493 lbs. shipped during 1889, against 246,238,457 lbs. in 1888, an increase of 68,572,036 lbs. for the year.

Live stock. — In live stock the receipts were 2,065,719 head in 1889, and 1,991,232 head in 1888, an increase of 74,487 head.

The receipts of wool in 1889 were 21,018,920 lbs., against 19,626,629 lbs. the previous year.

Groceries and dry goods. — The wholesale grocery and dry goods merchants all claim an increased business in their lines.

Boots and shoes. — Notably the boot and shoe trade has made rapid progress in the manufacture of their line of goods. There are 22 manufactories, and the output for the year was nearly 1,400,000*l*.

Drugs. — Although the leading drug establishment was burned in January, 1889, St. Louis still holds a position as one of the leading markets of the country.

St. Louis is still prominent as a hardware market, and the business in this line has been more extensive than ever, reaching to the very centres of iron and steel industries. *Hardware.*

The same may be said of the woodenware and saddlery lines of trade in which the city is prominent. *Woodenware.*

St. Louis has for several years held the foremost place and is said to be the largest manufacturer of tobacco in the world, the output exceeding any of the eastern cities, the receipts of tobacco for 1889 being 38,082 hogsheads against 27,140 hogsheads in 1888, an increase of 10,942 hogsheads during the year. The capital of one of the tobacco factories is 120,000*l*., the number of hands employed in its factory is 1,500. In 1889 the company sold 22,000,000 lbs. of tobacco. *Tobacco.*

The largest brewery in the world is situated in St. Louis. It would form a village by itself. Its buildings and yards occupy forty-five blocks. The wages of its 2,000 workmen are 600*l*. per day. The capital of the company is 1,000,000*l*. In 1889 the product was 25,000,000 gallons of beer, worth about 800,000*l*. Outside of the two largest breweries nearly all the rest are said to be controlled by an English syndicate, who have purchased a majority of the shares at an expense of about 140,000*l*. *Breweries.*

There are over 30 shoe factories, and 3 large stove factories, one of which has a capital of 200,000*l*.—the works cover 4 acres. The number of workmen is about 500, whose wages average 200*l*. a day. 600 tons of iron used and manufactured into 40,000 stoves, the aggregate value of which is 200,000*l*. *Shoe factories.*

The largest foundry has a capital of 250,000*l*., employs 700 men at an average of 85,000*l*. per annum. The annual consumption of material is 1,250 tons of wrought iron, and 60,000 tons of cast-iron. *Foundries.*

The largest range and furnace company has a capital of 100,000*l*., 300 workmen employed at a weekly wage of 660*l*. It turns out about 30,000 ranges annually, at a cost of 400,000*l*. The new waterworks, now under construction, will cost 600,000*l*., and will supply the city with over 100,000,000 gallons of water a day. *Ranges and furnaces.*

The new bridge across the Mississippi river with its approaches and terminal railway, to connect with all the lines entering the city and the Union Depot, will cost about 1,200,000*l*., and is expected to be ready for use in a few months—the bridge proper being already completed. *New bridge.*

The present terminals of the old or Eads Bridge have projected improvements to cost about 1,400,000*l*., of which 400,000*l*. is to be spent in the erection of a grand central station or depot. *Eads Bridge.*

The export trade of an interior city is not easily defined, as while a large portion is shipped direct on through bills of lading, a large portion oftentimes is billed to the seaboard, and foreign freight arrangements are made there. *Export of flour via Atlantic ports.*

The amount of flour shipped from St. Louis direct on through bills of lading was 388,128 barrels. This in an increase over the previous year, but does not give a proper idea of the export trade of the city, as a large amount was shipped to the care of eastern forwarders in order to have the necessary consular and other papers perfected, and a considerable quantity was shipped from interior towns for account by St. Louis millers and dealers to save freight.

British provinces. The trade with the British provinces has been small.

South and Central America. European trade. The trade with South and Central America has increased. The European trade has been quite large, but not up to expectations, in view of the quantity and superior quality of the wheat crops.

Stock flour at end of year. The stock of flour at the close of the year was less than 100,000 barrels. Prices have steadily declined during the year.

Foreign shipments of flour from St. Louis, viâ Atlantic seaports:—

Destination.	1889.	1888.
England	94,576	65,631
Scotland	137,885	59,705
Ireland	56,798	2,422
Germany	..	..
France	..	..
Holland	11,858	137
Belgium	24,719	..
South America	318	405
Mexico	102	..
Portugal	3,825	2,475
Canada	49,602	110,335
Cuba	8,440	12,147
Seaboard for export	..	300

NOTE.—Nearly all the above was shipped in sacks of various weights and is reduced to barrels for convenience of calculation.

Freight on grain to New Orleans.

AVERAGE Rates of Freight on Bulk Grain to New Orleans.

Month.	1888.	1889.
	Cents.	Cents.
January	7	7
February	7	7
March	7	6
April	5	5½
May	5	5
June	5	5
July	5	5
August	5½	5½
September	6	6
October	6½	6
November	6½	6½
December	7½	7

District—assessed valuations, real and personal. The State of Missouri, which comprises my district, except Jackson county, has 116 counties, with an assessed value, excepting railways, real estate at 111,704,509*l*., personal property at

38,320,918*l*., total 150,026,227*l*. Railways, bridges, and telegraph lines are assessed at 11,484,064*l*. Total assessed wealth of the State is 161,510.292*l*.

The city of St. Louis for the last five years has greatly improved in its structures and streets. The annual number of new structures is about 2,500. The appraised cost of the new buildings erected in 1889 was nearly 2,000,000*l*., and their real value much greater. In 1888 the taxable property of the city was 32,000,000*l*., and in 1889 it was 46.000,000*l*. One indication of the growth of a city is shown by the business of the banking clearing-house.

The clearings for 1889 reached the sum of 197,504,525*l*., the largest since the organisation of the clearing-house, and an increase of 96·10 per cent. over the previous year. <small>Bank clearings.</small>

The capital and surplus of the 21 banks increased from 3.092,173*l*. in 1888, to 3,763,643*l*. in 1889, and the proposed increase of capital of one bank, and new one to be opened March 1, will increase the banking capital to 4,000,0 0*l*. <small>Banking capital.</small>

The post-office statistics given on another page show a large increase in all departments. <small>Post-office.</small>

The year 1889 was favourable for transportation, the river being open to New Orleans all winter. <small>Traffic.</small>

The business of the rivers, as shown by the tonnage carried, compares with the previous year as follows:— <small>River transportation.</small>

	1889.	1888.
	Tons.	Tons.
Received by steamboats and barges..	543,900	597,955
,, ,, rafts	127,695	130,855
Shipped by steamboats and barges..	712,700	510,115
Total ..	1,384,385	1,238,925

The volume of business during the year was increased about 25 per cent. in package freights, on account of the low prices of produce and the increased demand at points along the Mississippi river.

Vessels enrolled at the port of St. Louis December 31, 1889. <small>Vessels enrolled at port.</small>

	Number.	Tons.
Steamers	103	40,246
Barges..	87	80,230
Total ..	193	120,476

UNITED STATES.

Shipments of grain to New Orleans.

Shipments of bulk grain by barges to New Orleans during 1889:—

	Bushels.
Wheat	1,672,361
Corn	13,315,952
Oats	89,707
Total	15,078,020

	Tons.
Bulk grain	428,204
Other freight	78,105
Total	506,309

CLEARING-HOUSE Statement.—Business of the Year 1888 compared with 1889.

	Clearings.		Balances.	
	1888.	1889.	1888.	1889.
	£ s.	£ s.	£ s.	£ s.
January	14,697,389 0	16,839,960 16	2,242,658 8	2,416,305 0
February	14,736,449 4	14,500,197 12	3,139,162 0	2,569,116 16
March	15,027,321 0	15,954,946 12	2,951,499 16	2,938,256 0
April	14,400,971 4	14,278,435 0	2,366,712 8	2,097,522 12
May	14,759,411 16	16,747,729 4	2,282,813 16	3,326,212 4
June	13,991,575 4	16,666,674 0	2,149,904 0	3,497,012 4
July	13,426,981 16	16,441,577 0	2,144,499 0	2,788,322 4
August	15,046,015 4	16,373,931 8	2,197,569 8	2,989,843 0
September	15,653,096 16	16,102,221 0	2,563,156 0	2,775,647 12
October	16,686,063 8	19,126,536 4	2,063,437 12	3,213,944 8
November	14,458,360 4	16,804,149 8	1,619,175 4	2,080,306 0
December	17,210,840 16	17,568,167 12	2,656,118 4	1,999,763 8
Aggregate	180,094,975 12	197,504,525 16	28,376,705 16	32,692,251 8

Increase of clearings in 1889, 9·6 per cent., 17,409,550*l.* 4*s.*

The clearings of 1889 are the largest of any year since the opening of the clearing-house.

COMPARATIVE Business in Leading Articles at St. Louis, Mo., for 1888–89.

Articles.		1888.	1889.
Flour, amount manufactured	Barrels	2,016,619	2,066,442
,, ,, handled	,,	3,773,155	4,249,261
Wheat, total receipts	Bushels	13,010,108	13,810,591
Corn, ,, ,,	,,	20,269,499	34,299,781
Oats, ,, ,,	,,	10,456,760	11,347,340
Rye, ,, ,,	,,	421,514	679,364
Barley, ,, ,,	,,	3,044,961	3,070,807
All grain received (including wheat reduced to flour)	,,	51,195,121	68,466,596
Cotton, receipts	Bales	521,156	544,189
Bagging, manufactured	Yards	12,000,000	13,000,000
Hay, receipts	Tons	107,884	166,346
Tobacco, receipts	Hogsheads	27,140	38,082
Lead, receipts in pigs	80 lb. pigs	1,853,781	2,018,483
Hog product, total shipments	Lbs.	246,238,457	314,810,593
Cattle, receipts	Head	546,875	508,190
Sheep, ,,	,,	456,669	358,495
Hogs, ,,	,,	929,230	1,120,930
Horses and mules, receipts	,,	58,458	78,104
Lumber and logs, ,,	,,	627,226,966	670,862,165
Shingles	Packages	66,285,500	111,080,500
Lath	,,	14,650,317	21,386,350
Wool, total receipts	Lbs.	19,626,629	21,018,920
Hides, ,, ,,	,,	31,814,049	29,732,042
Sugar, received	,,	138,561,200	150,262,050
Molasses, shipped	Gallons	3,807,070	2,131,080
Coffee, received	Bags	192,940	211,789
Rice, receipts	Packages	74,181	63,653
Coal, ,,	Bushels	67,676,875	65,403,025
Nails, ,,	Kegs	596,579	467,943
Potatoes,,	Bushels	1,219,893	992,919
Salt, ,,	Barrels	330,110	293,663
,, ,,	Sacks	24,649	21,319
,, ,,	Bushels, in bulk	254,700	304,080
Butter	Lbs.	11,109,733	12,822,101
Freight of all kinds received and shipped	Tons	13,455,760	14,909,443

Condensed Classification of Commodities Imported during the Years 1888-89, showing Values and Duty Paid.

Commodities.	1888. Value.	1888. Duties.	1889. Value.	1889. Duties.
	£ s. d.	£ s. d.	£ s. d.	£ s. d.
Ale and beer	4,091 16 0	1,147 10 6	4,458 8 0	1,553 7 10
Anvils	3,056 4 0	968 13 6	3,6·6 8 0	1,162 1 9
Barley	69,346 0 0	9,112 17 4	37,749 0 0	5,791 4 10
Chemicals	13,572 16 0	5,594 0 7	7,901 16 0	2,419 19 6
China and earthenware	24,716 4 0	13,923 5 0	31,034 0 0	17,710 2 10
Cutlery	19,765 12 0	9,295 8 0	21,335 0 0	10,559 12 10
Free goods	53,445 16 0	...	60,231 8 0	...
Glass and glassware	19,845 16 0	10,587 2 7	11,157 0 0	6,569 19 8
Guns and firearms	17,533 4 0	5,323 17 3	18,143 12 0	6,957 18 5
Hops	19,537 0 0	5,786 5 10	25,008 12 0	6,957 18 5
Manufacture of cotton	36,454 2 0	15,354 3 10	41,421 16 0	18,860 0 1
,, iron and steel	139,474 4 0	53,586 0 0	30,790 12 0	14,089 4 8
,, wool	30,289 8 0	20,888 9 10	21,900 0 0	19,514 6 10
Rice, granulated	45,153 8 0	9,030 13 10	25,637 12 0	5,341 12 0
Sugar	62,944 0 0	45,425 1 10	Refinery	closed.
Tobacco, cigars, and cigarettes	24,769 16 0	31,496 14 6	26,222 4 0	30,716 0 0
Wines and liquors	16,084 16 0	10,571 10 2	26,317 12 0	18,057 12 4
Liquors, reimported	13,510 12 0	12,012 10 6	...	...
Miscellaneous	101,631 0 0	30,981 13 7	256,843 0 0	82,497 2 10
Total	715,222 4 0	291,085 18 8	649,838 0 0	242,540 10 1

NOTE.—For convenience the above values are computed at 5 dols. to the 1*l*. sterling.

General Merchandise Imported into St. Louis through following Ports of Entry during 1889, showing Foreign Value and Estimated Duty.

Ports.	Foreign Value.	Duties.
	£	£
Baltimore	74,825	29,931
Boston	10,110	4,044
Detroit	32,167	12,867
Laredo	26,022	113
New Orleans	79,958	41,983
New York	254,019	94,547
Philadelphia	109,250	51,700
Portland	11,254	4,501
Port Huron	31,827	12,731
San Francisco	186	56
St. Paul	134	33
Port Townsend	79	31
Total	629,831	242,537

CHICAGO.

Internal Revenue Collections.

Designation.	1888.	1889.
	£	£
Lists (chiefly banks)	140	259
Spirit stamps	267,082	277,089
Tobacco	640,148	719,434
Cigars	28,376	28,839
Snuff	809	629
Beer	275,885	297,520
Special tax	28,286	29,670
Total	1,240,726	1,353,440
Increase during the year	..	112,714

Note.—There is a Bill pending in Congress to take off the tax on tobacco.

The following increase in the business of the Post-office for the past year, 1889, has been observed:— *Post-office statistics.*

	Increase.
Number of letter carriers	12
,, ,, registered letters	11,328
,, ,, mail letters	1,892,824
,, ,, postal cards	8,533
,, ,, local letters	485,277
,, ,, ,, postal cards	46,969
,, ,, papers and circulars delivered by carriers	1,559,182
,, ,, letters collected by carriers	15,020,981
,, ,, postal cards collected by carriers	8,158,854
,, ,, papers and circulars collected by carriers	3,684,828
Postage on drop matter	2,719

ST. PAUL.

Mr. Vice-Consul Morphy reports as follows:—

In many respects the past year was one which will occupy a prominent place in the history of the north-west. The vast strides made in the development of industries, the growth of population, and the material wealth of the country indicate an era of progress in respect of which the people may justly congratulate themselves. True, there was in some districts of North Dakota and South Dakota a partial failure of crops, but in Minnesota they have been good, and any fears of disastrous results to commerce, which may have been entertained in some quarters, were quickly dispelled.

The records of the cities of St. Paul and Minneapolis show a marked degree of improvement. The amount expended on buildings was in excess of that of any other season, and real estate, though not remarkably active, records the greatest volume of business it has ever shown. *General improvement in the cities of St. Paul and Minneapolis.*

UNITED STATES.

Bank clearings in St. Paul and Minneapolis.

Bank clearings exhibit a satisfactory increase over the previous year. In St. Paul they amounted to 209,409,381 dol. 3 c. as against 194,913,011 dol. 43 c. the year before. In Minneapolis the clearings were, in 1889, 239,707,573 dol.; in 1888, 215,626,250 dol. In St. Paul there are 14 banks with a total capital of 9,167,996 dol. 78 c., including surplus and undivided profits of 2,267,996 dol. 78 c. In Minneapolis the banking capital increased 360,000 dol., and now aggregates 7,220,000 dol., with a surplus of 878,500 dol., and undivided profits 704,300 dol.

A tabular statement of some of the principal items in connection with the trade and development of these cities is here given:—

ST. PAUL.

Tabular statement of the principal items in connection with the trade and development of St. Paul.

Items.		Number.
Population		211,000
Jobbing trade	Dollars	109,898,367
Manufacturing	,,	43,744,729
Bank clearings	,,	209,409,381
Imported goods	,,	1,098,849
Post-office business	,,	4,730,511
Assessed valuation taxable property	,,	127,669,159
Real estate transferred	,,	22,755,608
U.S. Internal Revenue	,,	2,804,338
Cost of public works	,,	2,310,633
Street railways, horse, cable and electric	Miles	65
Total graded streets	,,	439
,, paved ,,	,,	39
Area of city	Acres	35,483
Length of city east and west	Miles	10
Width of city north and south	,,	5
Daily passenger trains in and out		275
Daily U.S. Mail	Tons	90

Statistics of health department of St. Paul.

Statistics of the health department show the annual death rate of St. Paul to be 9·90 per 1,000 inhabitants, as against a rate of 11·80 for the year 1888. This is believed to be the lowest rate of any city of 200,000 inhabitants in the country. There was a total of 3,160 births, and 1,760 deaths, as against 3,342 births and 2,078 deaths in 1888.

Cost of year's building in St. Paul.

The cost of the year's building reached the sum of 7,939,493 dol., devoted largely to the erection of residences.

St. Paul waterworks.

One of the most important branches of the city departments is the waterworks. There has been laid, during the past year, 36 miles of pipe, making the total miles now laid 166½. During the year extensions have been made in the watersheds drained from 40 square miles, with a daily supply of 8,000,000 gallons, to 224 square miles, with an estimated daily supply of 44,000,000 gallons. About 21 miles of extensions are contemplated during the coming year.

CHICAGO.

In the matter of bridges the city has expended 530,000 dol. during the year. *Bridges.*

The record of losses by fire during the year has been unprecedentedly light, aggregating 285,340 dol. 54 c., as against 777,515 dol. 45 c. the previous year. *Losses by fire.*

Liquor licenses last year numbered 384, from which the receipts were as many thousand dollars. About 50 of those whose licenses have recently expired failed to have them renewed owing to the high tariff. *Liquor licenses.*

The total bonded indebtedness of the city is 7,000,000 dol.; total assets, 9,000,000 dol. *Bonded indebtedness.*

The custom duties collected at St. Paul last year amounted to 229,386 dol. 12 c., an increase of 51,699 dol. 23 c. over 1888. There was collected from all sources in the district of Minnesota outside of St. Paul 252,895 dol. 35 c., an increase of 41,967 dol. 35 c. over the previous year. The value of dutiable imports for the past year was 726,477 dol., free goods 372,372 dol. The value of domestic exports for the year was 1,406,479 dol., an increase of 430,000 dol. over the previous year. *Custom duties collected.*

MINNEAPOLIS.

Tabular statement of the principal items in connection with the trade and development of Minneapolis.

Items.		Number.
Population, estimated	..	225,000
Assessed valuation	Dollars	130,065,147
Bonded debt	,,	6,486,300
Banking capital	,,	7,220,000
Bank clearings	,,	239,707,573
Jobbing trade	,,	173,210,600
Jobbing capital	,,	22,834,500
Manufactures	,,	62,386,050
Retail firms, capital	,,	1,967,775
Real estate transfers	,,	49,559,160
Wheat consumed by home mills	Bushels	30,000,000
Wheat shipments	,,	12,603,970
Flour ,,	Barrels	6,096,411
Lumber, cut	Feet	275,855,648
Logs, scaled	,,	233,002,780
Annual capacity of mills	,,	500,000,000
Square miles in city	..	53½
Miles of streets	..	788
Miles of water mains	..	142

All in all, the record for Minneapolis is quite satisfactory, and the prospect of work to be done has a promise of better things and an enlarged field of operations that will bring a more bountiful return than the rich rewards of the past. Several of the great flouring mills have been improved by the introduction of new machinery, and the total capacity of all the mills is now 38,575 barrels daily. The recent sale of the Pillsbury and Washburn mills to an English syndicate will, it is said, in no way affect the policy of their management. *General record of Minneapolis.*

Purchase of mills by English syndicate.

Wheat production in Minnesota and Dakota.

The wheat production in Minnesota and Dakota last year was about 90,000,000 bushels; in 1888 it was 75,000,000 bushels; and in 1887, 95,000,000 bushels.

Educational interests.

Educational interests continue to receive very earnest attention. A magnificent building for the public library in Minneapolis has recently been completed, and formally opened, and an edifice for a like purpose is contemplated in St. Paul. The libraries in both cities have received many additions during the year.

Two new States formed out of Territory of Dakota.

Two States were newly created out of what was formerly the Territory of Dakota, called North Dakota and South Dakota. Since the Bill making them States passed the United States Congress the work of organisation has gone forward rapidly at their respective capitals, and their legislatures are doing much for the interests of the people.

Opening of Indian reservation.

By the proclamation of the President a large section of land in South Dakota, heretofore occupied as an Indian reservation, was a few weeks ago thrown open for settlement, and hundreds of people at once hastened to avail themselves of this opportunity of securing homesteads in a country towards which they had long looked with envious eyes.

Meeker Water Power.

An extensive scheme is now under way, with every prospect of being carried through to completion, for the utilisation of what is known as the Meeker Water Power, an event which will give an almost inconceivable impetus to the manufacturing and other industries here.

Alien Act amended.

The Alien Act was amended at the last session of the legislature of the State of Minnesota by Chapter 113 of the General Laws for 1889, allowing aliens to acquire lots or parcels of land not exceeding six lots of 50 feet frontage, by 300 feet in depth each, or, in lieu thereof, a parcel or trace of land of equal size within and forming a part of the platted portion of any incorporated city in the State. The Act, as a whole, is unpopular, and there is every reason to believe it will be repealed at the next session of the legislature.

DENVER.

Mr. Vice-Consul Pearce reports as follows:—

It will be seen from the statement which I have the honour to submit, that the State of Colorado has during the year 1889 shown unprecedented prosperity.

Population.

The population of Denver, the most important city in the State, shows an increase of 55,000, or from 95,000 in 1888 to 150,000 in 1889.

Value of new buildings.

The value of new buildings erected in Denver during the year amounts to the sum of 2,600,000*l.*; of this amount over 800,000*l.* was expended in the construction of large business blocks in the most important business centres of the city.

Transactions in real estate.

The transactions in real estate is said to represent the enormous sum of 12,078,419*l.*, an increase of 3,690,512*l.* over the previous year.

The records of the clearing-house show a total of 38,951,929*l*., an increase of 45·5 per cent. over 1888. *Clearing-house records.*

This increased prosperity may be said to be prevalent throughout the State generally, as we find from reliable figures that the value of taxable property in the State has increased 500,000*l*. during the year. *Value of taxable property.*

Denver has received no small attention by parties interested in manufacturing, for it is found that these interests show a value during 1889 of about 6,000,000*l*., or a gain of 36 per cent. over the previous year. *Manufacturing.*

One important feature during the year which has benefitted Denver perhaps more than any other of its numerous enterprises, is the construction of improved facilities for transportation. The old horse car was found to be too small for the requirements of the city, and 21 miles of cable railway has been constructed and equipped during the year. *Cable railways.*

There are now two distinct corporations holding franchises for cable railways in Denver: the Denver City Cable Railway Company, and the Denver Tramway Company. The former company at the present time represents 12 miles of double track cable road, the total cost of which, together with the necessary machinery, is estimated at 400,000*l*. The motive power is produced from two engines, each of 750 horse-power. 30 miles of rope is now in use, and this will be increased during the present year. This company also operates about 48 miles of single horse car track, a portion of which is used as feeders to the cable lines. The lines run about 10,000 car miles a day, and the horse lines about 5,400.

The Denver Tramway Company is a comparatively new organisation, and is composed entirely of Denver capitalists. This Company has constructed nine miles of double track cable road, which, together with their buildings and machinery, cost 140,000*l*. They have in operation one main and three branch lines. On the main line cars run every minute, and on the branches every three minutes, 19 hours a day; at a speed of eight miles an hour on the main line, and 12 miles on the branches.

This Company has also added to its plant four miles of single track electric road beginning at the terminus of one of their branch lines. This electric road cost 20,000*l*. The cars run at a speed of 18 miles to 20 miles an hour.

These two extensive systems of rapid transit running through the principal thoroughfares of the city, and reaching out as they do beyond the city limits in all directions, have been the means of building up the outlying districts, and enhancing the value of property to a remarkable degree.

The latest addition to the large amount of English capital invested in Denver and the State is the purchase of the two principal breweries by English capitalists, the consideration being 425,000*l*. These breweries produce annually 125,000 barrels of beer, of 32 gallons each, which, at 2*l*. per barrel, the selling price, realises the sum of 250,000*l*. The capital stock is 600,000*l*. *English capital.*

UNITED STATES.

Water companies.

A new water company has been organised, called the Citizens' Water Company, with a capital of 600,000*l*. Their supply of water will be drawn from the Platte river, about 25 miles from Denver. They have already completed the necessary arrangements at this point, and the work of laying pipes to the city will soon commence.

Railroads.

There has been no increase in railroad mileage during the year, but the Denver and Rio Grande Railway Company are rapidly pushing the work of widening their tracks to standard gauge, this, when completed, will make a new broad gauge system to the Pacific Coast.

An event of great importance to Denver, in connection with railroads, is the consolidation, recently consummated, of the Union Pacific Railway Company, with the Denver, Texas, and Fortworth Railroad Company. This gives a direct outlet for the great Union Pacific system to the Gulf of Mexico.

This new arrangement has made it necessary to make Denver the principal headquarters of the consolidated roads; and as a result of this combination, it has been determined to construct extensive railway repair shops in Denver, at an estimated cost of 200,000*l*. These shops will give employment to about 1,000 men.

Mining.

The total production of gold, silver, lead, and copper, during the year of 1889, from figures which I have been able to obtain from different sources, would appear to show an increase of 1,297,976*l*. over the previous year. The value of the entire product is estimated as follows:—

	£
Silver	3,868,367
Gold	1,733,040
Lead	1,064,000
Copper	72,000
Total	6,737,407

Coal.

Through the kindness of Mr. McNeil, State Inspector of Coal Mines, I have been able to give a statement showing the total production of coal for 1889, from the different counties in the State, together with a table showing the increase and decrease in the product of the several counties. I also append a statement showing the coal production for each year, from 1873 to 1889 inclusive.

It will be seen from these figures that the coal mining industry of Colorado is growing rapidly, and represents no small proportion of the value of the products of the State.

If we estimate the value of the coal output of the State on the same basis as that given in my last report, viz., 9*s.* 2*d.* per ton, we have a total value of 1,088,062*l*.

PRODUCTION of Coal by Counties in Colorado for the Year ending December 31, 1889. The month of December is partly estimated.

Counties.	Tons of 2,000 lbs.	Increase.	Decrease.
Arapahoe	900	..	600
Boulder	297,793	..	17,362
Douglas	300	..	..
Dolores	..	..	..
El Paso	54,066	9,952	..
Fremont	279,855	..	158,943
Gunnison	251,808	..	6,566
Garfield	144,627	29,627	..
Huerfano	309,023	149,413	..
Jefferson	6,600	..	2,400
Las Animas	876,990	170,535	..
La Plata	32,630	..	995
Mesa	..	..	300
Park	47,005	417	..
Pitkin	46,181	18,068	..
Weld	26,176	..	1,878
Total	2,373,954	..	..

Output for 1888, 2,185,477 tons; output for 1889, 2,373,954 tons; being an increase over 1888 of 188,477 tons.

COKE Manufactured during 1889.

Counties.	Tons of 2,000 lbs.	Increase.	Decrease.
Gunnison	42,858	2,158	..
Las Animas	119,436	..	1,298
Pitkin	22,125	6,125	..
Garfield	500	500	..
Total	184,919	..	..

The above increase and decrease of the coke production is in comparing 1888 with 1889.

UNITED STATES.

The following is a summary of the coal statistics for a number of years:—

Year.	Tons.
1873..	69,977
1874..	87,372
1875..	98,838
1876..	117,666
1877..	160,000
1878..	200,630
1879..	322,732
1880..	375,000
1881..	706,744
1882..	1,061,479
1883..	1,220,593
1884..	1,130,024
1885..	1,398,796
1886..	1,436,211
1887..	1,791,735
1888..	2,185,477
1889..	2,373,954

Petroleum. There has been no increase in the output of the oil wells near Florence, in Fremont county, the only developed oil region in the State. This is not due to a lack of oil, but to certain restrictions in the sale of the product, which are imposed by the Standard Oil Company.

Imports. Through the kindness of Mr. J. H. P. Voorhies, collector of customs at this port, I am able to send a list showing the value of the principal articles of import from Great Britain to Denver for 1889. It will be seen from this statement that the value of the imports has more than doubled during the year. This, in all probability, is due to the general prosperity of the State, and also to the geographical position of Denver as a distributing point.

The recent connection with the Atlantic seaboard and Europe by the Denver and Gulf Railway, and the Harrison Steamship Line, has given Denver many advantages which heretofore it did not possess. This direct connection with New Orleans, or Galveston, affords a saving in distance as against New York, or any of the Atlantic ports, of 900 miles; this, of course, reduces materially the cost of transportation, and enables Denver merchants to compete with Chicago, St. Louis, and New York.

The following is a record of imports from Great Britain for the past four years:—

	1886.	1887.	1888.	1889.
	£ s. d.	£ s. d.	£ s. d.	£ s. d.
Total value	3,201 0 0	5,043 12 0	8,109 12 0	17,585 7 0

CHICAGO.

RETURN of the Principal Articles of Import to Denver during the Year 1889.

	£	s.	d.
Ale and porter	250	15	0
Articles for use of churches and colleges	385	12	0
Books for public library	159	11	0
Bicycles, and parts of	44	16	0
Biscuits	16	1	0
Caustic soda	647	6	0
Earthenware	941	18	0
Furniture, finished	218	0	0
Gloves, kid or leather	30	12	0
Garden and other seeds	133	1	0
Household and personal effects	985	11	0
Hats	179	11	0
Jewellery	7	14	0
Manufactured silk	263	18	0
,, cotton	229	3	0
,, wool cloths	2,901	5	0
,, ,, clothing	282	13	0
,, ,, ,, and gentlemen's goods	1,720	8	0
,, carpets	330	9	0
,, glass	135	18	0
,, ivory	31	15	0
,, metal	168	5	0
Oil paintings	486	13	0
Precious stones	4,061	17	0
Paints	194	12	0
Pickles	178	3	0
Port wine	28	4	0
Saddlery	78	2	0
Tin plates	2,167	9	0
Varnish	121	15	0
Whiskey	64	9	0
Miscellaneous articles	139	16	0
Total	17,585	7	0

(927)

LONDON:
Printed for Her Majesty's Stationery Office,
By HARRISON AND SONS,
Printers in Ordinary to Her Majesty.
(1250   6 | 90 − H & S   927)

FOREIGN OFFICE.
1890.
ANNUAL SERIES.

No. 747.

DIPLOMATIC AND CONSULAR REPORTS ON TRADE AND FINANCE.

UNITED STATES.

REPORT FOR THE YEAR 1889
ON THE
TRADE OF THE DISTRICT OF THE CONSULATE-GENERAL OF NEW YORK.

REFERENCE TO PREVIOUS REPORT, Annual Series No. 545.

Presented to both Houses of Parliament by Command of Her Majesty,
JULY, 1890.

LONDON:
PRINTED FOR HER MAJESTY'S STATIONERY OFFICE,
BY HARRISON AND SONS, ST. MARTIN'S LANE,
PRINTERS IN ORDINARY TO HER MAJESTY.

And to be purchased, either directly or through any Bookseller, from
EYRE & SPOTTISWOODE, EAST HARDING STREET, FLEET STREET, E.C., and
32, ABINGDON STREET, WESTMINSTER, S.W; or
ADAM AND CHARLES BLACK, 6, NORTH BRIDGE, EDINBURGH; or
HODGES, FIGGIS, & Co., 104, GRAFTON STREET, DUBLIN.

1890.

[C. 5895—150.] *Price Twopence.*

New Series of Reports.

Reports of the Annual Series have been issued from Her Majesty's Diplomatic and Consular Officers at the following places, and may be obtained from the sources indicated on the title-page:—

No.		Price.	No.		Price.
631.	Berlin	1d.	689.	Trebizond	1d.
632.	Adrianople	1½d.	690.	Damascus	½d.
633.	Rome	1½d.	691.	Savannah (Georgia)	1d.
634.	Santiago	½d.	692.	Barcelona	2½d.
635.	Tahiti	½d.	693.	Santos	1d.
636.	Maranham	½d.	694.	San José	1d.
637.	Mexico	2d.	695.	Batavia	1d.
638.	Christiania	1d.	696.	Genoa	1½d.
639.	Copenhagen	1d.	697.	Calais	2d.
640.	Paris	1d.	698.	Marseilles	1d.
641.	Venice	1d.	699.	Brest	1d.
642.	Cherbourg	½d.	700.	Lisbon	2½d.
643.	New York	1d.	701.	Leghorn	2d.
644.	Patras	1d.	702.	Rio Grande do Sul	1d.
645.	Bourgas	½d.	703.	Tainan	1d.
646.	St. Petersburg	3d.	704.	Kewkiang	4d.
647.	Taganrog	½d.	705.	Fiume	1d.
648.	Baltimore	1½d.	706.	Odessa	2d.
649.	New Orleans	2d.	707.	Suakin	½d.
650.	New Orleans	1d.	708.	Hankow	½d.
651.	Samos	½d.	709.	Amoy	1d.
652.	Buda-Pesth	1½d.	710.	Buda-Pesth	1½d.
653.	Tripoli	½d.	711.	Corunna	2d.
654.	Buenos Ayres	½d.	712.	Mogador	2d.
655.	Paris	1d.	713.	Cadiz	½d.
656.	Cherbourg	1d.	714.	Cadiz	1d.
657.	Warsaw	½d.	715.	Rio de Janeiro	2½d.
658.	Rome	1½d.	716.	Newchwang	½d.
659.	Saigon	½d.	717.	Chinkiang	½d.
660.	Buenos Ayres	½d.	718.	San Francisco	6d.
661.	Galveston	1d.	719.	Bussorah	½d.
662.	Galatz	1½d.	720.	Beyrout	1d.
663.	Antwerp	1d.	721.	Adrianople	½d.
664.	Boston	1d.	722.	Nantes	½d.
665.	Madeira	½d.	723.	Caracas	1d.
666.	New Hebrides	½d.	724.	Mogador	½d.
667.	Riga	1d.	725.	Tientsin	1d.
668.	Charleston	1d.	726.	Foochow	1d.
669.	Algiers	2d.	727.	Port au Prince	½d.
670.	Stuttgart	1d.	728.	Callao	1d.
671.	Havre	3d.	729.	Puerto Plata	½d.
672.	The Piræus	1d.	730.	San Francisco	1d.
673.	Syra	1d.	731.	Philadelphia	2½d.
674.	Boulogne	1d.	732.	Pakhoi	1d.
675.	Taganrog	2d.	733.	Bilbao	1d.
676.	Wuhu	½d.	734.	Dunkirk	1d.
677.	Batoum	1d.	735.	Vienna	1d.
678.	Manila	1d.	736.	Nantes	1½d.
679.	Tamsui	1d.	737.	Paramaribo	1d.
680.	Kiungchow	1d.	738.	Honolulu	½d.
681.	Swatow	1d.	739.	Chicago	2d.
682.	Stettin	6d.	740.	Söul	1d.
683.	Bordeaux	2½d.	741.	Brindisi	1½d.
684.	Port Said	1d.	742.	Mozambique	1d.
685.	Coquimbo	½d.	743.	Caldera and Lota	1½d.
686.	Warsaw	1d.	744.	Nice	1½d.
687.	Ichang	1d.	745.	Aleppo	1d.
688.	Wênchow	1d.	746.	Hakodate	1d.

No. 747.

Reference to previous Report, Annual Series No. 545.

UNITED STATES.

NEW YORK.

Consul-General Booker to the Marquis of Salisbury.

My Lord,   *New York, April 23, 1890.*

I HAVE the honour to transmit, herewith, my Annual Report upon the Trade of New York, with some information in regard to other parts of my Consular district.

I am precluded from giving a good deal of information which would be interesting from the unusual delay in publishing the Reports of State Departments.

I have, &c.
Signed   WM. LANE BOOKER.

Annual Trade Report for the Year 1889.

General review of the trade. The trade of this port in 1889 was beyond the average of recent years, and it was entirely without inflation. The demand from the interior was to meet the actual requirements of the section of country drawing supplies from this city. Some of the jobbers complain that the profits grow smaller year by year, and attribute it to a disposition in the larger cities to combine various branches of business and thus crowd out the smaller retailers; be this so or not the prosperity in commercial circles has been very noticeable, in fact, excluding those engaged in the woollen and coal trades, all classes appear to have been fairly well satisfied with the result of their year's transactions. With this generally prosperous condition of things, it is somewhat remarkable to find but a very small falling-off in the number of failures, shown elsewhere; the liabilities are in fact heavier than in 1888, but this is due to a few failures with unusually large liabilities. The increased volume of trade is shown by the clearing-house returns of the New York city banks which, eliminating what come under stock transactions, exceeded those of 1888 by 24 per cent.

The total clearings were 7,394,271,543*l.*, of which 2,280,893,851*l.* represented stock transactions. The clearings in New York were 64 per cent. of those of the whole country, *i.e.*, the clearings of the cities having clearing-houses. The dispersion of money for

UNITED STATES.

railroad construction has been much less than in 1888, and very much less than in 1887, when there were constructed 13,000 miles of roads against about 7,000 in 1888, and 5,000 in the one under review. The construction in 1889 was almost entirely in branches connected with main lines, and in this State only 158 miles were built.

Imports of merchandise (excluding specie) exceeded those of 1888 by 6,295,100*l*., and exports by 9,473,956*l*.; customs receipts at this port in 1889 were 30,420,610*l*., a gain on 1888 of 3·52 per cent. The value of all dry goods marketed, that is, entered for consumption, and withdrawn from bonded warehouse was 28,004,526*l*., about 2,170,000*l*. more than in 1888. The gross and the net earnings of railroads have been far in excess of 1888, and dividends have in many instances been increased. The coal roads have been almost the only exception to the general prosperity. The report of the New York Railway Commissioner shows an increase in the gross earnings of the railroads of the State of about 3,000,000*l*. over those of 1888, the net earnings of about 2,700,000*l*., and in dividends 825,730*l*.

The money market showed important changes at different periods both in the demand for money, and in the rates of interest. In the first quarter call loans ranged from $1\frac{1}{2}$ to 5 per cent., and first-class commercial paper 4 to 5 per cent.; in the second quarter call loans from 2 to 6 per cent., commercial paper $3\frac{1}{2}$ to $4\frac{3}{4}$ per cent.; in the third quarter call loans 2 to 8 per cent., commercial paper $3\frac{1}{2}$ to 6 per cent.; and in the last quarter call loans ranged all the way from $1\frac{1}{2}$ to 12 per cent., and commercial paper $5\frac{1}{2}$ to $6\frac{1}{2}$ per cent.

There was at times during this quarter considerable stringency in money, arising mainly from the heavy demand from the west and south for crop movements.

Bank returns. The condition of the associated banks of the city at different periods of the year is shown in the following table:—

Associated Banks of New York City.

1889.	Loans.	Specie.	Legal Tenders.	Deposits.	Circulation.	Surplus over Reserve required against Deposits.
	£	£	£	£	£	£
January 5	80,820,165	15,868,695	6,701,118	84,236,778	999,203	1,510,620
March 31	86,730,780	16,587,470	7,088,995	90,214,960	884,338	1,122,725
June 29	85,996,410	14,896,355	9,327,990	90,641,380	813,165	1,564,000
September 28	84,318,210	14,332,244	7,352,717	85,968,785	813,310	192,765
December 28	81,320,930	15,565,505	5,385,066	82,136,423	768,658	416,465

Banking report. The Annual report of the Superintendent of the State banking department for the fiscal year ending September 30, 1889, has been presented to the Legislature, and from it I extract the following items of interest:—22 new State banks were authorised to do business during the year, with a total capital of 551,050*l*.; four of these, with a capital of 185,400*l*., are located in this city; and six, with a capital of 123,600*l*., at Brooklyn. Three of the 22 were converted from the national system. In 1879 there were 73 State banks, with 17,858,795*l*. total resources. Last year there were 149, with 5,050,376*l*. total resources.

Four new Trust Companies were authorised to do business during the year, two in New York city, and two in Brooklyn, with an aggregate capital of 515,000*l*. There are altogether under the supervision of the State banking department 30 Trust Companies and miscellaneous corporations, of which 21 are in this city, with a capital of 4,089,100*l*., and 6 in Brooklyn, with a capital of 721,000*l*. The savings banks of this city generally paid 3½ per cent. interest, a few paying 4 per cent. The following gives the rates of bankers' sterling exchange during the year 1889:— *Sterling exchange.*

Month.		At 60 Days.	At Sight.
		Dol. c.	Dol. c.
January	Highest	4 87	4 89½
	Lowest..	4 84½	4 89
February	Highest	4 87	4 89½
	Lowest..	4 86½	4 89
March	Highest	4 87	4 89½
	Lowest..	4 86½	4 89½
April	Highest	4 88	4 90
	Lowest..	4 87	4 89½
May	Highest	4 88	4 89½
	Lowest..	4 88	4 90
June	Highest	4 88	4 90
	Lowest..	4 87½	4 89
July	Highest	4 88	4 89½
	Lowest..	4 85½	4 87½
August	Highest	4 86	4 88½
	Lowest..	4 84	4 87
September	Highest	4 85½	4 89
	Lowest..	4 84½	4 88½
October	Highest	4 84	4 88½
	Lowest..	4 81½	4 86
November	Highest	4 82	4 86
	Lowest..	4 81	4 85½
December	Highest	4 81½	4 86
	Lowest..	4 80	4 84

In the following table, taken from Dun's Commercial Agency, will be found the number of failures in the past two years in New York and Brooklyn cities, and the States of my district, with the liabilities; also the number of persons engaged in trade in 1889 with the percentage of failures to traders:— *Failures.*

	Number of Failures.		Amount of Liabilities.		Number of Persons in Trade in 1889.	Percentage of Failures to Traders.
	1889.	1888.	1889.	1888.		
			£	£		
New York and Brooklyn Cities	585	690	3,574,426	3,516,455	57,140	1·02
New York, outside of New York and Brooklyn Cities	589	599	1,955,977	1,686,604	90,626	·65
Connecticut	137	137	334,680	160,634	...	·78
New Jersey	128	151	302,788	306,085	...	·22
Rhode Island	130	132	...	252,740	...	1·60
Delaware	15	26	32,177	66,785	...	·36

Dry Goods.

Dry goods—cotton.

Cottons.—The conditions mentioned in my last report respecting the different classes of goods coming under this head for the most part have to be confirmed to-day. Manufacturing here has on the whole been of a profitable nature, the New England and many of the mills in other States having paid their usual dividends, some of them larger dividends than usual, and machinery during the entire year having been well engaged, with fewer instances of strikes, or serious difficulty with work-people. The tendency has continued, as during some years previous in the New England mills, especially in Massachusetts and Rhode Island, to change the production into finer and lighter fabrics, leaving the coarser and heavier fabrics to southern mills. These last, on the whole, are said not to have proved as profitable as has previously been the case, though to this rule there are no doubt notable exceptions. Many of the heavy drills and sheetings manufactured by the southern factories find their way, through this city, to India and China markets, where their heavy and substantial character appear to meet with favour. Prices during the year have undergone slight variations, and neither manufacturers nor dealers are the holders of heavy stock.

It was mentioned in my last report that one or two of the Manchester printers had appeared in New York market with some attractive specimens of their work. This was probably the first public notice of this fact; but during the past season quite a sensation has been produced by the novelties sent out by the printers referred to, which have been exceptionally attractive in character, and have come into close competition with the finer classes of French satines. Meantime, American printers are doing excellent work, and are said to have had a very satisfactory year.

Worsteds and woollens.

The depression in these branches of trade has continued unrelieved during the last twelve months, the great question of duties on raw material having been, during the whole period, one of absorbing interest. That the demand for free wool is now made by a very large and constantly-increasing number of manufacturers is unquestionably the case, the carpet manufacturers being almost unanimous in this respect. On the other hand, the fact that the wool growers insist that the same protection which is extended to so many other interests should be equally accorded to them, makes their opposition to the admission of free wool most formidable, and it is impossible to predict what the result upon this point in Congress will finally be. But for the fact that the removal of the duty on wool is looked upon by Protectionists as the entering wedge, which would affect the whole fabric, it is not unlikely that the measure would receive a much greater support. During the year the interpretations of the Treasury have been adverse to the importers of Yorkshire worsted coatings, the importations of which, though, during the first half of the year, about equal to previous years, during the latter half of the year were curtailed; but the demand for mohair and alpaca fabrics for women's wear has been of increasing magnitude, and the goods have met with unusual favour.

Silks.— American manufacturers have more and more been getting possession of the market in plain goods, both black and coloured, and have also been doing a good deal in plushes, both silk and mohair, in which, until within a year or two, English manufacturers had almost the monopoly. The shipment of Yorkshire goods to this market, however, during the year have been very heavy, and there is as yet no indication here of the inability of English makers to compete for the trade, notwithstanding the excessive duty.

The following table shows the total grain shipments from this port, and the number of vessels engaged in the transport, with their nationality:—

Nationality.	Number of Vessels.	Number of Bushels.
British..	616	24,954,719
Belgian	70	4,236,672
German	167	3,837,335
French..	33	1,445,511
Dutch ..	21	644,082
Italian..	15	605,895
American	14	571,169
Danish..	21	598,265
Spanish	8	325,421
Austrian	10	289,139
Portuguese	9	235,162
Norwegian	6	162,899
Total ..	..	37,906,269

The past year has been an exceptionally profitable one to owners of steamships engaged in the carrying trade of this port. The regular lines have secured very satisfactory freights throughout the year, and more especially in the latter half. The demand for steamships elsewhere has kept the supply of ships not belonging to the regular lines within limits which have enabled them to secure cargoes at good freights. The sailing vessel is disappearing as a carrier of grain, and the number of "tank boats" has very largely reduced the volume of shipments of petroleum by sailing vessels, in fact, except at the height of the shipping season the tank boats are equal to the task of supplying the demand of the principal European receiving ports. The time is not far distant when the shipment of petroleum in barrels, for years one of the most profitable sources of freight for sailing vessels, will cease entirely. Sailing vessels are still employed largely as carriers of case oil to the East Indies, China, and Japan, and the demand for tonnage for this purpose was larger than in 1888, and rates much higher. Owing to the great falling-off in the supply of medium-sized sailing vessels, there has been a very good enquiry for them for general cargoes to Australia, New Zealand, and the west coast of South America, and freights have been higher than for many years. There has been also an active enquiry at highly remunerative rates throughout the year for ships to carry lumber cargoes to the River Plate.

Buffa'o. Buffalo is becoming every year a more important distributing point for produce and general merchandise.

The following table shows the receipts of principal articles by the Lake (Erie):—

Articles.		Quantity.
Barley	Bushels	1,474,570
Corn	,,	47,127,150
Copper	Tons	28,853
,,	Cakes and bars	..
,, ore	Tons	..
Flour	Barrels	5,480,710
Flax seed	Bushels	1,420,670
Feed	Sacks	810,720
Glucose	Barrels	15,457
Hoops	Number	..
Iron ore	Tons	298,060
Iron, pigs	,,	36,400
Lead, pigs	,,	265,130
Lard	Packages	217,520
Lumber	Feet	242,525,000
Lath	Pieces	10,033,500
Malt	Bushels	284,640
Oats	,,	14,309,300
Oatmeal	Barrels	30,000
Oil cake	Packages	301,340
Peas	Bushels	45,000
Pork	Barrels	41,180
Rye	Bushels	1,906,760
Seed	Bags	72,080
Staves	Number	200,000
Stave bolts	Cords	3,129
Shingles	Number	36,331,500
Posts	,,	15,000
Ties	,,	442,570
Timber	Cubic feet	24,450,000
Wheat	Bushels	26,051,600
Wool	Bales	53,310

4,237,085 tons of anthracite coal and 2,198,327 tons of bituminous were received in 1889 by rail and canal, the latter only bringing of this about 100,000 tons. In the same period 2,151,670 tons were sent to different points by the Lake. The customs receipts at Buffalo in 1889 were 175,800*l*., which varies little from the receipts of the three preceding years. The principal articles on which duty was paid were barley, dry-goods, tin-plates, timber, china and glassware. Eleven railroads, operating 11,700 miles, have their depôts in the city. The population of Buffalo, the largest city in the State after New York and Brooklyn, which was, at the census of 1880, 155,134, is now over 255,000. The wealth is estimated to have increased in the 10 years 90 per cent., city corporation property 168 per cent., custom-house receipts 68 per cent., manufacturing establishments 128 per cent., water supply 252 per cent., school property 132 per cent., banking capital 100 per cent., real estate valuations 83 per cent.

Canals. The New York canals were opened in 1889 for navigation on May 1, and closed December 1. The report of the Superintendent shows that 5,370,369 tons (2,000 lbs.) passed through, an increase on 1888 of 427,421 tons. The number of tons shipped by the canals, destined for this port, was 1,993,774. The average freights from Buffalo to New York in the past season were 4 c. (2*d*.) per bushel on wheat, and 3·6 c. on maize. Included in the traffic on the Champlain canal were 132,436 tons for Canada, and from Canada 199,022 tons came into the State. The fastest time ever made on the canals from Buffalo to West Troy, 345 miles, was 4½ days. The movements eastward by the canal included 15,318,376 bushels, wheat; 20,697,366 bushels, maize; 3,823,463 bushels, oats; 1,220,294 bushels, rye; 682,500 bushels, barley; 213,054 bushels, malt; 30,772 bushels, peas and beans; 8,454 barrels, flour; and 9,606 tons, pig-iron.

Railroads. There was a much more conservative feeling shown by the managers of the great trunk lines of railroads, who, with a better understanding among themselves, were able to maintain rates, and avoid the great demoralisation of 1888, thus enabling the various companies to make a very much better exhibit both in gross and net earnings; the increase in net earnings compared to the gross was due in a great measure to the absence of the disturbing influences of the preceding year, such as strikes, blizzards, &c. During the year 1,245,710 tons (2,000 lbs.) were sent westward to Buffalo, Pittsburg, &c., from this city, and 3,498,339 tons were received, originating at, or west of, Buffalo, Pittsburg, &c.

LABOUR.

Labour There has been no appreciable variation within my Consular district in the rates of wages in any branch of industry during the year, except in the cotton mills and ironworks, where there has been an advance varying from 5 to 10 per cent.

The State Board of Mediation and Arbitration reports for the year 1889 a marked and gratifying diminution in the number of strikes and lockouts as compared with previous years, as well as a change for the better in the character, duration, and consequences of such labour disturbances as have occurred. With the exception of surface street railroad tie-ups in New York and Brooklyn, and a surface street railroad tie-up at Rochester, the differences between employers and employés, as a rule, have not been of an uncompromising nature, but have yielded to settlement by conference and compromise. The favourable change is attributed largely to two causes; firstly to the general acceptance of arbitration in one form or another, as enforcing the true principle of settlement of disputes, especially in productive industries where the interests of capital and labour are mutual; and secondly to the power of investigation, vested in the Board, which has had the moral effect of deterring parties from making undue exactions and imposing unjust conditions. The Board, in its report to the Legislature, states:—" The constant effort of the Board has been, through a wide distribution of its reports among those whom they may concern, and by other available means, to impress the lesson of arbitration and infuse a spirit of compromise, and to induce settlements by local boards, or by direct negotiations, between the parties in interest, free from outside intervention. The tendency and growth in this direction have been encouraging. A conspicuous illustration of the fact is furnished by the shoe trade of Rochester, and merits special attention. That trade is one of the principal manufactures, if not the principal manufacture, of the city. It gives employment to over 5,000 hands, male and female. Two years ago, toward the close of 1887 and the opening of the season of 1888, in that industry, the employés, in one branch of the trade, desired certain changes in the scale that had prevailed during the previous year. The employers declined to submit the points at issue to arbitration, or to negotiate in any manner with their employés, and they posted notices in their factories which amounted to an ultimatum, and to which the employés affected refused to yield. In deference to the wishes of the Board, however, the employers assented to two conferences, for the purpose of allowing the employés to make statements of their side of the controversy, but nothing came of them. It could not be said that the differences took the form, strictly speaking, of either strike or lock-out, while they had the effect of both. For a period of about three months shoe manufacturers in Rochester were at a stand-still, and the trade suffered a check, not to say a blow, from which it took some time to recover. By the end of that period, such adjustments had been made as to enable a resumption of work, which has continued since. Again, towards the close of last year, 1889, the manufacturers desired a change in some particulars, but instead of posting an ultimatum they met and invited a conference with their employés. Representatives of both sides assembled, those of the employés embracing the two sexes. The latter made the proposition that in case of failure to agree the whole matter should be left to the decision of this Board, and the former were not averse, in that contingency, to such mode of settlement. After negotiations in several sessions, an understanding was ultimately reached, by which a strike or lock-out was averted, and harmonious relations were established for the current year. Another illustration of this fact is furnished by the agreement between the Brooklyn City Railroad Company and its employés, made December 27, 1886, which contains the following provision:—'Any difference or dispute arising between the parties hereto, under these arrangements, shall be submitted for settlement to arbitration. The company shall have the right to select one arbitrator and the employés one arbitrator; if the two so chosen fail to agree, the said arbitrators shall select a third arbitrator, and the decision of a majority so chosen shall be binding and final upon the parties hereto.' This agreement, with slight alterations, has been renewed from year to year, and a similar provision has recently been inserted in agreements between other surface street railroad companies in the city of Brooklyn and their employés. Kindred action on the part of employés in other cases has been productive of kindred results. The destructive policy of 'a word and a blow,' but 'the blow first,' is gradually being reversed, and the blow of a strike or lock-out is coming to be regarded in order only as a last resort after the word of reason has proved a failure."

Last year the Factory Inspection Law of this State was amended, and under the amended clauses no male under the age of 18, and no female under the age of 21, can be employed at labour in any manufacturing establishment for any longer period than 60 hours in each week, unless for the purpose of making necessary repairs to machinery, and further, that not more than 10 hours shall be exacted from, or permitted to be performed by any such male minor or female under 21 on any day unless for the purpose of making a shorter work-day on the last day of the week, and no labour shall be exacted from them between 9 p.m. and 6 a.m. No child under 14 years of age can be employed in any manufacturing establishment, and when children under 16 are employed, there must be placed on file an affidavit made by the parent or guardian stating the age, date, and place of birth of said child, and if said child has no parent or guardian, the affidavit shall be made by the child, said affidavit being open for the inspection on demand of the factory inspector or any of his deputies. No child under 16 shall be employed who cannot read and write simple sentences in the English language except during the vacation of the public schools in the city or town where the child lives. The inspector under the amended Act is also empowered to demand a certificate of physical fitness from some regular physician, in the case of children who may seem physically unable to perform the labour at which they may be employed, and shall have power to prohibit the employment of any minor that cannot obtain such a certificate. The amended Act also provides for suitable fire-escapes. The factory inspector in his annual report to the Legislature points out the insufficient force to properly perform the work delegated to the office. In this State there are 50,000 factories, and only 10 inspectors, while Massachusetts has 22 inspectors for 18,000 factories, and New Jersey 6 inspectors for less than 8,000 factories.

IMMIGRATION.

Immigration. There were 300,111 immigrants landed at this port in 1889, of the following countries and sex :—

Country.	Sex.		Totals.	
	Males.	Females.	In 1889.	In 1888.
England..	17,964	10,182	28,146	38,355
Ireland ..	19,864	18,776	38,640	44,307
Scotland..	4,182	2,094	6,276	10,986
Wales ..	391	242	633	1,269
Germany	39,042	28,908	67,950	78,145
France ..	3,022	1,725	4,747	5,437
Russia ..	17,580	10,272	27,852	33,052
Bohemia	3,032	2,229	5,261	3,982
Switzerland	4,701	2,429	7,130	7,305
Sweden ..	14,378	10,260	24,638	37,934
Norway ..	5,744	3,933	9,677	14,125
Belgium..	1,403	835	2,238	2,886
Holland ..	3,181	2,213	5,394	4,477
Italy ..	20,596	7,114	27,710	43,927
Spain ..	76	17	93	124
Portugal..	14	5	19	3
Denmark	4,435	2,838	7,273	7,698
Hungary	11,653	3,787	15,440	12,905
Austria ..	11,751	4,607	16,358	21,903
China ..	..	..	..	5
Australia	14	3	17	16
Turkey ..	201	53	254	184
Greece ..	106	2	108	378
All other countries	2,924	1,333	4,257	1,919
Total ..	186,254	113,857	300,111	370,822

Of the above, 57,447 were under 15 years of age; 211,631 between 15 and under 40 years; and 31,033, 40 years and over. The occupations of steerage passengers were as follows :—

Architects	68
Brewers ..	542
Butchers ..	1,249
Barbers ..	638
Bakers ..	1,335
Blacksmiths	1,646
Bar-tenders	204
Bricklayers	1,329
Carpenters	2,540
Cabinet-makers ..	1,102
Confectioners	232
Cigar-makers	852
Cooks	333
Coopers ..	437
Farmers ..	16,472
Florists ..	191
Gardeners..	1,082

NEW YORK.

Hatters	336
Ironmoulders	675
Labourers	92,665
Locksmiths	636
Laundrymen	0
Masons	2,491
Miners	3,991
Machinists	1,264
Millers	698
Musicians	779
Painters	1,271
Peddlers	5,002
Plasterers	513
Porters	373
Potters	339
Printers	408
Saddlers	537
Shoemakers	2,378
Spinners	454
Tailors	2,976
Tinsmiths	604
Tanners	396
Wagonsmiths	378
Weavers	920
Waiters	609
All other occupations	5,588
No occupation, including women and children	143,578

The destination of the immigrants, as recorded at the Castle Garden (landing depôt), was as follows:—

Alaska	0
Alabama	303
Arizona	67
Arkansas	325
Connecticut	7,271
Colorado	2,488
California	8,235
Delaware	243
District of Columbia	330
Dakota	5,311
Florida	258
Georgia	186
Indiana	2,288
Indian Territory	116
Illinois	24,574
Iowa	8,324
Idaho	143
Kentucky	657
Kansas	2,313
Louisiana	649
Maine	182
Maryland	1,448
Michigan	12,107
Missouri	4,828
Minnesota	10,667
Mississippi	41
Montana	1,033
Massachusetts	11,649
New Hampshire	171
North Carolina	50
Nebraska	5,029
Nevada	212
New Jersey	14,691
New Mexico	109
New York	96,901

UNITED STATES.

Ohio	10,807
Oregon	1,015
Pennsylvania	46,613
Rhode Island	2,660
South Carolina	105
Tennessee	419
Texas	2,833
Utah	1,429
Vermont	426
Virginia	231
West Virginia	255
Wisconsin	8,648
Washington	1,125
Wyoming	346

During the year 422 immigrants were prohibited from landing, and returned to the countries whence they came, under the provisions of the Act of Congress to regulate immigration; the prohibition includes convicts, lunatics, idiots, and all persons unable to take care of themselves without becoming a public charge.

Contract and labour law. Under the Act of Congress prohibiting the importation of foreign labourers under contract or agreement to perform labour in the United States, 26 immigrants were returned by the collector of the port. The majority of these were English, and the application of the law to most of them was open to question—one being a clerk of a mercantile house in Liverpool, who came out to adjust the accounts of the agency here; and the others ordinary immigrants, who had been given in London, with their passage tickets, letters to an agent of the Southern Pacific Railroad Company at Seguin, Texas, which on presentation would entitle them to free accommodation on their consenting to accept the first employment offered, unless a choice of more than one occupation was offered, when they were at liberty to accept which suited them best.

PRISONS.

Prisons. The condition of the State prisons, as appears from the annual report of the superintendent, is far from satisfactory. The contract system has been abandoned, and under existing regulations the bulk of the prisoners are without employment of any kind. Their labour is restricted under a law, which went into force June 6 last, to certain statutory purposes. Under this the total number of prisoners employed at one time in manufacturing one kind of goods, which are manufactured elsewhere in the State, shall not exceed 5 per cent. of the number of all persons within the State employed in manufacturing the same kind of goods as shown by the last United States census or State enumeration, except in industries in which not to exceed 50 free labourers are employed, provided that not more than 100 prisoners shall be employed in all the prisons of the State in the manufacture of stoves and iron hollow-ware, and that not more than 100 prisoners shall be employed in all the prisons in the manufacture of boots and shoes. Referring to this, and to the large deficiency in the earnings of the prisoners, the superintendent states:— "What compensation is there for this deficit of 369,274 dol. (76,070*l*.)? The convicts are immeasurably worse off than when they could earn their living. For six years, from 1881 to 1886, the convicts in the State prisons 'paid for their keep' by their labour. There was not a man among them who was not, by reason of such labour, a better man as a prisoner and a better man for the prospective freeman and citizen that he was to be. After this grand physical, financial, and moral demonstration of the value of systematic labour in the prisons, the position was abandoned in spite of the plain warnings of experience, and thereby the fiscal balance was changed from surplus to deficit. The criminals were deprived of the salutary influence of the most regenerating remedy that prison reformers ever found for relief and reform. Sickness, insanity, and death attacked the wretched imprisoned men as they never did before under the reform industrial system of management. The reports of the wardens, physicians, and chaplains show that the moral and sanitary condition of the prison population culminated in its highest excellence during the period in which work was most regular. Hence it appears that a prison population is like a free population; the best state of health, of morality, and prosperity attend the steady prosecution of industry. The great losses in the past in the prisons cannot be recouped, but it is not difficult to avoid now the paths which led to them."

New York State Finances.

The State is substantially out of debt. It has been reduced 39,140*l*. during the past fiscal year. The total funded debt on September 30 was 1,395,614*l*., against which there is a sinking fund of 920,125*l*., leaving a net debt of 475,489*l*. unprovided for but not due. The tax rate for the current fiscal year is 3·52 mills., which on the assessed valuation will yield 2,586,815*l*., of which 719,970*l*. is for the support of public schools. The city and county of New York pays over 45 per cent. of the State taxes.

State finances.

New York City Finances.

The total funded debt of the city of New York amounts to 29,218,841*l*., against which there is a sinking fund of 9,401,458*l*., leaving a net funded debt of 19,817,383*l*.

City finances.

Valuation and tax rates for the past five years are given in the following table:—

UNITED STATES.

Year.	Real Estate.	Personal.	City Tax.
	£	£	Per cent.
1889	274,305,127	42,078,152	1·95
1888	268,380,689	51,628,451	2·22
1887	258,425,300	52,148,655	2·16
1886	248,011,860	44,707,606	2·29
1885	240,699,285	41,750,816	2·40

City vital statistics.

VITAL Statistics, New York City.

	1889.	1888.
Births	37,527	34,023
Marriages	14,400	13,740
Deaths	39,679	40,175

Of the deaths reported 13,947 were of foreign birth, and 17,152 were under five years of age. The causes of death were principally as follows:—

	Number.
Phthisis	5,179
Pneumonia	4,075
Diarrhœal diseases	3,648
Bright's ,,	1,763
Diphtheria	1,686
Heart disease	1,970
Bronchitis	1,814
Scarlatina	1,242
Gastritis and peritonitis	421
Measles	470
Whooping cough	647
Malarial fevers	228

Annex A.—RETURN of all Shipping at the Port of New York in the Year 1889.

ENTERED.

Country.	Sailing. Number of Vessels.	Sailing. Tons.	Steam. Number of Vessels.	Steam. Tons.	Total. Number of Vessels.	Total. Tons.
Great Britain	1,214	639,939	1,495	2,662,599	2,709	3,302,538
United States	1,270	588,078	262	432,188	1,532	1,020,266
Germany	144	152,814	294	723,901	438	876,715
France	5	3,545	87	258,588	92	262,133
Sweden and Norway	199	141,412	172	72,595	371	214,007
Belgium	13	16,965	67	191,447	80	208,412
Italy	134	79,311	18	29,250	152	108,561
Mexico	...	...	...	...	...	133,478
Netherlands	9	8,950	69	124,528	78	25,976
Austria	38	25,976	...	...	38	92,476
Spain	21	6,872	56	85,604	77	53,360
Denmark	4	992	26	52,368	30	
Other European countries	22	9,990	2	2,108	24	12,098
South America	3	1,668	...	...	3	1,668
Central ,,	3	441	...	...	3	441
Other countries	1	350	...	...	1	350
Total	3,080	1,677,303	2,548	4,635,176	5,628	6,312,479
,, for the preceding year	3,033	1,620,362	2,329	4,217,431	5,362	5,837,793

NEW YORK.

CLEARED.

Country.	Sailing. Number of Vessels.	Sailing. Tons.	Steam. Number of Vessels.	Steam. Tons.	Total. Number of Vessels.	Total. Tons.
Great Britain	1,204	629,868	1,499	2,664,870	2,703	3,294,738
United States	781	361,645	252	415,693	1,033	777,338
Germany	112	118,856	282	694,354	394	813,210
France	6	4,254	83	246,699	89	250,953
Sweden and Norway	167	118,673	167	70,485	334	189,158
Belgium	3	3,915	79	225,736	82	229,651
Italy	139	82,271	18	28,436	157	110,707
Mexico	...	...	...	...	...	...
Netherlands	9	8,872	73	131,747	82	140,619
Austria	34	23,242	...	...	34	23,242
Spain	22	7,199	54	82,548	76	89,747
Denmark	2	496	23	46,326	25	46,822
Other European countries	19	8,268	3	3,162	22	11,790
South America	5	2,780	...	...	5	2,780
Central ,,	1	147	...	...	1	147
Other countries	...	...	...	...	...	...
Total	2,504	1,370,846	2,533	4,610,056	5,037	5,980,902
,, for the preceding year	2,536	1,462,687	2,304	4,150,533	4,840	5,513,220

Annex B.—RETURN of Principal Articles of Export from New York during the Years 1889–88.

Articles.		1889. Quantity.	1889. Value. £	1888. Quantity.	1888. Value. £
Agricultural implements	...	...	770,790	...	501,235
Bacon and hams	Lbs.	269,864,080	4,689,833	194,362,362	3,646,380
Beef, fresh	,,	110,561,262	1,806,208	71,628,226	1,401,166
,, canned	,,	31,107,216	475,705	20,660,630	353,047
Butter	,,	20,158,042	622,175	7,069,000	247,797
Cattle, live	Number	125,094	2,095,085	57,042	1,116,983
Cotton, domestic	Packages	164,030	1,861,208	173,986	2,013,610
,, raw	Bales	1,050,124	10,530,867	999,721	10,166,108
Cheese	Lbs.	70,616,136	1,275,310	68,296,464	1,286,999
Flour	Barrels	3,710,566	3,535,229	3,820,273	3,520,895
Hops	Lbs.	7,476,438	308,248	8,089,133	372,080
Indian corn	Bus. (56lbs.)	29,130,494	2,715,735	13,479,048	1,563,845
Lard	Lbs.	265,232,655	4,109,576	170,151,224	3,001,465
Oil cake and meal	,,	272,498,997	719,674	200,717,992	538,040
Oleomargarine	,,	42,954,590	841,215	23,528,706	515,440
Petroleum, refined	Gallons	392,551,146	6,174,605	322,991,600	5,453,295
,, crude	,,	50,123,443	773,780	41,645,879	639,325
,, lubricating	,,	11,585,652	209,180	21,468,777	801,915
Sewing machines	...	...	475,016	...	376,155
Sugar	Lbs.	7,614,695	128,827	13,508,232	204,885
Specie and bullion	...	...	14,781,236	...	9,238,385
Tallow	Lbs.	61,149,080	606,340	51,692,457	537,087
Wheat	Bus.(60lbs.)	10,853,078	2,014,328	12,352,445	2,386,080
Other articles	...	...	24,413,567	...	21,134,713
Total	...	...	86,033,737	...	71,016,930

UNITED STATES.

Annex B.—RETURN of Principal Articles of Import to New York during the Years 1889–88.

Articles.		1889. Quantity.	1889. Value.	1888. Quantity.	1888. Value.
			£		£
Cocoa	Bags	88,989	348,476	100,394	406,330
Coffee	,,	3,126,243	12,906,394	3,331,850	10,851,110
China, glass, and earthenware	...	...	1,916,856	...	1,790,390
Cotton	Bales	12,526	222,645	9,095	147,712
Dry goods—					
Manufactures of cotton	,,	...	4,393,605	...	4,277,388
,, flax	,,	...	3,945,785	...	3,457,360
,, silk	,,	...	9,043,710	...	8,122,372
,, wool	,,	...	8,263,770	...	7,597,538
,, miscellaneous	,,	...	2,509,800	...	2,486,002
Furs	Packages	22,888	1,292,157	21,087	1,110,240
Fruits	...	...	2,767,950	...	3,434,310
Hair	Packages	28,932	280,720	...	297,536
Hemp	Bales	494,492	2,587,855	419,143	1,737,842
Hides, dressed	...	...	646,810	...	790,240
,, undressed	...	...	3,460,270	...	3,709,575
Hops	Bales	10,100	161,390	7,179	120,115
India rubber	...	...	2,316,442	...	2,651,080
Jewellery, watches, and precious stones	...	...	2,709,100	...	2,354,030
Jute and jute butts	...	...	639,930	...	591,235
Linseed	...	...	653,715	...	340,265
Molasses	...	...	312,185	...	106,112
Paper stock	...	...	633,600	...	522,882
Metals—					
Cutlery	...	...	438,755	...	416,156
Iron, pig	Tons	23,778	70,875	64,207	194,066
,, spiegel		75,322	325,662	45,532	185,100
,, other	...	...	303,556	...	311,392
Metal goods	...	...	358,695	...	379,980
Steel	...	...	499,920	...	746,942
Tin plates	Boxes	2,312,171	1,718,385	2,026,366	1,567,585
,, slabs	Tons	14,220	1,338,940	36,500	1,601,245
Soda, ash	...	...	217,783	...	210,272
,, caustic	...	...	141,320	...	169,550
Spices	...	...	514,392	...	529,188
Stationery and books	...	...	1,100,790	...	1,100,215
Sugar	Tons	664,087	10,143,860	677,626	8,259,910
Specie and bullion	...	...	1,637,322	...	1,684,375
Tea	Packages	1,295,690	2,001,048	1,308,270	1,983,990
Tobacco and cigars	...	...	2,669,844	...	1,797,185
Wines, spirits, &c.	...	...	1,987,240	...	1,952,670
Wood	...	...	1,173,407	...	1,204,075
Wool	Lbs.	52,795,113	1,339,490	44,672,758	1,046,187
Other articles	...	...	13,564,845	...	14,995,463
Total	...	...	103,569,144	...	97,327,210

NEW YORK.

Annex C.—TABLE showing the Total Value of all Articles Exported from and Imported to New York to and from Foreign Countries during the Years 1889–88.

Country.	Exports. 1889.	Exports. 1888.	Imports. 1889.	Imports. 1888.
	£	£	£	£
Great Britain	40,090,215	32,634,000	22,268,820	22,372,990
British Possessions	6,138,228	5,785,500	7,056,865	6,399,085
Germany	6,991,392	8,019,385	14,468,825	13,662,325
France and Possessions	9,805,033	8,857,985	13,406,468	12,590,410
Belgium	2,928,263	3,095,865	1,204,945	1,350,295
Spain and Possessions	4,042,470	4,102,697	9,864,550	7,801,655
Netherlands and Possessions	2,988,487	2,566,050	3,710,397	2,776,320
United States of Colombia	516,540	1,010,320	1,119,321	1,152,665
Central American States	579,472	537,965	712,593	731,120
Italy	926,385	820,893	2,798,387	3,109,025
Brazil	1,333,458	986,520	10,227,777	9,659,845
China	642,100	629,505	2,038,877	2,217,650
Denmark and Possessions	681,664	497,935	164,495	87,825
Venezuela	1,385,900	773,580	2,568,990	1,872,545
Portugal and Possessions	434,036	606,430	247,965	267,545
Argentine Republic	1,453,835	941,890	525,656	555,675
Mexico	968,143	767,830	1,957,735	1,607,375
Hayti	1,191,158	943,313	701,185	596,760
Sweden and Norway	428,545	380,025	418,866	379,025
Japan	516,965	408,125	1,411,788	1,199,270
Chili	473,087	252,135	330,375	303,375
San Domingo	288,880	331,623	381,408	285,020
Uruguay	529,005	228,089	432,800	478,020
Austria	21,143	7,370	1,350,380	1,568,165
Russia	135,300	76,055	524,662	496,100
Peru	203,825	147,700	64,755	59,420
Switzerland	4,520	1,565	2,478,716	2,409,385
Other countries	335,588	536,630	1,131,563	1,336,020
Total	86,033,737*	71,016,930	103,569,144	97,327,210

* All but 3,588,000*l.* were domestic products.

UNITED STATES.

The Specie included in the Tables was Exported to and Imported from the following Countries during the Years 1889 and 1888.

Country.	Exports. 1889.	Exports. 1888.	Imports. 1889.	Imports. 1888.
	£	£	£	£
Great Britain	7,095,880	4,863,655	123,755	13,420
British Possessions	1,717	164,625	51,650	42,215
Germany	11,445	2,448,625	356,815	235,145
France and Possessions	5,755,530	106,485	341,012	608,300
Spain and Possessions	929,504	1,005,565	181,495	329,055
Netherlands and Possessions	6,352	4,230	16,660	15,750
United States of Colombia	23,423	147,940	391,905	244,525
Central American States	39,494	60,960	20,874	10,645
Brazil	100,428	3,450	235	435
China	..	275	..	..
Denmark and Possessions	6,138	4,610	5,232	515
Venezuela	546,442	138,840	17,310	35,500
Mexico	7,786	545	95,353	121,535
Hayti	196,376	136,945	10,345	19,430
San Domingo	57,787	141,165	13,044	5,570
Peru	..	6,285	..	..
Other countries	2,934	4,185	11,637	8,455
Total	14,781,236	9,238,385	1,637,322	1,690,495

PROVIDENCE.

Mr. Vice-Consul Stockwell reports as follows:—

General report on trade. Commercial operations generally during the year 1889 were unusually extensive and profitable. In all branches of trade, coal and woollen goods excepted, the volume of business was largely in excess of that for 1888. The bank clearings make a good index. During the year they amounted to 54,001,232*l.*, against 51,225,946*l.* for 1888, showing an increase in 1889 of 2,775,285*l.*

The important political events of the year are the repeal of the prohibitory law and the return to license, and the adoption of the Australian ballot system in State elections.

Definite plans have been adopted for the improvement of terminal facilities for railways, and for a better system of sewerage for the city of Providence. Work in both departments is progressing satisfactorily. The Department of Public Works has added during the year a new reservoir to increase the efficiency of the high service system. The city, now having three reservoirs to draw from, has an ample supply of water for domestic uses and for use of the fire department in any emergency.

An event of the year was the completion of a cable tramway, begun in 1888, from the Providence River, the centre of business, to the Pawtucket River on the east, through the better residence part of the city, heretofore without direct public conveyance.

Cotton and cotton goods. The cotton market has been active, and sales aggregated 226,051 bales for the year, the largest on record, against 178,502 in 1888. The lowest price during the year for middling-upland cotton laid down here was 10⅜ c. (5¼d.), and the highest 11⅞ c. (5¾d. to 6d.). The cotton goods business has been satisfactory, and stocks were well sold up at the close of the year. The sale of print cloths, both 64 and 56 squares, amounted to 1,427,500 pieces, against 2,460,500 pieces in 1888. Prices, 64 squares, ranged from 3½ to 4 c. (2d.).

The market for wool has been depressed, and prices have lagged, but there has been so little life in the trade that actual quotations give little information. This state of the market is attributed to the unsatisfactory condition of the goods market. It is stated by manufacturers that not enough wool is produced in this country to supply the demand. Foreign wools are shut out by a tariff considered too high, and hence cannot be bought to compete at home or in foreign markets with foreign goods. The free traders attribute the depression in wool and the woollen goods trade to the excessive tariff, while the protectionists find many other causes. Wool and woollens.

Labour has been well employed and paid for during the year. According to the Commissioner of Industrial Statistics the price of labour in all branches, trades, and operative work, is unchanged, except in the cotton industry, where there has been an advance of about 5 per cent. Woollen mills have been in operation most of the time, and a slight reduction in wages has resulted in some cases, but generally the scale remains the same, liable, however, to greater reduction if trade does not improve. Labour.

Port statistics are as follows:— Port statistics.

	£
Duties collected	60,040
Tonnage dues	86
Storage fees	250
Customs fees	150
Fines and penalties	14

TONNAGE of the Port.

	Number.	Tons.
Sailing vessels	78	12,014
Steam vessels	43	14,659
	121	26,673

Foreign importations into this port under Acts of Congress of July 14, 1870, and June 10, 1880, providing for bonded railway cars and boats, come to the value of 186,523l.

This shows the American price of the imports, or the cost laid down here; that is to say, the duties are added to the foreign or invoice price. The amount given in Annex C is the foreign price without the duties.

Importations into other ports, and transferred in bond to this port, not under Acts of Congress aforesaid:—

UNITED STATES.

Articles.		Quantity.
Brandy	Gallons ..	4,342
Wool	Bales ..	30,470
Tobacco	Lbs. ..	1,382

DIRECT Importations in Foreign and American Vessels.

	Articles.		Quantity.
	Lumber	Feet	2,793,000
	Laths	,, ...	11,255,000
	Shingles	,, ...	6,574,000
	Wood	Cords.. ..	933
	Logwood	Tons	3,821
	Pickets	,, ...	54,000
	Starch..	Casks.. ..	597
	Piling..	Pieces	3,136
	Brimstone	Tons	590
	Ice	,, ...	509
	Salt	Pounds ..	7,603,000
	Lime	Barrels ..	804
	Potatoes	Bushels	3,611
Receipts of domestic merchandise.	Domestic receipts—		
	Cotton	Bales.. ..	220,420
	Wool	,, and sacks	123,879
	Coal	Tons	1,054,314
	Iron and steel	,, ...	65,876
	Lumber	Feet	80,177,000
	Oils	Barrels ..	174,569
	Waste..	Tons	5,811
	Beef	,, ...	12,486
	Flour	Barrels ..	291,041
	Corn	Bushels ..	1,535,504
	Meal	,, ...	62,415
	Oats	,, ...	1,218,557
	Bran	,, ...	183,498
	Dry goods	Cases.. ..	52,156
	Print cloths	Bales.. ..	13,411
	Chemicals	Packages	66,858
	Liquors	Barrels ..	45,490

ANNEX A.

ENTERED.

Nationality.	Sailing.		Steam.		Total.	
	Number of Vessels.	Tons.	Number of Vessels.	Tons.	Number of Vessels.	Tons.
British	65	9,188	...	...	65	9,188
American	16	2,756	...	...	...	...
Austrian	1	790	...	...	...	...
Italian	1	446	...	...	...	...
Total	73	13,180	...	...	65	9,188
,, for the year preceding...	94	14,799	...	...	...	...

NEW YORK.

Cleared.

Nationality.	Sailing. Number of Vessels.	Sailing. Tons.	Steam. Number of Vessels.	Steam. Tons.	Total. Number of Vessels.	Total. Tons.
British	55	6,889	1	83	56	6,972
American	16	859	...	...	16	859
Austrian	1	790	...	...	1	790
Total	72	8,538	1	83	73	8,621
,, for the year preceding	64	7,709	...	...	64	7,709

Annex B.—Return of Principal Articles of Export from Providence for the Years 1889–88.

Articles.		1889. Quantity.	1889. Value.	1888. Quantity.	1888. Value.
			£		£
Coal	Tons	...	...	25	28
Oil	Gallons	...	...	268	5
,,	Barrels	4,380	17,635	...	...
Vessel	...	...	1,660	...	...
Total	...	...	19,295	...	33

Return of Principal Articles of Import into Providence during the Years 1889–88.

Articles.	Quantity. 1889.	Quantity. 1888.
	£	£
Dry goods	68,865	87,439
Chemicals	23,730	36,011
Metals and manufactures of	19,805	19,108
All others	32,080	3,687
Total	144,480	146,245

UNITED STATES.

Annex C.—TABLE showing the Total Values of all Articles Exported from Providence and Imported into Providence from and to Foreign Countries during the Years 1889–88.

Country.	Exports. 1889.	Exports. 1888.	Imports. 1889.	Imports. 1888.
			£	£
Austria	..	..	2,097	2,737
Belgium	..	..	..	..
British West Indies	..	..	13,675	16,789
Canada	..	..	9,014	8,931
Cuba	..	..	8,949	8,424
England	..	..	70,052	63,384
France	..	..	17,840	12,741
Germany	..	..	10,376	14,051
Greece	..	..	2,730	..
Hayti	..	..	..	7,509
Italy	..	..	2,176	5,068
Ireland	..	..	..	..
Japan	..	..	..	..
Netherlands	..	..	914	922
Scotland	..	..	1,265	1,709
Spain	..	..	..	134
Switzerland	..	..	5,180	3,358
Venezuela	..	..	..	400
All others	..	..	212	88
Total	..	..	144,480	146,245

NEW YORK.

RETURN of the Number of Seamen who have been Engaged, Discharged, Left Behind, Reported Dead, or Deserted, or who have been Relieved at the British Consulate-General, New York; and showing the Total Number of British and Foreign Sailors who were Engaged, Discharged, &c., from British Ships, with the Amount of Wages paid at the Consulate to Seamen on Discharge from their Ships, and from Hospital or Gaol; and also showing the Number of New Agreements entered into during the Year 1889.

Seamen.											Wages.			Agreements.
Engaged.	Discharged.	Left Behind.			Dead.			Deserted.	Relieved.	Nationality.		Total Number of Seamen.	Paid on Discharge from Vessels.	Paid on Discharge from Hospital or Gaol.	Total Wages Paid.	Number Opened
		In Hospital.	In Gaol.	Total.	At Sea.	On Shore.	Total.			British.	Foreign.					
14,277	10,343	186	15	201	61	35	96	4,111	200	17,316	11,912	29,228	Dollars. 418,515·31	Dollars. 5,132·60	Dollars. 423,647·91	296

(908)

LONDON:
Printed for Her Majesty's Stationery Office,
By HARRISON AND SONS,
Printers in Ordinary to Her Majesty.
(1250 7 | 90—H & S 908)